81

THE ATHENIAN BOULE

THE
ATHENIAN
BOULE

P. J. RHODES

OXFORD
AT THE CLARENDON PRESS
1972

Oxford University Press, Ely House, London W. 1

GLASGOW NEW YORK TORONTO MELBOURNE WELLINGTON
CAPE TOWN IBADAN NAIROBI DAR ES SALAAM LUSAKA ADDIS ABABA
DELHI BOMBAY CALCUTTA MADRAS KARACHI LAHORE DACCA
KUALA LUMPUR SINGAPORE HONG KONG TOKYO

PRINTED IN GREAT BRITAIN
AT THE UNIVERSITY PRESS, OXFORD
BY VIVIAN RIDLER
PRINTER TO THE UNIVERSITY

TO MY MOTHER
IN MEMORY OF
MY FATHER

PREFACE

In this book I give a detailed account of the organization and working of the Athenian boule, the council founded by Solon and remodelled by Cleisthenes which acted as a standing committee of the assembly. To make my analysis intelligible to the modern reader I have drawn the now-familiar distinction between legislative, administrative, and judicial functions, but this distinction would not have been familiar to the Athenians, and their boule was active in all three fields: this has inevitably led to some repetition and cross-reference. In a concluding chapter I summarize the history of the boule, and try to assess its importance in the machinery of the Athenian state.

The book has been revised from the thesis which I submitted for the degree of D.Phil. of the University of Oxford in the summer of 1968. Dr. D. M. Lewis suggested the subject and supervised my work for most of the time, and with his extensive knowledge of the material and keen eye for detail has been able to draw my attention to much that I should otherwise have missed, and to save me from more inadequacies than I care to think of. Mr. G. E. M. de Ste Croix provided valuable encouragement and guidance in 1964–5, when Dr. Lewis was in America. Before I submitted my thesis Mr. G. L. Cawkwell, Mr. W. G. G. Forrest, the late A. R. W. Harrison, and Mr. R. Meiggs read and helped me to improve substantial parts of it. Professor A. Andrewes and Professor R. J. Hopper served as examiners and made valuable comments, and Professor Andrewes has been generous with his help during the revision of the work for publication. At different stages my wife and Mr. M. D. Reeve helped me to avoid serious delays by their kindness in verifying references. Many others have helped me on a variety of points, and I have tried to acknowledge all specific debts in their place.

From 1963 to 1965 I held a Craven Fellowship at Oxford University, and a Hildebrand Harmsworth Senior Scholarship at Merton College, Oxford. As Craven Fellow I was able to visit Greece as a Student of the British School at Athens (and also to work in the libraries of the American School and the German Institute, and in the Epigraphical Museum), and to visit Germany as a *Gasthörer* and member of the Historisches Seminar of the Eberhard-Karls-Universität,

Tübingen. Since 1965 I have been a lecturer at the University of Durham, and my work on the boule has been continued with assistance from the University in the time that could be spared from my other responsibilities; the Joint Library of the Hellenic and Roman Societies and the Institute of Classical Studies in London has sent me books with admirable speed during term and has provided pleasant working conditions in vacation.

Most of the works which I have found helpful are cited in the notes. The foundation for inquiries of this kind was laid by the great German students of *Staatsaltertümer*; of more recent writers I owe most to Professor U. Kahrstedt and the late Professor A. H. M. Jones, and to the epigraphists who have worked on the inscriptions from the Agora, thanks to whom the volume of material bearing on Athenian institutions has been greatly increased in the last forty years, and it has become worthwhile to re-open old questions. In my thesis I tried to take account of work published to the end of 1967; revision was undertaken in the latter half of 1969, when I did my best to pay due attention to more recent publications, in particular the welcome *Selection of Greek Historical Inscriptions to the End of the Fifth Century B.C.,* of R. Meiggs and D. M. Lewis.

The Delegates of the Press have honoured me by their willingness to publish my work, and their staff has shown tact and skill in handling a difficult book and an obstinate author. Miss J. Martin and Mrs. I. Parkin did most of the typing, Dr. J. D. Thomas read the book in proof, and Mr. D. A. Scales compiled the indexes. The Managing Committee of the British School at Athens has given me permission to publish otherwise than under its auspices the results of work which I did as a Student of the School; the Johns Hopkins Press and the Publications Committee of the American School at Athens have given me permission to reproduce and adapt copyright diagrams.

To all the institutions and individuals named above I offer my sincere thanks. Thanks are due no less for help of a more intangible kind: I could repeat names mentioned above and add others; and I am very grateful to all who have encouraged me and borne with me while this book has been in the making.

P. J. R.

Durham
Long Vacation, 1971

CONTENTS

LIST OF TABLES

LIST OF PLANS

ABBREVIATIONS

1. *Literary Texts*

The following abbreviations should be noticed:

A.   Aeschines.
Ar.   Aristophanes.
Arist.   Aristotle.
A.P.   [Aristotle], *Athenaion Politeia* (see below).
D.   Demosthenes.
H.   Herodotus.
Isae.   Isaeus.
Is.   Isocrates.
L.S.   *Lexica Segueriana*, in vol. i of Bekker, *Anecdota Graeca* (see Bibliography).
O.O.   'Old Oligarch': [Xenophon], *Athenaion Politeia*.
Plat.   Plato.
Pl.   Plutarch.
T.   Thucydides.
X.   Xenophon.

Other abbreviations will, I hope, cause no difficulty. References in the form, 328 F 64, are to texts in Jacoby, *Die Fragmente der griechischen Historiker*. Books of Aristotle's *Politics* are numbered in manuscript order (as in the Oxford Text); speeches of Hyperides are numbered in the order of the Oxford and Loeb Texts; chapters of Plutarch's *Lives* are divided into sections as in the Teubner Text. Except in the case of the two works called *Athenaion Politeia*, for which see the list of abbreviations above, when a work wrongly attributed to an author is cited immediately after a genuine work of the same author, the spurious work is distinguished by an asterisk (e.g. D. XXI. *Mid.* 32–3, 54, *XXVI. *Aristog. ii.* 5). In most cases the question of authorship does not matter for my purposes, and I have been content to echo the judgements of editors. Among the works whose authorship I need not discuss I would rank the Aristotelian *Athenaion Politeia*: it is enough that the treatise was completed between 329/8 and 323/2 (e.g. Gilbert, p. xxii) and that it is a product of the Aristotelian school, and I would rather err on the side of caution than buttress a weak point by claiming Aristotle's authority for it.

2. *Epigraphic Texts*

In addition to the standard abbreviations, I use the following (see Bibliography for full details: in each case, unless a page is specified, the numeral following the abbreviation represents the serial number of an inscription):

Maier, *GMbi*   *Griechische Mauerbauinschriften* (texts are in vol. i).
HMA   Hill, revised Meiggs and Andrewes, *Sources for Greek History*

> *between the Persian and Peloponnesian Wars* (texts of inscriptions are in Section B).

M&L   Meiggs and Lewis, *A Selection of Greek Historical Inscriptions to the End of the Fifth Century* B.C.

P   Dow, *Prytaneis*: *Hesp.* Supp. i 1937.

Svt   Bengtson, *Die Staatsverträge des Altertums* (vol. ii).

I have adopted two other conventions, which I hope may help the reader to pick his way through the forest of references. (*a*) While for most purposes, including page numbers and line numbers, I use 'old style' arabic numerals (1234567890), for the serial numbers of inscriptions I use 'modern' numerals (1234567890). (*b*) A great many Athenian inscriptions have been published in the periodical *Hesperia*, and in almost all cases these inscriptions have been given serial numbers (a main series, running through each volume, of inscriptions from the Agora, and a few other independent series). In citing these texts I identify the inscriptions by serial number whenever available (in the main Agora series, except where otherwise indicated), and not by page number, and to alert the reader I identify the volume on these occasions by number only and not by year; but when citing pages of *Hesperia* I identify the volume (as in all other references to periodicals) by both number and year. Thus:

Hesp. x 1941, 320–6 = *Hesp.* x 1941, pp. 320–6.

Hesp. vi 3, 19–20   = *Hesp.* vi 1937, no. 3 in the series of inscriptions from the Agora, lines 19–20.

Hesp. vi (EM) 4   = *Hesp.* vi 1937, no. 4 in a series of inscriptions in the Epigraphical Museum.

The large number of publications in which texts are re-edited or reproduced from the editions of others makes for difficulties in citation. I have normally given one reference only, to the volume in which an up-to-date text has been most accessible to me (in particular, whenever possible I cite *SEG* rather than *Hesp.*), but in Index ii I incorporate a concordance of all texts which have been published in *IG* or in volume ii of *ATL*. The reader is warned that in quotations I adhere to the spelling on the stone even when my reference is to Tod.

3. *Periodicals*

In general I use the abbreviations of *L'Année philologique*, with the usual English divergences; but the publications of the German academies are abbreviated as *Abh. Berlin*, *Sb. Wien*, etc., and the *Mitteilungen des Deutschen Archäologischen Instituts, Athenische Abteilung*, as *AM*. Superior figures indicate the second and subsequent series of a periodical (e.g. *CQ*² xiii 1963).

4. *Other Modern Works*

Full details of all works cited will be found in the Bibliography. The following works are cited by author's name(s) only:

Bonner and Smith   *The Administration of Justice from Homer to Aristotle.*

Busolt and Swoboda *Griechische Staatskunde.*
Gilbert   *The Constitutional Antiquities of Sparta and Athens.*
Hignett   *A History of the Athenian Constitution.*
Jones   *Athenian Democracy.*
Lipsius   *Das attische Recht und Rechtsverfahren.*

Notice also:

ATL   Meritt, Wade-Gery, and McGregor, *The Athenian
                    Tribute Lists.*
Beazley, *A.R.V.*[2] *Attic Red-Figure Vase Painters*[2].
GG   *Griechische Geschichte.*
HG   *Histoire grecque.*
Kahrstedt, *S.S.A.* *Staatsgebiet und Staatsangehörige in Athen.*
Kahrstedt, *U.M.A.* *Untersuchungen zur Magistratur in Athen.*
Wade-Gery, *E.G.H.* *Essays in Greek History.*

CORRIGENDA

13 n. 12: Add reference to schol. Ar. *Vesp.* 300.

20 n. 3: The reference to *L.S.* should read: 296. 8.

40 n. 9: The reference should read: D.S. xi. 39. v.

73 n. 3: *Delete* reference to *P* 16.

124 n. 8: The reference should read: *IG* ii² 1678, aA 27–8.

129 l. 24: *For* admissions *read* admission.

135 n. 7: The reference should be to pp. 224–5.

137 n. 6: The reference should be to p. 135 n. 10.

142 n. 3: The reference to *Hesp.* xxxviii 1969 should be to pp. 459–94.

145 n. 5: The first reference should read: H. ix. 5. i–ii.

250: *Delete IG* ii² 284 (bef. 336/5). The inscription is listed as Tod 170 on p. 249.

254: *Delete HSCP* xlviii 1937, 105–11 (216/15). The inscription is listed as *IG* ii² 794 on p. 273.

261: *Delete IG* ii² 304 (bef. 336/5). The inscription forms a part of *SEG* xviii 11, listed on the same page.
Delete IG ii² 350 (331/0?). The inscription is listed as *SEG* xxi 320 on p. 263.
Delete IG ii² 343 (aft. 329). The inscription as revised in *Hesp.* ix 1940, 342–3, is listed on p. 262.

264: *In place of Hesp.* iv 68 (302/1) *read Hesp.* iv 6.
Delete IG ii² 568 (end C4). The inscription forms a part of *IG* ii² (Add.) 599+568, listed on p. 263.

265: *In place of Hesp.* ix. 23 (223/2) *read Hesp.* ix 23. i. The formulae should read: *E*; [ετ]δ; δ[τδ].

269: In paragraph 2, under *SEG* xxi 276 (334/3), the formulae should read: [*E*]; ετ[δ] ONLY.

270: In paragraph 5, the inscription entered as *IG* ii² 568 (end C4) should be entered as *IG* ii² (Add.) 559+568 (*c.* 303/2).

273: *Under IG* ii² 794 (216/15), *in the Contents column, delete* ? *and substitute* Honours for ephebi.

The table on p. 79 should be corrected in the light of the double entries deleted from Tables C and D, but the conclusions drawn from it will stand.

I · MEMBERSHIP AND ORGANIZATION

(i) *Qualifications and Appointment*

THE βουλή, or Council, which is the subject of this book, was established by Cleisthenes in his reforms of 508/7 B.C., though there was very probably an earlier boule created by Solon.[1] The Cleisthenic boule may first have met in 501/0, the year when the bouleutic oath was first sworn.[2] Membership was based on the ten new tribes created by Cleisthenes: each tribe was to provide 50 of the boule's 500 members.[3] Tribal representation of 50 was retained during the various tribal changes, so that there were 600 members after the creation of the two Macedonian tribes, 650 in the last quarter of the third century, and 600 again from 201/0;[4] but in A.D. 127, when a thirteenth tribe was again instituted, membership was reduced nominally to the original figure of 500 and in fact to about 520.[5] In the later years of the Roman Empire various changes were made, and totals are attested of 600, 750, and 300.[6]

As with other Athenian public offices appointment was made annually, from citizens who had reached the age of thirty:[7] though Aristotle writes of a 'retired' status for elderly citizens,[8] I know no evidence that

---

[1] On the Solonian boule see Ch. V, pp. 208–9.

[2] *A.P.* 22. ii; cf. appendix to Ch. IV, pp. 191–3.   [3] *A.P.* 21. iii.

[4] 600, Pl. *Demetr.* 10. vi; 650, *IG* ii² 687, 53, 847, 26; 600 again, *IG* ii² 1013, 7, 16, 1072, 10.

[5] e.g. *IG* ii² 4210. For the date, cf. J. A. Notopoulos, *TAPA* lxxvii 1946. The exact size of Hadrian's boule is uncertain: S. Dow, *Hesp.* Supp. i 1937, 196, assumed that 500 was the correct figure; P. Graindor, *Athènes sous Hadrien*, 83–5, envisaged a total of about 540, with tribal contingents varying between 40 and 42; A. E. Raubitschek, Γέρας Ἀντωνίου Κεραμοπούλλου, 242–55, believes in a boule of 13 × 40, or 520, and is followed in this by D. J. Geagan, *Hesp.* Supp. xii 1967, 95–6. Raubitschek argues that the wealthy patron who acted as ἐπώνυμος to the tribe (cf. p. 14 with n. 5, below) should be regarded as a member of the prytany only in those prytany-dedications where he is named with the prytanes and not apart from them, and claims that there were 40 prytanes in each of the twelve complete lists which have survived from this period. I offer my own analysis of these lists in Table A, p. 241: regular lists of 40 cannot be obtained without forcing the evidence, and it seems better to admit the possibility of variation.

[6] 600, *IG* ii² 3664 (*c.* A.D. 200—but at this time the boule retained its Hadrianic size, so if the date is right 600 must be a mason's error); 750, *IG* ii² 3669 (269/70); 300, *IG* ii² 3716, 4222 (C4). It has been suggested by D. J. Geagan, *Hesp.* Supp. xii 1967, 75, that from the third century all eligible citizens were admitted to the boule for life.

[7] X. *M.* i. ii. 35, D. XXII. *Andr. hyp.* i. 1; cf. 'Draco' in *A.P.* 4. iii, 'constitutions' of 411 in *A.P.* 30. ii, 31. i. It is possible that the age requirement was not that a man should have reached the age of thirty but that he should have entered on his thirtieth year (and so should have reached the age of twenty-nine): cf. Ch. IV, p. 172.

[8] Arist. *Pol.* iii. 1275 A (2–)15–19. Professor J. H. Oliver claimed that citizens were not

an upper age limit for holding public office was ever enforced in Athens. Evidence that men were invited to volunteer as candidates is slight and less than cogent,[1] but the lexicographers' statement that the Athenians κληροῦσι τὰς ἀρχάς from the ληξιαρχικὰ γραμματεῖα[2] is not enough to prove that all eligible citizens were automatically regarded as candidates.

Not all citizens above the age limit were eligible: those who had stayed in Athens in 411 to perform military service under the Four Hundred were debarred,[3] while prostitution disqualified a man for every aspect of public life, including μηδὲ γνώμην εἰπάτω μηδέποτε μήτε ἐν τῇ βουλῇ μήτε ἐν τῷ δήμῳ.[4] In the first case membership of the boule is linked with speaking in the assembly, and in the second public offices in general are linked with speaking in the boule and assembly, so we may probably add to our list the other offences quoted by Aeschines from the δοκιμασία ῥητόρων:[5] maltreatment of parents; desertion from the army or throwing away one's shield; squandering one's inheritance. According to Dinarchus ῥήτορες and στρατηγοί were required to have legitimate children and to own land within the boundaries of Attica,[6] and this too may have been required of bouleutae. It should be assumed, though it is not stated in our ancient authorities, that membership was open to the first three property-classes—but νῦν ἐπειδὰν ἔρηται τὸν μέλλοντα κληροῦσθαί τιν' ἀρχήν, ποῖον τέλος τελεῖ, οὐδ' ἂν εἷς εἴποι θητικόν.[7] (We may wonder also how far the other requirements were normally enforced: the career of Timarchus suggests that a man without alert enemies might be able to ignore his

expected to serve as bouleutae after the age of sixty (*The Athenian Expounders of the Sacred and Ancestral Law*, 55–6), but his promised development of this point seems not to have appeared. Socrates, born in 469/8 (Apollod. and Dem. Phal. *ap.* D.L. II. 44) was a member in 406/5 (X. *H.* I. vii. 15, etc.). Notice also Plat. *Legg.* VI. 755 A 4–B 2.

[1] Lys. XXXI. *Phil.* 33, Harp., Suid., *E.M.* ἐπιλαχών; cf. (on ἀρχαί in general) [Lys.] VI. *And.* 4, Is. XV. *Antid.* 150.

[2] Phot., Suid. s.v.

[3] And. I. *Myst.* 75. Cavalry service under the Thirty was probably made another bar to membership: Lys. XXVI. *Evand.* 10.

[4] A. I. *Tim.* 19–20, cf. 29.

[5] A. I. *Tim.* 28–30; cf. the questions asked at the δοκιμασία of archons (cf. Ch. IV, p. 176). A. I. 28–30 must in its present form be a product of the post-404 democracy, but the grounds of disqualification look older. On the quasi-official standing of ῥήτορες in the fourth century, see S. Perlman, *Athen.*² xli 1963, esp. 353–4.

[6] Din. I. *Dem.* 71.

[7] *A.P.* 7. iv. There were of course periods after the death of Alexander when the poorer citizens were deprived of all political rights, including membership of the boule. D. J. Geagan suggests, *Hesp.* Supp. xii 1967, 76, that under the Roman Empire membership of the boule was restricted to those who had performed ephebic service, and in commenting on *SEG* xxi 509, *a* 6, 18 (pp. 86–7), he conjectures that only these men were entitled to speak in the assembly. At any rate ephebic service and membership of the boule came to form two normal elements in the Athenian *cursus honorum*, but J. H. Oliver (*Hesp.* xxx 1961, 402–3) thinks that the requirements for οἱ ἐκκλησιάζοντες κατὰ τὰ νομιζόμενα may have been less strict than for membership of the boule.

disqualifications.) Prospective bouleutae will have been interrogated on these points in their δοκιμασία, conducted by their predecessors in office.[1]

Most Athenian offices a man could hold only once in his life, but we are told that a man might serve twice in the boule:[2] up to seventeen men are thought to have served twice in the fourth century;[3] I have not systematically checked the later lists, but I am not aware that any one served more often before the second century A.D., when (for example) the name of Vibullius Theophilus appears in three different lists.[4] Permission to serve twice was probably a concession granted because of the difficulty of finding 500 fresh bouleutae each year, and suggests that competition for places in the boule cannot have been very great.[5] For the fifth century we have no evidence, but it is likely that before the Peloponnesian War the citizen population of Athens was larger than at any time during the fourth century,[6] so it should certainly have been possible to enforce the fourth century's rule, and for a while before 431 an absolute ban on repetition may have been feasible.[7] Several prominent politicians are known to have served as bouleutae, sometimes at least in such crucial years that they must surely have chosen to stand at that particular time, and must unless the processes of fate were tampered with have been lucky

---

[1] Cf. Ch. IV, pp. 176–8. Physical infirmity apparently disqualified a man from the archonship (Lys. XXIV. *Pens. Inv.* 13): this too may have applied to bouleutae.

[2] *A.P.* 62. ii.

[3] They are listed in Table B, pp. 242–3; for Demosthenes see below, p. 4 with n. 8.

[4] *IG* ii² 1772, 6 (162/3); 1773, 13 (166/7); *SEG* xxi 610, 13 (end C2); cf. Geagan, *Hesp.* Supp. xii 1967, 75 (but Raubitschek, Γέρας Κεραμοπούλλου, 244, writes as if the old rule still applied): Geagan also cites Heliodorus Ἀρτέμωνος Κυδαθηναῖος, in *Hesp.* xi 15 (*c.* 160); *IG* ii² 1773 (166/7); 1776 (169/70); and also 2478 (mid C2)—but the last, a fragment with 9 names and no demotic, may not belong to a list of prytanes. Autobulus Αὐτοσόφου Συπαλήτ- τιος appears in *IG* ii² 2375 (before mid C4 B.C.) as well as in the two lists mentioned under his name in Table B, p. 242, but this list with 4 Συπαλήττιοι is probably not a list of bouleutae. It is likely that the oligarchic regimes of the late fourth and early third centuries had to relax this rule: cf. Ferguson, *Hellenistic Athens*, 25–6.

[5] In the democratic constitution imposed on Erythrae perhaps in 453 a man might serve once in four years (M&L 40, 12)—but *pace* Kahrstedt (*U.M.A.*, 135–6) this need have no implications for practice in contemporary Athens.

[6] Gomme, *Population of Athens*, 26, and Ehrenberg, *The Greek State²*, 31, have estimated the numbers of adult male citizens as follows (Gomme's figures do not include men over 60):

	Gomme	Ehrenberg
c. 480	35,000	25,000–30,000
c. 432	43,000	35,000–45,000
c. 400	22,000	20,000–25,000
c. 360	—	28,000–30,000
323	28,000	—
313	21,000	21,000

[7] So Larsen, *Representative Government*, 10–11. But against the larger citizen population must be set the lack until about the middle of the fifth century (pp. 5–6, 13–14 below) of payment to compensate for loss of earnings and so to encourage the poorer citizens to serve: a total ban on repetition is thus likelier in the 430s than in the 490s.

either in the lot or in the absence of competition. Cleon was bouleutes in a year before 424:[1] it is an attractive possibility that the year was 427/6,[2] when after the production of the *Babylonians* Cleon denounced Aristophanes in the bouleuterium,[3] the year to whose beginning may probably be ascribed the debates on the fate of Mytilene.[4] Hyperbolus was already a well-known figure when he became a bouleutes,[5] for it is suggested in the comedian Plato's *Hyperbolus* that his ἐπιλαχών is bound to be appointed to the seat in his place,[6] but Cleon's death may have made an office which would keep Hyperbolus in the public eye particularly desirable at this time. In the fourth century Androtion served twice;[7] Demosthenes was a member in 347/6, when the Peace of Philocrates was made with Philip[8] (Philocrates himself seems not to have been a member that year); Demades, who played so important a part in easing Athens' relations with Macedon in the years after Chaeronea, is found in a bouleutic list for which 336/5 has been suggested as the most likely date;[9] and Lycurgus, vital to Athenian administration during the reign of Alexander, was a member in or before 329/8.[10] But, inevitably in a council whose membership changed every year, many bouleutae were men who made no mark: of the 248 members listed in *SEG* xix 149, no less than 13 bear names which had not previously been found in Attica.

This prompts us to ask in more general terms how far the boule was representative of the Athenian people. We shall see later in this chapter that appointment was by lot, at any rate from the middle of the fifth century, and that seats were allocated to the demes in proportion to their size. The boule could thus have contained a fair cross-section of the citizen body, and it was indeed described by one scholiast as μικρὰ πόλις.[11] Nevertheless scholars have claimed to detect in it an undue bias towards

---

[1] Ar. *Eq.* 774–6.

[2] Stated as a fact by Wilamowitz, *Aristoteles und Athen*, i. 129 n. 11.

[3] Ar. *Ach.* 379–81: it is not certain that Cleon did this as a bouleutes.

[4] Cf. the chronological tables in Henderson, *Great War*, 494, Gomme, *Hist. Comm. Thuc.*, iii. 718.

[5] In 421/0: *IG* i² 84, 5 with 44.

[6] Plat. Com., frs. 166–7 (Kock).

[7] 'Before 378/7': *IG* ii² 61, 6–7 (for possible years before and after 378/7 see D. M. Lewis, *BSA* xlix 1954, 34); and in or before 356/5: D. XXII. *Andr.* 38 (for 356/5, B. R. I. Sealey, *REG* lxviii 1955, 89–92, G. L. Cawkwell, *C&M* xxiii 1962, 50–5; for 359/8, D. M. Lewis, *BSA* xlix 1954, 43–4, cf. E. Schweigert, *Hesp.* viii 1939, 12–17).

[8] D. XIX. *F.L.* 154, 234, A. II. *F.L.* 17, etc., cf. S. Perlman, *Athen.*² xli 1963, 343. It has been supposed on the basis of A. III. *Ctes.* 160, Pl. *Dem.* 22. i that he served again in 337/6, but Kahrstedt (*U.M.A.*, 136 n. 3) has shown that the evidence is far from compelling.

[9] *SEG* xix 149, 144; cf. the original publication by S. Charitonides, *Hesp.* xxx 1961. I am not convinced by the arguments of J. A. O. Larsen, *CP* lvii 1962, for an earlier date.

[10] *IG* ii² 1672, 302 (cf. Ch. II, p. 63 with n. 3, and Ch. III, p. 108 n. 4).

[11] Schol. A. III. *Ctes.* 4.

the rich: the Finnish scholar Professor Sundwall, applying somewhat haphazard tests to the known bouleutae of the fourth century, thought that the very rich occupied almost twice as many places as their numbers entitled them to, and that the very rich and the 'propertied' together filled up to 425 places in a boule of 500.[1] More recently, Professor Larsen has written:

> It is still possible to argue . . . that the poorer members of the community did not serve on the council. The evidence is difficult to interpret, and all will not agree, but there seems some reason to believe that a disproportionally large number of men of property served in the council. . . . Yet the number of those available for service was not such that the tendency can have been excessively great.[2]

A certain amount of bias towards the rich must have been inevitable. As we shall see, pay for bouleutae can hardly have been introduced before the 450s; we do not know how generous the fifth-century rate was, but in the 320s the daily fee of 5 obols was less than the 1 or $1\frac{1}{2}$ drachmae paid for attendance at the assembly,[3] and less than even an unskilled man could earn in a day's work.[4] Active membership of the boule must have involved some financial sacrifice for most men, and it is likely enough that many poorer citizens will have been reluctant to abandon their normal occupation for a year. Clearly we cannot place much reliance on arguments from the retention in theory of a law that was not observed in practice, but the fact that in the full, self-conscious democracy thetes remained legally debarred from holding public offices suggests that there were not large numbers of poorer citizens who wanted to participate as actively as this in the running of the state. For the fifth century we have no usable evidence,[5] but a number of bouleutae are known from the fourth century, and in particular we have in *SEG* xix 149 a list naming 248 of the members for one year (probably 336/5). The institution of trierarchy enables us to apply a simple test. Periander's symmory law of 357[6] made the richest 1,200 citizens liable for trierarchic service; Demosthenes in 354

---

[1] J. Sundwall, *Epigraphische Beiträge*, ch. i.

[2] J. A. O. Larsen, *Representative Government*, 11.

[3] *A.P.* 62. ii. G. T. Griffith, in *Ancient Society and Institutions*, 123, notes that the bias towards the rich must have been considerable before the introduction of pay for members.

[4] In the accounts of the Eleusinian epistatae for 329/8 unskilled labourers are paid $1\frac{1}{2}$ drachmae a day, skilled 2 or $2\frac{1}{2}$ drachmae (*IG* ii² 1672, cf. Jones, 143–4 n. 86); in the Erechtheum accounts of 409–7 unskilled workers received 3 obols and skilled 1 drachma (*IG* i² 373–4, cf. Gomme, *Hist. Comm. Thuc.*, ii. 45).

[5] Most of the bouleutae of 405/4 were sufficiently congenial to the Thirty to be reappointed for 404/3 (Lys. XIII. *Ag.* 20), but what happened in the last years of the Peloponnesian War when the fleet was absent from Athens cannot be regarded as typical.

[6] [D.] XLVII. *Ev. et Mnes.* 21.

contemplated extending the list to 2,000,[1] but in fact in 340 reduced it to 300;[2] before 340 trierarchs were roughly the richest 4 per cent of the citizens; after 340, the richest 1 per cent. If this list of half a boule is representative of the demos, we should expect it to contain about ten men who were liable for trierarchic service under Periander's law, two or three of whom would still be liable under Demosthenes' law. Our knowledge of Athenian trierarchs is of course very far from complete, but even so five of the men in this list are perhaps to be identified with known trierarchs,[3] and four to six others belong to families known to have supplied one or more trierarchs between 360 and 320.[4] Fortunes fluctuate, and are not evenly distributed in all branches of a family, but it seems likely that if we were more fully informed we should find men with trierarchic fortunes represented in more than their due proportion. At the other extreme, thirteen of the 248 bear names not otherwise found in Attica:[5] obscurity need not mean poverty,[6] but at least we are shown that the boule contained men who were inactive enough to leave no other trace of their existence.

We must turn now from the members of the boule to the mechanism by which they were appointed. Immediately before the revolution of 411 appointment was by lot, and this seems to have been regarded as an essential characteristic of a democratic boule, since both Thucydides and the *Athenaion Politeia* stress that the council expelled by the Four Hundred was εἰληχυῖαν τῷ κυάμῳ.[7] The successor to this council is said to have been appointed in a three-stage co-optation,[8] though the oligarchs may perhaps have intended that if their regime lasted the boule should in future be chosen or allotted from πρόκριτοι elected by tribesmen, with forty members from each Cleisthenic tribe.[9] Alcibiades on Samos was prepared

---

[1] D. XIV. *Symm.* 16.

[2] A. III. *Ctes.* 222, Hyp. fr. 134 (Kenyon), Din. I. *Dem.* 42.

[3] On all these bouleutae, see Charitonides' notes in *Hesp.* xxx 1961. I have also consulted J. K. Davies, *Athenian Propertied Families*, and bracket here and in the following footnote the three bouleutae whom he does not include in his Register. Trierarchs under Periander's law: Callias (*SEG* xix 149, 113), Philocrates (281) (discharges a trierarchic debt for someone else, *IG* ii² 1622, 247). Trierarchs under Demosthenes' law: Anytus (3), [Pythodorus (76)], Demades (144) (συντελής).

[4] Related to trierarchs under Periander's law: [Pythiades (14)], [Leontius (36)]. Related to trierarchs under Demosthenes' law: Athemion (7), Cleon (74), Timotheus (289), Autoclides (307).

[5] Homophron (9), Pythiades (14), Blepes (33), Blepsias (140), Midocrates (164), Damias (230), Eubiodemus (232), Onesion (256), Dipolis (260), Epagrus (274), Ergomeles (275), Euchirides (295), Calliphemus (315).

[6] Note that Pythiades (14) may come from a trierarchic family.

[7] T. viii. 69. iv, *A.P.* 32. i.   [8] T. viii. 67. iii.

[9] *A.P.* 31. i. I imagine that *A.P.* 31 is a regularization of the Four Hundred's position for future use; *A.P.* 30 is a promise made to appease those who were unhappy about the extreme

to accept the restriction of the franchise to 5,000, but ἐκέλευεν αὐτοὺς . . . καθιστάναι τὴν βουλὴν ὥσπερ καὶ πρότερον, τοὺς πεντακοσίους.[1] We may assume that a boule of 500 was appointed after the fall of the Four Hundred, but this may have been elective.[2] If this is correct, sortition will have been restored with the full democracy in 410,[3] and after the rule of the Thirty[4] it continued during the fourth century;[5] election probably returned during the later oligarchic interludes, but sortition is mentioned again in 256/5.[6] There is no direct evidence for the method of appointment before 412, or for any change of method, but since the archonship was elective in the time of Cleisthenes and sortition was introduced or reintroduced in 487/6[7] the possibility that Cleisthenes' bouleutae were elected ought not to be ruled out. But the introduction of the lot can hardly be later than the 450s.[8]

There is evidence from the late fifth and the fourth centuries that, at the same time as the bouleutae were appointed, ἐπιλαχόντες, or deputies, were appointed also, so that a man would be available to take the place of a member who died or was rejected in the δοκιμασία.[9] The comedian Plato's remark that the man who is ἐπιλαχών to Hyperbolus is bound to gain admission to the boule suggests that each ἐπιλαχών was made understudy to a particular member. A year as ἐπιλαχών should not have counted against the two years' actual membership which a man was allowed (unless he was called on to fill a vacancy), but all ἐπιλαχόντες must presumably have been eligible for actual membership, and if each member had his own understudy the Athenians will have needed to find a thousand eligible men each year. Yet it is probably because of the difficulty in finding bouleutae that men were allowed to serve twice in their lives, and we shall see shortly that even under this rule some small

oligarchy, a promise which few of the oligarchs intended to keep (i.e. an authentic document published by the Four Hundred but not a genuine statement of intent). I hope to discuss the revolutions of 411 more fully elsewhere.

[1] T. VIII. 86. vi.

[2] Hignett, 372, cf. 378, on And. I. Myst. 96. Cf. G. E. M. de Ste Croix, Hist. v 1956, 22.

[3] And. I. Myst. 96–8, with M&L 84; cf. B. D. Meritt, Athenian Financial Documents, 106–9.

[4] Who appointed congenial men as bouleutae: cf. X. H. II. iii. 2, 11 (quoted pp. 29–30), and Lys. XIII. Ag. 20.

[5] A.P. 43. ii, [D.] LIX. Neaer. 3, A. III. Ctes. 62.   [6] IG ii² 514, 5–6, 678, 11.

[7] A.P. 22. v. This is not the place for a discussion of the problems (see, most recently, N. G. L. Hammond, CQ² xix 1969), but I see no reason to doubt that election played some part in the appointment of archons before 487/6.

[8] We can safely argue (with Larsen, Representative Government, 9) from this clause in the decree for Erythrae, M&L 40, 8–9. G. T. Griffith, Ancient Society and Institutions, 123, regards appointment by lot as Cleisthenic.

[9] Harp., Suid., E.M. ἐπιλαχών, L.S. 256. 3, Schol. Ar. Thesm. 808–9 = Plat. Com., frs. 166–7 (Kock), A. III. Ctes. 62 with schol. citing Plat. Com.; perhaps cf. [D.] LVIII. Theocr. 29.

demes may occasionally have been unable to return a member.[1] We are entitled, I think, to wonder how regularly ἐπιλαχόντες were appointed and how numerous they were: perhaps they were appointed whenever there happened to be more candidates than seats, and one man may have been regarded as deputy to all members from his deme, or from a group of demes.

There is one aspect of appointment to the boule on which the American excavations in the Agora have greatly added to our store of information. We have a large number of inscribed lists of πρυτάνεις (one tribe's contingent of bouleutae), and also some lists of bouleutae from more than one tribe. In these lists the members are not merely given their demotics but are grouped by demes,[2] and in the early part of the boule's existence the numbers of bouleutae from the different demes show a considerable degree of consistency. Apart from a late fifth-century dedication by the prytanes of Erechtheis,[3] our evidence begins with lists set up by the prytany which had won the annual prize offered by the demos, early in the fourth century. These monuments gradually give way to decrees honouring a prytany and its officials (more than one prytany may now be honoured in the year), to which a list of members is appended: documents of this kind are found from the third to the first century. From about the time of Sulla these in turn give way to lists of prytanes and officials inscribed on a statue base.[4]

For the tribe Erechtheis,[5] in addition to the fifth-century dedication that I have mentioned, we have four fourth-century lists of the ten-tribe period, two of them more or less complete.[6] No changes in representation are apparent from these four lists, except that the small demes Παμβω-τάδαι and Συβρίδαι may have taken it in turns not to be represented.[7] From the end of the fourth century various changes will have been needed

---

[1] Cf. p. 11.

[2] For the few exceptions to this rule cf. p. 12 and nn. 1–2 below. In the fourth century the allocation of seats in the boule to demes is confirmed by A.P. 62. i.   [3] DAA 167.

[4] On the different kinds of prytany-inscription cf. S. Dow, Hesp. Supp. i 1937, 1–29.

[5] In working on this topic I compiled tables showing the deme-representation in all lists published to the end of 1967 and a few unpublished lists seen by Dr. D. M. Lewis which are or may be lists of bouleutae. These tables appear in the second volume of my D.Phil. thesis, a copy of which has been deposited in the Bodleian Library, Oxford; a forthcoming work by Dr. J. S. Traill, which will tabulate all the evidence now available, makes their inclusion here unnecessary. In these notes I shall therefore cite the most important texts only. Dr. Traill has read what I have written on the subject of deme-representation, and has enabled me to bring my observations up to date: I am very grateful for his co-operation.

[6] (Figures are based on texts known to me; Traill tells me that other fragments, not yet published, do not alter the general picture.) Hesp. xxxvi 34 (381/0), Hesp. xi 43 (367/6: complete), SEG xix 149 (?336/5: complete), IG ii² 1700 (335/4).

[7] There are noticeable differences between these and our one fifth-century list.

as the boule was enlarged or reduced to admit or exclude new tribes: Erechtheis lost three half-demes to Antigonis in 307/6 (and recovered two in 201/0), one deme to Ptolemais in 224/3, and one to Hadrianis in A.D. 126/7 (when the size of prytanies was reduced from 50 to about 40). A coherent pattern can still be made out in the third century B.C.; after that our evidence is slight, but the system seems to be breaking down.

For Aegeis there are five relevant documents from the ten-tribe period, and each of the two complete lists seems to have contained only 49 members.[1] In this tribe there are some changes in representation to note: about 350 there were two $Bατεεῖς$, four or more $Φηγαιεῖς$, two ʼ$Ιωνίδαι$, and one $Κυδαντίδης$; in our later lists representation of the first three was reduced to one, three and one, but the number of $Κυδαντίδαι$ was increased to two. In 341/0 there were six ʼ$Ερχιεῖς$, but in 336/5 we find six names and space for a seventh. We have one substantial list and two more fragmentary from the period of the Macedonian tribes,[2] differing inevitably from the earlier lists but not to a greater extent than the loss of some demes will justify; but fragments from the second century A.D. reveal no system at all.

Pandionis provides no less than eight documents earlier than 307/6, four of them complete lists.[3] In them we see $Κυδαθηναιεῖς$ move down from twelve representatives to eleven and then up again to twelve; $Ἀγγελῆθεν$ from three to two, and perhaps later up to three again; $Μυρρινούσιοι$ from seven down to six, and even to five; $Κυθήρριοι$ rise from no representatives, or perhaps one, to two; and possibly $Προβαλίσιοι$ from four to five. For our next complete list we have to wait until the middle of the second century, where we have a list not very different from those of the fourth century;[4] but a list published early in the reign of Augustus is markedly different from the earlier ones,[5] and thereafter there is no real system, though the lists of A.D. 166/7 and 169/70 are very similar.[6]

For Leontis we have five documents of the ten-tribe period, and of the two complete lists one again has only 49 names:[7] the blank space in this

[1] IG ii² 1747 (c. 350), 1749 (341/0: complete list of 49), SEG xix 149 (?336/5: complete list of 49+1 vacat), IG ii² 1700 (335/4), SEG xxi 520 (331/0 or 330/29).

[2] SEG xxiii 86 (304/3), P 10 (256/5: substantial), SEG xxi 595 (after mid C3).

[3] IG ii² 1740 (early C4: complete), SEG xxiii 87 (first qr. C4: complete), IG ii² 2370 (before mid C4), 1751 (after mid C4: complete), 1748 (348/7), SEG xix 149 (?336/5: complete), IG ii² 1700 (335/4), SEG xxiii 89 (before 307/6: so Gomme, Population of Athens, 51–2 n. 2, 58, misreported as 'after 307/6' by D. M. Lewis, BSA l 1955, 19 with n. 20).

[4] P 84 (155/4).   [5] P 116 (c. 20).   [6] IG ii² 1773, 1776.

[7] IG ii² 1742 (?370/69: so B. D. Meritt, Hesp. xvi 1947, 151: complete), 1744 (before mid C4), 1752 (after mid C4), SEG xix 149 (?336/5: complete list of 49+1 vacat), IG ii² 1700 (335/4).

list for the ninth Φρεάρριος is the only anomaly. In the next century, for which we have two complete lists and three smaller fragments, reasonable consistency seems to have been maintained,[1] and a list of about 160 suggests that the principle of deme-representation had not yet broken down entirely.[2]

Acamantis has left us a number of small fragments, but not much substantial information. One list, perhaps to be assigned to the end of the fourth century, seems to have contained no representatives of several small demes, and an unusually large number from some of the others.[3] The lack of system in the second century A.D. is shown by two full lists of consecutive years, 167/8 and 168/9, which are very different in composition.[4]

Little apart from fragments has survived from Oeneis, and we have only one complete list, in which the large deme Ἀχαρνεῖς accounts for 22 of the 50 members.[5] The representation of various demes seems to have changed about the middle of the fourth century.

Records for Cecropis are again numerous but fragmentary, and again there is only one complete list, this time of the second century A.D.[6] Nothing can fairly be noted apart from fluctuations in the number of Συπαλήττιοι.

For Hippothontis we are no better served in the fourth century, though it is clear even from the small fragments which survive that there were changes during the century. Fragments from the period of the Macedonian tribes show reasonable consistency, but in the second century three complete lists and a substantial fragment show considerable discrepancies.[7]

Aiantis began with only six well-attested demes, and lost one each to Ptolemais, Attalis, and Hadrianis. Epigraphic remains are poor, but though there was little scope for variation it is surprising to find two apparently identical lists as late as the first century B.C.[8]

In Antiochis, there were six Παλληνεῖς and two Εἰτεαῖοι in 335/4, seven Παλληνεῖς and one Εἰτεαῖος a year later.[9] As in other tribes there

---

[1] SEG xxiii 86 (304/3), Hesp. xxxvii 1968, 1–24 (303/2), Hesp. ix 22 (mid C3: complete), P 26 (c. 240–230), P 36 with Hesp. ix 1940, 78 (212/11 : 47+3 vacant).

[2] P 77 (complete).

[3] P 1 (after 307/6: so J. S. Traill, Hesp. xxxv 1966, 231; but see below, p. 11 n. 3).

[4] IG ii² 1774, 1775 (both complete).

[5] IG ii² 1745 (360/59).

[6] IG ii² 1782 (A.D. 177/8).

[7] P 64 (178/7: complete), Hesp. ix 24 (176–169), 25 (165/4–150: complete list of 49), SEG xii 101 (135/4).

[8] P 98 (before 60), 102 (c. 50).

[9] IG ii² 1700 (335/4), 1750 (334/3: complete).

is reasonable consistency in the third century, a breakdown in the second century, and no system at all under the Roman Empire.

Little survives from the five post-Cleisthenic tribes, but what information we have fits the pattern that has already emerged. In the fourth and third centuries, the figures are consistent enough to suggest that representation in the boule was organized on the basis not simply of tribes but of demes, and that the demes were given seats in proportion to their size—measured most easily by the numbers of citizens on their registers.[1] If there were general redistributions of seats based on up-to-date population figures, some tribes must have survived some redistributions without change (which is of course by no means unlikely); but some of the variations may represent more or less private arrangements made if a small deme was unable to fill all its seats:[2] in particular the non-representation of various demes of Acamantis in *P* 1 may have to be explained in this way.[3] Recently discovered inscriptions have made it clear that a tribe might on occasion have fewer than fifty members, though *DAA* 167[4] and *P* 36, with *Hesp.* ix 1940, 78,[5] are our only instances of a list with more than one vacancy. The difficulty experienced by small demes is reflected also in the practice of making some share a seat (Παμβωτάδαι and Συβρίδαι in Erechtheis; perhaps Τυρμεῖδαι and Ἱπποτομάδαι in Oeneis).[6] Such difficulties will have increased in the Hellenistic period, when more bouleutae had to be found (though the bouleuterium, which could with difficulty hold 500 members, was never enlarged[7]) and Athens' reduced political significance must have made membership less attractive: this no doubt is largely responsible for the breakdown of the representational system which is apparent in the second century, and for the lifting of the restriction on repeated terms of office by the second century A.D.; it may also have been one reason for the reduction of the boule to not far above its

---

[1] Totals of demesmen, adapted from the lists in *Prosopographia Attica*, were given by Gomme with the tables in his *Population of Athens*, 55–66. Revised totals will be given in Traill's forthcoming book.

[2] So Larsen, *Representative Government*, 8. The possibility of general redistributions, both for the fourth century and for the third, is rejected by S. Dow, *TAPA* xcii 1961, 71–2.

[3] *P* 1 used to be dated 327/6, with the famine from which Athens suffered invoked to explain the non-representation of some small demes. In *Hesp.* xxxv 1966, 231, Traill dated the list after 307/6: he tells me that he now ascribes it to 305/4 and believes that it contained no abnormalities. See the cautionary note of S. Charitonides, *Hesp.* xxx 1961, 36 n. 10.

[4] (Erechtheis, 408/7.) Here it seems that the demotics were inscribed on a pattern that would leave room for 50 members, and the names of some but not all of the prytanes were added under their demes. Raubitschek writes (*DAA*, p. 190): 'It must have been an intentional act on the part of these prytaneis whose names are omitted, to cancel their participation in the common dedication'; but the mystery remains.

[5] (Leontis, 212/11.) Under Κρωπίδαι we have one member and three vacancies.

[6] So Schoeffer, *RE*, v. 9, 28, s.v. δῆμοι.

[7] Cf. p. 31 and n. 1 below.

Cleisthenic total of 500. Yet in all but a very few late lists members continue to be grouped by demes,[1] and in half of the exceptions they are still given their demotics:[2] while this could be merely a matter of habit or fiction, it is possible that the demes were always involved in some way in appointments to the boule.

For the fifth century we have no evidence except *DAA* 167, which for all its difficulties does at least show that bouleutae could be grouped by demes before the regime of the Thirty. It is natural to suppose that Cleisthenes, who created the demes as political entities no less than the ten tribes, was responsible for this principle of deme-representation; and though it is dangerous to suppose that anything which fits our idea of Cleisthenes' policy must be the work of Cleisthenes there is no reason in this case to deny Cleisthenic authorship. As I have already remarked, though sortition had become established as an important principle before the end of the fifth century, it is possible that the demes originally elected their representatives.

Having secured appointment, the prospective bouleutae had to undergo a δοκιμασία, conducted certainly when the *Athenaion Politeia* was written and probably at all other times by their predecessors in office.[3] Presumably they were required to satisfy their examiners that they were citizens over 30 years old, and were not disqualified from membership on any of the grounds which I mention on pages 2–3 above: in effect they will have had to demonstrate fairly generally that they were satisfactory citizens, and intangible considerations of loyalty and thinking the right thoughts may have counted for more than the legal requirements.[4] When their appointment had been confirmed the new members took an

---

[1] In the following lists members are given their demotics but are not grouped by demes (all dates here and in the following footnote are A.D.):

PANDIONIS	*IG* ii² 1826	222/3
OENEIS	1803	215–20
HIPPOTHONTIS	1808	170–6
	1819	c. 200
PTOLEMAIS	*Hesp.* xi 25	180–92

[2] In the following lists members are not given their demotics:

ANTIOCHIS	*IG* ii² 1817	c. 220
ATTALIS	1824	221/2
	1825	222/3
	1827	223/4?
	1828	224/5
HADRIANIS	1832	231/2

[3] For δοκιμασίαι conducted by the boule, cf. Ch. IV, pp. 171–8. Notice in particular the questions asked at the archons' δοκιμασία, p. 176.

[4] Notice the arguments employed in Lys. XVI. *Mant.* (N.B. § 9), XXXI. *Phil.*

oath of loyalty to the state,[1] and the bouleutic year began with inaugural sacrifices, εἰσιτητήρια, of which we know scarcely more than that they were performed as usual by the Four Hundred when they entered office late in 412/11.[2]

Bouleutae, like other ἄρχοντες, wore a myrtle crown as a badge of office,[3] and were entitled to seats of honour in the theatre.[4] Though they were not required to remain in Athens during their year of office,[5] they were exempted from military service.[6] By 412/11 members were paid for their service in the boule: in that year the democratic boule, which still had nearly a month to serve, was given its salary up to the end of the bouleutic year, so that the Four Hundred could take over the running of the state.[7] When the *Athenaion Politeia* was written bouleutae were paid 5 obols a day,[8] with an extra obol as subsistence allowance for members of the tribe in prytany[9] and conceivably a larger allowance for the ἐπιστάτης of the day.[10] At this time the payment for attendance at the assembly was 1 or 1½ drachmae (lower rates having been introduced in the 390s),[11] and jurors were still receiving the 3 obols paid a hundred years earlier.[12] It is at any rate possible that the original rate of payment to bouleutae was lower than that of the 320s. Bouleutic pay was presumably instituted in the time of Pericles' supremacy:[13] his introduction of jury pay seems to have been the first instance of δημοσία τροφή,[14] and it

---

[1] For the content of the oath at different times see the appendix to Ch. IV, pp. 190–9.

[2] T. viii. 70. i; cf. also D. XIX. *F.L.* 190, XXI. *Mid.* 114.

[3] Lyc. *Leocr.* 122 (other ἀρχαί: Lys. XXVI. *Evand.* 8, D. XXI. *Mid.* 32–3, 54, *XXVI. *Aristog. ii.* 5).

[4] Ar. *Av.* 794 with schol., Hes. βουλευτικόν, Suid. βουλευτικός, Poll. iv. 122 (this last passage is oddly explained by W. A. McDonald, *Political Meeting-Places of the Greeks*, 147). For tokens which could have been used in this connection see M. Crosby, *Tokens*, 79–80, 112–13.

[5] Demosthenes in his year of office served on the first and second embassies to Philip of Macedon (A. II. *F.L.* 18–20, 94, D. XIX. *F.L.* 12–13, 154–5, etc.); in 411 the Four Hundred, who began by threatening fines for non-attendance ('future constitution' in *A.P.* 30. vi, cf. 'Draco' in *A.P.* 4. iii), found it convenient to grant leave of absence to their less enthusiastic members (cf. Lys. XX. *Poly.* 14, 16).

[6] Lyc. *Leocr.* 37.   [7] T. viii. 69. iv.

[8] Presumably this was payment for attendance, not an automatic daily grant.

[9] *A.P.* 62. ii.

[10] Foucart's restoration (*RPh*² xlii 1918) of a corrupt passage in *A.P.* 62. ii has won little favour, and does not seem very likely (cf. p. 24 below).

[11] *A.P.* 41. iii with Ar. *Eccl.* 184 sqq., etc.

[12] *A.P.* 61. ii with Ar. *Eq.* 797–800, etc. The view that Cleon had raised the fee from 2 obols rests on the emphasis given by Aristophanes to the τριώβολον and an emended version of schol. Ar. *Vesp.* 88.

[13] G. T. Griffith, *Ancient Society and Institutions*, 125, dates the introduction of bouleutic pay not long after 462.

[14] It is assumed that this is why jury pay was taken to be symbolic of the ἔμμισθος πόλις, as in *A.P.* 27. iii–iv. (On the date when jury pay was introduced, see H. T. Wade-Gery, *AJP* lix 1938, 131–4 = *E.G.H.*, 235–8, reaffirmed in *E.G.H.*, 197; Hignett, 342–3.)

should not have been necessary to introduce a salary in war time for an office which conferred exemption from military service on the holder.

In the Hellenistic and Roman periods rich officials were expected to contribute to the expenses of their office, and the poorer bouleutae no doubt counted on having rich colleagues who were prepared to bear the cost of the corporate sacrifices,[1] but against this we may set some special endowments from which the bouleutae benefited. About A.D. 120 Claudius Atticus and his wife established a special fund for bouleutae of their own tribe, presumably to subsidize the activities of the prytany,[2] and later they made similar endowments for other tribes;[3] on their death, however, these endowments were recovered by their son Herodes,[4] and from A.D. 138 we find individual tribes appointing a rich member to be their ἐπώνυμος, or patron.[5] In some later documents Athena Polias is linked with the human patron,[6] and it is assumed that a grant was made to the prytany from the Treasury of Athena. Another fund was endowed about A.D. 135–40 by a Cretan, Flavius Zenophilus, to provide gifts for bouleutae at some major festival, perhaps the Eleusinian Mysteries; we possess a decree of the Areopagus, of about 165, providing for the reinvestment of the accrued surplus and for additions to the list of recipients, among them Flavius' son Xenon.[7] Somewhat earlier, we have four decrees from the middle of the second century B.C. which reveal that the boule was given a καθέσιμον, or attendance fee, by the ἀγωνοθέτης of the Thesea:[8] presumably this payment was needed to secure the members' attendance at the festival.

Individual members who distinguished themselves in office were sometimes rewarded;[9] and at the end of the year the whole boule like any

---

[1] Cf. S. Dow, *Hesp.* Supp. i 1937, 14–15, on the treasurer of the prytanes. There might be other liabilities too: the second-century A.D. regulations of the Iobacchi make membership of the boule one of many offices for which, if he was appointed to it, a member of the guild was required to offer a worthy σπονδή (*IG* ii² 1368, 131).

We learn from Cassius Dio (LXIX. 16. ii) that under a law of Hadrian bouleutae were forbidden to engage in tax-farming.

[2] *P* 121, 12–15, with J. H. Oliver, *AJP* lxx 1949, 302.

[3] Cf. *IG* ii² 3597.

[4] Cf. Fronto, *Ad M. Caes.* iii. 3 (= i. 64, Haines).

[5] J. H. Oliver, *Hesp.* xi 1942, 30, cf. *AJP* lxx 1949, A. E. Raubitschek, Γέρας Κεραμοπούλλου, 242–55, D. J. Geagan, *Hesp.* Supp. xii 1967, 98–100. *Hesp.* xxxii 1963, 73–4, inscription I, *may* commemorate special help given by Hadrian.

[6] e.g. *IG* ii² 1817.

[7] *SEG* xii 95 with J. H. Oliver, *Hesp.* xxi 1952, 381–99.

[8] *IG* ii² 956, 14, with commentary; 957, 9; 958, 12; 959, 11.

[9] Towards the end of 343/2 the boule honoured its best speaker and invited the demos to join in the honours (*IG* ii² 223 A); in 290/89 the demos crowned the three best bouleutae of the year (*IG* ii² 2797); and about the same time the boule was honoured by one of its members (*SEG* xxi 360).

individual ἄρχων was subjected to a process of εὔθυναι,[1] and if it was found to have discharged its duties satisfactorily it was entitled to a δωρεά,[2] which seems to have taken the form of a gold crown.[3] Professor Kahrstedt rejected this view and tried to distinguish between a legally prescribed δωρεά, in the form of a cash donation for a sacrifice or dinner, and a merely customary crown.[4] However his argument that crowns were not legally provided for runs into difficulties with ὁ νόμος κελεύει in IG ii² 415, 28; and since the word δωρεά certainly could be used of a crown[5] as well as of various other honorific awards[6] it seems perverse to force a distinction between crown and δωρεά here.

When Androtion proposed that the boule in which he had served his second term[7] should receive the usual δωρεά, it was customary for the retiring boule to ask for its reward by putting the question on the assembly's agenda late in its own year of office.[8] The prosecution of Androtion by Euctemon and Diodorus seems to have had little immediate effect on this practice: the boule of 343/2 was certainly crowned in its year of office for successful management of the Dionysia,[9] and it may also have received the general award for satisfactory conduct before the end of the year.[10] But in the 330s there was further trouble over the award of a crown to an official who was still ὑπεύθυνος, when Aeschines prosecuted Ctesiphon for his proposal to crown Demosthenes. For individuals, Aeschines claims, there used at one time to be no restriction on ἔπαινοι and κηρύγματα, but when it was found that such votes of thanks were prejudicing the euthynae a law was passed διαρρήδην ἀπαγορεύοντα τοὺς ὑπευθύνους μὴ στεφανοῦν. A way round this provision was soon discovered: the proposer of an award had only to add the clause ἐπειδὰν λόγον καὶ εὐθύνας τῆς ἀρχῆς δῷ—but Ctesiphon had been careless enough to omit the saving clause and thus openly to break the law.[11] Inscriptions provide

---

[1] A. III. Ctes. 20, cf. And. II. Red. 19. In addition to this corporate responsibility of the boule, individual members could be attacked within a year in the γραφαὶ παρανόμων and νόμον μὴ ἐπιτήδειον θεῖναι for measures which they had proposed, even if their proposals were adopted by the boule and demos ([D.] LIX. Neaer. 4–5, etc., cf. Ch. II, pp. 62–3); and prytanes or proedri who had put an illegal or inexpedient motion to the vote could be prosecuted for that (cf. pp. 22–3, 27 below).

[2] It was laid down in particular that the boule was not entitled to this δωρεά unless it had built new triremes as required (A.P. 46. i: for the shipbuilding requirement cf. Ch. III, pp. 115–16).

[3] This is the natural inference from A. I. Tim. 111–12, D. XXII. Andr. 36, 38–9.

[4] Kahrstedt, S.S.A., 330.   [5] IG ii² 223 B, 13–14.

[6] e.g. IG ii² 672, 13–15; D. XXIII. Arist. 23, 89.

[7] D. XXII. Andr. 38. For the date see above, p. 4 n. 7.

[8] Ibid. 8.   [9] IG ii² 223 B, 5–6, 7–8.

[10] Cf. IG ii² 223 A, 1–3 (but this may be another reference to the crown awarded for the Dionysia).

[11] A. III. Ctes. 9–12.

us with a cluster of these saving clauses from the late 340s to the early 320s, all for awards to individuals,[1] and the clause then disappears apart from two instances in the third century.[2]

The prosecution of Ctesiphon, unsuccessful as it was, may well have resulted in a tightening of the law governing δωρεαί to individuals, but it is not clear how far we can argue from these awards to the δωρεά of the boule. When the *Athenaion Politeia* was written, the boule's crown had to be voted after its year of office was over,[3] so by the 320s the practice of the 350s had been abolished. In 343/2 the boule's crown for the Dionysia was voted immediately and without reference to euthynae, but we are not given the text of the decree conferring the boule's regular crown. It is tempting though perhaps fanciful to suppose that the honours with the saving clause resulted from an enactment after Androtion's proposal to crown the boule (it must be admitted that it is hard to find adequate grounds for exempting the boule's crown for the Dionysia from the general rule) and that more stringent precautions were introduced about 327.

(ii) *Subdivisions of the Boule*

A council of 500 was large enough to be unwieldy, and a standing committee was therefore instituted, comprising for one-tenth of the year at a time (later, one-twelfth, etc.) the fifty members from a single tribe. These were the πρυτάνεις, or 'presidents'.[4] During their prytany they lived and ate with the state secretaries in the θόλος or σκιάς, a circular building adjacent to the bouleuterium on the west side of the Agora.[5]

---

[1] The index in *IG* ii² IV. i, p. 51. i, s.vv. εὐθύνας δοῦναι, lists *IG* ii² 223 A, 13; B, 13; C, 13 (343/2); 330, 42 (336/5); 338, 18 (333/2); 410, 22 (*c.* 330); 415, 27 (*c.* 330/29); 354, 21 (328/7); and I can add Ἀρχ. Ἐφ. 1917, pp. 40–8, no. 92, 33–5 (328/7). There is a fifth-century example in *IG* i² 46, 19, but here it appears that officials concerned with the foundation of a colony were not to sail there until they had passed their euthynae in Athens.

[2] *IG* ii² 672, 35 (280/79); 780, 20 (252/1). Hellenistic prytanes were regularly honoured while still bouleutae and even, if theirs was the last prytany of the year, while still prytanes (cf. S. Dow, *Hesp.* Supp. i 1937, 7–8).   [3] *A.P.* 46. i.

[4] *A.P.* 43. ii, cf. lexica and scholia s.v. In the earliest passages cited by LSJ a πρύτανις seems to be a 'ruler' or 'chief'.

[5] On the Tholos and neighbouring buildings in general see pp. 30–5 below, and on the date of the Tholos and the possible implications of this see pp. 18–19.

The Tholos and its immediate surroundings are probably to be identified with the πρυτανικόν, where decrees honouring prytanes were regularly published in the third and second centuries (cf. E. Vanderpool, *Hesp.* iv 1935, R. E. Wycherley, *Testimonia*, p. 184). It should not be confused—as it frequently was by lexicographers and scholiasts—with the πρυτανεῖον, or town hall, where those whom the city wished to honour were entertained (cf. D. Levi, *ASAA* vi–vii 1923–4, S. Dow, *Hesp.* Supp. i 1937, 22–4, Wycherley, *Testimonia*, p. 166): it will be seen from pp. 17–19 that I am not prepared to accept Mr. MacDowell's compromise suggestion that the prytaneum was the original headquarters of the prytanes (commentary on And. I. *Myst.*, p. 69).

In addition to their bouleutic stipend of 5 obols a day (in the time of the *Athenaion Politeia*) they drew a one-obol subsistence allowance.[1]

This division of the boule into prytanies would help to ensure that Cleisthenes' ten new tribes played an important part in public life, and it is normally assumed that the division was his work. But we have very little evidence for the activities of the boule in the half-century after Cleisthenes' reforms, and I hope to suggest that until further changes were made in the constitution by Ephialtes its duties were limited to προβούλευσις, the preparation of business for the ecclesia. If this is so, Cleisthenes' boule will not by later standards have been busy, and a division into prytanies may not yet have been found necessary. Certainly there is no undisputed evidence that prytanies existed before Ephialtes.[2] Plutarch reports that the decree under which Miltiades led out the Athenians to Marathon was enacted in the prytany of Aiantis;[3] but it is possible that the text which Plutarch saw or read about, or at any rate this detail in it, was a fourth-century forgery.[4] In the Hecatompedon Inscription of 485/4 an official called ὁ πρύτανις is empowered to impose fines;[5] but members of prytanies in the boule are not known to have had this power. Of the inscribed Attic decrees whose prescript includes a mention of the tribe in prytany none is certainly earlier than the 450s, though Professor Wade-Gery has tried to locate the Phaselis Decree in the early 460s.[6]

[1] *A.P.* 62. ii; cf. p. 13 above.

[2] G. T. Griffith, *Ancient Society and Institutions*, 123, mentions the absence of early evidence for the epistates of the prytanes, but nevertheless thinks that the office, with at any rate the duty of presiding in the boule, was created by Cleisthenes.

[3] Pl. *Quaest. Conv.* 628 E–F.

[4] The decree of Miltiades is one of several documents purporting to be of the early fifth century of which texts seem to have become current in Athens about the middle of the fourth century (cf. C. Habicht, *Hermes* lxxxix 1961; on this decree, pp. 17, 20). It may be doubted whether a text of this kind (ordering immediate action on a single occasion), antedating Xerxes' sack of Athens, is likely to have survived; it is certain that if such a text did survive a later generation of Athenians would have been capable of adding such details as the tribe in prytany, in the interests of supposed verisimilitude (cf. the decree of Themistocles, M&L 23, whose staunchest champions must admit the overwhelming probability that Themistocles' patronymic and demotic have been added in this way: cf. M&L, p. 50). Professor Habicht makes the 'anachronistic' mention of the prytany his chief reason for condemning the text which Plutarch knew, thus begging the question which I am asking; the fairest comment is perhaps that of Macan (*Herodotus, IV–VI*, vol. ii, p. 219, cf. Hignett, *Xerxes' Invasion of Greece*, 14): 'It may be granted more probable that such a psephism was passed than that Miltiades was the mover, more probable that Miltiades was the mover than that the Aiantis was in office.'

[5] *IG* i² 4, 21–5.

[6] *E.G.H.*, 180–200, on M&L 31. I explain my reasons for doubt in Ch. IV, p. 204 n. 1. If this inscription can be dated *c.* 450 the earliest epigraphic reference to prytanes may be M&L 37 (458/7?) or HMA 21 (*c.* 457?). Another possible piece of evidence for prytanes before 462 is the 'Xanthippus Ostracon' as interpreted by A. Wilhelm, *Anz. Wien* lxxxvi 1949, but his explanation seems a little too ingenious to be credible. For other attempts to

Closer study of the Hecatompedon Inscription provides further reasons for doubt: the decrees are dated simply to an archon-year,[1] whereas later it was normal to date by the bouleutic calendar;[2] and they order the Treasurers of Athena, whose duties were later regulated by the bouleutic calendar, to check the contents of the Hecatompedon three times a month.[3] The special meeting of the demos in the Agora to hold an ostracism was presided over not by the prytanes but by the nine archons and the whole boule,[4] and Professor Kahrstedt used this fact as the chief peg on which to hang his argument that the prytany system was created in 462/1.[5] This point, however, is irrelevant. The ostracism-assembly was not a normal ecclesia, though a normal ecclesia had first to be held to decide whether there should be an ostracism-assembly.[6] It was, we may imagine, especially likely to get out of hand, and it may well have been given a larger presiding body simply for that reason.

Nevertheless the inscriptions that I have cited make the possibility that prytanies were a product of the Ephialtic reform worth considering, and I believe the case can be strengthened by a study of the building which was erected for the prytanes, the Tholos. This is dated by the excavators of the Agora c. 465,[7] and the Old Bouleuterium, to the north of it, they assign (with Cleisthenes in mind) to the end of the sixth century.[8] The Tholos and Old Bouleuterium replaced earlier buildings on the same site:[9] the complex CDE on the site of the bouleuterium is thought to have been begun (building C) about the time of Solon, enlarged (D) under Pisistratus, and altered (D abandoned and E built) in the last quarter of the sixth century; FGHI, on the site of the Tholos, were erected about 525, and at the end of the sixth century, about the time when the Old Bouleuterium was built, part of F was demolished and J was erected. These buildings, it is suggested, served more or less the same purpose as their successors, except that as there is no building suitable for the purpose the actual meetings of the Solonian boule must have been held in the open.[10]

solve this problem see A. E. Raubitschek, O. Broneer, E. Schweigert, *AJA*² li 1947, lii 1948, liii 1949. My disinclination to believe in pre-Ephialtic prytanes is not much weakened by Plat. *Gorg.* 516 D–E, or by Teleclides' comedy, Πρυτάνεις (Ath. XII. 553 E).

[1] *IG* i² 3, 16–17; 4, 26–7.
[2] On the bouleutic calendar see Additional Note A, pp. 224–9.
[3] *IG* i² 4, 17 sqq.
[4] Phil. 328 F 30, schol. Ar. *Eq.* 855, Pl. *Arist.* 7. iv–v, cf. [And.] IV. *Alc.* 7.
[5] *S.S.A.*, 125 n. 1, *U.M.A.*, 88, *Klio* xxxiii 1940, 10–11.
[6] Cf. *A.P.* 43. v.
[7] *Agora Guide*², 45; *c.* 470, *Hesp.* Supp. iv 1940, 126–8, 153.
[8] *Hesp.* vi 1937, 134–5, 212, cf. *Hesp.* Supp. iv 1940, 27, 153. On the date of the Old Bouleuterium, see further p. 30 n. 11 below.
[9] See my Plans A and B, and *Hesp.* Supp. iv 1940, 8–44, 153.
[10] *Hesp.* Supp. iv 1940, 43.

However, there is no evidence for any kind of prytany system in the Solonian boule: I should have expected the archons to preside, but in any case the use of tribal contingents of 100 seems unlikely. FGHI present a far more complicated unit than the later Tholos, and though these were no doubt public buildings it seems unsafe to insist that they must have stood in the same relationship to the buildings to the north of them as did the Tholos to the Old Bouleuterium. The smallest of changes in the excavators' date would be needed to make the Tholos a post-Ephialtic building, newly erected to serve the needs of the new standing committee made necessary by the extra duties acquired by the boule after Ephialtes' attack on the Areopagus.[1] The arguments I have used here cannot be decisive, but if I succeed in showing that there may have been no need for prytanies before Ephialtes, then we ought not to persist in ascribing the prytany system to Cleisthenes merely because it accords with our idea of what he was trying to do.[2]

When this subdivision of the boule was made the order of the prytanies during the year was determined by lot[3] in such a way that except in the penultimate prytany of the year it was not known in advance which would be the next tribe in prytany:[4] in other words, in the course of the year there must have been nine (more after the creation of the new tribes) separate sortitions to determine the order of prytanies. This is the earliest method of arranging the prytanies for which we have any evidence,[5] and its use continued under democratic regimes at any rate until the third century.[6] One year in which it seems likely that a different system was

---

[1] I have been helped in this matter by correspondence with Professor H. A. Thompson and Professor E. Vanderpool. Thompson tells me that the archaeological evidence would permit a date anywhere within the decade 470–460, and Vanderpool reminds me that the earlier buildings seem better suited than the Tholos to the needs of the prytanes—which remains a problem regardless of when prytanies were instituted and when the Tholos was built.

[2] On the pre-Ephialtic boule see the appendix to Chapter IV, pp. 190 sqq., and on the problem in general cf. Chapter V, pp. 209–10.

[3] A.P. 49. ii. For an allotment-machine which could have been used for this purpose, see Professor Dow's κληρωτήριον I, Hesp. Supp. i 1937, 198–202, 210–11.

[4] See W. S. Ferguson, Athenian Secretaries, 19–27. The decisive phrase is τοὺς π[ρ]υτάνει[ς οἳ ἂν τυγχάνω]σι πρυτανεύοντες μετὰ τ[ὴ]ν Οἰνη[ΐδα φυλήν] (IG ii² 553, 16–17).

[5] Kahrstedt (Klio xxxiii 1940, 9–10) maintained that the system was introduced at the time of the Peloponnesian War in place of a single sortition which had been used to determine the order for the whole year: but IG i² 166 is no longer restored with the text on which he relied (cf. SEG x 96), and all the fifth-century evidence we possess now seems compatible with the practice of separate sortitions (cf. B. D. Meritt, AJP lxix 1948, 69–70).

[6] The latest inscriptions I know which seem to betray ignorance of the next tribe in prytany are IG ii² 806, 1–3 (largely restored) (c. 230) and perhaps 808, 20–1 (239–229) (there is no positive evidence that any of the regimes under which Athens passed c. 300 used a different system). The order of prytanies in different years continued to vary as long as we have any evidence, and it may be assumed that the lot continued to be used (D. J. Geagan, Hesp. Supp. xii 1967, 96).

tried is 408/7: for this year four prytanies are known, the fifth and the seventh to the ninth, and the tribes which occupied them are Oeneis (VI), Leontis (IV), Pandionis (III) and Aegeis (II). While this could have resulted from the normal sortitions the coincidence is impressive and it may be that in this one year the prytanies were filled in reverse tribal order.[1]

The primary duty of the prytanes was to convene the boule and ecclesia. They fixed the agenda for the boule, as the whole boule did for the ecclesia, and were ultimately responsible for ensuring that the boule placed on the ecclesia's agenda matters which by law had to come before the demos.[2] It is possible (though our evidence is limited to two entries in the lexica) that they were required to give five days' notice of an ordinary meeting of the ecclesia,[3] specifying the time and place, and perhaps also the agenda.[4] They inevitably became the first recipients of envoys, messengers, and applicants for a hearing in the boule and assembly, and when the right of πρόσοδος πρὸς τὴν βουλὴν καὶ τὸν δῆμον was conferred on a foreigner the prytanes naturally figured among those who were to see that he was able to enjoy this right.[5] Demosthenes gives us an account of their arrangements to summon an extraordinary assembly in 339/8, when the news reached Athens that Philip II had occupied Elatea:

ἑσπέρα μὲν γὰρ ἦν, ἧκε δ' ἀγγέλλων τις ὡς τοὺς πρυτάνεις ὡς Ἐλάτεια κατείληπται. καὶ μετὰ ταῦθ' οἱ μὲν εὐθὺς ἐξαναστάντες μεταξὺ δειπνοῦντες τούς τ' ἐκ τῶν σκηνῶν τῶν κατὰ τὴν ἀγορὰν ἐξεῖργον καὶ τὰ γέρρ' ἀνεπετάννυσαν, οἱ δὲ τοὺς στρατηγοὺς μετεπέμποντο καὶ τὸν σαλπικτὴν ἐκάλουν· καὶ θορύβου πλήρης ἦν ἡ πόλις. τῇ δ' ὑστεραίᾳ, ἅμα τῇ ἡμέρᾳ, οἱ μὲν πρυτάνεις τὴν βουλὴν ἐκάλουν εἰς τὸ βουλευτήριον, ὑμεῖς δ' εἰς τὴν ἐκκλησίαν ἐπορεύεσθε, καὶ πρὶν ἐκείνην χρηματίσαι καὶ προβουλεῦσαι πᾶς ὁ δῆμος ἄνω καθῆτο. καὶ μετὰ ταῦτα ὡς ἦλθεν ἡ βουλὴ καὶ ἀπήγγειλαν οἱ πρυτάνεις τὰ προσηγγελμέν' ἑαυτοῖς καὶ τὸν ἥκοντα παρήγαγον κἀκεῖνος εἶπεν, ἠρώτα μὲν ὁ κῆρυξ "τίς ἀγορεύειν βούλεται;"[6]

[1] Tod 92 with W. S. Ferguson, *Athenian Secretaries*, 26 n. A, B. D. Meritt, *TAPA* xcv 1964, 203. W. K. Pritchett, *BCH* lxxxviii 1964, 467–70, refuses to make the inference.

[2] *A.P.* 43. iii–vi, 44. iv, cf. 45. iv, D. XXI. *Mid.* 8–9. In citizenship grants under some fourth-century and third-century regimes the prytanes were ordered to δοῦναι περὶ τοῦ δεῖνος τὴν ψῆφον ἐν τῇ πρώτῃ ἐκκλησίᾳ (presumably to order and organize the meeting, as the proedri now presided) : references given at *IG* ii² IV. i, p. 61, s.v. πρυτάνεις. Cf. also M&L 46, 35–7, 40 ; 69, 26–31, 33–8.   [3] *L.S.* 296–8, Phot. πρόπεμπτα.

[4] Our best evidence for advance publication of agenda is in connection with νομοθεσία (D. XXIV. *Tim.* 23, cf. 18, XX. *Lept.* 94), but in a system where for example ἱκετηρίαι were permitted at one ecclesia in each prytany (*A.P.* 43. vi) there must surely have been some notice of what matters were to come up on which occasions. The last sentence of *A.P.* 43. iii might be read as evidence that the boule received advance notice of matters to be discussed, and in the law for rebuilding the walls usually dated to 337/6 the boule is to be given the opportunity to study in advance the συγγραφαί on which it will have to vote (*IG* ii² 244, 6–9).

[5] References in *IG* i², p. 369. ii–iii, s.v. πρύτανις, *IG* ii² IV. i, p. 60. ii (paragraphs 6–7) s.vv. πρυτανεία κτλ.

[6] D. XVIII. *Cor.* 169–70. ἀνεπετάννυσαν is Girard's conjecture, cf. schol. Ar. *Ach.* 22 ; the MSS. read ἐνεπίμπρασαν.

In the fourth century it is to be assumed that a part of their duty in convening meetings was delegated to a board of three bouleutae from each tribe known as συλλογεῖς τοῦ δήμου, though the only attested duties of the συλλογεῖς are religious;[1] from the late third to the early first century the activities for which prytanes are honoured include taking care of the συλλογὴ τῆς βουλῆς καὶ τοῦ δήμου.[2]

Until the institution of the proedri early in the fourth century[3] the prytanes also presided at the meetings of the boule and ecclesia.[4] In the bouleuterium they had seats facing the other members,[5] and similar arrangements must have been made when the boule met elsewhere, and also at the various meeting-places of the ecclesia.[6] With the presidency went responsibility for good order at meetings, and therefore control of the Scythian τοξόται;[7] it also involved the right to declare a meeting closed, and in Aristophanes' *Acharnians* we find Dicaeopolis taking advantage of the grounds on which an assembly might be dissolved:

> ΔΙ.   ἀλλ' ἀπαγορεύω μὴ ποεῖν ἐκκλησίαν
> τοῖς Θρᾳξὶ περὶ μισθοῦ· λέγω δ' ὑμῖν ὅτι
> διοσημία 'στὶ καὶ ῥανὶς βέβληκέ με.
> ΚΗ.   τοὺς Θρᾷκας ἀπιέναι, παρεῖναι δ' εἰς ἔνην·
> οἱ γὰρ πρυτάνεις λύουσι τὴν ἐκκλησίαν.[8]

In judicial matters as in legislative the co-operation of the prytanes was needed if an item was to come before the boule or ecclesia: in Clinias' tribute-decree the prytanes are threatened with heavy penalties if they fail to bring charges before the boule,[9] and Aristophanes shows us a charge made the subject of a φάσις to the prytanes.[10] The decree of Dracontides, probably to be dated to 438/7, required Pericles to submit οἱ λόγοι τῶν χρημάτων to the prytanes, though both under this decree and under Hagnon's he was ultimately to be tried by δικασταί.[11] A rider to Thudippus' assessment decree of 425 is restored to provide that assessments

---

[1] Cf. Ch. III, pp. 129–30.

[2] *P* 23 (235/4) to *Hesp.* xvii 12 (95/4).   [3] Cf. pp. 25–8.

[4] e.g. Ar. *Ach.* 167–73, X. *H.* i. vii. 14–15. Before the creation of the prytanes I imagine that presidency of the ecclesia and probably of the boule also rested with the archon, or with the college of archons (cf. Hignett, 150–1); and I do not see why this practice should not have lasted until the reforms of Ephialtes.

[5] Cf. p. 33.   [6] For the ecclesia see Ar. *Ach.* 23–6, cf. 40–2, *Eccl.* 86–7.

[7] e.g. Ar. *Ach.* 54 with schol. (ecclesia), *Eq.* 665 (boule).

[8] Ar. *Ach.* 169–73; cf. *Eq.* 674.   [9] M&L 46, 35–7.

[10] Ar. *Eq.* 300–2. In Lucian, *D. Meretr.* 15. ii, a foreigner who has committed a drunken assault is to be denounced to the prytanes—but it is not clear what powers the prytanes are here thought to possess or how closely Lucian is following Athenian procedure of any period. See J. Delz, *Lukians Kenntnis der athenischen Antiquitäten*, 150, D. J. Geagan, *Hesp.* Supp. xii 1967, 103.

[11] Pl. *Per.* 32. iii: for the date see F. J. Frost, *JHS* lxxxiv 1964.

which have been the subject of a διαδικασία are to be reported by the prytanes and the secretary of the boule to the appropriate court for confirmation.[1] Here the prytanes are being used not for their primary purpose but as an executive committee, and there are of course many instances of this outside the judicial sphere. In 434/3 when the city settled its debt to the Other Gods the boule was to convene the thirty logistae to reckon up the sums due, and payment was to be made by 'the prytanes with the boule'.[2] In a largely restored decree of about 420 a payment is to be made by the colacretae serving under the prytany of Aegeis; if they fail in this they are to be punished and compelled to pay by the tribe next in prytany, or else the prytanes of that tribe will themselves be punished.[3] It is at first sight surprising that the prytanes should be blamed by Amphitheus in the *Acharnians* for not giving him ἐφόδια for his journey to make peace with Sparta[4]—the prytanes could not on their own authorize payment from the public treasuries—but their fault is presumably that they have failed to put the question to the assembly.

In addition to their general responsibility as bouleutae, members were liable to praise or blame for their conduct as prytanes. Nicias in 415 assured 'the prytanis' that he need not be afraid of breaking the law in giving the demos a second chance to decide whether it was to undertake the Sicilian campaign;[5] and we read that at the Arginusae trial the prytanes were afraid of breaking the laws by putting Callixenus' proposal to the vote.[6] In the previous paragraph I have mentioned some instances of the prytanes' being threatened with penalties if they failed to perform some specific act, and more could be given.[7] *IG* i² 95 has been restored tentatively by Mr. A. G. Woodhead to yield provisions for the boule and

---

[1] M&L 69, 51–4. There is a more unusual appearance of a prytanis in the judicial sphere in *Hesp.* v 10, 116–17, cf. 12–13, where courts confiscating property are attended by a κυρωτὴς παρὰ πρυτάνεων; Meritt (comm. on 12–13) would make a similar restoration in *IG* ii² 1678, aA 27.

[2] M&L 58 A, 7–13. Cf. M&L 87, 37–42, where the prytanes are to supervise the deletion of certain records.

[3] *SEG* x 96. I am not happy about this restoration: l. 5 seems to entail an unfortunate situation in which the new prytany's colacretae will be liable to punishment if they do not deal promptly with a payment left to them by the slackness of their predecessors, who themselves will escape punishment; and there is no good parallel to the punitive power ascribed to the prytanes in ll. 7–8.

[4] Ar. *Ach.* 53–4.   [5] T. vi. 14.   [6] X. *H.* i. vii. 14–15.

[7] The prytanes are to be fined if they fail to set in motion the machinery for the reassessment of the Delian League at the time of the Great Panathenaea (M&L 69, 26–31), and Thudippus' decree itself seems to have been enacted under a similar sanction (ibid. 33–8; cf. Additional Note B, pp. 229–30); cf. M&L 46, 35–7. The document in Demosthenes' speech *Against Timocrates* which outlines the procedure for an annual ἐπιχειροτονία τῶν νόμων states that both prytanes and proedri may be prosecuted (by ἔνδειξις to the thesmothetae) if they prevent the lawful appointment of nomothetae (D. XXIV. *Tim.* 22).

ecclesia to call a past prytany to account before the end of 418/17, but I find some of the details of his restoration unconvincing.[1]

By way of encouragement, early in the fourth century the boule held a contest for the best prytany of the year: a fragment reads, ἐπα[ινέσαι καὶ] ἀναγράψαι [δικαιο]σύνης ἕνεκα ὅτι ἔκρινεν αὐτὸς ἡ βολὴ νικᾶν τὰς ἄλλας φυλὰς ὡς ἄριστα πρυτανεύσαντας τῆι πόλει.[2] Later, but still before the middle of the century, this contest seems to have been taken over by the demos: we have a dedication by the members of Leontis, νικήσαντες δ(ό)ξαν τῶι δήμωι,[3] and another inscription has a similar format though the words after νικήσαντες are lost.[4] In the Hellenistic period honours were multiplied, and we know of years when two or even three prytanies might be favoured;[5] already by the 340s references to the contest have disappeared from the headings of prytany-lists.[6] The standard decrees in honour of prytanes published with the Hellenistic lists show that the various prytanies reported to the ecclesia on the discharge of their own duties,[7] and to the boule on the conduct of the officials of the boule and the prytany:[8] though this practice is not mentioned in the briefer documents of the fourth century there is no reason to believe that it was a late innovation.

For some purposes a single head of state was needed, and to meet this requirement one of the prytanes was picked by lot to serve for 24 hours as ἐπιστάτης, a position which a man might occupy only once in his life.[9] In his day of supremacy he was continuously on duty, and picked one τριττύς to remain in the Tholos with him.[10] He had charge of the keys to the temples used as state depositories, and of the public seal: we see him using the latter when alternative proposals for the use of the ἱερὰ ὀργάς are placed in separate, sealed vessels, and Delphi is to be asked which

---

[1] *Hesp.* xviii 1949, 78–83 = *SEG* xii 32; cf. Ch. IV, p. 161.

[2] *IG* ii² 1142 (beg. C4). [3] *IG* ii² 1742, 2 (370/69?).

[4] *IG* ii² 1743, 1. In *Hesp.* xvi 41 we find dedications by prytanies of 362/1, 361/0, 370/69 and 363/2, but we are not told what occasioned them; the preamble to *Hesp.* xxxvi 34 (381/0) seems not to have named the awarding body; in *DAA* 167 (408/7) Raubitschek restores a formula similar to that in *IG* ii² 1743.

[5] In 164/3 the prytanes of Erechtheis (*SEG* xvi 96), Ptolemais (*P* 80) and Hippothontis (*SEG* xvi 95) were honoured.

[6] e.g. *IG* ii² 1749, 1750.

[7] Prytany 'first' decrees (see below, p. 76 n. 2), *passim*.

[8] Prytany 'second' decrees, *passim*.

[9] *A.P.* 44. i, cf. lexica and scholia. Under the Roman Empire one man seems to have served as ἐπιστάτης for the whole prytany: P. Graindor, *Athènes de Tibère à Trajan*, 68 n. 2, D. J. Geagan, *Hesp.* Supp. xii 1967, 102–3.

[10] Until the proedri were created to preside in the boule and ecclesia it will not have been possible for them to remain in the Tholos for the whole 24 hours—but doubtless it was only intended that they should be available there when not otherwise occupied with public business.

proposal should be adopted.[1] He may have received extra remuneration for this one day, but Foucart's proposal of a ten-obol supplement would be uncharacteristically high.[2] While the prytanes presided in the boule and ecclesia he will have been chairman of the bench,[3] but Xenophon's account of the Arginusae trial shows that when any problem arose the opinion of his colleagues had to be taken into account.[4]

Neither 50 nor 49 is a product of 3, so the τριττὺς τῶν πρυτάνεων which remained on duty with the epistates for the full 24 hours cannot have been a mathematical third. Some have therefore suggested that the word should be understood in its Cleisthenic sense, of the bouleutae from one τριττύς of the tribe in prytany[5]—and these τριττύες were very far from mathematical thirds, as the following table shows:[6]

Tribe	ἄστυ	παραλία	μεσόγειος
Erechtheis	16	23	11
Aegeis	10	16	24
Pandionis	12 (one deme)	19	19
Leontis	16?21	20?15	14
Acamantis	17	16	17
Oeneis	6?10	22?18	22 (one deme)
Cecropis Hippothontis Aiantis	(too little information available)		
Antiochis	10 (one deme)	27+	13−

A refinement of this view has recently been suggested by Dr. W. E. Thompson, who has noticed that the arrangement of many surviving prytany-lists does not follow the Cleisthenic trittyes but does nevertheless seem to incorporate a threefold division which bears some relationship to those trittyes but comes nearer to a mathematically equal division. These groups, he suspects, are the τριττύες τῶν πρυτάνεων to which the *Athenaion*

---

[1] *IG* ii² 204, 39–40. In A.D. 38/9(?) the public seal is used by the herald of the Areopagus (*IG* iv² 83, 17–19). There is a note on the seal by W. P. Wallace, *Phoen.* iii 1949.

[2] *RPh*² xlii 1918, 55–9 (on *A.P.* 62. ii). Cf. p. 13 above.

[3] Cf. schol. Plat. *Gorg.* 473 E, s.v. ἐπιψηφίζειν.

[4] X. *H.* I. vii. 14–15.

[5] Busolt and Swoboda, 973 with n. 2, Kahrstedt, *U.M.A.*, 38 with n. 3, cf. D. M. Lewis, *Hist.* xii 1963, 35 with n. 122, cf. 32 with n. 98. The view that lists of prytanes were regularly arranged by (Cleisthenic) trittyes rests on a suggestion of A. Milchhöfer, *Sb. Berlin* 1887, iv, 43, elaborated by him (*Abh. Berlin* 1892, 10–11, 12, etc.) and by R. Loeper (*AM* xvii 1892, 336 sqq.).

[6] The table is based on the fourth-century lists of the ten-tribe period. Some attributions of demes to trittyes are uncertain, and figures for some demes are not constant throughout the century, but this summary must be a fair approximation to the truth. Compare Table 1 (based on figures supplied by J. S. Traill) of C. W. J. Eliot, *Phoen.* xxii 1968, 7, which with its companion tables supersedes his earlier table (*Coastal Demes of Attika*, 143).

Politeia refers.[1] His article, based on a small number of inscriptions only, applies the principle successfully in Aegeis, Pandionis, and Leontis; he notes that it does not work for Erechtheis but could work for Acamantis.

Study of the fragmentary lists provides some confirmation, and suggests also that this principle of division may not have been abandoned immediately on the creation of the Macedonian tribes.[2]

There is not enough regularity to indicate a thorough, official system, but there is far too much to be attributed to coincidence, and it does appear that some tribes may have had a convention for dividing their prytanies into trittyes, which often had its effect on the arrangement of membership lists.

By the time of the *Athenaion Politeia* the prytanes' duty of presiding in the boule and assembly had passed to a board of nine πρόεδροι. Each day the new epistates of the prytanes picked one member by lot from each tribe except his own and designated one of these as their epistates: a man might be πρόεδρος once in each prytany, and epistates once in the year.[3] Inscriptions (and the later writers I have cited) provide ample confirmation of the *Athenaion Politeia*'s account: in and after the fourth century the ἐπιστάτης named in the prescripts of decrees represents a deme that does not belong to the tribe in prytany; as an alternative to ὁ δεῖνα ἐπεστάτει we find the formula τῶν προέδρων ἐπεψήφιζεν ὁ δεῖνα, which after a period of coexistence with the older formula becomes standard from the late 340s onwards;[4] 22 decrees from 333/2 to the 220s follow this formula with a list of συμπρόεδροι—one from each tribe except that in prytany and that of the epistates, given in tribal order.[5] Nevertheless strange views of the proedri are found in scholia: more than once they are said to be ten members of the tribe in prytany, given full presidency of the state for

---

[1] *Hist.* xv 1966. In *Phoen.* xxi 1967, esp. 83–4 n. 18, C. W. J. Eliot reacted unfavourably to this suggestion, overstressing (to my mind) the exceptions which have to be allowed. Thompson has returned to the subject in *Mnem.*[4] xxii 1969. In reply to Eliot's linguistic arguments he suggests that these divisions were formed deliberately by modifying the Cleisthenic τριττύες, and came to be known as τριττύες for that reason (*Mnem.* 1969, 140): this may be the correct explanation, or a part of it, but I do not think Eliot's linguistic arguments exclude the possibility that whatever the word ought to have meant τριττύς came in fact in Athens to mean specifically a third part of a tribe.

[2] For a fuller discussion of the problem, with an analysis of all texts substantial enough to be of use, which survive from the ten-tribe period and the following twelve-tribe period, see my article, "τριττὺς τῶν πρυτάνεων", in *Hist.* (forthcoming).

[3] *A.P.* 44. ii–iii, Poll. viii. 96, Eust. *Od.* xvi. 455, Harp., Suid. ἐπιστάτης, *L.S.* 244. 31, 290. 8, cf. A. I. *Tim.* 104, II. *F.L.* 84. The number of tribes determined the number of proedri, so that in the twelve-tribe periods, for example, there were eleven proedri (e.g. *IG* ii² 502, 5 sqq.). The ban on repeated service as epistates seems ultimately to have broken down: Stratophon was twice epistates of the proedri in 106/5 (*IG* ii² 1011, 63 sqq., 73 sqq.).

[4] S. B. Smith, *CP* xxv 1930, 267.

[5] S. Dow, *Hesp.* xxxii 1963.

seven days;[1] less far from the truth, a scholiast on Demosthenes remarks that there was a board of ten proedri, one from each tribe, among whom the presidency rotated.[2]

The exact date of their institution is uncertain. The epigraphic evidence has been analysed by Glotz[3] and Dr. D. M. Lewis,[4] and I have nothing to add to the latter's discussion. 403/2 is the last year in which the epistates named in decree prescripts is certainly a member of the tribe in prytany;[5] 378/7 gives us our first certain epistates of the proedri[6] and also our first instance of the alternative formula τῶν προέδρων ἐπεψήφιζεν.[7] Literary evidence may, however, enable us to continue the presidency of the prytanes some way into this uncertain period. Lysias, describing in 399 the procedure by which the Thirty tried the traitors whom Agoratus denounced, says: οἱ μὲν γὰρ τριάκοντα ἐκάθηντο ἐπὶ τῶν βάθρων, οὗ νῦν οἱ πρυτάνεις καθέζονται (in the boule);[8] and later in the 390s Aristophanes uses language which ought to imply that the prytanes still preside:

$$\text{δεῖ σε καταλαβεῖν ἔδρας}$$
$$\text{ὑπὸ τῷ λίθῳ, τῶν πρυτάνεων καταντικρύ.[9]}$$
$$(\textit{ΥΠΟ ΤΩΙ ΛΙΘΩΙ}· \text{ὑπὸ τῷ βήματι.)[10]}$$

Scholars have argued fiercely as to whether this reorganization represents an attempt to reduce the power of the prytanes, which was felt to be excessive, or simply an attempt to lessen the burden of the office and share out work more fairly among the bouleutae.[11] If the latter explanation is the more likely, the most obvious occasion for the change is provided by the creation of the Second Athenian League, in whose foundation-documents the proedri make their first undoubted appearance. The establishment of an allied συνέδριον in permanent session in Athens was bound to lead to extra work for the boule and ecclesia, and provides

---

[1] Schol. A. III. *Ctes.* 3, 4, D. XXII. *Andr. hyp.* ii. 7 (which adds an annual five-day interregnum), *E.M. ἐπιστάται*.

[2] Schol. D. XXII. *Andr.* 5.   [3] *REG* xxxiv 1921.

[4] *BSA* xlix 1954, 31–4.   [5] Tod 97, *IG* ii² 2, *Hesp.* x 78.   [6] Tod 123, 124.

[7] Tod 124, 6.   [8] Lys. XIII. *Ag.* 37.   [9] Ar. *Eccl.* 86–7.

[10] Schol. Ar. *Eccl.* 87. Dr. Lewis says he is inclined to discount these passages, as the prytanes would still need to be well placed at meetings (cf., e.g., D. XVIII. *Cor.* 169): his caution may be justified with regard to the passage from Aristophanes, but the Thirty, before whose regime the proedri had certainly not come into existence, must surely have occupied the presidential benches.

[11] Cloché delivered a powerful blow against the view that the boule was thought to be growing too powerful (*REG* xxxiv 1921), but the idea has persisted (e.g. S. B. Smith, *CP* xxv 1930, and cf. A. Andrewes, *Ancient Society and Institutions*, 13–14). Avoidance of that continuity and access to the best information which we should regard as essential seems almost wilful, but I am reluctant to believe in an attack on the boule when in a fairly well-documented period there are no traces of controversy on the matter. Compare my remarks in Ch. V, pp. 218–19, with notes referring to my discussions of related problems.

a sufficient motive for the transfer of one of the prytanes' duties to a new board.

The duty of the proedri was simply to preside, and with the presidency went the necessary powers of discipline in the boule and ecclesia.[1] Like the prytanes before them they could be punished for putting an illegal motion to the vote;[2] and in the *Athenaion Politeia* we find listed among the cases which came before the courts of the thesmothetae a γραφὴ προεδρική and a γραφὴ ἐπιστατική,[3] but we know nothing of these apart from their titles, and cannot even be sure that the epistates against whom the latter charge was directed was the epistates of the proedri. Aeschines includes the proedri in the general charge of corruption with which he begins the speech *Against Ctesiphon*,[4] and about 337 Hyperides attacked the proposal of one Philippides to honour a board of proedri who had put to the vote an illegal pro-Macedonian motion.[5]

The epistates of the proedri and the epistates of the prytanes were both involved in the consultation of the Delphic Oracle on the use of the ἱερὰ ὀργάς at Eleusis. The epistates of the proedri was to roll up the pieces of tin on which the alternative proposals were engraved, shake them in a bronze hydria, and draw one to be placed in a gold hydria leaving the other to be placed in one of silver; his colleague would then seal them with the public seal, to await the verdict of Apollo.[6] The proedri appear later in the decree, where editors have given us the following text:

$$\pi\text{-}$$
[αρασχεῖν δὲ ὅρους λιθίνους,] ὁπόσων ἂν προσδέηι, τοὺς πωλη-
[τὰς ποιήσαντας μετὰ τῆς] βουλῆ[ς μ]ίσθωμα, τούς τε προέδρος
[τῆς βουλῆς μετὰ τῶν πωλητῶν] συγγράψαι καθότι ἐξεργασθήσ-
[ονται, ἐπιμελεῖσθαι δ' ὅπως ἐπι]σταθήσονται τῆς ἱερᾶς ὀργ-
[άδος οἱ ὅροι, καθὰ δείξου]σιν οἱ αἱρεθέντες.[7]

This makes strange reading. The normal duty of proedri was to put other men's proposals to the vote, not to help in drawing up proposals themselves, and to ἐπιμελεῖσθαι that the provisions of a decree were carried out would be even further from their normal line of duty. Moreover, proedri served only for one day, and this makes it very unlikely that οἱ πρόεδροι τῆς βουλῆς, without further specification, should be given either

---

[1] For what little is known about discipline after the institution of the proedri, see Ch. IV, pp. 144-7.
[2] Cf. the νόμος in D. XXIV. *Tim.* 50.   [3] *A.P.* 59. ii.
[4] A. III. *Ctes.* 3.   [5] Hyp. II. *Phil.*, esp. 4-6.
[6] *IG* ii² 204, 31-9.   [7] *Ibid.* 65-70.

of these tasks.[1] We should perhaps come nearer to the required sense by restoring

τούς τε προέδρος

[χρηματίσαι τῶι βουλομένωι] συγγράψαι,

but a new subject would then be needed for [ἐπιμελεῖσθαι] in the following line, and more work will be needed to produce an acceptable text.

We should perhaps note here that proedri are found also in connection with the enactments of the fourth-century nomothetae: *IG* ii² 140 has a decree-like prescript, including the formula τῶν προέδρων ἐπεψήφιζεν but ending with δεδόχθαι τοῖς νομοθέταις;[2] decrees calling for the enactment of a νόμος require the proedri to raise the question with the nomothetae;[3] and the involvement of proedri with the nomothetae is confirmed by our literary sources.[4] Common sense suggests that here we have the nomothetae organized after the manner of the boule and ecclesia with their own proedri and epistates, and one inscription makes it fairly clear that this is correct:

εἰὰν δὲ μ-

[ὴ ἐπιψηφ]ίσωσιν οἱ [πρ]όεδροι καὶ [ὁ]

[ἐπιστά]της τῶν νομοθετῶν, ὀφειλέ-

[τω ἕκαστ]ος αὐτῶν Χ δραχμὰς ἱερὰς

[τῆι Ἀθην]ᾶι.[5]

The nomothetic system was probably in continuous existence from the restoration of 403/2, but we have no means of telling how the proedri of the nomothetae were appointed, nor whether they antedate or post-date the creation of the proedri of the boule.

I conclude this section with a note on the organization of the boule under the oligarchic constitutions of 411 and 404. Thucydides' choice of words is not an infallible guide in these matters, but for what it is worth he tells us that the five men who formed the nucleus of the Four Hundred in 411 were πρόεδροι,[6] and that after entering office the Four Hundred πρυτάνεις ἑαυτῶν ἀπεκλήρωσαν.[7] We possess part of what is thought to be a decree of the Four Hundred, revealing a single epistates with whom

---

[1] It is scarcely more likely that the poletae should have performed these duties: cf. Ch. III, pp. 96–8 (on the poletae in general), 124.

[2] (For νομοθεσία and νόμοι cf. Ch. II, pp. 49–52, and Table H.) Cf. *SEG* xii 87 and (restored) *IG* ii² 333; also the νόμος in D. XXIV. *Tim.* 71.

[3] *IG* ii² 222, 41–6; 330, 18 sqq.; vii 4254 = *SIG*³ 298, 35–41.

[4] A. III. *Ctes.* 39, νόμος in D. XXIV. *Tim.* 33.

[5] *IG* ii² 222, 48–52.

[6] T. viii. 67. iii.

[7] T. viii. 70. i: retention of the lot by an oligarchic boule is a little surprising.

other men were associated, and this is normally restored with reference to Thucydides' five proedri:

[βολῆ]ς ἐπεστάτε [– 17 –]
[– 3 – κ]αὶ μετ' αὐτὸ π[ρόδρευον —]
[room for 4 names and demotics before proposer of motion].[1]

I am loth to rely on Thucydides' terminology, but if we are to be guided by his choice of words we should note that the proedri were pre-eminent oligarchs around whom the boule was built, and that when he came to write of a subdivision the word he chose was πρυτάνεις :[2] the fact that we are again dealing with five men does not commit us to the existence of proedri of the fourth-century type. A presiding board of five, with a chairman, appears also in the 'future constitution' put out by the Four Hundred to appease their opponents, but these presidents are given no title.[3] If this provision does reflect the actual practice under the Four Hundred, I believe that is purely coincidental.[4]

The Five Thousand reverted to a boule of 500,[5] and a decree of this boule is quoted from Caecilius in the *Lives of the Ten Orators*: ἔδοξε τῇ βουλῇ, μιᾷ καὶ εἰκοστῇ τῆς πρυτανείας· Δημόνικος Ἀλωπεκῆθεν ἐγραμμάτευε, Φιλόστρατος Παλληνεὺς ἐπεστάτει· Ἄνδρων εἶπε.[6] There was, then, a prytany system in which prytanies lasted at least twenty-one days, and a single man was designated ἐπιστάτης, but beyond this we cannot go.[7]

The Thirty, appointed in 404 οἳ τοὺς πατρίους νόμους συγγράψουσι,[8] . . . τούτους μὲν ἀεὶ ἔμελλον συγγράφειν τε καὶ ἀποδεικνύναι, βουλὴν δὲ καὶ τὰς

---

[1] M&L 80, 4–8 (not printing a supplement to l. 5). Dr. Lewis has noted (*ap.* G. E.M. de Ste Croix, *Hist.* v 1956, 18 n. 85a) that if reference to a prytany is wanted ll. 1–2 might be restored:

[– 8 –]ην[– 14 – ἔδοξεν]
[τῆι βολ]ῆι· ἦν τε[τάρτη τῆς πρυτανείας] ;

but this is said in M&L, p. 249, to be 'probably wrong'. Ferguson, *Mélanges Glotz*, i. 354, linked the restoration of π[ρόδρευον] with *A.P.* 30; but even if that chapter reflects an actual constitution, which I do not believe, the title πρόεδρος does not appear there or elsewhere in the *A.P.*'s account of the year 411.

[2] Kahrstedt, *Klio* xxxiii 1940, 12, therefore preferred to restore π[ρυτάνεις? ἔσαν] in l. 5. Notice also *A.P.* 29. iv, where we are told that salaries were abolished for all but the nine archons and τῶν πρυτάνεων οἳ ἂν ὦσιν.

[3] *A.P.* 30. iv–v: sortition is again specified.

[4] Cf. p. 6 n. 9 above.   [5] Cf. p. 7.

[6] [Pl.] X. *Or.* 833 D–834 B : I quote from 833 E (ἔδοξε and Παλληνεύς are emendations, but are certain). See on this prescript de Ste Croix, *Hist.* v 1956, 16–17.

[7] The secretary and epistates belonged to the same tribe, which was not possible before the fourth-century changes in presidency and secretaryship (cf. Ch. III, pp. 134–5); and a count of days within the prytany was not used in the prescripts of decrees under the democracy until the 360s (cf. Additional Note A, p. 226). Failure to specify the prytany by name or number may well be due to careless transmission of the text.

[8] X. *H.* ii. iii. 2.

ἄλλας ἀρχὰς κατέστησαν ὡς ἐδόκει αὐτοῖς.[1] The Thirty seem to have been more interested in demolishing old stelae than in setting up new, and we have no epigraphic evidence for the organization of their boule, but it appears that at any rate in judicial sessions of the boule the Thirty themselves presided,[2] and this should have eliminated the need for any kind of prytany system.

(iii) *Meetings and Meeting-Places*

The boule met daily except on holidays and days of ill omen.[3] In all it is said to have had sixty holidays a year;[4] days mentioned are the Plynteria,[5] the Μέση of the Thesmophoria,[6] and the Cronia;[7] Athenaeus records a fourth-century decree in which the boule gives itself five days' holiday for the Apaturia,[8] and we have already noticed that in the second century the Agonothetes of the Thesea might give the bouleutae a καθέσι-μον for the festival.[9]

The basic meeting-place of the boule was the βουλευτήριον, on the west side of the Agora.[10] The building identified by the excavators as the Old Bouleuterium was built about the end of the sixth century to house Cleisthenes' new boule, damaged during the Persian Wars, and restored soon afterwards:[11] for the buildings which it replaced, which were probably

[1] X. *H.* II. iii. 11.

[2] Cf. the trials of Theramenes (X. *H.* II. iii. 23–56, esp. 50) and of Agoratus' victims (Lys. XIII. *Ag.* 37: see p. 26 and n. 10 above).

[3] *A.P.* 43. iii, Lucian, *Pseudol.* 12. I agree with D. W. Bradeen (*TAPA* lxxxvi 1955, 27) that in the immediately post-Cleisthenic period meetings were probably less frequent.

[4] Schol. Ar. *Vesp.* 663. The Athenians had more festivals than other cities: cf. O.O. iii. 2, 8, T. II. 38. i, [Plat.] *Alc. ii.* 148 E.   [5] Pl. *Alc.* 34. i.   [6] Ar. *Thesm.* 79–81.

[7] D. XXIV. *Tim.* 26.   [8] Ath. IV. 171 E.   [9] Cf. p. 14 and n. 8 above.

[10] Texts concerning the bouleuterium are collected by R. E. Wycherley, *Testimonia*, pp. 128–37; concerning the Metroum, ibid., pp. 150–60; concerning the Tholos, ibid., pp. 179–84. For excavation reports see on the bouleuteria and Metroum H. A. Thompson, *Hesp.* vi 1937, 115–224; on the Tholos and on the whole complex of buildings H. A. Thompson, *Hesp.* Supp. iv 1940; and for a recent summary see *Agora Guide*[2], pp. 45–50. The buildings under discussion are illustrated in my Plans A–F; I shall not give references for activities and their dates which can be found in the Chronological Index in *Hesp.* Supp. iv 1940, 153–6.

[11] Originally, with Cleisthenes in mind, Thompson dated the Old Bouleuterium to the last decade of the sixth century. Recently he has been worried by the absence of clear evidence of Persian destruction around the building and by the free use of second-hand blocks in the interior foundations, and has considered the possibility that the Old Bouleuterium was not built until the 470s (this lower dating is mentioned by R. E. Wycherley, *J. Hist. Stud.* i 1967–8, 255 with n. 21); in July 1969, however, he told me that he thought the evidence on balance favoured the earlier date, though he would now put the building after rather than before 500. The problem will be discussed in *The Athenian Agora*, vol. xiv (forthcoming), by Professor Thompson and Professor Wycherley. (Thompson and Wycherley have been generous with their help on this matter: in particular I would thank Professor Wycherley for keeping me up to date over a period of some years, and for letting me have a copy of the article cited and of the projected note on the date of the Old Bouleuterium in their forthcoming book.)

used by the Solonian boule, see above, pp. 18–19. About the end of the fifth century work began on a New Bouleuterium immediately to the west of the Old: this was finished after a change in plan, early in the fourth century. The actual chamber was very slightly smaller in the new building than in the old,[1] and though the excavators claim that seating accommodation could be provided for 500 members it seems highly unlikely that seats were available for every member of the enlarged boulae of the Hellenistic period.

The boule seems from an early date to have been linked with the cult of the Mother of the Gods, and a temple erected to the north of the Old Bouleuterium at the same time as that building is thought to have been the temple of the Mother.[2] This was not rebuilt after the Persian sack, but the cult persisted, and the statue of the Mother by Phidias[3] or his pupil Agoracritus[4] was perhaps housed in the Old Bouleuterium. When the New Bouleuterium was built the Old was left standing until after 150, apparently used as a cult centre and record office,[5] and our evidence suggests that by about the middle of the fourth century the Old Bouleuterium was becoming known as the Μητρῷον.[6] In the third quarter

[1] The foundation measurements of the Old Bouleuterium are reported as 23·30 × 23·80 m. (*Hesp.* 1937, 128); the external measurements of the actual building are 22·74 × 23·30 m., and the internal measurements of the chamber 21·26 × rather less than 16·09 m. (*Hesp.* Supp. 1940, fig. 62, reproduced in this book as Plan C). W. A. McDonald, *The Political Meeting Places of the Greeks*, 171, reports what are in fact the foundation measurements as those of the walls.

The New Bouleuterium was built on foundations measuring 22·50 × 17·50 m. (*Hesp.* 1937, 142); the external measurements of the building are 21·40 × 16·90 m. and the internal measurements 20·12 × 15·62 m. (*Hesp.* 1937, plate viii: until the porch was added shortly before 275 the building comprised nothing but the chamber). McDonald compromises between the foundations and the walls, and reports the dimensions as 22·50 × 16·90 m. (op. cit., 172).

Thompson thought that the Old Bouleuterium 'might have accommodated about 700 persons' (*Hesp.* 1937, 134, cf. McDonald, op. cit., 172), but I would modify his restoration (cf. pp. 32–5 with p. 32 n. 6 and Plan E). On the excavators' allowance of ½ m. of bench per member my plan has comfortable room for 50 prytanes on the benches against the south wall, and about 490 places on the other benches—but some deduction must be made for aisles providing access to the seats. The maximum for the New Bouleuterium after wooden benches had given way to stone is calculated as 'just over 500' with an allowance of ½ m. per member (*Hesp.* 1937, 160).

This compares with internal measurements of about 21½ × 13¾ m. for the chamber of the House of Commons (S. Rossiter [ed.], *Blue Guide: London*⁹, plan on pp. 16–17), which at present has 630 members and seats for 602 (ibid., 18).   [2] *Hesp.* 1937, 135–40.

[3] Paus. I. 3. v, Arr. *Peri.* 9.   [4] Plin. *N.H.* xxxvi. 17.   [5] *Hesp.* 1937, 206–10.

[6] From *c.* 450 (HMA 34, 7 sqq.) to 342 ([D.] VII. *Hal.* 33) but not thereafter we find references to stelae ἐν τῶι βουλευτηρίωι, while throughout the fourth century (And. I. *Myst.* 95 [400] to *IG* ii² 487, 19–20 [304/3]) stelae might be erected ἔμπροσθεν τοῦ βουλευτηρίου. In 353/2 a νόμος was to be published ἔμπροσθεν τοῦ Μητρωίου (*IG* ii² 140, 34–5); from 343 (D. XIX. *F.L.* 129) until the third century A.D. documents were kept ἐν τῶι Μητρωίωι, but late in the fourth century A.D. Julian, v. 159 A–B, uses the past tense for this practice.

The area in front of the bouleuterium/Metroum is probably denoted also by the ἔμπροσθεν

of the second century B.C. a larger Metroum was built on the site of the Old Bouleuterium and the pre-480 temple of the Mother, and this no doubt continued to serve the dual purpose of temple and record office, perhaps until the Herulian sack in A.D. 267. Professor Thompson's argument from the anti-tyranny law of 337/6[1] that when that law was carried the Areopagus used to meet in the Old Bouleuterium is not convincing.[2]

To the south of the bouleuteria lay the Tholos, whose erection I have discussed on pp. 18–19. Since the prytanes and state secretaries ate there a kitchen was needed, and four different structures were added to the north side of the building for this purpose, the earliest being contemporary with the main building. A porch was added to the main (east) entrance to the Tholos about the time of Augustus, and an annexe was built on the west side in the third century A.D. Other changes in the buildings occupied by the boule may be noticed more briefly: the Tholos was damaged and repaired on several occasions, the first being not long after the building's completion, and the whole area was damaged in the Sullan sack and the sack of the Herulians; at some time marble benches on the theatre pattern were installed in the New Bouleuterium (previously the seats were probably of wood);[3] and various ornamental additions were made to the open space between the New Bouleuterium and Metroum and the Tholos.[4] After the Herulians' sack the Bouleuterium was abandoned,[5] and for a time the Metroum also was neglected; but the Tholos was repaired and when that was abandoned at the beginning of the fifth century A.D. the Metroum was brought into use again. By the seventh or eighth century the whole region was desolate.

Some details can be pieced together of the internal arrangements of the bouleuterium.[6] (We do not know the exact date of the New Bouleuterium's completion, and cannot be sure which of the two buildings is

τοῦ συνεδρίου or πρὸς τῶι συνεδρίωι found in three inscriptions of the third century B.C. (*Hesp.* vi 2 A, 12; vii 18, 39–40; vii 19, 5); but Professor Wycherley in his note on συνέδριον (*Testimonia*, pp. 126–8) seems too willing to apply to a building uses of the word which probably refer to a meeting.

The area in front of the Old Bouleuterium could also be regarded (more loosely) as in front of the New Bouleuterium, but it seems likely that from about the 340s the Old Bouleuterium was becoming known as the Metroum.   [1] *SEG* xii 87, 24–6.

[2] *Hesp.* xxii 1953, 52. On this passage see also Meritt, *Hesp.* xxi 1952, 358, xxii 1953, 129, Wycherley, *JHS* lxxv 1955, 118–21, *Testimonia*, p. 127. βουλευτήριον in this law must surely refer to the council-chamber of the Areopagus, and συνέδριον to meetings of the Areopagus in its βουλευτήριον or anywhere else.

[3] *Hesp.* 1937, 158–60.   [4] Cf. Plans C and D.   [5] *Hesp.* 1937, 171–2.

[6] Cf. W. A. McDonald, *Political Meeting Places of the Greeks*, 131–8. I reproduce his plan of the New Bouleuterium (plate xviii) as Plan F, and suggest a similar reconstruction of the internal arrangements of the Old Bouleuterium in Plan E. (Until stone benches were installed it is assumed that the seats in the New Bouleuterium, as in the Old, were arranged to form three sides of a rectangle: *Hesp.* 1937, 134, 150.)

referred to in some of our texts; but since the two council chambers were almost identical in dimensions it is unlikely that there were any differences of real significance for the scanty information available to us.)[1] There was a βῆμα from which men spoke, in full view of the rest of the chamber, and large enough for two men to stand on together.[2] At the end of the fifth century there were special benches for the prytanes, presumably facing the rest of the chamber, with room in front of them for the two tables on which the Thirty required members to place their votes.[3] Whereas there were fifty prytanes there can never have been more than twelve proedri, so after the change in presidency the space that had to be set aside for presiding officers will have been smaller. I imagine that in so small a chamber the prytanes will then have sat with the other members, though a part of the members' seating may have been set aside as the πρυτανικὸν μέρος.[4]

At the entrance to the chamber was a κιγκλίς, which could be used to separate members from non-members: if Aristophanes' sausage-seller is to be trusted, it was possible to listen to the proceedings from outside the κιγκλίς,[5] but a man who wished to speak to the boule would have to pass inside.[6] The κιγκλίς is probably to be distinguished from the δρύφακτοι, which appear to have been barriers separating the members' seats from the front part of the chamber. When the sausage-seller gave his good news about the price of pilchards,

> ἐκεκράγεσάν τε τοὺς πρυτάνεις ἀφιέναι·
> εἶθ' ὑπερεπήδων τοὺς δρυφάκτους πανταχῇ.[7]

There are interesting details in Xenophon's account of the 'trial' of Theramenes. Critias, not trusting the boule to condemn his opponent, talked to his colleagues in the Thirty and then went out and ἐπιστῆναι ἐκέλευσε τοὺς τὰ ἐγχειρίδια ἔχοντας φανερῶς τῇ βουλῇ ἐπὶ τοῖς δρυφάκτοις.[8]

---

[1] McDonald applies all the evidence to the New Bouleuterium: this is certainly wrong for some passages.   [2] Ant. VI. *Chor.* 40.

[3] Lys. XIII. *Ag.* 37: cf. p. 26 and n. 10 above.

[4] From 410/09 each member had to sit in the seat allotted to him (Phil. 328 F 140): at that time prytanes certainly sat apart from the other members, and they apparently occupied special seats, perhaps front benches or, say, 'right wing' benches later (cf. Din. II. *Arist.* 13). A location for the presidential benches is suggested at no. 4 in Plans E and F: McDonald failed to allow for the change in presidency. The seven νομοφύλακες instituted in the late fourth century sat with the proedri (Phil. 328 F 64 b). (For a machine which could have been used for the allotment of seats see Dow's κληρωτήριον III, *Hesp.* Supp. i 1937, 204–5, 211–12.)

[5] But contrast [D.] XXV. *Aristog.* i. 23, Harp. ἀπεσχοινισμένος. Perhaps there was an outer barrier at the entrance to the precinct and/or to the vestibule (of the Old Bouleuterium), and this too was called a κιγκλίς (cf. *Hesp.*vi 1937, 134, 213, McDonald, 172. The bases of two pairs of posts which may have supported such a κιγκλίς are marked K on Plan C, and there is a similar pair, not shown on the plan, due south of the west wall of the Old Bouleuterium).

[6] Ar. *Eq.* 625 sqq., esp. 641–2.   [7] Ibid. 674–5.   [8] X. *H.* II. iii. 50.

When Critias had announced the exclusion of Theramenes from the three thousand who were entitled to a trial by the boule, and his condemnation by the Thirty, Theramenes sought refuge at the ἑστία,[1] but Satyrus came in with the Eleven and dragged him away. ἡ δὲ βουλὴ ἡσυχίαν εἶχεν, ὁρῶσα καὶ τοὺς ἐπὶ τοῖς δρυφάκτοις ὁμοίους Σατύρῳ καὶ τὸ ἔμπροσθεν τοῦ βουλευτηρίου πλῆρες τῶν φρουρῶν.[2] Pollux seems to have regarded the κιγκλίς and δρύφακτοι as distinct, since he remarks that the courts had both,[3] and McDonald's arrangement of the barriers seems the most reasonable.[4] (Mention of the φρουροί employed by the Thirty reminds us that even under the fifth-century democracy the Scythian archers were used to keep order in the boule.[5] Where were these stationed? Even the φρουροί of the Thirty were apparently out of the members' sight until they were called in, so it is likely that when meetings were in progress there was a contingent of archers in the outer vestibule of the Old Bouleuterium,[6] which could be summoned into the chamber if the prytanes thought it necessary.)

There are several other references to the ἑστία βουλαία, where men could seek sanctuary. Mantitheus and Apsephion, bouleutae accused of mutilating the Hermae in 415, went to sit at the ἑστία;[7] Andocides, when he attempted to return to Athens under the regime of the Four Hundred, was brought before the boule and on being denounced by Pisander leaped to the ἑστία and took hold of the sacred emblems.[8] Men might also swear by the ἑστία βουλαία.[9] McDonald locates this ἑστία, with the βῆμα, in the 'orchestra' of the bouleuterium.[10] ἐν αὐτῷ τῷ βουλευτηρίῳ Διὸς βουλαίου καὶ Ἀθηνᾶς βουλαίας ἱερόν ἐστι καὶ εἰσίοντες οἱ βουλευταὶ προσεύχονται:[11] Pausanias in his visit to Athens saw in the bouleuterium statues of Zeus βουλαῖος, Apollo, and Demos, and paintings of the thesmothetae (late fourth century) and Callippus (third century).[12] In the first century A.D. Zeus, Athena, and Hestia shared a priest,[13] who was given a front seat in the Theatre of Dionysus,[14] and Zeus βουλαῖος might receive dedications either with Hestia βουλαία[15] or alone.[16] McDonald locates the

---

[1] X. *H.* II. iii. 52, cf. D.S. XIV. 4. vii, 5. iii, [Pl.] *X. Or.* 836 F.

[2] X. *H.* II. iii. 55. [3] Poll. VIII. 17, cf. 124.

[4] See Plans E and F: δρύφακτοι, no. 3; κιγκλίς, nos. 5 (E), 8 (F). [5] Ar. *Eq.* 665.

[6] Cf. Plans B, C, E. The New Bouleuterium had nothing corresponding to this vestibule until a porch was added on the south side shortly before 275, but the force of Scythian archers was disbanded early in the fourth century (cf. Busolt and Swoboda, 979–80) and it is not known that their police duties at meetings of the boule passed to any other body (for the ecclesia, cf. Ch. IV, pp. 146–7). [7] And. I. *Myst.* 44.

[8] And. II. *Red.* 15. [9] A. II. *F.L.* 45, Din. fr. 8 (Burtt) = ²xviii. 1 (Sauppe).

[10] See Plans E and F: ἑστία, no. 1: βῆμα, no. 2. [11] Ant. VI. *Chor.* 45.

[12] Paus. I. 3. v. [13] *IG* ii² 3543. [14] *IG* ii² 5054.

[15] *Hesp.* xii 16 and 17 (CI B.C.). [16] *IG* ii² 1813, 16 (*c.* A.D. 200).

statues near the entrance to the chamber, no doubt correctly, and identifies them with the ἱερόν,[1] but the members' religious act on entering the chamber does not rule out the more attractive possibility that the ἱερόν was in fact the altar in the 'orchestra'.[2]

Though the bouleuterium was the headquarters of the boule, meetings could be and frequently were held elsewhere.[3] Government had to continue and decisions had to be made while Athens was abandoned during the Persian Wars, and there is nothing unlikely in the statement (in the story of the rejected Persian peace terms) that the boule met on Salamis.[4] In the emergency which followed the mutilation of the Hermae the boule spent the night on the Acropolis—with the exception of the prytanes, who went to the Tholos.[5] In 434/3 the newly created Treasurers of the Other Gods were to take over the treasures of the various sanctuaries in the presence of the boule on the Acropolis;[6] in 371 the boule was in session on the Acropolis when news of the battle of Leuctra arrived.[7] On other occasions the boule's business took it to the Piraeus: the second decree for Methone, in 426/5, refers to τὰς ἐν τῶι νεορίοι ἕ[δρας], presumably of the boule,[8] and in 325/4 the boule was ordered to meet συνεχῶς on the quay to deal with the dispatch of a colony to the Adriatic.[9] In the confused circumstances of 319 there was a meeting of the boule in the Piraeus which is not known to have been concerned with naval business,[10] and other meetings in the Piraeus decreed honours for the officials of a prytany,[11] and for a priest.[12] During the period of the Mysteries the boule met at Eleusis,[13] and on the first day after the Mysteries, in accordance with a 'Solonian' law, it met in the city Eleusinium.[14] References are found in late inscriptions to meetings in the Theseum (to honour ephebi),[15] and in the Panathenaic Stadium (to honour prytanes' officials)[16] or adjourned from there to the Theatre of Dionysus (to

---

[1] *Meeting Places*, 135, cf. Plan F, nos. 6 and 7.

[2] Schol. A. II. *F.L.* 45, s.vv. καὶ τὴν ἑστίαν κτλ., Bachmann, *Anecdota Graeca*, i. 181. 9; cf. McDonald, *Meeting Places*, 137 n. 51, D. M. MacDowell, commentary on And. I. *Myst.* 44.

[3] McDonald, *Meeting Places*, 141–7, discusses meeting-places other than the bouleuterium.

[4] H. IX. 4. ii–5. i., Lyc. *Leocr.* 122, Aristid. XLVI. *Quatt.* 217. 11 sqq. (pp. 286–7, Dindorf).

[5] And. I. *Myst.* 45   [6] M&L 58 A, 18–21.

[7] X. *H.* VI. iv. 20.   [8] M&L 65, 53–4.

[9] Tod 200, 247 sqq. We may wonder how formally such a meeting was organized and how many members attended it.

[10] Pl. *Phoc.* 32. iv. Athens had lost most of her ships in 322 (D.S. XVIII. 15. ix, Pl. *Demetr.* 11. iv, *Marm. Par.* 239 B 9).

[11] *P* 44, 3.   [12] *IG* ii² 783, 4.

[13] *IG* ii² 1072, 3, cf. McDonald, *Meeting Places*, 145 (citing Graindor, *Album d'inscriptions attiques d'époque impériale*, 28).

[14] And. I. *Myst.* 111, cf. *P* 36, 30–1. (On *IG* ii² 794, 4, see Pélékidis, *REG* lxiii 1950, 112–17.)

[15] *IG* ii² 1039, 3.   [16] *Chron. Hell. Ath.*, 114, ll. 6–7.

honour ephebi again,[1] and to make a grant of citizenship),[2] and Pollux writes of the boule's meeting in the Stoa Basileos for the δοκιμασία of the archons.[3] Plutarch twice tells the story of Cimon's attempt to return from ostracism and fight with his tribe at Tanagra in 457: in the *Pericles* it is Pericles' friends who refuse to admit him to the ranks,[4] but in the *Cimon* the boule is said to have ordered the generals not to admit him.[5] If there is any truth at all in the story the version which blames Pericles' friends must surely be the correct one: the other story seems to envisage a meeting of the boule at Tanagra, but any formal meeting to consider such a question is unlikely, and in any case the bouleutae, being exempt from military service,[6] ought not to have been at Tanagra.

Meetings of the boule were proclaimed by the herald, and it may be that a further signal was given by the lowering of a flag: ἐπειδὴ τὴν βουλὴν εἰς τὸ βουλευτήριον ὁ κῆρυξ ἀνείποι ἰέναι καὶ τὸ σημεῖον καθέλοι, τῷ αὐτῷ σημείῳ ἡ μὲν βουλὴ εἰς τὸ βουλευτήριον ᾖει, οἱ δ᾽ ἐκ τῆς ἀγορᾶς ἔφευγον, δεδιότες εἰς ἕκαστος μὴ συλλειφθείη.[7] But references in Aristophanes to a σημεῖον for the δικαστήρια[8] and for the assembly[9] do not help us to decide what the σημεῖον was or how it was used.

Before a meeting began a purificatory sacrifice was offered, of small pigs, whose blood was used for the ritual cleansing of the meeting-place.[10] (This is attested only for the assembly, but where evidence is available the parallel between procedure in the boule and in the assembly is so close that in matters of formality it seems safe to apply to the boule texts in which only the assembly is mentioned.[11]) The herald then recited a curse[12] and prayer[13] at the dictation of the secretary: the curse, we are told,[14] and the rest of the prayer, we may assume, were the same for boule and assembly. Liable to the curse were those who took bribes to speak

---

[1] *IG* ii² 1043, 4–5.

[2] *IG* ii² 893, 5–7, restored by Meritt (*AJP* lxxviii 1957) to read

$$[βου]λὴ$$
$$[καὶ ἐκκλησία ἐν τῶι] θεάτρωι μεταχθε[ῖ]σα ἐκ$$
$$[Παναθηναϊκοῦ σταδίο]υ$$

(letters underlined read by Lolling but not by Meritt), 'this being an abbreviated form . . . probably implying that the deliberations had been begun with a meeting of the Council in the Panathenaic stadion and concluded with a meeting of the Assembly in the theater' (p. 397). I should like to see a more secure parallel to this odd formula.

[3] Poll. viii. 86 (*not* in *A.P.*).

[4] Pl. *Per.* 10. i.   [5] Pl. *Cim.* 17. iv–v.   [6] Cf. p. 13 and n. 6 above.

[7] And. I. *Myst.* 36.   [8] Ar. *Vesp.* 689–90.   [9] Ar. *Thesm.* 277–8 and schol.

[10] A. I. *Tim.* 23, cf. Ar. *Ach.* 44 and schol., *Eccl.* 128 and schol., Harp., Suid., Phot. καθάρσιον, Suid. περιστίαρχος, Poll. viii. 104.

[11] Cf. A. G. Woodhead, *Hist.* xvi 1967, 134.

[12] Din. II. *Arist.* 16, Lyc. *Leocr.* 31.

[13] Din. II. *Arist.* 14.   [14] D. XIX. *F.L.* 70.

against the interests of the city,[1] who betrayed the city,[2] who deceived the boule and demos,[3] or who (as late as 380!) negotiated with the Mede.[4] But our best evidence for the prayer and curse is a parody in Aristophanes' *Thesmophoriazusae*, and from this we can reconstruct the general sense of the original:

Let us pray to (various deities) that this meeting in the boule/ecclesia may go as well as possible, to the benefit of the city of Athens and individually of ourselves, and that whoever acts and speaks in the best interests of Athens may prevail.[5]

Let us pray to the Olympian Gods, the Pythian, the Delian, and all the other gods, that if any one devises evil against the demos of Athens, or negotiates with the Mede with a view to harming Athens, or plans to set up a tyranny, or to bring the tyrant back,[6] or deceives the boule and demos of Athens, or betrays the city, or takes bribes to speak against the interests of Athens,[7] or debases the coinage, he and his house may come to a miserable end.

But on the rest of us may the gods pour many blessings.[8]

References to bringing back the tyrant and to negotiating with the Mede guarantee the antiquity of part of the prayer; but although we know of no clause which must be later than the Persian Wars it is not unlikely that other specific imprecations will have been incorporated later.

The detailed πρόγραμμα for meetings of the boule was produced by the prytanes,[9] just as the πρόγραμμα for the ecclesia was produced by the boule as a whole, but there were general principles governing the order of business. Aeschines (writing of the ecclesia) tells us:

προχειροτονεῖν κελεύει (sc. ὁ νομοθέτης) τοὺς προέδρους περὶ ἱερῶν τῶν πατρίων καὶ κήρυξι καὶ πρεσβείαις καὶ ὁσίων,[10] καὶ μετὰ ταῦτα ἐπερωτᾷ ὁ κῆρυξ· "τίς ἀγορεύειν βούλεται τῶν ὑπὲρ πεντήκοντα ἔτη γεγονότων;" ἐπειδὰν δὲ οὗτοι πάντες εἴπωσι, τότ' ἤδη κελεύει λέγειν τῶν ἄλλων Ἀθηναίων τὸν βουλόμενον, οἷς ἔξεστιν.[11]

The distinction between those over fifty and the younger citizens is found also in Plutarch,[12] and elsewhere Aeschines ascribes to Solon a law no longer observed, requiring men to speak in descending order of age in

---

[1] Din. I. *Dem.* 47, II. *Arist.* 16.   [2] D. XXIII. *Arist.* 97.
[3] D. XVIII. *Cor.* 282, XXIII. *Arist.* 97, Din. I. *Dem.* 47.
[4] Is. IV. *Paneg.* 157, cf. Pl. *Arist.* 10. vi.   [5] Cf. Ar. *Thesm.* 295-311.
[6] Cf. ibid. 331-9.   [7] From texts cited above, nn. 1-3.
[8] Cf. Ar. *Thesm.* 347-51. There is a considerable overlap with the specific strand of the νόμος εἰσαγγελτικός (cf. Ch. IV, p. 163); and compare also the bouleutic oath (appendix to Ch. IV, p. 194).   [9] Cf. p. 20 and n. 2 above.
[10] Compare the order in which items are listed for the third and fourth assemblies of the prytany, in *A.P.* 43. vi; and also the 'future constitution' of 411 (*A.P.* 30. v). For the προχειροτονία held before the ecclesia settled down to serious debate, cf. Ch. II, p. 58 n. 4. There is no evidence for προχειροτονία in the boule.
[11] A. I. *Tim.* 23.   [12] Pl. *An Seni*, 784 C-D.

both boule and ecclesia.[1] The age distinction is not observed in mock assemblies: Aristophanes' heralds open the debate with a simple τίς ἀγορεύειν βούλεται;[2] while Lucian adds the warning that the invitation does not of course apply to the ἄτιμοι: τίς ἀγορεύειν βούλεται τῶν τελείων θεῶν οἷς ἔξεστιν;[3] In one of Lucian's divine assemblies the gods are to be graded according to quality, with those whose statues were by Phidias and the like ranking very low and not being permitted to speak; but this turns out to be a matter of Solonian property-classes: Hermes says: μανθάνω ὅτι πλουτίνδην κελεύεις ἀλλὰ μὴ ἀριστίνδην καθίζειν, καὶ ἀπὸ τιμημάτων,[4] and various Greek deities object to being placed among the ζευγῖται.[5]

Priority of religious matters in the order of business is confirmed by inscriptions.[6] Foreigners who were given the right of access to the boule and demos were commonly given a guarantee that they were to be brought forward πρῶτον μετὰ τὰ ἱερά;[7] while in a decree concerning the public doctors' sacrifices to Asclepius the probouleuma reads χρηματίσαι περὶ τούτων ἐν ἱεροῖς,[8] and in a decree of Athenian cleruchs on Lemnos five envoys who are being sent to Athens on ceremonial business ποιήσονται τὴν πρόσοδον ἐ[ν ἱεροῖς πρός τε τὴν βουλὴν] καί τὸν δῆμον.[9]

On questions concerning the δοκιμασία or the punishment of a named individual the boule voted by ballot: we see this method employed to decide whether an invalid passed or failed the δοκιμασία for his subsistence grant,[10] to reach a verdict on an εἰσαγγελία,[11] and in the trial of

---

[1] A. III. Ctes. 2. ἰσηγορία in the ecclesia has recently been discussed by G. T. Griffith (Ancient Society and Institutions, 115–38) and A. G. Woodhead (Hist. xvi 1967). Mr. Griffith would date the appearance of freedom of speech for all citizens to the period immediately after 462 (p. 125), while Mr. Woodhead has stressed that there must always have been freedom of speech in the Cleisthenic boule and its Solonian predecessor (cf. Griffith, p. 122). On Aeschines' allegation of priority for older citizens see Griffith's remarks, pp. 119–20.

[2] Ar. Ach. 45, Thesm. 379, Eccl. 130; cf. D. XVIII. Cor. 170 (but if the longer formula was in use Demosthenes would no doubt have shortened it here for rhetorical effect).

[3] Lucian, Deor. Conc. 1, Jupp. Trag. 18. On these passages in Lucian see J. Delz, Lukians Kenntnis der athenischen Antiquitäten, 121–4. [4] Lucian, Jupp. Trag. 7.

[5] Ibid. 10. I do not imagine that the right to address the assembly was even formally defined in terms of these property-classes.

[6] Cf., e.g., L. Robert, BCH lviii 1934, 513.

[7] IG i² 59, 19; post-403/2 references collected IG ii² iv. i under lemmata cited at p. 62. i s.vv. πρῶτον μετὰ τὰ ἱερά. [8] IG ii² 772, 14–16.

[9] IG ii² 1224 ab, 17–18. Wade-Gery and Meritt wrote of the arrangements for the carrying of Thudippus' assessment-decree (M&L 69, 33–8): 'It seems that on the second day the adjourned business came πρῶτον, not merely πρῶτον μετὰ τὰ ἱερά' (AJP lvii 1936, 387–8 n. 28). It would perhaps be fairer to say that if the matter could not be settled in one day the assembly would be adjourned, and business would naturally be resumed where it had been interrupted. For a short discussion of this passage, see Additional Note B, pp. 229–30.

[10] Lys. XXIV. Pens. Inv. 26. But voting was by show of hands in the δοκιμασία of archons (A.P. 55. iv), and surely in that of bouleutae also. [11] [D.] XLVII. Ev. et Mnes. 42.

members on matters of internal discipline;[1] when the question of whether to expel a member was raised the boule voted first with olive leaves and afterwards by ballot.[2] The normal democratic practice, which the Thirty failed to uphold, was that each voter had two ψῆφοι, one black and one white, and to guarantee the secrecy of the ballot placed one into each of two καδίσκοι.[3] The word ψήφισμα suggests that voting on all substantial motions should originally have been by ballot, but this was too cumbersome a procedure to be employed except when ψηφίσματα were few, and it is unlikely that it had been employed for this purpose even then.[4] Most decisions were made by show of hands, with a count probably not taken unless the will of the meeting was not clear, and in Athenian practice ψηφίζειν and χειροτονεῖν were used to distinguish not voting procedures but types of decision. χειροτονεῖν is the regular word used in literary and epigraphic texts for all kinds of appointment, and in inscribed decrees the verb διαχειροτονεῖν was used in open clauses, within otherwise specific motions, on which a fairly straightforward decision was needed.[5]

Though the Old and New Bouleuteria could both accommodate five hundred members, one may wonder how well the meetings of the boule were attended. We have already seen that membership of the boule did not oblige a man to spend the whole year in Athens,[6] and even the most conscientious members may have found that other public duties, perhaps duties due to their membership of the boule, sometimes prevented them from attending meetings. And of course not every member was conscientious. Demosthenes in his attack on Androtion distinguishes between the inactive members who keep quiet and make no proposals, and for the most part do not even go to the bouleuterium, and οἱ λέγοντες or πολιτευόμενοι, who are the men responsible for the unsatisfactory conduct of the whole boule;[7] and Plato in the Laws expects his bouleutae to be busy only when they are members of the reigning prytany.[8] A further indication of low attendance is that although from 307/6 until the reign of Hadrian the number of members was never less than 600, and rose to 650 in the last quarter of the third century B.C., it was never felt necessary to enlarge the New Bouleuterium.[9]

[1] νόμος in A. I. Tim. 35.   [2] A. I. Tim. 112.   [3] Cf. Lys. XIII. Ag. 37.
[4] Cf. Busolt and Swoboda, 454–5. For voting by show of hands in the ecclesia at the end of the fifth century cf. X. H. I. vii. 7, Lys. XII. Erat. 75.
[5] M&L 65, 5 sqq.; IG i² 88, 1–5; M&L 78, b 2–3; Tod 114, 13 sqq.; 166, 5 sqq.; IG ii² 674, 13–20. Compare the boule's vote on whether to fine Theophemus 500 drachmae or refer the case to a δικαστήριον for a heavier penalty ([D.] XLVII. Ev. et Mnes. 42).
[6] Cf. p. 13 and n. 5 above.   [7] D. XXII. Andr. 36–8.
[8] Plat. Legg. VI. 758 B.   [9] Cf. p. 31 above.

Except when secrecy was specified, meetings of the boule were open to the public. Demosthenes in his speech *On the Chersonese* refers to what he has recently heard a man saying in the boule;[1] and in the speech *On the Embassy* he mentions the report which he made to the boule on returning from the second embassy to Philip of Macedon, and says: καὶ ταυτὶ πολλοὶ συνίσασιν ἃ μέλλω λέγειν· τὸ γὰρ βουλευτήριον μεστὸν ἦν ἰδιωτῶν.[2] Aeschines, complaining of sharp practice by Demosthenes, tells us that he εἰσελθὼν εἰς τὸ βουλευτήριον καὶ μεταστησάμενος τοὺς ἰδιώτας ἐκφέρεται προβούλευμα εἰς τὴν ἐκκλησίαν, προσλαβὼν τὴν τοῦ γράψαντος ἀπειρίαν.[3] Menexenus went to listen to the debate when he heard that the boule was to choose the orator who would deliver the funeral oration, but he was thwarted, for the matter was postponed until the next day.[4] Our only problem here is to find room for ἰδιῶται in an already crowded bouleuterium. The passage which I have quoted from Demosthenes' speech *On the Embassy* ought to mean that the public was admitted into the Chamber; but in the *Knights* the sausage-seller follows Cleon to the bouleuterium, hears Cleon's speech, and only when he has decided to address the boule himself bursts in through the κιγκλίς.[5] There was probably space in which some members of the public could stand in the aisle on the south side of the chamber in the Old Bouleuterium and on the east side in the New;[6] if the ἰδιῶται were kept beyond the κιγκλίς they will have been outside the chamber altogether, able to hear the proceedings only with difficulty, and if the βῆμα is correctly located in the 'orchestra' perhaps unable to see the speakers. It is more likely that ἰδιῶται were allowed inside the chamber,[7] but the problem cannot finally be solved on the limited evidence available.

The boule was entitled, when it chose, to meet in secret, and we have a number of references, of varying reliability, to these secret meetings.[8] According to Diodorus, Themistocles outlined his plans for rebuilding the walls of Athens after the Persian Wars[9] and for fortifying the Piraeus[10] at secret meetings of the boule—but in each case the boule is entrusted with the kind of decision which we should expect the ecclesia to reserve

---

[1] D. VIII. *Chers.* 4.

[2] D. XIX. *F.L.* 17 (the scholiast *ad loc.* thinks that the ἰδιῶται were mingling with the members).

[3] A. III. *Ctes.* 125. μεταστησάμενος τοὺς ἰδιώτας surely means 'having the public removed' (cf. Budé and Loeb translations), but Professor Jones oddly translates it as 'pushing aside the ordinary members' (*Athenian Democracy*, 120).

[4] Plat. *Menex.* 234 A–B.   [5] Ar. *Eq.* 625 sqq.   [6] Cf. Plans E and F.

[7] ἰδιῶται could certainly enter the chamber when a meeting was not in progress: cf. Ant. VI. *Chor.* 40.

[8] References collected by G. E. M. de Ste Croix, *CQ*[2] xiii 1963, 115 n. 1.

[9] D. S. xv. 39. v.   [10] Ibid. 42. v.

for itself,[1] and the stories thus have a suspicious ring.[2] But although we have no trustworthy example this early, secret sessions had become enough of an institution by the 420s (no doubt they were found particularly useful in war time) for Aristophanes to offer a parody: the sausage-seller in the *Knights*, after informing the boule that pilchards are at their lowest price since the outbreak of the war, suggests in secret that the members should lay hands on all available containers and go to buy up the whole stock.[3] We hear of two secret meetings before the sailing of the Sicilian expedition in 415. When information was laid about the profanation of the Mysteries the prytanes held what might be called a 'secret' assembly, comprising only those citizens who had themselves been initiated into the Mysteries, to hear the detailed accusation;[4] and when Dioclides offered to give the names of those who were involved in the mutilation of the Hermae a secret discussion in the boule resulted in the decision to arrest Andocides and others. (Since they were summoned afterwards, the generals must have been excluded from this meeting.)[5] Far less plausibly, Diodorus writes of a secret meeting attended by the generals, which discussed what should be done with Sicily after the island had been conquered.[6]

Andocides, after his failure to secure recall from exile under the Four Hundred, tried to win the favour of the restored democrats, and to this end he made secret proposals to the boule of a plan to relieve Athens' corn shortage.[7] Another secret session took place in 404 in the course of the complicated plot to eliminate troublesome democrats: Theocritus claimed at a secret meeting of the boule that a plot was being formed but that he himself did not dare name the conspirators; this was to be done by Agoratus.[8] By 396 some of the Athenians were growing increasingly dissatisfied with their post-war dependence on Sparta, and one Demaenetus, who was alleged to have obtained the backing of the boule at a secret meeting, sailed from the Piraeus to join Conon (who was commanding Pharnabazus' fleet). When he had gone there was a panic in Athens, and the boule convened an assembly, οὐδὲν προσποιούμενοι μετεσχηκέναι τοῦ πράγματος.[9] After Philip's capture of Amphipolis in 357 there was some talk of secret negotiations or secret promises which he had

---

[1] Cf. Ch. II, p. 84 n. 3.
[2] Perhaps Ephorus misunderstood the use of ὑπειπών in T. I. 90. iv (so Gomme, *Hist. Comm. Thuc.*, i. 258, after Pfister). The Piraeus story is dubious in the extreme, and our confidence in it is not increased by Cicero's application of part of the mechanism to a different story about Themistocles (Cic. *Off.* II. 49).
[3] Ar. *Eq.* 647–50.
[4] And. I. *Myst.* 11–12.
[5] Ibid. 45.　　　[6] D.S. XIII. 2. vi.　　　[7] And. II. *Red.* 3, 19, 21.
[8] Lys. XIII. *Ag.* 21.　　　[9] *H.O.* 6. i–ii (Bartoletti).

violated,[1] but Mr. de Ste Croix has shown that the nature of ancient democracy excludes the possibility of Athens' being party to a secret agreement.[2] In 340/39 to divert the Amphictyonic Council's attention from the misdeeds of Athens Aeschines had urged a sacred war against Amphissa. He reported to the boule and ecclesia, and was thanked as Athenian representatives commonly were, but Demosthenes prevailed on one of the bouleutae to sponsor a motion at a secret meeting, which after its ratification by the ecclesia dissociated Athens from Aeschines' policy and the war against Amphissa.[3] Finally, before the outbreak of the Lamian War, Leosthenes was elected στρατηγός and τῇ βουλῇ διαλεχθεὶς ἐν ἀπορρήτοις obtained money and a supply of arms.[4] His supplies must in the last resort have been voted by the assembly, but it is perfectly credible that he outlined his plans at a secret meeting of the boule.[5]

A few general references may be added. In the first speech *Against Aristogiton* we are told that thanks to the κιγκλίς the boule is master of its secrets and ἰδιῶται are excluded; likewise the Areopagus and other ἀρχαί can keep intruders away.[6] Lysias, attacking a prospective bouleutes at his δοκιμασία, suggests that he is not a man who will be able to keep secrets.[7] And there is a disturbing passage in Aristophanes' *Ecclesiazusae*:

> γυναῖκα δ' εἶναι πρᾶγμ' ἔφη νουβυστικὸν
> καὶ χρηματοποιόν· κοὔτε τἀπόρρητ' ἔφη
> ἐκ Θεσμοφόροιν ἑκάστοτ' αὐτὰς ἐκφέρειν,
> σὲ δὲ κἀμὲ βουλεύοντε τοῦτο δρᾶν ἀεί.[8]

This is comedy, it is true, but we may well wonder how safe a secret was when it had been entrusted to several hundred Athenians. Certainly it is unlikely to have remained a secret for very long, but this probably did not matter. The more reliable accounts of secret meetings all deal with matters that were bound in any case to be made public before long, and where the advantage to be derived from secrecy was surprise action, usually against offending citizens or a foreign state: once the action had taken place, the object of the exercise was achieved.

We see in some of the texts cited above that non-members could be given permission to address the boule, either at a public or at a secret meeting. Any Athenian citizen could write to the prytanes to request an

---

[1] D. II. *Ol. ii.* 6.   [2] *CQ*² xiii 1963.
[3] A. III. *Ctes.* 125, quoted p. 40.   [4] D.S. XVII. 111. iii, cf. XVIII. 9. ii–iii.
[5] Professor F. W. Mitchel wants to believe in a secret agreement with the Aetolians, negotiated on behalf of the boule (*Phoen.* xviii 1964, 16–17), but see de Ste Croix's article, cited n. 2 above.
[6] [D.] XXV. *Aristog. i.* 23, cf. Harp. ἀπεσχοινισμένος. On the implications of this for the internal arrangements of the bouleuterium, cf. p. 33 and n. 5 above.
[7] Lys. XXXI. *Phil.* 31.   [8] Ar. *Eccl.* 441–4.

audience,[1] and foreigners who were honoured by the Athenians were frequently given the right of πρόσοδος πρὸς τὴν βουλὴν καὶ τὸν δῆμον.[2] Heralds and envoys from other states were brought before the boule,[3] and Athenian envoys were expected to report to the boule on their return to Athens:[4] Aristodemus, sent to negotiate with Philip in 348, failed to do this, and ἐνταῦθ᾽ ἠγανάκτουν πολλοὶ ὅτι τὴν πρεσβείαν οὐκ ἀπήγγειλεν ὁ Ἀριστόδημος. . . . τελευταῖον δ᾽ εἰς τὴν βουλὴν εἰσελθὼν Δημοκράτης ὁ Ἀφιδναῖος ἔπεισε τὴν βουλὴν ἀνακαλέσασθαι τὸν Ἀριστόδημον.[5] Large numbers of Attic decrees have their origin in reports made by men who have come before the demos in this way, and who have their requests granted or are honoured for doing their duty.[6] Generals on duty away from Athens sometimes sent written reports from which decrees resulted,[7] and foreign rulers also were apt to send letters to the boule and demos.[8]

More needs to be said about the relations between the boule and the generals. It has often been said that the generals occupied a specially privileged position with regard to the boule,[9] but the evidence must be examined carefully in the light of what has been said above. Plutarch tells us that Nicias ἄρχων μὲν ἐν τῷ στρατηγίῳ διετέλει μέχρι νυκτός, ἐκ δὲ βουλῆς ὕστατος ἀπῄει πρῶτος ἀφικνούμενος,[10] and writes of Pericles ὁδόν τε γὰρ ἐν ἄστει μίαν ἑωρᾶτο τὴν ἐπ᾽ ἀγορὰν καὶ τὸ βουλευτήριον πορευόμενος,[11] but Nicias may well have served a year in the boule, and what is said of Pericles could be said of any πολιτευόμενος who habitually went to listen to debates. In the fifth and fourth centuries the generals were often coupled with the boule and/or prytanes as the authorities who were to protect honorands from injustice.[12] As supreme military officials they often figure among those who took the oath to a treaty: our earliest oath of this

[1] Schol. Ar. Pax 905, cf. [Lys.] VI. And. 29, 33, O.O. iii. 3; request to be in writing, D. XXIV. Tim. 48, cf. Is. VII. Areop. 15; ἱκετηρία to the boule, A. I. Tim. 104.

[2] References IG i², p. 369. i. s.v. πρόσοδος, IG ii² IV. i, 59. ii, s.v. πρόσοδος.

[3] e.g. M&L 52, 12–14, D. XIX. F.L. 185. For two foreign representatives who did not get beyond the boule see H. IX. 5. ii, X. H. VI. ix. 20.

[4] SEG x 86, 40–2, cf. D. XIX F.L. 18–19. [5] A. II. F.L. 16–17.

[6] e.g. Athenian ambassadors, IG ii² 40, 207;

generals, IG ii² 108, Tod 143, IG ii² 187, 408, 414, (cf. Hesp. ix 1940, 340–1), IG ii² 735;

religious functionaries, IG ii² 47, 330, 365, 403, 410, 661, 689, 775, 780, 783, 807, 839, 976, SEG xviii 22, 26, xix 124;

other officials, on their religious and other duties, IG ii² 491, 665, 668, 781, 929, 941, 949, 1011, 1039, 1042, 1043, SEG xiv 64, 65, prytany decrees passim (on religious reports cf. Ch. III, p. 132);

ἰδιῶται, Tod 108 (probably), IG ii² 70, 243, 276 (probably a metic), 502 (a δημόσιος); foreigners, Tod 122, 124, 126, 131, 133, 134, 135, 146, 147, 159, 167, 168, 175, 178.

[7] e.g. Tod 168, cf. Lyc., fr. 105 (Sauppe).

[8] e.g. Tod 133, 167, IG ii² 387, 486, cf. [D.] XII. Ep. Phil.

[9] e.g. Hignett, 246–7, W. Schwahn, RE, Supp. vi. 1079. [10] Pl. Nic. 5. i.

[11] Pl. Per. 7. v, cf. Praec. Ger. Reip. 800 c (βῆμα and bouleuterium).

[12] e.g. SEG x 53, 105, M&L 90, Tod 173, 178, 181.

kind, to the Chalcidian alliance of 446/5, was taken by the boule and the δικασταί,[1] but the oath in a proxeny decree of about 430,[2] and the oath to the alliance with Halieis in 424/3,[3] were sworn to by the generals and the boule. The truce with Sparta in 423 was sworn to by three generals,[4] and the Peace of Nicias in 421 by seventeen Athenians including some of the generals;[5] the Bottiaean alliance of 422 by the boule, the generals, and other ἀρχαί,[6] and the Argive alliance of 420 by the boule and ἔνδημοι ἀρχαί under the supervision of the prytanes.[7] In 394 we find the beginning of what was to be the fourth-century pattern: the oath to Eretria was taken by the boule, the generals, and the ἱππεῖς.[8] Thereafter the oath was usually taken by the boule, the generals, and the ἱππεῖς or various military officials; occasionally the boule was omitted.[9]

Nothing that I have yet mentioned proves that the generals ever enjoyed a privileged status vis-à-vis the boule, though it does show that the boule and generals were often required to co-operate. There is, however, some evidence that the generals enjoyed special privileges in the latter half of the fifth century. In the alliance with Perdiccas of Macedon, possibly to be dated about 436, the words [—τὸς στρατ]εγὸς χρεματί-σαντα[ς —] are plausibly restored;[10] in the second decree for Methone we read: ἄλλο δὲ προχρεμα[τίσαι το]ύ[το]ν μεδέν, ἐὰμ μέ τι οἱ στρατε[γ]οὶ δέοντα[ι];[11] and, most important, the truce of 423 with Sparta orders the generals and the prytanes to convene an ecclesia for the Athenians to deliberate about peace.[12] In 431, when the Athenians' patience was strained by the Peloponnesians' invasion of Attica, Pericles ἐκκλησίαν . . . οὐκ ἐποίει αὐτῶν οὐδὲ ξύλλογον οὐδένα, τοῦ μὴ ὀργῇ τι μᾶλλον ἢ γνώμῃ ξυνελθόντας ἐξαμαρτεῖν,[13] but a year later, when morale was sapped by the plague, we read of him ξύλλογον ποιήσας (ἔτι δ' ἐστρατήγει).[14] On the first passage, Gomme remarks:

There is no evidence that the strategoi had the power . . . to disallow the regular ekklesiai; what Perikles refused to do was to summon a special meeting, which in a crisis the strategoi could do and which they did next year (59. iii), and to address the people in any way.[15]

---

[1] M&L 52, 3–4. In ll. 64–9 the boule is ordered to appoint three of its members to join with Hierocles in sacrificing for Euboea; and so that this can be done as soon as possible hοι στρατεγοὶ συνεπιμελόσθον καὶ τὸ ἀργύριον ἐς ταῦτα [π]αρεχόντον.

[2] SEG x 54, 10–11.　　　　[3] SEG x 80, 27–30.　　　　[4] T. iv. 118. xi–119. ii.

[5] T. v. 19. ii, cf. 24. On the Athenian signatories see A. Andrewes and D. M. Lewis, JHS lxxvii 1957.　　[6] Tod 68, 8–9.　　[7] T. v. 47. ix.　　[8] Tod 103, 10–12.

[9] As in IG ii² 21, 11–13; Tod 122, 16 sqq.; 144, 38 sqq.

[10] SEG x 86, 13.　　　　[11] M&L 65, 55–6.　　　　[12] T. iv. 118. xiv.

[13] T. ii. 22. i, cf. Pl. Per. 33. vi.　　　　[14] T. ii. 59. iii.

[15] Hist. Comm. Thuc., ii. 76. I agree that regular meetings of the assembly are unlikely to have been suspended; but contrast de Ste Croix, Dover, Brunt, cited on p. 45 n. 3 below.

On the second, he doubts whether this was their legal right:

As strategos, or rather as one of the ten strategoi, . . . he could request the prytaneis to call a special meeting of the ekklesia. It is not clear whether the prytaneis were bound to accede to the request, but little men were in any case not likely to oppose a popular politician.[1]

Hignett preferred to believe that Pericles' personal *auctoritas* influenced the decisions of the prytanes and boule,[2] but I think Gomme's stronger view or a modification of it must be correct: convening the ecclesia and arranging its agenda at this time may have been the joint prerogative of the prytanes (on behalf of the boule) and the generals; the possibility of their disagreeing was perhaps not envisaged.[3]

Other passages are less cogent in themselves, but may be adduced in support of this view. A decree which Professor Meritt refers to the collection of tribute and dates about 430 is restored to read:

$$[\pi\epsilon\rho\grave{\iota} \; \delta\grave{\epsilon}]$$
$$[\tauο\acute{\upsilon}\tauο\nu \; \tau\grave{\epsilon}\nu \; \beta ολ\grave{\epsilon}\nu \; \grave{\epsilon}\chi σ\epsilon\nu\epsilon\gamma\kappa\acute{\epsilon}]\nu \; \grave{\epsilon}\pi\acute{\alpha}\nu\alpha\gamma\kappa\epsilon\varsigma \; \grave{\epsilon}\varsigma \; \tauο[\nu \; \delta\acute{\epsilon}μο\nu \; \kappa\alpha]-$$
$$[\grave{\iota} \; \chi\rho\epsilonμ\alpha\tau\acute{\iota}σ\alpha\iota \; \tauο\hat{\iota}\varsigma \; σ\tau\rho\alpha\tau\epsilon\gammaο]\hat{\iota}\varsigma \; hό\tau\alpha\nu \; \delta\acute{\epsilonο\nu\tau\alpha\iota.}[4]$$

The proxeny decree for Potamodorus and Eurytion is restored to order the generals and prytanes to guarantee their πρόσοδος to the boule and demos.[5] A decree of 415 perhaps orders an assembly to be convened for the generals and other officers of the Sicilian expedition[6]—but this reflects the importance of the expedition rather than the privileged status of its officials. I can think of no reason why the generals should not at any time have drafted a motion to be put via the boule to the ecclesia on behalf of the whole college, even if they possessed no special privileges,[7] but it remains a fact that the only two instances we possess of decrees enacted on a γνώμη στρατηγῶν are dated to the latter half of the fifth

[1] Ibid. 167. The assumption that the prytanes were bound to be 'little men' is unfortunate.

[2] Pp. 246–7; he believed that the generals were *ex officio* members of the boule, but had no special powers beyond that.

[3] For more recent discussions of this topic see Jones, 124–5, G. E. M. de Ste Croix, *Hist.* v 1956, 3 n. 12, K. J. Dover, *JHS* lxxx 1960, 74–5, P. A. Brunt, *Phoen.* xix 1965, 265. H. D. Westlake, *Individuals in Thucydides*, 33, considers only Pericles' standing *vis-à-vis* his fellow generals.

Hignett seems to have exaggerated the involvement of the generals with the boule: they did not attend the secret meeting which considered the Hermocopid scandal, and I have little confidence in the secret meeting which Diodorus makes them attend to decide what to do with Sicily when it has been conquered (cf. p. 41 and nn. 5–6 above).

[4] *SEG* xii 26, 7–9.

[5] *SEG* x 84, 32–4.

[6] Tod 77 A, 14–19 (but no restorations in the cautious text of M&L 78, *c* 5–10).

[7] Cf. Ch. II, pp. 52–7, 63, on προβούλευσις.

century—the alliance with Perdiccas, perhaps about 436,[1] and a proxeny decree, to 416/15.[2] Proposals emanating from the generals are clearly more likely at a time when they participated in the duties of the boule and prytanes. Numerous enactments are attributed to Pericles himself,[3] but I am not convinced that to have carried each of them in his own name he must have been a general with privileged access to the boule and ecclesia: the alliance with Perdiccas is our only useful piece of evidence dated outside the Peloponnesian War, and its date is scarcely firm.[4]

For the fourth century there is not much evidence. A few motions arising from a general's report[5] prove nothing, and we are left with a passage in Plutarch's life of *Phocion*: γράψαντος δὲ τοῦ Ἀλεξάνδρου περὶ τριήρων ὅπως ἀποστείλωσιν αὐτῷ, καὶ τῶν ῥητόρων ἐνισταμένων, τῆς δὲ βουλῆς τὸν Φωκίωνα λέγειν κελευούσης, "λέγω τοίνυν ὑμῖν", εἶπεν, "ἢ τοῖς ὅπλοις κρατεῖν ἢ τοῖς κρατοῦσι φίλους εἶναι."[6] Obviously the point of the anecdote is the remark that Phocion made; if Plutarch happens to have described the circumstances correctly we need only suppose that Phocion along with other πολιτευόμενοι had gone to hear the debate in the boule, and was seen by the members and invited to speak.[7] I am not prepared to argue from this passage that he possessed special privileges.

In later Athenian history the generals, and in particular the στρατηγὸς ἐπὶ τὰ ὅπλα, acquired greater political power.[8] From the second century onwards prescript formulae show that they were able to convene meetings of the boule and ecclesia,[9] and under Roman domination the importance of the στρατηγὸς ἐπὶ τὰ ὅπλα seems to have increased still further. Under the Sullan regime this general was the author of decrees of the boule to honour the ephebi,[10] and the same practice is found in a decree of the

---

[1] HMA 66 (revised from *SEG* x 86), 47 sqq.

[2] *IG* ii² 27, cf. *Hesp.* viii 1939, 68.

[3] References HMA, p. 377.

[4] Three other texts illustrate the relations of the generals and the boule during the Peloponnesian War. In Thudippus' assessment-decree the generals are to apply to the boule, directly rather than via a court unless the ecclesia decrees otherwise, if they want an extra collection from the allies (M&L 69, 44–50); in a naval decree of about 409/8 the generals are to apply to the boule if they need more oars (*SEG* x 131, 10–12); and about the same time we find the ecclesia ratifying an on-the-spot agreement made by the generals with Clazomenae (M&L 88). None of these texts suggests anything approaching *ex officio* membership of the boule.

[5] Cf. p. 43 n. 6 above: the last inscription cited is of the third century, the others are of the fourth.

[6] Pl. *Phoc.* 21. i.

[7] In that case he must have been inside the chamber (cf. p. 40)—but it is unwise to rely too much on the background details of a story of this kind.

[8] On the στρατηγὸς ἐπὶ τὰ ὅπλα see now D. J. Geagan, *Hesp.* Supp. xii 1967, 18–31; he discusses the general's relationship with the boule and ecclesia on pp. 27–9, cf. p. 92.

[9] *IG* ii² 897, 4–6; 911, 6–7; 954, 2; cf. *SEG* xv 108, 50–4.

[10] *IG* ii² 1039.

boule and ecclesia carried early in the reign of Hadrian.[1] Hadrian's law on olive oil confirms 'the general's' right to convene the boule or ecclesia:

> ἐὰν δὲ τῶν ἐκ τοῦ πλοίου τις
> μηνύσῃ, ἐπάναγκες ὁ στρατηγὸς τῇ ἐξῆς
> ἡμέρᾳ βουλὴν ἀθροισάτω, εἰ δ' ὑπὲρ τοὺς
> πεντήκοντα ἀμφορεῖς εἴη τὸ μεμηνυ-
> μένον, ἐκκλησίαν.[2]

From the beginning of the third century we have a decree proposed by the ἄρχων [τῶν Εὐμολπιδῶν],[3] from which it would be dangerous to make any inference about automatic rights of access, and a decree with a very striking prescript:

> βουλὴ συνήχθη ἐπὶ τοῖς
> [εὐαγγ]ελίοις, ἀναδειχθέντος [Αὐτοκράτορος Καίσαρος Ποπλίου]
> [Σεπτιμίου Γέτα Εὐσεβοῦς Σεβαστοῦ]· ἐν ᾗ ἀνεγνώσθη
> [γνώμ]η [τ]ῶν συνεδρίων διὰ τῶν ἀρχόν[τ]ων, ἀναγνόν-
> [τος τοῦ] στρατηγοῦ Ἀλκαμένους Λαμπτρέως γνώμην τὴν ἀναγεγραμμένη[ν]·
> [ἡ ἐξ Ἀρείου] πάγου βουλὴ καὶ ἡ βουλὴ τῶν Φ καὶ ὁ δῆμος ὁ Ἀθηναί-
> [ων μετὰ] τῶν ἀρχόντων, τοῦ τε ἐπωνύμου ἄρχοντος Φλ. Διογενοῦς
> [Μαραθων]ίου κα[ὶ τ]οῦ ἐπὶ τὰ ὅπλα στρατηγοῦ καὶ ἐπιμελητοῦ γυ-
> [μνασιαρχί]ας θε[οῦ] Ἀδρι[α]νοῦ καὶ ἀ[ντ]άρχοντος τοῦ ἱερωτάτου ἀγ-
> [ῶνος τοῦ Π]ανελληνίου [Μα]ρ. Αὐρ. Ἀλκαμένους Λαμπτρέως καὶ τοῦ κήρ-
> [υκος τῆς ἐξ] Ἀρείου π[ά]γου βουλῆς καὶ ἀγωνοθέτου τῶν τῆς Σεβα-
> [στῆς οἰκίας (?) ἀ]γώνω[ν Τρύ]φωνος τοῦ Θεοφίλου Ὑβάδου γνώμην ἀπο-
> [φαίνου]σιν κατὰ [τὰ] πάτρια.[4]

No privileged access is revealed in the decrees honouring M. Ulpius Eubiotus.[5] It has been suggested that by this time the right to propose decrees was limited to the στρατηγὸς ἐπὶ τὰ ὅπλα, the Areopagus (through its herald), and other senior officials of the state,[6] but this is going beyond the evidence. It is not clear from the prescript which I quote above who attended which of the three meetings which must have taken place, but at any rate the στρατηγὸς ἐπὶ τὰ ὅπλα seems to have become an *ex officio* member of the boule, with the right to call meetings and propose motions.

---

[1] *IG* ii² 1072 (A.D. 136/7). In *IG* iv² 82–4 (A.D. 38/9?) the same man is author of the decree of the Areopagus and of the decree of the boule and demos, but there is no reason why he should not have been a bouleutes.

[2] *SEG* xv 108, 50–4.

[3] *IG* ii² 1078/9 (c. A.D. 220).

[4] *IG* ii² 1077, 5–17 (A.D. 209/10).

[5] *Hesp.* Supp. vi 31/2 with *SEG* xxi 506/5 (A.D. 229/30 or 230/1).

[6] See W. Dittenberger, *Hermes* xii 1877, 15–16, H. Swoboda, *RM²* xlv 1890, 309–10, cf. *Die griechischen Volksbeschlüsse*, 190–3, W. S. Ferguson, *Klio* ix 1909, 328, P. Graindor, *Athènes de Tibère à Trajan*, 70. (Kirchner at *IG* ii² 3618 has rejected Dittenberger's restoration of [γνώμῃ] στρατηγοῦ in *IG* iii 726.) Cf. now D. J. Geagan, *Hesp.* Supp. xii 1967, 86–7.

We cannot safely assert that ordinary bouleutae lost the right to make proposals and speak to them, though if they retained the right they doubtless exercised it less often than in the more enthusiastically democratic past.

In the next three chapters we shall examine first the boule's part in the making of laws and decrees, secondly the administrative powers which it exercised within the framework of the laws and decrees, and finally its judicial powers. In the fifth and last chapter I shall attempt an outline of the boule's history, and a more general assessment of its importance in the Athenian state.

II · LEGISLATION

(i) νόμοι

THERE are two words commonly used of enactments of the Athenian people, νόμος and ψήφισμα. The orators of the fourth century regularly claim that νόμοι have, or ought to have, greater authority than ψηφίσματα, and Hyperides attributes this rule to Solon:[1] νόμοι were somehow more than mere human enactments, and they ought therefore to be more basic, more general, and more permanent than ψηφίσματα; it was characteristic of an extreme democracy that it allowed ψηφίσματα to prevail over the νόμοι.[2] The application of this principle in Athenian practice presents a number of difficulties,[3] but I believe that the attempt to distinguish between νόμοι and ψηφίσματα belongs to the restored democracy of 403/2, and that before then any part of the Athenian 'statute book' might be called a νόμος, and any part which had been enacted by vote of the ecclesia (as opposed to a special legislative commission like that held by Solon) might also be called a ψήφισμα: νόμος referred to the law as a part of the Athenian code, while ψήφισμα referred to the mode of its enactment.[4]

In the last years of the Peloponnesian War a programme of revising and consolidating the law-code was undertaken, and this was resumed on the fall of the Thirty.[5] Documents quoted in Andocides' speech *On the Mysteries* show that a special procedure was created for making changes in the νόμοι, totally different from the ordinary voting of the ecclesia.[6] Other documents, quoted by Aeschines and Demosthenes, show that about the middle of the fourth century there existed a procedure for the 'correction' of the νόμοι, by adding new provisions and removing inconsistencies.[7] νομοθεσία was presumably regarded as more solemn and

[1] Hyp. III. *Ath.* 22.

[2] A. I. *Tim.* 177 (Sauppe's text), D. XX. *Lept.* 92, XXII. *Andr.* 49, XXIII. *Arist.* 86–7, 218, XXIV. *Tim.* 29–30, *LIX. *Neaer.* 88, [Plat.] *Def.* 415 B, Arist. *Pol.* IV. 1292 A 4–7, 23–5, 32–7, cf. *A.P.* 41. ii fin.

[3] For a sensible discussion of the difference between νόμοι and ψηφίσματα in Athens see U. Kahrstedt, *Klio* xxxi 1938, 1–19, and (briefly) M. Ostwald, *Nomos and the Beginnings of the Athenian Democracy*, 1–3.

[4] The inclusion of περὶ νόμων θέσεως in the list of the boule's interests in O.O. iii. 2 will then refer to the part played by the boule in the making of decrees of the demos (*pace* Ostwald, op. cit. 2 n. 3, which I cannot accept).   [5] Lys. XXX. *Nic.*, esp. 2–5.

[6] And. I. *Myst.* 83–4, 87.   [7] A. III. *Ctes.* 38–9, D. XXIV. *Tim.* 20–3.

binding than the enactment of ψηφίσματα, but the measures which have
survived suggest that the Athenians failed to live up to this ideal. Finance
seems the clearest example of a topic which ought to have been dealt
with by νόμος, but even here there are difficulties.[1] In Demetrius of
Phalerum Athens had another νομοθέτης of the Solonian type;[2] on the fall
of his regime we find another revision of the laws in progress;[3] but thereafter no alternative to ψηφίσματα is found until the reign of Hadrian.[4]

The greater part of this chapter will be concerned with the part played
by the boule in legislation by ψήφισμα, but something must first be said
about the fourth-century procedure for the enactment of νόμοι.[5] The
decree of Tisamenus, quoted by Andocides, assigns definite duties to the
boule in the revision of the law-code in 403/2. The nomothetae appointed
by the boule are to make and publish proposals for new laws, and any
private citizen who wishes may submit proposals to the boule; these
proposals are to be scrutinized (δοκιμάζειν) by the boule and a second
board of nomothetae, 500 in number, elected by the demes; and any
proposal which passes this scrutiny is presumably to be accepted as law
without further formality.[6] This is a once-for-all procedure, a part of the
reconstruction of the democracy, which led to the publication of a de-
finitive law-code and so made the fourth-century attempt to distinguish
between νόμοι and ψηφίσματα possible. Andocides' speech is our only
source for this aspect of the legal revision, and we do not know how the
co-operation of the boule with the two boards of nomothetae was
organized.

In 403/2 the boule was involved but not the assembly; in the regular
'correction' attested by Aeschines and Demosthenes the assembly has to
decide each year whether nomothetae are needed, and if so to appoint

---

[1] The distinction is acknowledged but belittled in three decrees which authorize expenditure not provided for in the annual μερισμός and order the nomothetae to make the necessary
change (IG ii² 222, 41–6; 330, 15–23; vii 4254 = SIG³ 298, 35–41 [not 39–45]); in Tod 167,
39–44, no νόμος is needed, presumably because what is ordered is only a temporary adjustment. The theoric fund was regulated by a mixture of νόμος (D. III. Ol. iii. 10–11) and
ψήφισμα ([D.] XLIV. Leoch. 38); Apollodorus attempted to divert theoric monies to the
stratiotic fund by ψήφισμα ([D.] LIX. Neaer. 4–5), and the change achieved by Demosthenes
seems likely to have been by ψήφισμα (Phil. 328 F 56 a); Hegemon's measure weakening the
position of financial officials was a νόμος (A. III. Ctes. 25).
[2] Syncellus, 521; Dem. Phal. 228 ττ 1–2, F 45, etc.; cf. S. Dow and A. H. Travis, Hesp.
xii 1943.   [3] IG ii² 487.
[4] SEG xv 108. The title νομοθέτης was borne by Tib. Claudius Novius in A.D. 61 (IG ii²
1990, 6) and by Annius Pythodorus from 118/19 to 124/5 or after (Inscr. de Délos, 2535–7),
but we know nothing of their activities.
[5] This is not the place for a full discussion of the subject, though one is badly needed. The
only recent studies of nomothetic procedure are by U. Kahrstedt, Klio xxxi 1938, 1–19, and
K. M. T. Atkinson, BRL xxiii 1939 (briefly reviewed by A. W. Gomme, CR liv 1940, 38);
cf. A. R. W. Harrison, JHS lxxv 1955, 35.   [6] And. I. Myst. 83–4.

them; it also appoints five συνήγοροι to defend the existing laws, and has read to it any new proposals.[1] Procedural details are hard to disentangle. Our literary texts seem to envisage a quasi-judicial activity, occurring at the beginning of the year, to decide whether a particular proposal is or is not in accordance with the idea of law;[2] but the few inscribed νόμοι surviving from the fourth century show that νομοθεσία could occur at any time during the year, and far from bearing indications of judicial activity they have prescripts closely modelled on the prescripts of decrees, naming the proposer, and the ἐπιστάτης τῶν προέδρων who put the question.[3] The most puzzling text for our present purposes is the decree of Epicrates, under which Timocrates was enabled to submit irregularly to the nomothetae the debt law to which Demosthenes objected: τοὺς πρυτάνεις τοὺς Πανδιονίδος καθίσαι νομοθέτας αὔριον, τοὺς δὲ νομοθέτας εἶναι ἕνα καὶ χιλίους ἐκ τῶν ὀμωμοκότων, συννομοθετεῖν δὲ καὶ τὴν βουλήν.[4] The prytanes are mentioned in connection with the nomothetae by Aeschines also,[5] but this is the only passage which orders the boule to participate in the work of the fourth-century nomothetae. The day in question was that of the Cronia, and Demosthenes tells us in the text that this was one of the boule's holidays,[6] but he makes no more direct reference to the last clause of the decree. The boule is not linked with the nomothetae in our surviving prescripts, and in the absence of further evidence we must assume that this partnership was exceptional.[7]

[1] D. XXIV. *Tim.* 20–3, XX. *Lept.* 94, 137. A. III. *Ctes.* 38–9 seems to move rather awkwardly from a meeting of the ecclesia to appoint nomothetae, to the resulting meeting of the nomothetae to pass judgement on the laws.

[2] Great as the difficulties are, I cannot believe in the complex procedure outlined by Mrs. Atkinson, whereby a man who wanted to change the law had to undertake a γραφή against the old law and persuade the ecclesia to adopt his proposal in a ψήφισμα, before the appointment of nomothetae was even discussed, and it is suggested that the decision of the nomothetae may have required ratification by the ecclesia. It seems reasonably clear that the assembly's involvement was limited to deciding (by ψήφισμα) that νομοθεσία was needed and setting the machinery in motion.

[3] For a list of surviving νόμοι and their formulae see Table H: *SEG* xii 87 was enacted in the ninth prytany of 337/6. I have argued in Ch. I (p. 28) that the proedri mentioned in connection with νόμοι are proedri of the nomothetae, to be distinguished from those of the boule.

[4] D. XXIV. *Tim.* 27. The dating, with which Demosthenes is concerned, is confirmed by his own words in § 26. (The problem here is that nomothetae exist on 11. i [Hec.], or if they do not exist they are appointed to meet on the following day, whereas the appointment for the year ought not to be made until a later assembly. If they do already exist on the 11th, the nomothetae may perhaps be those of the previous year, still in office.) The reference to the boule is not confirmed, but the documents in this speech are in general acceptable, and the decree ought if possible to be explained rather than dismissed as a forgery.

[5] A. III. *Ctes.* 40. The easiest inference from these two passages is that the prytanes on behalf of the ecclesia drew up a πρόγραμμα specifying the dates of the nomothetae's meetings and the topics to be discussed. [6] D. XXIV. *Tim.* 26.

[7] Another instance of the boule's combining with a heliastic panel is found in the trial of Cleophon, for which see the appendix to Ch. IV, p. 182.

Normally, despite Mrs. Atkinson's efforts to avoid this conclusion, νομοθεσία must have been a process in which the legislative organs of the state surrendered their right of final decision to a judicial body: the boule's part would be limited to the preparatory work for the original decree of the ecclesia, which appointed the nomothetae and ordered them to pass judgement on a certain part of the Athenian law-code. It was a cumbersome procedure, not often used if we may trust the evidence of epigraphic survival, and it failed to eliminate that confusion which had led to the compilation of an organized code of νόμοι. Isocrates writes in his *Panathenaic* that the laws are full of confusion,[1] and in the trial of Ctesiphon in 330 Demosthenes and Aeschines were able to cite different, conflicting laws on the proclamation of crowns.[2] Whenever it was possible, the Athenians continued to express their will in ψηφίσματα, to which we must now turn.

(ii) *Decrees of the Boule and Demos*

It was a basic principle in Athens, that no decree might be enacted by the ecclesia without prior consideration by the boule: οὐκ ἔξεστιν οὐδὲν ἀπροβούλευτον οὐδ' ὅ τι ἂν μὴ προγράψωσιν οἱ πρυτάνεις ψηφίσασθαι τῷ δήμῳ.[3] This much is clear, but how the principle was interpreted is less certain. We need to know, first of all, to what extent this rule represents a limitation of the ecclesia's sovereignty, preventing the demos from decreeing whatever it wished; that is, how far the boule was able if it chose to control the course of Athenian voting. At one extreme, Hartel[4] claimed that since the ecclesia was sovereign it must specifically have authorized every 'prior' discussion in the boule, so that each probouleuma will have been commissioned by the ecclesia (a procedure which is occasionally attested in inscriptions). Miller,[5] reacting against this, argued that the principle can have served no purpose unless it was strictly applied: hence he believed that the ecclesia could not even commission a probouleuma on a subject unless given the opportunity by the boule's placing on the agenda some topic to which this subject was relevant. Whether commissioned by the ecclesia or not, the boule's deliberations

---

[1] Is. XII. *Panath.* 144.

[2] D. XVIII. *Cor.* 120–1, A. III. *Ctes.* 32 sqq. Aeschines' argument, that there can be no contradiction as a procedure of διόρθωσις exists to eliminate contradictions, is not wholly convincing.

[3] *A.P.* 45. iv, cf. Pl. *Sol.* 19. i, *X. Or.* 835 F–836 A, D. XXII. *Andr. hyp.* i. 2, *hyp.* ii. 9.

[4] W. Hartel, *Studien über attisches Staatsrecht und Urkundenwesen.*

[5] H. A. E. O. Miller, *De Decretis Atticis Quaestiones Epigraphicae.*

frequently resulted in a positive motion which could be put to the ecclesia for approval, and this leads to our second major problem: did the boule usually make up its own mind, and produce a definite recommendation, on any subject which it invited the ecclesia to debate,[1] or did it do this for matters of routine only, preferring to put controversial questions on the agenda without proposals of its own?[2]

Hartel's extreme view of προβούλευσις depended on a perverse interpretation of the formula in decree prescripts, and was adequately refuted by Miller, but it is less easy to choose between Miller's position and the compromise view of Gilbert,[3] that any business could be initiated either in the boule or by the ecclesia's commissioning a probouleuma.

There are a few passages which might be used to support Miller's view: in the parody of an assembly which opens the *Acharnians*, Dicaeopolis and Amphitheus are helpless ἢν μὴ περὶ εἰρήνης γε πρυτανεύσητέ μοι (but we must not lean too heavily on this, as the resulting situation is important for Aristophanes' dramatic purposes).[4] According to Demosthenes, a private citizen who wants to secure a law or decree[5] or an embassy with a report to make[6] must first go to the boule, which will make a probouleuma at the proper time. At some time between 345 and 331 one Hierocles was seen with sacred vestments, and was denounced to the prytanes as a temple robber; the prytanes brought him before the ecclesia, and there a motion was made by Aristogiton, that if Hierocles admitted his guilt he should be put to death without more ado; if not, he should stand trial. This motion is described as πρῶτον μὲν ἀπροβούλευτον, ἔπειτα δεινότατον, and we are told that it was successfully attacked in a γραφὴ παρανόμων.[7] No doubt the first objection was merely an excuse, and the attack concentrated on the δεινότης of the motion, but it is far from clear what was amiss with this motion that was not also amiss with many others, such as that made by Demosthenes after Philip's occupation of Elatea in 339.[8] Perhaps the probouleuma was so worded that it could be said not to cover Aristogiton's motion, or perhaps other factors of which we know nothing made the legal case better than it appears to us.

---

[1] As has been supposed by B. D. Meritt, *Documents on Athenian Tribute*, 32–3, and G. L. Cawkwell, *REG* lxxv 1962, 458, and *CQ*² xiii 1963, 133.

[2] The view of A. H. M. Jones, 118, cf. A. W. Gomme, *JHS* lxxix 1959, 183.

[3] G. Gilbert, pp. 295–6; cf. his pp. 293–4 n. 4, citing exchanges between himself and Hartel.

[4] Ar. *Ach.* 51–60.

[5] D. XXIV. *Tim.* 48, confusing (no doubt deliberately) the procedures for decree-making and νομοθεσία.

[6] D. XIX. *F.L.* 185, cf. schol. 17.

[7] [D.] XXV. *Aristog. i, hyp.* 1–2 (probably deriving its information from Lycurgus' lost speech).

[8] D. XVIII. *Cor.* 170 with 173.

In the literary texts we find that rights of access to the people are commonly exercised as Demosthenes thought they should be: Murychides in 479,[1] the Spartan ambassadors to Athens in 420/19,[2] the Theban herald bringing the news of Leuctra,[3] and the Spartan ambassadors in 369[4] all went first to the boule. Aristodemus was summoned before the boule in 347/6 when he did not come of his own accord to report on his mission to Philip;[5] the 'first embassy' sent to Philip in 346 reported to the boule on its return,[6] and so too did the 'second embassy'.[7] Even in the emergency resulting from the news that Philip had occupied Elatea in 339, normal probouleutic practice was followed: the messenger arrived with his news in the evening and reported to the prytanes; they immediately left their dinner, some to clear the Agora, others to summon the generals and the trumpeter; the following morning the boule met, and only after that an assembly was held, at which the prytanes and the messenger explained the situation.[8]

The assembly in Aristophanes' *Acharnians* is at first sight somewhat irregular. None too early, the prytanes jostle their way in;[9] without specifying the subject for debate, the herald proclaims, τίς ἀγορεύειν βούλεται;[10] Amphitheus is disposed of,[11] and the herald then calls on the ambassadors returned from the Great King.[12] The herald here must represent the prytanes,[13] and we may assume that the appearance of these ambassadors and of the King's Eye has been placed on the agenda by the boule: their audience ends with the herald's announcement:

$$\text{τὸν βασιλέως ὀφθαλμὸν ἡ βουλὴ καλεῖ}$$
$$\text{ἐς τὸ πρυτανεῖον.}^{14}$$

Theorus, an Athenian sent to the Thracian king Sitalces, is now called forward by the herald,[15] and when Dicaeopolis proclaims an unfavourable omen the herald on behalf of the prytanes dissolves the assembly.[16]

Our evidence is enough to show that it was normal to approach the ecclesia by way of the boule—it is not for nothing that the right frequently conferred upon foreigners was πρόσοδος πρὸς τὴν βουλὴν καὶ τὸν δῆμον—

---

[1] H. IX. 5. i–ii. There are no procedural indications in Herodotus' account of earlier negotiations (VIII. 140–4), and I am not disposed to place much faith in Plutarch's version of this story (*Arist.* 10. ii–vi). On the boule and the generals see Ch. I, pp. 43–8.

[2] T. v. 45. i.   [3] X. *H.* VI. iv. 20.   [4] Cf. X. *H.* VII. i. 2, 11.

[5] A. II. *F.L.* 16–17.   [6] A. II. *F.L.* 45–6.   [7] D. XIX. *F.L.* 17–18, 31.

[8] D. XVIII. *Cor.* 169–70.   [9] Ar. *Ach.* 40–2.   [10] Ibid. 43–5.

[11] Ibid. 46–60: though no subject for debate has been mentioned, this attempt to raise a topic from the floor of the house is quickly ruled out of order.   [12] Ibid. 61.

[13] He can order silence (ibid. 59, 64), call for the archers (54), and on the prytanes' behalf dissolve the assembly (173).

[14] Ibid. 124–5.   [15] Ibid. 134.   [16] Ibid. 173.

but we cannot yet exclude the possibility that there was some direct access to the assembly.

We must now consider the information given in *A.P.* 43. iv–vi on the matters discussed at different assemblies. The agenda of the κυρία ἐκκλησία (the principal of the four regular assemblies in each prytany) included:

a vote of confidence in the public officials;

περὶ σίτου καὶ περὶ φυλακῆς τῆς χώρας χρηματίζειν;[1]

an opportunity for those who wished to make εἰσαγγελίαι;

reading of inventories of confiscated property and of lists of inheritance-suits;

and in the sixth prytany only:

a vote on whether an ostracism should be held;

συκοφαντῶν προβολαί up to a limit of three charges against citizens and three against metics;

and (presumably προβολαί again) against those who had failed to keep their promises to the people.

In the second assembly, any one who wished might make a ἱκετηρία; and in the remaining two regular assemblies other business was transacted.[2]

A possible interpretation of this, and perhaps the most natural, is that the agenda drawn up by the boule would simply enjoin the hearing of εἰσαγγελίαι, προβολαί, and ἱκετηρίαι, and that individual charges and requests did not have to be submitted in advance to the boule.[3] προβολή was not a trial procedure, but a method of initiating a case: the word seems usually to be used of complaints made in the assembly, after which a normal trial might follow;[4] but we have no further evidence on how a προβολή could be made. εἰσαγγελία, however, was fundamentally a trial procedure: though it might end with an ordinary hearing in a δικαστήριον, it was essentially a trial by boule and/or ecclesia, and I shall argue in Chapter IV that while proceedings most commonly began in the boule they could be initiated in the ecclesia, which if it did not

---

[1] On debates περὶ φυλακῆς τῆς χώρας see Additional Note C, pp. 231–5.

[2] A. Reusch, *De Diebus Contionum Ordinarium apud Athenienses*, 71–9, predicted that the division of business between the second, third, and fourth assemblies in Poll. viii. 96 would not be found in the *A.P.*: it is interesting to note that this has only partly been borne out. Professor Jones argues (108 with n. 77) from a similar clause in the 'future constitution' of 411 (*A.P.* 30. v) that the items for discussion at the third and fourth assemblies were picked by lot from those put forward; Wilamowitz thought that the selection was made by προχειροτονία (cf. p. 58 n. 4 below).

[3] For ἱκετηρίαι, at any rate, Wilamowitz thought that each individual supplication had first to receive the boule's approval: *Aristoteles und Athen*, ii. 252–3.

[4] Is. XV. *Antid.* 314, *L.S.* 288. 18, *E.M.* προβάλλεσθαι, cf. Poll. viii. 46; but in Poll. viii. 87 οἱ θεσμοθέται εἰσάγουσι.

reject the charge out of hand would either delegate the trial to the boule or, to retain ultimate control, commission a probouleuma on the matter. For ἱκετηρίαι there is a little epigraphic evidence, which will have to be considered later in this chapter:[1] for the moment we should note that a decree of the demos can be enacted either περὶ ὧν ὁ δεῖνα ἔδοξεν ἐν τῇ βουλῇ ἔννομα ἱκετεύειν or περὶ ὧν ὁ δεῖνα ἔδοξεν ἐν τῷ δήμῳ ἔννομα ἱκετεύειν; there is one instance of the latter formula in an undoubted probouleuma,[2] which is most easily explained if the request was first made in the ecclesia and then referred to the boule for consideration.

Proof is impossible, but it seems likely that the provision for εἰσαγγελίαι, προβολαί, and ἱκετηρίαι did provide some opportunities for direct access to the people, though the rule of προβούλευσις will have prevented action from being taken until the matter had been referred to the boule.

Further indications are hard to come by, and when inscriptions attest the ecclesia's commissioning of a probouleuma they do not reveal the circumstances in which this occurred. Where an inscription gives the text of a rider appended to an original motion, it appears that debates must have kept fairly well to the point, and that the opportunity of smuggling in fresh business was rarely taken. Many riders involve more or less straightforward additions and corrections, and of those that are more substantial only two can be regarded as perhaps strictly irrelevant to the motions which they supplement:[3] in M&L 49 it is likely but not certain that the audience with the boule which Phantocles secures for himself has some connection with the colony at Brea; in M&L 73 it is possible to argue for the relevance of Lampon's intercalation proposal,[4] but there is no apparent connection between his regulations for the Πελαργικόν and the main decree.[5] In the case of Lampon's rider, there is a further point to note. Lampon is to συγγράψαι and to bring his proposals before the boule, and the boule must bring these proposals before the assembly: the boule cannot be ignored altogether, or no place for Lampon's proposals will be provided in the agenda, but it is deprived of the right not to proceed with the matter, whose importance we shall consider below.[6]

With certain reservations, then, it seems that Miller's account of probouleusis is to be accepted: εἰσαγγελίαι, προβολαί, and ἱκετηρίαι gave

---

[1] See pp. 72–3 and p. 73 n. 1. [2] IG ii² 192.
[3] See my classified list of riders, Table J.
[4] M&L 73, 53–4, with commentary, p. 221.
[5] P. Guillon, BCH lxxxvi 1962, 467–75, thinks he can find one.
[6] Cf. pp. 57–8. When the συγγραφεῖς of 411 made their report, the democratic constitution had not yet been upset, and to minimize the obstacles to its being upset they πρῶτον μὲν ἔγραψαν ἐπάναγκες εἶναι τοὺς πρυτάνεις ἅπαντα τὰ λεγόμενα περὶ τῆς σωτηρίας ἐπιψηφίζειν (A.P. 29. iv).

citizens some chance of direct access to the ecclesia, and a Lampon might strain considerations of relevance to ensure that his proposals had a hearing, but in general the ecclesia was prepared to let the boule decide what it should debate. The permanent standing orders of *A.P.* 43. iv–vi probably came into being as guarantees that certain topics should be debated at specified times rather than as precautions against their being debated at other times, but Demosthenes' insistence on doing things in good order and at the proper time shows that they could also be viewed as restrictions which the people were on the whole prepared to accept as a condition of living under the rule of law. If a citizen wanted some action to be taken, his best policy might well be to seek the co-operation of a member of the boule, as Demosthenes did in 340/39, when to reverse a decision of the ecclesia he εἰσελθὼν εἰς τὸ βουλευτήριον καὶ μεταστησάμενος τοὺς ἰδιώτας ἐκφέρεται προβούλευμα εἰς τὴν ἐκκλησίαν, προσλαβὼν τὴν τοῦ γράψαντος ἀπειρίαν.[1]

When we consider the practical working of this system, we have a good deal of material, but it is hard to interpret. Thucydides locates all debates in the ecclesia, mentioning the boule only for the device by which Alcibiades secured a change of alliance in 420/19,[2] and when it was paid off by the oligarchs in 411.[3] The boule plays a slightly greater part in Xenophon, but for most of our information we have to turn to the orators, often personally involved in the events which they describe, more concerned to show that what happened was right or wrong than to explain the full course of events. Decrees are sometimes mentioned by later writers, especially Plutarch, but details which are not essential to the point which he wished to illustrate could all too easily become garbled.

We know of two occasions when a foreign envoy came before the boule and the boule refused to make a probouleuma. In 479 Mardonius sent Murychides to the boule on Salamis, and a bouleutes who proposed that he should be brought before the ecclesia was stoned to death;[4] in 371 after the battle of Leuctra the Thebans sent a herald to Athens, and the boule refused him the customary invitation to the prytaneum and sent

---

[1] A. III. *Ctes.* 125. For other probouleumata obtained in this way see *A.P.* 29; (cf. p. 63 with n. 3, and p. 74), D. XXIII. *Arist.* 9, 14; cf. also p. 60 n. 1 below.

[2] T. v. 45, cf. Pl. *Nic.* 10. iv–vi, *Alc.* 14. vi–ix.

[3] T. viii. 69–70. i. Further details would have been particularly welcome of the debates on the alliances offered by Corinth and Corcyra in 434/3, on the fate of Mytilene in 427 (when Cleon, author of the original decree, was probably a bouleutes—cf. Ch. I, p. 4), and on the institution of the πρόβουλοι in 413. Professor Andrewes, noticing Thucydides' silence on the Spartan gerousia, shows insufficient surprise at his near-silence on the Athenian boule (*Ancient Society and Institutions*, 4–5).

[4] H. ix. 5. i–ii, cf. Lyc. *Leocr.* 122, D. XVIII. *Cor.* 202, 204.

him away without a reply.[1] Refusal to act is spectacular only when it involves a rebuff of this kind, but it must often have happened that the boule's discussion of a subject led to the conclusion that there was no need for a debate in the ecclesia.

On other occasions, the boule would place a subject on the agenda by means of an open probouleuma, which did not recommend any particular course of action. The clearest example of this is a proposal of 349/8: ἔγραψε ψήφισμα ἐν τῇ βουλῇ Ἀπολλόδωρος βουλεύων, καὶ ἐξήνεγκε προβούλευμα εἰς τὸν δῆμον, λέγον διαχειροτονῆσαι τὸν δῆμον εἴτε δοκεῖ τὰ περιόντα χρήματα τῆς διοικήσεως στρατιωτικὰ εἶναι εἴτε θεωρικά.[2] But this probouleuma is not genuinely open: surplus moneys at this time did go to the theoric fund, so that Apollodorus' invitation to the demos to decide between two alternatives was equivalent to a straightforward proposal that surplus moneys should henceforth be diverted to the stratiotic fund. If this oblique method was adopted in the hope that Apollodorus should evade personal responsibility for the proposal, it failed, for after the ecclesia had voted in favour of the stratiotic fund Apollodorus was successfully indicted in a γραφὴ παρανόμων.[3]

A few years earlier, in 354/3, ζητηταί had been appointed to help recover sums due to the state. Euctemon made a μήνυσις to these ζητηταί, and was brought before the boule; a probouleuma was made, and in the ecclesia, after a προχειροτονία,[4] he spoke, and proposed a motion against

---

[1] X. *H.* VI. iv. 20: another instance of the boule's refusal to act at II. ii. 15. G. T. Griffith, *Ancient Society and Institutions*, 129, believes that the boule's right to prevent action was restricted during the fifth century: I imagine that the right remained, but was exercised only when the boule was confident that public opinion was on its side. J. A. O. Larsen, *Representative Government*, 16–17 with 198 n. 38, thinks that such negative action was 'not rare'.

[2] [D.] LIX. *Neaer.* 4.

[3] Ibid. 5. The only ground of illegality which we know is that Apollodorus as a state debtor was temporarily ἄτιμος and so not entitled to sponsor decrees.

[4] The procedure of προχειροτονία is first found in the fourth century. The clearest statement of what it involved is given by Harpocration and Suidas s.v. (Suidas omits the final sentence): ἔοικεν Ἀθήνησι τοιοῦτό τι γίγνεσθαι, ὁπόταν τῆς βουλῆς προβουλευσάσης εἰσφέρεται εἰς τὸν δῆμον ἡ γνώμη· πρότερον γίνεται χειροτονία ἐν τῇ ἐκκλησίᾳ πότερον δοκεῖ περὶ τῶν προβουλευθέντων σκέψασθαι τὸν δῆμον, ἢ ἀρκεῖ τὸ προβούλευμα. ταῦτα δ' ὑποσημαίνεται ἐν τῷ Λυσίου πρὸς τὴν Μιξιδήμου γραφήν. (Cf. *A.P.* 43. vi, where there is a clear lacuna before χρηματίζουσιν, A. I. *Tim.* 23, D. XXIV. *Tim.* 11–12.) Acceptance without debate would be possible only if the probouleuma incorporated a specific motion; if, as seems to have occurred in the case of Euctemon, there was an open element in the probouleuma, the προχειροτονία must have determined not whether the probouleuma should be accepted at once or discussed but whether the matter should be discussed or rejected outright. The remark of the *A.P.* might perhaps refer to matters which so obviously had to be discussed that no προχειροτονία was necessary.

Lipsius, *LSKP* xvii 1896, 405–12, found acceptance without debate incredible, and thought that προχειροτονία always involved a choice between discussion and outright rejection, and this could perhaps be correct. Nevertheless, I believe he was wrong to base this view on what we are told of the procedure for deciding whether to hold an ostracism in *A.P.* 43. v,

the opposition of Androtion and others; for this he was attacked in a γραφὴ παρανόμων, but was acquitted.[1] Certainty is impossible, but it seems likely that here we have a genuinely open probouleuma—that the demos should hear what Euctemon had to say and decide as it saw fit.[2] The probouleuma for the extraordinary assembly after Philip's occupation of Elatea in 339, when no one but Demosthenes had any advice to give, must also have been open.[3]

On other occasions the boule did sponsor a definite proposal. The clearest example of the ecclesia's adopting a probouleuma is an incident to which I have already alluded: in 340/39 Aeschines, as a delegate to the Amphictyonic Council, had distracted attention from the sins of Athens by arousing indignation against Amphissa; an extraordinary meeting was to be convened, at which the punishment of Amphissa would be discussed. Aeschines and his colleagues reported to the boule and assembly, and their action was approved. But a bouleutes who was co-operating with Demosthenes secured a new probouleuma at a secret meeting of the boule (probably addressed by Demosthenes), to prevent Athens from

cf. *L.R.C. κυρία ἡ ἐκκλησία* = Dem. Phal. 228 F 4 (in both of which the original reading is *ἐπιχειροτονίαν*) and *L.R.C. ὀστρακισμοῦ τρόπος* = Phil. 328 F 30, cf. schol. Ar. *Eq.* 855. Whatever is the correct technical term here, there is an important distinction between this decision and the *προχειροτονία* which somehow preceded a debate: this decision was an end in itself, in that it could commit the demos to action on a later occasion, whereas the *προχειροτονία*, if successful, would be followed by a debate at the same meeting of the assembly. Wilamowitz, *Aristoteles und Athen*, ii. 254–6, thought that *προχειροτονία* should be referred particularly to the limitations in *A.P.* 43. vi, and was a vote by which the ecclesia decided which of the items offered to it by the boule it would discuss, and in what order.

[1] D. XXIV. *Tim.* 11–14.   [2] Cf. Wilamowitz, op. cit. ii. 255 n. 5.

[3] D. XVIII. *Cor.* 169 sqq., cf. A. III. *Ctes.* 142 sqq., Pl. *Dem.* 18, D.S. xvi. 84–85. i: on the nature of this probouleuma see p. 234.

For other possible open probouleumata in literary texts see A. II. *F.L.* 16–17; ibid. 45–6 with 53, cf. III. *Ctes.* 66–7, D. XIX. *F.L.* 234 (in these two cases I imagine that the probouleuma was that the demos should hear the envoys' report and decide as it saw fit); and also the debate on 16. xii (Scir.) 347/6 (D. XIX. *F.L.* 17–18, 31 [denied A. II. *F.L.* 121–2], 35). In the latter case it is far from clear what happened: Mr. Cawkwell believes that on learning that Philip was beyond Thermopylae the boule met again, suppressed the original probouleuma, and issued another more appropriate to the changed circumstances (*REG* lxxv 1962, 458); but Demosthenes' *ἔπεισα ταῦτα τὴν βουλήν* (§ 18) is perhaps a little weak for inclusion in the probouleuma, and it is possible that the probouleuma, though including a pro-Phocian motivation-clause indicating what kind of action was envisaged, was open in that it did not contain a definite proposal (cf. p. 61 n. 6, below), and that such probouleumata did not need to be read out in full. (On this point we have only the evidence of parodies: in Ar. *Thesm.* 372–9 a short open probouleuma is read out, and cf. *Eccl.* 394–8; in Lucian, *Deor. Conc.* 1, the probouleuma is not read.)

For open probouleumata in inscribed decrees see Table G: the clearest instance is the first decree in Tod 189. Larfeld, *Handbuch der griechischen Epigraphik*, ii. ii. 675–6, thought that open probouleumata were very rare and that most 'non-probouleumatic' decrees were carried against a probouleuma. This assumption cannot be checked, but if it is correct and the criteria I shall use in this chapter for identifying non-probouleumatic decrees are sound the boule must have been 'defeated' alarmingly often in the fifth and fourth centuries.

taking part in the war against Amphissa, and at the very end of a meeting of the assembly Demosthenes διεπράξατο ἐπιψηφισθῆναι καὶ γενέσθαι δήμου ψήφισμα.[1] The ecclesia might if it wished reject a probouleuma, and either take no action at all, or adopt an alternative proposal made from the floor of the house.[2] In 369 Spartan ambassadors were sent to Athens to work out the details of the alliance made after Leuctra, and the boule proposed that Sparta should have the leadership on land and Athens at sea; but one Cephisodotus, who failed to realize how Leuctra had changed the balance of power in Greece and was afraid that this arrangement would give too much power to Sparta, persuaded the assembly to approve instead the alternation of the whole command between Athens and Sparta every five days.[3] Twenty years later the rejection of a probouleuma led, so far as we can tell, to no action at all: Phocion had been sent to Euboea to help Plutarch of Eretria against Callias of Chalcis; on the news that he was blockaded in Tamynae the boule proposed the sending of reinforcements, but οὐκ ἐδόκει, προϊούσης τῆς ἐκκλησίας καὶ λόγων γιγνομένων, τῆς τῶν ἱππέων βοηθείας ἤδη δεῖν, ἀλλ' ἀνεπεπτώκει τὰ τῆς ἐξόδου.[4]

An additional factor to be taken into account in the middle of the fourth century was the Second Athenian League. For matters requiring action from Athens as well as her allies, the Athenian ecclesia seems to have been the sovereign body,[5] with the Athenian boule and the allied

[1] A. III. Ctes. 125–7 (Demosthenes' practice may have been sharp, but it can hardly have been illegal, or we should have heard much more about it). For other decrees which are or may be ratified probouleumata see D. XIX. F.L. 286; perhaps A. II. F.L. 19; and perhaps D.S. xvII. 111. iii; many inscribed texts contain a clear indication that this procedure has been followed, in the probouleumatic formula (cf. p. 65 and Table C). The friends who sponsored decrees on Demosthenes' behalf after Chaeronea may well have been bouleutae: Pl. Dem. 21. iii gives a sensible compromise between D. XVIII. Cor. 248 and A. III. Ctes. 159, though in Din. I. Dem. 78–80 we have one post-Chaeronea decree γραφέντος ὑπὸ Δημοσθένους.

[2] In Ar. Thesm. 431–2 the speaker, having outlined her proposal from the floor of the ecclesia (under an open probouleuma), promises to draft the final version with the help of the secretary. At the second assembly to discuss peace with Philip, on 19. ix. (Elaph.) 347/6, Demosthenes had a ready-drafted motion with him in case Philocrates let him down (A. II. F.L. 67–8).

[3] X. H. vii. i. 1–14. G. L. Cawkwell has suggested (CQ² xiii 1963, 133) that we have another motion carried against a probouleuma in 344/3—[D.] VII. Hal. 19–20—but though the motion was proposed from the floor of the house I am not satisfied that there was a specific probouleuma with which it conflicted.

[4] D. XXI. Mid. 162–3. It has been suggested that news of Phocion's victory arrived while the assembly was in progress: Schaefer, Demosthenes und seine Zeit², ii. 82, Cawkwell, CQ² xii 1962, 128–9.

[5] The final decision on new alliances was taken by the ecclesia, though we should perhaps conclude from the συνέδριον's declared willingness to abide by the decision of the ecclesia in 346—A. II. F.L. 60—that even at this late stage the allies could not be committed without their formal approval. In any case, they could still refuse the oath to a new member.

συνέδριον as parallel probouleutic bodies: in 368 the boule asked the συνέδριον to submit a δόγμα to the ecclesia;[1] in 362/1 the συνέδριον submitted a δόγμα to the boule, as a result of which a probouleuma was made.[2] The συνέδριον is involved in the most fully documented of all Athenian debates, that leading to the Peace of Philocrates in 346. The Macedonian ambassadors failed to reach Athens in time for an assembly before the Dionysia;[3] on their arrival, during the festival, Demosthenes was the author of a probouleuma for assemblies on 18 and 19. ix (Elaph.) to discuss the possibility of peace and alliance:[4] a δόγμα of the allies, that there should be a discussion of peace alone after the return of the Athenian envoys sent under the decree of Eubulus to secure Greek support against Philip,[5] was ignored. So far as we can recover the text of the probouleuma, it seems to have been formally open, though by specifying peace and alliance it indicated the kind of decision wanted:[6]

τοὺς πρυτάνεις μετὰ τὰ Διονύσια τὰ ἐν ἄστει καὶ τὴν ἐν Διονύσου ἐκκλησίαν προγράψαι δύο ἐκκλησίας, τὴν μὲν τῇ ὀγδόῃ ἐπὶ δέκα, τὴν δὲ τῇ ἐνάτῃ . . . καὶ τὸ μὲν τῶν συμμάχων δόγμα κελεύει . . . ὑπὲρ εἰρήνης μόνον ὑμᾶς βουλεύσασθαι, Δημοσθένης δὲ καὶ περὶ συμμαχίας κελεύει.[7] . . . τῇ μὲν προτέρᾳ τῶν ἐκκλησιῶν συμβουλεύειν τὸν βουλόμενον, τῇ δ' ὑστέρᾳ τοὺς προέδρους ἐπιψηφίζειν τὰς γνώμας.[8]

Philocrates, who seems not to have been a member of the boule, proposed a peace and alliance with Philip, from which Phocis and Halus were to be excluded;[9] the allies submitted a δόγμα recommending peace only, which any of the Greeks might join within three months.[10] When Philip's envoys were interrogated on 19. ix (Elaph.) it was made clear that peace on the allies' terms would not be acceptable to him;[11] in spite of the probouleuma, further debate ensued, and Philocrates' proposal was finally adopted in an amended form.[12]

[1] Tod 133, 8–13.   [2] Tod 144, 12–16.   [3] A. III. *Ctes.* 67–8.
[4] A. II. *F.L.* 61, 65, cf. III. *Ctes.* 68. What I have identified as a probouleuma Aeschines calls a ψήφισμα. D. M. Lewis believes that the assemblies for 18 and 19. ix were fixed by decree of the demos at the abortive assembly on 8. ix—*BSA* l 1955, 25–6—but having been thwarted once the Athenians will probably have waited until the envoys arrived before committing themselves again to a date, and I suspect that on their arrival Demosthenes was the author of a probouleuma appropriating for the discussion of the peace terms an assembly previously arranged for other business.   [5] A. II. *F.L.* 60.
[6] I should perhaps stress that there could be different degrees of openness in probouleumata: compare the probouleuma of Demosthenes which was not read out on 16. xii (Scir.) 347/6 (p. 59 n. 3 above) and the open probouleuma at the assembly in the *Thesmophoriazusae* (ibid.), in each case indicating a line of action but not offering a definite suggestion.
[7] A. II. *F.L.* 61.   [8] Ibid. 65.
[9] D. XIX. *F.L.* 159, A. II. *F.L.* 67–8, cf. 64. I cannot share Mr. Cawkwell's view (*REG* lxxiii 1960, 434–5) that 'the proposal of Philocrates was the Council's προβούλευμα'.
[10] A. III. *Ctes.* 69–70.   [11] D. XIX. *F.L.* 321, A. III. *Ctes.* 71–2.
[12] D. XIX. *F.L.* 159.

The vote of the assembly was not the only risk which a motion had to run. A motion might be ruled out of order by the prytanes or proedri, though in both of the cases known to us public opinion prevailed over the objection. There is a good deal to puzzle us in the trial of the generals after Arginusae, and it is perhaps a mistake to look for complete regularity in such exceptional circumstances, but it seems certain that Socrates and perhaps some of his colleagues were reluctant to put to the vote Callixenus' probouleuma for a single decision on the fate of all the generals accused; nevertheless this was put to the vote, and was carried against Euryptolemus' alternative proposal for a fairer trial.[1] On 25. ix (Elaph.) 347/6 Demosthenes was one of the proedri, and tried to rule out of order a motion (proposed from the floor of the house) which would admit Cersobleptes of the Odrysians to the Second Athenian League in time for him to participate in the Peace of Philocrates: the motion was in the end put to the vote, but was presumably defeated.[2] Despite the powers of the prytanes and proedri, an ἀπροβούλευτον ψήφισμα might on occasion be put to the vote. I have noted already that it is hard to find anything procedurally wrong with Aristogiton's decree against Hierocles,[3] but we have a clearer case in Androtion's proposal that the boule in which he served his second term of office should be crowned.[4] The proposals to reward loyal democrats in 403 present a number of problems,[5] but we are told that Thrasybulus' proposal to make Lysias an Athenian citizen was successfully attacked in a γραφὴ παρανόμων, διὰ τὸ ἀπροβούλευτον εἰσαχθῆναι:[6] scholars assume rather too readily that the proposal was ἀπροβούλευτον because there was no boule to approve it.

The γραφὴ παρανόμων is first met in 415,[7] and may have been instituted by Ephialtes.[8] One instance of its use gives us a further piece of information about probouleumata. Cersobleptes' mercenary leader Charidemus had been made an Athenian citizen, and in 353 Aristocrates sponsored a probouleuma conferring further benefits on him; before the ecclesia could vote on this, Euthycles announced his intention of prosecuting Aristocrates, and Demosthenes wrote a speech for Euthycles to deliver at the trial. This took place after the new year, and one of the arguments which he anticipated was: οἶμαι τοίνυν αὐτὸν κἀκεῖνον ἐρεῖν τὸν λόγον, . . .

---

[1] X. H. i. vii, esp. 14–15, 34; cf. M. i. i. 18, iv. iv. 2, Plat. Apol. 32 B–C, Gorg. 473 E–474 A
*Axioch. 368 D–E.   [2] A. II. F.L. 82–4, cf. III. Ctes. 73–4.
[3] [D.] XXV. Aristog. i, hyp. 1–2. Cf. p. 53.
[4] D. XXII. Andr. 5–6, cf. hyp. i. 2, hyp. ii. 9.
[5] See most recently D. Hereward, BSA xlvii 1952, esp. 111–13, on Tod 100.
[6] [Pl.] X. Or. 835 F–836 A; ἀπροβούλευτον again in P. Oxy. xv. 1800, frs. 6+7, restored to refer to Thrasybulus' general proposal of A.P. 40. ii; cf. also A. III. Ctes. 195.
[7] And. I. Myst. 17.   [8] e.g. Lipsius, 36, 383, Glotz and Cohen, HG, ii. 140.

ὡς ἄκυρόν ἐστι τὸ ψήφισμα· προβούλευμα γάρ ἐστιν, ὁ νόμος δ' ἐπέτεια κελεύει τὰ τῆς βουλῆς εἶναι ψηφίσματα, ὥστε κἂν αὐτοῦ νῦν ἀποψηφίσησθε, ἤ γε πόλις φλαῦρον οὐδὲν πείσεται κατὰ τὸ ψήφισμα τοῦτο.[1] With the aid of a slightly confused scholium[2] we may conclude that a decree of the boule requiring some action to be taken will lapse unless the action is taken by the end of the bouleutic year, though the result achieved by such action will remain valid indefinitely: as a special case of this, any probouleuma not voted on by the ecclesia will automatically lapse at the end of the year. If the boule wished to recommend a number of decrees to the people, it had to provide enough assembly time for them in its own year of office.

Thus we learn from our literary sources that the boule could normally prevent action by refusing to make a probouleuma; or, if it wished the ecclesia to debate a subject, it could raise the question either with an open probouleuma or with a specific recommendation of its own: alternative motions could be proposed in the ecclesia, and a motion might finally be carried in an amended form. A specific proposal recommended by the boule must presumably always have stood in the name of a member (though he might be acting on behalf of a non-member);[3] if a citizen with a specific proposal to make obtained permission to address the boule, the result might instead be an open probouleuma, that the demos should hear what this man had to say, and decide as it saw fit,[4] but normally a proposal in the name of a non-member will have received its first airing in the ecclesia.

But we cannot tell from literary texts alone whether open probouleumata were the rule or the exception, whether the ecclesia played an active part in the conduct of public affairs or was content as a rule to adopt the boule's suggestions. These texts, where they give us enough detail, show a heavy bias towards genuine debates in the assembly and towards decrees proposed by non-bouleutae, but this is inevitable: the evidence is mostly for controversial issues in the fourth century, where the

[1] D. XXIII. *Arist.* 92.

[2] Schol. D. XXIII. *Arist.* 92.

[3] Cf. A. III. *Ctes.* 125, where Demosthenes' guileless accomplice is ὁ γράψας; and almost certainly *A.P.* 29. i: εἰπόντος τὸν μὲν πρὸ τοῦ ψηφίσματος λόγον Μηλοβίου, τὴν δὲ γνώμην γράψαντος Πυθοδώρου (on which see p. 74). I should conclude from *IG* ii² 1672, 302, that Lycurgus was a member of the boule in or before 329/8 (cf. Ch. I, p. 4 with n. 10, and Ch. III, p. 108 n. 4).

[4] There is no undoubted instance of this, but it is the most likely form of probouleuma when a decree is the work of συγγραφεῖς (commissioned by the demos at a previous assembly?) or follows a γνώμη στρατηγῶν (for the powers of the generals *vis-à-vis* the boule and ecclesia see Ch. I, pp. 43–8), or for the proposals envisaged by Lampon in his rider to M&L 73. Decrees of the demos with special origins are listed in Table E.

boule's suggestions are least likely to have been adopted without change by the ecclesia, and since our most voluble informant is Demosthenes we ought not to be surprised at the prominent appearance of his own decrees in many years when he was not a bouleutes. For a fairer estimate of the part played by boule and ecclesia we must turn to the preserved texts of inscribed decrees, selected not for their importance to the orators but by the chance of discovery.

Athenian decrees contain a number of formulaic expressions, evolved to record standard procedures.[1] Those which may be informative for our purpose are (I print in bold type the abbreviations which I shall use in referring to these formulae):

1. Minute-headings: βουλῆς ψηφισμα(τα) or δήμου ψηφισμα(τα).[2] (**BΨ/ΔΨ**)
2. Records of meeting: βουλή, ἐκκλησία, or ἐκκλησία κυρία, with or without the place of meeting specified, are the most common.[3] (**B/E**)

> ΔΨ and E are of course proper to any enactment of the demos, whatever its origins; BΨ and B are proper to enactments of the boule.[4]

3. Enactment-formulae:
   i. ἔδοχσεν τôι δέμοι (**ετδ**) is found in the very earliest Attic decrees (at beginning *or* end).[5]
   ii. ἔδοχσεν τêι βολêι καì τôι δέμοι (**ετβκτδ**) replaces it, and appears as the standard formula for all decrees of the demos from *c.* 469–458 (462/1?) to 405/4.[6]
   iii. From 403/2 onwards both ετδ[7] and ετβκτδ[8] are found, and it is widely believed that the difference in formula represents a difference in procedure (see below).
   iv. ἔδοξεν τῆι βουλῆι (**ετβ**) is the proper formula for a decree of the boule alone.

---

[1] For an exhaustive analysis of the formulae in inscriptions known *c.* 1900 (none has since been attempted) see Larfeld, *Handbuch der griechischen Epigraphik*, II. ii, esp. 601–81. In vol. I, 465–87, and in his *Griechische Epigraphik*[3] (*HdA*, vol. I. v) he compares the formulae employed in different states. For a brief modern discussion see Klaffenbach, *Griechische Epigraphik*[2], 70–5. (I repeat my list of formulae and abbreviations in the introductory note to Tables C–L, pp. 244–5.)

[2] Found occasionally from the late third to the early first century.

[3] Found frequently but not invariably from 336/5 onwards: *IG* ii[2] 330, etc.

[4] BΨ and B could be misapplied to probouleumata ratified in the ecclesia; cf. p. 77 n. 4 below.

[5] M&L 14 (C6), *IG* i[2] 3, 4 (485/4).

[6] M&L 23 (purporting to be of 480, but inscribed later), *IG* i[2] 5 (*c.* 475–450?—D. M. Lewis *per epistulam*), M&L 31 (*c.* 469–450), HMA 21 (*c.* 457?), etc. The only apparent exception is ετδ given by all MSS. of Thucydides for the one-year truce with the Peloponnesians in 422—T. IV. 118. xi. *SEG* x 86, 47, restored [ετ]δ in the decree for an alliance with Perdiccas of Macedon, but the longer line of the latest text allows [ετβκτ]δ: *ATL*, iii. 313 n. 61 = HMA 66, cf. more cautious text at *Svt* 186.

[7] Decree *ap.* And. I. *Myst.* 83 (403/2), Tod 114 (387/6), etc.

[8] In *IG* ii[2] 243 (337/6) a careless mason cut ετδκτβ.

4. Motion-formulae:

i. δεδόχθαι/ἐψηφίσθαι τῶι δήμωι (δ/ψτδ) is the phrase used to record a motion in the ecclesia; as such it can appear in a rider to a motion, which in effect is a separate motion, separately voted on.[1]

ii. δεδόχθαι/ἐψηφίσθαι τῆι βουλῆι (δ/ψτβ) is the phrase used to record a motion in the boule.[2]

iii. A special case of ii is the probouleumatic formula. (PF) The basic pattern, on which many variations are possible, is δεδόχθαι/ἐψηφίσθαι τῆι βουλῆι τοὺς προέδρους οἳ ἂν τυγχάνωσι προεδρεύοντες ἐν τῶι δήμωι χρηματίσαι περὶ τοῦ δεῖνος, γνώμην δὲ ξυμβάλλεσθαι τῆς βουλῆς εἰς τὸν δῆμον ὅτι δοκεῖ τῆι βουλῆι . . .[3]

There is sometimes an indication that the probouleuma has been commissioned by the ecclesia (CPF): ἐπειδὴ ὁ δῆμος ἐψήφισται τὴν βουλὴν προβουλεύσασαν ἐξενεγκεῖν εἰς τὸν δῆμον περὶ τοῦ δεῖνος, δ/ψτβ τοὺς προέδρους . . .

iv. δεδόχθαι/ἐψηφίσθαι τῆι βουλῆι καὶ τῶι δήμωι (δ/ψτβκτδ) is, if my interpretation of the formulae is correct, a somewhat improper phrase. Though common elsewhere, it is very rare in Athenian decrees before the time of the Roman Empire.[4]

δεδόχθαι and ἐψηφίσθαι appear to be interchangeable, δεδόχθαι being by far the commoner. These formulae are grammatically presented as part of the speaker's motion, dependent on the εἶπε which they follow either immediately or after a clause giving the reasons for the enactment: they thus seem to report that the speaker asked the demos/boule to resolve/vote that . . .

5. Commissioning of probouleuma: περὶ τοῦ δεῖνος, τὴν βουλὴν προβουλεύσασαν ἐξενεγκεῖν εἰς τὸν δῆμον εἰς τὴν πρώτην ἐκκλησίαν . . . (CP)

6. Mention of probouleuma: περὶ ὧν ἡ βουλὴ προεβούλευσεν . . . (MP)

7. Rider-formulae:

i. τὰ μὲν ἄλλα καθάπερ τῆι βουλῆι introduces the rider to a probouleuma. (RP)

ii. τὰ μὲν ἄλλα καθάπερ ὁ δεῖνα introduces the rider to an individual's motion. (RI)

iii. τὰ μὲν ἄλλα καθάπερ αἱ χσυγγραφαί in a decree where for ὁ δεῖνα εἶπε we have τάδε οἱ χσυγγραφὲς χσυνέγραφσαν.

(iv. One enactment of the nomothetae was regarded as an amendment of the existing law on the subject with which it dealt: τὰ μὲν ἄλλα καθάπερ τὸν Χαιρημονίδο νόμον περὶ τῆς ἀπαρχῆς.[5])

---

[1] ἐψηφίσθαι δὲ Ἀθηναίων τῶι δήμωι in rider, Tod 97. i (403/2), cf. IG ii² 19, 26; ἐψηφίσθαι Ἀθηναίοις, Tod 100 (403?); ψτδ, IG ii² 47, 23 sqq. ('beg. C4'); δτδ, Tod 114 (387/6); etc.

[2] Tod 133 (369/8), etc.

[3] Tod 124 (378/7); cf. IG ii² 79, 82 ('before 378/7'), etc.

[4] Preserved in M&L 94 (405/4), IG iv² 84 (c. A.D. 40–2), ii² 1072 (A.D. 116/17); restored in IG ii² 895 (188/7) (unnecessarily; not in new text, SEG xxi 436), Kerameikos, iii. A 5 (c. 100), IG ii² 1040. i and ii (mid 40s). It is a common formula in other states, and if not standard it at any rate became common in Athens under the Roman Empire (cf. J. Delz, Lukians Kenntnis der athenischen Antiquitäten, 138, D. J. Geagan, Hesp. Supp. xii 1967, 66).

[5] IG ii² 140.

Down to 404/3 there is a single form of enactment-formula in use, and motion-formulae are not found at all. But after 403/2 there are two enactment-formulae available for decrees of the demos and the motion-formulae also begin to appear. Many decrees were not inscribed with both an enactment- and a motion-formula, and many more are so mutilated that we cannot safely restore both formulae, but for the decrees where both are preserved or restorable the correlations are:[1]

		Motion	
		PF	δ/ψτδ
Enactment	ετβκτδ	80	10
	ετδ	14	92

It is clear that we have here two main patterns: $\epsilon\tau\beta\kappa\tau\delta$+PF and $\epsilon\tau\delta$+ $\delta/\psi\tau\delta$. In the first case the procedure followed seems obvious—it is hard to imagine that decrees following this pattern are anything but probouleumata ratified verbatim in the ecclesia. It has commonly been believed that decrees following the second pattern are not ratified probouleumata, and in the next few pages I shall do what I can to test this theory.

I begin with an examination of two documents where the procedure followed is fairly clear. *IG* ii² 360 contains five decrees in honour of Heraclides of Salamis, the logical sequence of which is as follows:

(a) (decree iii) Between 330/29 and 328/7 Telemachus carried a motion in the ecclesia, calling on the boule to make a probouleuma so that Heraclides might obtain what benefit he could from the Athenian demos.

(b) (decree iv) In the boule Cephisodotus referred to decree iii and to Hera-clides' having supplied corn promptly and at a fair price, and sponsored a probouleuma recommending that he be praised and given a gold crown worth 500 drachmae; εἶναι δ' αὐτῶι καὶ εὑρέσθαι παρὰ τοῦ δήμου ὅ τι ἂν δύναται ἀγαθόν (62–3).[2]

(c) (decree ii) In the ecclesia Telemachus briefly referred to Heraclides' ser-vice to Athens and recommended praise and a gold crown; he then pro-posed the sending of an envoy to Heraclea to protest against the theft of Heraclides' sails.

(d) (decree v) In or after 328/7 Phyleus in the boule referred to Heraclides' old service to Athens and to the fact that it prompted the ecclesia to commission a probouleuma; he then remarked on Heraclides' contribution

---

[1] Three decrees require special notice:

Tod 100	403?	ετδ; ἐψηφίσθαι Ἀθηναίοις	
IG ii² 672	280/79	E; [ετ]βκτδ; δτδ	two copies of same decree
Hesp. x 1941, 338–9		E; [ετδ]; (stone ends)	
IG ii² 839	221/0	ετβ; PF	

[2] For an analysis of ἄλλο ἀγαθόν clauses see Table L.

εἰς σιτωνίαν, and he recommended that he be praised and given a gold crown worth 500 drachmae; εἶναι δ' αὐτῶι καὶ εὑρέσθαι ἀγαθὸν παρὰ τοῦ δήμου ὅτου ἂν δοκεῖ ἄξιος εἶναι (75).

(e) (decree i) This has a normal prescript dating it to 325/4. In the ecclesia Demosthenes referred to Heraclides' general goodwill and his two specific services to Athens, and recommended that he be praised and given a gold crown; also that he be made πρόξενος and εὐεργέτης and granted the privileges commonly associated with this status, and that this decree καὶ τοὺς ἄλλους ἐπαίνους be published.

Decree iv declares its dependence on iii, and it is economical to assume that ii is dependent on iv and i on v: they briefly repeat the provisions of the probouleuma (but not in full—each time we must go back to the probouleuma to find out how much money is to be spent on the crown) and then grant further benefits as authorized in lines 62–3 and 75. The inscription ends with ὁ δῆμος in two crowns and ἡ βουλή in two crowns, which supports the view that we have two probouleumata plus two decrees arising from them, not two probouleumata ratified by the ecclesia plus two wholly independent decrees of the ecclesia.[1]

From the procedural point of view, instead of decrees ii and i we might have had two riders, τὰ μὲν ἄλλα καθάπερ τῆι βουλῆι, adding the clauses that are found only in ii and i. What we have here is a second way of amending a proposal, by producing a new motion which briefly reaffirms the old and adds further items, *and which does not contain any indication of its history*:[2] if the stone stopped short at line 45 and we had only the two final decrees of the demos, there would be no means of telling that these had been expanded from probouleumata. There is no enactment-formula, but the final decrees and the initial motion calling for a probouleuma all have the motion-formula which I should expect to be non-probouleumatic, δ/ψτδ—and here, with all the relevant decrees preserved, we can see that in a sense they are non-probouleumatic, as they are not simple repetitions of a probouleuma.

Another way in which an 'independent' decree of the demos can arise from a probouleuma is illustrated by Tod 189. The stone carries two decrees:

(i) an open probouleuma, with ετβ and PF, providing for the demos to listen to the Citians' request for a temple and make up its own mind;

---

[1] Mr. G. L. Cawkwell has suggested to me that *IG* ii² 360 comprises one commissioning of a probouleuma and four probouleumata ratified by the ecclesia. My analysis is, I believe, confirmed by the fact that we are told of only two acts on account of which Heraclides deserved to be honoured.

[2] Cf. A. Billheimer, *AJA*² xlii 1938, 467 n. 3. Larfeld, *Handbuch der griechischen Epigraphik*, II. ii. 676–7, thought that amendment by reformulation was rare; but we cannot tell.

(ii) the resulting decree of the demos, containing a new prescript, with $\epsilon\tau\delta$ and $\delta\tau\delta$, granting the request.

Again there is no clue in the second decree to the circumstances in which it was enacted. Thus the only distinction which we can attempt to base on the formulae is between those which ratify probouleumata verbatim, with or without riders, and all others (whether revised from a probouleuma like *IG* ii² 360. i and ii *or* framed in response to an open probouleuma like Tod 189. ii *or* carried in opposition to the wishes of the boule) : *I shall use the words 'probouleumatic' and 'non-probouleumatic' in accordance with this distinction.*

Several tests must be applied before we can confidently use the formulae to make even this distinction. First, it is very likely that wherever we find the ecclesia commissioning a probouleuma on some subject the decree in which it does this will be non-probouleumatic: there would be no point in the boule's recommending that the ecclesia order the boule to make a recommendation.[1] This happens four times after 403/2: in three of the decrees the formulae in which we are interested are preserved, and they are all of the non-probouleumatic kind.[2]

Likewise, we should not expect a decree to be probouleumatic as I have defined the word when its preamble mentions a probouleuma in such words as $\pi\epsilon\rho\grave{\iota}$ $\mathring{\omega}\nu$ $\mathring{\eta}$ $\beta o\upsilon\lambda\grave{\eta}$ $\pi\rho o\epsilon\beta o\acute{\upsilon}\lambda\epsilon\upsilon\sigma\epsilon\nu$: a probouleuma relevant to the subject of the decree has been made, but if the preamble is to make sense the text of the decree as we have it must have come from the floor of the house (though it may be either a mere amplification of a probouleuma, as in *IG* ii² 360, or an outright contradiction of a probouleuma). Of the six instances of this, four have straightforward non-probouleumatic formulae.[3] Tod 144 combines $\epsilon\tau\beta\kappa\tau\delta$ with $\delta[\tau\delta]$; the proposer's name is

---

[1] J. Tréheux has, however, suggested that this is the procedure underlying a Lampsacene document of *c.* 100 B.C. (*SEG* xiii 458) which he published in *BCH* lxxvii 1953, 426–43 (discussion of procedure, 438–40), and the arguments used against his interpretation by J. and L. Robert, *REG* lxvii 1954, 159–62, no. 209, have failed to convince W. G. G. Forrest (*Phoen.* xxi 1967, 14 with n. 9). The inscription comprises two decrees: the first, with the formulae ΨB; $\epsilon\tau\beta\kappa\tau\delta$; $\delta\tau\beta\kappa\tau\delta$, commissions a probouleuma and cites a law which permits the demos to do this; the second, with the formulae ΨB; $\epsilon\tau\delta$; $\delta\tau\beta\kappa\tau\delta$, begins with a reference to the demos' having commissioned a probouleuma. It seems to me that the content of the decrees makes the procedure followed so clear that there is no need to base an argument on the formulae: the first decree is the measure by which the demos commissioned the probouleuma, and the second is the resulting probouleuma, which we may assume from its publication as the second and last decree of this document to have been ratified verbatim by the ecclesia. If this is correct the secretary will have been very careless in his adding of minute-headings and enactment-formulae—but such carelessness did happen. (My interpretation of this document is very close to that of the Roberts.)

[2] Tod 154 (357/6), *IG* ii² 193 (before 353/2), 360. iii (330/29), *Chron. Hell. Ath.* 104–8 (204/3)—see Table D. Cf. G. Klaffenbach, *Griechische Epigraphik*², 74.

[3] *IG* ii² 336 (334/3), 338. i (333/2), 352 (after 318/17), *Hesp.* Supp. vi 31/2. ii (A.D. 229/30 or 230/1)—see Table D.

followed by orders to the herald to vow sacrifices to the principal deities
if what the Athenians decide turns out well;[1] and then

$$[\dot{\epsilon}\pi\epsilon\iota]\text{-}$$
$$[\delta\dot{\eta}\ \delta]\dot{\epsilon}\ o\dot{\iota}\ \sigma\dot{\nu}\mu\mu\alpha\chi o\iota\ \delta\acute{o}\gamma\mu\alpha\ \epsilon\dot{\iota}\sigma\dot{\eta}\nu\epsilon\iota\gamma\kappa\alpha\nu\ \epsilon\dot{\iota}s\ \tau[\dot{\eta}\nu\ \beta o\upsilon\lambda]\text{-}$$
$$[\dot{\eta}\nu\ \delta]\dot{\epsilon}\chi\epsilon\sigma\theta\alpha\iota\ \tau\dot{\eta}\nu\ \sigma\upsilon\mu\mu\alpha\chi\acute{\iota}\alpha\nu\ \kappa\alpha\theta\dot{\alpha}\ \epsilon\dot{\iota}\sigma\alpha\gamma\gamma\acute{\epsilon}\lambda[\lambda o\nu\tau\alpha\iota\ o]\text{-}$$
$$[\dot{\iota}\ A\rho]\kappa\acute{\alpha}\delta\epsilon s\ \kappa\alpha\dot{\iota}\ A\chi\alpha\iota o\dot{\iota}\ \kappa\alpha\dot{\iota}\ \dot{}H\lambda\epsilon\hat{\iota}o\iota\ \kappa\alpha\dot{\iota}\ \Phi\lambda\epsilon[\iota\acute{\alpha}\sigma\iota o\iota,\ \kappa\alpha]\text{-}$$
$$[\dot{\iota}\ \dot{\eta}\ \beta o]\upsilon\lambda\dot{\eta}\ \pi\rho o\ddot{\upsilon}\beta o\acute{\upsilon}\lambda\epsilon\upsilon\sigma\epsilon\nu\ \kappa\alpha\tau\dot{\alpha}\ \tau\alpha\ddot{\upsilon}\tau\acute{\alpha},\ \delta\epsilon\delta\acute{o}[\chi\theta\alpha\iota\ \tau\hat{\omega}\iota\ \delta]\text{-}$$
$$[\dot{\eta}\mu\omega\iota\ \epsilon\hat{\iota}]\nu\alpha\iota\ \sigma\upsilon\mu\mu\acute{\alpha}\chi o\upsilon s\ \kappa\tau\lambda.$$

The allies' δόγμα, we are told, recommended the acceptance of the
alliance; the probouleuma may have incorporated the substance of
the δόγμα or it may simply have commended the δόγμα to the demos;
and the demos accepted the recommendation—but with a preamble
which, whether or not what follows it was taken over verbatim from the
δόγμα or the probouleuma, cannot itself have formed part of the text
until the assembly-stage. But the probouleuma was at least permissive
and probably favourable to the alliance, so that here we have a decree
which is in accordance with a probouleuma, yet is technically non-
probouleumatic.

There remains *IG* ii² 660. ii, which is restored to read:

$$[\ddot{\epsilon}]\delta o\xi\epsilon\nu\ \tau\hat{\epsilon}\iota\ \beta o\upsilon\lambda\hat{\epsilon}\iota\ \kappa\alpha\dot{\iota}\ \tau\hat{\omega}\iota\ \delta\dot{\eta}\mu\omega\iota,\ [\quad -\ 23\ -\quad \epsilon\hat{\iota}]\text{-}$$
$$[\pi]\epsilon\nu.\ \pi\epsilon\rho\dot{\iota}\ \dot{\omega}\nu,\ \ddot{\omega}\sigma\pi\epsilon\rho\ \dot{o}\ \pi\rho\epsilon\sigma\beta\epsilon\upsilon\tau\dot{\eta}s\ \tau[\hat{\omega}\nu\ T\eta\nu\acute{\iota}\omega\nu\ \alpha\dot{\iota}\tau\epsilon\hat{\iota},\ \pi\rho o\beta\epsilon\beta o\acute{\upsilon}\lambda\epsilon\upsilon\tau]\text{-}$$
$$[\alpha]\iota\ \tau\hat{\epsilon}\iota\ \beta o\upsilon\lambda\hat{\epsilon}\iota,\ \tau o\dot{\upsilon}s\ \pi\rho o\acute{\epsilon}\delta\rho o\upsilon s\ o[\dot{\iota}\ \ddot{\alpha}\nu\ \lambda\acute{\alpha}\chi\omega\sigma\iota\ \kappa\tau\lambda.]$$

Here an external reference to the probouleuma seems to turn into the
probouleuma referred to. Something must have dropped out, and a restoration to give perfect sense is impossible, but the difficulties are
reduced if we read: ὁ πρεσβευτὴς τ[ῶν Τηνίων ἐπαγγέλλει, ἐψηφίσθα]ι τῆι
βουλῆι κτλ. The inscription will then cease to be relevant here.[2]

A further test can be based on the fact that a man could not be a
member of the boule, and ought not to have been able to sponsor a

---

[1] Cf. p. 75.

[2] Tod 193 also seems to have a preamble which has been over-condensed. It reads:

$$\ddot{\epsilon}\delta o\xi\epsilon\nu\ [\tau\hat{\eta}\iota\ \beta o\upsilon\lambda]\hat{\eta}\iota\ \kappa\alpha\dot{\iota}\ \tau\hat{\omega}\iota\ \delta\dot{\eta}\mu\omega\iota\cdot\ N\acute{o}\theta[\iota\pi\pi o s\ \Lambda\upsilon\sigma\acute{\iota}o\upsilon\ \Delta\iota o]\text{-}$$
$$\mu\epsilon\iota\epsilon\acute{\upsilon}[s\ \epsilon\hat{\iota}\pi\epsilon\cdot\ \pi]\epsilon\rho\dot{\iota}\ \dot{\omega}\nu\ \dot{o}\ \delta\hat{\eta}\mu o s\ \pi\rho\acute{o}[\tau\epsilon\rho o\nu\ \dot{\epsilon}\psi\dot{\eta}\phi\iota\sigma\tau\alpha\iota\ \dot{\epsilon}\pi\grave{\iota}]$$
$$[\tau\hat{\eta}s\ \text{—}]s\ \pi\rho\upsilon\tau\alpha\nu\epsilon\acute{\iota}\alpha s\ \tau[o\dot{\upsilon}s\ \pi\rho o\acute{\epsilon}\delta\rho o\upsilon s\ o\dot{\iota}\ \ddot{\alpha}\nu\ \lambda\acute{\alpha}\chi]\text{-}$$
$$[\omega\sigma\iota\nu\ \dot{\epsilon}\nu\ \tau\hat{\omega}\iota\ \delta\dot{\eta}\mu]\omega\iota\ \pi\rho o\epsilon\delta[\rho\epsilon\acute{\upsilon}\epsilon\iota\nu\text{— stone ends}].$$

Most of this is restored, but what is on the stone makes the restorations disturbingly likely:
yet it should be the boule in its probouleumatic formula, not the ecclesia, which gives order
to the proedri in this way. I offer this reconstruction *exempli gratia*:

$$\ldots\ \pi\epsilon\rho\dot{\iota}\ \dot{\omega}\nu\ \dot{o}\ \delta\hat{\eta}\mu o s\ \dot{\epsilon}\psi\dot{\eta}\phi\iota\sigma\tau\alpha\iota\ \dot{\epsilon}\pi\dot{\iota}\ \tau\hat{\eta}s\ \text{—}\ \pi\rho\upsilon\tau\alpha\nu\epsilon\acute{\iota}\alpha s\ \langle\tau\dot{\eta}\nu\ \beta o\upsilon\lambda\dot{\eta}\nu\ \pi\rho o\beta o\upsilon\lambda\epsilon\acute{\upsilon}\sigma\alpha\sigma\alpha\nu\ \dot{\epsilon}\xi\epsilon\nu\epsilon\gamma\kappa\epsilon\hat{\iota}\nu\ \epsilon\dot{\iota}s$$
$$\tau\dot{o}\nu\ \delta\hat{\eta}\mu o\nu\ \pi\epsilon\rho\dot{\iota}\ \dot{}P\eta\beta o\acute{\upsilon}\lambda o\upsilon\ \ddot{o}\ \tau\iota\ \ddot{\alpha}\nu\ \alpha\dot{\upsilon}\tau\hat{\eta}\iota\ \delta o\kappa\epsilon\hat{\iota}\ \ddot{\alpha}\rho\iota\sigma\tau o\nu\ \epsilon\hat{\iota}\nu\alpha\iota,\ \dot{\epsilon}\psi\eta\phi\acute{\iota}\sigma\theta\alpha\iota\ \tau\hat{\eta}\iota\ \beta o\upsilon\lambda\hat{\eta}\iota\rangle\ \tau o\dot{\upsilon}s\ \pi\rho o\text{-}$$
$$\acute{\epsilon}\delta\rho o\upsilon s\ \kappa\tau\lambda.$$

probouleumatic decree, for more than two years of his life.[1] The fourth century has left records of some prolific authors of decrees, and it may be helpful to examine the formulae used in their decrees.[2]

Aristophon is the author of five measures with significant formulae between 363/2 and 336/5: none of them incorporates the probouleumatic formula, but some have ετβκτδ rather than ετδ.[3] The orator Lycurgus is the author of a probouleumatic decree in 336/5,[4] and of a decree of the boule in or perhaps before 329/8: he is responsible in other years for a νόμος, and for four decrees with non-probouleumatic formulae (the formulae in a fifth are lost). We have no less than eleven prescripts of decrees in the name of Demades, who is attested as a member of the boule in a list perhaps to be dated 336/5 (none of his surviving decrees belongs to this year). Of the three decrees dated in the oligarchic year 320/19, one has ετδ and δτδ, a second ετβκτδ and no motion-formula, and the restoration of the third is uncertain; the other decrees all have formulae of the non-probouleumatic kind. Even under the democratic constitution Demades was entitled to serve twice in the boule, and there will of course have been fewer eligible citizens to man the boule under the oligarchic constitution which followed the Lamian War.[5] For Demosthenes Δημοσθένους Παιανιεύς it is surprising to find that there is only one decree preserved on stone: its enactment-formula is restored as ετδ. We have the prescripts of at least sixteen decrees proposed by Stratocles Εὐθυδήμου Διομεεύς, and in all except one, where the restoration of Stratocles' name is doubtful, the prescript formulae are non-probouleumatic. Finally, we may note that Pandius is the author of a probouleumatic decree for Dionysius of Syracuse in 369/8; in the following year the same man is author of a decree with non-probouleumatic formulae by which Athens makes an alliance with Dionysius.[6]

This test provides a fair amount of confirmatory evidence and, except in the case of Aristophon, nothing that need conflict with the theory that

---

[1] Cf. Kahrstedt, U.M.A., 291–2 with 292 n. 1. He thought that in such cases the proposer offered his motion to the boule, which then accepted it as a probouleuma—but I believe that if the boule chose formally to adopt a proposal rather than to commend it to the demos in an open probouleuma a bouleutes should figure as the nominal proposer: cf. p. 63 with n. 3, and p. 74.

[2] I list in Table F the decrees of Aristophon, Lycurgus, Demades, Demosthenes, and Stratocles, with their prescript formulae.

[3] Cf. Tod, vol. ii, p. 128. Aristophon is notorious as the man who claimed to have been acquitted in 75 γραφαὶ παρανόμων (A. III. Ctes. 194).

[4] We have no list of the bouleutae from his tribe in that year.

[5] For the possibility that the ban on more than two years' service was lifted under the oligarchy cf. Ch. I, p. 3 with n. 4.

[6] Tod 133 (369/8) (PF); 136 (368/7) ([ετδ]; δτδ).

ετδ and δ/ψτδ are formulae proper to non-probouleumatic decrees. Aristophon is the only one of the orators from whom we have several decrees who was active before 350, and here I must anticipate my conclusion, that the distinction between the two main patterns of formula was not firmly established in the first half of the fourth century, but that at that time there was still a tendency to use ετβκτδ with any enactment of the demos (as in the fifth century).

Just as there are two ways of introducing a decree, there are two ways of introducing a rider to a decree: the mover of the rider may use either τὰ μὲν ἄλλα καθάπερ τῆι βουλῆι (**RP**) or τὰ μὲν ἄλλα καθάπερ ὁ δεῖνα (**RI**). RP is as unmistakable as the probouleumatic formula, and we should expect to find this used with probouleumatic decrees; RI, it has been suggested, ought to be the proper formula for riders to non-probouleumatic decrees.[1] In the fifth century we have very little to go on: of the 17 reliable instances of RP, four follow a decree containing what looks like bouleutic language, and of the seven inscribed instances of RI three are found in the second rider to a decree, taking the form of a rider *to the first rider* (which has the RP formula).[2] From 403/2 there are 26 clear

[1] Jones, 112–13, M&L, p. 131 (commentary on no. 49, 32–5); but on p. 188 (commentary on no. 68, 26–7) they remark: 'It is not . . . certain that [RI] was never used to amend a probouleuma.'

[2] Professor Meritt has worked on the assumption that all Athenian decrees were probouleumatic (even as I define the term), that the first rider to any decree must be introduced by RP, and that RI must always introduce a second or subsequent rider (*Documents on Athenian Tribute*, 32–3 with n. 36, *ATL*, i. 213): Tod 167 is admitted as an exception.

There is a rider to Cleonymus' tribute-decree, M&L 68, beginning at l. 25, which must (as has been known for some time) be καθάπερ ὁ δεῖνα, and this is the first and only rider of which traces are preserved, but to fit the decree to his presuppositions Meritt restored a previous rider with RP in the lacuna after l. 9 (*ATL* D 8, 10). A new fragment has been discovered, which makes it clear that ll. 26–7 (M&L enumeration) should read καθάπερ Κλεόνυμ[ος], and in view of this Meritt has withdrawn his first rider (*AJP* lxxxviii 1967; withdrawal of first rider, p. 32) but without discussing the principle which had led him to suggest it. Nevertheless the dating of the decree to Cleonymus' year in the boule, 426/5, appears sound. Cleonymus was the author of a probouleumatic decree for Methone in the first prytany of 426/5 (M&L 65, 32–56, (notice 51 sqq.); dated from M&L 72, 5); in the Cecropid prytany of one year he was the author of M&L 68. i, 68. ii, and *SEG* x 73 (the last two on the same day). Cecropis held the second prytany of 426/5 (M&L 72, 3–4); in Cleonymus' decree for Methone, in the first prytany of that year, we read that priority is to be given in the second prytany to one or more debates on the other cities, and it is tempting to see in M&L 68 the decrees resulting from these debates (cf. Meritt, *AJP* 1967, 31–2). There is no reason why a decree which is technically non-probouleumatic should not stand in the name of a bouleutes.

There is no second rider in which RP is found; Tod 167 provides the only other RI in what is demonstrably a first rider; but there are only nine inscribed examples of RI in all.

Some mention ought to be made of two fifth-century documents where we seem to have riders without an orthodox rider-formula. M&L 44, the first decree for the priestess of Athena Νίκη, contains two motions introduced by the name of the proposer alone: Meritt has argued (*Hesp.* x 1941, 307–15) that these are both riders to an original motion which was inscribed on a superimposed block of stone, now lost; but for doubts about this see M&L,

examples of RP:

to a decree with PF or other bouleutic language   14[1]

to a decree with ετβκτδ ONLY   3

to a decree with no other indication of origin   8[2]

to a decree which should be non-probouleumatic (*IG* ii² 276—
see below)   I

RI occurs only twice after 403/2—in Tod 139, with no other indication of origin, and in Tod 167, which contains bouleutic language yet ought not to be probouleumatic (see below).

In the first of our two problem decrees, *IG* ii² 276, the relevant formulae are:

[περὶ ὧν ἔδοξε Ἀσκληπιό]δωρος [Πο]λυ[– 14 – ἐν τῆι βο]υλῆι ἔννομα ἱ[κετεύειν, ψ]τδ (3–6);
τὰ μὲν ἄλλα καθάπερ τῆι βο[υλῆι] (24–5).

The ἱκετεύειν-clause does not prove that the decree is probouleumatic: a probouleuma could apparently contain either ἔδοξεν . . . ἐν τῆι βουλῆι or ἔδοξεν . . . ἐν τῶι δήμωι (in the latter case the probouleuma was probably commissioned by the ecclesia); when the boule is mentioned the boule ought in some way to have been involved, but the resulting decree might bear the same relationship to the probouleuma as in *IG* ii² 360 (discussed above, pp. 66–7)—that is, it could be in general accord with the probouleuma but not be a verbatim ratification of it. ἔδοξεν . . . ἐν τῆι βουλῆι

pp. 110–11. In M&L 52 we have first a motion by Diognetus; in l. 40 a motion of Anticles begins, introduced simply by Ἀντικλῆς εἶπε; and in l. 70 Archestratus proposes a rider καθάπερ Ἀντικλῆς. The relationship between the motions of Diognetus and Anticles is uncertain: the manner in which Anticles prescribes the oath suggests that his may be the earlier of the two motions, but Meritt, *Documents on Athenian Tribute*, 33 n. 36, regarded Anticles' motion as a first rider; M&L, p. 141, regard Anticles' as an independent decree moved at the same assembly as Diognetus'.

In *IG* ii² 448. i a rider is introduced with the unparalleled τάδε Πανφίλου Εὐφ[ι]λήτου.

[1] Including *IG* ii² 235 (340/39), with a new enactment-formula (ετ[δ]), and *IG* ii² 373 (322/1), where the rider has a complete new prescript (*E*; ετδ) with the date in both archontic and bouleutic calendars. The latter must surely and the former may possibly have been enacted on a later occasion than the original decree (perhaps on the resumption of an adjourned assembly?). This process has developed further in *IG* ii² 682 (after 256/5) and perhaps *SEG* xxi 359 (beg. C3): here a probouleumatic decree is followed by a pseudo-rider, not embodying one of the old formulae, to the decree as previously enacted (τὰ μὲν ἄλλα πράττειν κατὰ τὸ πρότερον ψήφισμα). With this we may compare *IG* ii² 140, a νόμος which was framed as an amendment to an already existing νόμος.

[2] I include among these decrees *IG* ii² 289. E. Schweigert linked with this the prescript-fragment *IG* ii² 372, where the formulae are *E*; ετδ (*Hesp.* viii 1939, 173–5, cf. *SEG* xxi 300; this is one of Demades' decrees, cf. Table F). Since the fragments are very different in colouring and do not join, his case is not compelling, and the evidence for Demades' career and for the association of RP with probouleumatic decrees makes it safer to keep the two fragments apart.

(After I had written this note Dr. D. M. Lewis drew my attention to J. Pečírka, *LF* lxxxix 1966, 262–6, cf. *The Grant of Enktesis*, 57, who dissociates the fragments on epigraphic grounds.)

would then have the same procedural implications as περὶ ὧν ἡ βουλὴ προεβούλευσεν (pp. 68–9 above).[1] We are left, therefore, with a direct clash between ψτδ and RP, and I am inclined to pin my faith on the motion-formula: the reference to the boule suggests a decree which is at any rate in substantial agreement with the intention of the probouleuma; in such cases attention could easily be concentrated on the boule, where the business had originated, rather than on the author of the final motion, and so RP could easily be misapplied.[2]

In Tod 167 we have the reverse phenomenon, RI with a decree which looks as if it should be probouleumatic. The prescript contains no formulae which can help us, but the clause beginning in line 53 ought to be part of a probouleuma:

> χρηματίσαι τοὺς προέδ[ρους]
> [οἳ] ἂν λάχωσι προεδρεύειν ἐν τῶι δήμωι [τῆι]
> [ὀγ]δόηι ἐπὶ δέκα πρῶτον μετὰ τὰ ἱερά   (55–7)

is bouleutic language, not ecclesiastic language.[3] But the original motion stands in the name of Androtion, and the rider is introduced with τὰ μὲν ἄλλα καθάπερ Ἀνδροτίων. Androtion appears as ἐπιστάτης in a decree dated 'before 378/7',[4] and was bouleutes again in or before 356/5:[5] he

---

[1] ἔδοξεν ... ἐν τῆι βουλῆι:

| IG ii² 318 | 346/5 | PF |
| 276 | before 336/5 | (discussed in text) |

ἔδοξεν ... ἐν τῶι δήμωι:

IG ii² 196	before 353/2	PF
218, 22 sqq.	346/5	in RP; cf. above for probouleuma
336. iii*	333/2	(no indication of origin: date Dow, Hesp. xxxii 1963, 341–2),
502*	302/1	E; ετδ

*ἐν τῶι δήμωι restored to fit στοιχηδόν arrangement; ἐν τῆι βολῆι has same number of letters, but that spelling is unlikely as late as this.

Tod 166 (348/7) has [περὶ ὧν οἱ Ὀλύνθιοι ἔδοξαν ἔννομα ἱκετεύειν ἔν τε τῶι δήμωι καὶ ἐν τοῖς συμμ]άχοις restored (!) and an open proposal which might but need not belong to a probouleuma.

Tod 189. ii (333/2), a non-probouleumatic decree published with an open probouleuma, has ἔδοξαν ἔννομα ἱκετεύειν αἰτοῦντες τὸν δῆμον χωρίου ἔνκτησιν.

In IG ii² 404 (before mid C4) the ἱκετεύειν-clause cannot safely be restored.

[2] Most of the ἱκετεύειν-clause is restored, and we ought perhaps not to rule out the possibility that it has been restored wrongly.

[3] An open clause in a probouleuma seems particularly likely in financial matters: cf. IG ii² 223 A, 13, P 16; and notice also as examples of the caution prescribed in finance the three orders from the ecclesia for νομοθεσία to adjust the μερισμός: IG ii² 222, 41–6; 330, 15–23; SIG³ 298, 35–41.

[4] IG ii² 61, 6–7. D. M. Lewis lists possible years before and after 378/7 in BSA xlix 1954, 34.

[5] D. XXII. Andr. 38. For 356/5, B. R. I. Sealey, REG lxviii 1955, 89–92, G. L. Cawkwell, C&M xxiii 1962, 40–5; for 359/8, D. M. Lewis, BSA xlix 1954, 43–4, cf. E. Schweigert, Hesp. viii 1939, 12–17.

ought not, therefore, to have been a member of the boule yet again and capable of sponsoring a probouleumatic decree in 347/6. This decree figures prominently in Laqueur's discussion of 'concealed riders':[1] though Athenian documents seem to have been so carelessly drafted that arguments from lack of logical cohesion can have little force, we have seen that decrees could be amended and expanded by reformulation, and it may be that Androtion from the floor of the assembly has taken over and partially reformulated the probouleuma. A prominent politician could easily concentrate the amender's attention on his part in the making of the decree, and RI was therefore used—but correctly, I would submit, as Androtion's decree was technically non-probouleumatic.

We must also consider here Pythodorus' decree of 412/11 in *A.P.* 29. i–iii. In § i we read τὴν δὲ γνώμην γράψαντος Πυθοδώρου; in § ii the text is preceded by ἦν δὲ τὸ ψήφισμα τοῦ Πυθοδώρου τοιόνδε; and in § iii Κλειτοφῶν δὲ τὰ μὲν ἄλλα καθάπερ Πυθόδωρος εἶπεν. But the principal advocate of the decree was Melobius (εἰπόντος τὸν μὲν πρὸ τοῦ ψηφίσματος λόγον Μηλοβίου [§ i]), and the most likely explanation is that the motion stood in Pythodorus' name because he was a bouleutes and the more prominent oligarch Melobius was not—but if Pythodorus was a bouleutes we should expect to find RP rather than RI. There has certainly been some editorial work to fit the decree into the accompanying text,[2] and it is conceivable that an original RP has been changed to RI, but Pythodorus' decree remains a greater obstacle to the theory under discussion than any inscribed text.

We must admit, then, that in certain contexts the two rider-formulae might fairly easily be misapplied. Nevertheless, the evidence that RP means what it says, and should be found in riders to probouleumatic decrees, is good: there are several clear examples, and the only instance of its use with a non-probouleumatic decree is easily explained. The case for linking RI with non-probouleumatic decrees is weaker: the formula is found only ten times in all, and though its epigraphical instances are compatible with the theory the decree in *A.P.* 29 is more disturbing. The very fact that RI is the rarer formula may be significant: a proposal made and perhaps published in advance by the boule will have been easier to amend than one produced from the floor of the assembly without any advance notice.[3]

---

[1] *Epigraphische Untersuchungen.* See A. Billheimer, *AJA*[2] xlii 1938, for a detailed reply.

[2] And notice τοιόνδε here (29. ii), but ταύτην 4. i, τάδε 30. i, τήνδε 31. i, τάσδε 39. i.

[3] In *SEG* x 84, 30 sqq., Meritt claims to have detected a rider added while the probouleuma was still before the boule: *Hesp.* x 1941, 320–6.

Professor Jones has tried to use as an indication of a decree's origin another common piece of decree-language. He believes that the phrase αὐτίκα μάλα can only have been inserted in a motion when it was under discussion in a body competent to order immediate action, and that any decree of the demos which contains this phrase must be non-probouleumatic.[1] This seems to be extracting too much from the language. It is frequently necessary to specify that action of some kind be taken as soon as possible after the motion ordering it has been carried, for example if men have to be appointed for some particular task, or if instructions are being given to men in some official position. Immediate action on the part of the assembly itself is necessary if an otherwise specific motion has an open clause in it—the boule or a lay citizen may equally well propose that the demos should decide at once whether it wishes to do one thing or another. Such clauses could be included in Athenian decrees either with αὐτίκα or αὐτίκα μάλα, or with ἤδη (not before the early third century), or with no expression of immediacy: there is in fact no surviving instance of this use of αὐτίκα in an undisputed probouleuma,[2] but clauses with ἤδη or no temporal adverb, but in other respects indistinguishable from the clauses with αὐτίκα, are found in probouleumata.

There is one use of αὐτίκα which may perhaps bear Jones's interpretation. Three decrees of the early fourth century begin with orders to the herald to vow αὐτίκα μάλα that special sacrifices will be performed if what the demos does turns out well. All three decrees have the non-probouleumatic kind of enactment-formula, δ/ψτδ, though in the two where a motion-formula survives it is ετβκτδ.[3] The vow was presumably to be made at the assembly enacting the decree, and if the proposal had come from the boule we should perhaps expect a specific reference to the assembly, e.g. εὔξασθαι μὲν τὸν κήρυκα ἐν τῶι δήμωι αὐτίκα μάλα κτλ. But even if this interpretation is correct, it affects only three decrees which may be considered non-probouleumatic on other grounds, and in general I am not satisfied that clauses containing αὐτίκα μάλα provide any indication of the origins of a decree.

There remains the major obstacle to a distinction between probouleumatic and non-probouleumatic decrees, the fact that in a certain number of inscriptions an enactment-formula of one kind is combined with

---

[1] Jones, 113 with 156 n. 96. In Table K I give a classified list of the relevant decrees, showing that the phrase is used in some certainly non-probouleumatic decrees.

[2] But IG ii² 174 orders proclamation [ἐν τῶι αὐτί]κα μάλα ἐν ἄστει [ἀγωνι].

[3] IG ii² 30 (386/5), Tod 144 (362/1), Tod 146 (362/1). See Table K, § 2, and for Tod 144 cf. pp. 68–9.

a motion-formula of the other kind. I consider first those in which the enactment-formula is $\epsilon\tau\beta\kappa\tau\delta$ and the motion-formula $\delta/\psi\tau\delta$:[1]

Tod 100	403?	Citizenship *or* lesser rewards for metics of Phyle	ἐψηφίσθαι Ἀθηναίοις
IG ii² 70	before 378/7	To inscribe Phocian decree requesting citizenship for Antiochus *et al.*	*
Tod 123	378/7	Prospectus of Second Athenian League	
142	363/2	Regulations for Iulis	*
144	362/1	Alliance with Arcadians and others	
146	362/1	Cleruchy at Potidaea	*
147	361/0	Alliance with Thessalians	*
IG ii² 134	354/3	Honorific decree	
138	353/2	Honorific decree	[δτδ] not certain
Tod 168	347/6	Renewal of Mytilenaean alliance	*
IG ii² 672	280/79	Honorific decree	Second copy, *Hesp.* x 1941, 338–9, has [ετδ]
790 +*Hesp.* xi 47	235/4	Honours for prytanes	

The last two examples can be dismissed as the products of carelessness: in the first case we have [ετ]βκτδ in one copy but [ετδ] in a second; and it seems to have been a matter of legislative etiquette, very rarely broken, that decrees in honour of a prytany were not recommended to the ecclesia by the boule,[2] so that the use of ετβκτδ in *IG* ii² 790 is probably due to a simple error. The remaining ten decrees all belong to the period

---

[1] See Table D for details of formulae. The decrees marked with an asterisk are based on someone's report, and the probouleuma *may* have been that the demos should hear what the man in question had to say and make up its mind accordingly.

[2] It was normal Hellenistic practice to publish a (non-probouleumatic) decree of the demos honouring the prytany ('first' decree) and a decree of the boule honouring the officials of the prytany ('second' decree)—cf. S. Dow, *Hesp.* Supp. i 1937, 3 with n. 2. Dow makes inferences as to the origins of decrees from the nominatives in 'citations' (op. cit. 22, 76): I would rather suppose that after the demos had voted to honour a prytany (under a probouleuma that it should hear the prytany's report) the boule also voted to honour the prytany, in a separate, unpublished decree. Cf. Pritchett's review of Dow, *AJP* lx 1939, 260.

The only known exceptions to normal practice are *P* 84. i (155/4), where the prytany is honoured in a decree of the boule; *SEG* xvi 100 (104/3), where the 'first' and 'second' decrees are both probouleumatic; and *Kerameikos*, iii. A 5 (*c.* 100), where the 'second' decree (the only one surviving) is probouleumatic. Etiquette did not prevent Euctimenus Εὐδήμου Εἰτεαῖος, who in 140/39 was both treasurer and secretary of his prytany, from proposing the 'first' and 'second' decrees in honour of that prytany: *Hesp.* xvii 9.

403–345: for this same period we have 13 decrees with ϵτδ and no motion-formula,[1] ten with δ/ψτδ and no enactment-formula, and only five with ϵτδ and δ/ψτδ. The evolution of the two main formulaic patterns took some time—we have no dated example of the probouleumatic formula before 378/7[2]—and these ten 'crossbred' decrees are products of the evolutionary process.

My own inclination is to rely on the motion-formula and class these decrees as non-probouleumatic.[3] The motion-formula, as a part of the basic text of the document, ought to be more reliable than the enactment-formula added by the secretary when preparing the text for publication; and in the development of Attic documentary language the new formula, not included in the published texts of the fifth century, ought to be more reliable than the form of enactment-formula which in the fifth century had been universal but after about 345 was to be used with a certain kind of decree only. These 'crossbreeds' include some decrees of great importance, but there are important decrees which according to all surviving indications ought to be non-probouleumatic, and in view of the possibility of amendment by reformulation we ought not to be surprised at this.[4]

Fifteen decrees combine ϵτδ with the probouleumatic formula:[5]

SEG xvi 52	339/8	?	*
SIG[3] 287	332/1	Honours Phanodemus for Oropus νομοθεσία	
IG ii[2] 772	270/69	Public doctors to make customary sacrifice	
661	269/8	Honours for epimeletae of mysteries	*

---

[1] I include here *IG* ii[2] 26 (394–387), whose formulae are ϵτδ; ἐπαινέσαι μέν; ἐψηφ[ίσθαι δέ —].   [2] Tod 124.   [3] Cf. Jones, 115–16.

[4] Mr. R. Meiggs has suggested to me that these 'crossbreeds' are probouleumatic decrees with δ/ψτδ inserted to emphasize the demos' approval of them: he could follow Miller (who believed that ϵτβκτδ and/or PF is a guarantee of a probouleumatic decree; only those with ϵτδ *and* δ/ψτδ are non-probouleumatic) in leaning heavily on *IG* ii[2] 109 (363/2), where δτδ seems uniquely to be dependent on the δοκεῖ τῆι βουλῆι of the probouleumatic formula. Against this I would cite Tod 144, one of the most substantial decrees with mixed formulae, which can hardly be probouleumatic as I define the term (cf. p. 68).

For carelessness in the application of formulae, cf.

IG ii[2] 32	385/4	ϵτ[β]; RP
839	221/0	[Δ]Ψ; E; ϵτβ; PF
847	215/14	BΨ; E; ϵτβκτδ; PF
1072	A.D. 209/10	B; δτβκτδ

A striking example of secretarial carelessness has now been published in *Hesp.* xxxviii 2 (220/19), where decree i combines BΨ with δτδ and decree ii combines E and ΔΨ with δτβ (in each case the motion-formula is correct). For other possible misapplications of ϵτβ, cf. pp. 82–5.

[5] See Table C for details of formulae. The decrees marked with an asterisk are again based on some one's report. On *Hesp.* xi 56 see further Additional Note C, esp. p. 234.

IG ii² 735	before mid C3	Honorific decree	*
798	250/49	Honours for [agonothetes?]	
Hesp. xi 56	247/6	Appeal for contributions to stratiotic fund	
Hesp. xxxvi 6	*c.* 170	Honorific decree	
Hesp. ii 16	161/0	Honours for cosmetes of ephebi	[ετδ] not certain
SEG xv 104. i, ii	127/6	Ephebic decrees	*
IG ii² 1011. i, ii	107/6	Ephebic decrees	*
1028. i, ii	100/99	Ephebic decrees	*

Here I have no hesitation in relying on the motion-formula.[1] The probouleumatic formula is our one unmistakable guide, and with these documents not concentrated in any one period it seems unnecessary to look beyond secretarial carelessness for an explanation.

The distinction between probouleumatic and non-probouleumatic decrees comes fairly well out of these tests. Sometimes we have to postulate carelessness, occasionally we have to resort to an explanation which it is to be feared may be tidier than the facts of the case; but it seems in general to be true that the difference between the two formulaic patterns corresponds to a difference between two types of enactment, that from the fourth century the Athenians chose to differentiate verbatim ratifications of a probouleuma from other enactments of the demos. The distinction appeared gradually during the first half of the fourth century, and is likely to have been a matter of secretarial tradition rather than specific regulation. The rules were somewhat slackly applied—which will surprise no one who is familiar with Athenian decrees—but the distinction was made.[2]

We can return at last to the question which gave rise to these investigations. Did the ecclesia play an active part in legislation, or was it content to adopt proposals made by the boule? I have listed in Table C those inscribed decrees which I believe to be probouleumatic, and in Table D those which I believe to be non-probouleumatic. The distribution of the two classes in different periods is remarkable, as can be seen from the table on p. 79.[3]

---

[1] Cf. Klaffenbach, *Griechische Epigraphik*², 74–5.   [2] Cf. Jones, 114.

[3] I include decrees earlier than 403/2 for completeness' sake only: the figures signify nothing as we cannot guess at the origins of most fifth-century decrees. 403 and 321 are obvious dividing-points; the next line could be drawn anywhere between about 285 and about 260 to yield the same result; 200 and 100 are of course purely arbitrary. So many decrees are only approximately dated, or are tied to magistrates whose date is insecure, that

Date	Probouleumatic		Non-probouleumatic			Totals	
	sub-stantial	all	sub-stantial	all except prytany-decrees	all	sub-stantial	all
(to 404/3	9	20	5	*	6	14	26)
403/2–322/1	11	107	15	*	101	26	208
321/0–263/2	2	79	3	85	93	5	172
262/1–201/0	1	65	0	14	28	1	93
200/199–101/0	1	91	0	13	46	1	137
from 100/99	0	16	0	3	4	0	20
Totals (from 403/2)	15	358	18		272	33	630
(Final Totals	24	378	23		278	47	656)
		+1 undated					+1

* No prytany-decrees with relevant formulae are known before 285/4.

In the fourth and early third centuries the total of all decrees and the substantial decrees (see below) alone are fairly evenly divided between probouleumatic and non-probouleumatic (the slightly greater emphasis on non-probouleumatic decrees between the Lamian and the Chremonidean War perhaps suggests that until Athens learned to live with her humiliation the demos tried to make frantic activity a substitute for effective action). At this time (and probably in the fifth century also, when a good many decrees stood in the name of prominent citizens) there must have been a reasonable nucleus of politically-minded Athenians, and the ecclesia took a fairly active interest in legislation, even though in proportion to the whole citizen body attendance was low except in times of crisis.[1] But once the Athenians became aware of their insignificance

it seems unwise to attempt further precision. A survey of *dated* decrees from the troubled period 321/0–263/2 yields the following results:

321/0–319/18   decrees of both kinds (especially non-probouleumatic)
318/17   no probouleumatic decrees; 5 non-probouleumatic
317/16–308/7   no probouleumatic decrees; 1 non-probouleumatic
307/6–302/1   many decrees of both kinds (especially non-probouleumatic)
301/0–263/2   decrees of both kinds (no probouleumatic before 291/0)

I have marked with an asterisk in Tables C and D those decrees which I am regarding as substantial for the purposes of these statistics. Alliances, tribute regulations, and the like clearly are matters of substance, while at the other extreme purely honorific decrees (though it may be of great significance that at a particular time the political climate is favourable to a particular man, and a bitter controversy may underly a motivation-clause, as in the rider to Tod 116) cost the state little and are easily drafted; but in many cases it is hard to give a verdict.   [1] Ar. *Ach.* 19–22; contrast D. XVIII. *Cor.* 169.

political life lost its attractions, and it appears that from early in the third century the ratification of honorific probouleumata took up more and more of the assembly's time. After 322/1 documents of real substance are very rare, and other indications of an active ecclesia are wanting: we have two pseudo-riders, but no more true riders to decrees, and only one instance of the assembly's commissioning a probouleuma.[1]

An active assembly did not make the boule merely a cog in the machine, or deprive the boule of initiative except in routine and uncontroversial matters.[2] Policy could not very easily be made by an assembly of some thousands, and we may assume that most citizens went to hear and to vote (and to draw their attendance-money) rather than to make speeches and offer proposals. The boule did discuss policy,[3] and the principal politicians did think it worth their while to attend its non-secret sessions.[4] Yet a council of a few hundred must still have been too large a body for the corporate discussion of policy, and even a prytany of fifty would be somewhat unwieldy. In the Roman Senate a subject was named and members were invited to offer *sententiae*, from which the presiding magistrate chose a motion to put to the vote; the same procedure was followed in Athens when an open probouleuma was submitted to the ecclesia,[5] and was presumably followed in the boule and prytany. The boule was entitled to make recommendations on any subject, and whether it did on important and perhaps controversial matters may well have depended on who were bouleutae at the time. Men with political ambitions did serve in the boule, but some selections of five hundred citizens may have included no one who was prepared to offer bold suggestions.

But many bold suggestions were made in the boule. If the RP formula is a reliable indicator the fifth-century decrees drafted in the boule include an alliance with Egesta,[6] the second Methone decree,[7] Thudippus' assessment-decree of 425,[8] and the decrees for Samos at the end of the Peloponnesian War;[9] in the fourth century the probouleumatic formula guarantees the bouleutic origin of a number of important decrees—alliances with Chalcis in 378/7,[10] with Corcyra in 375/4,[11] with Thracian kings[12] and with Neapolis[13] in 357/6. In 369/8 the boule asked

---

[1] *IG* ii² 845 (204/3).   [2] As Professor Jones believes (p. 118).
[3] e.g. D. VIII. *Chers.* 4.
[4] Non-members in the boule: D. VIII. *Chers.* 4, XIX. *F.L.* 17 and schol., A. III. *Ctes.* 125, Plat. *Menex.* 234 A–B. Cf. Ch. I, p. 40.
[5] Cf. D. XVIII. *Cor.* 170, 173; A. III. *Ctes.* 2, Pl. *An Seni*, 784 C–D; Lucian, *Jupp. Trag.* 18 and schol., *Deor. Conc.* 1; Ar. *Thesm.* 372–9.   [6] M&L 37.
[7] M&L 65. ii.   [8] M&L 69.   [9] M&L 94+Tod 97.
[10] Tod 124.   [11] Tod 126.   [12] Tod 157.   [13] Tod 159.

the συνέδριον of the Second Athenian League to report to the assembly its views on the possibility of an alliance with Dionysius I of Syracuse; but the report seems to have been unfavourable, since in the following year the author of the boule's decree, now no longer a member of the boule, drafted a decree by which Dionysius became an ally of Athens alone.[1] Other decrees for which responsibility can probably but less certainly be assigned to the boule include one concerning judicial relations with Siphnos[2] and one containing regulations for the Panathenaea.[3] Other important measures reached their published form in the assembly, such as the final alliance with Dionysius which I have mentioned above, and the regulations imposed on Clazomenae in 387/6[4] and on Eretria thirty years later.[5] They may result from the initiative of a man who does not belong to the boule, and has been allowed in the probouleuma to put his suggestion to the people; or they may have been produced in response to a purely open probouleuma. But sometimes they represent a probouleuma which has been revised in the assembly: in the Peloponnesian alliance of 362/1, for instance, the preamble cannot have been written until the matter came before the assembly, but the δόγμα of the allies and the probouleuma of the boule to which it alludes must surely have favoured the alliance.[6] A non-probouleumatic decree is not necessarily a sign that the boule has refused to commit itself. We have noticed occasions when the boule committed Athens to inaction, though in circumstances which must have made its decision generally welcome;[7] more controversially, it committed Athens to another bout of aggressive nationalism when Philip of Macedon was assassinated, by ordering sacrifices in thanksgiving.[8] It seems wise to conclude that the boule always could give a lead, and that in the fifth and fourth centuries it often but by no means always did so, but as Athens declined into the Hellenistic period there were fewer important decisions to be taken, and the political apathy of the city as a whole left such decisions as there were to the boule. This system, or lack of it, will not have made for coherent policy, but an annual change in bouleutic membership would in any case have prevented this. Policies were on the whole the policies of individual men, and their carrying out depended on the continuing popularity of these men and of what they stood for with the boule and demos.

---

[1] Tod 133, 136. [2] SEG xvii 19. [3] IG ii² 334.
[4] Tod 114. [5] Tod 154. [6] Tod 144; cf. pp. 68–9.
[7] pp. 57–8 with p. 58 n. 1 above.
[8] A. III. Ctes. 160, cf. 77, Pl. Dem. 22.

(iii) *Decrees of the Boule*

We shall be studying in the next two chapters the various kinds of decision which could be made by the boule, but there are some matters which, since they concern published decrees, can usefully be considered here.

A few Athenian decrees incorporate a provision for filling gaps, if it should later be found that there are some matters which the decree has left unsettled. In the fifth century there were at any rate some occasions when the demos reserved for itself the right to make any necessary additions and corrections: we find this in a decree of 415 for the dispatch of the Sicilian expedition, and in a rider to the decree of 409 honouring Thrasybulus.[1] But it seems likely that in the decree of 424/3 for Potamodorus and Eurytion the right to make supplementary decisions of this kind was delegated to the boule,[2] and in the fourth century this became standard practice.[3] In one of our fourth-century examples, Cephisophon's decree for a colony to the Adriatic, the proviso is added that the boule's supplementary decrees may not run counter to the original enactment:

ἐὰν δέ του προσδέει τόδε τὸ ψήφισμα τῶν περὶ τὸν ἀπόστολον, τὴν βουλὴν κυρίαν εἶναι ψηφίζεσθαι, μὴ λύουσαν μηθὲν τῶν ἐψηφισμένων τῶι δήμωι.[4]

Such a delegation of power to the boule may be regarded as a special case of the instructions to the prytanes and boule (*inter alios*) to see that the provisions of a decree are carried out.[5]

More surprisingly, we have a number of documents of the early fourth century which have been inscribed as decrees of the boule alone

---

[1] M&L 78, *c* 10–12 (where the sense is clear though M&L decline to restore); 85, 36–8. The same principle seems to be taken for granted in Thudippus' assessment-decree of 425 (M&L 69, 42–4).

[2] *SEG* x 84, 39–40. The same seems to be implied by the Neapolis decree of 407/6 as restored by Merritt and Andrewes (*SEG* xii 37, 56), but I would restore ηό τι ἄν δοκεῖ ἀγαθ[ὸν ηô δέονται] to produce an ἄλλο ἀγαθόν clause of my first type (Table L); M&L (no. 89) decline to restore, and print both suggestions in the *apparatus* on p. 275. The decree concerning the goddess Bendis (*c.* 430) contained a clause giving the boule some kind of authority or duty, possibly that of filling gaps in the original decree: for different reconstructions see *SEG* x 64 a, 36 (Roussel), 64 b, 27 (Ferguson); xvii 5, 23 (Bingen—who offers no restoration of this clause); xxi 52, 23 (Sokolowski).

[3] *SEG* xiv 47, B 3 sqq.; Tod 157, 34–6; *IG* ii² 204, 85–6; 435, 7–9; Tod 200, 264–9 (the clause added in [*IG* ii² 1629], 272 sqq. is presumably a supplementary decision made under this provision by the boule).

[4] Tod 200, 264–9. Cf. *SIG*³ 736, 180–94, the final clause of a law of Andania of 92 B.C.

[5] The commonest form of this is an order to protect honorands from injustice and to see that they enjoy the right of πρόσοδος to the boule and demos that has been conferred upon them: HMA 80, 2–9; *SEG* x 53, 17 sqq.; 105, 14–19; etc. For the coupling of the generals with the boule and prytanes in responsibilities of this kind cf. Ch. I, pp. 43–4; on the provisions for stopping gaps in decrees see further Additional Note C, pp. 231–5.

yet record decisions which would not normally be delegated by the ecclesia. Most of them are proxeny decrees,[1] and for these two ways of removing the anomaly have been suggested: it may be that the boule was simply ordering the publication or re-publication of an award already made by the ecclesia;[2] or these decrees may be probouleumata ratified by the ecclesia, but published with the wrong formulae by secretaries who took the text from the records of the boule.[3] Either of these explanations is possible. We know that under the regime of the Thirty various honorific stelae were demolished, and that after the democratic restoration such honours were confirmed and new stelae were erected.[4] One of the proxeny decrees with the formula ετβ specifically orders the replacement of an old stele at the expense of one of the beneficiaries,[5] and some of the others ought perhaps to be explained in this way.[6] We have seen already that the early fourth century was a time of uncertainty in the use of formulae, and it is not impossible that some of the documents published as decrees of the boule are in fact probouleumata ratified by the ecclesia: we shall notice shortly an alliance with Eretria, which can hardly be explained in any other way.[7] There is one proxeny decree in which it seems that both explanations are applicable.

[1] The proxeny inscriptions to be considered here are Tod 98, _IG_ ii² 49, 13, _Hesp._ vii 11, _IG_ ii² 32, 63, 77, 95; compare the citizenship award in _IG_ ii² 17. The questions which I discuss are treated by A. Lambrechts, _Texst en Uitzicht van de Atheense Proxeniedecreten_, chs. ii A 4 (French summary, pp. 141–2) and ii B 2 a (French summary, pp. 142–3): she seems far too eager to give precise dates to different formulaic practices.
[2] So Kirchner, in his notes on _IG_ ii² 13, 32, 63; cf. 17 and 77; also Lambrechts, ii A 4. Heydemann, _De Senatu Atheniensium_, 17–18, thought that the boule could give this permission only if no public expense was involved. [3] Francotte, _MB_ iv 1900, 55 sqq.
[4] Tod 98, _IG_ ii² 9; cf. the confirmation of the honours for Samos, M&L 94+Tod 97.
[5] Tod 98.
[6] The question is bedevilled by formulaic ambiguity. In the fifth and early fourth centuries a decree conferring a proxeny might use either the formula εἶναι αὐτὸν πρόξενον or ἀναγράψαι αὐτὸν πρόξενον (_IG_ i² index s.v. πρόξενος, p. 368. iii; _IG_ ii² iv. i index s.v. πρόξενος καὶ εὐεργέτης, p. 58. i–ii: Miss Lambrechts, ii B 2 a, violently redates decrees so as to make the second formula standard until 389/8 and the first standard from 388/7). Of the decrees listed in n. 1 above, _IG_ ii² 13, 32, 63, 77. i and 95 all have the ἀναγράψαι formula (ἀναγράψαι αὐτὸν εἶναι πρόξενον in 63), while 77. ii alone has the εἶναι formula. In 77 (where both decrees have the enactment-formula ετβ κατὰ τὸ τοῦ δήμου ψήφισμα) it is clear that decree i is ordering the publication of decree ii—(ἀναγράψαι αὐτὸν πρόξενον) . . . [κατὰ τὸ ψήφισ]μα ὃ ἐνίκησε περὶ αὐτοῦ πρό[τερον] (5–8)—and so we see that the ἀναγράψαι formula could be used not only for the award but alternatively for the publication of an award already made. (Compare _IG_ ii² 17, where decree ii, whose prescript cannot be recovered, makes a grant of citizenship and orders its publication, and decree i (ετβ) introduces with the words [ἀναγράψαι Σθόρυι] . . . τὰ ἐψηφι[σμένα περὶ Σθόρυος τῶι] δήμωι (8–11) a modification of the publication order.)
It must be admitted that towards the middle of the fourth century the boule did refer a mere publication order to the assembly: _IG_ ii² 172 (PF) deals with the renewal of a hereditary proxeny where the original stele has disappeared.
[7] Tod 103. The words [ἐλέσθαι δὲ πρ]έσβες αὐτίκα μάλ[α] τὴ[ν βουλήν] (17–18) tell us nothing about the origin of the decree (cf. p. 75).

In *IG* ii² 32 the enactment-formula is ετβ, but ratification by the ecclesia is proved by the subsequent appearance of a rider to the probouleuma (RP); and though the prescript dates the document to 385/4 there are provisions for the possibility that the honorand may be unjustly treated ἐν τῶμ πόλε[ων ὅσων Ἀ]θην[αῖοι κρατ]ὅσ[ι]ν, which is scarcely meaningful in the years following the Peace of Antalcidas. We cannot for every decree say which explanation is the right one,[1] but at any rate there is no need to suppose that the boule acquired the right to confer proxenies for a short time after the democratic restoration.

Three other documents need to be considered. I have already mentioned the Athenian alliance of 394/3 with Eretria:[2] its enactment-formula is ετβ, but very good evidence indeed would be needed to satisfy us that at this time the demos could delegate or surrender its right to conclude treaties.[3] In the same year the Athenians honoured Dionysius of Syracuse, in another decree whose enactment-formula is ετβ:[4] nothing more concrete than ἐπαινέσαι has survived, and there is no reason why the boule should not have praised Dionysius and his family, but a head of state would normally be praised by the demos or not at all, and lesser honours would not be published if those of the demos were not.[5] It seems safest to assume that the surviving fragment is either a ratified probouleuma or an independent decree of the boule below which a decree of the demos was also inscribed. Finally, we must look at the appointment of heralds. About 398–390 Eucles was made herald of the boule and demos, and some thirty years afterwards his son Philocles was appointed to the post. The two relevant decrees have been inscribed on the same stele: the second embodies the probouleumatic formula, but in the first [ἔδοξεν τει βουλει] used to be restored to fit the στοιχηδόν arrangement;[6] Dr. D. M.

---

[1] I have placed in my Table C only those decrees where we have some reason to presume ratification by the demos, and have listed the others among decrees of the boule in Table G.

[2] Tod 103.

[3] See for example S. Accame, *La Lega ateniese*, 234–5. Special delegations of power to the boule are discussed by P. Cloché, *REG* xxxiv 1921, 254–8, and G. E. M. de Ste Croix, *CQ*² xiii 1963, 114–15 with 115 n. 2. Though it may not always have been clear how extensive the power conferred was (cf. Ch. IV, pp. 171 with n. 1, 180 with n. 4, and 186–8) it seems that duties specially delegated were of the same order as the boule's regular duties, subsidiary to the major decisions of the ecclesia, and there is no evidence that the demos was willing to surrender its right to take these major decisions.

[4] Tod 108. Tod accepts this as a decree of the boule alone (vol. ii, p. 25).

[5] For the question of who might honour whom see Francotte, *MB* iii 1899, 246–81, iv 1900, 55–75, 105–13; and see further on the honours conferred by the Athenians Heydemann, *De Senatu Atheniensium*, 11–21, and Kahrstedt, *S.S.A.*, 332–3. Most of the honorific decrees inscribed in the name of the boule honour the officials of a prytany when the demos has honoured the prytany as a whole; but it is likely that when the demos had honoured a prytany the boule would add its own honours but not publish the decree (cf. p. 76 n. 2 above).

[6] *IG* ii² 145.

Lewis, noticing that this formula contained one letter too many, merely changed the spelling to [ἔδοξεν τῆι βολῆι].[1] It is not, I think, impossible that an appointment of this kind should have been delegated to the boule, but it would be surprising if the boule had been able to make the original appointment on its own authority but had been obliged to gain the demos' approval for the transfer of the office to Eucles' son, and I feel sure that the correct restoration is [ἔδοξεν τῶι δήμωι].[2]

The prescripts of decrees do not, then, force upon us the conclusion that for a short time at the beginning of the fourth century the boule enjoyed legislative powers normally reserved for the ecclesia. It must be admitted that Cloché believed the boule's judicial powers were temporarily enhanced at this time,[3] and some have seen in the institution of the proedri and the reform of the secretarial system in the first third of the century an attack on the boule which could be more easily explained if the boule had for a time been enjoying greater powers than in the fifth century.[4] I remain unconvinced. The cumulative effect of these arguments does not seem to me to outweigh the strong presumption that after two unhappy experiments with oligarchy the demos would have insisted on the full restoration of its sovereignty,[5] or that if this full restoration were delayed we should have clearer traces of its eventual achievement.

In the later history of Athens, however, when formulae had become more stereotyped, inscriptions provide almost all the information we have on the government of the city, and decrees of the boule on matters normally decided by the demos may if they show a consistent pattern be used as pointers to a more oligarchic regime. The publication in 155/4 of a decree in honour of a prytany as a decree of the boule is probably due to clerical carelessness rather than to a departure from normal procedure, as this is an isolated exception.[6] The two decrees concerned with the

[1] BSA xlix 1954, 36–7.

[2] Elections in general, like other acts of the demos, were held under a probouleuma (A.P. 44. iv): I imagine that except when there was an obvious candidate, such as the retiring herald's son, the probouleuma will have been open, simply providing that a man be elected to a specified office.

[3] See appendix to Ch. IV, p. 184.

[4] See my remarks in Ch. V, pp. 218–19, with notes referring to my discussions of related problems.

[5] There are however signs that disagreement persisted as to who should count as members of the demos (in addition to the vexed question of how generously non-citizens who had helped the democrats could be rewarded, notice Phormisius' proposal to restrict citizenship to landowners: D.H. 525–33. Lys. 32–3). Archinus' irregular use of the boule to condemn a man to death (A.P. 40. ii, cf. appendix to Ch. IV, p. 180) probably sprang from a desire for rapid action rather than constitutional dogmatism; the circumstances in which Thrasybulus brought forward his ἀπροβούλευτον ψήφισμα are not clear (cf. p. 62).

[6] P 84. i. It is possible that the ecclesia ratified the honours voted for the priest of Asclepius in 94/3 (SEG xviii 29: the ecclesia honoured the ephebi at this time).

shrine of the Hero Doctor (or Hero the doctor?) present an interesting contrast. Both arose from a πρόσοδος of the priest to the boule: in 221/0 he asked for a new οἰνοχόη to be made from the old dedications in the shrine, and his request was granted in a probouleumatic decree;[1] towards the end of the second century the shrine's plate was again in poor condition, and this time a decree of the boule was enough to authorize the work for which the priest asked.[2] The second inscription cannot be precisely dated: it could conveniently be located in the mildly oligarchic regime which Ferguson believed to have been set up in 103/2,[3] but whatever change was made in Athens at that time the demos clearly did not lose the power to vote decrees.[4] Perhaps the boule had acquired or usurped the right to grant this permission, but we may here be dealing with another misapplied formula. We are on firmer ground in dealing with the regime established by Sulla. It is generally believed that the oligarchy which he established lasted from 83 to 48, and for this period there are no dated decrees of the demos, while the boule was responsible for some matters which at other times were referred to the assembly: an ephebic inscription emanating from the boule alone, *IG* ii[2] 1039, seems to belong to the early years of this period,[5] and in 52/1 the boule gave permission to the priest of Asclepius to rebuild the shrine at his own expense.[6] Democratic government was restored by Caesar;[7] another ephebic document marks a return to oligarchy in 39/8;[8] and decrees of the demos reappear under the Roman Empire.[9] Another tendency in late decrees we noticed at the end of chapter I: though ordinary members of the boule and ecclesia may never have lost the right to sponsor proposals, under the Roman Empire decrees were apt to stand in the name of such senior officials as the στρατηγὸς ἐπὶ τὰ ὅπλα.[10] But published decrees of all kinds are rare after Sulla's settlement, and they became

---

[1] *IG* ii[2] 839.

[2] *IG* ii[2] 840. S. Dow, *Hesp.* Supp. i 1937, 100 with n. 2, suggests a date *c.* 124/3, but his argument is not such as to rule out a date some twenty years later.

[3] W. S. Ferguson, *Klio* iv 1904; *Hellenistic Athens*, 427 sqq. with 427–8 n. 4.

[4] See Tables C and D, where decrees of the demos continue until 94/3.

[5] On the general structure of decrees honouring ephebi cf. O. W. Reinmuth, *Hesp.* xxiv 1955, 226–8.   [6] *IG* ii[2] 1046.

[7] In *IG* ii[2] 1042 (*c.* 41/0) the 'acceptance decree' is of the boule alone, but the two decrees which follow it are probouleumatic decrees of the demos.

[8] *IG* ii[2] 1043.

[9] e.g. *IG* iv[2] 84 (A.D. 38/9?). On changes in the Athenian constitution from 91 until the Sullan settlement see Ferguson, *Hellenistic Athens*, 440 sqq., 454 sqq. On the restoration of democracy under Caesar and return to oligarchy under Antony see Kirchner's notes on these inscriptions in *IG* ii[2], following Kolbe, *Die attischen Archonten*: their view has been generally accepted, though Ferguson dated the democratic interlude *c.* 70–54/3 (*Klio* ix 1909, 323–30, 340).

[10] Cf. Ch. I, pp. 46–8.

rarer still under the Roman Empire as the affairs of the city became steadily less important.[1]

In times of democratic government the decrees of the boule remained subsidiary to those of the ecclesia. Its honours were conferred on lesser functionaries or were added to those voted by the ecclesia; in more serious matters policy and many details were decided by the ecclesia, though often on the recommendation of the boule, but the boule had a large part to play in ensuring that these decisions were carried out, as we shall see in the next two chapters.

[1] On decree-making under the Empire cf. P. Graindor, *Athènes sous Auguste*, 100–5, *Athènes de Tibère à Trajan*, 62–7, *Athènes sous Hadrien*, 86–90; and now D. J. Geagan's study of the post-Sullan constitution, *Hesp.* Supp. xii 1967, esp. 32–6, 64–7, 71–81, 83–90. Geagan does not consider the possibility that minute-headings (βουλῆς ψηφίσματα etc.) may have been misapplied (see p. 77 n. 4, above), and I cannot share his faith in the reliability of genitives after ἀγαθῆι τύχηι as a guide to the origins of a decree: whether it is on the demos of Athens or the boule and demos that good fortune is invoked in a decree surely tells us nothing about the procedure by which that decree was enacted. I agree with Geagan, 66–7, against Delz, *Lukians Kenntnis der athenischen Antiquitäten*, 138–9, that the formula δτβκτδ (cf. p. 65 and n. 4, above) should not be taken to imply that there were now joint sessions of the boule and ecclesia. Geagan does not make his own view of the extent to which the different decree-making bodies were independent of each other entirely clear: on pp. 79–80 he seems to accept Keil's view (*Beiträge zur Geschichte des Areopags*, 29) that the boule 'had the ability to formulate decrees in the name of the whole community'; on p. 85 he writes that 'the *demos*, like the *boule*, was able to pass valid decrees by itself, although probably subject to the approval of the other corporations' (i.e. Areopagus and boule).

Decrees of the boule and ecclesia continue into the reign of Hadrian, with *IG* ii² 1072 (116/17) and probably 1073 and 1075; later still we have a non-probouleumatic decree in *IG* ii² 1078/9 (*c.* 220), and a decree which is thought to be probouleumatic but does not exhibit any of the older formulae in *Hesp.* Supp. vi 31/2 with *SEG* xxi 506/5. ii (229/30 or 230/1). Beside these, however, we find resolutions of the Areopagus (ὑπομνηματισμοί to *c.* 200, e.g. *IG* iv² 83 [38/9?]; ἐπερωτήματα from *c.* 150 or δόγματα from *c.* 200, e.g. *Hesp.* Supp. vi 31 etc., iii [229/30 or 230/1]—see Geagan, 42–8), and at any rate in the first of the cases cited the resolution of the Areopagus came last and determined the wording of the dedication (*IG* iv² 82–4: Geagan, 33–5, after Keil). Meritt has suggested (*Hesp.* xxxii 1963, 29) that the third-century document contained as its first item a decree of the Sacred Gerousia, established under Marcus Aurelius.

Dedications (listed by Geagan in his Appendix I, pp. 140–59) show that honours could be awarded or permitted by the Areopagus, boule, and ecclesia together, or by one or two of these bodies alone: Geagan notes (pp. 63, 68, 82–3) that honours of the boule, the demos, or the two together are found particularly in the time of Augustus; there is a further group of honours by the demos in the time of Claudius and of honours by the boule in the time of Hadrian.

III · ADMINISTRATION

(i) Finance

FINANCE was a matter of great concern to the Athenians. Objects of public expenditure were by modern standards few, but so too were sources of public income, and if the state lacked the money to pay for its immediate needs those needs could not be met. Demosthenes threatened that a temporary shortage of money, which might occur under Timocrates' new debt law,[1] would bring the boule, ecclesia, and lawcourts to a standstill:

τὰς δ' ὀκτὼ (sc. πρυτανείας) τί ποιήσομεν; εἶπε, Τιμόκρατες· οὐ σύνιμεν καὶ βουλευσόμεθ' ἐάν τι δέῃ; εἶτ' ἔτι δημοκρατησόμεθα; οὐ δικάσει τὰ δικαστήρια τά τ' ἴδια καὶ τὰ δημόσια; καὶ τίς ὑπάρξει τοῖς ἀδικουμένοις ἀσφάλεια; οὐκ εἴσεισιν ἡ βουλὴ καὶ διοικήσει τὰ ἐκ τῶν νόμων; καὶ τί λοιπὸν ἔσθ' ἡμῖν ἀλλ' ἢ καταλελύσθαι;[2]

This was in 353 B.C.: five years later we hear of a crisis in which lack of money to pay the jurors did prevent the courts from meeting.[3] Athenian financial business had to be transacted with very great care, and although all major decisions were taken by the demos and often governed by special regulations[4] a good deal of work was delegated to the boule. περὶ πόρου χρημάτων is second only to περὶ τοῦ πολέμου in the Old Oligarch's list of matters which were the concern of the boule,[5] and Lysias wrote of the boule's being tempted to miscarriages of justice when it was short of money for the needs of the state: ἡ βουλὴ ἡ ⟨ἀεὶ⟩ βουλεύουσα, ὅταν μὲν ἔχῃ ἱκανὰ χρήματα εἰς διοίκησιν, οὐδὲν ἐξαμαρτάνει, ὅταν δὲ εἰς ἀπορίαν καταστῇ, ἀναγκάζεται εἰσαγγελίας δέχεσθαι καὶ δημεύειν τὰ τῶν πολιτῶν καὶ τῶν ῥητόρων τοῖς ⟨τὰ⟩ πονηρότατα λέγουσι πείθεσθαι.[6] Aristophanes represents Cleon as bringing the city an ample supply of money when he was a bouleutes:

καὶ πῶς ἂν ἐμοῦ μᾶλλόν σε φιλῶν ὦ Δῆμε γένοιτο πολίτης;
ὃς πρῶτα μὲν ἡνίκ' ἐβούλευόν σοι χρήματα πλεῖστ' ἀπέδειξα
ἐν τῷ κοινῷ, τοὺς μὲν στρεβλῶν τοὺς δ' ἄγχων τοὺς δὲ μεταιτῶν,
οὐ φροντίζων τῶν ἰδιωτῶν οὐδενός, εἰ σοὶ χαριοίμην.[7]

---

[1] Cf. Ch. IV, pp. 148–51. [2] D. XXIV. *Tim.* 99. [3] D. XXXIX. *Boe. Nom.* 17.
[4] e.g. M&L 58 B, 15–19. [5] O.O. iii. 2. [6] Lys. XXX. *Nic.* 22.
[7] Ar. *Eq.* 773–6.

It seems fair to conclude from these passages that the boule was regarded as generally responsible for the financial well-being of Athens.

The boule's earliest appearance in financial matters concerns the tribute from the Delian League, which accounted for much of the money flowing into Athens in the second half of the fifth century. Clinias' decree, probably to be dated to 447 B.C.,[1] begins:

$$[- \tau \grave{\epsilon}] \mu \ \beta-$$
$$o\lambda \grave{\epsilon} \nu \ \kappa a \grave{\iota} \ \tau \grave{o}s \ \mathring{a} \rho \chi [o \nu \tau a s \ \grave{\epsilon} \nu] \ \tau \hat{\epsilon} \sigma-$$
$$\iota \ \pi \acute{o} \lambda \epsilon \sigma \iota \ \kappa a \grave{\iota} \ \tau \grave{o}s \ [\grave{\epsilon} \pi \iota \sigma \kappa \acute{o}] \pi o s \ \grave{\epsilon}-$$
$$\pi \iota \mu \acute{\epsilon} \lambda \epsilon \sigma \theta a \iota \ h\acute{o}\pi [o s \ \mathring{a} \nu \ \chi \sigma] \upsilon \lambda \lambda \acute{\epsilon}-$$
$$\gamma \epsilon \tau a \iota \ ho \ \phi \acute{o} \rho o s \ \kappa [a \tau \grave{a} \ \tau \grave{o} \ \acute{\epsilon}] \tau o s \ h-$$
$$\acute{\epsilon} \kappa a \sigma \tau o \nu \ \kappa a \grave{\iota} \ \mathring{a} \pi \acute{a} [\gamma \epsilon \tau a \iota] \ \mathring{A} \theta \acute{\epsilon} \nu a-$$
$$\zeta \epsilon.[2]$$

The boule was thus the principal authority in Athens concerned with the collection of tribute.[3] Clinias ordered that the allied cities were to send to Athens with their tribute a sealed tablet stating the sum which they were sending, and the tribute was to be brought to the boule and the tablet read there.[4] If any one obstructed the payment of tribute or the sending of a cow and panoply to the Panathenaea the boule was to act as a court of first instance (since it was not competent to inflict a penalty appropriate to so serious an offence), and through the prytanes to recommend a suitable penalty to a δικαστήριον.[5] The boule is mentioned several times in the less certain passages at the end of the inscription. In Cleonymus' decree of 426/5 the boule is less prominent,[6] but if the ecclesia is to be given an annual report on which states have paid their tribute and which have defaulted,[7] it is likely enough that individual payments continue to be made in the presence of the boule, as under the earlier decree of Clinias. That the boule was still involved is confirmed by a passage in the second decree, entrusting the boule with the appointment of heralds to convey to the allied cities the order to appoint ἐκλογεῖς who will be responsible for their city's tribute.[8]

---

[1] This is not the place to discuss Professor H. B. Mattingly's attempt to down-date various documents assigned to the mid fifth century, in a series of articles published since 1961 (a recent summary in *Ancient Society and Institutions*, 193–223; on M&L 46 see *Hist.* x 1961, 150–69). Though his warning that we should not be too confident in assigning dates on a basis of letter-forms is not to be ignored, I do not think he has succeeded in showing that 'the forms of sigma and rho have put many decrees in contexts where they do not really make full sense' (*JHS* lxxxi 1961, 132).   [2] M&L 46 (*ATL* D 7), 5–11.

[3] Cf. O.O. iii. 2, giving ⟨περὶ τῶν ἐν⟩ τοῖς συμμάχοις as one of the topics discussed by the boule and φόρον δέξασθαι as one of the boule's responsibilities.

[4] M&L 46, 11–18.   [5] Ibid. 31–43: cf. Ch. IV, pp. 151–2, 189–90.

[6] M&L 68. On the date see Ch. II, p. 71 n. 2.

[7] M&L 68, 11–16.   [8] Ibid. 52–7.

Thudippus' assessment-decree of the following year again reveals the importance of the boule in the finances of the Delian League :[1]

The boule is to appoint eight heralds to summon representatives from the cities,[2] and ten τάκται to list and assess the cities liable to tribute.[3] Appeals are to be addressed to a board of εἰσαγωγεῖς and the polemarch,[4] who will bring them before a court of 1,000 jurors established by the thesmothetae[5] to make new assessments [χσ]ὺν τêι [βο]λêι . . . [καθάπερ ἐπὶ τês τελευτ]αίας ἀρχês, and the τάκται must abide by the verdict in these cases. The boule is to meet daily to check and ratify the assessments thus arrived at, and the decree and assessment are to be published on the Acropolis and in the bouleuterium.[6]

The heralds work under the orders of the τάκται (for their route) and the ecclesia (for what they are to say).[7]

hότ[αν χσυντάχσει hε βολè τ]èν τάχσι[ν τô] φό[ρ]ο the generals are to see that it is paid : each year they shall make an estimate of their expenses, and apply directly to the boule (unless the demos votes that they should first apply to a court) if they need an extra levy.[8]

The principle, that no assessment should be reduced unless a city was genuinely unable to pay, and the procedure to be followed in making the assessment, were laid down by the demos, but it was left to the boule to see that the assessment was made as the demos had laid down. Assessment by the boule and a special court is mentioned also in special rubrics in the quota lists dated to 430/29 and 429/8.[9] The exact significance of these and other rubrics has been much disputed, but it is probable that something like Thudippus' procedure already existed, with figures proposed in the first instance by the τάκται and disputes adjudicated by the special court and the boule. In addition to the assessments by court and boule we have a block of assessments made by the τάκται of a previous year

---

[1] M&L 69 (ATL A 9; cf. translation and commentary in ATL, iii. 70–8). The rider-formula in l. 51 shows that this decree was drafted in the boule.   [2] M&L 69, 4–7.

[3] Ibid. (text of ATL, ii) 8–12 (M&L leave unrestored gaps in ll. 8, 9). The number is restored from [And.] IV. Alc. 11.

[4] For the elimination of the archon from the ATL text, see ATL, iv, p. ix n. 10.

[5] In line 16 ATL restore [νομο]θέτα[ι] after Meritt and West, The Athenian Assessment, 44, cf. 59. This was challenged by Kahrstedt (GGA cxcvii 1935, 51–2, U.M.A., 284 n. 2, Klio xxxi 1938, 9, cf. Wade-Gery, CR xlix 1935, 186, Nesselhauf, Gnomon xii 1936, 297; Meritt defends the restoration in AJP lvi 1935, 323, Epigraphica Attica, 132–6 with 150 nn. 26–7) on the grounds that nomothetae are not attested for the fifth-century democracy. In view of the task to be performed by these officials I feel certain that [θεσμο]θέτα[ι] must be the correct restoration, even though it requires the crowding of five letters into four spaces (so Wade-Gery, op. cit.).M&L decline to restore, but favour [θεσμο]θέτα[ι] in their apparatus (p. 192).

[6] M&L 69, 12–26 (M&L leave another gap in l. 14).

[7] Ibid. 40–4: in the ATL, ii, text of 38–40 the heralds are under the boule's jurisdiction; M&L revert to the text of ATL, i, in which this jurisdiction is over the prytanes, if they fail to expedite the passage of the decree (cf. Meritt and West, The Athenian Assessment, 61).

[8] Ibid. 44–50.

[9] ATL, list 25, iii. 60–1, list 26, ii. 43–4. For a recent discussion of the rubrics, see F. A. Lepper, JHS lxxxii 1962.

(probably 434/3), apparently for states paying on a voluntary basis and not as regular members of the League.[1] It is to be noticed that both in the rubrics and in Thudippus' decree the boule is specifically mentioned with the special court in connection with the problematic or disputed cases, a fact to which the authors of *ATL* have not paid sufficient attention in their account of the procedure followed.[2] Possibly in each disputed case the boule was required to confirm the court's decision, but at any rate the boule must at some stage have been involved in the dispute as well as being responsible for ratifying the final assessment which the τάκται produced after all disputes had been settled.

The work supervised by the boule was a more or less straightforward assessment of the tribute which the allied cities might be expected to pay, with some special consideration shown to the 'volunteer' states, but the decision that a state was to be given special privileges and concessions had to be made by the demos. The first decree for Methone, carried in 430/29, records an invitation to the demos to decide whether a special assessment should be made at once or Methone should be made to pay simply the ἀπαρχή on her current assessment of tribute: the latter alternative was in fact chosen.[3] Two years later another cautious proposal may have resulted in the decision that Aphytis too should pay only the ἀπαρχή on her tribute.[4] The pattern that emerges is that the demos laid down policy and authorized special departures from it, but the boule was in general responsible for carrying out this policy and for making the lesser, 'ministerial' decisions necessary for this purpose.

In the fifth century any surplus money was likely to find its way into the sacred treasuries, especially that of Athena, and the boule's concern with these was therefore a matter of more than purely religious importance. The *Athenaion Politeia* tells us that the treasurers of Athena παραλαμβάνουσι δὲ τό τε ἄγαλμα τῆς Ἀθηνᾶς καὶ τὰς Νίκας καὶ τὸν ἄλλον κόσμον καὶ τὰ χρήματα ἐναντίον τῆς βουλῆς,[5] and this is no doubt true of the latter half of the fifth century as well as of the fourth, since in creating the unified board of treasurers of the Other Gods in 434/3 Callias enacted

παρὰ δὲ τὸν νῦν ταμιὸν καὶ τὸν ἐπιστατὸν καὶ τὸν hιεροποιὸν τὸν ἐν τοῖς hιεροῖς, hοι νῦν διαχειρίζο[σι]-
ν, ἀπαριθμεσάσθον καὶ ἀποστεσάσθον τὰ χρέματα ἐναντίον τες βολ[ε̂]-
ς ἐμ πόλει, καὶ παραδεχσάσθον hοι ταμίαι hοι λαχόντες παρὰ τὸν νῦ[ν]
ἀρχόντον.[6]

---

[1] Cf. Lepper, op. cit. 32–4.   [2] *ATL*, iii. 77.
[3] M&L 65 (*ATL* D 3), 5–9, 29–32.   [4] *ATL* D 21, 17–18 (largely restored).
[5] *A.P.* 47. i, cf. Poll. viii. 97. For these treasurers' control of all sacred treasures at this time, see W. S. Ferguson, *Treasurers of Athena*, 118.   [6] M&L 58 A, 18–22.

As well as simplifying the administration of the sacred treasures, Callias provided for the payment of money due to the Other Gods, now that the 3,000 talents due to Athena had been paid:[1] the thirty logistae[2] were to be convened at the discretion of the boule to work out accurately how much was due, and the prytanes with the boule were to pay the debts and cancel the record.[3]

An inscription of 353/2 again attests the boule's interest in the treasurers of Athena.[4] An inventory was to be made of the treasures in the Chalcothece, in the presence of all those who had served as treasurers of Athena since 362/1, and of various high officials of state (and perhaps the whole boule):[5] the prytanes were to name the day, and the actual list was to be written down by a δημόσιος, copied by the public secretaries, and published in front of the Chalcothece.[6] The inscription continues:

> ἐπειδὰν δὲ ταῦτα παρασκ[ευα]-
> σθε͂ι, τοὺς πρυτάνε[ι]s προγράψαι περὶ τούτων [ἐ]ν [βουλε]-
> [υ]τηρίωι, ὅτ[α]ν οἷόν τε ἦι, ἀκούσασαν [δὲ τὴν] βου[λὴ]ν [ἀ]ντα-
> [ν]αγιγνωσκομένων τ[ῶν ? ἀναγεγραμμένων ἐν τῆι] χαλκο[θ]-
> [ήκ]ει πρὸς τὰ ἀναγεγρ[αμμένα ἐν ταῖς στήλαις ἐ]άν τ[ινο]-
> [s] δέηι προβουλεύσασ[αν ἐξενεγκεῖν εἰς τὸν δ]ῆμον, ὅ[πως]
> [ἂ]ν ἀκούσας ὁ δῆμος βου[λεύσηται πῶς πληρ]ωθήσετ[αι τὰ]
> [ἐ]λλείποντα, ὅ[π]ω[s] ἂ[ν] ἔχ[ηι κάλλιστα καὶ ε]ὐσεβέστ[ατα τ]-
> [ὰ π]ρὸς τὴν θεόν.[7]

---

[1] M&L 58 A, 2–7. The background to these decrees is not directly relevant to the present study, but I believe that both the 3,000 talents paid to Athena and the smaller sum paid to the Other Gods represent the repayment, with interest, of sums borrowed at the time of the Samian War. The authors of *ATL* regard the 3,000 talents as the total of a planned series of payments made for building purposes from the tribute (*ATL*, iii. 118–32, 326–41, B. D. Meritt, *Hesp.* xxiii 1954, 185–231, H. T. Wade-Gery and B. D. Meritt, *Hesp.* xxvi 1957); Gomme believed that until 434/3 there was a substantial surplus in the state treasury, which Callias transferred to Athena for safer keeping (*Hist.* ii 1953–4, iii 1954–5, *Hist. Comm. Thuc.*, ii. 26–32). Professor Mattingly has attempted to revive the old date of 422/1 for these decrees (*PACA* vii 1964, *BSA* lxii 1967, 14–17, *BCH* xcii 1968).
[2] On the logistae, see p. 111 below.   [3] M&L 58 A, 7–13.
[4] *IG* ii[2] 120; for the date see E. Schweigert, *Hesp.* vii 1938, 281–9, publishing as (ACR) 16 a new fragment of *IG* ii[2] 1438, which mentions the inventory made in accordance with this decree (*B*, 13–14; Wilhelm's restoration of these lines, *SEG* xix 129).
[5] Too little survives of this part of the inscription to allow a continuous text to be reconstructed. The suggestion that the whole boule attended the ἐξετασμός was made by W. Bannier, *PW* xlii 1922, 838–9, cf. J. Tréheux, 'Recherches sur la topographie et l'histoire de l'Acropole d'Athènes', 26 with n. 1, 42 n. 1; rightly, I think, Tréheux regards *IG* ii[2] 120 as a decree of the boule (its publication was paid for from the boule's expense-account: ll. 20–2), and in ll. 32–3 they restore the heading τάδε ἐ[ξήτασεν ἡ βο]υλὴ ὄντα ἐν τῆ[ι χαλ]κοθήκει (Bannier, 839, cf. *SEG* i 16; Tréheux, 36, 43–7, 55). I am indebted to Dr. D. M. Lewis for lending me a copy of Tréheux's unpublished thesis.   [6] *IG* ii[2] 120, 7–24.
[7] Ibid. 24–32. Tréheux, op. cit. 39 (cf. 16–17, 54–5) offers as his text of l. 27:

> [ν]αγιγνωσκομένων τ[ῶμ περ]ιό͞ν[των ἀπὸ τῶν ἐν τῆ⟨ι⟩] χαλκο[θ]-
> or . . . ἐκ τῶν ἐν τῆι] . . .

and comments: 'L'intention du Conseil est claire. Il veut, pour aviser aux moyens de le

Here we have a case, which must be one of many, where the boule was expected to initiate any necessary legislation in a matter of which its administrative duties gave it special knowledge.[1] During the Four Years' War at the end of the fourth century we see a further development. At this time the city made deposits in and withdrawals from the treasury of Athena, though the fifth-century formality of treating withdrawals as borrowings, on which interest had to be computed, was not repeated. In the eleventh prytany of 306/5 forty talents were allocated to Polyclitus and others under a decree of the boule, and in the following prytany a part of this was repaid under the terms of the same decree;[2] a transfer to the stratiotic fund in the same year was authorized by a decree of the demos,[3] and another decree of the demos in 305/4 covered the depositing of money by individual Areopagites and the ταμίας τῶν στρατιωτικῶν.[4] Ferguson assumed that when the treasurers of Athena were used as bankers in the fourth century 'payments from such funds were made on vote of the Council or the *demos* and certified by the Chairman of the prytany for the time being':[5] unfortunately it is not at all clear when orders could be issued by the boule and when they remained the prerogative of the ecclesia. These payments belong to a period traditionally regarded as 'democratic', but Ferguson pointed out that this was 'much less radical and consistent' than the democracy of before 322.[6] It is most unlikely that the boule would have been allowed to release money from the treasury of Athena in the Demosthenic era.

The boule was involved also in the finances of the Eleusinian cult: a rider to a decree of the second half of the fifth century calls for the appointment of five epistatae to take charge of the χρέματα of the Two Goddesses;

[τὸς δὲ] h̄ειρεμένο-
[s] προσιόντας πρὸς τὲν βολέν, ἐάν τι ὀφελ-
ό[μ]ενον ἐ̂[ι] τοῖν θεοῖν, φρά[ζ]εν καὶ ἀ[ν]απρά-
[τ]τεν. . . .

ἀναλίσκεν δὲ ὅ τι ἂν [μά]-
λιστα δέει μετὰ τôν h̄ιερέον καὶ τês β[ολ]-
ês βουλευόμενος τὸ λοιπόν.[7]

combler, apprécier le déficit de la collection (ll. 30–1, τὰ ἐλλείποντα) entre 362/1 et la date de l'ἐξετασμός. Il comparera donc la consistance du lot dans les dix années écoulées, telle que la décrivent les παραδόσεις, avec ce qu'il en *reste* effectivement au début de 353/2.'

[1] Tréheux, op. cit. 60–149, combines *IG* ii² 1438 with 1440 and smaller fragments to make a single document of 349/8 (date, p. 125): on this occasion a more extensive ἐξετασμός was held, ordered again by the boule (pp. 101–2), and supervised over several days by the prytanes (pp. 106–11).   [2] *IG* ii² 1492, 103–18.   [3] Ibid. 118–24.   [4] Ibid. 124–31.

[5] Ferguson, *Treasurers of Athena*, 134; for 'certification' (epistates named) see ll. 95, 110 of the inscription.   [6] Ferguson, *Hellenistic Athens*, 99.

[7] HMA 41, 14–17, 28–30. The decree is dated after 432, Mattingly, *Hist.* x 1961, 171–3; c. 448, Meritt and Wade-Gery, *JHS* lxxxiii 1963, 111–14.

Assistance in the recovery of sums due depends on the general rule that all public debts whether sacred or secular were to be discharged in the presence of the boule;[1] consultation of the boule before the treasurers could spend money from their own funds is at first sight a little startling, but it should surprise us no more than the power of initiative granted to the boule in connection with the Chalcothece inventory: the sacred treasuries were very much a matter of public concern. The actual offering of first-fruits at Eleusis also lay within the scope of the boule. In a decree perhaps to be dated to 416/15[2] the boule was commissioned to send heralds to the allied cities to warn them that contributions were required of them, τὸ μὲν νῦν ἔναι hος τάχιστ, ατὸ δὲ [λ]οιπὸν hόταν δοκεῖ αὐτεῖ,[3] and to the other Greek cities hόποι ἂν δοκεῖ αὐτεῖ δυνατὸν ἔναι, inviting them to contribute too.[4] The offerings were to be given to the Eleusinian hieropoei, and when the prescribed sacrifices had been made the remainder was to be sold and dedications made with the proceeds by the hieropoei in conjunction with the boule,[5] while a record of the offerings was to be kept both at Eleusis and in the bouleuterium.[6] In or after 403/2 the Eleusinian cult was reorganized by a law of Chaere-

[1] D. XXIV. *Tim.* 96; see Ch. IV, pp. 148–51, for the part played by the boule in the collection of public debts.

[2] M&L 73. The decree has been variously dated between 445 and 415, though most scholars place it in the last decade of this period. In particular, there has been disagreement as to whether it should precede or follow *IG* i² 311, which records the handing over by the hieropoei to the epistatae of the proceeds from the sale of corn offered at Eleusis in the quadrennium 422/1–419/18: the arguments on both sides are summarized by Ziehen in Prott and Ziehen, *Leges Graecorum Sacrae*, II. i, pp. 21–2, who fails to convince me that M&L 73 is the earlier inscription. The American calendar specialists agree in dating the decree in or after 418 (Dinsmoor, *Archons of Athens*, 335–41, suggested 416/15, and this is currently accepted by Meritt, *CW* lvi 1962–3, 41 n. 2, with *AJP* lxxxv 1964, 416 n. 7, cf. Meritt and McGregor, *Phoen.* xxi 1967, 88–9); recently arguments for 422/1 have been presented by P. Guillon (*BCH* lxxxvi 1962) and Mattingly, having first accepted these (*BCH* lxxxvii 1963, 391) would now revert to Ziehen's date of 423/2 (*PACA* vii 1964, 53–5, ix 1966, 66 n. 42, 76).

[3] M&L 73, 22–4.

[4] Ibid. 30–2. Heralds are again dispatched by the boule in M&L 68, 51–6 (426/5), [*SEG* x 136, 15–17 (407/6)—wholly restored]] and Tod 137, 14 sqq. (367/6); in the *ATL*, ii, text of the assessment-decree of 425/4 the heralds are under the jurisdiction of the boule, but M&L revert to the text of *ATL*, i, in which the boule's jurisdiction is not over the heralds (cf. p. 90 n. 7, above; the heralds are to get their orders from the τάκται and the ecclesia). In Clearchus' coinage-decree, however, the heralds are dispatched by the demos (M&L 45 = *ATL* D 14, § 9: fr. iii [Aphytis], ll. 23–4, reads ἐλέσθαι τὸ[ν δῆμον], with the o clearly visible in *ATL*, ii, pl. vi). It seems fashionable to assume that the boule began as a powerful body and was gradually weakened to the profit of the ecclesia (e.g. A. G. Woodhead, *Hist.* xvi 1967; see my remarks in Ch. V, pp. 213–5, esp. p. 215), but at any rate in matters of this kind I should expect what in the early fifth century was a prerogative of the demos to be delegated to the boule as the volume of diplomacy increased; and if I am right we have here very slight support for an early dating of M&L 45 and a late dating (i.e. 425–415 rather than *c.* 445) of M&L 73.

[5] M&L 73, 36–44. On the hieropoei, see pp. 127–30 below.

[6] M&L 73, 27–30.

monides,[1] and this law in turn was modified in 353/2.[2] The law of 353/2 leaves the demos to decide by decree how the ἀπαρχή is to be collected, but appears to give the boule general oversight over the subsequent proceedings.

A decree carried during the Archidamian War reveals yet other sacred treasuries which were penetrated by the boule.[3] After providing for contributions to the cult of Apollo to be exacted from the ἱππεῖς, [hoplites], and τοξόται, it lays down that the boule should choose two of its members to act as treasurers of Apollo at the same time as the treasurers of the Mother were chosen (again, presumably, from the boule);[4] these treasurers, together with the priest, were to be responsible for the τέμενος.[5] A little while later, the boule may have been involved in the melting down of golden νίκαι for emergency coinage.[6]

A Hellenistic postscript is provided by two decrees concerned with the shrine of the Hero Doctor (or Hero the doctor?). Both began with a πρόσοδος of the priest to the boule. In 221/0 he asked for a new οἰνοχόη to be made from the old dedications in the shrine, and his request was granted in a probouleumatic decree:[7] the work was to be entrusted to a committee of two Areopagites, three other citizens, the priest, the στρατηγὸς ἐπὶ τὴν παρασκευήν, and the ἀρχιτέκτων ἐπὶ τὰ ἱερά;[8] and the finished vessel was to bear the inscription ἡ βουλὴ ἡ ἐπὶ Θρασυφῶ[ντ]ος ἄρχοντος ἀπὸ τῶν ἀναθημάτων ἥρωι ἰατρῶι[9]—surprisingly, in view of the absence of bouleutae from the committee. Under a more oligarchic regime at the end of the second century, when the shrine's plate was found to be in poor condition, the priest asked for it to be attended to by a committee whose lay members should be three bouleutae and a δημόσιος, and this was granted in a decree of the boule.[10] Temple treasuries thus remained matters of public interest, and the ecclesia's approval of the dedicatory inscription giving the credit for work done to the boule, though apparently

---

[1] IG ii² 140, 8–10. Substantial fragments of Chaeremonides' law have now been discovered and await publication.

[2] IG ii² 140; Elter's restorations incorporated in IG ii² Addenda, SIG³ 200; most recent text Sokolowski, Lois Sacrées (Suppl.), 13 (cf. SEG xxi 253).

[3] IG i² 79: discussed by B. D. Meritt, Greek Historical Studies, 123–4, with revised text of ll. 7–9 at 124 n. 34 (cf. SEG xxi 441).

[4] IG i² 79, 9–11.   [5] Ibid. 15–18.

[6] SEG xxi 80 with W. E. Thompson, Mnem.⁴ xix 1966, 338–9. The inscription is dated to 404/3, but the decree of the boule which is cited could be earlier.

[7] IG ii² 839.

[8] On the στρατηγὸς ἐπὶ τὴν παρασκευήν and the ἀρχιτέκτων ἐπὶ τὰ ἱερά, cf. below, pp. 125–6. The general worked with a committee of Areopagites and other citizens to check the treasures of Asclepius in 247/6 (IG ii² 1534, 149–51) and in 215/14 (IG ii² 1539).

[9] IG ii² 839, 36–7, cf. the more fragmentary decrees 841 and 842.

[10] IG ii² 840. For the date see Ch. II, p. 86 and n. 2.

unjustified in the context where we find it, fairly reflects the importance of the boule at an earlier period.

Rents and taxes were another financial concern of the boule. The appropriate contracts were made by the πωληταί under the boule's supervision:

ἔπειθ᾽ οἱ πωληταὶ ι᾽ μέν εἰσι, κληροῦται δ᾽ εἷς ἐκ τῆς φυλῆς. μισθοῦσι δὲ τὰ μισθώματα πάντα, καὶ τὰ μέταλλα πωλοῦσι καὶ τὰ τέλη μετὰ τοῦ ταμίου τῶν στρατιωτικῶν καὶ τῶν ἐπὶ τὸ θεωρικὸν ᾑρημένων ἐναντίον τῆς [βουλῆς]· καὶ κυροῦσιν, ὅτῳ ἂν ἡ βουλὴ χειροτονήσῃ, καὶ τὰ πραθέντα μέταλλα τά τ᾽ ἐργάσιμα τὰ εἰς τρία ἔτη καὶ τὰ συγκεχωρημένα τὰ εἰς [ι᾽]* ἔτη πεπραμένα. καὶ τὰς οὐσίας τῶν ἐξ Ἀρείου πάγου φευγόντων καὶ τῶν ἄλλων ἐναντίον τῆς βουλῆς πωλοῦσιν, κατακυροῦσι δ᾽ οἱ θ᾽ ἄρχοντες. καὶ τὰ τέλη τὰ εἰς ἐνιαυτὸν πεπραμένα ἀναγράψαντες εἰς λελευκωμένα γραμματεῖα τόν τε πριάμενον καὶ [ὅσου] ἂν πρίηται τῇ βουλῇ παραδιδόασιν. . . . ἀναγράψουσι δὲ καὶ τὰ χωρία καὶ τὰς οἰκίας τἀπογραφέντα καὶ πραθέντα ἐν τῷ δικαστηρίῳ· καὶ γὰρ ταῦθ᾽ οὗτοι πωλ[οῦσιν].¹

The details of the *Athenaion Politeia*'s account belong to the author's own time: it is likely that the theoric fund was not set up until the late 350s,² and possible that it was controlled by a single commissioner until the 330s;³ it is likely also that the appearance in this context of the treasurer of the stratiotic fund was an innovation of the Lycurgan period.⁴ The poletae, however, were officials of respectable antiquity: they are alleged to have existed at the time of Solon,⁵ and are epigraphically attested from the middle of the fifth century, making contracts for the erection of stelae⁶ and for various public works.⁷ In its essentials the procedure outlined by the *Athenaion Politeia* was in existence by the end of the fifth century, and I see no reason to doubt that the boule's supervision of the poletae goes back to the Ephialtic reforms.⁸ Presumably what we are told

---

¹ *A.P.* 47. ii–iii (cf. Harp., Suid. πωληταί, *L.S.* 291. 17): the asterisked [ι᾽] is printed in Kenyon's Oxford Text; but Miss M. Crosby has shown that, whereas a term of ten years is compatible with the literary evidence, surviving mine leases point to a term of seven years for categories other than ἐργάσιμα (*Hesp.* xix 1950, 199–201, cf. R. J. Hopper, *BSA* xlviii 1953, 226, 237), and M. H. Chambers reads γ᾽ and accordingly regards this as an error for ζ᾽ (*TAPA* xcvi 1965, 36–7). ² See p. 105 and n. 6 below.

³ See Additional Note D, p. 235. The office clearly was collegiate when *A.P.* 47 was written. ⁴ Cf. pp. 107–8 and Additional Note D, p. 240.

⁵ *A.P.* 7. iii. The latest dated evidence for their existence is *IG* ii² 463, 36, 1589, 1 (both 307/6), but they now appear in *Hesp.* xxxvii 23, 5 (assigned to beg. C2 and published without comment): cf. p. 100 n. 1, below.

⁶ Down to 405/4 only (references *IG* i², p. 369. iii, s.v. πωλητής: notice ἀπομισθοσάντο[ν ℎοι πολεταὶ ἐν τêι βο]λêι [M&L 85, 34–5]; οἱ δὲ πολεταὶ ἀπομι[σθο]σ[άντον κατὰ τὸν ν]όμον [M&L 86, 8–9]'. After the restoration of the democracy in 403/2 the reference to the poletae disappears, and for much of the fourth century it was customary to state how much would be spent on the stele; later the treasurer was ordered to disburse simply τὸ γενόμενον ἀνάλωμα (references *IG* ii² iv. i, pp. 37–8, s.v. ἀναγραφή).

⁷ On contracts for public works see below, p. 124.
⁸ Cf. Ch. IV, pp. 204–5, and Ch. V, p. 211.

of the mines is true of state contracts in general, and the decision to place the contract with one man or partnership rather than another rested with the boule (Andocides παρελθὼν . . . εἰς τὴν βουλήν rather than πρὸς τοὺς πωλητάς outbid Agyrrhius for the collection of the πεντηκοστή,[1] and Aeschines remarks that the boule πωλεῖ τὸ πορνικὸν τέλος[2]), while the poletae probably drew up a detailed contract for the boule's approval. Another example of the poletae's activity is provided by a decree possibly to be dated to 432/1, in which the state assumes responsibility for the collection of the drachma contributed to Apollo Δήλιος by each of the ναύκληροι mooring at Phalerum.[3] The *Athenaion Politeia* states that the sale of confiscated property had to be ratified by the nine archons: why this was so, and what were the distinct responsibilities of the boule and the archons, is far from clear, but the fact is now confirmed by an inscription of 370/69.[4]

The leasing of sacred lands was a duty of the basileus, and he too worked under the supervision of the boule.[5] Any fundamentally new decision, however, had to be made by the demos, as we see from a decree of 418/17:[6]

Adusius proposes that the ἱερόν of Codrus, Neleus, and Basile shall be fenced and the τέμενος leased according to the (appended) συγγραφαί, boundary officers shall be sent to mark the boundaries of these ἱερά, and (the revenue from) the τέμενος shall defray the cost of the fencing. All this shall be done in the current bouleutic year, and anyone who fails in this may be fined 1,000 drachmae.[7]

A rider, also in the name of Adusius, adds that the basileus and poletae shall lease the τέμενος for twenty years, and the lessee shall fence the ἱερόν at his own expense; each year the rent for the τέμενος shall be paid to the apodectae in the ninth prytany, and they shall pass the money to the treasurers of the Other Gods in accordance with the law;[8] if the basileus or any one else fails to do his duty in the Aegeid prytany[9] the offender shall be fined 10,000 drachmae. Further clauses concern the removal of the mud from the ditch (in the current bouleutic year), the recording of the lessee's name, and the publication of the decree.[10]

---

[1] And. I. *Myst.* 134.   [2] A. I. *Tim.* 119.   [3] *SEG* xxi 37, 6–7.

[4] *SEG* xix 133, 1–2 (cf. *Hesp.* v 9, 4–5, with commentary suggesting that the ratification might be made by any one of the archons, with his σύμβουλοι or πάρεδροι).

[5] *A.P.* 47. iv. Presumably the poletae also were involved, as in *IG* i² 94, 11–13.

[6] *IG* i² 94, most recently studied (for its topographical interest) by R. E. Wycherley, *BSA* lv 1960.

[7] *IG* i² 94, 1–11.   [8] See p. 99 n. 3 below.

[9] Aegeis was not in prytany when the decree was passed, and the decree must therefore belong to the ninth prytany, when it would be known by elimination that Aegeis would hold the tenth and last prytany of the year (cf. Ch. I, p. 19 with n. 4). On the interpretation of ll. 18–20 see B. D. Meritt, *CQ* xl 1946, 45–6.

[10] *IG* i² 94, 11–28.

The inscription ends with the συγγραφαί, in accordance with which the lessee is to fence the ἱερόν in the current bouleutic year, to plant at least two hundred olive shoots in the τέμενος, and to control the ditch and rainwater within a specified area; the lease is to be for twenty years.[1]

In the fourth century the leasing of a special tract of land and the setting aside of its rent to finance the lesser Panathenaea required the complicated procedure of νομοθεσία;[2] the law laid down that the prytanes were to convene a meeting of the boule specifically for the making of the relevant contracts.[3]

In some times of crisis the state resorted not to extra taxes but to appeals for voluntary contributions, and the boule was involved in these no less than in more formal arrangements. In the middle of the fourth century we hear of three such appeals, apparently for men to serve extra trierarchies: the last of the three was for the Olynthian war of 349–8, and Demosthenes claims that Midias made his offer not at the proper time— ἐν τῇ βουλῇ γιγνομένων ἐπιδόσεων παρὼν οὐκ ἐπεδίδου τότε—but later, at a meeting of the ecclesia when there seemed a risk of his being sent on a cavalry expedition to Euboea.[4] About a hundred years later a decree invited contributions of between 50 and 200 drachmae to the stratiotic fund,

$$[\H\"o\pi\omega\varsigma\ \H\alpha\nu\ \chi\rho\eta\mu\H\alpha\tau\omega\nu]$$
$$[\pi]o\rho\iota\sigma\theta\H\epsilon\nu\tau\omega\nu\ \H\epsilon\chi\epsilon\iota\ \H o\ \tau\alpha\mu\H\iota\alpha\varsigma\ \mu\epsilon\rho\H\iota\zeta\epsilon\iota\nu\ \tau\H\alpha\ [\delta\epsilon\H o\mu\epsilon\nu\alpha,\ \H\iota\nu\alpha\ \kappa\alpha\tau\H\alpha\ \tau\H o]-$$
$$[\nu\ \kappa]\alpha\tau\H\alpha\lambda\omega\pi\omega\nu\ \chi\rho\H o\nu\omega\nu\ \tau\omega\H\upsilon\ \H\epsilon\nu\iota\alpha\upsilon\tau\omega\H\upsilon\ \sigma\upsilon\nu\kappa[\omega\mu\iota\sigma\theta\H\omega\sigma\iota\nu\ \omega\H\iota\ \H\epsilon\kappa\ \gamma\H\eta\varsigma]$$
$$[\kappa]\alpha\rho\pi\omega\H\iota\ \mu\epsilon\tau'\ \H\alpha\sigma\phi\alpha\lambda\epsilon\H\iota\alpha\varsigma.^{5}$$

Contributions were to be offered to the boule or the generals within the month of Munychion.[6]

When the time for actual payment came, different officials were involved. Records of contracts were kept by a δημόσιος on behalf of the boule, and it was his duty to give the lists of sums currently due to the ἀποδέκται, the official receivers of public revenue, one appointed by lot from each tribe.[7] As after 454 the tribute from the Delian League was paid to the Hellenotamiae in the presence of the boule,[8] so the apodectae

---

[1] *IG* i² 94, 29–38.

[2] *SEG* xviii 13; cf. original publication and commentary by D. M. Lewis, *Hesp.* xxviii 1959, 239–47. For a discussion of the *Néa* see L. Robert, *Hellenica* xi–xii 1960, 189–203, suggesting that the revenue in question comprises the customs dues from Oropus.

[3] *SEG* xviii 13, 11–15.   [4] D. XXI. *Mid.* 161–2.

[5] *Hesp.* xi 56, 9–12.   [6] Ibid. 17–19.   [7] *A.P.* 47. v.

[8] In view of Thucydides' contempt for technicalities and the pre-454 context of the passage this cannot be inferred with certainty from T. i. 96. ii. Pollux, indeed, would have imperial revenue like domestic paid in the first instance to the apodectae (viii. 97): ἀπο-δέκται δὲ ἦσαν δέκα, οἳ τούς τε φόρους καὶ τὰς εἰσφορὰς καὶ τὰ τέλη ὑπεδέχοντο, and this is accepted in *ATL*, iii. 12–13. But despite the Cleisthenic origin alleged for the apodectae in

received domestic dues in the boule's presence, and noted any cases of failure to pay. They then surrendered the records, and it became the responsibility of the boule to take action against defaulters.[1] The apodectae were receiving officers only, and they were required immediately to μερίζειν the sums which they received to the various ἀρχαί entitled to spend public money: having recorded their allocations, on the day after they had transacted their business for the prytany they read out the list in the boule, which discussed any allegations of offences in connection with the μερισμός.[2] Androtion thought, or was believed by Harpocration to have thought, that the apodectae were created by Cleisthenes to take the place of the colacretae, but the decree of 418/17 concerning the τέμενος of Codrus, Neleus, and Basile is our earliest evidence for the existence of the apodectae,[3] and, though it is the last dated document in which the colacretae appear, they probably continued in existence until the revolution of 411;[4] moreover, while the apodectae were receivers the colacretae were spenders of public money.[5] When the apodectae were instituted, and how control was exercised over the revenue before then, we cannot say; but the μερισμός of the *Athenaion Politeia* seems to be a substitute, probably introduced in the law-code of 403/2, for the fifth-century practice whereby all duly authorized public expenditure was made from a central treasury.[6] The changes made in Athens' financial organization in the third quarter of the fourth century, to which we shall

Andr. 324 F 5 they are not mentioned before 418/17 (p. 99 with n. 3 below) and if in the 440s they did exist and receive tribute their absence from M&L 46, 16–22, is surprising.

[1] *A.P.* 48. i, cf. *E.M.* ἀποδέκται, *L.S.* 198. 1, 427. 13. For the part played by the boule in the collection of fines and overdue debts see Ch. IV, pp. 148–51.

[2] *A.P.* 48. ii. Cf. also Ch. IV, pp. 147–8 with p. 148 n. 1.

[3] *IG* i² 94, 15–18, where they are to pass their receipts to the treasurers of the Other Gods κατὰ τὸν νόμον: Dr. D. M. Lewis suggests that the νόμος may be simply M&L 58 A, which established this board of treasurers.

[4] *IG* i². 94, 28: they appear also in M&L 73, 51–2 (perhaps to be dated to 416/15—cf. p. 94 n. 2 above); an allusion in Ar. *Av.* 1541 (414) does not guarantee their continued existence. The 'future' constitution of 411 provides for an enlarged board of 20 Hellenotamiae in charge of all non-sacred moneys (*A.P.* 30. ii), and we do find that in and after 410 the Hellenotamiae numbered 20 (M&L 84 with Meritt, *Athenian Financial Documents*, 98–103) and made payments which earlier would have been made by the colacretae (cf. p. 102 with n. 5 below). It is likely therefore that in or perhaps shortly before 411 the imperial and city treasuries were finally merged (the fact that the treasuries could have been merged earlier than 411 is noted by W. K. Pritchett, *BCH* lxxxviii 1964, 474 with n. 3—but I do not find his speculations about the Hellenotamiae on pp. 474–80 attractive), and though the authors of *ATL* believe that under the democracy the colacretae were revived to handle jury pay there is no evidence for this. (Like the poletae, the colacretae are said in *A.P.* 7. iii to have existed in the time of Solon.)
For recent discussions of financial organization in the late fifth century see *ATL*, iii. 359 sqq., and Jacoby's commentary on Andr. 324 F 5.

[5] Cf. again p. 102 with n. 5 below.

[6] But see p. 100 with n. 5, below on *SEG* x 138.

come shortly, left the apodectae in existence, but they are not attested after 323/2.[1] The third-century decree appealing for contributions to the stratiotic fund suggests at first sight that the μερισμός to different spending authorities continued, but that revenue was under the control of the single ταμίας τῶν στρατιωτικῶν;[2] however, in payment orders in Hellenistic decrees μερίσαι seems to be synonymous with δοῦναι,[3] and μερίζειν in this decree need not imply an allocation of revenue in the fourth-century manner.

On a few occasions the apodectae were made directly responsible for an item in the state's expenditure, and it is assumed that Athens' financial position had become so critical that there were no funds immediately available, and money had to be obtained from the apodectae as soon as they were able to collect it. Our earliest example of this is a decree, largely restored, dating from 407/6: in it the generals are ordered to borrow money from the apodectae and transmit it directly to the ναυπηγοί; the sum is to be repaid by the trieropoei in due course.[4] Meritt suggests that at this time the correct procedure would have been for the Hellenotamiae to disburse the necessary sums from the combined state and imperial treasury to the trieropoei, and for these to pass on the money to the ναυπηγοί.[5] In two decrees of c. 386 the apodectae are made directly responsible for the cost of publication:

$$μερίσαι\ δὲ\ τ-$$
$$ὸ\ ἀργύριον\ τὸ\ εἰρημένον\ τὸς\ ἀποδέ-$$
$$κτας\ ἐκ\ τῶν\ καταβαλλομένων\ χρημά-$$
$$[τ]ων,\ ἐπειδὰν\ τὰ\ ἐκ\ τῶν\ νόμων\ μερ[ίσω]-$$
$$σι.[6]$$

---

[1] Their last dated appearance is in *IG* ii² 365, *b* 6; 1631, 324–5 (both 323/2), but they are now found in *Hesp.* xxxvii 23, 4 (assigned to beg. C2 and published without comment): cf. p. 96 n. 5 above. On the question of their continued existence in the heyday of the theoric officials, and on the relationship to them of the antigrapheus, see Additional Note D, p. 239.

[2] *Hesp.* xi 56, 9–10, cf. 1–2 (247/6).

[3] See the examples given in *IG* ii² iv. i, p. 38. i–ii, s.vv. ἀναγραφή etc., and cf. pp. 109–10 below on *IG* ii² 674.

[4] *SEG* x 138, 4–9. For the trieropoei and ναυπηγοί, cf. pp. 115–17 below.

[5] B. D. Meritt, *Classical Studies presented to E. Capps*, 246–52, cf. *ATL*, iii. 361. For immediate use of income a little earlier cf. M&L 84, 3 (410/9).

Dr. D. M. Lewis has suggested to me that we have here a foreshadowing of the fourth-century μερισμός—with emergency arrangements being made because the shipbuilding grant is temporarily exhausted. But revenue from a specified source could be allocated in advance for a particular purpose as early as 434/3 (M&L 58 A, 4–7) and if similar arrangements had been made here for a particular consignment of new ships I do not think this decree need presuppose a significant departure from fifth-century practice.

[6] Tod 116, 18–22 (386). This decree is our earliest clear evidence for the fourth-century μερισμός.

[ἐς δ]ὲ τὴν ἀναγραφ[ὴν τῆς]
[σ]τή[λης μερίσαι] τὸς [ἀπ]οδέκτα[ς τριάκ]-
[ο]ν[τα] δ[ραχμὰς] τῶι γραμματεῖ τ[ῆς βολῆ]-
[ς].¹

There seems to have been a similar shortage of money a few years later, in 378/7.² After a period in which the sacred treasurers defrayed publication costs these costs were normally met from a fund created perhaps c. 376 to cover the running expenses of the ecclesia, τὰ κατὰ ψηφίσματα ἀναλισκόμενα τῶι δήμωι,³ but the μερισμός was so nicely calculated that a small additional burden imposed on the ecclesia's expense-account necessitated an adjustment to the μερισμός, which like the earmarking of revenue from a new lease for the lesser Panathenaea had apparently to be made not by ψήφισμα but by νόμος. Thus in 344/3 the ecclesia voted Pisithides of Delos a maintenance grant of a drachma a day, to be paid for from this fund, and ordered the nomothetae to provide for an appropriate addition to the fund's annual allowance.⁴ In 347/6, however, a decree had sufficed not only to order that Spartocus and his brothers should be given gold crowns each Great Panathenaea from the assembly's expense-account but also to state that for the present the apodectae were to advance the money from (I imagine, what they would normally allocate to) the stratiotic fund.⁵ Presumably this was merely a temporary adjustment, and the assembly's expense-account ultimately bore the cost of the crowns given in 346.

The second speech *Against Boeotus* gives us a final reminder of the boule's concern with all matters of revenue. Boeotus has claimed that when his grandfather, Pamphilus, had died his father, Mantias, collected from the bouleuterium the surplus that remained from Pamphilus' confiscated

---

¹ Tod 117, 14–17 (386/5). A. C. Johnson, *CP* ix 1914, 417–23, proposed to restore a similar mention of the apodectae in two other decrees which he assigned to this date, *IG* ii² 33 and 81 (cf. W. B. Dinsmoor, *AJA*² xxxvi 1932, 158 with n. 4); but the verb δόναι makes it more likely that in these cases a treasurer or treasurers paid.

² *IG* ii² 40, 21–3. Johnson proposed to associate this decree with those cited above, but it seems settled in 378/7, and the verb μερίσαι should guarantee the restoration of the apodectae (Kirchner, *IG* ii² iv. i, p. 37. ii, s.vv. ἀναγραφή etc., against Wilhelm in *IG* ii² Add.). Johnson recognized in his notes on *IG* ii² 301 and 520 that μερίσαι was not an appropriate verb for treasurers: *CP* ix 1914, 424–5, 428.

³ The fund is attested, with variations of title, from the second quarter of the fourth century. Its first dated appearance is in 368/7 (*IG* ii² 106, 18–19), but the ταμίας τοῦ δήμου, who administered it, is mentioned in *IG* ii² 21 (*c.* 376?—Johnson, *CP* ix 1914, 421) and Tod 129 (*c.* 375–3), and the fund was probably set up about 376. For payment for stelae in the first quarter of the century, see p. 103 n. 7 below; and on the fund after 323 see pp. 108–10.

⁴ *IG* ii² 222, 41–6. We have two other decrees calling on the treasurer of the demos to make a payment and on the nomothetae to see that he is reimbursed: *IG* ii² 330, 15–23 (335/4); *IG* vii 4254 = *SIG*³ 298, 35–41 (not 39–45) (329/8).

⁵ Tod 167, 39–44.

property after his debt to the state had been paid:[1] Mantitheus in reply
to this states that Pamphilus' property was not enough to clear the debt,
so there cannot have been any surplus.[2] Yet again, we find the boule
mentioned in the special field of naval debts: in 342/1 a man who had
been ταμίας τῶν τριηροποιϊκῶν in 363/2 made a payment to the boule,[3] while
the debts collected by the epimeletae in 323/2 were paid to the ταμίας τοῦ
νεωρίου in the presence of the boule, as prescribed by a law of Diphilus.[4]

We turn now from public revenue to public expenditure. From the
beginnings of our evidence about the middle of the fifth century until 411
or perhaps shortly before then all payments for Athenian as opposed to
imperial purposes appear to have been made by the colacretae.[5] Payment
for imperial purposes was made by the Hellenotamiae,[6] and it is clear that
in Athenian book-keeping the city and imperial funds were distinct,
though the two collections of money may have been kept in the same
place.[7] Ultimate control rested with the ecclesia, which could order
regular or once-for-all payments, but the colacretae, the officials who
actually made the payments, served for a term of one prytany, and the
prytanes for whose term they served could be ordered by the ecclesia
to see that a specified payment was made.[8] In 411, or possibly in the
period of financial crisis between the Sicilian disaster and the revolution,
the empire's funds were merged with those of the city, and in the last
years of the Peloponnesian War an enlarged board of twenty Hellenotamiae[9] provided the money for such domestic purposes as the erection
of stelae[10] and the award of gold crowns.[11]

[1] [D.] XL. *Boe. Dot.* 20.   [2] Ibid. 22.
[3] *IG* ii² 1622, 566–72.   [4] *IG* ii² 1631, 505–11.

[5] They are best described as ταμίαι τῶν πολιτικῶν χρημάτων (schol. Ar. *Av.* 1541 = Andr.
324 F 36). (Notes in scholia and lexica are conveniently assembled by J. Oehler, *RE*, xi.
1068.) They were responsible for jury pay (Hes., Suid. κωλακρέται, *L.S.* 190. 15, 275. 22, cf.
Ar. *Vesp.* 695, 725, *Av.* 1541) and for various other stipends—for theori (Andr. 324 F 36), for
heralds (M&L 69, 50–1), for hieropoei (*IG* i² 84, 22–3), and for the priestess of Athena
Νίκη (M&L 71)—and also for the publication of documents (e.g. M&L 37, 11–14; 69,
22–6; 73, 48–52) and for various other state payments (e.g. *IG* i² 80, 7–9; 336, 4–5; *SEG* x 84,
26–30, 41 sqq.; 243, ii. 24–5; *SEG* xxi 52, 20–2).

[6] Cf. HMA 79, M&L 72, where the sacred treasurers provide money either for the
Hellenotamiae or for generals in immediate need.

[7] The authors of *ATL* write of a single fund, τὸ δημόσιον, from which the colacretae or
Hellenotamiae made payments as appropriate (*ATL*, iii. 360–1), but records of borrowing
from the sacred treasuries show that the fifth-century Athenians were careful to note which
sums of money belonged to whom, and as long as the city's officials were distinct from those
which she supplied to the Delian League it seems more realistic to think in terms of two
separate funds.

[8] *SEG* x 84, 26–30, and 96 (but here I have doubts about the restoration: see Ch. I,
p. 22 n. 3), with A. Wilhelm, *Sb. Wien* ccxvii. 5. 1939, 52–72; cf. Wilamowitz, *DLZ* xix
1898, 383, on M&L 71.   [9] Cf. p. 99 n. 4 above.
[10] M&L 85, 34–6; 86, 4–9; 94, 38–40.   [11] M&L 85, 10–12.

In the fourth century, with its μερισμός, we reach a more advanced level of financial organization. Whereas previously, so far as we can tell, every payment from the public treasury was earmarked for a particular purpose, various ἀρχαί were now given an annual allowance for their ordinary expenses, which presumably was theirs to spend without further interference, so long as they could satisfy the boards of logistae in the check made every prytany, and in the final examination after their year of office.[1] A few of the allocations are known: in 357/6 Midias as treasurer of the Paralus had 12 talents to spend;[2] in the 320s the ἱερῶν ἐπισκευασταί received ½ talent a year[3] and the epimeletae of the Great Dionysia 1⅔ talents;[4] and an order to the ἀγορανόμοι in a decree of 320/19 shows that the delegation of spending power was continued by the regime set up after the Lamian War.[5] I have already had cause to mention the ecclesia's expense-account, and the fact that the sum allocated to it left very little room for manœuvre.[6] How large that sum was we do not know, but perhaps for a short time before this account was created stelae were paid for from a fund of ten talents in the hands of the treasurers of Athena.[7]

The boule also had an expense-account which received an allowance in the μερισμός, τὰ κατὰ ψηφίσματα ἀναλισκόμενα τῆι βουλῆι. The uses of this fund about which we can be most certain are to finance the

[1] On the logistae cf. p. 111 below.

[2] D. XXI. *Mid.* 174 (on the date I follow G. L. Cawkwell, *C&M* xxiii 1962).

[3] *A.P.* 50. i.

[4] *A.P.* 56. iv (at an earlier date they had been expected to defray their expenses out of their own pockets).

[5] *IG* ii² 380, 14–17. We have seen that the use of the verb μερίζειν continued into the Hellenistic period, but with a weakened meaning (p. 100 and nn. 2 and 3 above).

[6] Cf. p. 101 and n. 5 above.

[7] On the assumption that at any one time there should be only one source of payment for stelae W. B. Dinsmoor, *AJA²* xxxvi 1932, 158–9 (modifying the views of A. C. Johnson, *CP* ix 1914, 417–23), suggested that payments were made by the joint sacred treasurers from 404/3 until 387/6, by the apodectae in 386/5, by the treasurers of Athena from 385/4 to 377/6 (from a special ten-talent fund in the last two years of this period: Tod 123 is dated to 378/7; the other decrees mentioning the fund are *IG* ii² 22, 84, Tod 139, *IG* ii² 173), and by the treasurer of the demos from 376/5. The succession of joint sacred treasurers–treasurers of Athena–treasurer of the demos may be accepted; but one of the three likely references to the apodectae seems later than 386/5, and it is easier to believe that they might make a direct payment in any emergency (cf. p. 101 and nn. 1 and 2 above); and it is an obstacle (though perhaps not fatal) to Dinsmoor's view of the ten-talent fund that many have thought the content of Tod 139 to be better explained by a date in the 360s (see Tod's commentary).

There is no justification beyond the actual sum involved for the attempt of some scholars to identify the ten-talent fund with the proceeds of the levy imposed on metics (*IG* ii² 505, 14–15) (R. Thomsen, *Eisphora*, 241 with n. 264, cites earlier discussions and is undecided on this point—but thinks citizens as well as metics contributed to the ten talents). For a recent discussion of the fund see S. Accame, *La Lega ateniese*, 65–6 (not aware of Johnson and Dinsmoor); Jones simply identifies the fund with the ecclesia's expense-account (102 with 154 n. 33).

publication of the boule's decrees[1] and the making of crowns awarded by
the boule.[2] Professor Kahrstedt has tried to identify various other expenses
which were paid from this account:[3] it is certainly likely that the boule's
corporate religious observances were paid for in this way,[4] but I am
less happy about his other identifications. The cost of meals in the
Tholos may have been defrayed from this account rather than by direct
grant,[5] but there is no real evidence either way;[6] it is not inherently
likely that the herald's salary was a charge on the boule;[7] and the fact
that the boule held the δοκιμασία of the ἀδύνατοι[8] tells us nothing about
the payment of their maintenance grant. We do not know how or by
whom the bouleutae's own stipends were paid. But if assembly pay was
given to the first 6,000 to arrive[9] and was successful in attracting citizens
to the assembly, then at Agyrrhius' final rate of 3 obols the forty guaranteed assemblies in the year will have cost 20 talents. If the special fund
of 10 talents is a reliable guide to the size of the ecclesia's expense-account
the money cannot have come from that source, and we may therefore
assume that stipends for bouleutae were not paid through the boule's
expense-account.

It will be seen from this survey that the boule's control of finance
depended on its supervision of a large number of financial boards. It
watched over the activities of the sacred treasurers, of the poletae, and
of the apodectae; in the fifth century it controlled the colacretae, and in
the fourth it appointed a board of logistae (as we shall see at the end of

---

[1] e.g. *IG* ii² 120, 21–2.

[2] e.g. *IG* ii² 223 A, 7; B, 15; Kahrstedt (*S.S.A.*, 332–3) has noticed that although in the
Demosthenic period the boule could award gold crowns it later awarded only green crowns,
except in those oligarchic periods in the first century when the boule made awards which at
other times would have been ratified by the demos (cf. Ch. II, p. 86). This is presumably
due to Athens' comparative poverty and to the great increase in honours in the Hellenistic
period, rather than to any deliberate desire to reduce the boule's financial independence.

[3] *U.M.A.*, 193.

[4] e.g. *IG* ii² 223 B, 5; *P* 10, 10 sqq.

[5] *U.M.A.*, 193 with n. 6: Kahrstedt should have specified the Tholos, not the Prytaneum.

[6] The ἀείσιτοι in 'second' prytany decrees thank not the prytanes but the prytanes'
treasurer, and the payments specifically attributed to him are for sacrifices, not for board
residence. We cannot rule out (as Kahrstedt did, *S.S.A.*, 223) the possibility that the prytanes
received a separate allowance for expenses of this kind, which their treasurer administered;
but since in *IG* ii² 674, 16–21, sacrifices of the prytanes were to be charged to the boule's
expense-account it is certainly possible that the prytanes' expenses were always considered to
form a subsection of the boule's.

[7] Philocles was appointed *c.* 368–358 by the boule and demos (*IG* ii² 145. ii), and I argue
in Ch. II, pp. 84–5, that the appointment of his father *c.* 398–390, [κηρυκεύεν ... τ]ῆι βολῆι καὶ
τῶι δήμω[ι τῶι Ἀθηναίων], was made by the demos (*IG* ii² 145. i).

[8] Cf. Ch. IV, pp. 175–6.

[9] This is the figure for the quorum at an ὀστρακοφορία or an assembly to ratify a grant of
citizenship.

this section[1]) to examine in each prytany the accounts of those who received an allocation of public money for their expenses. Each of these officials or boards was involved only at one point in the state's finances: the boule was involved at every point, and it alone could see the whole picture. Only the boule had access to the information which would show whether extra taxation was needed, or whether the city could afford some new charge on its resources, and this must be the reason for the boule's financial predominance.

From about the middle of the fourth century, however, we find major state treasurers at work, who were able to challenge the supremacy of the boule in this field.[2] The first clear allusion to a stratiotic fund, τὰ στρατιω-τικά, concerns the year 373:[3] it is likely that before the creation of the theoric fund about twenty years later any surplus revenue after other charges had been met was made over to the stratiotic fund if Athens was at war;[4] a stratiotic allowance may also have been included in the regular μερισμός, but there is no evidence of this.[5] In the years immediately after the Social War the theoric fund, τὰ θεωρικά, was created or at any rate reorganized,[6] and this received all surplus revenue[7] until Demosthenes redirected surpluses to the stratiotic fund in 339/8.[8] Estimates

---

[1] p. 111 below.

[2] I am greatly indebted to Dr. D. M. Lewis for letting me see his unpublished essay on Eubulus and Lycurgus, and notes on it by Messrs. G. E. M. de Ste Croix, A. R. W. Harrison, and G. L. Cawkwell.

[3] [D.] XLIX. Tim. 12, 16; cf. for 362 [D.] L. Poly. 10. Glotz's view that the fund was a creation of the 340s (RH clxx 1932) has been answered by G. L. Cawkwell, Mnem.[4] xv 1962, who thinks it possible that a stratiotic fund existed as early as the 390s. A ταμίας στρατιωτικῶν first appears in 344/3 (IG ii² 1443, 12–13), but there is no reason why the office should not be as old as the fund.

[4] According to [D.] LIX. Neaer. 4, when Apollodorus made his illegal proposal in 349/8 the laws prescribed ὅταν πόλεμος ᾖ, τὰ περιόντα χρήματα τῆς διοικήσεως στρατιωτικὰ εἶναι, but Athens had been formally at war with Philip since his capture of Amphipolis in 357 (Is. V. Phil. 2, A. II. F.L. 21, 70, 72, III. Ctes. 54) and in 349/8 surplus money was clearly going to the theoric fund. Presumably the creation of the latter fund after the Social War had in fact upset the arrangement to which the speaker alludes.

[5] I would however infer a μερισμός to the stratiotic fund from Tod 167, 39–44 (347/6). The fund is mentioned also in 349/8 (IG ii² 207, bcd 11) and its treasurer in 344/3 (cf. n. 3 above), and as at this time surpluses went to the theoric fund an allocation in the μερισμός seems inevitable.

[6] J. van Ooteghem, LEC i 1932, cf. G. L. Cawkwell, JHS lxxxiii 1963, 55–6 with n. 53, relying on Justin, vi. ix. 1–5 and schol. A. III. Ctes. 24 (in edition of F. Schultz, 1865, or ap. NJhb xciii 1866 (i), 27); J. J. Buchanan, Theorika, 48–53, prefers the attribution to Agyrrhius in Harp. θεωρικά. Eubulus seems at any rate to have been responsible for the name θεωρικά (Philinus, fr. 3 [Sauppe] ap. Harp. s.v.) and for the important position held by the theoric officials in the 340s (A. III. Ctes. 25).

[7] Apollodorus' attempt to divert surpluses to the stratiotic fund in 349/8 was thwarted by a γραφὴ παρανόμων ([D.] LIX. Neaer. 4–6). According to Libanius (D. I. Ol. i. hyp. 5) the death penalty was threatened for repetitions of this proposal.

[8] Phil. 328 F 56 a: the change is unlikely to have outlasted the settlement of 338/7 (but for a different view see F. W. Mitchel, TAPA xciii 1962, 224–5 with 224 n. 33).

of the sums distributed from the theoric fund to enable citizens to attend the festivals have varied between 15 talents or less and not much under 100 talents,[1] but the fund was not used only for this purpose, and it is clear that the sums passing through it were considerable.[2] Aeschines, in a context where some exaggeration is to be expected, claims:

διὰ δὲ τὴν πρὸς Εὔβουλον γενομένην πίστιν ὑμῖν οἱ ἐπὶ τὸ θεωρικὸν κεχειροτονημένοι ἦρχον μέν, πρὶν ἢ τὸν Ἡγήμονος νόμον γενέσθαι, τὴν τοῦ ἀντιγραφέως ἀρχήν, ἦρχον δὲ τὴν τῶν ἀποδεκτῶν, καὶ ⟨ἦρχον τὴν⟩* νεωρίων ἀρχήν, καὶ σκευοθήκην ᾠκοδόμουν, ἦσαν δὲ καὶ ὁδοποιοί, καὶ σχεδὸν τὴν ὅλην διοίκησιν εἶχον τῆς πόλεως.[3]

Other texts confirm the use of the theoric fund for public works.[4] The fund must have become as important to Athens as the sacred treasuries had been in the second half of the fifth century, and in this sense it could fittingly be called κόλλαν . . . τῆς δημοκρατίας,[5] but unfortunately it is not clear how its development affected the balance of control in public finance. There is no evidence of a departure from the principle that any expenditure of public money had ultimately to be authorized by the people, and I imagine that the theoric officials became important in two main ways. First, as the custodians of the fund on which any new commitment to spend public money was likely to depend, they would doubtless advise whether the city could afford a suggested venture; and this could affect many aspects of public life, as when Eubulus insisted in 346 that Athens could not afford not to make peace with Philip of Macedon. Secondly, they may have been associated with the work of some other departments, such as that of the apodectae, though there must still have been other men (retaining old titles or bearing new ones) to do much of the routine work.[6] This may be illustrated by A.P. 47. ii,[7] where we read that (in the 320s) the theoric board and the treasurer of the

[1] References given by G. E. M. de Ste Croix, CR² xiv 1964, 191.

[2] In 349/8 Demosthenes thought that the large-scale expedition he wanted to send to Olynthus could be financed from the theoric fund (D. I. Ol. i. 19–20, III. Ol. iii. 10–11), and in 346 Eubulus thought it necessary to warn the Athenians that if they did not make peace on terms acceptable to Philip the theoric moneys would have to be diverted to the stratiotic fund (D. XIX. F.L. 291).

[3] A. III. Ctes. 25 (the asterisked insertion is my own; Kaibel suggested καὶ νεωρίων ἦρχον; the Teubner and Budé editors retain the manuscripts' text unchanged). The powers of the theoric officials, their term of office, and whether there was a single man, ὁ ἐπὶ τὸ θεωρικόν, or a board, have all been disputed: see Additional Note D, pp. 235–40.

[4] Phil. 328 F 56 a, Harp. θεωρικά. Since Demosthenes spent 10 talents ἐκ τῆς διοικήσεως on the walls (A. III. Ctes. 31), and διοίκησις was the business of the theoric officials (A. III. Ctes. 25; Hyp. V. Dem., col. 28, referred by D. M. Lewis ap. G. L. Cawkwell, JHS lxxxiii 1963, 58 n. 68, to Demosthenes as a theoric official) it is likely that the fund also financed Eubulus' work on the fortifications (schol. D. III. Ol. iii. 29).

[5] Pl. Quaest. Plat. 1011 B.   [6] See Additional Note D, pp. 237–40.

[7] Quoted on p. 96. Similarly in 307/6 ὁ ἐπὶ τῇ διοικήσει combined with the poletae to make a wall-building contract: IG ii² 463, 36.

stratiotic fund combined with the poletae to make mine leases and tax
contracts in the presence of the boule. Bouleutae and poletae were
appointed by lot, and changed from year to year; theoric officials were
elected, even after their position had been weakened by the law of
Hegemon,[1] and at any rate before that law was passed there is no reason
to doubt the likelihood that the same man could be elected again and
again. Whether the fund was administered by a board from the beginning
or, as I imagine, there was a single official, ὁ ἐπὶ τὸ θεωρικόν, until the law
of Hegemon was passed, the men who were elected to these posts will, if
they combined with other financial boards as they combined with the
poletae, have gained that general knowledge of the state's finances, and
therefore that right to advise on all matters in which finance was involved,
which had previously been the preserve of the boule—with the added
possibility of reappointment. Formally, the boule will have lost power by
losing its monopoly of information, and there will inevitably have been
a tendency for the new officials to replace the boule as the ultimate source
of financial wisdom.

Demosthenes was ἐπὶ τὸ θεωρικόν in 337/6,[2] and very shortly afterwards
the office was in some way weakened by Hegemon, but another rival for
the boule's financial supremacy appeared in Lycurgus. What constitutional position he held must remain a mystery, but for τρεῖς πενταετηρίδας,[3]
or twelve years,[4] he was concerned with πρόσοδοι[5] and ἡ διοίκησις,[6] and
could be described as a ταμίας.[7] Hegemon's law, or another, had prevented the holding of some post or posts ἐπὶ τὰ δημόσια χρήματα for more
than four years, and so Lycurgus is said after his first quadrennium to
have directed affairs through one of his friends.[8] One is tempted to think
of the treasurer of the stratiotic fund, who by the 320s had acquired with
the theoric board the right to share in the making of mine leases and tax
contracts, but Demades' tenure of this office may well have fallen within
Lycurgus' first quadrennium.[9] No other office mentioned in the *Athenaion
Politeia* could fit Lycurgus' position, and it has been suggested that he was

---

[1] *A.P.* 43. i.   [2] A. III. *Ctes.* 24.   [3] [Pl.] *X. Or.* 841 B, decree *ap.* 852 B.
[4] D.S. xvi. 88. i.   [5] Decree *ap.* [Pl.] *X. Or.* 852 B, D.S. xvi. 88. i.
[6] ταχθεὶς δὲ ἐπὶ τῇ διοικήσει τῶν χρημάτων, Hyp., fr. 118 (Kenyon); cf. [Pl.] *X. Or.* 841 c,
D.S. xvi. 88. i, D. *Ep. iii.* 2. D.H. 660. Din. 11 describes Menesaechmus as μετὰ Λυκοῦργον τὴν
διοίκησιν τῶν δημοσίων χρημάτων παραλαβών.
[7] [Pl.] *X. Or.* 841 B, decree *ap.* 852 B.   [8] [Pl.] *X. Or.* 841 c.
[9] *IG* ii² 1493/4/5 with F. W. Mitchel, *TAPA* xciii 1962, esp. 219–25, arguing that Demades
was treasurer of the stratiotic fund for the Panathenaic quadrennium 334–330 (cf. Additional
Note D, p. 237): he was at any rate treasurer in 334/3. If we are to be tied to Panathenaic
quadrennia for Lycurgus, which at any rate in the case of an extraordinary appointment does
not seem inevitable, I should prefer to think that the twelve years began in 334 and that
Lycurgus did not live to the end of the third quadrennium (cf. [Pl.] *X. Or.* 842 F).

styled ὁ ἐπὶ τῇ διοικήσει, which is perhaps used as a formal title by Hyperides in referring to Lycurgus, and is found in one inscription that seems to be earlier than 307/6.[1] Probably a post was created specially for Lycurgus, and was described in various ways on different occasions; but we then have to resolve the difficulty of his being unable to hold such a post for more than four years.[2] Lycurgus increased the revenues of the state, and was responsible for expenditure on the navy and on public works;[3] like the theoric officials he was probably given access to the financial activities supervised by the boule,[4] but whatever his constitutional power he seems to have played much the same part in the state's finances as Aeschines ascribed to them, and the result will have been the same: real financial control was passing from a changing, democratic council to men of experience and proved ability. The tributes to Lycurgus show that the change was justified by results.

We are far from adequately informed about financial control after the death of Alexander, and most of our knowledge comes from publication orders in decrees. The ecclesia's expense-account continued in existence until 302/1, and throughout this period payments were made from it by the ταμίας τοῦ δήμου.[5] Before 302/1, however, other financial officials also made payments from this fund for the erection of stelae: several times payments are made by ὁ ἐπὶ τῇ διοικήσει, first found as a regular

---

[1] For Hyperides see p. 107 n. 6 above. In *Hesp.* xxix 3 = *SEG* xix 119 [Ξενοκλῆς Ξ]εινίδος Σ[φήττιος] is said to have been κ⟨α⟩τ[ασταθεὶς δ' ἐπ]ὶ τῆι διοι[κήσει τῆς π]όλεως (κ⟨α⟩ὶ [ἡιρημένος ἐπ]ί, D. M. Lewis) (7–9), and in the course of his activities he ἐμέρισε[ν τὰ εἰς τὸ ἱ]ερὰ θῦσαι [τὸ γένος τὸ Κ]ηρύκων (10–13). Xenocles was active from 346/5 to 306/5 (*PA* 11234, cf. Meritt's commentary on this inscription), but Meritt thinks the letters 'too well cut to fit comfortably into the last years of the century' (Dr. Lewis tells me that he concurs) and regards ὁ ἐπὶ τῇ διοικήσει as the title borne first by Lycurgus and then by his friends, and Xenocles as one of these friends.

[2] Possibly this is an element which later misunderstanding has allowed to enter the tradition, but *SEG* xix 119 would seem to confirm it, and we have so little detailed information on Lycurgus' position that it is dangerous to reject anything we are told. One could nevertheless perhaps argue against this element from *IG* ii² 1672, 11, recording an order issued by Lycurgus in 329/8 (certainly after the end of his first quadrennium) that an architect should be paid in advance.

[3] Hyp., fr. 118 (Kenyon), [Pl.] *X. Or.* 841 c–d, 842 f, decree *ap.* 851 f–852 e, cf. *IG* ii² 457, b (1–)3–9.

[4] ὁ ἐπὶ τῇ διοικήσει worked with the poletae in 307/6 (p. 106 n. 7 above). If Lycurgus' office was extraordinary rather than established, this may have seemed a sufficient reason for its omission from the *Athenaion Politeia*; if Lycurgus' own tenure was limited to one quadrennium any constitutional power will have passed with the office to his deputy—but it was the right of every citizen to request an audience with the boule and to address the assembly, and Lycurgus will surely have exercised this to the full. He was the author of a decree of the boule in or before 329/8 (*IG* ii² 1672, 302), but the safest inference from this is that he was a member at the time (Ch. II, p. 63 with n. 3; cf. Ch. I, p. 4 with n. 10). Mitchel, *TAPA* xciii 1962, 222 n. 26, confuses the right of πρόσοδος with the members' right to propose motions.

[5] e.g. *IG* ii² 393, 11–15 (322/1–319/18); 448, 85–7 (318/17); 505, 62–4 (302/1).

title in 307/6,[1] and there are four decrees of about 302 in which this fund is drawn on by the treasurer of the stratiotic fund.[2] To add to our confusion there is one other reference to the ταμίας τοῦ δήμου:

εἰς δὲ τὴν ἀναγραφὴν τῆς στήλης
δοῦναι τὸν ταμίαν τοῦ δήμου ΔΔΔ δ-
ραχμὰς ἐκ τῶν κοινῶν χρημάτων.[3]

τὰ κοινὰ χρήματα perhaps refers to the ecclesia's expense-account. Thereafter that account disappears from the record, apart from two occasions when payment for stelae is made from it by οἱ ἐπὶ τῇ διοικήσει.[4] Otherwise the officials are named, but the funds from which they pay are not: in 299/8 payment is made by ὁ ἐξεταστὴς καὶ οἱ τριττύαρχοι;[5] from 295 to 288 by ὁ ἐπὶ τῇ διοικήσει; from 288 to 263 by οἱ ἐπὶ τῇ διοικήσει; and from 263 to 229 by the single official again. From 229 to 169 payment could be made either by οἱ ἐπὶ τῇ διοικήσει or by the treasurer of the stratiotic fund, except in the case of prytany documents, where ὁ ἐπὶ τῇ διοικήσει persisted (probably as one tribe's representative on the board[6]). Thereafter we find only the treasurer of the stratiotic fund mentioned.[7] The treasurer of the boule is not mentioned as paying for stelae after 323,[8] but the office continued to exist and to qualify its holder for mention in prytany documents until the first century B.C. (the ταμίας τῆς βουλῆς does not normally figure among the ἀείσιτοι of the Christian era).[9] One document, however, a prytany decree of 275/4, suggests that the boule's expense-account was not the independent fund which it had been in the fourth century:

ὅπως ἂν δὲ καὶ τὰ Χαλκεῖα θύσωσιν τῆ(ι) Ἀθηνᾶι τεῖ Ἀρχη[γετίδι τ]-
ῆς πόλεως καὶ ἔχει καλῶς καὶ εὐσεβῶς τῆι βουλεῖ καὶ τῶι δήμωι τὰ π[ρὸς τοὺς]
[θεούς,] διαχειροτονῆσαι τὸν δῆμον, ὁπόσον δεῖ αὐτοῖς μερίσαι εἰς τὴ[ν διοικησ]-
[ιν τῆς θυσίας·] ὅ τι δ' ἂν διαχειροτονοῦντι τῶι δήμωι δόξει, μερίσαι τὸ[ν ταμίαν τ]-
[ῶν στρατιωτικῶν] καὶ τοὺς ἐπὶ τῆι διοικήσει. πόρον δὲ ὑπάρχειν ἐ[κ τῶν εἰς τὰ]
[ψηφίσματα ἀναλισκ]ομένων ὑπὸ τῆς βουλῆς.[10]

---

[1] e.g. IG ii² 463, 36 (307/6—but we have no reference to his paying for stelae in this first year); 500, 40–3 (302/1). On this overlap cf. W. K. Pritchett, Hesp. x 1941, 270–3.

[2] IG ii² 806, 6–9; 809, 4–8; Hesp. viii 12, 5–9; ix 45, 29–32—with E. Schweigert's commentary on Hesp. ix 45, p. 351. [3] IG ii² 558, 29–31 (c. 303/2).

[4] IG ii² 657, 70–3 (285/4); 672, 16–17 (280/79). IG ii² 675 is linked with 525 and dated to 306/5 by W. K. Pritchett, AJP lviii 1937, 329–33; for 806, 809 cf. n. 2 above.

[5] IG ii² 641, 29–32, 643, 9–12. [6] W. S. Ferguson ap. S. Dow, Hesp. Supp. i 1937, 13 n. 1.

[7] On financial officials from 295 see S. Dow, Hesp. Supp. i 1937, 11–13, B. D. Meritt, Hesp. xxxii 1963, 18 n. 36.

[8] At the end of the third century an honorific decree almost certainly of the boule (IG ii² 863: it ends with the 'citation', ἡ βουλὴ [τὴ]ν ἱέρειαν, ll. 10–11) was to be paid for simply by ὁ ταμίας (ll. 7–9). Kirchner quotes the opinion of Hartel and Fellner that this was the ταμίας τῆς βουλῆς, but in view of the absence of any parallel after 323 the ταμίας τῶν στρατιωτικῶν is more likely. [9] For the history of the office see p. 141 n. 4 below.

[10] IG ii² 674, 16–21. A different interpretation underlies the remarks of D. J. Geagan, Hesp. Supp. xii 1967, 116 n. 179.

This is a 'first' prytany decree, in which the demos honours the members of the prytany, and in it the demos is invited to consider the sum which the treasurers shall provide for one of the prytanes' sacrifices, and lays down that this sum shall be provided from the boule's expense-account. μερίζειν, as I have already remarked,[1] seems to have been divorced from the principle of an allocation to independent spending authorities, and this text seems to suggest that the payments were made by the state's financial officers[2] from a central fund, very much as in the fifth century, but that within that fund individual payments might be debited to particular accounts. This would make the work of such officers as the ταμίας τῆς βουλῆς and the ταμίας τῶν πρυτάνεων simply one of routine, in so far as public money was concerned, but in the Hellenistic period it was doubtless a large part of their duty to add to the official allowance from their own pockets, and to encourage other bouleutae to do likewise.[3]

Since the ecclesia's expense-account continued in existence until 301 it is likely that other independent funds survived with it.[4] A major reorganization seems to have been begun after 307, from which Athens emerged with the treasurer of the stratiotic fund and a board or a single officer (according to the complexion of the current regime) ἐπὶ τῇ διοική-σει as the principal state treasurers. Orders governing payment for stelae suggest that at first some distinction was drawn between the two accounts, but from 229 the distinction seems to have disappeared, and in later documents the ταμίας τῶν στρατιωτικῶν is the only paying officer mentioned. Financial control seems to have been concentrated in fewer hands than before 350, though traces of the old independent funds may have survived as separate accounts with the central treasury. We have no evidence on the formal relationship between these Hellenistic treasurers and the boule, but a few men, active in a wide field, will inevitably have been in a stronger position than the various limited boards of the classical democracy, and we need have no doubt that ultimate financial direction now lay not with the boule but with the treasurers.

Returning to the classical period, we read in the *Athenaion Politeia* that the boule συνδιοικεῖ ταῖς ἀρχαῖς[5] and κρίνει . . . τὰς ἀρχὰς . . . τὰς πλείστας, καὶ μάλισθ' ὅσαι χρήματα διαχειρίζουσιν.[6] συνδιοικεῖ will be further illustrated in the remaining sections of this chapter, and κρίνει in Chapter IV,

---

[1] Cf. p. 100 and n. 3 above.

[2] Notice that here and in *Hesp*. xi 56 (cf. p. 98) the treasurer of the stratiotic fund still exists, though at this time he is not involved in payment for stelae.

[3] Cf. Ch. I, p. 14 and n. 1.

[4] The ἀγορανόμοι still had funds at their disposal in 320/19 (cf. p. 103 and n. 5 above).

[5] *A.P.* 47. i, 49. v.   [6] *A.P.* 45. ii.

but this is perhaps the best place to mention the various boards of λογισταί found in Athens. In the first three quota-lists of the Delian League we have a reference to a board of thirty logistae, who checked the sums paid from the tribute to Athena.[1] The thirty appear again in the first financial decree of Callias, where they are to reckon up the sums due to the Other Gods and the boule is to be responsible for convening them;[2] and logistae, this time with no number stated, recorded the sums which the state borrowed from the sacred treasuries in and after 433, and computed the interest due.[3] The author of the *Athenaion Politeia* knew two boards of logistae: ten were appointed by lot from the boule to examine officials' accounts every prytany,[4] while on retiring from office at the end of the year officials had to present their accounts to ten logistae and their ten συνήγοροι, appointed by lot from the whole citizen body.[5] Logistae of this kind are not attested in the fifth century, nor logistae like the thirty, available for general accounting duties, in the fourth; but the insistence in some texts on the number of the thirty suggests that other logistae may have existed simultaneously with them, and Lysias' reference, immediately after the democratic restoration of 403/2, to an examination of accounts in each prytany at any rate gives no grounds for thinking that this was an innovation. Logistae are not mentioned after the *Athenaion Politeia*, and may well have seemed unnecessary in the financial framework of Hellenistic Athens.

In the heyday of the democracy, however, there were elaborate precautions against the misappropriation of public money. For important duties boards rather than single officials were commonly appointed, each board was strictly limited in its scope, and every holder of a public appointment was required to present his accounts for examination—if only to prove that he had neither received nor spent any public money.[6] Charges of embezzlement in high places were made:[7] Phidias was accused after completing the chryselephantine statue of Athena,[8] and Pericles as one of the epistatae may have been accused in the same connection;[9] Antiphon's choregus laid an εἰσαγγελία against three private

---

[1] *ATL* list 1, 2, cf. postscript; list 2, 1; list 3, 1.   [2] M&L 58 A, 7–9.

[3] M&L 72. The similarity of function makes it as good as certain that we are dealing with the same board again. Logistae, again with no number stated, reckoned up the expenditure of the Eleusinian epistatae: HMA 41, 22–8.

[4] *A.P.* 48. iii, Poll. VIII. 99, cf. Lys. XXX. *Nic.* 5.

[5] *A.P.* 54. ii, cf. scholia and lexica. Phot., *E.M.* εὔθυνα confuse these with the εὔθυνοι, on whom see Ch. IV, p. 148 n. 1; M. A. Levi, *Comm. Stor. Resp. Ath.*, (ii.) 378, identifies them with the logistae who examined accounts each prytany.   [6] A. III. *Ctes.* 9–23, esp. 22.

[7] Though little trust can be placed in such general charges as A. III. *Ctes.* 9–10.

[8] Phil. 328 F 121, cf. Pl. *Per.* 31. ii–v, D.S. XII. 39. i–ii, Suid. Φειδίας.

[9] Pl. *Per.* 32. iii–iv with F. J. Frost, *JHS* lxxxiv 1964.

citizens and the secretary to the thesmothetae for embezzlement,[1] and after he had been appointed to the boule uncovered malpractices on the part of the poristae, the poletae, the practores, and their secretaries.[2] The boule's concern with finance was largely supervisory, in its direct oversight of certain operations and its appointment of the logistae who conducted the interim examination each prytany, and its members will have been tempted more to connivance at the misdeeds of others than to embezzlement of public money passing through their own hands. Timarchus, for instance, when serving on the boule in 361/0, was accused of misappropriating 1,000 drachmae in conjunction with one of the treasurers of Athena:[3] perhaps he had been bribed to overlook or to help conceal a fraud practised by the treasurer. Other suggestions that the bouleutae were open to bribery can easily be found: the Old Oligarch agrees unhesitatingly with a suggestion that the boule and demos are so overburdened with work that a man has to offer a bribe to be sure that an item of business will be placed on the agenda;[4] and Mnesilochus in the *Thesmophoriazusae*, when told that he is to be fastened to the plank, pleads:

> ὦ πρύτανι πρὸς τῆς δεξίας, ἥνπερ φιλεῖς
> κοίλην προτείνειν, ἀργύριον ἤν τις διδῷ,
> χάρισαι βραχύ τί μοι καίπερ ἀποθανουμένῳ.[5]

Such remarks from a critic of the democracy and a comedian do not of course tell us a great deal—neither does Aeschines' allegation (in 330) that Demosthenes had employed bribery to obtain his place in the boule in 347/6[6]—but it is unlikely that a society in which a man's enemies could regularly be charged with corruption was entirely blameless, and the possibility that politicians would take bribes to work against the interests of Athens was taken seriously enough for the offence to be listed in the νόμος εἰσαγγελτικός.[7] Again, in a decree honouring a bouleutes it was felt to be worth stating that he ἀδωροδοκήτως βεβούλευκεν.[8]

We cannot tell from a few passages how successful the precautions against embezzlement were, but I imagine that the division of Athens' financial business into a large number of separate operations performed by separate officials, while reducing the opportunities for any one man to make away with a large sum, will have meant that if a man could conceal a fraud in his own accounts he was unlikely to be found out later. We shall notice in Chapter IV, in connection with the charges levelled

---

[1] Ant. VI. *Chor.* 35. [2] Ibid. 49. [3] A. I. *Tim.* 110.
[4] O.O. iii. 1–3. [5] Ar. *Thesm.* 936–8. [6] A. III. *Ctes.* 62.
[7] Hyp. IV. *Eux.* 8; cf. Ch. IV, p. 163. [8] *IG* ii² 223 A, 11.

against Androtion, a tendency to think that what mattered was to pin the responsibility for the embezzlement to someone, who if he were innocent could be left to seek restitution from the guilty;[1] and in the speech *Against Androtion* we find Demosthenes arguing that embezzlement by the ταμίας τῶν τριηροποιϊκῶν cannot be used by the boule as a defence against the charge of failing to build the required number of triremes.[2] The appearance of such attitudes suggests that the Athenian system was not particularly successful either in preventing dishonesty or in exposing it when it occurred; bouleutae, as I have remarked, will have had better opportunities to turn a blind eye to the peculation of others than to take public money directly.

(ii) *Army and Navy*

Whether to fight or to make peace is one of the most obvious decisions to be reserved for a popular assembly, as no state can fight a war without a reasonable amount of popular support;[3] and in Athens a constitutional document inscribed at the end of the fifth century but incorporating earlier measures included the making of war (and no doubt the concluding of peace) among actions which might not be taken ἄνευ τὸ δέμο τὸ Ἀθεναίον πλεθύοντος.[4] Professor Larsen, connecting the whole document with the original imposition of an oath on the boule, believes that in the few years between Cleisthenes' reform and the imposition of the oath the boule was able on its own authority to make peace and war, and to do the other things which it was later forbidden to do,[5] but I believe that what may have been stated in writing for the first time about the beginning of the fifth century must long before then have been customary. Under the rule of προβούλευσις, as interpreted at Athens, the boule could in theory deny the people the chance to make peace or war, but I do not believe that it would have occurred to the bouleutae to prevent a debate

---

[1] Cf. Ch. IV, p. 157. ὁρῶ γὰρ ὡς τὰ πόλλ' ἐνίους οὐκ εἰς τοὺς αἰτίους, ἀλλ' εἰς τοὺς ὑπὸ χεῖρα μάλιστα τὴν ὀργὴν ἀφιέντας (D. VI. *Phil. ii.* 34—on a different matter).

[2] D. XXII. *Andr.* 17–20.   [3] Notice, for example, T. III. 27–8.

[4] *IG* i² 114, l. 35 in the enumeration of H. T. Wade-Gery, *BSA* xxxiii 1932–3, 113–22. I discuss this inscription in the appendix to Ch. IV, pp. 195–9, and argue:

(i) that δῆμος πληθύων means simply 'people in assembly', and that clauses in which this phrase rather than δῆμος alone is used are likely to be older than 450 B.C., but that the whole document need not represent a single enactment, with a single date; and

(ii) that the imposition of an oath (whose text was given at the beginning of this inscription) on the boule in 501/0 does not justify the inference that anything which the boule then swore not to do it had previously been allowed to do (that is, I regard the oath as consolidating Cleisthenes' reform, not as modifying it).

[5] *Representative Government*, 15–18.

for which there was a genuine desire.[1] It was the demos again which decided major questions of strategy: the Sicilian expedition of 415[2] and the Euboean war of 349/8[3] will suffice as examples. Specific questions of tactics, naturally, had to be decided by the generals on the spot, though they were accountable like any other officers of state for their decisions. It seems to have been the particular responsibility of the boule to ensure that all the necessary equipment, both human and inanimate, was available for fighting a war.

For the army the boule's responsibility was slight. Hoplites were expected to provide their own armour (in the Lycurgan period they were each presented with a shield and a spear at the end of their first year of service as ephebi[4]), and were called up by the generals, without a special δοκιμασία.[5] But the registers on which the call-up was based were the ληξιαρχικὰ γραμματεῖα, and the boule checked the enrolment of citizens in these when they came of age.[6] The boule was also involved to some extent in the young citizens' period of national service as ephebi. Though the institution is likely to be older, the ephebia is first directly attested in 334/3, and it was no doubt extensively reorganized after Chaeronea:[7] as described in the *Athenaion Politeia* it constituted a serious programme of military training, apparently for all young citizens of hoplite census,[8] and on the completion of their first year's training the ephebi gave a display of their prowess to the ecclesia before going out to guard the frontiers of Attica during their second year.[9] Our only clue to the involvement of the boule at this time is the inscription of 334/3 for the ephebi of the tribe Cecropis, from which it appears that honours were decreed by their tribe, the boule, and two demes.[10] In the Hellenistic period ephebic service ceased to be compulsory, and became little more than a hobby of the aristocratic, providing physical education and a lengthy programme of religious observances,[11] and the parade before the assembly now gave way to an ἀπόδειξις before the boule.[12] For the cavalry the boule checked

---

[1] Though Aristophanes was prepared to consider it as a comic possibility: *Ach.* 26–39. Cf. Ch. II, pp. 57–8 and p. 58 n. 1.

[2] T. vi. 8–26.   [3] D. XXI. *Mid.* 162–3.   [4] *A.P.* 42. iv.

[5] [Lys.] XIV. *Alc. i.* 6, XV. *Alc. ii.* 7, cf. D.S. xi. 81. iv.

[6] *A.P.* 42. i–ii, etc. I discuss this δοκιμασία in Ch. IV, pp. 171–4.

[7] *IG* ii² 1156, 1189. On the date of the institution see the discussions cited in Ch. IV, p. 173 n. 6.

[8] So Beloch, *Klio* v 1905, 351; *GG²*, iii. ii. 402; Gomme, *Population of Athens*, 11; Jones, 82. *A.P.* 42 and Lyc. *Leocr.* 76 imply that ephebic service was compulsory for all Athenians: I find it incredible that the thetes should have been subjected to a two-year programme of hoplite training, but my incredulity is not shared by Pélékidis, *Histoire de l'éphébie attique*, 113–14, cf. Forbes, *Greek Physical Education*, 128 with n. 1.   [9] *A.P.* 42. iii–v.

[10] *IG* ii² 1156, 64.   [11] Cf. Pélékidis, op. cit., part iii.

[12] The earliest instance is *Hesp.* vii 20, 17–18 (258/7).

the lists drawn up by the καταλογεῖς, and held a δοκιμασία also of the πρόδρομοι and ἄμιπποι (special classes of foot-soldiers who fought with the cavalry); it also checked the fitness of the horses themselves for use in battle.[1]

The boule's main duty in enabling the city to fight its wars was the provision of ships and equipment for the navy:

ἐπιμελεῖται δὲ καὶ τῶν πεποιημένων τριήρων καὶ τῶν σκευῶν καὶ τῶν νεωσοίκων, καὶ ποιεῖται καινὰς [[δὲ]]* τριήρεις ἢ τετρήρεις, ὁποτέρας ἂν ὁ δῆμος χειροτονήσῃ, καὶ σκεύη ταύταις καὶ νεωσοίκους· χειροτονεῖ δ' ἀρχιτέκτονας ὁ δῆμος ἐπὶ τὰς ναῦς. ἂν δὲ μὴ παραδῶσιν ἐξειργασμένα ταῦτα τῇ νέᾳ βουλῇ, τὴν δωρεὰν οὐκ ἔστιν αὐτοῖς λαβεῖν· ἐπὶ γὰρ τῆς ὕστερον βουλῆς λαμβάνουσιν. ποιεῖται δὲ τὰς τριήρεις, δέκα ἄνδρας ἐξ αὐ[τῆς] ἑλομένη τριηροποιούς.[2]

The corrupt δὲ which I asterisk in this passage has been emended by some editors to yield a numeral (4 or 10), in which case our author will be specifying a fixed annual quota of new ships.[3] There are two other texts which seem to point to a fixed annual quota: Diodorus credits Themistocles with a target of twenty ships a year after the Persian Wars,[4] and the Anonymus Argentinensis is restored in lines 9–11 with a decision of the boule[5] or order to the boule[6] to build ten ships a year (at what date is not clear, but the text is part of a commentary on Demosthenes, XXII. *Against Androtion*). Diodorus' note comes at the end of a series of stories, involving many improbabilities, about Themistocles' successes after the Persian Wars, and although it cannot be dismissed as obviously false it would be dangerous to rely at all heavily on it. The Anonymus Argentinensis has been much discussed in recent years for its remarks on Athenian finance and building in the time of Pericles, and the controversy has emphasized that the length of line and the reliability of the author are alike uncertain. The version produced in 1957 runs as follows:

[— θαλάσσης δ' ὅπως ἂν κρατ]ῶσι, τὴν βουλὴν τῶν παλαιῶν τριή-
[ρων ἐπιμελεῖσθαι ὥστε ὑγιεῖς παραδι]δόναι, καινὰς δ' ἐπιναυπηγεῖν ἑκάσ-
[του ἐνιαυτοῦ πρὸς ταῖς ὑπαρχούσαις δ]έκα.

(This is followed by a fresh lemma.) δ]έκα has been read by all editors,[7] but their confidence does not seem justified by the photograph which

---

[1] A.P. 49. i–ii, etc. For these δοκιμασίαι see again Ch. IV, pp. 174–5.   [2] A.P. 46. i.

[3] The δὲ was first deleted by Kenyon, followed by Blass, Sandys, Opperman, and Mathieu and Haussoulier, cf. Gilbert, 278–9 n. 3; δ' was read by Keil; δέκα by Thalheim, Kolbe, and Wilcken, cf. Busolt and Swoboda, 1032, Miltner, RE, vii A, 121.

[4] D.S. xi. 43. iii.   [5] ATL, i, T 9, and ii, D 13, as amalgamated in HMA, p. 51.

[6] H. T. Wade-Gery and B. D. Meritt, Hesp. xxvi 1957, 164, using a markedly longer line than previous reconstructions.

[7] e.g. Keil, Anonymus Argentinensis, 74–5; Kolbe, AM xxvi 1901, 411–13; Wilcken, Hermes xlii 1907, 387–9, cf. 399–402. Keil dotted the ε, but nowhere discussed the reading; Wilcken printed the ε as certain. The usual interpretation is accepted in a recent study by S. K. Eddy, GR&BS ix 1968.

Professors Wade-Gery and Meritt published in 1957,[1] and examination of this and of a new photograph which has been taken for me suggests that, while the κ and α cannot be seriously doubted, the first surviving letter is not likely to be ε (and ought perhaps to be ο), and between this and the κ there is an appreciable space, which could have contained a narrow letter (there are marks in the space which could but need not be part of an ι). I would therefore read]ο[.]κα.[2] But even if δ]έκα is correct it is not inevitable that this should denote the number of triremes to be built in a year: in 1901 Kolbe restored the text with a reference to the ten trieropoei.[3] It may be significant that neither *hypothesis* to Demosthenes' speech *Against Androtion* attempts to give a figure for the boule's shipbuilding requirements;[4] and we cannot extract from *IG* ii² 1611 information on the numbers of ships actually built in different years before the Social War, for we do not know the names, classification, and building-dates of all the 283 ships[5] which ought to have been mentioned in the complete text, and we do know that lines 106 sqq. do not exhaust the list of ἐξαίρετοι.[6] Two doubtful texts and a story in Diodorus are a poor basis for a general theory. There may well have been times when a programme was adopted that would cover several years, but I think it more likely that the normal practice was for the demos to be asked to approve a figure each year.

Our only other references to the men and procedures involved in ship-building are found in fifth-century inscriptions. A decree dated *c.* 435 mentions officials called νεοροί, who are involved in some way with men who have lost equipment, and contains two references to [ηοι ναυπ]εγοὶ ηοι ἐκ τὸ νεορίο.[7] Another document, slightly later, has a reference to [τρι]εροποιοί;[8] the next part of the inscription is concerned with the numbers of men required for certain tasks; we then meet [ηο τρι]έραρχος

---

[1] *Hesp.* xxvi 1957, facing p. 164.

[2] I have obtained this photograph through the co-operation of Professor J. Schwartz and Mr. R. G. Maber, and Dr. J. D. Thomas has kindly examined with me this photograph, another taken for Professor B. R. I. Sealey (lent to me by Dr. D. M. Lewis), and the photograph published in *Hesp.* xxvi 1957. Schwartz's opinion, based on an examination of the papyrus, is that 'le *kappa* est absolument sûr et il est précédé d'une lettre ronde que l'on est tout naturellement porté à lire *epsilon*.'

[3] Cf. p. 115 n. 7 above. He accepted Keil's readings and restored:

τριή-
[ρων τῶν ἔτι πλωΐμων ἐπιμελ]ε[ῖ]σθαι, καινὰς δ' ἐπιναυπηγεῖν ἑκατὸ[ν]
[ἑλομένην ἐξ αὐτῆς ἄνδρας δ]έκα.

[4] Cf. D. XXII. Andr., hyp. i. 1, hyp. ii. 8.   [5] *IG* ii² 1611, 9.

[6] G. L. Cawkwell, *C&M* xxiii 1962, 41–2, arguing against D. M. Lewis, *BSA* xlix 1954, 44. Even if full details of the ἐξαίρετοι had survived, we do not know when any of the πρῶται, δεύτεραι, and τρίται were built.

[7] *IG* i² 74, cf. *SEG* x 41: ναυπεγοί, ll. 23, 31.   [8] *IG* i² 73, 4.

καὶ ho κυ[βερνέτες] ;[1] and the inscription ends with penalties for offenders, to be imposed by [hοι ἐπιμε]λόμενοι τὸ νεορίο, and orders for publication. Neither inscription mentions the boule. More sense can be extracted from a decree of c. 409/8:

τ[ὸ]ς κοπέας hὸς ἔγαγον ο[ἴκοθεν δ]-
[όντον τοῖς τριε]ροποιοῖς, κ[α]ὶ hοι τριεροποιοὶ ε[ὐθὺς παρ]-
[αλαβόντες τιθ]έντον ἐς τὸ να[υ]πέγιον· καὶ ἐὰν δέ[ονται ἄλλ]-
[ο τινὸς hοι στ]ρατεγοί, χρόσθο[ν φρ]άζοντες τêι β[ολêι καὶ h]-
[άμα ἀποδιδόν]τες τὲν τεταγμέ[νεν] τιμέ[ν]· καὶ hο[ι ναυπεγοὶ]
[λογιζέσθον το]ῖς τριεροποιο[ῖς τὰ τε]ταγμέν[α].[2]

I have mentioned already for its financial significance the decree of 407/6 which seems to have ordered the generals to borrow money from the apodectae and give it to the ναυπηγοί for shipbuilding, and the trieropoei to repay this in due course.[3] The decree continues by ordering [the generals] to see that those responsible go to Macedon to [man the ships],[4] and [the boule] to see that the newly built ships are to be brought to Athens and [dispatched with an expedition to Ionia].[5] Where so much depends on restoration we must be extremely cautious, but mention of the trieropoei and the boule provides a link with the *Athenaion Politeia*, and there are no indications that this aspect of Athenian naval organization underwent any substantial change between the late fifth century and the late fourth. The number of ships to be built, and the choice of the ἀρχιτέκτονες whose expert knowledge would be required, were left to the demos, but the work done by the ναυπηγοί was supervised by the boule through ten of its members appointed as trieropoei, who *inter alia* administered the funds made available for shipbuilding.[6] I am not eager to extend outside the period of the Peloponnesian War the involvement of the generals in work of this kind.[7]

The ἐπιμεληταὶ τῶν νεωρίων had duties somewhat analogous to those of the sacred treasurers:[8] it is now established that they existed at the

---

[1] Ibid. 13–14.   [2] *SEG* x 131, 8–13.
[3] *SEG* x 138, 4–9: cf. p. 100 and nn. 4–5 above. Cf. *SEG* x 226, 11 sqq. (largely restored), where the sacred treasurers in 431/0 provide money for the ναυπεγοί and trieropoei.
[4] *SEG* x 138, 9–14.   [5] Ibid. 14–20.
[6] The funds must have been voted by the assembly—presumably a special vote for each consignment of ships in the fifth century and in the fourth an allocation in the μερισμός (which can have been a regular sum only if there was a regular quota). Meritt and Wade-Gery restore in ll. 17–18 of the Anonymus Argentinensis a note that money for building triremes was voted by the boule (*Hesp.* xxvi 1957, 164, cf. 177); earlier editors (e.g. Wilcken, *Hermes* xlii 1907, 407–9) did not attempt to restore a full text of this section.
[7] Cf. Ch. I, pp. 43–6.
[8] There is a full treatment of the epimeletae by G. Glotz, *DA*, ii. i. 669. i–673. i. For the boule's interest in the dockyards cf. O.O. iii. 2.

end of the fifth century,[1] but they are best known from the records which they published in the second and third quarters of the fourth century, which show them to be custodians of ships, equipment, and all that the dockyards contained. These things they received from their predecessors and handed on to their successors; they supplied them to trierarchs and attempted to recover them from trierarchs. They did not maintain a large treasury, but any money which they exacted went either directly[2] or indirectly[3] to the apodectae, to be used in the general μερισμός. Actual decisions as to what should be done with the equipment in the dockyards seem normally to have emanated from the boule. In 357/6 when various trierarchs were having difficulty in obtaining ships' equipment from their predecessors they complained to the ἀποστολεῖς and the boule, and the boule decreed that they were to recover the equipment in any way possible; when one of the previous year's trierarchs, Theophemus, still refused to surrender his equipment he was prosecuted by εἰσαγγελία before the boule for impeding the dispatch of the fleet.[4] From the navy lists we see that a decree of the boule authorized trierarchs to take over hanging tackle for their ships;[5] another decree of the boule authorized a ship which had been returned after repair to be taken over by another trierarch;[6] and a quadrireme was provided, very probably for Miltiades' voyage to the Adriatic, in a decree of the boule apparently passed under a clause allowing it to fill any gaps which appeared in the original decree of the demos.[7] The boule of 335/4 provided 256 ὑπο-ζώματα for the ships,[8] while the boule of 326/5 sold 214 ὑποβλήματα in accordance with a law of Hegemon;[9] other sales were made on the orders of the boule,[10] and we may suspect either a standing or a particular order from the boule when the epimeletae sold rotten equipment and bought new.[11] Unsound equipment did not always have to be sold: we have four references to the boule's authorizing the ταμίας τῶν τριηροποιϊκῶν to take 56 masts for the slaves clearing the cliff, the wood for 37 yard-arms and 16 masts for the slaves assigned to the stadium, and 406 worm-eaten and useless oars for slaves.[12] The second decree for Methone refers to τὰς ἐν τôι νεορίοι ἕ[δρας], presumably of the boule,[13] and it is likely that the boule

---

[1] *SEG* x 142, 5, 6 (*c.* 406).   [2] e.g. *IG* ii² 1627, 214–16.
[3] e.g. *IG* ii² 1628, 339 sqq. Further references, *DA*, II. i. 672. ii with n. 156.
[4] [D.] XLVII. *Ev. et Mnes.*, esp. 33, 41–2. On the misdeeds of Theophemus see Ch. IV, pp. 154–6.   [5] *IG* ii² 1609, 111.   [6] *IG* ii² 1623, 200 sqq.
[7] *IG* ii² 1629, 272 sqq.; cf. the enabling clause, 264–9.
[8] *IG* ii² 1627, 49–51; 1628, 231–3; 1629, 358–61.   [9] *IG* ii² 1628, 297 sqq.
[10] *IG* ii² 1629, 417–20, 1133–6; 1631, 196–9, 326 sqq.   [11] *IG* ii² 1629, 430–6.
[12] *IG* ii² 1627, 374–95; 1628, 533–51; 1629, 1010–29; 1631, 237–51.
[13] M&L 65, 53.

watched the epimeletae as closely as it watched the state's financial officers.

No clear distinction can be drawn between the rights of the boule and those of the demos in this aspect of naval administration. In the 320s various items of military equipment in 'the large building by the gates' were for some reason the responsibility of the epimeletae;[1] in 323/2 they were transferred to the general for the Piraeus κατὰ ψήφισμα βουλῆς καὶ δήμου.[2] The various trierarchs in Miltiades' Adriatic fleet were authorized by a decree of the demos to take two extra ὑποζώματα τῶν ἐγλυθέντων.[3] We may have another example of intervention by the assembly in the rubric, τάδε ἀπελάβομεν σκεύη παρὰ τριηράρχων κατὰ ψήφισμα δήμου, ὃ εἶπεν Δημόφιλ Ἀχαρνεύς,[4] but the circumstances are not disclosed, and Demophilus' decree may have been of fairly general application.[5]

On one occasion the boule made a special appointment for naval matters. One of our naval documents, very unlike the usual records of the epimeletae, contains a list of exactions from officials who had defaulted over a period of thirty years: τάδε παρὰ τῶν ἀρξάντων ἐν τοῖς νεωρίοις εἰσπέπρακται ἐπὶ Εὐβούλου ἄρχοντος καὶ Λυκίσκου καὶ Πυθοδότου καὶ Σωσιγένους (345/4–342/1).[6] Most of the ἄρξαντες were epimeletae or ταμίαι τῶν τριηροποιϊκῶν, but in the middle of the list we find Μνησικλῆς Κολλυ, αἱρεθεὶς ἐκ τῆς βουλῆς: ἐπὶ Ἀρχίο (346/5).[7] Another man mentioned is Εὐθύμαχος Ε[—], ταμίας γενόμενος ἐς τὰ νεώρια [ἐπὶ Θε]μιστοκλέου[s ἄρχο] (347/6):[8] this man seems to have done work which would normally have been done by the epimeletae, and, since the epimeletae are not attested between 348/7 and 334/3 or later, Dr. D. M. Lewis has suggested that in the heyday of the theoric officials the epimeletae may for a time have been replaced by other officials.[9]

A decree of the assembly, preserved in one of the navy lists, illustrates the responsibility of the boule when a fleet was sent out:[10]

The epimeletae were to give the trierarchs their ships and equipment, and the trierarchs were to be ready to sail by a specified date: gold crowns were offered to the first three. A court was to meet on two specified days under the general for the symmories, to hear pleas from the trierarchs.

(After a statement of the aim of the colony, there is a lacuna in the text.)[11]

---

[1] IG ii² 1627, 279 sqq.; 1628, 501 sqq.; 1629, 976 sqq.　　　[2] IG ii² 1631, 212 sqq.
[3] IG ii² 1629, 11–15, 31–6, 53–7, 99–104, 113–23, 133–8, 152–7, 277–97 marg.
[4] IG ii² 1631, 655–8.
[5] Similarly the decree cited in [D.] XLVII. Ev. et Mnes. 21 probably made general provisions for the working of Periander's law.
[6] IG ii² 1622, 379–85.　　　[7] Ibid. 420–2.　　　[8] Ibid. 444–8.
[9] See Additional Note D, pp. 239–40.　　　[10] IG ii² 1629 = Tod 200, 165–170–271 (325/4).
[11] The lacuna must have included detailed provisions as to the fleet which Miltiades was to take with him: cf. ll. 165–9.

Any one who failed to do his duty would be fined 10,000 drachmae. The boule was to ἐπιμελεῖσθαι τοῦ ἀποστόλου, punishing disorderly trierarchs according to the laws, and for this purpose was to meet on the jetty every day until the fleet sailed. The demos was to elect ten ἀποστολεῖς to take charge of the dispatch καθάπερ τῆι βουλῆι προστέτακται.[1] For the efficient discharge of their duty the boule and prytanes might be awarded a gold crown. The boule might fill any deficiencies which appeared in the decree, so long as it did not annul the original provisions, and the decree was placed in the category, εἰς φυλακὴν τῆς χώρας.

ἀποστολεῖς seem to have been an extraordinary appointment, and are attested only in the fourth century. At the time of Theophemus' defiance of authority, in 357/6, they and the epimeletae were the εἰσάγουσα ἀρχή for trierarchs' disputes over equipment,[2] and when Theophemus lost his διαδικασία but made no attempt to return the equipment he was reported to the ἀποστολεῖς and the boule[3]—whereupon the boule tried to enforce the law and the ἀποστολεῖς dropped out of the picture. Aeschines[4] and the lexicographers[5] add nothing to our knowledge of this office. Crowns for efficient trierarchs were awarded by the boule-and-demos,[6] but it was the boule that decided who should receive them, and which inefficient trierarchs should be prosecuted in a δικαστήριον (for a heavier penalty than the boule itself could impose).[7] The summoning of the trierarchs from the list of those liable seems throughout the history of this liturgy to have been the duty of the generals (later, of the general for the symmories).[8] For a fifth-century dispatch we have fragments of decrees relating to the Sicilian expedition of 415: it is possible that the allied cities were to tell the boule how many sailors they could provide,[9] and the boule was to make a probouleuma(?) on whether the ships should be fitted out at the expense of the trierarchs, ἀπὸ τὸ τιμέματος, or of the state.[10]

The burdens of trierarchy were heavy, and attempts to avoid or mitigate them gave rise to a large number of lawsuits. I discuss this side of the

---

[1] τῆι βουλῆι is, I think, best interpreted as a dative of the agent, so that this clause will place the ἀποστολεῖς under the supervision of the boule.

[2] [D.] XLVII. *Ev. et Mnes.* 26.   [3] Ibid. 33.

[4] A. II. *F.L.* 177. The office is not mentioned by Demosthenes, *pace* Jacoby and others: the passages cited in the commentary on Phil. 328 F 63 refer to dispatches but not to dispatchers.

[5] Texts conveniently assembled at Phil. 328 F 63 and commentary.

[6] Cf. *IG* ii² 1953.   [7] D. LI. *Cor. Tri.* 4. Cf. Ch. IV, pp. 153–4.

[8] Ar. *Eq.* 912–18 with schol., D. XXXV. *Lacr.* 48, XXXIX. *Boe. Nom.* 8, *A.P.* 61. i; cf. the 'decree of Themistocles', M&L 23, 18–23, with the remarks of M. H. Jameson, *Hist.* xii 1963, 395–7: when the preliminary lists had been drawn up the boule and the generals were to πληροῦν the ships (ll. 35–40).

[9] Tod 77 A, 5–6 (not restored at M&L 78, *b* 5–6).

[10] Tod 77 A, 10–12 (not restored at M&L 78, *c* 1–3).

boule's naval activity in Chapter IV,[1] and here I will simply anticipate my main conclusions. Usually but not invariably cases involving failure to return equipment were decided by a δικαστήριον, but when the ship itself came in question the case was heard by the boule. When Theophemus was charged by his successor with failing to surrender equipment an appeal was made to the boule after the court's judgement had proved ineffectual; but there was no higher authority than the boule, and when its decree was ignored the trierarch could only go back with further complaints. Naval matters were among those issues of public importance which could be made the subject of an εἰσαγγελία to the boule, and we shall see that restrictions on the boule's power of punishment did not prevent it from decreeing a penalty in excess of its own powers for certain offences.

I end this section with a puzzle. In § 17 of the speech *Against Androtion* Demosthenes begins to consider an argument which may be put forward by Androtion, that the failure to build the required number of ships should be blamed not on the boule but on the ταμίας τῶν τριηροποιϊκῶν, who absconded with two and a half talents. He points out that the boule is given its δωρεά not for good intentions but for results, and if the ships have not been built the reason for this is irrelevant; but in any case, ὅτι τοίνυν οὐδ᾽ αἴτιος ἄλλος οὐδεὶς ἀνθρώπων ἐστὶν τοῦ μὴ πεποιῆσθαι τὰς ναῦς, τοῦτο σαφῶς ὑμῖν ἐπιδείξω· ἀνελοῦσα γὰρ ἡ βουλὴ τὸν νόμον, τοῦτον ἐχειροτόνησεν αὐτή.[2] The scholiast's explanation of the passage seems to be the only one possible:

ΑΝΕΛΟΥΣΑ ΚΤΛ. ἐὰν δὲ στίξωμεν ἄχρι τοῦ "τὸν νόμον", τοιοῦτόν ἐστι, καταφρονήσασα ἡ βουλὴ τοῦ νόμου κελεύοντος γνώμῃ τοῦ δήμου χειροτονεῖσθαι τὸν ταμίαν, αὐτὴ ἑαυτῇ τοῦτον ἐχειροτόνησε καθ᾽ ἑαυτήν φησι.[3]

The ταμίας τῶν τριηροποιϊκῶν does not figure in the *Athenaion Politeia*'s list of elected financial officers,[4] or indeed anywhere in that treatise, but there were other elected treasurers in Athens, such as the treasurers of the Paralus and the Ἄμμωνος,[5] and so long as his office was not deemed to be περὶ τὴν ἐγκύκλιον διοίκησιν there is no reason why the scholiast should not be right about this treasurer. The boule can hardly have made the appointment without reference to the demos (given so excellent a reason for not crowning the boule, Demosthenes would surely devote more than

---

[1] Pp. 153–8.
[2] D. XXII. *Andr.* 20. The final αὐτή is Jurinus' generally accepted emendation for the αὐτήν or αὐτῇ of the MSS.
[3] Schol. D. XXII. *Andr.* 20 (not in Sauppe; 679. 15, Dindorf; quoted O.C.T. app.).
[4] *A.P.* 43. i.
[5] *A.P.* 61. vii, cf. D. XXI. *Mid.* 171.

one sentence to it) : perhaps it was normal for a free election to be held under an open probouleuma, but on this occasion the boule had recommended a candidate for the approval of the ecclesia.[1]

(iii) *Public Works*

ἔκρινεν δέ ποτε καὶ τὰ παραδείγματα καὶ τὸν πέπλον ἡ βουλή, νῦν δὲ τὸ δικαστήριον τὸ λαχόν· ἐδόκουν γὰρ οὗτοι καταχαρίζεσθαι τὴν κρίσιν. καὶ τῆς ποιήσεως τῶν Νικῶν καὶ τῶν ἄθλων τῶν εἰς τὰ Παναθήναια συνεπιμελεῖται μετὰ τοῦ ταμίου τῶν στρατιωτικῶν.[2]

It appears from the inscriptions relating to public works that the change to which the author alludes must have been made not long before the *Athenaion Politeia* was written, and that there may have been an earlier change which he does not mention. In the fifth century many matters of detail were decided by the ecclesia, with the boule playing simply its normal probouleutic part. The first decree for Athena Νίκη enacted that the ἱερόν of the goddess should be given a door to be designed by Callicrates and that a temple and stone altar should be built to his design;[3] the rider of Hestiaeus ordered the boule to elect three of its members to co-operate with Callicrates in drawing up the ξυγγραφαί and submitting them to the boule,[4] and may perhaps have ended by requiring the boule to submit them to the demos.[5] Another decree of the mid fifth century gave Callicrates the commission for protective work on the Acropolis, and specified that the work was to be completed in sixty days.[6] The demos is more clearly concerned with details in two slightly later decrees. The proposer of a decree dated about 435 left it to the assembly to decide whether the [doorway] to the temple (of Athena Νίκη?) should be of [bronze] or ivory [and gold],[7] and a decree of 422/1

---

[1] In Ch. II, pp. 85–6, I argue from *IG* ii² 145 that the herald of the boule and demos was appointed by the ecclesia, which could accept a recommendation made in a specific probouleuma.

Dr. D. M. Lewis has suggested the following alternative solution. There is some evidence to support a theory that the office rotated among the tribes:

I	346/5	*IG* ii² 1622, 387–90;
V	332/1	*IG* ii² 1627, 23–4, 374–5; 1628, 3–6, 83–6;
IX	328/7	*IG* ii² 1628, 11–14; 1629, 275; 1632, 14–15;

(but the treasurers for 363/2 and 359/8 were both from X). Such an officer would probably be appointed by lot, and the boule's offence would then lie in having a man elected. But this is incompatible with the scholium cited on p. 121 n. 3 above, and Demosthenes' emphasis seems to me to be on the part played by the boule rather than on the fact of election.

[2] *A.P.* 49. iii : in 60. i the athlothetae appointed to manage the Panathenaea τοὺς ἀμφορεῖς ποιοῦνται μετὰ τῆς βουλῆς.

[3] M&L 44 (= Tod 40), 1–13.   [4] Ibid. 14 sqq.
[5] So Tod, vol. i, p. 80.   [6] HMA 45.   [7] *IG* i² 88, 1–5.

gave detailed instructions for the building of a bridge.[1] About 432/1, when the state agreed to make a contribution of up to 500 drachmae towards the building of a shrine to Apollo Δήλιος, the architect was to be summoned before the boule and ecclesia.[2] In 421/0, however, the boule may have been made fully responsible for having an altar set up to Hephaestus.[3]

In the fourth century, when the ὅροι of the ἱερὰ ὀργάς at Eleusis needed to be replaced, a committee of five bouleutae and ten other citizens was appointed to decide where the ὅροι should be sited,[4] and according to the restorations in the *Corpus* the proedri and the poletae were to make συγγραφαί for the work, and to see that the ὅροι were placed correctly.[5] συγγράφειν and ἐπιμελεῖσθαι, however, were duties which did not normally fall either to the proedri or to the poletae, and we must reject this restoration and admit that it is not clear who did have these duties on this occasion.[6] Only in the wall-building νόμος usually dated to 337/6[7] do we find the 'previous' procedure of the *Athenaion Politeia*: both for the repair of the walls[8] and for work in the harbour[9] συγγραφαί were to be drawn up by the regular salaried architects (met here for the first time), and by any one else who wished, and the boule was to decide which συγγραφαί should be adopted. When further work on the walls was undertaken in 307/6 an architect was to be elected by the demos,[10] but there are also three references to architects (plural),[11] and the text is not sufficiently complete to show any difference in function between the one architect and the architects, nor even to make it certain that the boule was no longer required to approve the συγγραφαί. At one point in the decree editors have given us the restoration,

ὅ[ρκωι πι]σ[τῶ]σαι ἐν τῆι [β]ουλ[ῆι κ]ατὰ [τὸν ν]όμ[ον],[12]

but since the previous line mentions contractors and the two following lines seem to be concerned with the punishment of offenders I imagine

---

[1] *IG* i² 81.   [2] *SEG* xxi 37, *a* 7–10.   [3] *IG* i² 84, 38–9.
[4] *IG* ii² 204, 5–12, cf. 69–70, 74 sqq. (352/1).
[5] Ibid. 67–70.   [6] Cf. Ch. I, pp. 27–8.
[7] *IG* ii² 244. G. L. Cawkwell, *JHS* lxxxiii 1963, 66 with n. 109, would prefer to date this a little earlier and connect it with the activities of Eubulus, and his argument may be strengthened by the appearance of the antigrapheus in l. 23 (cf. Additional Note D, p. 238).
[8] *IG* ii² 244, 6–10.   [9] Ibid. 40–2.   [10] *IG* ii² 463, 6–7, cf. 9.
[11] Ibid. 21, 32, 117. In the *IG* text the architects, both singular and plural, are linked with ὁ ἐπὶ τῇ διοικήσει, though the only evidence for this is that in l. 9 the architect is followed by καί and that in l. 36 ὁ ἐπὶ τῇ διοικήσει is combined with the poletae. An additional fragment (*Hesp.* ix 9) makes it clear that at any rate the division of the work into sections (117–18) was made by the architects alone, and all the restorations of this combination disappear in the latest text, Maier, *GMbi* 11.   [12] *IG* ii² 463, 23, retained by Maier.

that some kind of report or the checking of accounts is more likely than the pledging of oaths.

Until the end of the fourth century (after which we have no further evidence) contracts for public works were made by the poletae, one of the many boards working under the supervision of the boule.[1] The poletae placed the contract for making the door to the ἱερόν of Athena Νίκη,[2] and also the contract for Callicrates' work on the Acropolis—in the latter case ὅπος ἄριστα καὶ εὐτελέστατα σκευάσαι.[3] Cheapness was always important for a state whose finances were as precarious as Athens', and we find a further reference to economy in the second decree of Callias[4] and a clear desire to spend [ὀ]λιγίστον χρεμάτον in the surviving part of the 'spring-house decree'.[5] The poletae again worked with the boule to make the contract[6] (but probably not to supervise the work) when the ὅροι were renewed at Eleusis, but by the end of the fourth century a change seems to have taken place. In two documents dated after the middle of the century, one (very fragmentary) relating to the temple of Zeus Σωτήρ in the Piraeus,[7] the other a contract for work on Delos,[8] there are references to the placing of a contract in a δικαστήριον, and it may be that it is to the placing of contracts rather than to the approval of the architects' plans that we should refer the Athenaion Politeia's all too brief note on the boule and παραδείγματα. In 307/6 the boule may not have been involved, but the poletae were, in conjunction with the new financial officer: [— καθ' ἃς ἐξέδοσαν τὰ ἔργα] οἱ πωληταὶ καὶ ὁ ἐπὶ τεῖ διοικήσει Ἅβρω[ν Λυκ]ούργου Βουτ[ά]δης.[9]

The Athenaion Politeia seems also to have credited the boule with the supervision of public buildings: ἐξετάζει δὲ (sc. ἡ βουλὴ) καὶ τὰ οἰκο-δομήματα τὰ δημόσια πάντα, κἄν τις ἀδικεῖν αὐτῇ δόξῃ, τῷ τε δήμῳ τοῦτον ἀποφαίνει καὶ καταγνοῦσα παραδίδωσι δικαστηρίῳ.[10] If the reference is to buildings already standing we have no evidence which can be used to check the statement, but it is at any rate possible that the author's allusion is to work in progress. In the fifth century the immediate supervision of any major public work was entrusted to an annually

---

[1] Cf. pp. 96–8.   [2] M&L 44, 5–8.   [3] HMA 45, 8–11.

[4] M&L 58 B, 10–11, has ATL's restoration [εὐτελέστατα]; Wilhelm's text (quoted in the apparatus) does not, but he agreed that further expenditure on the Acropolis was to be severely limited.   [5] ATL D 19/HMA 69, 7.

[6] IG ii² 204, 66–7. Cf. Ch. I, pp. 27–8 and p. 28 n. 1.   [7] IG ii² 1669, 8, 21, etc.

[8] IG ii² 1678, 27–8. This must antedate the loss of Delos in 314.

[9] IG ii² 463, 36. Cf. pp. 106–7 with 106 n. 7 above.

[10] A.P. 46. ii. On the καταγνοῦσα of the papyrus text see Ch. IV, p. 159 n. 1. The ἱερά whose ἐπιμέλεια is credited to the boule in O.O. iii. 2 are probably religious buildings rather than ceremonies.

changing board of epistatae: these were presumably elected by the
demos, though I know no direct evidence for this period.[1] The records
which the various boards have left on stone show that financial control
played an important part in their work.[2] This makes it very likely that the
boule watched over their activities: at any rate the logistae appointed
from the boule will have examined their accounts every prytany.[3] The
second decree of Callias is restored by the authors of *ATL* to make οἱ
ἐπιστάται co-operate with the treasurers of Athena and with the architect
in finishing the work on the Acropolis[4] (the text as restored by Wilhelm
would have the same general effect[5]); and, given a narrow fragment of a
contemporary decree which mentions the making of a doorway, the boule,
and one or more architects, Meritt restores on the basis of ten letters a 62-
letter line, requiring the epistatae to supervise the work as the boule shall
direct, and the epimeletae and the architect to co-operate with them![6]

In the fourth century we have clearer evidence for the popular election
of epistatae and for supervision by the boule. The wall-building νόμος to
be associated with Eubulus or Demosthenes contains the provision,

$$[\chi ειροτονῆσαι \ δὲ \ τὸν \ δῆμον \ αὐτίκα \ μάλα \ ἐπιστάτας \ δύο]$$
$$[ἄνδ]ρας \ ἐξ \ Ἀθηναίων \ ἀπάντων, \ οἵτινες \ ἐπιμελήσονται \ τῶν \ ἔργων.[7]$$

[When the work was complete,] the boule was to be given 500 drachmae
for a dedication and the [teichopoei and architects 300] from the teicho-
poeic fund.[8] Meanwhile the boule was required to meet for one day on the
λογισμός before payments were made, and to discuss some aspect of the
work one day in each prytany.[9] The boule was again involved in 307/6,
possibly to check accounts,[10] and the decree of this year may also confirm
the *Athenaion Politeia*'s claim that the boule had punitive powers in connection with public buildings.[11]

There already existed in the time of Demosthenes permanent, salaried
city architects:[12] in the Hellenistic period the office seems to have been
divided into departments. As early as 346 one ἀρχιτέκτων was responsible

---

[1] But the Eleusinian epistatae are known to have been elected: HMA 41, 7–13.

[2] *IG* i[2] 335 sqq., e.g. M&L 54 (chryselephantine Athena), 59 (Parthenon), 60 (Propylaea).

[3] Cf. p. 111 above. The boards of epistatae seem to have kept their accounts by the
bouleutic calendar: see Additional Note A, p. 227.

[4] M&L 58 B, 2–12.

[5] Extracts in M&L *apparatus*, p. 157, cf. *SEG* xii 18 and his article in *JHS* lxviii 1948.
I cannot, however, see why the *treasurers* should require the architect to produce a παράδειγμα:
Wilhelm offers this restoration of ll. 8–9 without comment in his final sentence (p. 129).

[6] *SEG* x 44, 3–6.

[7] *IG* ii[2] 244, 28–9. For the election of ἐπιστάται τῶν δημοσίων ἔργων cf. A. III. *Ctes.* 14.

[8] *IG* ii[2] 244 38–40. [9] Ibid. 26–7, 36–7. [10] Cf. pp. 123–4 and p. 123 n. 12 above.

[11] *IG* ii[2] 463, 25: cf. Ch. IV, p. 159 and n. 5. [12] *IG* ii[2] 244, 6, 40–1.

for the allocation of theatre seats,[1] but I know no instance of the title ἀρχιτέκτων ἐπὶ τὸ θέατρον vel simile quid. In inscriptions from the late third century onwards we find an ἀρχιτέκτων ἐπὶ τὰ ἱερά, who was responsible for religious buildings and properties, and the partitioning of the generals' duties, begun in the fourth century,[2] had by then produced a στρατηγὸς ἐπὶ τὴν παρασκευήν, who had the unmilitary duty of co-operating with this architect.[3] Twice in the third century this general was assisted by a committee on which the Areopagus and the demos as a whole were represented in checking the treasures of Asclepius,[4] and four decrees concerned with the repairing and recasting of temple plate entrusted the work to similar committees. When the priest of the Hero Doctor asked for a new οἰνοχόη to be made from the old dedications in the shrine, the priest, the στρατηγὸς ἐπὶ τὴν παρασκευήν and the ἀρχιτέκτων ἐπὶ τὰ ἱερά, as specialists, were to be joined by five laymen, two from the Areopagus and three from the whole citizen body, and (surprisingly) the finished vessel was to be dedicated in the name of the boule.[5] The same pattern is suggested by two other, more fragmentary decrees,[6] and at the end of the second century the shrine's plate was attended to by the three specialists and three bouleutae.[7] Another decree, of 161/0, calls on the ecclesia to appoint five citizens to work with the priest, the general, and the architect in order to repair a sanctuary, and this if it is correctly restored contains the latest example of the old kind of bouleutic control:

[—] ἐναντίον τῆ[ς βουλῆς παρ]αλαβεῖν δὲ αὐτοὺς καὶ τα[—].[8]

As we might expect, the boule was responsible for its own buildings and equipment: in a decree of 181/0 the boule honoured three of its members whom it had appointed to attend to bedding and other items in the Tholos.[9] In general, however, the boule now appears only in oligarchic

---

[1] D. XVIII. Cor. 28, cf. A. II. F.L. 55. This architect appears twice in inscriptions, IG ii² 456, 32–3; 792, 7–9.

[2] A.P. 61. i, cf. W. S. Ferguson, Klio ix 1909, 314–23. Professor Hammond suggests that the partitioning was begun in the fifth century, shortly after the Persian Wars (CQ² xix 1969, esp. 116–17, 142), but I think it dangerous to postulate a silence (apart from an uncertain reading in Lys. XXXII. Diog. 5) of more than a century.

[3] The office is not mentioned in A.P. 61. i. Ferguson noted that IG ii² 1487, 80–4, shows six στρατ[ηγῶν τῶν ἐπὶ τὴν τοῦ πολέμου παρασκ]ευὴν κεχει[ροτονημένων] in 307/6, and ll. 91 sqq. record the handing over of military equipment by generals to the treasurers of Athena in 306/5. Shortly afterwards the treasurers of Athena were abolished (cf. Ferguson, Treasurers of Athena, 126) and στρατηγὸς ἐπὶ τὴν παρασκευήν became a regular office (apparently so in IG ii² 682, 21–4 [296/5]). Ferguson suggested that this general was primarily responsible for military stores, some of which were kept in the temples, and through this came to be concerned with everything that was kept in the temples.   [4] Cf. p. 95 n. 8 above.

[5] IG ii² 839 (221/0): on the decrees concerning this shrine cf. pp. 95–6 above.

[6] IG ii² 841, 842.   [7] IG ii² 840.   [8] Hesp. xvi 64; I quote l. 15.

[9] Hesp. Supp. iv 1940, 137–41.

periods, providing the lay members of the superintending committee, or giving permission which at other times would have been given by the demos. In 52/1 the boule allowed the priest of Asclepius to do some necessary rebuilding at his own expense,[1] while the two 'oligarchic' inscriptions for ephebi contain decrees of the boule allowing the ephebi to set up a statue of their cosmetes[2] and after the time of Sulla a number of prytanies were permitted by the boule to set up a statue of their treasurer.[3]

Evidence in this section is very scanty, but we have seen the boule involved in the fifth and fourth centuries in the adoption of συγγραφαί, the making of contracts, and at any rate enjoying some financial oversight in conjunction with separate boards of epistatae. Lay representation of some kind continued at any rate to the end of the second century, but there seems to have been a gradual development from the fifth-century practice, whereby the work required might be specified in some detail by a decree of the ecclesia, towards the establishment of a Public Works department, headed by a general and salaried architects, which settled the details with the lay committee. Inscriptions do not attest the boule's close involvement after the fourth century, but in the Hellenistic period important buildings commonly owed their existence to private munificence rather than public expenditure, and there was therefore less need for detailed supervision of the work by the people's representatives.[4]

(iv) *Religion*

Much has been said already, in the sections on finance and public works, which illustrates the importance of the boule in religious affairs. It took a close interest in the coined and non-monetary treasures of the various temples, to the extent of assisting the sacred treasuries to recover sums due to them and (at least in one case) being consulted on expenditure. When temples were built or repaired the boule could be involved in the adoption of plans, and would play some part in making the contracts and supervising the work.

In the administration of festivals we commonly find priests co-operating with boards of ἱεροποιοί, usually ten in number, and these hieropoei were often provided by the boule. Hieropoei are attested at Eleusis from early in the fifth century, making sacrifices[5] and exacting dues from

---

[1] *IG* ii² 1046.   [2] *IG* ii² 1039. ii, 1043. ii.   [3] e.g. *P* 97.

[4] But in the second century A.D. the boule built the ἀγορανόμιον and dedicated it to Antoninus Pius: *IG* ii² 3391 with H. S. Robinson, *AJA*² xlvii 1943, 304–5, D. J. Geagan, *Hesp.* Supp. xii 1967, 78.

[5] *IG* i² 5, 2 (*c.* 475–450).

initiates;[1] in the law perhaps to be dated to 416/15[2] they were to receive first-fruits,[3] to combine with the architect in choosing the site for the granaries,[4] and after the sacrifices had been made to sell the remaining offerings and make a dedication in conjunction with the boule.[5] These men were styled ἱεροποιοὶ Ἐλευσινόθεν[6] or ἱεροποιοὶ Ἐλευσῖνι:[7] there is no fifth-century evidence on how they were appointed. Between 422 and 418 there were also epistatae, who were in charge of the χρήματα of the goddesses and received the proceeds from the sale of what was not needed for sacrifices;[8] but a century later the offerings were apparently received in the first instance by the epistatae, who provided the hieropoei (now designated ἱεροποιοὶ ἐκ βουλῆς) with what was needed for the sacrifices.[9] In the meantime the cult had been reorganized by a law of Chaeremonides, which had been modified in 353/2, and the modified law seems to have given the boule general responsibility for the offering of first-fruits and the performance of various rites.[10] Elter restored in the law of 353/2 a provision for the boule to appoint ten of its members as hieropoei,[11] and though this has not been retained in Sokolowski's recent text[12] Eleusinian hieropoei were certainly appointed by the boule in 341/0.[13]

The Eleusinian hieropoei were not the only ones provided by the boule. A decree of 421/0 regulating the Hephaestia provides for ten hieropoei to be appointed by lot from the δικασταί[14] and another ten by lot from the boule.[15] The hieropoei (presumably of both kinds) were to make the distributions of meat, and to take charge of the πομπή with power to impose fines of up to 50 drachmae or to prosecute the disorderly

---

[1] SEG x 6, 89–92 (c. 460).

[2] M&L 73: see above, p. 94 and especially n. 2.

[3] M&L 73, 8–10, 16–18, 34–5.   [4] Ibid. 10–12.   [5] Ibid. 40 sqq.

[6] Ibid. 9–10, 17–18. The title is given as ἱεροποιοὶ Ἐλευσινόθεν Ἐλευσινάδε by Oehler, RE, viii. 1585, but Ἐλευσινάδε is surely to be read with παραδιδόναι.

[7] IG i² 311, 18–19 (422–418).   [8] HMA 41 (after 450), IG i² 311.

[9] IG ii² 1672, 279 sqq.   [10] Cf. pp. 94–5 and p. 95 nn. 1–2 above.

[11] IG ii² 140 Add., cf. SIG³ 200, 25–6.   [12] Lois Sacrées (Suppl.), 13, cf. SEG xxi 253.

[13] IG ii² 1749, 80–4, honouring τοὺς ἱεροποιοὺς τοὺς τὰ μυστήρια ἱεροποιήσαντας Ἐλευσῖνι. All ten were members of the tribe Aegeis (which was presumably in prytany at the time of the festival); one of them was the treasurer of the prytany, and another was also a συλλογεὺς τοῦ δήμου. The honours for the συλλογεῖς were proposed by a ἱεροποιός; the honours for the hieropoei by a συλλογεύς; and honours for the ἱεροποιός who had proposed the honours for the συλλογεῖς by another ἱεροποιός: the proposer of the honours for the hieropoei also proposed the honours for the treasurer of the prytany. A friendly set of men.

Demosthenes addressed to (hypothetical) dicasts the following comment on Midias: ἐχειροτονήσατε τοῦτον . . . μυστηρίων ἐπιμελητὴν καὶ ἱεροποιόν ποτε καὶ βοώνην (D. XXI. Mid. 171). It is perhaps unwise to insist from this passage on the same mode of appointment to all three offices, but it is at any rate possible that before 353/2 the Eleusinian hieropoei were not appointed by the boule, and that Midias held office under the old dispensation.

In 329/8 the Eleusinian epistatae spent 70 drachmae on sacrificing an ἀρεστήριον to each of the two goddesses, in accordance with a decree of the boule proposed by Lycurgus (IG ii² 1672, 302).   [14] IG i² 84, 19–21.   [15] Ibid. 23–5.

in a δικαστήριον. Hieropoei κατ' ἐνιαυτόν received money from the treasurers of Athena for a hecatomb at the Great Panathenaea in 410/09,[1] and about 335 a decree provided for the administration of the Lesser Panathenaea by τοὺς ἱεροποιοὺς τοὺς διοικοῦντας τὰ Παναθήναια τὰ κατ' ἐνιαυτόν[2] (who like the hieropoei for the Hephaestia had punitive powers[3]). In neither of these cases do we know how the appointment was made. A decree of about 330 honoured the priest of Dionysus, certain other priests, and ten ἱεροποιοὶ αἱρεθέντες ὑπὸ τῆς βουλῆς for their sacrifices to Dionysus and the other gods, for the health and safety of the boule and demos of the Athenians and their children, their wives and their other possessions.[4] The author of the *Athenaion Politeia* knew two boards each of ten sortitive hieropoei:

τοὺς ἐπὶ τὰ ἐκθύματα καλουμένους οἳ τά τε μαντευτὰ ἱερὰ θύουσιν, κἄν τι καλλιερῆσαι δέῃ, καλλιεροῦσι μετὰ τῶν μάντεων;[5]

τοὺς κατ' ἐνιαυτὸν καλουμένους, οἳ θυσίας τέ τινας θύουσι καὶ τὰς πεντετηρίδας ἁπάσας διοικοῦσιν πλὴν Παναθηναίων:[6]

He goes on to list the quadrennial festivals involved—the Delian, the Brauronia, the Heraclea, and the Eleusinia (for none of which are hieropoei epigraphically attested); [νῦν] δὲ πρόσκειται [καὶ 'Η]φαίσ[τια] ἐπὶ Κηφισοφῶντος ἄρχοντος (329/8). Blass's restoration has been generally accepted, and has the advantage of mentioning a festival for which hieropoei are known to have existed, but there is no apparent reason why an old-established festival should have been brought into the cycle at this date. A more obvious candidate for admissions is the Amphiarea at Oropus, attested in 329/8,[7] but it seems impossible that Ἀμφιάρεια is what the scribe wrote.[8]

Hieropoeic duties seem also to have been performed by the συλλογεῖς τοῦ δήμου, a board probably of three men from each tribe, attested in the fourth century.[9] We possess a dedication by the συλλογεῖς of 324/3, who

---

[1] M&L 84, 6–7.   [2] IG ii² 334: title in ll. 31–2.   [3] Ibid. 34–5.
[4] IG ii² 410.   [5] A.P. 54. vi.   [6] A.P. 54. vii.   [7] IG vii 4254 = SIG³ 298.
[8] In reply to suggestions by Foucart and Wilhelm that Ἀμφιάρεια should be restored Keil quoted (in *Hermes* xxx 1895, 474) a letter from Kenyon stating that the restoration was impossible; and Dr. J. D. Thomas tells me that he would read ['Η]φαίστ[ια] from the 1891 facsimile. More recently Dr. D. M. Lewis has favoured the Amphiarea, and the suggestion has been mentioned by Dr. J. K. Davies, *JHS* lxxxvii 1967, 35 with n. 36.
[9] Cf. Ch. I, p. 21. For the number compare the three from Aegeis in 341/0 (IG ii² 1749, 75–9: cf. p. 128 n. 13 above) with Poll. viii. 104, Hes., Phot. τριάκοντα. Glotz, *The Greek City*, 189, suggested that one of the three was appointed from each trittys; but the three men named as συλλογεῖς in IG ii² 1749, 79, represent only two of W. E. Thompson's τριττύες τῶν πρυτάνεων, and only one Cleisthenic trittys.
IG ii² 1425, 126–30, records gold crowns dedicated by the συλλογεῖς in the treasury of Athena in 370/69 and 369/8 ('and perhaps annually thereafter'—D. M. Lewis, *BSA* xlix 1954, 45); IG ii² 2821 records a further dedication in 351/0.

have accorded special honours to one of their number who [ἱ]εροποίησεν τῆι Ἀθ[ηνᾶι]¹ and to another who [ἱεροποίησεν τῶι Διΐ] τῶι 'Ολυμπίωι,² and the connection of the συλλογεῖς with the Olympiea is confirmed by an inscription recording receipts from the sale of sacrificial victims' hides in the quadrennium 334/3–331/0: most of the money is provided by epi-meletae and hieropoei, but that from the Olympiea is paid by the συλλογεῖς τοῦ δήμου.³ Three decrees enacted in 335, two of the ecclesia and one of the boule, honour Phyleus, elected to an office of the boule and demos, and two συνάρχοντες.⁴ Köhler, with what has been described as *felici acumine*,⁵ made extensive restorations on the assumption that these three men were a tribal contingent of the thirty συλλογεῖς, being honoured for their hieropoeic duties, but how even Athenian laxity could describe the tribal contingent of a bouleutic sub-committee as χειροτ[ονηθέντες ἱεροποιεῖν τῆι τε] βουλῆι καὶ τῶι δήμωι⁶ I do not understand. The office was elective, and almost certainly triumviral, but that seems to be all that we can say about it.

Demosthenes performed hieropoeic duties when he was a member of the boule in 347/6:

εἴασε μέν μ' (sc. ὁ Μειδίας) εἰσιτητήρι' ὑπὲρ τῆς βουλῆς ἱεροποιῆσαι καὶ θῦσαι καὶ κατάρξασθαι τῶν ἱερῶν ὑπὲρ ὑμῶν καὶ ὅλης τῆς πόλεως, . . . περιεῖδε δὲ ταῖς σεμναῖς θεαῖς ἱεροποιὸν αἱρεθέντ' ἐξ Ἀθηναίων ἁπάντων τρίτον αὐτὸν καὶ καταρξά-μενον τῶν ἱερῶν.⁷

The boule certainly had its own religious observances, which we shall consider below,⁸ and it may well be that particular bouleutae were made responsible for these and designated hieropoei. The ἱεροποιοὶ ταῖς σεμναῖς θεαῖς are mentioned in the lexica also: according to Photius⁹ they were τὸν ἀριθμὸν ἀόριστοι, while the *Etymologicum Magnum*¹⁰ gives their number as ten.

Clearly there were large numbers of hieropoei in Athens, and we prob-ably ought not to look for any definite policy behind their different modes of appointment. In general their duties seem to have covered those aspects of festival administration which were not the responsibility of the priests themselves, and at any rate for some festivals the hieropoei were bouleutae.¹¹ On some occasions the boule as a whole was involved in a festival: it met in Eleusis during the celebration of the Mysteries and (in

¹ *IG* ii² 1257 A. ² *IG* ii² 1257 B. ³ *IG* ii² 1496, 82–3, 113–14.
⁴ *IG* ii² 330. ⁵ Kirchner in *IG* ii² i. i, p. 135. ⁶ Cf. ll. 6–7, 33–4.
⁷ D. XXI. *Mid.* 114–15. ⁸ Cf. pp. 131–3. ⁹ s.v. ἱεροποιοί.
¹⁰ s.v. ἱεροποιοί. The conclusion is based on a fragment of Dinarchus' speech *Against Lycurgus*, fr. 4 (Burtt) = ²viii. 1 (Sauppe); D. XXI. *Mid.* 115 is quoted without the words τρίτον αὐτόν.
¹¹ In the fifth century the boule also provided some religious treasurers: cf. p. 95 and nn. 4 and 5 above.

accordance with a 'Solonian' law) in the city Eleusinium on the day after their completion;[1] and in 343/2 the administration of the Dionysia was a task for which the whole boule could be honoured.[2]

The boule appointed θεωροί to attend the Pythian festival at Delphi,[3] and it was represented also on other, less regular religious commissions: when peace was made with Chalcis in 446/5 it was ordered to appoint three of its members to join Hierocles in sacrificing for Euboea;[4] it contributed five of the fifteen men who in 352/1 determined the boundaries of the ἱερὰ ὀργάς,[5] and one of the three sent to consult the Delphic oracle in conditions of elaborately secured arbitrariness on the future use of the ὀργάς.[6] (This latter decree gives us a fascinating glimpse of the *naïveté* of Athenian public life even in the fourth century. The alternative uses of the land were written out on identical pieces of tin, which were wrapped in the same way and placed in a hydria; this was shaken, after which the first piece to be drawn out was placed in a gold hydria and the other in one of silver; the epistates of the prytanes sealed these with the public seal, and any other Athenian citizen might come forward and add his seal: Apollo was asked simply whether the instructions in the gold hydria or those in the silver should be followed.[7] A similar lack of modern organization is found in the provisions for the future care of the sacred places:

[— ἐπι]μελεῖσθαι [δ]ὲ τῆς ἱερᾶς ὀργάδος καὶ τῶν ἄλλω-
[ν ἱερῶν ἁπάντ]ων τῶν Ἀθήνησιν ἀπὸ τῆσδε τῆς ἡμέρας εἰς τὸν
[ἀεὶ χρόνον οὔ]ς τε ὁ νόμος κελεύει περὶ ἑκάστου αὐτῶν καὶ τ-
[ὴν βουλὴν τὴν] ἐ[ξ] Ἀρείου πάγου καὶ τὸν στρατηγὸν τὸν ἐπὶ τῆ-
[ν φυλ]ακὴ[ν τῆς χ]ώρας κεχειροτονημένον καὶ τοὺς περιπολά-
[ρχ]ους καὶ τοὺς [δη]μάρχους καὶ τὴν βουλὴν τὴν ἀεὶ βουλεύου-
[σαν] καὶ τῶν ἄλλ[ων Ἀθ]ηναίων τὸμ βουλόμενον τρόπωι ὅτωι ἂν
[ἐπ]ίστω[ν]ται.[8])

Another concern of the boule was the appointment of judges for the musical and dramatic festivals. After it had drawn up a short list, in consultation with the choregi, the names of the candidates from the different tribes were placed in separate hydriae, which were sealed by the prytanes, counter-sealed by the choregi, and deposited on the Acropolis in the care of the treasurers of Athena: one judge could thus be chosen by lot from each tribe.[9]

The boule itself had various religious duties to perform. The bouleuterium contained statues of Zeus βουλαῖος and Athena βουλαία, to whom

[1] See Ch. I, p. 35 nn. 13 and 14.   [2] *IG* ii² 223 B, 7–9, cf. 5–6.   [3] D. XIX. *F.L.* 128.
[4] M&L 52, 64–9.   [5] *IG* ii² 204, 5–6.   [6] Ibid. 42 sqq.
[7] Ibid. 23–42. (For the sequel see Andr. 324 F 30, Phil. 328 F 155.)
[8] *IG* ii² 204, 16–23.
[9] Is. XVII. *Trap.* 33–4, with Pickard-Cambridge, *Dramatic Festivals of Athens*², 95–8.

the members prayed on entry, and a Hestia βουλαία, by which oaths were taken and where sanctuary might be sought.[1] The year began with εἰσιτητήρια, inaugural rites;[2] and meetings of the boule began with a purification ceremony and with the herald's reciting the standard curse and prayer at the secretary's dictation.[3] Probably in the boule no less than in the ecclesia sacred business was given priority at meetings.[4] In addition to matters which we have already considered, this will have involved hearing reports from a large number of officials on the discharge of their religious duties.[5] Such reports are attested from priests,[6] from a priest and hieropoei,[7] from a priest and epimeletae,[8] from the epimeletae of the Mysteries,[9] from a hierophant,[10] from the men elected to supervise the repair of the statue of Athena Νίκη,[11] from the ἀρχιθέωρος to the Nemean festival,[12] and from an agonothetes.[13] Reports were delivered on their religious duties also by other officials, whose duties were not primarily religious: by an archon,[14] by the cosmetes of the ephebi,[15] by the demarch of Eleusis,[16] and above all by the prytanes.[17] Due performance of their sacrifices was one of the grounds on which prytanes were honoured in the Hellenistic period, and these sacrifices are regularly mentioned in the honorific decrees. They were offered

Ἀπόλλωνι τῶι Προστατηρίωι (καὶ τῆι Ἀρτέμιδι τῆι Βουλαίαι) (καὶ τῆι Φωσφόρωι)
καὶ τοῖς ἄλλοις θεοῖς οἷς πάτριον ἦν,
ἐφ' ὑγιείαι καὶ σωτηρίαι τῆς βουλῆς καὶ τοῦ δήμου (τῶν Ἀθηναίων) (καὶ παίδων
καὶ γυναικῶν) (καὶ τῶν φίλων καὶ συμμάχων).[18]

[1] Cf. Ch. I, p. 34.
[2] D. XXI. *Mid.* 114–15 (quoted p. 130), XIX. *F.L.* 190 (quoted p. 133), cf. T. VIII. 70. i. Cf. Ch. I, p. 13.   [3] Cf. Ch. I, pp. 36–7.   [4] Cf. Ch. I, p. 38.   [5] Cf. Ch. I, pp. 42–3.
[6] e.g. *IG* ii² 689, 775, 976, *SEG* xviii 22, 26. (I make no claim to completeness for the list of references in this and the following ten notes. The decrees cited are, inevitably, late: honours were not awarded, or at any rate their award was not published, on such slight pretexts before the Hellenistic period.)   [7] *IG* ii² 410.
[8] *IG* ii² 783 (a decree of the boule).   [9] *IG* ii² 661.   [10] *SEG* xix 124.
[11] *IG* ii² 403.   [12] *IG* ii² 365.   [13] *IG* ii² 780.   [14] *IG* ii² 668, 781, 929.
[15] *IG* ii² 1011, 1039, 1042, 1043.   [16] *IG* ii² 949.   [17] Prytany 'first' decrees, *passim.*
[18] Cf. S. Dow, *Hesp.* Supp. i 1937, 8–11. Artemis appears commonly but by no means invariably; the friends and allies of the Athenians are added to the list of beneficiaries from *c.* 200. Two third-century inscriptions add further sacrifices:

[ἔθυσαν δὲ καὶ]
[τὰ Στήνια καὶ τὰ] Χαλκεῖα κα[τὰ τὰ πάτρια ὑπέρ τε τῆς βουλῆς]
[καὶ τοῦ δήμου].   (P 4, 6–8)

[ἔθ]-
υσαν δὲ καὶ τὰ Στήνια παρ' α[ὐ]τῶν τεῖ Δήμητρι καὶ τεῖ Κόρηι ὑπὲρ τ[ῆς βουλῆ]-
ς καὶ τοῦ δήμου.   (*IG* ii² 674, 6–8)

Artemis βουλαία (of whom there was an altar in the precinct of the Tholos: *Hesp.* vi 3, 19–20), Artemis Φωσφόρος, and αἱ Φωσφόροι seem to have been particularly associated with the Tholos: see H. A. Thompson, *Hesp.* Supp. iv 1940, 137–41. In the second century A.D. an official with responsibilities for the Tholos acted also as ἱερεὺς Φωσφόρων: cf. p. 142 n. 6 below. See also on sacrifices in the Tholos or its precinct Paus. I. 5. i.

In the period of subjection to Macedon, from 262 to 229, sacrifices to the Σωτῆρες might be added, and the Macedonian royal house might be included among the beneficiaries—to be deleted later. The record becomes more elaborate as we proceed later into the Hellenistic period, but, as Professor Dow observes, sacrifices cost money, and it may be doubted if the expansion of the record reflects any increase in the actual programme of sacrifices.

A boule which had been crowned for a successful year of office might set up a dedication, such as that to the twelve gods by the boule of 357/6,[1] the statue of δημοκρατία erected by the boule of 333/2,[2] or the dedication to [Hephaestus] by the following year's boule;[3] and we have a record of φιάλαι dedicated at Eleusis by the bouleutae of 336/5, 334/3, and 333/2.[4] Prytanies also could make special dedications, apart from the record that they had been deemed worthy of honours.[5] In the second century the agonothetes of the Thesea gave the whole boule a καθέσιμον for the festival and the prytanes money for a sacrifice.[6] A decree of 129/8, resulting from a πρόσοδος to the boule by its treasurer, regulated the cult of Apollo: among those who were to perform sacrifices were the treasurers of the sitonic fund and the treasurer of the boule, while the prytanes in office at the time were to offer the ἐξαμηναῖον, and were to receive the money for this from the treasurer of the stratiotic fund.[7] Theophrastus' μικροφιλότιμος, the man who glories in petty distinctions,

ἀμέλει δὲ καὶ συνδιοικήσασθαι παρὰ τῶν πρυτάνεων, ὅπως ἀπαγγείλῃ τῷ δήμῳ τὰ ἱερά, καὶ παρεσκευασμένος λαμπρὸν ἱμάτιον καὶ ἐστεφανωμένος παρελθὼν εἰπεῖν, "ὦ ἄνδρες Ἀθηναῖοι, ἐθύομεν οἱ πρυτάνεις [τὰ ἱερὰ] τῇ Μητρὶ τῶν θεῶν τὰ Γαλάξια, καὶ τὰ ἱερὰ καλά, καὶ ὑμεῖς δέχεσθε τὰ ἀγαθά." καὶ ταῦτα ἀπαγγείλας ἀπιὼν διηγήσασθαι οἴκαδε τῇ αὑτοῦ γυναικί, ὡς καθ' ὑπερβολὴν εὐημέρει.[8]

Earlier writers are less specific. Antiphon's choregus includes in the list of his activities before he was compelled to retire from the boule,

εἰς τἆλλα ἱερὰ πάντα εἰσιὼν μετὰ τῆς βουλῆς, καὶ θύων καὶ εὐχόμενος ὑπὲρ τῆς πόλεως ταύτης, καὶ πρὸς τούτοις πρυτανεύσας τὴν πρώτην πρυτανείαν ἅπασαν πλὴν δυοῖν ἡμέραιν, καὶ ἱεροποιῶν καὶ θύων ὑπὲρ τῆς δημοκρατίας.[9]

Demosthenes tells us that

πάντες οἱ πρυτάνεις θύουσιν ἑκάστοτε κοινῇ καὶ συνδειπνοῦσιν ἀλλήλοις καὶ συσπένδουσιν. . . . ἡ βουλὴ ταῦτα ταῦτα, εἰσιτητήρι' ἔθυσε, συνειστιάθη.[10]

[1] IG ii² 2790. [2] IG ii² 2791 with A. E. Raubitschek, Hesp. xxxi 1962, 238–43.
[3] IG ii² 2792. [4] IG ii² 1544, 47–50. [5] e.g. Hesp. xvi 41.
[6] IG ii² 956, 14–15; 957, 9–10; 958, 12–13; cf. restoration of 959, 11–12.
[7] SEG xxi 469 C, 58–61. [8] Theoph. Char. xxi. 11.
[9] Ant. VI. Chor. 45. [10] D. XIX. F.L. 190.

Though the original object of sacrifices was to feed the gods, they made available a considerable amount of meat on which human beings could feast. Thus a decree of about 430 is restored to provide for a distribution of sacrificial meat to all the citizens.[1] But often particular persons had their share guaranteed before the general distribution was made: a decree of the early fourth century concerning the cult of Asclepius reserved the meat from the first ox for the prytanes, the nine archons, the hieropoei, and the πομπεῖς;[2] and the decree of about 335 regulating the Lesser Panathenaea stipulated five portions for the [prytan]es, [three] for the nine archons, [one] for the hier[opoei], [three] for the generals and taxiarchs, and the customary allowance for the πομπεῖς and [canephori].[3] In 215/14 the epimeletae of the Mysteries were honoured in a probouleumatic decree for the proper discharge of their duty, including the distribution of meat to the boule;[4] they had also had the ζεῦγος for the conveyance of the sacred objects made at their own expense, and had presented the boule with the sum allocated to them for this.[5] About A.D. 135–40 a Cretan, Flavius Zenophilus, endowed a fund to provide gifts for bouleutae, perhaps at the Mysteries; some thirty years later the surplus was reinvested, and Flavius' son and various religious officials were added to the list of recipients.[6]

(v) Secretaries and Attendants

Three public secretaries are mentioned in the Athenaion Politeia:

κληροῦσι δὲ καὶ **γραμματέα τὸν κατὰ πρυτανείαν καλούμενον**, ὃς τῶν γραμμάτων ἐστὶ κύριος καὶ τὰ ψηφίσματα τὰ γιγνόμενα φυλάττει, καὶ τἆλλα πάντα ἀντιγράφεται, καὶ παρακάθηται τῇ βουλῇ. πρότερον μὲν οὖν οὗτος ἦν χειροτονητός, καὶ τοὺς ἐνδοξοτάτους καὶ πιστοτάτους ἐχειροτόνουν· καὶ γὰρ ἐν ταῖς στήλαις πρὸς ταῖς συμμαχίαις καὶ προξενίαις καὶ πολιτείαις οὗτος ἀναγράφεται· νῦν δὲ γέγονε κληρωτός.

κληροῦσι δὲ καὶ **ἐπὶ τοὺς νόμους** ἕτερον, ὃς παρακάθηται τῇ βουλῇ, καὶ ἀντιγράφεται καὶ οὗτος πάντας.

χειροτονεῖ δὲ καὶ ὁ δῆμος **γραμματέα τὸν ἀναγνωσόμενον** αὐτῷ καὶ τῇ βουλῇ, καὶ οὗτος οὐδενός ἐστι κύριος ἀλλὰ τοῦ ἀναγνῶναι.[7]

From just before the middle of the fifth century until 368/7 there is evidence for a secretary who served for one prytany only, and seems to have been appointed in such a way that all tribes were represented in the

---

[1] SEG xxi 38, 7–8. [2] IG ii² 47, 35 sqq. [3] IG ii² 334, 10–16.
[4] IG ii² 847, 25–6. The inclusion of this in a decree of the demos reflects the dominant position which the boule had by now acquired in the enactment of decrees.
[5] Ibid. 17–20. [6] SEG xii 95 (J. H. Oliver, Hesp. xxi 1952, 381–99).
[7] A.P. 54. iii–v.

course of the year and the secretary was never a member of the tribe in prytany.[1] This secretary appears to have been a member of the boule,[2] and there is no reason to doubt his identification with the γραμματεὺς τῆς βουλῆς who was commissioned to publish decrees,[3] and in conjunction with whom the ἀναγραφεῖς τῶν νόμων were to republish the text of Draco's homicide law in 409/8.[4] This secretary is presumably the γραμματεὺς κατὰ πρυτανείαν in his former state, though that title is not attested for the prytany-ly secretary.[5] The *Athenaion Politeia*'s observation that this post was filled by leading citizens has been generally accepted, but the precise significance of καὶ γὰρ ἐν ταῖς στήλαις . . . οὗτος ἀναγράφεται is disputed.[6] My own view is that the prescripts of decrees are to be interpreted as a kind of running headline from the secretary's minute book, which was the source of texts inscribed at public or private expense, and the headings in larger letters which often precede a prescript, naming an eponymous officer or a date or the subject-matter of a decree, were added primarily for purposes of identification; once the archontic year had been made the boule's term of office the archon became the most convenient eponymous magistrate even in the proceedings of the boule and ecclesia, and was therefore preferred to the secretary in identificatory headings.[7] What our author is saying, I suggest, is, 'Look around and see what men held this office under the old system'; whether he also regarded the disappearance of the secretary from headings as a sign of his reduced importance, we cannot tell. The last year for which secretaries serving for one prytany only are attested is 368/7.[8] By 363/2 the secretary named in prescripts of decrees is an annual officer;[9] he bears the title γραμματεὺς κατὰ πρυτανείαν,[10] and is not a member of the boule.[11] The change from

---

[1] W. S. Ferguson, *The Athenian Secretaries*, chs. vi–vii.

[2] In 403/2 Cephisophon appears both as author of a probouleumatic decree (Tod 97. i) and as secretary (Tod 97. ii).   [3] e.g. M&L 31, 24; 37, 12; 52, 58–9; 69, 24.

[4] M&L 86, 6–7, giving the new readings of Dr. R. S. Stroud.

[5] This title used to be restored in the passage cited in n. 4 above (e.g. Tod 87).

[6] See Ferguson, *The Athenian Secretaries*, ch. viii, suggesting that the secretary had himself named for purposes of ostentation in the headings of inscriptions recording alliances and grants of proxeny or citizenship; Brillant, *Les secrétaires athéniens*, ch. 1, § ii, arguing that the secretary was named in the heading to date a document, and in the prescript when it was inscribed at public expense to guarantee the official nature of the publication (on this last point I should prefer to say that the whole prescript was the mark of a text derived from the official records, whoever was responsible for publication).

[7] (On the assimilation of the bouleutic to the archontic year see Additional Note A, pp. 214–5.) The secretary is named in two headings shortly after the reorganization: *IG* ii² 119 (360/59), Tod 157 (356/5).

[8] Tod 134, contr. 131, 135, 136.   [9] *IG* ii² 109, 110, 111 = Tod —, 143, 142.

[10] *IG* ii² 223 C with 224, 225 (343/2).

[11] *IG* ii² 1749, 63–5, with 228–9 (341/0). κληρωτὸς ὑπὸ τῆς βουλῆς (Poll. viii. 98) seems to be a simple misquotation from *A.P.* 54. iii.

election (from among the bouleutae) to sortition was presumably made at the same time.[1]

One other secretary is mentioned before the reorganization of the 360s. The γραμματεὺς τῆς πόλεως who παρελθὼν ἀνέγνω τοῖς Ἀθηναίοις the letter which Nicias sent from Syracuse in the winter of 414/13[2] is clearly the elected Reader of the *Athenaion Politeia*. The title he is given by Thucydides is not found elsewhere, and it is economical to identify him with the γραμματεὺς τῆς βουλῆς καὶ τοῦ δήμου, for whom no duties are attested, but who appears among the ἀείσιτοι listed in prytany documents of all periods.[3]

After the reorganization we meet a greater number of secretaries, and have one major problem in identification. Between 363/2 and 322/1 the publication of decrees might be entrusted either to the γραμματεὺς κατὰ πρυτανείαν (that is, to the eponymous secretary under the new system)[4] or to the γραμματεὺς τῆς βουλῆς (whose title was borne by the eponymous secretary under the old system).[5] Ferguson and Brillant regarded these as

---

[1] Ferguson discovered that this office normally rotated among the tribes in their official order, and in *Klio* xiv 1914–15 he suggested that the regular cycles beginning with tribe VII in 356/5 were preceded by a cycle in which each tribe took by lot one of the ten years 366/5–357/6, and that 366 was therefore a likely year for the institution of annual secretaries. This may be right, but many have doubted it.   [2] T. vii. 10.

[3] He is first found as γραμματεὺς τῆι βουλῆι καὶ τῶι δήμωι in *IG* ii[2] 1740 (early C4) and the title is used also in *IG* ii[2] 1747 (*c.* 350), *Hesp.* iii 54 (where γτδκτβ [*sic*] was restored by Wilhelm, *Abh. Berlin* 1939, xx, and [independently] by Raubitschek, *Hesp.* xi 1942, 305–6) (same year as *IG* ii[2] 1747, though Raubitschek's argument for a date after 355 is weak—cf. p. 142 n. 3 below), and in *Hesp.* xxxvii 1968, 1–24 (303/2). In *IG* ii[2] 1700 (335/4) and *Hesp.* x 11 (324/3) he is styled γραμματεὺς τῶι δήμωι; in *P* 10 (256/5) he is called γραμματεὺς τοῦ δήμου (but the usual version of the title is found in *P* 9, another inscription of the same year), and this form occurs in two other third-century documents, *P* 13 and 34. (It is not clear which secretarial office was held by the γραμματεύς of *SEG* xxiii 87, 62–4 [first qr. C4] and the γραμματεὺς βουλῆς of *IG* ii[2] 1744, 18–21 [before 350].)

Some scholars have claimed to find supporting evidence for the identification of this secretary with the Reader in *IG* ii[2] 223 A, 10 (343/2):

ἀναγ[νῶ]ναι τόδε τὸ ψήφισμα τὸν γραμματέα τῶι δήμωι

(so Brillant, *Les secrétaires athéniens*, 113, Schulthess, *RE*, vii. 1725). They may be right to interpret τὸν γραμματέα τῶι δήμωι as a title, but we have seen that this was not the usual form of the title, and it seems to me equally likely that the author of the decree intended τὸν γραμματέα as the title (ἀναγνῶναι makes it clear which secretary is meant) and τῶι δήμωι as indirect object.

According to *A.P.* 54. v οὗτος οὐδενός ἐστι κύριος ἀλλὰ τοῦ ἀναγνῶναι, but modern scholars have disagreed. Brillant, op. cit., 110–11, 122, claimed that the actual reading aloud of documents would be performed by the herald under the guidance of this secretary, whose duties would make him a highly influential Keeper of the Statute Book. Dow, *Hesp.* Supp. i 1937, 16, identified him with the γραμματεὺς τῆς βουλῆς (cf. p. 137 n. 7 below) and claimed that in the Hellenistic period this was 'a political office': one holder of the office, Euthymachus, was earlier ὑπογραμματεύς and later a member of the boule (Dow, op. cit., 103–4, on *P* 48). Contrast, however, K. J. Dover in his commentary on T .vii. 10 (regarding γραμματεὺς τῶι δήμωι as the normal fourth-century version of the title).

[4] e.g. *IG* ii[2] 222, 27–8.   [5] e.g. Tod 147, 42–3; 166, 11.

alternative titles for the same secretary,[1] while Schulthess argued that in this period the duties of publication were divided between two secretaries.[2] One text in particular seemed to support Schulthess's view:

καὶ ἐπειδὰν τὸ οἴκημα ἀ-
[νοι]χθεῖ ἐξετάζεν κατὰ ἔθνος ἕκαστα καὶ ἐπιγράφεν τ-
[ὸν] ἀριθμόν, ἀντιγράφεσθαι δὲ τὸγ γραμματέα τὸν κατὰ
[πρ]υτανείαν καὶ τοὺς ἄλλους γραμματ⟨τε⟩έας τοὺς ἐπὶ τοῖ-
[ς δ]ημοσίοις γράμμασιν· ἐπειδὰν δὲ ἐξετασθῆι πάντα κ-
[αὶ] ἀναγραφῆι, τὸγ γραμματέα τῆς βουλῆς ἀναγράψαντα
[ἐν] στήληι λιθίνηι στῆσαι ἔμπροσθεν τῆς χαλκοθήκη[ς].[3]

It was very hard to believe that the author of the decree ordering an inventory to be made of the treasures in the Chalcothece could have referred to the same secretary by two different titles in the space of four lines—yet we now know that this is what happened. A document published by the treasurers of Athena has been found on the Acropolis, which refers to the stele set up in 353/2 by Philocedes in front of the Chalcothece:[4] this must surely be the stele whose erection by the γραμματεὺς τῆς βουλῆς was ordered in the decree quoted above; but Philocedes is very probably to be restored as the eponymous secretary in two decrees of 353/2,[5] and we have seen that the eponymous secretary was the γραμματεὺς κατὰ πρυτανείαν.[6] The γραμματεὺς τῆς βουλῆς and the γραμματεὺς κατὰ πρυτανείαν must therefore be identical.[7]

We are thus dealing with a single office, which had been held, probably by bouleutae, for a prytany at a time, and was now made annual and in its new form was not held by bouleutae. Some have supposed that the object, or at any rate one object, of the change was to weaken the boule by taking a powerful office out of its hands.[8] However, a good deal of political writing survives from the fourth century, and I have not found any suggestion that the boule had to be watched because there was a danger of its becoming too powerful:[9] the author of the *Athenaion*

---

[1] *The Athenian Secretaries*, chs. iii–iv; *Les secrétaires athéniens*, ch. iii.

[2] *RE*, vii. 1711–22.   [3] *IG* ii² 120, 13–19 (353/2).   [4] *SEG* xix 129, 13–14.

[5] *IG* ii² 138, 139.   [6] Cf. p. 136 n. 10 above.

[7] The conclusion was first drawn by Pritchett and Meritt, *Chron. Hell. Ath.*, 2 n. 6. Schweigert in publishing as *Hesp.* vii (ACR) 16, what is now *SEG* xix 129, failed to draw the obvious conclusion from it (*Hesp.* vii 1938, 286–7). The list of ἀείσιτοι in *P* 1 (305/4?) includes both the γραμματεὺς κατὰ πρυτανείαν and the γραμματεὺς τῆς βουλῆς καὶ τοῦ δήμου, and Schweigert was misled by Dow's identification, in *Hesp.* Supp. i 1937, 35, of the latter (the elected Reader?—cf. p. 136 and n. 3 above) with the γραμματεὺς τῆς βουλῆς (who in the fourth century published decrees) into thinking that the γραμματεὺς τῆς βουλῆς and γραμματεὺς κατὰ πρυτανείαν must be distinct.

[8] e.g. Brillant, *Les secrétaires athéniens*, 28, Glotz and Cohen, *HG*, iii. 164.

[9] See my remarks in Ch. V, pp. 218–19, with notes referring to my discussions of related topics.

Politeia, indeed, discusses the change in the secretaryship without mentioning the boule, and seems to have thought that it was the secretaryship which was weakened by the change. The extra detail which found its way into the prescripts of decrees during the fourth century suggests that the Athenians were beginning to treat their records more seriously, and the chief secretaryship was becoming too arduous for its duties to be performed by a member of the boule who after only one prytany would surrender them to another novice. Professional expertise was not yet thought necessary, or the office would not have been made sortitive, but dissociation from the boule and a longer period of tenure suggest an improvement in efficiency and perhaps a slightly fairer spreading of the state's burdens.[1]

A few of the fourth-century prytany documents discovered in the Agora include in their lists of officials the second of the three secretaries mentioned in the *Athenaion Politeia*, the ἐπὶ τοὺς νόμους.[2] Ferguson originally supposed that the ἐπὶ τοὺς νόμους did for νόμοι what the γραμματεὺς κατὰ πρυτανείαν did for ψηφίσματα,[3] but Brillant later persuaded him that this secretary was to be identified with the ἐπὶ τὰ ψηφίσματα found in fourth-century lists but not in the *Athenaion Politeia*.[4] In 1941, however, Professor Meritt showed that ἐπὶ τοὺς νόμους and ἐπὶ τὰ ψηφίσματα were distinct offices,[5] which ought in view of their titles to have been more or less parallel, though one is mentioned in the *Athenaion Politeia* and the other is not.[6] Other secretaries found in the fourth-century lists are the ἀναγραφεύς[7] and the ἀντιγραφεύς,[8] whose exact duties in connection with the public records are unknown, and there may have been yet others, not

---

[1] The office was one which a man might hold in middle life: Dieuches, secretary in 349/8 (*IG* ii² 206, 2–3; 208, 3–4; 209, 2–3), was 40 years old at the time (*IG* ii² 2409, 50, with D. M. Lewis, *BSA* 1 1955, 32–3).

[2] *Hesp.* x 11 (324/3); *P* 1 (305/4?) (Meritt, *Hesp.* x 1941, 45–6, substitutes ἐπὶ τ[οὺς νόμους] for Dow's ἐπὶ τ[ὸ ἀνάθημα]); *Hesp.* xxxvii 1968, 1–24 (303/2). Poll. viii. 98, in contradiction to the *Athenaion Politeia*, states that this secretary was elected by the boule.

[3] *The Athenian Secretaries*, ch. xv.

[4] *Les secrétaires athéniens*, ch. vi. Ferguson announced his conversion to this view in *Athenian Tribal Cycles*, 160–1 n. 1.

[5] *Hesp.* x 1941, 45–6, suggesting that both were included in *Hesp.* x 11 and *P* 1; both are now found in *Hesp.* xxxvii 1968, 1–24; ἐπὶ τὰ ψηφίσματα appears also in *IG* ii² 223 C.

[6] What their duties were, we cannot say, but the only two νόμοι in which the publication-clause survives were, like contemporary decrees, published by the γραμματεὺς τῆς βουλῆς (*IG* ii² 140, 31; *SEG* xii 87, 23–4).

[7] *IG* ii² 1700, *Hesp.* x 11, *P* 1, *Hesp.* xxxvii 1968, 1–24: it is probably the holder of this office who is honoured in *IG* ii² 415 (*c*. 330?) for his attention to the ἀναγραφὴ τῶν γραμμάτων (cf. S. Dow, *HSCP* lxvii 1963, 39–40). He is not to be confused with the ἀναγραφεῖς τῶν νόμων of the late fifth century (Lys. XXX. *Nic.* 2, cf. 25; M&L 86, 5–6) and the man or men probably given the same title in 304/3 (cf. *IG* ii² 487).

[8] *IG* ii² 1700, *P* 1, *Hesp.* xxxvii 1968, 1–24. On this "ἀντιγραφεὺς τῆς βουλῆς" and the earlier "ἀντιγραφεὺς τῆς διοικήσεως" see Additional Note D, pp. 237–9.

considered worthy of inclusion in these lists: we have seen that the inventory of treasures in the Chalcothece was to be compiled by τὸγ γραμματέα τὸγ κατὰ πρυτανείαν καὶ τοὺς ἄλλους γραμματέας τοὺς ἐπὶ τοῖς δημοσίοις γράμμασιν.[1] Various authorities had their γραμματεύς or ὑπογραμματεύς:[2] the men were apparently drawn from a pool, and at the beginning of the fourth century were forbidden to serve twice in the same office, in case they should become too influential.[3] Aeschines held some secretarial office which brought him into contact with the boule and assembly, but it may be merely in order to denigrate him the better that Demosthenes styles him ὑπογραμματεύς.[4]

The secretaries ἐπὶ τοῖς δημοσίοις γράμμασιν, and especially the γραμματεὺς κατὰ πρυτανείαν, bore general responsibility for the public records. In addition to publishing current documents on stone stelae, this could involve bringing the bouleutic oath up to date,[5] or correcting an unfortunate phrase in an already published decree;[6] combining with the codifiers of the laws to republish a text from the ἄξονες (at the end of the fifth century),[7] or giving a copy of an honorific decree to the person honoured.[8] In 405, when the Athenian triremes at Samos were presented to the Samians, the names of the trierarchs responsible for them were to be registered with the secretary and the generals.[9] Some duties may have given a strong secretary the opportunity to influence the course of events: in the *Thesmophoriazusae* a speaker in the assembly outlines her general plan for dealing with Euripides, and ends by offering to work out the details in conjunction with the secretary;[10] and if when the boule had made up its mind on a judicial matter a case had to be referred to a δικαστήριον the secretary was responsible for that.[11] Those secretaries who were concerned with the work of the boule and ecclesia ate with the prytanes in the Tholos, at public expense,[12] and as ἀείσιτοι they joined with the prytanes in the Hellenistic period to honour the treasurer of the

---

[1] *IG* ii² 120, 15–17.

[2] e.g. the ὑπογραμματεύς (Ant. VI. *Chor.* 35) or γραμματεύς (*A.P.* 55. i–ii) of the thesmothetae; the γραμματεύς of the Eleven (Poll. VIII. 102; *IG* ii² 1631, 377 sqq., 389 sqq.).

[3] Lys. XXX. *Nic.* 29. The rule seems not to have been in force in the Periclean period: Satyrus χουνεγραμμάτευε in *ATL*, lists 12, 36 and 13, 2 (443/2 and 442/1); and Anticles was probably secretary to the epistatae of the Parthenon throughout the period of the work (*IG* i² 339–53; esp. 349, 1; 351, 55; 352, 1–2; 353, 1–3; in the earlier lists he χουνεγραμμάτευε but no colleague is named).

[4] D. XIX. *F.L.* 70, cf. 237, 249, [Pl.] *X. Or.* 840 A, F.　　　　　[5] M&L 45, § 12.
[6] *SEG* xii 37, 58.　　　　[7] M&L 86, 4–7.　　　　[8] Tod 97, 22–3.
[9] M&L 94, 25–8.　　　　[10] Ar. *Thesm.* 431–2.　　　　[11] M&L 69, 51–4.

[12] D. XIX. *F.L.* 249, cf. 314; the scholiast on § 249 says that in the Tholos ἐσιτοδοτοῦντο ἀπὸ τοῦ δημοσίου γραμματεῖς οἱ χειροτονηθέντες ἀπὸ (ὑπὸ?—P. J. R.) τῆς πόλεως. Kahrstedt, *S.S.A.*, 336, combined these ἀείσιτοι with those whom the state entertained as a mark of distinction in the Prytaneum; but see S. Dow, *Hesp.* Supp. i 1937, 22–4.

prytany (for his attention to the regular sacrifices) and were themselves honoured by the boule.[1]

Some of the constitutional changes at the end of the fourth century and the beginning of the third affected the secretaries. It is now known that there were two periods when the eponymous character and publicatory duties of the γραμματεύς κατὰ πρυτανείαν passed to a (probably elected) ἀναγραφεύς—from 321/0 to 319/18 and from 294/3 to 292/1.[2] In the first of these periods we also find a γραμματεύς in decree prescripts, who served only for one prytany and was probably a member of the reigning prytany. At other times the γραμματεύς κατὰ πρυτανείαν retained the position which he had occupied since the 360s. Surprisingly, he does not appear in the lists of ἀείσιτοι included in prytany documents from about 260: the highest honours are paid to the treasurer and secretary of the prytany, both elected by and from the prytanes,[3] and the only other secretaries mentioned are the γραμματεύς τῆς βουλῆς καὶ τοῦ δήμου (probably the Reader, and certainly not the eponymous secretary) and a ὑπογραμματεύς.[4] The list was normally completed by the treasurer of the boule, the herald (from c. 250), the ἱερεὺς τοῦ ἐπωνύμου, and (from the 220s) the αὐλητής;[5] the ἀντιγραφεύς was occasionally added at the end of the list.[6] The ἀναγραφεύς and the secretaries ἐπὶ τοὺς νόμους and ἐπὶ τὰ ψηφίσματα disappear from the records until the late second century, when greatly expanded lists of officials include all these and more besides:[7] the γραμματεύς κατὰ πρυτανείαν is now admitted to the list, but is regularly placed towards the end, and there is also a new secretary, ἐπὶ τὸ ἀπόρρητον. Sulla's occupation of Athens marks the end of an era in prytany documents,[8] and it is not until the reign of Marcus Aurelius that we again find a regular pattern in the lists of ἀείσιτοι.[9] Religious functionaries now predominate, but some of the Hellenistic officials survive: we have the

[1] S. Dow, *Hesp.* Supp. i 1937, 13–19.

[2] W. B. Dinsmoor, *Archons of Athens*, 16–28; most recently S. Dow, *HSCP* lxvii 1963, 37–54, B. D. Meritt, *Hesp.* xxxii 1963.

[3] The fact of election is attested for the treasurer in prytany 'second' decrees, *passim*; for the secretary in *Hesp.* iii 16, 8–9.   [4] Once called ὑπογραμματεὺς τοῦ [δήμου]: *P* 84.

[5] *Hesp.* xxxvii 1968, 1–24 (303/2), includes in its list of officials not only the regular κῆρυξ τῆι βουλῆι καὶ τῶι δήμωι but also a κῆρυξ ἐπὶ το[— c. 6½ —]. The priest is first found in *Hesp.* xxxiii 26 (c. 250); the αὐλητής in *P* 28 (c. 229–7).

[6] *P* 86 (145/4); restored in *Hesp.* xxxiii 37 (c. 150). His restoration at a higher place in the list in *P* 58 (before 178/7) seems less likely, but some additional officer must be found to fill this place.

[7] *SEG* xii 101, *Hesp.* xxxii 21 (both 135/4); *Hesp.* x 77 (131/0); *Kerameikos*, iii. A 5, *Hesp.* xxxiv 5 (both c. 100); *Hesp.* xvii 12 (95/4).   [8] Cf. S. Dow, *Hesp.* Supp. i 1937, 25–6.

[9] The principal lists of the intervening period are *P* 110, 116, *SEG* xviii 53 (Augustan); *Hesp.* xi 2, *IG* ii² 1759, *Hesp.* xi 13, *IG* ii² 1769 (CC1–2 A.D.). One official in *SEG* xviii 53 is described as γρ[αμματεὺς] τοῦ σ[υνεδρίου] γ[ενόμενος]. On the post-Sullan ἀείσιτοι in general, see now D. J. Geagan, *Hesp.* Supp. xii 1967, 103–12.

γραμματεὺς βουλῆς καὶ δήμου, the γραμματεὺς κατὰ πρυτανείαν (now more often called περὶ τὸ βῆμα),[1] the ἀντιγραφεύς, and the ὑπογραμματεύς. Sometimes a γραμματεὺς βουλευτῶν is found.[2]

The treasurers I have had occasion to mention in the first section of this chapter. The treasurer of the boule was responsible for the boule's expense-account, τὰ κατὰ ψηφίσματα ἀναλισκόμενα τῇ βουλῇ, and when this had ceased to exist as a separate fund presumably continued to administer and to augment public money spent on the boule's account.[3] (In the mid fourth century the office seems to have been shared between two men.[4]) In Hellenistic prytany documents the elected treasurer of the prytany, who has seen to the expenditure on sacrifices, is the most important single individual. Expenditure for the other activities of the prytany, notably for the meals provided in the Tholos, may have come within his scope, but we have no evidence on the matter.[5] The growing prominence of religious observances in the duties of the prytanes makes the inclusion of priests among the ἀείσιτοι natural; the herald and the αὐλητής were professionals, holding office for long periods, whose services were needed at meetings of the boule and ecclesia.[6]

Humbler officials also were attached to the boule. The records made by the poletae and cancelled after settlement by the apodectae were in the custody of a δημόσιος, or public slave, who worked for the boule,[7] and we have other references to the δημόσιος in charge of records in the

---

[1] IG ii² 1077, 2 with 50 (col. iii) shows that περὶ τὸ βῆμα was a title of the eponymous secretary.

[2] e.g. Hesp. xvi 87 B (A.D. 177/8 or 188/9), IG ii² 1796 (c. 180), 1808 (end C2). See Geagan, Hesp. Supp. xii 1967, 101, who notices especially IG ii² 1775 (168/9): the heading names ὁ γραμματεὺς τῶν βουλευτῶν τῆς Ἀκαμαντίδος φυλῆς Φιλούμενος Ἔρωτος Κεφαλῆθεν, and there follows a full list of 40 members, not including this man. But normally this office seems to have been held by one of the prytanes.

[3] Cf. pp. 103–4, 109–10.

[4] The treasurers of the boule are mentioned in the plural in IG ii² 120, 20–2 (353/2), and there are two of them in IG ii² 223 C, 7–9 (343/2); in IG ii² 1700, 218–19 (335/4) we find one ταμίας τῆς βουλῆς and one ταμίας τῶν εἰς τὸ ἀνάθημα. Thereafter the boule's funds were regularly administered by a single treasurer (A. C. Johnson, CP ix 1914, 418, explained as an error the apparent mention of a single treasurer of the boule in IG ii² 24, b 8–10 (early C4), but increasing financial centralization lessened the importance of this officer (cf. pp. 109–10 and S. Dow, Hesp. Supp. i 1937, 18). On the treasurer after Sulla see Geagan, Hesp. Supp. xii 1967, 98–9, 115–16: he appears in P 108 (c. 40 B.C.) and (restored) in P 110 (29/8–22/1); the ταμίας τῆς βουλῆς καὶ τοῦ δήμου in P 116 (c. 20) Geagan regards as an erroneous description of him; in the Christian era, when the boule was largely dependent on private benefactions (cf. Ch. I, p. 14) no comparable treasurer is regularly listed, but we do find a ταμίας, not further specified, in IG ii² 1759 (A.D. 90–100) and 1799 (c. 180), and a [ταμί]ας φυλῆς in IG ii² 1827 (C3).

[5] Cf. p. 104 and n. 6 above.

[6] Cf. S. Dow, Hesp. Supp. i 1937, 15–16 on the priest (who might but need not be a member of the boule), 17–18 on the herald and αὐλητής.

[7] A.P. 47. v, 48. i.

Metroum.[1] In the fifth century a place in the theatre seems to have been allocated to βουλῆς ὑπηρέται,[2] and in an inscription of about 350 a ὑπηρέτης is mentioned along with the γραμματεὺς τῶι δήμωι καὶ τῆι βουλῆι (sic).[3] In the first century B.C. our lists of ἀείσιτοι begin to include a λειτουργός,[4] later styled λειτουργὸς ἐπὶ τὴν Σκιάδα;[5] from the 160s A.D. we commonly find an official entitled ἐπὶ Σκιάδος,[6] and one list ends with several οἰκέται τῆς Θόλου.[7] The Tholos seems at all times to have been a depository of standard weights and measures,[8] and we possess two copies of a decree of the late second century B.C. entrusting to a δημόσιος the set of weights and measures which was deposited in the Tholos:[9] he was under the supervision of the prytanes and the στρατηγὸς ἐπὶ τὰ ὅπλα, μαστιγοῦντες καὶ κολ[άζοντ]ες κατὰ τ[ὴν] ἀξίαν τοῦ ἀδικήματος.[10]

There must have been other attendants also, of whom no trace is preserved. Since meals were eaten in the Tholos, for instance, it must have been someone's duty to cook them, but I have found no reference to an official cook. Nevertheless, by modern standards the boule's staff was small, and the bouleutae no doubt often had to do for themselves what modern Members of Parliament and senior civil servants would expect to have done for them. A good example of this is provided by the arrest of Agoratus in 405/4: when Theocritus had laid his information

---

[1] D. XIX. F.L. 129; IG ii² 463, 28–9; 583, 5–7. In IG ii² 120, 11–13, Eucles the δημόσιος was to write down what was found in the Chalcothece.   [2] IG i² 879.

[3] Hesp. xi 1942, 305–6, re-editing Hesp. iii 54. A. E. Raubitschek ad loc. suggests that he had taken the place of the old antigrapheus, mentioned after the secretary in IG ii² 1740 (early C4); but there is far too little evidence to make this a safe inference, and his date of 355/4 for the disappearance of the old antigrapheus rests on a dubious chronology for Eubulus (see Additional Note D, pp. 235–7). Wilhelm, Abh. Berlin 1939, xx, restored [ὑπ]ηρέτης Βίων in IG ii² 2411, 4, and argued that each tribe in the boule had its ὑπηρέτης. (He also made the restoration of secretary and ὑπηρέτης in Hesp. iii 54.) In the list of 303/2 eight [ὑπηρέται τῆ]ς βουλῆς have been added in a different hand: Hesp. xxxvii 1968, 1–24, with Traill's commentary, p. 24. ὑπηρέται are found in Hesp. xxxviii 1969, 459–64 (281/0), and one is restored in Hesp. xxxvi 38, 15 (c. mid C3).

In L.S. 248. 7, E.M. ἐκφυλλοφορία, the origin of this unusual method of voting on the fate of a bouleutes (for which see Ch. IV, pp. 144–6) is ascribed to the fact that a ὑπηρέτης had once tampered with the ordinary ballots.

[4] P 105 (40–30 B.C.), P 108 (45–30 B.C.), Hesp. xi 2 (late C1 A.D.).

[5] IG ii² 1759 (A.D. 90–100), Hesp. xi 11 (first half C2).

[6] e.g. Hesp. xii 23 (165/6?); IG ii² 1774 (167/8); Hesp. xi 18, IG ii² 1775 (both 168/9); 1794, 1797 (c. 180). The man who is styled ἐπὶ Σκιάδος in the last two inscriptions elsewhere bears the title ἱερεὺς Φωσφόρων καὶ ἐπὶ Σκιάδος: IG ii² 1795, 1796, 1798, Hesp. iii 43 (all c. 180); SEG xiv 92 (182/3); in IG ii² 1077 (209/10) the title ἱερεὺς Φωσφόρων alone is used. On the development of this office see now D. J. Geagan, Hesp. Supp. xii 1967, 14–15, 110: the δημόσιος gives way to a metic λειτουργός between c. 56/5 and 14/13 B.C., and the office is first held by a citizen in A.D. 168/9. For the cult of the Phosphori cf. p. 132 n. 18 above.

[7] IG ii² 1799, 25 sqq. (c. 180): six names are preserved.

[8] Cf. H. A. Thompson, Hesp. Supp. iv 1940, 141–2.

[9] IG ii² 1013, 37–43 (the other copy, in which this passage has not survived, is published as Hesp. vii 37).   [10] IG ii² 1013, 45–7.

at a secret meeting of the boule, and it was decided to arrest and question Agoratus, οἱ αἱρεθέντες τῶν βουλευτῶν went to the Piraeus to look for him; he frustrated his pursuers by providing guarantors, and then took sanctuary; armed with a fresh resolution of the boule, οἱ ἐκ τῆς βουλῆς returned, and Agoratus agreed to go with them.[1]

In this chapter we have seen many committees of the boule at work, and other public committees on which the boule was represented: a man who volunteered for service in the boule could if he chose spend a very busy year and acquire considerable experience of public affairs. In the fourth century bouleutic committees were a common enough phenomenon to be thought worthy of caricature by Sophilus, who suggested that to improve the state of the fish market the boule should appoint two or three ὀψονόμοι.[2]

[1] Lys. XIII. *Ag.* 21–9, cf. Ch. IV, pp. 164–5. In Ar. *Thesm.* a τοξότης is available to the prytanis to fasten Mnesilochus to his plank (ll. 931, 940): obviously the bouleutae would always make use of attendants for work of this kind.

[2] Sophilus, fr. 2 (Kock), *ap.* Ath. VI. 228 B.

IV · JURISDICTION

EVIDENCE for the boule's judicial activity is largely confined to a period from about the middle of the fifth century to the death of Alexander the Great. In this chapter I discuss the scope of the boule's jurisdiction under four main heads:

   (i) internal discipline,
  (ii) 'official' jurisdiction,
 (iii) εἰσαγγελία,
 (iv) δοκιμασία;

and in an appendix I re-examine the question of when and why limits were set to the punitive powers of the boule.

(i) *Internal Discipline*

Evidence for the discipline of bouleutae is very slight. The most important passage is to be found in Aeschines' speech *Against Timarchus*, where it is alleged that while serving as a bouleutes Timarchus combined with one of the treasurers of Athena to embezzle 1,000 drachmae. The matter came before the ecclesia (we are not told why), and Pamphilus suggested that ἐὰν μὲν ἡ βουλὴ καταγνοῦσα τουτουὶ ἀδικεῖν καὶ ἐκφυλλοφορήσασα δικαστηρίῳ παραδῷ it should be entitled to the customary δωρεά, but if it failed to do this it should lose its reward.[1]

μετὰ ταῦτα ὡς ἐπανῆλθεν ἡ βουλὴ εἰς τὸ βουλευτήριον, ἐξεφυλλοφόρησε μὲν αὐτόν, ἐν δὲ τῷ ψήφῳ κατεδέξατο. ὅτι δ' οὐ παρέδωκε δικαστηρίῳ οὐδ' ἐξήλασεν ἐκ τοῦ βουλευτηρίου, ἄχθομαι μὲν λέγων, ἀνάγκη δ' ἐστὶν εἰπεῖν ὅτι τῆς δωρεᾶς οὐκ ἔτυχε.[2]

The scholiasts and lexicographers have duly noticed the phenomenon of ἐκφυλλοφορία, but they tell us nothing that cannot be learned from the text of Aeschines:[3] the boule, on finding one of its members guilty of an offence (which in any case lay within its jurisdiction—see below, pp. 148–51), could vote first by using leaves and afterwards by an orthodox ballot

---

[1] A. I. *Tim.* 110–11.   [2] Ibid. 112.
[3] In *L.S.* 248. 7, *E.M.* ἐκφυλλοφορία, the origin of this strange practice is ascribed to the fact that a ὑπηρέτης had once tampered with the ordinary ballots.

to expel him, and might then prosecute him in a δικαστήριον (as it was obliged to do if it wanted a heavier penalty than a 500-drachmae fine in a case within its competence—see p. 147). We do not know what the fate of Timarchus would have been if the boule had not relented, but it is dangerous to assume from this passage that any bouleutes convicted of an offence would be expelled. We merely note that the charge lay within the boule's competence, and if found guilty Timarchus was liable to any penalty the boule was entitled to inflict, including expulsion.

The choregus whose defence was written by Antiphon was driven out of the bouleuterium when the basileus accepted a charge of φόνος against him,[1] but this again is a special case. Once the charge had been accepted an alleged homicide was automatically deemed polluted until a court had aquitted him, and it is not clear whether the boule would formally have expelled him or his membership would simply have fallen into abeyance, to be resumed if and when he was subsequently acquitted.

Dinarchus wrote a κατὰ Πολυεύκτου, ἐκφυλλοφορηθέντος ἐκ τῆς βουλῆς, ἔνδειξις,[2] and this is cited (without reference to the boule) in a confused note of Harpocration and Suidas on the word παλιναίρετος. The charge against Polyeuctus apparently involved συκοφαντία, and we may perhaps combine Dionysius' title for the speech with the lexicographers' note to suggest that Dinarchus was attacking Polyeuctus for trying to exercise the rights of a bouleutes, which he had lost when prosecuted on a charge of συκοφαντία; presumably restoration of bouleutic membership was possible, and presumably the point at issue was that Polyeuctus' rights had not yet been restored.

Callixenus, the author of the probouleuma under which the Arginusae generals were tried,[3] was one of those who were later made to provide guarantors and were imprisoned by their guarantors to await trial:[4] we are not told whether the Athenians' change of heart occurred in the same bouleutic year as the condemnation of the generals, but Callixenus was still under arrest when Cleophon was condemned after Aegospotami, so this incident is probably not evidence for the judicial status of current bouleutae. Nor can we rely on the two occasions in the fifth century when a bouleutes found himself in trouble for proposing the acceptance of peace terms. In 480/79 the man who was prepared to entertain Mardonius' offer was lynched;[5] in 405/4 Archestratus was imprisoned for proposing the acceptance of the terms which Sparta offered after Aegospotami,[6] but

---

[1] Ant. VI. *Chor.* 49.   [2] D.H. 651. *Din.* 10.   [3] X. *H.* I. vii. 8.
[4] Ibid. 35.   [5] *H.* IX. 5. i–ii, cf. Lyc. *Leocr.* 122, D. XVIII. *Cor.* 202, 204.
[6] X. *H.* II. ii. 15.

we do not know the outcome of this, and in any case various acts of dubious legality occurred in the months before Athens' capitulation.[1]

We are left with the meagre knowledge that the boule could expel a member against whom a criminal charge was laid, but except when the member was tainted with the pollution of a homicide charge there is nothing to suggest that this expulsion was automatic or obligatory. Indeed, the point most worthy of notice is that in the face of Pamphilus' threats the boule was capable of refusing to expel Timarchus and prosecute him in a δικαστήριον for a penalty beyond its own competence (it does not follow from this that Timarchus was not punished at all). We should always be alert for misleading truths in the orators, and it is possible that the boule of 361/0 lost its crown for some totally different reason; but Aeschines could at any rate suggest that in this matter the boule had defied public opinion and so had forfeited its reward. Though the ecclesia might have the last word at the end of the year, it apparently could not order the expulsion of a bouleutes whose colleagues were not prepared to expel him.

Further evidence for the discipline of bouleutae comes from a set of νόμοι inserted in the same speech of Aeschines by an ancient editor who was careless enough not to realize what point Aeschines was trying to make.[2] This does not in itself prove that what he inserted are not Athenian laws at all, and they are not inherently implausible:

> Speakers in the boule or ecclesia must keep to the subject, must treat each subject separately, must not speak twice on the same subject at the same meeting; must avoid invective, must not interrupt another speaker, must not speak except from the βῆμα, must not assault the epistates. For each offence the proedri may impose a fine of up to 50 drachmae, or for a greater penalty they may refer the matter to the next meeting of the boule or ecclesia.

From 410/09 bouleutae were required to sit not where they chose at meetings but in the place allotted to them.[3] Keeping order in the boule and ecclesia seems to have been a serious problem, to judge from the various devices employed at different times. In the fifth century both bodies were policed by the Scythian archers under the control of the prytanes;[4] three tantalizing passages in speeches of the fourth century refer to the προεδρεύουσα φυλή chosen by lot for a single assembly[5] (whether this is to be regarded as one tribe of bouleutae or the whole of

---

[1] e.g. the condemnation of Cleophon—p. 182 below.
[2] A. I. *Tim.* 35.
[3] Phil. 328 F 140.
[4] Ar. *Eq.* 665 (boule); *Ach.* 54 with schol., etc., Plat. *Protag.* 319 c (ecclesia).
[5] A. I. *Tim.* 33 with schol., III. *Ctes.* 4 with schol., [D.] XXV. *Aristog. i.* 90.

one tribe in the assembly is disputed,[1] but the latter alternative is perhaps the more likely); and in the Hellenistic period the ephebi attended the assembly under arms.[2] Such policing could have its sinister side, as we learn from Xenophon's account of the condemnation of Theramenes.[3]

(ii) 'Official' Jurisdiction

κρίνει δὲ τὰς ἀρχὰς ἡ βουλὴ τὰς πλείστας, καὶ μάλισθ' ὅσαι χρήματα διαχειρίζουσιν· οὐ κυρία ἡ κρίσις ἀλλ' ἐφέσιμος εἰς τὸ δικαστήριον. ἔξεστι δὲ καὶ τοῖς ἰδιώταις εἰσαγγέλλειν ἣν ἂν βούλωνται τῶν ἀρχῶν μὴ χρῆσθαι τοῖς νόμοις· ἔφεσις δὲ καὶ τούτοις ἐστὶν εἰς τὸ δικαστήριον ἐὰν αὐτῶν ἡ βουλὴ καταγνῷ.[4]

This follows immediately after the paragraph in the *Athenaion Politeia* which tells the story of Eumelides and Lysimachus and claims that in consequence of that incident the boule lost all its rights of final jurisdiction and was reduced to the level of a court of first instance.[5] Outside the *Athenaion Politeia*, however, we have no evidence that the boule's right to impose penalties up to a fine of 500 drachmae was subject to appeal, though reference to a δικαστήριον was needed for a more severe penalty, and it seems best to assume that the *Athenaion Politeia* has distorted the facts.[6] It seems to have been standard Athenian practice that authorities other than the δικαστήρια should have punitive powers up to a certain limit.[7]

The Athenians did not share the English view that the judiciary should be independent of the legislative and executive authorities. The involvement of the boule in decree-making and administration made it seem natural that the boule should be given judicial powers with which to enforce its decisions, and we shall see that these powers covered the activities of public officials, and of anyone else who had public duties to perform. Many offences would come to light through the boule's supervision of the state's administration, which we examined in Chapter III, and we should notice particularly here the fourth-century board of ten

---

[1] Gilbert, 290 with n. 4. [2] Earliest dated inscription, *IG* ii² 1006, 20–1 (122/1).
[3] X. *H.* ii. iii. 50, 55. [4] *A.P.* 45. ii.
[5] For this story and its implications see the appendix to this chapter, pp. 179 sqq.
[6] Notice especially [D.] XLVII. *Ev. et Mnes.* 43: ταῖς πεντακοσίαις, ὅσου ἦν κυρία κατὰ τὸν νόμον. M&L 73, 57–9, and Tod 200, 234–6, are less decisive. Lipsius, 198 with n. 67, was prepared to believe in an appeal against any verdict of the boule on an official, but see Bonner and Smith, ii. 240–3. (For δοκιμασίαι see pp. 171–8 below.)
[7] The apodectae could settle ἔμμηνοι δίκαι involving sums up to 10 drachmae (*A.P.* 52. iii), and in the νόμος of A. I. *Tim.* 35 the proedri could fine up to 50 drachmae; it seems that in the later fifth and fourth centuries the archons retained limited punitive powers (e.g. νόμος ap. [D.] XLIII. *Mac.* 75, cited by Wade-Gery, *E.G.H.*, 185 n. 2; and cf. Hignett, 222–3).

λογισταί appointed from the boule every prytany to make an interim examination of officials' accounts.[1]

That the boule could take action in an official case either on its own initiative or on receipt of a charge from any citizen is made clear by Antiphon's speech *On the Choreutes*: the choregus had first laid an εἰσαγγελία before the boule, charging the secretary to the thesmothetae and three private citizens with peculation;[2] while in the following year he uncovered further malpractices on the part of the πορισταί, πωληταί, and πράκτορες, and as a πρύτανις brought them before the boule: ὅτι πρυτανεύων πυθόμενος αὐτοὺς δεινὰ καὶ σχέτλια ἐργάζεσθαι εἰσῆγον εἰς τὴν βουλήν, καὶ ἐδίδαξα ὡς χρὴ ζητοῦντας ἐπεξελθεῖν τῷ πράγματι.[3] The condemnation of the Arginusae generals provides another instance of the boule's starting proceedings on its own initiative: the demos which had elected the generals exercised its right to depose them,[4] but the machinery which resulted in their condemnation was set in motion when they reported on the battle to the boule, which decided on the proposal of Timocrates to arrest them and bring them before the ecclesia:[5] the ecclesia ordered the boule to make a probouleuma on how they should be tried; Callixenus on the boule's behalf recommended that a single vote be taken in the ecclesia on the fate of all the accused; objections were made and an alternative proposal put up, but they were ultimately condemned under this probouleuma.[6]

Most official cases, as the *Athenaion Politeia* acknowledges, were financial. A δημόσιος attached to the boule kept lists of sums due to the state, classified according to the date when payment was due, and a defaulter

[1] A.P. 48. iii, Poll. VIII. 99; cf. Lys. XXX. *Nic.* 5. The boule was only slightly involved in the process of εὔθυναι which all officials had to undergo on retirement. The annual board of ten λογισταί and ten συνήγοροι was appointed from the whole demos to look into the strictly financial side, and referred men to the δικαστήρια for conviction or clearance; the ten εὔθυνοι and twenty πάρεδροι who received miscellaneous complaints were bouleutae, but if they found there was a case to answer they referred the charges to the δικαστήρια or the δικασταὶ κατὰ δήμους. Cf. Ch. III, p. 111.

Another check which the boule made each prytany in the fourth century concerned the μερισμός. After the apodectae had completed their allocation of revenue to the various spending authorities the boule was given the opportunity to consider any offences (A.P. 48. ii). Cf. Ch. III, pp. 99–100.

The boule's concern with weights and measures committed it to another regular inspection: the Tholos was one of four places where a standard set was kept (IG ii² 1013, 37–47; cf. Ch. III, p. 142), and this inscription of the late second century makes it the duty of the boule to compel the ἀρχαί if they do not συνεπισχύωσι τοῖς ἰδιώταις (6–7) and to check in the month of Hecatombaeon each year that the traders are using correct measures (16–18).

[2] Ant. VI. *Chor.* 35: on the use of the word εἰσαγγελία here cf. p. 170 n. 1 below.

[3] Ibid. 49. Cf. Lipsius, 198–9 with n. 69.

[4] X. *H.* I. vii. 1.   [5] Ibid. 3.

[6] Ibid. 4–24. The involvement of the ecclesia makes this act of rough justice analogous to the procedure called εἰσαγγελία, on which see pp. 162–71 below.

had to make double repayment or might be imprisoned: καὶ ταῦτα εἰσπράττειν ἡ βουλὴ καὶ δῆσαι κυρία κατὰ τοὺς νόμους ἐστίν.¹

The orators provide us with several laws or proposed laws about state debts. Andocides tells us that in the last years of the Peloponnesian War defaulting contractors and other men in debt to the state became ἄτιμοι; contractors and their guarantors had to pay in the ninth prytany of the year, and if they defaulted their debt was doubled and their property could be confiscated or sold to pay it.² Cephisius, one of Andocides' prosecutors in 400, had defaulted on a contract, and only the amnesty and recodification of the laws on the fall of the Thirty made it safe for him to appear in Athens: ὁ γὰρ νόμος οὕτως εἶχε (sc. before 403)· κυρίαν εἶναι τὴν [τε] βουλήν, ὃς ἂν πριάμενος τέλος μὴ καταβάλῃ, δεῖν εἰς τὸ ξύλον.³

In 353, to save Androtion from the consequences of the embezzlement of which he was guilty at the time of his embassy to Mausolus of Caria, Timocrates introduced a νόμος which was milder than the existing law governing state debts:

εἴ τινι τῶν ὀφειλόντων τῷ δημοσίῳ προστετίμηται κατὰ νόμον ἢ κατὰ ψήφισμα δεσμοῦ ἢ τὸ λοιπὸν προστιμηθῇ, εἶναι αὐτῷ ἢ ἄλλῳ ὑπὲρ ἐκείνου ἐγγυητὰς κατα-στῆσαι τοῦ ὀφλήματος, οὓς ἂν ὁ δῆμος χειροτονήσῃ, ἦ μὴν ἐκτείσειν τὸ ἀργύριον ὃ ὤφλεν. τοὺς δὲ προέδρους ἐπιχειροτονεῖν ἐπάναγκες, ὅταν τις καθιστάναι βούλη-ται. τῷ δὲ καταστήσαντι τοὺς ἐγγυητάς, ἐὰν ἀποδιδῷ τῇ πόλει τὸ ἀργύριον ἐφ' ᾧ κατέστησε τοὺς ἐγγυητάς, ἀφεῖσθαι τοῦ δέσμου. ἐὰν δὲ μὴ καταβάλῃ τὸ ἀργύριον ἢ αὐτὸς ἢ οἱ ἐγγυηταὶ ἐπὶ τῆς ἐνάτης πρυτανείας, τὸν μὲν ἐξεγγυηθέντα δεδέσθαι, τῶν δὲ ἐγγυητῶν δημοσίαν εἶναι τὴν οὐσίαν. περὶ δὲ τῶν ὠνουμένων τὰ τέλη καὶ τῶν ἐγγυωμένων καὶ ἐκλεγόντων, καὶ τῶν τὰ μισθώσιμα μισθουμένων καὶ ἐγγυω-μένων, τὰς πράξεις εἶναι τῇ πόλει κατὰ τοὺς νόμους τοὺς κειμένους. ἐὰν δ' ἐπὶ τῆς ἐνάτης ἢ δεκάτης πρυτανείας ὄφλῃ, τοῦ ὑστέρου ἐνιαυτοῦ ἐπὶ τῆς ἐνάτης πρυτανείας ἐκτίνειν.⁴

Under this proposal the defaulting debtor had to provide guarantors for his repayment of τὸ ἀργύριον ὃ ὤφλεν, whereas under the existing law, Demosthenes protests, defaulters on sacred debts had to repay tenfold, and some other public debts were doubled.⁵ It is not clear to the modern reader whether Demosthenes' substitution of τὸ τίμημα τὸ γιγνόμενον would have been needed to ensure that in such cases the multiple and not the simple debt was due.

But a relaxation of some kind was being proposed for certain classes of public debtor. Hitherto all men in debt to the state had been treated as defaulting contractors: τοὺς ἔχοντας τὰ θ' ἱερὰ καὶ τὰ ὅσια χρήματα

---

¹ A.P. 48. i.   ² And. I. Myst. 73–4.   ³ Ibid. 92–3.
⁴ D. XXIV. Tim. 39–40, largely confirmed in the text of §§ 41–95.
⁵ Ibid. 82–3, cf. 86.

καταβάλλειν εἰς τὸ βουλευτήριον, εἰ δὲ μή, τὴν βουλὴν αὐτοὺς εἰσπράττειν χρωμένην τοῖς νόμοις τοῖς τελωνικοῖς.[1] A scholiast offers us this account of the νόμοι τελωνικοί:

ἰστέον δὲ ὅτι ἐγγυητὰς παρεῖχον οἱ τελῶναι ἐξ ἀρχῆς, ἵνα ἕως τῆς ἐνάτης πρυτανείας εἰ μὴ καταβάλοιεν, τὰ διπλᾶ ἀνάγκην ἔχοιεν ἢ οὗτοι ἢ ἐκεῖνοι καταβαλεῖν. καὶ γὰρ καὶ πάντες οἱ χρεωστοῦντες τοῦτο ἐποίουν· ὡς εὐθὺς ὅσοι ἐχρεώστουν τῇ πόλει, ἀνάγκην εἶχον δοῦναι ἐγγυητάς, ὅτι πρὸ τῆς ἐνάτης πρυτανείας καταβαλοῦσι, καὶ ἔμενον ἄτιμοι, ἕως οὐ κατέβαλον. εἰ δὲ παρεγένετο ἡ ἐνάτη πρυτανεία καὶ μὴ κατέβαλον, τότε καὶ ἐδεσμοῦντο καὶ τὰ διπλᾶ κατέβαλον, καὶ ἐγγυητὰς οὐκέτι ἐξῆν αὐτοῖς παρασχεῖν περὶ τῶν διπλῶν.[2]

We know that for the mid fourth century, if not for the time of Andocides, this concentration on the ninth prytany is an oversimplification: the payment on some contracts had to be made in several instalments during the year.[3] Nor does it seem credible that contractors became ἄτιμοι unless their payments were overdue. The fourth-century law governing public contracts should perhaps be reconstructed as follows:

Those who became public debtors by undertaking to collect a tax, or by some other form of contract, had to provide guarantors when the contract was made.[4] If they fell behind with their payments, they incurred a multiple debt and lost their civic rights until that debt was discharged (this much was probably automatic); and to ensure that the debt was discharged the boule had the right to order their imprisonment until payment was made, and the confiscation of their guarantors' property.[5] The boule's agents in this work were the ten πράκτορες, with whom all offenders were registered.[6]

(It is not clear how this law differed from that in force before 403. Mr. MacDowell suggests that the change lay in accepting double re-payment as an alternative to imprisonment;[7] perhaps in the fifth century

---

[1] D. XXIV. Tim. 96.

[2] Schol. D. XXIV. Tim. 40 (ἐξῆν αὐτοῖς, Sauppe; ἐξῆν αὐτῆς, Dindorf). The apodectae had judicial functions in ἔμμηνοι δίκαι involving the τελῶναι: A.P. 52. iii (cf. p. 147 n. 7 above).

[3] In 369 Xenoclides, who had bought the right to collect the 2 per cent corn tax, had to pay an instalment in the bouleuteriι m eveιy prytany ([D.] LIX. Neaer. 27); in 343/2 Mixodemus was guarantor to three men whι defaulted on prytany-ly payments (Hesp. v 10, 118–52); and cf. A.P. 47. iii.   [4] Cf. And. I. Myst. 134.

[5] Agyrrhius spent many yearι in prison ἕως τὰ χρήματα ἀπέτεισεν ἃ ἔδοξε τῆς πόλεως ὄντ' ἔχειν (D. XXIV. Tim. 134–5); ιn the bouleutic oath not to imprison any citizen offering three guarantors from his own property-class an exception was made ἐάν τις . . . τέλος πριά-μενος ἢ ἐγγυησάμενος ἢ ἐκλέγων μὴ καταβάλῃ (ibid. 144). Mixodemus in Hesp. v 10 (cf. n. 3 above) has had an apartment house confiscated and sold to pay the debts of the three men he was backing. In [D.] XL. Boe. Dot. 20 we read of the collection from the bouleu-terium of the surplus proceeds of a sale of confiscated property, after the debt to the state had been paid.

[6] A. I. Tim. 35, [D.] XLIII. Mac. 71; cf. two fragmentary inscriptions, IG i² 75, ii² 45. In the amnesty after Aegospotami, the boule and πράκτορες were ordered to cancel records of out-standing debts (And. I. Myst. 77–9).   [7] Commentary on And. I. Myst. 93.

imprisonment was prescribed (and so may have been regarded as penal) for all who defaulted on a state debt, while in the fourth it was left to the boule as a precautionary measure so that the offender's person could be held as security for his payment.)[1]

Timocrates proposed to leave this law untouched for contractual debtors, but to grant a certain measure of relief to others, from whom immediate payment could be demanded: Demosthenes in his attack mentions fines, and restitution of stolen or misappropriated property,[2] which perhaps are the προσκαταβλήματα said to be exacted because the revenue from τέλη was insufficient.[3] ἀτιμία was automatic in these cases, as with contractual default; imprisonment depended on the charge: in some cases it followed automatically upon conviction, in others it was left to the discretion of the courts;[4] exaction as with contractual debts was the responsibility of the boule and πράκτορες. Demosthenes is determined to upset Timocrates' proposal by fair means or by foul, and the incomplete state of our knowledge makes it hard to judge which of his arguments are fair,[5] but it appears that the main effect of Timocrates' law would have been that in the case of fines and misappropriation of public property immediate payment was replaced by a contractual obligation to pay by the ninth prytany.

One financial matter in which the boule had jurisdiction was the collection of tribute from the Delian League. Clinias' decree gave the boule primary jurisdiction over anyone in Athens or the allied states who committed an offence in connection with the tribute or with the allied states' duty to send a cow and panoply to the Panathenaea: trial before the boule was to be a first hearing only; if the boule convicted, the case was to be referred to the heliaea and the prytanes were to arrange

---

[1] On precautionary and penal imprisonment cf. Bonner and Smith, ii. 275, E. Ruschenbusch, *Untersuchungen zur Geschichte des athenischen Strafrechts*, 13. In the fourth century, at any rate, the boule seems to have had powers of precautionary imprisonment only (cf. p. 179 n. 3 below); Ruschenbusch, op. cit. 29 with n. 87, thinks that the introduction even of precautionary imprisonment at the boule's discretion was a late addition to the procedures against state debtors.

[2] Fines, D. XXIV. *Tim.* 60, 63–5 (another νόμος of Timocrates, though the clause providing for imprisonment until the fine has been paid was probably not an innovation), 103, 105; restitution of stolen property, 105, 114–15; of misappropriated public property, 111–12, cf. 135.

[3] D. XXIV. *Tim.* 97–8 with schol. It is possible that the term also covers other items of revenue which could not be calculated in advance, such as πρυτανεῖα (Jones, 102 with 154 n. 29).

[4] Cf. Lipsius, 944–7.

[5] Imprisonment in connection with κλοπή (cf. n. 2 above) is an obvious red herring. κλοπή was an ἰδία δίκη (§ 114), and the optional five days ἐν τῇ ποδοκάκκῃ were a mark of disgrace, not a precaution against the offender's absconding without paying his debt. See Ruschenbusch, *Untersuchungen zur Geschichte des athenischen Strafrechts*, 13 with n. 15.

a debate on a suitable penalty.[1] The only judicial proceedings mentioned in the surviving part of Cleonymus' decrees were to be heard in the δικαστήρια, but a record of the ἐκλογεῖς in the different cities was to be kept in the bouleuterium, and it is not unlikely that the boule retained some jurisdiction.[2] Thudippus' decree of 425 is concerned with the assessment of tribute, not with its collection, and the quasi-judicial part played by the boule in making assessments has been discussed above, in Chapter III;[3] but we should notice here that the boule was given some jurisdiction, either over the prytanes if they failed to expedite the passage of the decree or (less probably) over the heralds sent out to announce the revision of the assessment.[4] Another League matter probably entrusted to the jurisdiction of the boule was the ban on local weights, measures, and silver coinage: Clearchus added to the bouleutic oath a clause in which the members swore to enforce his decree.[5]

The boule does not seem to have enjoyed similar powers in connection with the Second Athenian League: in the early years of the League, when Athens was careful not to trespass on the rights of the members, we should expect the allies to be involved in the collection of συντάξεις and the punishment of offenders; later the exaction of overdue payments seems to have been regulated by decree of the assembly.[6]

Most financial irregularities were probably uncovered by the boule in the course of its administrative work. The case of Androtion and his colleagues, however, began when a private citizen gave information to a board of ζητηταί set up to inquire into sums due to the state,[7] and it was always possible for a private citizen to initiate a financial case by φάσις.[8] Aristophanes mentions three such φάσεις, in the *Acharnians*, against the Megarian who tries to sell his children as pigs and the Boeotian who has Copaic eels and other luxuries to sell,[9] and in the *Knights*, where the Paphlagonian threatens to φαίνειν the sausage-seller to the prytanes for not paying the tithe on his tripe.[10] Early in the fourth

---

[1] M&L 46, 31–43. Since each of the prytanes could be fined a sum which must be restored as 1,000 or 10,000 drachmae if they failed to bring the case before the boule, any 'suitable' penalty would obviously be in excess of the boule's 500-drachmae limit. See pp. 189–90 below, where I quote the text. [2] M&L 68, 54–6. [3] pp. 90–1.

[4] M&L 69, 38–40. On the text, see Ch. III, p. 90 n. 7. [5] M&L 45, § 12.

[6] Cf. Tod 142, 11 sqq., 156, 16 sqq. For jurisdiction left to or shared with the allies in the early years of the League, see Tod 123, 41–6, 51–63.

[7] D. XXIV. *Tim.* 11–14, cf. *hyp.* ii. 1–3.

[8] On φάσις in general, see Lipsius, 309–16, Ruschenbusch, *Untersuchungen zur Geschichte des athenischen Strafrechts*, 70–3.

[9] Ar. *Ach.* 818 sqq., 908 sqq. The authority to whom these φάσεις would be made is not specified. [10] Ar. *Eq.* 300–2.

century the boule was involved when a ship on which a man had lent money was denounced by φάσις as belonging to a Delian,[1] and when the σιτοπῶλαι were accused of buying more than the 50 φορμοί of corn allowed by the law:[2] in each case there was talk in the boule of putting the accused to death ἄκριτοι, but the cases were ultimately referred to the δικαστήρια. Less reliable is the boule's verdict against Callimachus under the Ten in 403, though this case ought still to have come before the boule under the democracy: Patrocles claimed that money in the possession of Callimachus belonged to the state; an argument developed, and when one of the Ten appeared Patrocles made a φάσις to him; when this man brought the disputants before his colleagues they referred the case to the boule, which gave its verdict against Callimachus.[3]

In naval matters evidence is fairly plentiful, though the interaction of boule and δικαστήρια is complex. The navy lists give several instances of trierarchs who had failed to maintain their ships in good condition, and were ordered by a δικαστήριον, when they admitted their liability, to provide a new ship at their own expense, breaking up the old and depositing its ἔμβολος in the dockyard.[4] Again, it was a δικαστήριον which ruled that a ship had been damaged by storm (and so presumably released the trierarch from the obligation to provide a replacement).[5] In one instance only, in 334/3, a δικαστήριον doubled the trierarch's debt and ordered him to provide two new triremes;[6] but in 326/5[7] and probably in the following year also[8] men who failed to replace their ships had the debt doubled by the boule. Some decisions of the ecclesia seem no more fundamental than matters decided by the boule or δικαστήρια, and on one occasion it took a decree of the demos to establish that three horse-transports were unfit for war service.[9] We have seen in Chapter III that the boule had considerable responsibilities when an expedition was sent out; the boule decided the award of crowns to

---

[1] Is. XVII. Trap. 42.

[2] Lys. XXII. Frum. 2. On this speech see R. J. Seager, Hist. xv 1966, and on the implications of these two cases for the judicial powers of the boule see below, pp. 180, 184.

[3] Is. XVIII. Call. 5–6.

[4] IG ii² 1623, 6 sqq., 26 sqq., 118 sqq., 129 sqq.; 1629, 545 sqq.,* 572 sqq.,* 1085–92; 1631, 184–6. (In the two cases marked (*) the trierarch ὡμολόγησεν as elsewhere, but there is no reference to the punishing authority, or to the ἔμβολος of the old ship.)

[5] IG ii² 1629, 646–9; 1631, 116 sqq., 141–3, 342–7.

[6] IG ii² 1623, 144 sqq.

[7] IG ii² 1628, 339–44, cf. 484–8; 1629, 859–63, cf. 788–92; 1631, 60–1.

[8] IG ii² 1631, 430–3.

[9] IG ii² 1627, 241–8 with 271–4; 1628, 460–4 with 492–4; 1629, 722–9 with 805–7; 1631, 100–5.

efficient trierarchs, and prosecuted the inefficient in a δικαστήριον (for heavier penalties than it was competent to inflict).[1]

The δικαστήρια appear from the lists to have been the regular authorities for dealing with ships' equipment, and there are many references to a trierarch's having his debt doubled by a δικαστήριον.[2] Further light is thrown on the situation by a decree of the boule, whose text is given in one of the lists.[3] In 325/4 one Sopolis had been convicted in a δικαστήριον of failing to surrender the equipment for ten triremes on behalf of his brother, who had been ταμίας, and had been ordered to pay 'more than double'.[4] There were in the dockyards some lengths of timber suitable for making into oars, which belonged to Sopolis, and these together with the rest of his property had been confiscated; Polyeuctus, who had made the ἀπογραφή, is granting the legally permitted remission, and in this decree orders the ἐπιμεληταὶ τῶν νεωρίων to allow 3 drachmae against Sopolis' debt for each of the lengths of timber which he has deposited: if the epimeletae or the secretary of the Eleven fail to comply with this decree, each of them will incur a fine of 3,000 drachmae, εἶναι δὲ καὶ εἰσαγγελίαν αὐτῶν καθάπερ ἐάν τις ἀδικεῖ περὶ τὰ ἐν τοῖς νεωρίοις. The boule is thus revealed as the principal judicial authority in naval matters, which could enact an adjusting measure after a court had passed sentence; we shall see that the εἰσαγγελία referred to would naturally have been heard by the boule, with reference to a δικαστήριον for the penalty, and it is interesting to notice that the boule could specify in a decree a penalty more severe than it could on its own authority inflict.[5]

The boule's powers and weaknesses are clearly illustrated by the case of Theophemus, which is described in detail in the speech *Against Evergus and Mnesibulus*.[6] In 357/6 a naval expedition was sent out in some haste, presumably to take part in the Social War, and was threatened by a serious shortage of equipment. Chaeredemus therefore carried a decree (whether in the boule or ecclesia is uncertain) providing for the recovery

---

[1] D. LI. *Cor. Tri.* 4: cf. Ch. III, p. 120. But in 361, when trierarchs who had made over their duties to contractors were held responsible for Athens' defeat by Alexander of Pherae, the case probably went as an εἰσαγγελία to the assembly (cf. p. 180 n. 2 below).

[2] *IG* ii² 1623, 50 sqq.,* 60 sqq., 87 sqq., 91 sqq., 105 sqq., 136 sqq., 218 sqq.; 1628, 621 sqq., 631 sqq.; 1629, 1100 sqq.; 1631, 289 sqq., 297 sqq., 304 sqq., 312 sqq., 319 sqq. (In the case marked (*) the punishing authority is not named.)

[3] *IG* ii² 1631, 350–403.

[4] Probably to be interpreted as twice the original debt plus a fine (Boeckh, *Urk. Seew.*, 212).

[5] Boeckh (*Urk. Seew.*, 536–7) thought this would be possible only if full powers for the collection of naval debts had been delegated to the boule. There must obviously have been some legal basis for the boule's passing an adjusting decree of this kind, but I suspect that the ordering of a penalty in excess of the boule's 500-drachmae limit indicates a gap in the law which no one had thought of plugging.

[6] [D.] XLVII. *Ev. et Mnes.*

of equipment in the possession of ex-trierarchs:[1] it is probably this decree which ordered the confiscation of the property not only of those who refused to surrender state-owned equipment but also of those who possessed equipment of their own and would not sell it.[2] Under Periander's symmory law of the previous year trierarchs were authorized to collect equipment directly from their predecessors, and another decree laid down the principles on which defaulting trierarchs were to be allocated to their successors: in accordance with this decree ἡ ἀρχὴ παραλαβοῦσα παρὰ τῆς προτέρας ἀρχῆς (surely the epimeletae[3]) allotted Demochares and Theophemus to the speaker.[4] The speaker demanded his equipment from them, without success. He then summoned them before the ἀποστολεῖς and epimeletae, who at that time brought διαδικασίαι over equipment into court:[5] Demochares and Theophemus were both convicted, but while the former discharged his debt the latter did nothing about it.[6]

The speaker's next step was to complain to the ἀποστολεῖς and the boule, of whom the boule seems to have been the more important, as the ἀποστολεῖς do not play an active part in the affair. Other trierarchs in a similar plight complained to the boule at the same time, and after some debate the boule authorized them to recover the equipment due to them in any way possible: εἰσπράττεσθαι τρόπῳ ᾧ ἂν δυνώμεθα.[7] The speaker thinks it worth mentioning that the decree was not challenged in a γραφὴ παρανόμων, which suggests that a measure of this kind was unusual,[8] and even after being given *carte blanche* he proceeded with great caution. Being unable to find Theophemus he went to the man's brother Evergus and asked him to tell Theophemus about the decree; a few days later he went with witnesses to be assured by Evergus that he and Theophemus held their property separately, not in common, and to discover (a little belatedly) where Theophemus lived.[9] He then took a ὑπηρέτης from the ἀρχή and went to Theophemus' house, sending the woman who opened the door to find Theophemus;[10] when he arrived the speaker produced the text of the boule's decree and asked for the inventory of the equipment. When Theophemus replied with threats the boy

---

[1] § 20.   [2] § 44.
[3] The navy lists published by the ἐπιμεληταὶ τῶν νεωρίων constitute a record of the παραλαμβάνειν and παραδιδόναι of these officials (cf. the headings of *IG* ii² 1607, 1611, 1623), so it must surely be the epimeletae and not the boule (as Kahrstedt would prefer, *U.M.A.*, 2) to whom the speaker refers as ἡ ἀρχή.
[4] §§ 21-2.   [5] § 26.   [6] § 28.   [7] § 33.
[8] Perhaps the arrangements for the transfer of equipment directly from one trierarch to another were an innovation, and Theophemus and his fellow offenders were taking advantage of uncertainties caused by the new law. See pp. 156-7 below.   [9] § 34.   [10] § 35.

(i.e. the ὑπηρέτης) was sent out into the street to fetch witnesses.[1] In the presence of these witnesses the speaker asked Theophemus either to accompany him to the ἀποστολεῖς and the boule (if he disputed the claim) or to hand over the equipment: if he refused, the speaker would have to take security for it. Theophemus remained unco-operative, so the speaker laid hands on 'the person' standing by the door;[2] Theophemus stopped him; he went inside to take something as security; Theophemus assaulted him.[3]

The speaker gave an account of the incident to the boule, and displayed his bruises. The boule took a serious view of the matter, recognizing that this was not simply a private injury but defiance of public authorities,[4] and told the speaker to proceed against Theophemus by εἰσαγγελία, ὡς ἀδικοῦντι καὶ διακωλύοντι τὸν ἀπόστολον. Not surprisingly, Theophemus was found guilty;[5] but when the boule was voting on whether to fine him 500 drachmae (plus, we may assume, double the debt for the equipment) or to press for a heavier penalty in a δικαστήριον, the speaker declared that he would be satisfied with a fine of 25 drachmae.[6] We may wonder if the speaker is telling less than the whole truth —perhaps Theophemus was fined 25 drachmae for assault and a larger sum for impeding the dispatch of the expedition, or perhaps the boule was less easily softened than the speaker—for the dispute was prosecuted with increasing violence when the speaker returned from the expedition.[7] They entered lawsuits against each other; Theophemus contrived to have his charge heard first, and secured a verdict against the speaker; and when his damages had not been paid he seized the speaker's property with considerable violence. The speaker replied by charging Theophemus' principal witnesses with perjury, and [Demosthenes], XLVII, was written in support of that charge.

A stone has been found in the Agora bearing, on one face, part of a law or laws concerning trierarchs, naval equipment, and ship-builders, inscribed in the old Attic alphabet and, on the reverse, part of the Athenian sacrificial calendar, inscribed in the Ionic alphabet: it is therefore to be assumed that the naval law was published or republished in the revision of the laws begun in 410,[8] and this fragment probably belongs to a collec-

---

[1] [D.] XLVII. 36.   [2] § 37.   [3] § 38.   [4] § 41.   [5] § 42.

[6] § 43. The verb used is προστιμηθῆναι, denoting an additional penalty.

[7] We are not told that Theophemus surrendered the equipment even now, but it is to be presumed that he did: the inventory was produced in the course of the hearing (§ 43), and the speaker was somehow enabled to leave Athens with his ship (§ 45).

[8] Hesp. iv 1935, 1–32, nos. 1–2; text of the naval law (1) reprinted as SEG x 142. For the revision of the law code cf. Lys. XXX. Nic. 2–5, and on its publication see S. Dow, Proc. Mass. Hist. Soc. lxxi 1953–7.

tion of all the naval laws then in force. Lines 3–8 have been restored by Professor Oliver to yield the following provisions:

If any [man in debt to the state does not surrender to the trierarch succeeding him the hanging or] wooden equipment, the trierarch may [summon such an offender before the ἀρχή of the epim]eletae in the presence of two κλητῆρες and make his claim [; . . .] the epimeletae shall bring the case before the δικαστήριον on the following day; if [the defaulter does not enter a διαδικασία, he shall surrender the equipment] to the injured party, the execution being as from a [private debtor; if he does not give security when the trierarch asks for it, he shall pay] the δημόσιον such a sum as the δικαστήριον may assess.

That is, we are offered provision for a διαδικασία and procedure for dealing with a defaulting ex-trierarch which corresponds to that followed in 357/6 except in two respects: there is no mention of the ἀποστολεῖς, who in 357/6 but not for long afterwards played some part in bringing disputed cases to trial,[1] and jurisdiction remains with the δικαστήριον instead of passing to the boule if the original court order is ignored.

It is clear enough from the stone that we are dealing with trierarchs who bring disputes over equipment through the epimeletae to the δικαστήρια, but it is not clear that in the fifth century equipment passed directly from one trierarch to another without the intervention of the dockyard officials. It would at least be compatible with [Demosthenes], XLVII. 21 if direct transfer was introduced for the first time by Periander's symmory-law of 358/7, and this might help to explain why several trierarchs were in the same plight as the speaker:[2] Oliver may be right to restore provision for defiance in line 8, since proposers of fifth-century decrees seem commonly to have been pessimistic in this respect, but defiance after a court had pronounced judgement ought not in practice to have been common.

Theophemus very probably gave way after the εἰσαγγελία, but one thing which stands out very clearly is the impotence of the boule (as of other courts) in the face of straightforward defiance: with trierarchic debts treated as private debts rather than as debts to the state, imprisonment was evidently impossible, and though the decrees of the boule indemnified the new trierarch for any acts which he committed in the attempt to recover the equipment (at any rate, they should have indemnified him, but Theophemus found a court which

---

[1] [D.] XLVII. 26, with Lipsius, 114. Since ἀποστολεῖς were an extraordinary commission (Ch. III, p. 120) the duty was probably assigned specifically to the ἀποστολεῖς of that year.
[2] [D.] XLVII. 33. Cf. p. 155 n. 8 above.

thought otherwise) it seems that in the last resort little or nothing could be done if a trierarch retained state-owned equipment with sufficient obstinacy.

The difficulty of enforcing verdicts is further illustrated by the case of Androtion and his fellow ambassadors, who retained the proceeds from the sale of enemy goods. A decree moved, presumably in the ecclesia, by Aristophon provided for the appointment of ζητηταί before whom μηνύσεις might be laid against any one holding public moneys, whether sacred or secular. Euctemon denounced the trierarchs Archebius and Lysithides; he came before the boule, which made a probouleuma; in the ecclesia after a προχειροτονία he repeated his charge. Androtion and his colleagues protested that they, not the trierarchs, had the money, but Euctemon ἔδωκε γνώμην that the state should hold the trierarchs responsible, and leave it to them to enter a διαδικασία against the ambassadors who had been sailing on their ship; this decree was attacked in a γραφὴ παρανόμων, but without success.[1] The main object of the proceedings—and Demosthenes describes Euctemon's γνώμη as ὡς δυνατὸν δικαιοτάτην[2]—was not to lay the blame on the right man but to establish that some one was in debt to the state: if the men picked on were innocent, they nevertheless became responsible for repayment unless and until they could persuade a court to transfer the responsibility to those who had actually taken the money.

To sum up what we have seen of the boule's jurisdiction in naval matters—the principles on which court cases were distinguished from the boule's cases are not wholly clear, but though its powers of punishment were limited the boule seems to have been regarded as the senior authority, which could make an adjustment after a court had given its verdict, or would be consulted if a court's verdict had proved ineffective. Serious naval offences could be made the subject of an εἰσαγγελία, but the boule's involvement was not limited to cases brought to its attention in this way.

Of the boule's powers in connection with public works we read in the *Athenaion Politeia*: ἐξετάζει δὲ καὶ τὰ οἰκοδομήματα τὰ δημόσια πάντα, κἄν τις ἀδικεῖν αὐτῇ δόξῃ, τῷ τε δήμῳ τοῦτον ἀποφαίνει καὶ καταγνοῦσα παρα-

---

[1] D. XXIV. *Tim.* 11–14. I take it that § 9 is to be referred to this: Androtion was condemned by the boule, which made a probouleuma to bring Euctemon before the assembly; by the assembly, which enacted Euctemon's decree; and by the courts, which upheld the legality of the decree and found against Androtion in the διαδικασία. Since what we should expect to be a legal process found its way to the assembly, Euctemon's μήνυσις was presumably regarded as or converted into an εἰσαγγελία (for such conversion see p. 170 n. 1 below).

[2] D. XXIV. *Tim.* 13.

δίδωσι δικαστηρίῳ.¹ That the boule should have had powers in this field is extremely likely: we should expect it to have been able to impose fines up to 500 drachmae on its own authority, or to refer to a δικαστήριον for a heavier penalty, and we know that elsewhere this treatise regularly fails to mention the boule's limited final jurisdiction. The difficulty lies in τῷ τε δήμῳ ... ἀποφαίνει: since it is the boule which παραδίδωσι δικαστηρίῳ, condemnation by the ecclesia can scarcely have been required before the case was transferred to a court,² yet we have no parallel for the boule's being required to inform the ecclesia of actions in which the ecclesia did not participate. Foucart suggested that in some cases special action may have been required (i.e. by decree of the ecclesia) to rectify the consequences of an offence.

We have very little other evidence on judicial activity in connection with public works. The *Lexica Segueriana* mention the possibility of φάσις to the archon³—on what authority, we do not know. In the wall-building activity of 337/6 ἐπιβολαί were imposed and courts presided over by the tribally elected τειχοποιοί;⁴ and there remains only a tantalizing line from the decree of 307/6 for wall-building:

[—]ξ [. . . συλλ]αβοῦσαν κολ[άζ]ειν τ[ὸ]ν μὴ πειθαρχοῦν[τα].⁵

It is possible that the feminine noun to be supplied is βουλήν,⁶ but there is too much missing to permit a reliable reconstruction.

We are a little better informed in religious matters. An Eleusinian law of the fifth century fixed a fine of 500 drachmae for offences concerning the Πελαργικόν, and in such cases ordered the basileus to εἰσαγγέλλειν to the boule.⁷ When an uproar broke out in 415 over the profanation of the Eleusinian Mysteries and the mutilation of the Hermae the first public mention of the affair was made in the ecclesia: the boule was made αὐτοκράτωρ to inquire into the whole affair, but as far as we can tell all sentences were imposed by the δικαστήρια.⁸ Shortly before Andocides' trial in the autumn of 400, a branch was placed in supplication

---

¹ *A.P.* 46. ii. καταγνοῦσα is the reading of the papyrus: Kaibel and Wilamowitz, followed by most subsequent editors, proposed καταγνόντος, but Opperman and the Budé editors retain καταγνοῦσα. See also, for the emendation, B. Keil, *AM* xx 1895, 46–7 n. 2; against it, P. Foucart, *RPh²* xviii 1894, 247–8 (who appreciated the real difficulty), Lipsius, 197 n. 61, 981, Kahrstedt, *U.M.A.*, 207 n. 2. For καταγνοῦσα of a case to be referred to a δικαστήριον, cf. M&L 46, 38 (quoted below, p. 169), A. I. *Tim.* 111 (quoted above, p. 144), D. XXIV. *Tim.* 63.   ² As the champions of the emendation believe.

³ *L.S.* 315. 16.   ⁴ A. III. *Ctes.* 27.

⁵ *IG* ii² 463, 25. The *xi* was read by early editors, but not by Koehler (*IG* ii 167): it is still printed in the most recent text (Maier, *GMbi* 11).

⁶ So Kahrstedt, *U.M.A.*, 226 n. 2. The surviving portion of the inscription mentions no body which is likely to have been specified as ἡ ἀρχή.

⁷ M&L 73, 57–9.   ⁸ Cf. pp. 186–8 below.

on the altar in the Eleusinium during the celebration of the Mysteries. Meanwhile Cephisius made an ἔνδειξις of Andocides for taking part in the festival while ἄτιμος,[1] and when the basileus made his customary report to the prytanes they said they would bring him before the boule, and warned Andocides and Cephisius to attend. The boule met in the Eleusinium, and Callias drew attention to the branch on the altar; the herald asked who had put it there, and no one answered, though Andocides and Cephisius were standing by and Callias could see them;[2] there being no answer, the herald went in again to the boule. When the herald told the boule that there was no answer, Callias mentioned a νόμος πάτριος, that any one who had committed this offence could be put to death ἄκριτος,[3] and said he had heard that Andocides was guilty; Cephalus pointed out that Callias had no right to lay down the law— he was a Κῆρυξ, and not an Ἐξηγητής—and that the stele in the Eleusinium prescribed not the death penalty but a fine of 1,000 drachmae: but since Andocides was accused, he should be summoned before the boule. ἐπειδὴ δὲ ἀνεγνώσθη ἡ στήλη κἀκεῖνος οὐκ εἶχεν εἰπεῖν ὅτου ἤκουσεν, καταφανὴς ἦν τῇ βουλῇ αὐτὸς θεὶς τὴν ἱκετηρίαν.[4] Both the ἔνδειξις of Andocides for attending the Mysteries while ἄτιμος, which was ultimately referred to a δικαστήριον in which all the δικασταί were initiates,[5] and the illegal supplication were matters with which the boule was prepared to concern itself, and since our fragmentary Eleusinian decrees involve the boule in various ways there is no need for Mr. MacDowell's surprise at this fact.[6]

Bouleutic interest in another religious offence is attested by a passage in the *hypothesis* to the first speech *Against Aristogiton*:

Πυθάγγελος καὶ Σκάφων ἰδόντες Ἱεροκλέα φέρονθ' ἱερὰ ἱμάτια . . . ἀπάγουσι πρὸς τοὺς πρυτάνεις ὡς ἱερόσυλον, οἱ δὲ τῇ ὑστεραίᾳ καθιστᾶσιν εἰς τὴν ἐκκλησίαν.... ἐνταῦθ' Ἀριστογείτων γράφει ψήφισμα πρῶτον μὲν ἀπροβούλευτον, ἔπειτα δεινό-τατον, κελεῦον, ἐὰν μὲν ὁμολογῇ τὰ ἱμάτι' ἐξενεγκεῖν, ἀποθανεῖν αὐτὸν αὐτίκα, ἐὰν δ' ἀρνῆται, κρίνεσθαι.

---

[1] Cf. And. I. *Myst.* 121: this is the charge in connection with which the speech was written. ἔνδειξις was a formal pointing-out that a man was using rights to which he was not entitled (cf. Lipsius, 331–7, MacDowell, edition of this speech, p. 13 and commentary on § 111, Ruschenbusch, *Untersuchungen zur Geschichte des athenischen Strafrechts*, 67–70): when the rights in question were secular the charge was not heard by the boule.

[2] And. I. *Myst.* 112. This is more commonly taken to mean that Cephisius could see Andocides: e.g. Budé and Loeb translations, MacDowell's commentary.

[3] On some charges, presumably those for which there was a fixed penalty, a man who confessed his guilt could be punished without a formal trial (D. XXIV. *Tim.* 65, cf. *XXV. *Aristog.* i, *hyp.* 1). We cannot tell certainly from Lysias' verbal jugglings whether the σιτοπῶλαι of Lys. XXII. *Frum.* admitted their guilt, but even if they did they claimed the authority of the σιτοφύλακες for what they had done (§§ 5–6).

[4] And. I. *Myst.* 110–16.   [5] Ibid. 29.   [6] Commentary on § 111.

Aristogiton's decree was successfully attacked in a γραφὴ παρανόμων, and he was fined 5 talents.[1] The author of our speech concentrates on general abuse of Aristogiton, claiming that the facts had been adequately rehearsed by Lycurgus,[2] and Lycurgus' speech is presumably the source of the detailed account in the *hypothesis*. We may assume that the prytanes brought Hierocles before the boule as well as the ecclesia, and I suspect that the ἀπαγωγή may have resulted in a formal εἰσαγγελία.[3]

Finally, more unusual irregularities in the running of the state might be referred to the boule by the ecclesia. *IG* i² 95 has been tentatively restored by Mr. A. G. Woodhead to yield provisions for the boule and ecclesia to call a past prytany to account in the year 418/17.[4] On the general import of the decree he may well be right, but I am unhappy about the restoration of lines 9–12:

τὲν δ' ἐκκλεσίαν ποιὲν [περὶ τὲς Αἰαντί]-
[δος τὸς πρυτάνες] τὲς Αἰγεῖδος πρυταγ[είας εὐθὺς ἀφ' ἐς ἅ]-
[ν προβολεύσει hε βο]λὲ περὶ τούτον πέν[τε ἐμερόν, hόπος ἅ]-
[ν δικάζεν ἐχσει τει βολ]ει [τ]ει ἐπὶ Ἀντιφ[όντος ἄρχοντος].

If the boule is to make a probouleuma and bring the matter before the ecclesia, it is odd to set a time limit so that the *boule* may δικάζειν within the current year, and in any case the expression τει βολει τει ἐπὶ Ἀντιφόντος ἄρχοντος ought not to have been possible before the archontic and bouleutic years were made conterminous after the fall of the Four Hundred.

Another tentatively restored inscription from the end of the fifth century has a rider calling on the boule to inquire into the bribery used to obtain a decree:

[— τὲν βολὲν βολεῦσ]αι ἐν τει πρότει hέδ-
[ραι ἐν τοι βολευτερί]οι καὶ κολάζεν τὸν [δ]ορο-
[δοκεσάντον καταφσ]εφιζομένεν, καὶ ἐς δικασ-
[τέριον αὐτὸς ἐσάγε]ν, καθότι ἂν δοκει αὐτε[ι].[5]

This makes better sense: the initial verdict is to be the boule's, and the case is presumably to be referred to a δικαστήριον for a penalty more severe than the boule can impose.

---

[1] [D.] XXV. *Aristog. i, hyp.* 1–2, Din. II. *Arist.*, 12.   [2] [D.] XXV. *Aristog. i.* 14.

[3] ἀπαγωγή—physically taking the accused to the authorities—was permitted when an offender was caught in the act. See in general Lipsius, 317–31, Ruschenbusch, *Untersuchungen zur Geschichte des athenischen Strafrechts*, 67–70, and compare the right of arrest possessed by all British citizens who see a man committing an 'arrestable' offence. (I am grateful to Mr. C. D. Drake for explaining the current law to me.)

Though Aristogiton's decree was first proposed in the ecclesia, it is not clear from the *hypothesis* in what way it was technically ἀπροβούλευτον: see Ch. II, p. 53.

[4] *Hesp.* xviii 1949, 78–83 = *SEG* xii 32.   [5] M&L 85, 41–4. In l. 44 M&L follow Lipsius, 184 n. 23, in restoring παραδιδόσα]ν, but the infinitive of *IG* and Tod seems preferable.

In finance, in naval matters, and in religion the claims made for the boule by the *Athenaion Politeia* have been borne out, though in public works evidence for jurisdiction on the part of the boule and of other authorities is almost wholly lacking. Whereas we do our best to keep justice separate from the executive powers, so that even our rulers must obey the rule of law, the Athenians believed that executive authority should be reinforced by judicial power. The infliction of severe penalties was reserved for the people, or for representatives of the people sitting in a δικαστήριον, but the boule, which itself was the city in microcosm, was given enough power to deal with all but the most serious offences which it was likely to uncover in the course of its administrative duties.

(iii) εἰσαγγελία[1]

In examining the boule's official jurisdiction I have already mentioned several times the procedure known as εἰσαγγελία. According to the *Athenaion Politeia* εἰσαγγελία was instituted by Solon to enable the Areopagus to try τοὺς ἐπὶ καταλύσει τοῦ δήμου συνισταμένους:[2] though this formulation is more at home in the fourth century than in the sixth, Cylon before Solon and Pisistratus after remind us that the danger of tyranny at that time was very real, while Solon's poems show his awareness of the explosive situation with which he was dealing. That he provided for εἰσαγγελίαι to the Areopagus on major charges of public importance, such as attempting to set up a tyranny, does not seem inherently unlikely. Some have thought that εἰσαγγελίαι were partly or wholly transferred to the boule and ecclesia by Cleisthenes, but I shall argue in the appendix to this chapter that no change was made until the reforms of Ephialtes.[3]

The nature and content of the νόμος εἰσαγγελτικός in the period of the orators have been much disputed. The first strand in the lexicographers' account (derived according to the *Lexicon Rhetoricum Cantabrigiense* from

---

[1] See especially, H. Hager, *JP* iv 1872, Lipsius, 176–211, Bonner and Smith, i. 294–309. In addition to those treated in this section, there were certain other charges to which the word εἰσαγγελία was proper (see, e.g., Harp. s.v.). Ruschenbusch, *Untersuchungen zur Geschichte des athenischen Strafrechts*, 65, 73–4, stresses that the different εἰσαγγελίαι should have had a common origin; but in the classical period these other εἰσαγγελίαι were so much like γραφαί that they could be called γραφαί (e.g. Isae. XI. *Her. Hagn.* 6, 15, contr. 28, 31, 32, 35, [D.] LVIII. *Theocr.* 32, *A.P.* 56. vi), and εἰσαγγελία *tout court* denoted the procedure which I discuss here. On the different uses of this term see further p. 170 n. 1 below.

[2] *A.P.* 8. iv. εἰσαγγελία appears also in the 'Draconian' constitution (*A.P.* 4. iv), apparently for charges against the ἀρχαί.

[3] pp. 199–201 below.

Caecilius) reserves this process for ἄγραφα δημόσια ἀδικήματα.[1] The other strand in our tradition enumerates specific offences which were to be dealt with by εἰσαγγελία (I print in bold type those parts of the law which are quoted by Hyperides) :

(i) ἐάν τις τὸν δῆμον τὸν Ἀθηναίων καταλύῃ . . . ἢ συνίῃ ποι ἐπὶ καταλύσει τοῦ δήμου ἢ ἑταιρικὸν συναγάγῃ,[2]

(ii) ἢ ἐάν τις πόλιν τινὰ ἢ χώριον ἢ φρούριον προδῷ ἢ ναῦς ἢ πεζὴν ἢ ναυτικὴν στρατιάν,[3]

(iii) ἢ ῥήτωρ ὢν μὴ λέγῃ τὰ ἄριστα τῷ δήμῳ τῷ Ἀθηναίων χρήματα λαμβάνων καὶ δωρεὰς παρὰ τῶν τἀναντία πραττόντων τῷ δήμῳ,[4]

(iv) ἢ εἰς τοὺς πολεμίους ἄνευ τοῦ πεμφθῆναι ἀφικνῆται ἢ μετοικῇ παρ' αὐτοῖς ἢ στρατεύηται μετ' αὐτῶν ἢ δῶρα λαμβάνῃ.[5]

This does not exhaust the list of offences which might be dealt with by εἰσαγγελία, and Hager and Thalheim tried to add further clauses to the νόμος, so as to bring within its scope all charges which were in fact the subject of εἰσαγγελίαι. Hager added dockyard offences, on the basis of the bouleutic decree preserved in a navy-list: εἶναι δ' εἰσαγγελίαν αὐτῶν εἰς τὴμ βουλὴν καθάπερ ἐάν τις ἀδικεῖ περὶ τὰ ἐν τοῖς νεωρίοις,[6] and trading offences, from the title of a speech by Dinarchus: κατὰ Πυθέου περὶ τῶν κατὰ τὸ ἐμπόριον εἰσαγγελία.[7] Thalheim proposed to add also deceiving the people by false promises, παραπρεσβεία, and actions endangering the Second Athenian League.[8]

Bonner and Smith have attacked the whole principle underlying the search for additional clauses, arguing that the purpose of the νόμος εἰσαγγελτικός was to ensure the use of this procedure in certain cases, not to rule it out in others.[9] Certainly the degeneration of εἰσαγγελία into a means of dealing with petty crime, of which Hyperides complains,[10] suggests that there was no finite list of offences to which it could be applied. Though terms like conspiracy against the demos invited misinterpretation, I think we should accept the non-specific strand in the tradition, allowing εἰσαγγελίαι for ἄγραφα δημόσια ἀδικήματα as well as for

[1] Poll. VIII. 51, L.S. 244. 14, Harp., L.R.C. εἰσαγγελία (cf. Suid. εἰσαγγελία, schol. Plat. Rep. VIII 565 c).
[2] Hyp. IV. Eux. 7–8, Poll. VIII. 52, L.R.C. εἰσαγγελία.
[3] Hyp. § 8, Poll., L.R.C., cf. Lys. XXXI. Phil. 26.
[4] Hyp. § 8, Poll., L.R.C.
[5] Poll., L.R.C. (μετοικῇ is Houtsma's emendation of νικοίη in the MS. of the L.R.C.).
[6] IG ii² 1631, 398–401. Cf. p. 154 above.
[7] D.H. 651. Din. 10 (εἰσαγγελία is added from Harp. ἀντιβληθέντος), D. XXXIV. Phorm. 50.
[8] T. Thalheim, Hermes xxxvii 1902. The first two of these charges would probably be covered by the law as quoted by Hyperides.
[9] Bonner and Smith, i. 307.
[10] Hyp. IV. Eux. 1–3.

specified acts of treason and corruption.[1] Any major public offence was liable to be tried by this means, and it may be that the listing of eisangeltic offences did not keep pace with accepted practice.

The procedure followed has been disputed no less hotly than the range of charges to which it was applicable. One case of which we have a detailed account, that of the trierarch Theophemus in 357/6, has already been discussed. When Theophemus assaulted a man who was trying to take security for the return of trierarchic equipment (which the boule had authorized him to recover in any way possible), the injured man began by making a comparatively informal complaint to the boule, which regarded the assault as a public offence rather than a private injury, and told him to make an εἰσαγγελία: the prytanes were to set aside two days for Theophemus' trial ὡς ἀδικοῦντι καὶ διακωλύοντι τὸν ἀπόστολον. The trial took place, plaintiff and defendant spoke, and on a secret ballot the defendant was found guilty; the boule had then to vote by show of hands whether to fine Theophemus 500 drachmae (the most it could do on its own authority) or to pass the case to a δικαστήριον, but the plaintiff was content with an 'additional penalty' of 25 drachmae.[2] Hearing by the boule constituted a full trial, and if it was satisfied with a penalty within its own competence the case need go no further; if a heavier penalty was thought appropriate the case must go before a δικαστήριον. No mention is made of the ecclesia.

εἰσαγγελία certainly could involve the ecclesia, as we see from the unsavoury career of Agoratus at the end of the Peloponnesian War.[3] Lysias claims that as the democratic leaders objected to the peace terms which Theramenes brought back from Sparta he decided to eliminate them from politics before the terms were discussed in the ecclesia:

---

[1] German scholars have rejected the non-specific strand, and have tried to deduce from the trial of relevant cases when 'the νόμος εἰσαγγελτικός' was enacted (Lipsius, for instance, dated 'the νόμος' about the middle of the fourth century, and supposed that the non-specific rule applied to εἰσαγγελία before this date: this is now repeated by Berneker in Der Kleine Pauly, ii. 218). But this is to make too rigid a thing of 'the νόμος': before 410 any measure providing for εἰσαγγελία was a νόμος εἰσαγγελτικός; the revision of the laws at the end of the fifth century probably resulted in the compilation of a list of offences which at that time were eisangeltic, and which we may call the νόμος εἰσαγγελτικός; but a procedure existed in the fourth century for altering the νόμοι, and unless the compilation of the late fifth century was so framed as to limit εἰσαγγελία to certain charges (which is unlikely) an ordinary ψήφισμα would probably have sufficed to make further offences eisangeltic. (But the decree in IG ii² 1631 is merely bringing an offence under an already existing heading.)

The offences specified as eisangeltic bear a strong resemblance to those for which men were solemnly cursed in the prayer which began all meetings of the boule and ecclesia (cf. Ch. I, pp. 36–7). The oaths taken by archons, bouleutae, and (no doubt) other officers of state may be regarded as distant relatives.

[2] [D.] XLVII. Ev. et Mnes. 41–3.

[3] Lys. XIII. Ag. (cf. XII. Erat. 48).

Agoratus was Theramenes' main tool, but was to appear as an unwilling witness.[1] At a secret meeting of the boule (which in 405/4 was corrupt and oligarchically inclined) Theocritus gave news of a conspiracy, but would not himself reveal any name except that of Agoratus.[2] The boule resolved that some of its members should go down to the Piraeus to fetch Agoratus: they met him in the agora and tried to arrest him, but Nicias and others offered themselves as guarantors.[3] The bouleutae took the guarantors' names and returned to Athens; Agoratus and his friends took refuge by the altar at Munychia, but he refused to escape from Attica.[4] The boule enacted another decree (presumably, that Agoratus was to be interrogated at once), and οἱ ἐκ τῆς βουλῆς came to Munychia. Agoratus left the altar and went with them—of his own free will, Lysias claims.[5] He was taken to the boule, and there he denounced his guarantors, Theramenes' opponents, and others;[6] and was produced before an assembly in the theatre at Munychia, where he repeated his denunciations.[7] This assembly voted that his victims should be arrested and tried in a δικαστήριον[8] (but granted ἄδεια to one Menestratus at the request of a relative of Critias[9]). At this stage in the affair peace was made with Sparta and the Thirty came into power. Ignoring the decree of the assembly, they arranged for the trial to be held in a boule whose members voted under the watchful eyes of the Thirty:[10] Agoratus[11] and Menestratus[12] were released as public benefactors, and their victims were condemned to death. To prove Agoratus' involvement in the affair, Lysias cites the decrees of the boule and demos περὶ ὧν Ἀγόρατος κατείρηκεν, and remarks that the formal verdict acquitting Agoratus read, διότι ἔδοξε τἀληθῆ εἰσαγγεῖλαι:[13] likewise Menestratus was released, δόξαντα τἀληθῆ εἰσαγγεῖλαι.[14] The man who at first was arrested to face a charge of conspiracy was transformed by turning state's evidence into the prosecutor of his victims,[15] and had the democracy not been overthrown the case would have passed through all three bodies competent to hear εἰσαγγελίαι—boule, ecclesia, and a δικαστήριον. Nor can the ecclesia have been eliminated from the procedure after the fall of the Thirty: in the case of Ergocles, in 388, the ecclesia apparently met twice on consecutive days, to discuss verdict and penalty;[16] in the εἰσαγγελία against Lycophron in 333 Hyperides' speech was delivered before δικασταί, but ἐν τῷ δήμῳ τὸ πρῶτον αὐτοὶ εὐθὺς ᾐτιάσαντο;[17]

---

[1] §§ 1–19. (In fact the ecclesia probably agreed to the terms before these events took place.)   [2] §§ 20–2.   [3] § 23.   [4] §§ 24–8.   [5] § 29.
[6] §§ 30–1.   [7] § 32.   [8] §§ 34–5.   [9] § 55.   [10] §§ 35–7.
[11] § 38.   [12] § 56.   [13] § 50.   [14] § 56.
[15] εἰσαγγεῖλαι is surely technical here, pace Lipsius, 208.
[16] Lys. XXVIII. Erg., especially § 9.   [17] Hyp. I. Lyc. 3.

and the *Athenaion Politeia* and the lexica record that time was provided for the hearing of εἰσαγγελίαι at the κυρία ἐκκλησία of each prytany.[1]

It has been suggested that the three-stage procedure intended in the case of Agoratus was obligatory, at any rate in cases where a fine imposed by the boule was inadequate. Ferguson wrote: 'The Council lacked the power to submit an *eisangelia* involving treason to a dikastery without the *thesmothetae* first laying it before the *demos*',[2] and took the reference of Antiphon's case directly from the boule to a δικαστήριον as an indication of the constitutional irregularity of the regime of the Five Thousand. Reference of the case immediately from the boule to a δικαστήριον he described as 'an aggrandisement of the Council', but Clinias' tribute-decree, probably in the 440s, provides for immediate reference from the boule to the heliaea,[3] and since the full judicial power of the demos resided with those of its members who sat in the δικαστήρια[4] I am not convinced that this by-passing of the ecclesia need ever have appeared undemocratic. The details of known εἰσαγγελίαι are hard to reconcile with Ferguson's theory.

The relations of the boule and ecclesia provide the most difficult problem. The trials of Antiphon, Agoratus, and Theophemus all began in the boule, and this practice was at any rate commonly observed. Isocrates in listing the ways in which it is possible to proceed against συκοφάνται mentions γραφὰς μὲν πρὸς τοὺς θεσμοθέτας, εἰσαγγελίας δ' εἰς τὴν βουλήν, προβολὰς δ' ἐν τῷ δήμῳ,[5] which ought to mean that the boule was the normal recipient of εἰσαγγελίαι. Yet there is evidence to suggest that an εἰσαγγελία might be begun in the ecclesia, and Harpocration thought that ἡ πρώτη κατάστασις could be made to the boule or the ecclesia.[6] Pythonicus first mentioned the profanation of the Mysteries

---

[1] *A.P.* 43. iv, Poll. VIII. 95, Harp., Suid. κυρία ἐκκλησία, L.R.C. κυρία ἡ ἐκκλησία. It is stated elsewhere that the thesmothetae τὰς εἰσαγγελίας εἰσαγγέλλουσιν εἰς τὸν δῆμον (*A.P.* 59. ii, Poll. VIII. 87, Phot. θεσμοθέται, cf. schol. Plat. *Phaedr.* 235 D). That the thesmothetae should have presided at an eisangeltic session of the ecclesia is unlikely, and what is needed is a statement that they were the εἰσάγουσα ἀρχή when an εἰσαγγελία was referred to a δικαστήριον, which is what the Plato scholiast seems to mean. Blass (*A.P.*, 4th edition) and Lipsius (207 n. 99) read ⟨ἃς⟩ εἰσαγγέλλουσιν, and Dr. D. M. Lewis has suggested ⟨τοῖς⟩ εἰσαγγέλλουσιν. The appearance of προβολαί later in the list may possibly be a sign of more serious corruption, but many if not most of the cases which were the subject of προβολαί (informal complaints in the ecclesia, which need have no legal consequence—cf. Lipsius, 211–19) would come to the courts of the thesmothetae, and carelessness on the part of the author is a more likely explanation.

[2] W. S. Ferguson, *Mélanges Glotz*, i. 349, cf. T. Thalheim, *RE*, v. 2140. Lipsius, 184, 206, also cited by Ferguson, does not support the part of his account which I have quoted. For the condemnation of Antiphon see [Pl.] *X. Or.* 833 D–834 B, with G. E. M. de Ste Croix, *Hist.* v 1956, 16–17, and p. 182 below, with notes.

[3] M&L 46, 37–9 (quoted below, p. 189). [4] Cf. p. 169 with n. 5, and pp. 197–8.

[5] Is. XV. *Antid.* 314. [6] Harp. εἰσαγγελία.

in 415, Andocides says, in the ecclesia,[1] and this constituted an εἰσαγγελία;[2] Isocrates in a far less detailed account writes of an εἰσαγγελία
to the boule,[3] and it is not disputed that the boule was made αὐτοκράτωρ
and received the later charges.[4] It seems likely from Andocides' wording
that Pythonicus had not given prior notice of his allegations, but it also
appears that the item on the agenda under which his allegations were
made was the dispatch of the Sicilian expedition. But time was, as I have
said, provided expressly for τὰς εἰσαγγελίας ... τοὺς βουλομένους ποιεῖσθαι
in the κυρία ἐκκλησία of each prytany,[5] and this may point the way to
a solution. I have discussed in Chapter II the rule of προβούλευσις, by
which any matter on which the ecclesia voted had first to be discussed
by the boule, and suggested there that the provision for εἰσαγγελίαι and
προβολαί in the κυρία ἐκκλησία and ἱκετηρίαι in a second assembly constituted a partial exception to the rule: under these items a matter could
be given its first airing in the ecclesia, but since it had not yet been discussed by the boule the ecclesia could only reject the matter out of hand
or provisionally accept it and refer it to the boule for further consideration.[6] If this is correct, the beginnings of an εἰσαγγελία will have been
similar to the beginnings of a decree: like any other business transacted
by the ecclesia it had to be discussed by the boule before the ecclesia
could reach a final decision; normally the boule would be the first public
authority to discuss it, but it was possible for the question to originate
in the ecclesia and be referred back to the boule. This I believe was
intended to be the main characteristic of eisangeltic procedure in
the post-Ephialtic democracy, that εἰσαγγελίαι were heard not by the
ordinary courts but by the final authorities in Athens, the boule and
demos.

But we know that the δικαστήρια did come to be involved in εἰσαγγελίαι, at any rate by the end of the fifth century. Some instances have
already been mentioned, and many more could be added. Timotheus,
on a charge which was very probably the subject of an εἰσαγγελία, was
fined 100 talents by voters who had taken an oath;[7] Aristophon, very
probably on an εἰσαγγελία, was acquitted in a δικαστήριον by two
votes;[8] and Philocrates, certainly on an εἰσαγγελία, was condemned in a

---

[1] And. I. *Myst.* 11.   [2] Ibid. 27.
[3] Is. XVI. *Big.* 6. (Lipsius, 195 with n. 57, follows Isocrates, regarding Andocides' version
as rhetorical exaggeration.)
[4] Cf. pp. 186–8 below.   [5] Cf. p. 166 and n. 1 above.
[6] Cf. Ch. II, pp. 52–7.
[7] Din. I. *Dem.* 13–14 = III. *Phil.* 17, Nep. XIII. *Timoth.* 3. v, cf. Is. XV. *Antid.* 101.
[8] Hyp. IV. *Eux.* 28, cf. schol. A. I. *Tim.* 64, where Hager (*JP* iv 1872, 85–6) accepted
Meier's παρ' ὀλίγον for παρανόμων.

δικαστήριον.[1] Hyperides implies in the opening of his speech *For Euxenippus* that in the days when εἰσαγγελίαι were directed against prominent men (who normally did not remain in Athens to await the verdict) on serious charges the cases regularly came before a δικαστήριον.[2] Just as the boule's hearing was a full trial, and the verb καταγιγνώσκειν could be used of its condemnation,[3] it appears from the acquittal of Aristophon and indeed from the general remarks of Hyperides that the court's hearing also was a full trial, not merely a meeting to sentence a man who had already been convicted. The same was presumably true of εἰσαγγελίαι heard by the ecclesia, and a man threatened with a serious penalty by this means will thus have had at least two chances of acquittal, though on charges carrying a fixed penalty beyond the competence of the boule the hearing in the boule may have been purely formal.[4]

Many cases were referred by the boule to the δικαστήρια, some to the ecclesia, and it was at any rate possible for all three bodies to be involved. A clue to the explanation is perhaps provided by a passage in Aristophanes' *Wasps*:

ἔτι δ' ἡ βουλὴ χὠ δῆμος ὅταν κρῖναι μέγα πρᾶγμ' ἀπορήσῃ
ἐψήφισται τοὺς ἀδικοῦντας τοῖσι δικασταῖς παραδοῦναι.[5]

I believe that Ephialtes, or whoever deprived the Areopagus of the right to hear εἰσαγγελίαι, intended that they should be heard instead by the boule, with reference to the demos sitting in its judicial capacity as the undivided ἡλιαία—but his measure providing for this probably specified no more than 'boule and demos'. The development of the separate δικαστήρια and reduction of the archons' judicial power are poorly attested,[6] but I suspect that the old concept of the heliaea as a judicial session of the ecclesia lingered for some time after it had become normal for the heliaea to be divided into δικαστήρια. Perhaps the last active

---

[1] Hyp. IV. *Eux.* 29, cf. the inscription recording the sale of his property, *Hesp.* v 10, 45–50, 105–15.

[2] Hyp. IV. *Eux.* 1–2. Cf. also the νόμος in D. XXIV. *Tim.* 63 (n. 4 below).

[3] Cf. p. 159 n. 1 above.

[4] When a case was referred to the ecclesia, the boule would make a probouleuma in the normal way. For procedure when a case was referred to a δικαστήριον, Timocrates' *habeas corpus* law (D. XXIV. *Tim.* 63) is our best guide: the boule's κατάγνωσις was given to the thesmothetae by the chief secretary, the γραμματεὺς κατὰ πρυτανείαν, and (subject to the limitations in the bouleutic oath—cf. pp. 194–5) the accused could be kept under arrest to await his trial; prosecution was not taken over by the boule but remained the responsibility of private citizens. If the charge did not carry a fixed penalty, the boule's κατάγνωσις could probably include a recommendation (cf. M&L 46, 39–41, where the prytanes are to arrange a debate in the boule on the penalty in an official case).

[5] Ar. *Vesp.* 590–1.

[6] Cf. p. 204 and n. 1.

occurrence of the old sense of the word is its restoration in Clinias' tribute decree:

$$[\hat{h}\hat{o}\ \delta'\ \mathring{a}\nu]$$
καταγνôι h[ε βολέ, μὲ τιμᾶν αὐτ]ôι κυρία ἔστο [ἀλλ' ἐσ]-
φερέτο ἐς τ[ὲν ἐλιαίαν εὐθύ]ς.[1]

Shortly afterwards we find a reference to 'the heliaea of the thesmo-thetae',[2] and it is presumably this that is intended when Thudippus' assessment-decree mentions [τῆς ἐλιαίας καὶ τ]ôν ἄλλον δικαστερίον.[3] It is assumed that when the change was complete the courts of the thesmo-thetae, meeting in the building of the old heliaea, retained the name of the heliaea also. With the name, they must have retained also some of the aura of the old heliaea, and must still have been thought of as judicial sessions of the demos: at any rate it is abundantly clear that the δικαστήρια acquired the right to inflict those heavy penalties which were reserved in the laws reissued at the end of the fifth century for the δῆμος πληθύων.[4]

A rule that εἰσαγγελίαι were to be heard by the boule and demos would thus become open to two interpretations. Provision that εἰσαγγελίαι might receive their first airing in the ecclesia, probably made when εἰσαγγελίαι were taken away from the Areopagus, will have suggested that δῆμος should be interpreted as the ecclesia, yet before the end of the fifth century it seems to have been accepted that the full judicial powers of the demos were vested in the separate δικαστήρια.[5] While this development was taking place, the boule was acquiring the official jurisdiction which we have examined in the previous section.[6] If the laws concerning εἰσαγγελία did contain fairly general provisions as well as a list of major public offences which ought to be dealt with by this means, the line between εἰσαγγελίαι and other charges heard by the boule will have become blurred—and some of the laws giving the boule official jurisdiction may

---

[1] M&L 46, 37–9 (447?).

[2] M&L 52, 75–6 (446/5); cf. Ant. VI. *Chor.* 21 (419), where the same court is called the heliaea of the thesmothetae and a δικαστήριον.

[3] M&L 69, 49. A reference to the heliaea in line 14 is said to be to the building (*ATL*, iii. 71).

[4] *IG* i² 114 (on this inscription see pp. 195–9). I translate δῆμος πληθύων as 'people in assembly'.

[5] In the Hermocopid investigation a δικαστήριον condemned to death (And. I. *Myst.* 66), but this right is reserved for the δῆμος πληθύων in *IG* i² 114, 37 (= l. 36, Wade-Gery, *BSA* xxxiii 1932–3). Cf. pp. 197–8.

[6] The boule's acquisition of official jurisdiction cannot of course be dated. I believe that the process was started by Ephialtes (cf. pp. 201 sqq.) and greatly encouraged by the need to administer the Delian League, and that the situation in the fourth century will have been more nearly static than in the fifth.

have specified reference to the δικαστήρια.[1] It was clear enough what charges might be laid before the boule, but it may sometimes have been less clear, especially with offences which were covered by more than one law, whether what was going on was or was not an εἰσαγγελία. If an εἰσαγγελία was first made in the assembly, the law being followed was clear, and by ordering a probouleuma the assembly could retain ultimate control; but the assembly's time was valuable and the volume of public business tended to increase: the assembly may frequently have ordered the boule not to report back but to refer cases to a δικαστήριον for a heavy penalty, and the boule will have tended to use the δικαστήρια for εἰσαγγελίαι of which it was the first recipient, except in a few cases of major importance. In this way εἰσαγγελίαι will have been assimilated procedurally to the boule's official jurisdiction,[2] and I believe the lines which I quoted from the *Wasps* refer to the beginnings of this transference to the δικαστήρια of the μεγάλα πράγματα which should have been judged by the boule and demos.[3]

εἰσαγγελίαι on major charges of public importance might be submitted

---

[1] Many factors will have assisted the confusion. It takes time for a technical vocabulary to become established and recognized, and verbs whose general meaning was obvious, like γράφεσθαι, εἰσαγγέλλειν, μηνύειν, and φαίνειν, could easily be used in contexts where they were not technically correct. Dr. Ruschenbusch has made the interesting suggestion (*Untersuchungen zur Geschichte des athenischen Strafrechts*, 73–4) that εἰσαγγέλλειν was the original term for any verbal denunciation to the authorities, and tended to survive for all charges older than the rule that such denunciations must be submitted in writing: if he is right, this will do much to explain uses of the term which by the standard of the fourth-century νόμος εἰσαγγελτικός were non-technical.

It is, I think, likely that charges of νόμοις μὴ χρῆσθαι against a magistrate, though heard by the boule, were not covered by the νόμος εἰσαγγελτικός of the fourth century; yet εἰσαγγέλλειν is used of these in *A.P.* 45. ii, and εἰσήγγειλα is used in Ant. VI. *Chor.* 35, for what is presumably an instance of this charge. More clearly incorrect is εἰσήγγελλε in Lys. X. *Theomn.* i. 1, in a case which should have been an ἔνδειξις: here the Budé editors have suggested the more innocuous ἐπήγγελλε. Lipsius, with *A.P.* 45. ii particularly in mind, was brought to the conclusion (196–7): 'Von dieser probuleutischen Tätigkeit des Rats bei Eisangelien über Verbrechen wider den Staat ist nun aber zu scheiden seine selbständige Strafgewalt. . . . Von Anzeigen über Vergehen, die von Beamten oder Privaten an ihn gelangen, ist εἰσαγγέλλειν der herkömmliche Ausdruck.' It is perhaps safer to say that there was a tendency to use εἰσαγγέλλειν, technically incorrectly, of cases heard by the boule which were not even thought to be covered by the νόμοι εἰσαγγελτικοί.

It appears also that a laying of information might be converted into an εἰσαγγελία, or be treated as an εἰσαγγελία in retrospect. The speaker of [D.] XLVII. *Ev. et Mnes.* consulted the boule informally and was told to εἰσαγγέλλειν (§§ 41–2); Agoratus began by being arrested on an eisangeltic charge, but was finally released διότι ἔδοξε τἀληθῆ εἰσαγγεῖλαι (Lys. XIII. *Ag.* 50).

[2] This in turn will have encouraged the use of εἰσαγγελία for cases that were not of major importance. The assimilation of other procedures to that of the γραφή is noticed by Ruschenbusch, *Untersuchungen zur Geschichte des athenischen Strafrechts*, 53–64: in the case of εἰσαγγελία the tendency to use a δικαστήριον instead of the assembly illustrates the development, but the involvement of the boule survived as a distinguishing characteristic of this procedure.

[3] Cf. Lipsius, 184, Bonner and Smith, i. 300–1.

either to the ecclesia or to the boule. If the ecclesia was the recipient it could not immediately give the charge a full hearing: it could reject it out of hand, or else it had to refer the case to the boule, when it might commission a probouleuma or order reference to a δικαστήριον or leave the boule discretion to decide further procedure.[1] If the boule was the recipient, it had this discretion in any case. The boule then considered the charge, and if it acquitted, the trial was over. If it convicted, the heaviest penalty it could impose was a fine of 500 drachmae, enough to prevent further waste of time in routine matters, but not enough for the major offences which εἰσαγγελία was intended to cover. In these cases a second hearing was required, before the ecclesia or a δικαστήριον, to reconsider the verdict and if necessary to pass sentence (if the charge carried no fixed penalty, the boule could make suggestions). The boule also had jurisdiction in a variety of official cases, to which the word εἰσαγγελία was not technically appropriate: here too its punitive power was limited to a fine of 500 drachmae, but it could refer the case to a δικαστήριον if a heavier penalty seemed desirable. Confusion inevitably resulted, and the similarity of procedure obliterated the distinction between two originally very different forms of trial.

(iv) δοκιμασία

I conclude with a note on a quasi-judicial activity of the boule, the holding of various δοκιμασίαι (checks on a man's qualifications for some duty or privilege). Most δοκιμασίαι were held in the δικαστήρια, but in the time of the *Athenaion Politeia* there were four kinds in which the boule was involved: the δοκιμασία of the ἔφηβοι on their enrolment; that of the ἱππεῖς, πρόδρομοι, ἄμιπποι, and of the horses used by the cavalry; that of the ἀδύνατοι entitled to a subsistence grant; and that of the next year's archons and bouleutae.

According to the *Athenaion Politeia* an Athenian came of age at eighteen, and was subjected to a δοκιμασία before enrolment in his deme. The process began with a διαψήφισις in the deme to exclude any who were under age, or were not free and of citizen birth: a candidate rejected on the criterion of freedom might appeal to a δικαστήριον, and if the court upheld the deme's judgement he would be sold as a slave. The candidates

---

[1] This last, rather than enhanced punitive power, is perhaps what was intended when the boule was made αὐτοκράτωρ in a judicial matter (cf. p. 180 n. 4 and pp. 186–8 below)—but I suspect that the implications of this term were never openly formulated.

were then vetted by the boule on the criterion of age, and if the demesmen had accepted anyone under age they might be punished by the boule.[1]

For administrative convenience δοκιμασία and registration did not follow immediately after a man's birthday, but took place in an annual ceremony, probably early in the new year.[2] Whereas the *Athenaion Politeia* seems to insist that a man must have reached his eighteenth birthday,[3] the most natural inference from Demosthenes' first speech *Against Aphobus* is that he was enrolled after his seventeenth birthday, in the course of his eighteenth year.[4] Ages could be specified in Athens by either means: bouleutae[5] and dicasts[6] were men who 'had reached the age of thirty'; διαιτηταί were men 'in their sixtieth year'.[7] Dr. Pélékidis tries to support the rule of the *Athenaion Politeia* from the epitaph of Dexileos of Thoricus, but something has gone wrong with his calculations:[8] if Dexileos had completed two years' service as an ἔφηβος before he became one of the πέντε ἱππεῖς (which is not certain), those two years should have contained his eighteenth and nineteenth birthdays, so that he would have been registered in his eighteenth year. Since διαιτηταί held office for a year they were more naturally described as men 'in their sixtieth year'; but specification that a certain birthday should have been reached is the more convenient rule in cases where a man who has become eligible will remain eligible for life, and also for ephebic registration, which took place when a man had reached a specified age. Unless in Athenian counting a man was 'one' when he was born and his 'eighteenth' birthday was what we should call his seventeenth (and his 'sixtieth' year was, in our counting, the year between his fifty-eighth and his fifty-ninth birthdays), there is a clash between the *Athenaion Politeia* and what we learn from Demosthenes, and the circumstantial detail of the forty-two age-groups suggests that the *Athenaion Politeia* should not be wrong.

---

[1] *A.P.* 42. i–ii. On this δοκιμασία, see Ch. Pélékidis, *Histoire de l'éphébie attique*, part ii, ch. 2.
[2] Cf. Lys. XXI. *Pec. Acc.* 1; D. XXX. *Onet. i.* 15 is not decisive against this.
[3] ἐγγράφονται . . . ὀκτωκαίδεκα ἔτη γεγονότες (*A.P.* 42. i); κἄν τις δόξῃ νεώτερος ὀκτωκαίδεκ' ἐτῶν εἶναι (*A.P.* 42. ii). It has now been argued by J. M. Carter, *BICS* xiv 1967, that these expressions mean not 'at the age of 18' but 'in the 18th year'; but the fact that the διαιτηταί were the men of the 42nd age-group (*A.P.* 53. iv–v, originally given a perverse interpretation by Kenyon) proves that the *A.P.* is not reckoning ages in the same way for the ephebi and for the διαιτηταί. If a man is registered after his 18th birthday, he will belong to the 42nd age-group in the year in which his 60th birthday falls.
[4] D. XXVII. *Aphob. i.* 19, contr. 21–3, 63, 69. Cf. B. R. I. Sealey, *CR*² vii 1957, 195–7.
[5] X. *M.* 1. ii. 35.
[6] Heliastic oath *ap.* D. XXIV. *Tim.* 150.
[7] *A.P.* 53. iv.
[8] Tod 105, with Pélékidis, op. cit. 94 n. 2. Dexileos was born in 414/13 and killed in 394/3; Pélékidis misdates his birth in 413/12 but makes him 21 years old at his death!

According to the *Athenaion Politeia* there was a possibility of reference from the deme-assembly to the courts on the criterion of freedom, and compulsory reference to the boule on the criterion of age. In Aristophanes' *Wasps* Philocleon includes the following in his list of the delights enjoyed by dicasts:

παίδων τοίνυν δοκιμαζομένων αἰδοῖα πάρεστι θεᾶσθαι.[1]

The *Athenaion Politeia*'s account may be incomplete, and it may be that both courts and boule were entitled to take notice of all criteria for citizenship, but any connection between the δικαστήρια and this δοκιμασία would provide a sufficient excuse for this remark in comedy.[2]

The names of those accepted as citizens were placed on the ληξιαρχικὸν γραμματεῖον,[3] which apparently differed from the ἐκκλησιαστικὸς πίναξ.[4] Inclusion in the first preceded inclusion in the second, and it has been inferred from a passage in Xenophon that registration on the ἐκκλησιαστι- κὸς πίναξ came when a man was twenty (or in his twentieth year).[5] It is not necessary for our present purposes to examine the problems connected with the institution of the ἐφηβεία, but if this two-year gap between registration as a citizen and inclusion on the lists of those entitled to attend the assembly is to be accepted, we have an additional reason for dissenting from Wilamowitz's view that this system of two years' compulsory training was first devised in the years after Chaeronea:[6] the δοκιμασία of young citizens goes back at any rate as far as Aristophanes' *Wasps*, and is unlikely to be a more recent creation than Cleisthenes' deme organization; and the antiquity of the oath sworn by the ἔφηβοι is generally acknowledged.[7] In the ephebic system as recorded in the *Athenaion Politeia* the young citizens displayed their prowess after their

[1] Ar. *Vesp.* 578.

[2] There are several references in Lysias to the δοκιμασίαι of young citizens, but they throw no light on the procedure: X. *Theomn.* i. 31, *XI. *Theomn.* ii. 12, XXI. *Pec. Acc.* 1, XXVI. *Evand.* 21, XXXII. *Diog.* 9.

[3] *IG* i² 79, 5–7, Isae. VII. *Her. Apoll.* 27, Lyc. *Leocr.* 76, Lucian, *Jupp. Trag.* 26 with schol., Harp. ληξιαρχικὸν γραμματεῖον. Professor Habicht argues from *IG* i² 79 that in the fifth century the thetes were excluded from the ληξιαρχικὰ γραμματεῖα (*Hermes* lxxxix 1961, 5–6), but he has been sufficiently answered by Meritt (*Greek Historical Studies*, 123–4) and Jameson (*Hist.* xii 1963, 399–400).

[4] [D.] XLIV. *Leoch.* 35. Were the πίνακες perhaps instituted when assembly-pay was introduced?

[5] X. *M.* III. vi. 1 (οὐδέπω εἴκοσιν ἔτη γεγονώς: if pressed, this would support the *A.P.* view that registration followed the eighteenth birthday—but see p. 172 n. 3 above, for a suggestion that the phrase should mean 'in the 20th year'), cf. Lucian, *Jupp. Trag.* 26. See Gilbert, 199.

[6] Wilamowitz, *Aristoteles und Athen*, i. 193–4. Recent arguments for an earlier origin: O. W. Reinmuth, *TAPA* lxxxiii 1952; Ch. Pélékidis, op. cit., part i.

[7] Tod 204, 5–20, cf. Lyc. *Leocr.* 76, Poll. VIII. 105–6, Stobaeus, *Flor.* XLIII. 48.

first year's training at an assembly held in the Theatre of Dionysus;[1] but later, when the ἐφηβεία had ceased to be compulsory and became the preserve of the rich, they made their ἀπόδειξις not to the whole demos but to the boule.[2]

In addition to the regular vetting of men at the age of eighteen, special checks were made from time to time when it was suspected that unqualified men had found their way on to the lists of citizens. Any such διαψήφισις was an extraordinary event, and the procedure may have been different on different occasions, but the boule was not involved in the one check for which information is available: in the διαψήφισις ordered by a law of Demophilus in 346/5 the assemblies of the separate demes were to vote on each member of the deme, and any rejected by their deme could appeal to a δικαστήριον.[3]

The boule also performed various δοκιμασίαι in connection with the cavalry, which enabled Xenophon to make the generalization, ἡ πόλις . . . προσέταξε δὲ τῇ βουλῇ συνεπιμελεῖσθαι τοῦ ἱππικοῦ.[4] The *Athenaion Politeia* lists its functions as follows:[5] it held a δοκιμασία of the cavalry's horses, with the power to withhold the fodder grant from a man who was not feeding his horse adequately and to brand and reject those horses which could no longer do what was required of them; it vetted the special forces known as πρόδρομοι and ἄμιπποι, presumably checking their physical ability to do their duty; and it checked the cavalry lists compiled by a board of ten elected καταλογεῖς: every man listed apparently had to appear in person before the boule. The lists of the καταλογεῖς were presented to the boule by the hipparchs and phylarchs, and we now have an inscription of 282/1 in which the cavalry honours the hipparchs and phylarchs, who *inter alia* have taken care of the τιμήσεις and δοκιμασίαι, and have held the τῶν σωμάτων δοκιμασία with the boule.[6] The boule's rejection of unfit horses is attested also by Xenophon[7] and Hesychius,[8] though Photius ascribes it to the generals[9] and Pollux is non-committal.[10] Its δοκιμασία of the cavalry also is mentioned by Xenophon,[11] but in the complaint that Alcibiades had insinuated himself into the cavalry

---

[1] *A.P.* 42. iv.

[2] Earliest dated inscription *Hesp.* vii 20, 17–18 (258/7).

[3] [D.] LVII. *Eub., hyp.* The speech gives us a fascinating account of the proceedings in the assembly of the deme Halimus (§§ 9–14); § 8 shows that Eubulides was a member of the boule as well as demarch (cf. *IG* ii² 218, 6 sqq. [346/5]).

[4] X. *Hipparch.* i. 8.   [5] *A.P.* 49. i–ii.

[6] Threpsiades and Vanderpool, *AΔ* viii 1963, 103–9, no. 1 = *SEG* xxi 525.

[7] X. *Oec.* ix. 15, *Hipparch.* i. 13, cf. iii. 9–14.

[8] Hes. τρυσίππιον.

[9] Phot. ἵππου τρόχος.

[10] Poll. VII. 186.   [11] X. *Oec.* ix. 15.

without undergoing a δοκιμασία, the words, οὔτε ὑφ' ὑμῶν δοκιμασθείς, are addressed to δικασταί.[1]

A late archaic vase-painter of the Brygan circle (*c.* 500?) has given us a representation of one of these δοκιμασίαι: three young horsemen are submitting themselves and their horses to a commission of two men, identified by Körte as bouleutae, and a secretary; a man with a staff, perhaps one of the hipparchs, is also present.[2] Körte, writing before the discovery of the *Athenaion Politeia*, distinguished between the annual review of the existing cavalry, and the check on new entrants, assuming that the former took place in the presence of the whole boule but new entrants were vetted by a small sub-committee, and that the δοκιμασία-painter's vase illustrates the latter.[3] Clearly the detailed examination, whether of old cavalrymen protesting their inability to continue in the service or of new recruits, must have been carried out by a few men, but this was probably followed by a parade in the presence of the whole boule, after which a vote was taken. In any case the δοκιμασία-painter could hardly be expected to depict the whole boule.

The boule's concern for the cavalry's horses is analogous to its concern for the navy's ships, and its power over cavalrymen who failed to take good care of their horses may be compared with that over trierarchs who failed to return ships and equipment in good condition. The other δοκιμασίαι seem to have been checks that men were fit and competent to perform their special tasks. These tasks of the boule fit in with its general duty to ensure that equipment and men with special responsibilities were available whenever the state needed them.

A third form of δοκιμασία held by the boule was that of the invalids with property of less than three minas, who were entitled to a subsistence grant from the state:[4] they apparently had to undergo this examination annually.[5] Grants to war invalids are said to have been instituted in the sixth century, by Solon or Pisistratus,[6] but though such grants may

---

[1] [Lys.] XIV. *Alc. i.* 10, cf. 1. [Lys.] XIV. *Alc. i.* 8, XV. *Alc. ii.* 7, Lys. XVI. *Mant.* 13, Harp., Suid. δοκιμασθείς mention the δοκιμασία of the cavalry without specifying the examining authority.   [2] Berlin 2296; Beazley, *A.R.V.*[2], i. 412, no. 1; illus. *AZ* xxxviii 1880, pl. 15.

[3] G. Körte, *AZ* xxxviii 1880. We have no evidence on the organization of the cavalry as early as this vase, and it is at any rate possible that in the pre-Ephialtic period the examining authority was not the boule. (For my view of the boule between Cleisthenes and Ephialtes cf. pp. 194 sqq.) W. Helbig, *Mém. Ac. Inscr. et Belles-Lettres*, xxxvii. 1. 1904, ch. vi, discussed this vase and three others depicting Athenian cavalry, quoted from Hauser a date of 485–455 for the vases, and suggested that they are to be linked with a reorganization of the Athenian armed forces shortly after 477. He would identify one at least of the inspectors as a hipparch, and Körte's hipparch as an ordinary member of the public (op. cit. 230–1).

[4] *A.P.* 49. iv, A. I. *Tim.* 103–4 with schol.   [5] Lys. XXIV. *Pens. Inv.* 7, 26.

[6] Pl. *Sol.* 31. iii–iv, cf. schol. A. I. *Tim.* 103, whose rate of 3 obols is perhaps due to a confusion with jury pay (so Boeckh, Jacoby).

perhaps have been made this early to a few men on some specific occasion (probably as σίτησις ἐν πρυτανείῳ rather than a cash grant) this regular system of δημοσία τροφή must be a creation of the Periclean or post-Periclean democracy. In the time of Lysias the grant was 1 obol *per diem*;[1] in the reign of Alexander, 2 obols;[2] and Philochorus' figure of 9 drachmae a month probably reflects a commutation made in the twelve-tribe period when there were as many prytanies as months:[3] an invalid's grant was always less than the wage which an unskilled but able-bodied citizen could earn. The boule's task will have been to check that the invalids' property was worth less than three minas, and that their disabilities were such as to hinder them from earning their living. Lysias wrote a speech for an invalid to address to the boule,[4] when an unnamed enemy objected that he must be an able-bodied man as he could ride on horseback (though he could walk only with two sticks),[5] and that in any case he did not need the money (yet his father had left nothing, until recently he had had to keep his mother, he had no children, and though he plied a trade he could find no assistant who could take over when he grew too old to continue with it).[6]

Finally, there is the δοκιμασία of bouleutae and archons, of which we read: δοκιμάζει δὲ καὶ (sc. ἡ βουλὴ) τοὺς βουλευτὰς τοὺς τὸν ὕστερον ἐνιαυτὸν βουλεύσοντας καὶ τοὺς ἐννέα ἄρχοντας. καὶ πρότερον μὲν ἦν ἀπο-δοκιμάσαι κυρία, νῦν δὲ τούτοις ἔφεσίς ἐστιν εἰς τὸ δικαστήριον.[7] Later in the *Athenaion Politeia*[8] the δοκιμασία of the archons is described in greater detail, and is said to take place ἔν τε τῇ βουλῇ καὶ πάλιν ἐν δικαστηρίῳ. Prospective archons were asked about their ancestry and family shrines, their treatment of their parents, their payment of taxes,[9] and their military service. Accusations might be brought, and the candidates were given the opportunity to reply: οὕτω δίδωσιν ἐν μὲν τῇ βουλῇ τὴν ἐπι-χειροτονίαν, ἐν δὲ τῷ δικαστηρίῳ τὴν ψῆφον. ἐὰν δὲ μηδεὶς βούληται κατ-ηγορεῖν, εὐθὺς δίδωσι τὴν ψῆφον. This ballot used to be a pure formality

---

[1] Lys. XXIV. *Pens. Inv.* 13, 26.   [2] *A.P.* 49. iv, Hes. ἀδύνατοι.

[3] Philochorus, 328 F 197 a, with Jacoby's commentary. (F 197 b, from *L.S.* 345. 15, has the figure of 5 obols!) Earlier in the fourth century the grant was being paid once a prytany (A. I. *Tim.* 104).

[4] Lys. XXIV. *Pens. Inv.* (boule, § 1, etc.).   [5] §§ 4–5, 10–12.

[6] §§ 4–6.   [7] *A.P.* 45. iii.   [8] *A.P.* 55. ii–iv, cf. Poll. VIII. 85–6.

[9] The papyrus reads [καὶ] τὰ τέλη τελεῖ. Most editors have followed Kaibel and Wilamowitz in inserting ⟨εἰ⟩ before τελεῖ from *L.R.C.* θεσμοθετῶν ἀνάκρισις, and in referring this to payment of taxes; but Gilbert, 219, compared *A.P.* 7. iv and thought that the question referred to membership of a Solonian property-class. The latter must be the interpretation of Pollux, who paraphrases: καὶ τί τὸ τίμημά ἐστιν αὐτοῖς (VIII. 86: τί is Koch's suggestion in *RE*, v. 1271, for εἰ); but the orthodox interpretation is confirmed by Cratinus Junior, fr. 9 (Kock), and Dinarchus, II. *Arist.* 17–18.

when no objections were brought, with one man giving 'the vote of the court', but before the *Athenaion Politeia* was written it had been made a genuine vote, in case a candidate colluded with his objectors. Three stages are thus envisaged in the development of this δοκιμασία: in the first, it was conducted by the boule alone, from whose decision no appeal was possible; later it was begun in the boule but afterwards referred to a δικαστήριον—apparently whether the boule accepted or rejected the candidate, since provision was made for a purely formal vote if no objections were brought; finally, the court was required to vote seriously regardless of what had happened in the boule. This double δοκιμασία of the archons seems to be confirmed by a reference to the thesmothetae in Demosthenes' speech *Against Leptines*: δὶς δοκιμασθέντας ἄρχειν, ἔν τε τῇ βουλῇ καὶ παρ' ὑμῖν ἐν τῷ δικαστηρίῳ.[1]

Reference from the boule to a δικαστήριον after the equivalent of an acquittal would be unique, and some scholars have refused to believe in it.[2] The *Athenaion Politeia*'s second stage would seem to guarantee it, but this in itself is hard to credit. In all other instances of ἔφεσις to a δικαστήριον the court's power to give the final decision is taken very seriously, and is regarded as an important element in the democracy, and it does not seem likely that a reformer would at the same time give the right of final decision in all δοκιμασίαι to the δικαστήρια and in the case of the archons provide for a purely token vote in cases where no objection had been lodged. But if ἔφεσις did become obligatory in all cases, there would be more point in an argument provided by Lysias for a man who attacked Evander (very probably the archon of 382/1) at his δοκιμασία in the boule:

ἂν δὲ καὶ ἐπὶ τοιόνδε λόγον τράπωνται, ὡς ὁ χρόνος οὐκ ἐγχωρεῖ ἄλλον ἐπικληρῶσαι, ἀλλὰ ἀνάγκη, ἐὰν αὐτὸν ἀποδοκιμάσητε, ἄθυτα τὰ πάτρια ἱερὰ γίγνεσθαι, τάδ' ἐνθυμήθητε, ὅτι πάλαι ὁ χρόνος παρελήλυθεν. ἡ γὰρ αὔριον ἡμέρα μόνη λοιπὴ τοῦ ἐνιαυτοῦ ἐστιν, ἐν δὲ ταύτῃ τῷ Διὶ τῷ σωτῆρι θυσία γίγνεται, δικαστήριον δὲ παρὰ τοὺς νόμους ἀδύνατον πληρωθῆναι. εἰ δὲ ταῦτα πάνθ' οὗτος ὥστε γενέσθαι διαπέπρακται, τί προσδοκῆσαι ⟨δεῖ⟩ δοκιμασθέντ' αὐτὸν ποιήσειν;[3]

[1] D. XX. *Lept.* 90 (ascribing the rule to Solon, as usual).

[2] e.g. Lipsius, 271, Kahrstedt, *U.M.A.*, 62. Reference of all archontic δοκιμασίαι to a court is accepted by Bonner and Smith, ii. 243–4, and also by Wade-Gery, *E.G.H.*, 194–5, whose view is slightly different from that advocated in the text. He believes that confirmation by the heliaea was always required when the boule accepted a candidate, but originally the boule's rejection was final: in the time of the *Athenaion Politeia* 'the Archon designate must (before he can take office) be scrutinized twice, by Boulê and lawcourt: two fences must be taken but only the second need be cleared', but 'formerly, the Archon had to *clear* both fences'. He would date the introduction of appeal against the boule's rejection late and thinks that in Lys. XXVI. *Evand.* 14–15 'it is perhaps rather implied that there is none'.

[3] Lys. XXVI. *Evand.* 6–7. M. Just suggests that ἔφεσις could be initiated only by a candidate whom the boule rejected: *Hist.* xix 1970, 132–40.

When Evander's friends try to defend his appointment on the grounds that it is now so late in the year that if he is rejected there will be no time to appoint another man before the inaugural ceremonies of the new year, the objector is to reply that it is in any case too late to complete the panel of archons in time for the new year,[1] since a court cannot be convened to ratify the boule's acceptance of his in time.[2]

That double δοκιμασία for archons was the rule in the fourth century must, I think, be accepted; whether the *Athenaion Politeia*'s second stage ever existed is doubtful (perhaps the purely formal vote when no objection was made belongs to the period before ἔφεσις was introduced).[3] The nature of the questions officially prescribed suggests that the institution is an old one, older than the full democracy in which the δικαστήρια played so important a part, and probably older than the Cleisthenic boule of five hundred.[4] If this δοκιμασία goes back to the sixth century, we should expect it to be conducted by the ex-archons in the Areopagus rather than the boule of four hundred, and its transfer to the boule and δικαστήρια may have been a part of Ephialtes' reform.[5]

Double δοκιμασία is mentioned only for the archons, and the vetting of four or five hundred bouleutae must have been an arduous business which the Athenians would not duplicate unnecessarily. Here ἔφεσις is likely to have meant optional appeal or perhaps automatic reference to a court for those men whom the outgoing boule rejected, and I imagine that the original check will always have been made by the outgoing boule.[6]

---

[1] This has happened on previous occasions (§ 8).

[2] The passage is normally taken to mean that there will be no time for an appeal before the new year if the boule rejects Evander, but it is Evander and his friends who are stressing the dire consequences of his rejection; the objector's reply ought to be that this argument is irrelevant as Evander will not be able to play his part in the inaugural sacrifices even if he is accepted. § 8 will to some extent be a red herring, as the sacrifices will be presided over by the basileus whether Evander is ultimately allowed through or not.

[3] If pressed, the wording of *A.P.* 55. iv might point to the conclusion that in the author's day the boule did not vote unless objections were raised, but this is more probably an unfortunate condensation.

[4] This does not, of course, rule out changes: πόθεν τῶν δήμων must be post-Cleisthenic. Kahrstedt (*U.M.A.*, 61–2) thought that the archaic state with its small ruling class did not need δοκιμασίαι, and suggested that their introduction might be linked with that of the bouleutic oath; but I do not think that a formal, rather than genuinely fact-finding, interrogation before the swearing of the archontic oath would be impossible in the sixth century.

[5] Cf. p. 205 below.

[6] We have two speeches of Lysias written for delivery at the δοκιμασία in the boule of a prospective bouleutes: XVI. *Mant.* (so Blass, *Attische Beredsamkeit*², i. 517), XXXI. *Phil.* (cf. § 2); and cf. XXVI. *Evand.* 10–11.

APPENDIX

The Punitive Powers of the Boule

The normal picture of the boule's history as a lawcourt is based principally on the following passage in the *Athenaion Politeia*:

ἡ δὲ βουλὴ πρότερον μὲν ἦν κυρία καὶ χρήμασιν ζημιῶσαι καὶ δῆσαι καὶ ἀποκτεῖναι. καὶ Λυσίμαχον αὐτῆς ἀγαγούσης ὡς τὸν δήμιον καθήμενον ἤδη μέλλοντα
ἀποθνῄσκειν Εὐμηλίδης ὁ Ἀλωπεκῆθεν ἀφείλετο, οὐ φάσκων δεῖν ἄνευ δικαστηρίου
γνώσεως οὐδένα τῶν πολιτῶν ἀποθνῄσκειν· καὶ κρίσεως ἐν δικαστηρίῳ γενομένης
ὁ μὲν Λυσίμαχος ἀπέφυγεν καὶ ἐπωνυμίαν ἔσχεν ὁ ἀπὸ τοῦ τυπάνου, ὁ δὲ δῆμος
ἀφείλετο τῆς βουλῆς τὸ θανατοῦν καὶ δεῖν καὶ χρήμασιν ζημιοῦν, καὶ νόμον ἔθετο,
ἄν τινος ἀδικεῖν ἡ βουλὴ καταγνῷ ἢ ζημιώσῃ, τὰς καταγνώσεις καὶ τὰς ἐπιζημιώσεις
εἰσάγειν τοὺς θεσμοθέτας εἰς τὸ δικαστήριον, καὶ ὅ τι ἂν οἱ δικασταὶ ψηφίσωνται,
τοῦτο κύριον εἶναι.[1]

In this appendix I try to show that there was never a time when the
boule's judicial powers were unlimited: after working backwards through
the evidence for the powers which the boule exercised, I shall re-examine
the nature of the bouleutic oath, and the so-called Charter of the
Democracy, *IG* i² 114, and conclude with the suggestion that the boule
first acquired judicial powers (apart from the discipline of its members
and the δοκιμασία of its successors) in the reforms of Ephialtes, and that
a limit was set to these powers from the beginning.

I remarked at the beginning of this chapter that the result attributed
to Eumelides' rescue of Lysimachus is too drastic: the boule was in the
fourth century able to impose fines up to 500 drachmae,[2] and to imprison
in certain circumstances.[3] But it could not impose fines above this limit,
and it could not pass the death sentence. Midias could say to the boule,
ἀγνοεῖτ᾽, ... ὦ βουλή, τὸ πρᾶγμα; καὶ τὸν αὐτόχειρ᾽ ἔχοντες ... μέλλετε καὶ
ζητεῖτε καὶ τετύφωσθε; οὐκ ἀποκτενεῖτε;[4] but Demosthenes is representing

---

[1] *A.P.* 45. i.   [2] See p. 147 and n. 6 above.

[3] The boule could order the arrest of the generals accused of misconduct at Arginusae
(p. 148), of defaulting state debtors (pp. 148–51), and of men whom it found guilty on an
εἰσαγγελία, whose case it intended to refer to a δικαστήριον for a heavy penalty (D. XXIV.
Tim. 63); but it swore not to imprison a man who could provide three guarantors from his
own property-class except on a charge of treason or conspiracy against the demos or under the
νόμοι τελωνικοί (p. 194 with n. 4). These are all cases of precautionary imprisonment, to
ensure that a man discharged a debt or stood trial (cf. p. 151 n. 1 above): I imagine that it
was left to the boule to decide in any case for which it was responsible whether these precautions were necessary (so Lipsius, 813, on εἰσαγγελίαι).

If we refer 45. i to penal imprisonment only, however, the *Athenaion Politeia* seems to be right
in denying that the boule possessed such powers in the author's day; but I have suggested on
pp. 150–1 that in the fifth century imprisonment may have been automatic, and regarded
as penal rather than precautionary, when a man defaulted on a debt to the state.

[4] D. XXI. *Mid.* 116.

Midias' conduct as outrageous, and although he does not complain on this particular score the passage cannot be used as a serious indication that the boule could order a man to be put to death. About 386 the boule was tempted to have offending corn-dealers executed ἄκριτοι (that is, without a trial in the proper form),[1] and there is a similar case as early as 393, where a man charged before the boule says, παρὰ μικρὸν ἦλθον ἄκριτος ἀποθανεῖν, τελευτῶντες δὲ ἐπείσθησαν ἐγγυητὰς παρ' ἐμοῦ δέξασθαι.[2] (These men, whom it would have been improper for the boule to condemn to death, were not citizens but foreigners.[3] We know of one occasion in the fourth century when the boule did pass sentence of death on a Cean:[4] it is natural that the rights of aliens should have been less than those of citizens, though likely that the boule's greater power over aliens was simply inferred from the absence of any clearly stated restriction in the laws, so that public opinion was unhappy about the exercise of these powers except in moments of such strong feeling as would be aroused by the killing of an Athenian πρόξενος.) On the restoration of the democracy in 403/2 Archinus brought before the boule a man who was failing to respect the amnesty, and secured his condemnation to death: πείσας ἄκριτον ἀποκτεῖναι.[5] We must not place too much faith in the ἄκριτον here, since the procedure would certainly have been irregular at the time when the *Athenaion Politeia* was written and the word may have been used anachronistically, but it is at least very likely that this condemnation was in fact irregular.[6] The obligation to accept guarantors in most cases instead of arresting a man until his trial or the payment of his debt, was written into the bouleutic oath,[7] and there is no evidence that in the fourth century the boule possessed the right of penal, as opposed to precautionary, imprisonment.

These limitations are known to have existed in the fourth century, and though there is no indication of date in the passage which I have quoted

---

[1] Lys. XXII. *Frum.* 2.

[2] Is. XVII. *Trap.* 42. We should not see in D. LI. *Cor. Tri.* 8–9 another instance of temptation to the boule, in 361. Though the speech is addressed to the boule the case alluded to here probably came before the ecclesia as an εἰσαγγελία (Lipsius, 190–1 n. 41, Gernet, Budé edition of D.'s *Plaidoyers Civils*, iii. 62–3 n. 3).

[3] Lys. XXII. *Frum.* 5, Is. XVII. *Trap.* 3–4.

[4] Tod 142, 37–41. Perhaps the boule had been made κυρία to inquire into this matter—in which case there may have been more doubt than ever as to what the boule's powers were (cf. p. 171 n. 1 above, and pp. 186–8 below).   [5] *A.P.* 40. ii.

[6] Though the letter of the law gave him a convenient excuse to attack Thrasybulus' citizenship decree (*A.P.* 40. ii, A. III. *Ctes.* 195, [Pl.] *X. Or.* 835 F–836 A), Archinus was prepared to upset the original arrangement made with the oligarchs who had withdrawn to Eleusis (*A.P.* 40. i), and until the new code of νόμοι had been ratified there was genuine uncertainty as to what was law (cf. And. I. *Myst.* 81).

[7] D. XXIV. *Tim.* 144–8, cf. pp. 194–6 below.

from the *Athenaion Politeia*,[1] it has been thought that another passage
provides a *terminus post quem*. After listing the eleven μεταβολαί which the
constitution has undergone, the author writes: ἁπάντων γὰρ αὐτὸς αὑτὸν
πεποίηκεν ὁ δῆμος κύριον, καὶ πάντα διοικεῖται ψηφίσμασιν καὶ δικαστηρίοις,
ἐν οἷς ὁ δῆμός ἐστιν ὁ κρατῶν. καὶ γὰρ αἱ τῆς βουλῆς κρίσεις εἰς τὸν δῆμον
ἐληλύθασιν.[2] This implies, it has been said, that the transference of the
boule's κρίσεις to the demos occurred in or after the eleventh μεταβολή,
and Wilamowitz[3] and Sandys[4] accordingly supposed that the boule
possessed unrestricted judicial powers at least until 403. But other
references to the judicial activity of the boule show that this simple
solution cannot be accepted.

It is certain that the boule appointed by the Thirty was frequently
used as a lawcourt with full condemnatory powers. We are told that it
gladly condemned the informers who were first charged before it;[5]
Critias denounced Theramenes to the boule,[6] and when he was afraid
that the boule would acquit him struck his name off the roll of the three
thousand privileged citizens and pronounced his condemnation on behalf
of the Thirty;[7] Agoratus' victims were condemned by the boule, with the
Thirty sitting on the prytanes' benches to see how the bouleutae voted.[8]
At first the boule was the only judicial body, but a law enacted shortly
before the condemnation of Theramenes reserved for the three thousand
the right to a trial before the boule, and gave the Thirty full powers over
all other Athenians.[9] (The Eleusinians whom the Thirty exterminated in
preparation for their flight from Athens were condemned by an assembly
of the three thousand;[10] Demaretus was killed under the regime of the
Ten, it is not clear by whom.[11]) If it had not been possible immediately
before the oligarchy for the boule to condemn to death, the precedent
will have been useful both to Archinus and to those fourth-century
accusers who urged the boule to exceed its powers; but the democrats
took care to annul the acts of the Thirty,[12] and there can be no question

---

[1] The story in its present form belongs to the period when it was held that the full judicial
power of the demos was vested in the δικαστήρια, but οὐ . . . ἄνευ δικαστηρίου γνώσεως in *A.P.*
45. i could be a fourth-century paraphrase of an earlier οὐκ ἄνευ τοῦ δήμου.

[2] *A.P.* 41. ii. It is not clear how widely κρίσεις should be interpreted: its coming shortly
after δικαστηρίοις should mean that strictly judicial matters are at any rate included; if the
δοκιμασία of bouleutae and archons (45. iii) and the choice of παραδείγματα and the Panathenaic πέπλος (49. iii) are to be included as well, it would be dangerous to assume that all
these changes must have taken place at the same time.

[3] *Aristoteles und Athen*, ii. 195–7: change between 386 (Lys. XXII. *Frum.*) and 352 (D.
XXIV. *Tim.*).   [4] Commentary[2] on *A.P.* 45. i, ὁ ἀπὸ τοῦ τυπάνου.

[5] X. *H.* II. iii. 12.   [6] D.S. XIV. 4. v, X. *H.* II. iii. 23.

[7] X. *H.* II. iii. 50–1.   [8] Lys. XIII. *Ag.* 36–8.

[9] X. *H.* II. iii. 51, *A.P.* 37. i.   [10] X. *H.* II. iv. 8–10.

[11] *A.P.* 38. ii.   [12] D. XXIV. *Tim.* 56.

of the boule's having legally retained rights given it by the oligarchs: if about the turn of the century the boule possessed unlimited judicial powers, these powers must have been granted or re-granted by the democrats after the fall of the Thirty.

Immediately before the oligarchy, in the years after the fall of the Four Hundred, it appears that it had not been possible for the boule to condemn to death. After Athens' defeat at Aegospotami in 405 Cleophon attacked the boule as disloyal, and Satyrus, one of the bouleutae, persuaded the boule to arrest Cleophon and bring him before a δικαστήριον. Nicomachus, one of the men engaged in revising the Athenian law-code, produced on the day of the trial a law permitting the boule to sit with the jury, and this device enabled the boule to secure Cleophon's condemnation.[1] We have already seen that the trial of the generals who failed to pick up survivors after the battle of Arginusae in 406 was initiated by the boule. The generals were first deposed by οἱ ἐν οἴκῳ—presumably the ecclesia—and one of them was prosecuted in a δικαστήριον for peculation and misconduct, but the proceedings which led to their condemnation by a riotous assembly began when they reported on the battle to the boule, and were arrested to be produced before the demos.[2] The trial of Antiphon and Archeptolemus is ascribed by Caecilius to the archonship of Theopompus,[3] who replaced Mnasilochus on the fall of the Four Hundred early in 411/10.[4] If we follow Professor Meritt in associating the restoration of the full democracy with the battle of Cyzicus,[5] this trial will have taken place under the regime of the Five Thousand, and this seems to be borne out by various peculiarities in the document preserved for us.[6] It appears from the decree that Antiphon and Archeptolemus were denounced to the boule by the generals, and the boule voted that they should be arrested, and prosecuted in a δικαστήριον by the generals and ten bouleutae.[7]

We thus have three instances, two from the full democracy and one from the intermediate regime of 411/10, of the boule's transferring a case in which it was hostile to the accused to an organ of the demos, either the

---

[1] Lys. XXX. *Nic.* 10–11, cf. XIII. *Ag.* 12.   [2] X. *H.* I. vii. Cf. p. 148 above.
[3] Decree quoted [Pl.] *X. Or.* 833 E–F.   [4] *A.P.* 33. i.
[5] *Athenian Financial Documents*, 106–9.

[6] We are given the date within the prytany, not otherwise found in dating a decree before 368/7 (Tod 136); and the secretary and ἐπιστάτης are from the same tribe, which under the democracy could not occur before the reorganization of the secretarial office between 368/7 and 363/2 (Tod 136, contr. *IG* ii² 109). Cf. Additional Note A, p. 226, and Ch. III, pp. 134–5.

[7] I hope to discuss elsewhere the general nature of the constitution of the 5,000, but I may remark here that I am not persuaded by Mr. G. E. M. de Ste Croix's arguments (*Hist.* v 1956) that the property qualification applied only to office-holding and not to membership of the ecclesia.

ecclesia or a δικαστήριον. (There is also a rider to a decree of 409, ordering the boule to investigate a charge of using bribery to secure a decree, and to produce the offenders in a δικαστήριον, καθότι ἂν δοκεῖ αὐτεῖ.[1]) Cloché pointed out[2] that in the two later cases the boule appears to have been more hostile to the accused than the populace as a whole, and took special measures to secure a conviction. In these circumstances we must surely believe that if the boule had been entitled to pass sentence it would have done so, and that the boule's powers were therefore already at this time restricted. In all these cases the boule at least retained the power of arrest,[3] but the charges all concern treasonable activity (Cleophon accused the boule of treasonable conspiracy, and was probably himself condemned as a traitor[4]), and the boule was entitled to arrest men awaiting trial on these charges even in the time of Demosthenes.[5] There is nothing here to suggest that in the last years of the Peloponnesian War the boule's powers were greater than in the fourth century.

Confirmation that by the late fifth century the boule's powers were limited is commonly drawn from a badly mutilated inscription published as *IG* i² 114 and subsequently studied by Professor Wade-Gery.[6] I shall have more to say about this tantalizing document below, in considering the nature of the bouleutic oath, but here it will be sufficient to remark that the document was almost certainly inscribed very soon after the fall of the Four Hundred; that much of it is concerned with the boule and with steps that may not be taken ἄνευ τō δέμο τō Ἀθεναίον πλεθύοντος; and that among these steps seem to be the infliction of the death penalty (l. 36) and some other form of penalty (θοὰν ἐπιβαλēν, l. 41), while the sum of 500 drachmae, which was the limit up to which the boule could impose fines in the fourth century, also makes an appearance (l. 31).[7] The

---

[1] M&L 85, 38 sqq.

[2] P. Cloché, *REG* xxxiii 1920 (except where otherwise stated, all references to Cloché are to this article). This is the most important study of the problems examined in this appendix.

[3] Compare also the arrest of Archestratus, with what result we do not know, for proposing in the boule that the terms offered by Sparta after Aegospotami be accepted (X. *H.* II. ii. 15).

[4] No charge specified, Lys. XXX. *Nic.* 10–11. πρόφασιν μὲν ὅτι οὐκ ἦλθεν εἰς τὰ ὅπλα ἀναπαυσόμενος, Lys. XIII. *Ag.* 12—but the penalty for ἀστρατεία or λιποταξία was not death but ἀτιμία (A. I. *Tim.* 29, III. *Ctes.* 176, Lys. X. *Theomn.* i. 1, D. XV. *Rhod. Lib.* 32, cf. XXI. *Mid.* 58) without loss of property (And. I. *Myst.* 74), and the charge was heard not in a regular court but by the generals and soldiers ([Lys.] XIV. *Alc.* i. 5, XV. *Alc.* ii. 1, D. XXXIX. *Boe. Nom.* 17). Doubtless this was one of the charges made against Cleophon, but it was probably not the only one.

[5] D. XXIV. *Tim.* 144–8.

[6] *BSA* xxxiii 1932–3, 113–22. I cite by Wade-Gery's line numbers throughout; to obtain the correct reference in *IG* i² 114, add one.

[7] The evidence of this inscription must be used with extreme caution, as fragment a is very badly preserved: I assume that letters read both in *IG* i² and by Wade-Gery were safely identifiable thirty to forty years ago, and I report some readings of Dr. D. M. Lewis; I also report some readings of my own (I claim no authority for these, but think it useful to record what

precise significance of the document is disputed, but it would be generally accepted that it testifies to restrictions on the powers of the boule, which ought to have been observed at the time when the document was inscribed or reinscribed.

Cloché, accepting that the boule's powers were limited between 410 and 404, but believing that the story of Eumelides and Lysimachus should be dated after the eleventh μεταβολή in the constitution, suggested that the boule lost its full powers at some time before 410, but recovered them after the fall of the Thirty, only to lose them again early in the fourth century. The final change he dated before 386, recognizing that it would not have been proper for the boule to pass sentence on Lysias' corn-dealers, but he overlooked the parallel case of the speaker of Isocrates' *Trapeziticus*, not later than 393: if the boule's powers were increased in 403, it cannot have retained these additional powers for more than ten years.[1] The only piece of evidence which suggested to Cloché that the boule possessed full judicial powers at any time after 403 is *Athenaion Politeia*, 41. ii. It would be surprising if the author regarded the removal of so recently granted a power as an important part of the democracy's development, and I believe that a proper reading of the text need not indicate that he associated the reduction of the boule's powers with the eleventh μεταβολή at all. The eleventh change is the last, and since Athens' constitutional history has been represented as the development of democracy with occasional setbacks it is not unnatural that at the end the author should summarize what has taken place. It is the final result of the whole process, that the demos has made itself κύριος and administers everything by decrees and δικαστήρια, that even the κρίσεις of the boule have passed to the demos. The introduction of assembly pay, which follows in § iii, happens to be a change made after 403, but I believe it is mentioned not for that reason but to illustrate the growth in the power of the demos. I am not satisfied that this passage can be used to date the restriction of the boule's powers, and if I am right there is nothing which obliges us to believe that the boule of the democracy possessed unlimited judicial powers at any time after 410.[2]

could be seen in 1964 by a non-expert examining the stone carefully but—deliberately—without expert help). I was unable to make out any part of the word δραχμάς in l. 31 (traces of the first letter seemed most like a κ; beyond that I could identify nothing, nor more than faint traces of [θ]α[νατ]ō[ι] in l. 36; θοὰν ἐπιβαλε[ν] is clearly legible on the better-preserved fragment b. See further on the readings p. 196 nn. 3, 5, and p. 197 n. 1 below.

[1] He agreed that the death sentence passed at the instance of Archinus very shortly after the restoration in 403 was probably illegal.

[2] For other suggestions that the boule was deprived of various powers in the early part of the fourth century see my remarks in Ch. V, pp. 218–9, with notes referring to my discussions of related problems.

The oligarchs of 411, like those of 404, made the boule rather than the assembly of all qualified citizens the sovereign body: ἐλθόντας δὲ αὐτοὺς τετρακοσίους ὄντας ἐς τὸ βουλευτήριον ἄρχειν ὅπῃ ἂν ἄριστα γιγνώσκουσιν αὐτοκράτορας, καὶ τοὺς πεντακισχιλίους δὲ ξυλλέγειν ὁπόταν αὐτοῖς δοκῇ.[1] These men chose all magistrates themselves, and all organs of popular government were suspended. Judicial functions, like all others, were discharged by the Four Hundred: Andocides was arrested and brought before them, and though he saved his life by seeking refuge at the ἑστία he was imprisoned;[2] Thucydides writes in general terms of executions, imprisonments, and exiles.[3]

It is when we turn to the situation before the revolution that our troubles begin. In Aristophanes' *Thesmophoriazusae*, whose production is commonly assigned to the Dionysia of 411,[4] the following lines occur:

> EYP.   τῇδε θἠμέρᾳ κριθήσεται
>   εἴτ' ἔστ' ἔτι ζῶν εἴτ' ἀπόλωλ' Εὐριπίδης.
> ΜΝΗΣ.   καὶ πῶς; ἐπεὶ νῦν γ' οὔτε τὰ δικαστήρια
>   μέλλει δικάζειν οὔτε βουλῆς ἐσθ' ἕδρα,
>   ἐπεὶ τρίτη 'στὶ Θεσμοφορίων, ἡ Μέση.[5]

Some have seen in this a sign that as late as 411 the boule was competent to condemn to death, but we must beware of making illicit deductions from the words of a comedian, and I believe that another interpretation is equally possible. Aristophanes has to introduce the fact that the Thesmophoria are being celebrated, and that the women are planning revenge on Euripides: when Euripides says that today will decide his fate, Mnesilochus replies that this is impossible as the courts are not sitting today; the courts seem to have sat daily except on public holidays,[6] and another body which notoriously met daily except on public holidays was the boule;[7] I therefore suggest that the fact that the courts are not sitting is the strict reply to Euripides, and a reference to the boule is added simply to emphasize that today is the third day of the Thesmophoria, and to prepare the way for Aristophanes' festival.[8] There is, however, in this play another passage which may be relevant. In lines 929–46 Mnesilochus is sentenced to be bound to a plank (so that he may represent Andromeda chained to the rock, and provide an opportunity for a parody of Euripides'

---

[1] T. VIII. 67. iii.   [2] And. II. *Red.* 13–15.   [3] T. VIII. 70. ii.

[4] V. Coulon in the introduction to the Budé edition of Aristophanes (vol. i, p. vi), M. Platnauer (*O.C.D.*, 93. i), K. J. Dover (*O.C.D.*², 113. i), and W. Kraus (*Der Kleine Pauly*, i. 578) all give this date without hesitation. See further p. 190 below.

[5] Ar. *Thesm.* 76–80.   [6] Cf. Ar. *Vesp.* 661–3.   [7] *A.P.* 43. iii, cf. Ch. I, p. 30.

[8] Professor P. A. Brunt has suggested to me that, if this passage has any implications for the powers of the boule, arrest pending trial may suffice.

Andromeda), and this sentence is pronounced by a πρύτανις on behalf of the boule:

> ἔχοντα ταῦτ' ἔδοξε τῇ βουλῇ σε δεῖν,
> ἵνα τοῖς παριοῦσι δῆλος ᾖς πανοῦργος ὤν.[1]

Fastening to a plank seems to be not merely a brutal and spectacular form of imprisonment, but the preparation for execution by ἀποτυμπανισμός,[2] and though the punishment has its part to play in the plot the involvement of the boule does not. This passage does therefore seem to suggest that the boule possessed greater powers at the time of the *Thesmophoriazusae* than later—yet if we take it seriously we find that it presupposes a meeting of the boule on a day when, according to the other passage discussed, no meeting should have been held; and this should perhaps warn us against trying to find significance where none may have been intended.

We shall find that the *Thesmophoriazusae* is unique if it does imply that the boule's judicial powers were unlimited. The next instance which we meet as we work back is the Hermocopid and Mysteries scandal of 415. The charge of profaning the Mysteries was first made by εἰσαγγελία in the ecclesia,[3] whereupon the prytanes cleared the meeting of non-initiates so that evidence could safely be heard.[4] It is presumably this assembly which gave the boule its special commission, since the boule had already been made αὐτοκράτωρ when Teucrus wrote from Megara to offer information on both charges.[5] After further information had been offered, one of the bouleutae proposed that those charged with profanation be tried in a δικαστήριον, and was overwhelmingly defeated in the earliest recorded γραφὴ παρανόμων.[6] Some men who had been denounced fled from Attica and were condemned to death in their absence;[7] Andocides' father, who remained in Athens,[8] appears thanks to this γραφὴ παρανόμων to have avoided trial altogether. Presumably as soon as each set of names had been produced and the men denounced had fled a trial was rapidly held, and since Speusippus on receipt of the fourth μήνυσις had proposed that the trial be held in a δικαστήριον it is likely that those trials which were not blocked were held in a δικαστήριον.

The charge of mutilating the Hermae could first be pressed when Teucrus offered information to the boule.[9] A board of ζητηταί was appointed, apparently to help in the investigation of both charges,[10] and

---

[1] Ar. *Thesm.* 943–4.   [2] Cf. Bonner and Smith, ii. 279–87.
[3] And. I. *Myst.* 11, cf. 14, 27.   [4] § 12.   [5] § 15.
[6] § 17. We do not know what was illegal about this proposal.
[7] § 13, cf. 15, 16, 25.   [8] § 19.   [9] § 15.   [10] Profanation, § 14.

recommended vigorous action, so that every meeting of the boule was expected to issue in arrests.[1] Dioclides made an εἰσαγγελία to the boule, which promptly suspended the decree forbidding the torture of citizens.[2] Two bouleutae who were accused fled from Attica, after which at a secret meeting the boule decided to arrest the others whom Dioclides denounced, and made a military disposition of the citizens.[3] Andocides was induced by his fellow prisoners to turn state's evidence;[4] further arrests were made and his account was investigated by the boule and ζητηταί;[5] Dioclides admitted his perjury and a δικαστήριον sentenced him to death,[6] while four men whom Andocides denounced went into exile— and were no doubt condemned in absence to death.[7]

So much can be learned from Andocides. Alcibiades seems primarily to have been suspected of profaning the Mysteries,[8] and was accused before the boule. Without success he demanded from the ecclesia an immediate trial; after he had sailed for Sicily it was decided to recall him, the Salaminia was sent to fetch him and other suspects, and in due course he and they were condemned *in absentia*. The language of Isocrates implies that this was the work of the boule: συστήσαντες τὴν βουλὴν καὶ τοὺς ῥήτορας ὑπ' αὐτοῖς ποιησάμενοι.[9] The account of Thucydides, who as usual eschews technical language, leads us to suspect that some organ of the demos was responsible:

ὧν (sc. the fall of the Pisistratids) ἐνθυμούμενος ὁ δῆμος ὁ τῶν Ἀθηναίων . . . χαλεπὸς ἦν τότε καὶ ὑπόπτης ἐς τοὺς περὶ τῶν μυστικῶν τὴν αἰτίαν λαβόντας, καὶ πάντα αὐτοῖς ἐδόκει ἐπὶ ξυνωμοσίᾳ ὀλιγαρχικῇ καὶ τυραννικῇ πεπρᾶχθαι.[10] . . . (Andocides then gave information about the mutilation of the Hermae.) ὁ δὲ δῆμος ὁ τῶν Ἀθηναίων ἄσμενος λαβών, ὡς ᾤετο, τὸ σαφές . . . τὸν μὲν μηνυτὴν εὐθὺς καὶ τοὺς ἄλλους μετ' αὐτοῦ ὅσων μὴ κατηγορήκει ἔλυσαν, τοὺς δὲ καταιτια-θέντας κρίσεις ποιήσαντες τοὺς μὲν ἀπέκτειναν, ὅσοι ξυνελήφθησαν, τῶν δὲ δια-φυγόντων θάνατον καταγνόντες ἐπανεῖπον ἀργύριον τῷ ἀποκτείναντι.[11] . . . (This matter being settled, there was renewed suspicion of Alcibiades on the profanation charge,) ὥστε βουλόμενοι αὐτὸν ἐς κρίσιν ἀγαγόντες ἀποκτεῖναι πέμπουσιν οὕτω τὴν Σαλαμινίαν ναῦν ἐς τὴν Σικελίαν ἐπί τε ἐκεῖνον καὶ ὧν περὶ ἄλλων ἐμεμήνυτο.[12] . . . (These men escaped to the Peloponnese.) οἱ δὲ Ἀθηναῖοι ἐρήμῃ δίκῃ θάνατον κατέγνωσαν αὐτοῦ τε καὶ τῶν μετ' ἐκείνου.[13]

It is likely enough that the boule, as investigating authority, was responsible for the decision to recall Alcibiades to stand his trial, but there is nothing here to conflict with the impression given by Andocides, that no sentences were passed by the boule.

[1] § 36. [2] § 43. [3] §§ 44–5. [4] § 61. [5] §§ 64–5. [6] §§ 65–6.
[7] §§ 67–8. [8] Is. XVI. *Big.* 6–7, Pl. *Alc.* 19–20 (esp. 20. v), 22. iv, T. VI. 28. i, 61. i.
[9] Is. XVI. *Big.* 7. [10] T. VI. 60. i. [11] Ibid. iv.
[12] Ibid. 61. iv, cf. 53. i. [13] Ibid. 61. vii.

The boule's special commission covered both charges, and apparently enabled it to suspend the decree against torture, and to give general emergency instructions to the citizens (if the suspicion of political conspiracy found in Thucydides is authentic, the charges may have been such as to justify the boule's arrests even under fourth-century law), but whenever an actual or prospective condemnation is attributed to a particular judicial body that body is a δικαστήριον. If even a boule which was αὐτοκράτωρ was prepared to hand over to the courts men accused of profanation, it is highly unlikely that the boule without special powers was entitled to condemn to death.[1] It is quite likely that a hurried decree of the ecclesia had made the boule αὐτοκράτωρ without specifying how far it might exceed its normal powers, and I have suggested above that the intention was probably to give the boule a free hand in procedure rather than to raise any restrictions on its powers of punishment,[2] but the fact that the boule referred these charges to the δικαστήρια remains good evidence.

In a decree regulating the offering of first-fruits at Eleusis (the dates suggested for it range from 445 to 415, but most scholars are now agreed in placing it near the end of this period[3]) the following rule is laid down for offences concerning the Πελαργικόν:

ἐὰν δέ τις παραβαίνει τ ∶ ∶ ∶ οὗτον τι, ἀποτινέτο πεντακοσίας δραχμάς, ἐσαγγελλέτο δὲ h[ο] βασιλεὺς ἐς τὲν βολέν.[4]

The fixing of the fine at 500 drachmae may of course be purely coincidental—500 is a convenient round number—but it is at any rate possible that this sum was chosen because it already represented the maximum penalty which the boule might impose without referring the case to a δικαστήριον.

Professor Kahrstedt made use in this connection of two lines from Aristophanes' *Wasps*, which I have interpreted as a comment on the use of the δικαστήρια to hear εἰσαγγελίαι:

ἔτι δ᾽ ἡ βουλὴ χὠ δῆμος ὅταν κρῖναι μέγα πρᾶγμ᾽ ἀπορήσῃ
ἐψήφισται τοὺς ἀδικοῦντας τοῖσι δικασταῖς παραδοῦναι.[5]

If the boule and demos voted to transfer cases to the δικαστήρια, he claimed, it must still have been possible for them in 422 to vote that

---

[1] Mr. MacDowell in his commentary on And. I. *Myst.* 66 points out that Dioclides was not guilty of mutilating the Hermae and we do not know the charge on which he was condemned; but his implication in the affair ought to have been sufficient to bring him within the scope of the boule's special powers.   [2] Cf. p. 171 n. 1 and p. 180 n. 4 above.
[3] See Ch. III, p. 94 n. 2.   [4] M&L 73, 57–9.
[5] Ar. *Vesp.* 590–1, cf. Kahrstedt, *U.M.A.*, 208 with n. 2. For my view of this passage, see pp. 168–70 above.

a case should not be transferred to a δικαστήριον, and to pass judgement on the spot. But whether or not my view of this passage is correct, the conjunction in it of boule and demos makes it very difficult to draw any conclusion as to the rights of the boule alone. Aristophanes himself was prosecuted in the boule by Cleon, after the production of his *Babylonians*,[1] but we have no detailed information on what took place.

The Athenian settlement with Chalcis in 446/5 involved an oath to be taken by the boule and dicasts on behalf of Athens:

> οὐκ ἐχσελῶ Χα-
> λκιδέας ἐχ Χαλκίδος οὐδὲ τὲν πόλιν ἀνά-
> στατον ποέσο οὐδὲ ἰδιότεν οὐδένα ἀτιμ-
> όσο οὐδὲ φυγεῖ ζεμιόσο οὐδὲ χσυλλέφσο-
> μαι οὐδὲ ἀποκτενῶ οὐδὲ χρέματα ἀφαιρέ-
> σομαι ἀκρίτο οὐδενὸς ἄνευ τô δέμο τô Ἀθ-
> εναίον.[2]

Bonner and Smith insist that if protection of this kind was given to the allies, *a fortiori* Athenian citizens must have been safeguarded against severe penalties inflicted ἄνευ τοῦ δήμου: we have already seen that in the fourth century, when the boule's right to punish citizens was undoubtedly limited, it could still sentence a Cean to death.[3] Shortly before this, about 447, the decree of Clinias which laid down more stringent regulations for the collection of tribute from the allies and their bringing a cow and panoply to the Panathenaea, specified a procedure for dealing with offenders in which the boule's power was certainly limited:

> ἐὰν δέ τις Ἀθ[εναῖος ἒ χσύμμαχος ἀδικεῖ περὶ τὸ]-
> ν φόρον hὸν δεῖ [τὰς πόλες γραφσάσας ἐς γραμματεῖ]-
> ον τοῖς ἀπάγοσ[ιν ἀποπέμπεν Ἀθέναζε, ἔστο αὐτὸν γ]-
> ράφεσθαι πρὸς [τὸς πρυτάνες τôι β]ολομένο[ι Ἀθενα]-
> ίον καὶ τôν χσ[υμμάχον· hοι δὲ πρυτά]νες ἐσαγ[όντον]
> ἐς τὲμ βολὲν [τὲν γραφὲν hέν τι]ς ἂγ γράφσετα[ι ἒ εὐθ]-
> υνέσθο δόρο[ν χιλίαισι δραχμ]ε͂σ[ι h]έκαστος· [hô δ' ἂν]
> καταγνôι h[ε βολέ, μὲ τιμᾶν αὐτ]ôι κυρία ἔστο [ἀλλ' ἐσ]-
> φερέτο ἐς τ[ὲν ἐλιαίαν εὐθύ]ς· ὅταν δὲ δόχσει [ἀδικε͂]-
> ν, γνόμας πο[ιέσθον hοι πρυ]τάνες hό τι ἂν δοκ[εῖ αὐτ]-
> ὸμ παθὲν ἒ ἀ[ποτεῖσαι. καὶ ἐ]άν τις περὶ τὲν ἀπα[γογὲ]-
> ν τ̂ες βοὸς ἒ [τ̂ες πανhοπλία]ς ἀδικεῖ, τὰς γραφὰ[ς ἐνα]-
> ι κατ' αὐτô κ[αὶ τὲν ζεμίαν κ]ατὰ ταὐτά.[4]

---

[1] Ar. *Ach.* 379–81.
[2] M&L 52, 4–10.
[3] Cf. p. 180 and n. 4 above.
[4] M&L 46, 31–43. Cf. p. 152 n. 1 above. πο[ιέσθον], restored by M&L in l. 40, is my suggestion for earlier editors' πο[ιόντον]; cf. T. III. 36. ii. The prytanes are surely expected to hold a debate in the boule rather than to make proposals on their own account.

The fine to which each of the prytanes would be liable for failing to bring a case before the boule must be restored as 1,000 or 10,000 drachmae, and we may assume that any defaulting allies would be very heavily penalized. This decree does not prove that the boule's powers were already limited in other cases within its jurisdiction, but it does at any rate make it seem reasonably likely.

From the middle of the fifth century to 411 there is no text except in the *Thesmophoriazusae* which could justify the view that the boule's powers were unlimited or at all greater than in the fourth century, while there are texts which seem to point in the other direction. Their import is not so clear that the conclusion could stand against a good contrary instance, but we must ask how good a contrary instance the *Thesmophoriazusae* provides. Neither of the passages discussed provides indubitable evidence of a powerful boule; but if the play does reflect a powerful boule it might be argued that the boule in question is not that of the democracy. The play is normally assigned to the Dionysia of 411, before the democracy was overthrown,[1] but 410 has had its champions,[2] and if this is the correct date the play will have been completed and produced under the regime of the Five Thousand. The condemnation of Antiphon and Archeptolemus shows that the δικαστήρια had been revived under this regime,[3] but the 'moderates' may have allowed the boule greater powers than it possessed under the democracy, and Aristophanes may have credited the boule with greater powers than the 'moderates' allowed it (the example of the Four Hundred will still have been very recent). I believe that 410 is a possible, but not certain, date for the *Thesmophoriazusae*, but that if it belongs to 411 it does not compel us to believe that the boule possessed greater powers then than later.[4] I therefore think it is a serious possibility that the restrictions on the boule's judicial powers go back as far as the middle of the fifth century.

Before the middle of the fifth century we have no mention of the boule's discharging judicial functions, but Cloché attempted to show from Herodotus that the original restriction of its powers antedates even the Persian Wars. In 479 Mardonius sent Murychides to Athens to offer peace terms; when a member of the boule proposed that these terms be

---

[1] Cf. p. 185 n. 4 above.

[2] Most recently, B. B. Rogers, in his edition of the *Thesmophoriazusae*.

[3] Cf. p. 182.

[4] The play has no *hypothesis*; much of the information in the scholia can be manipulated to yield either date; enough uncertainty remains to make the political situation which the play seems to reflect a factor that must be taken into account. The case for 411 is conveniently presented by Wilamowitz, *Aristoteles und Athen*, ii. 343 sqq.; the case for 410, in Rogers's edition, pp. xxxiii–xlii (1920 reprint). I hope to reconsider the arguments elsewhere.

submitted to the ecclesia this so angered his colleagues that he was stoned to death, and Murychides was sent away without a reply.[1] Cloché rightly saw no legal significance in the lynching, but he emphasized that the boule was already obliged to consult the ecclesia on questions of peace and war. Now in *IG* i² 114 the declaration of war is one of the steps which may not be taken ἄνευ τὸ δέμο πλεθύοντος,[2] and if this requirement already existed in 479 we may suspect, he argued, that the boule's judicial restrictions already existed too, and may plausibly ascribe this restriction of the boule to the oath imposed on that body probably in 501/0 and still sworn by the bouleutae in the time of the *Athenaion Politeia*: ἐφ' Ἑρμο-κρέοντος ἄρχοντος τῇ βουλῇ τοῖς πεντακοσίοις τὸν ὅρκον ἐποίησαν ὃν ἔτι καὶ νῦν ὀμνύουσιν.[3] He noted the institution of the strategia about the same time as an indication of the 'democratic advance' of the period.

These arguments are open to a number of objections.[4] Cloché must surely have been mistaken to argue from the demos' sovereignty in peace and war to a restriction of the boule's judicial powers: peace and war is one of the first issues in which a popular assembly acquires sovereignty, since in war every citizen has a part to play and those who wage war must be sure of popular support; even in the Homeric poems an occasional assembly is necessary, and the institution of the hoplite army led inevitably to the hoplites' demanding certain political powers. But is it right to regard consultation before sentence of death is passed as one of the basic citizen rights? The American *Declaration of Independence* regards life, liberty, and the pursuit of happiness as inalienable human rights, and the twentieth-century scholar may be pardoned (if not positively lauded) for treating the death sentence as a major issue; but a society which allowed the immediate killing of an adulterer caught in the act might well not share our views.[5]

Cloché is by no means alone in regarding the imposition of the bouleu-tic oath as a means of lessening the powers of the boule. Professor Larsen

---

[1] H. ix. 5. i–ii, cf. Lyc. *Leocr.* 122, D. XVIII. *Cor.* 202, 204.

[2] l. 35 (Wade-Gery). On this inscription cf. pp. 183–4 above, 195–9 below.

[3] *A.P.* 22. ii. On the date see, e.g., T. J. Cadoux, *JHS* lxviii 1948, 115–16, G. V. Sumner, *CQ²* xi 1961, 35–7.

[4] Some of which have already been made by W. Peremans (*LEC* x 1941, 193 sqq.). Cloché's reply (*LEC* xii 1943–4) deals only with the interpretation of *IG* i² 114 by J. Sencie and W. Peremans (*LEC* x 1941, 329 sqq.).

[5] It is important to distinguish between the decisions of individual magistrates and corporate bodies. Solon gave the people the right to appeal against a magistrate's verdict, but the Areopagus retained considerable inappellable powers until 462/1 (similarly in Rome the right of *provocatio ad populum* against a magistrate's decision was granted very early, but senatorial *quaestiones* passed capital sentences in the second century B.C. until prevented by a law of C. Gracchus).

has written, 'It is natural to believe that when the bill (*IG* i² 114) states that the *boule* cannot act on certain questions without consulting the "entire *demos*," this means that the right to take final action on these questions formerly belonged to the *boule* and is now being taken away from it.'[1] He reaches the startling conclusion that before the oath was imposed 'the *boule* was so powerful that it can almost be said that Athens for a few years possessed a representative government'.[2] We may well wonder if this is correct. In some circumstances this kind of explanation would be acceptable, and we may be sure, for instance, that the requirement added in 410 that the bouleutae should sit in the places allocated to them[3] was directed against a real evil. But what we know of the two decades before Marathon does not make a major restriction of the powers of the five hundred, less than ten years after their establishment by Cleisthenes, very likely; and unless they had been alarmed by some actual abuse of power it is hard to see why Athenian democrats should ever have wanted to reduce the boule's powers. To the political theorist the boule was a characteristic organ of democracy:

αὕτη (sc. ἡ τῶν προβούλων ἀρχή) γὰρ οὐ δημοκρατική· βουλὴ δὲ δημοτικόν· δεῖ μὲν γὰρ εἶναί τι τοιοῦτον ᾧ ἐπιμελὲς ἔσται τοῦ δήμου προβουλεύειν, ὅπως ἀσχολῶν ἔσται. . . . καταλύεται δὲ καὶ ἡ τῆς βουλῆς ἡ δύναμις ἐν ταῖς τοιαύταις δημοκρατίαις ἐν αἷς αὐτὸς συνιὼν ὁ δῆμος χρηματίζει περὶ πάντων. τοῦτο δὲ συμβαίνειν εἴωθεν ὅταν εὐπορία τις ᾖ μισθοῦ τοῖς ἐκκλησιάζουσιν· σχολάζοντες γὰρ συλλέγονταί τε πολλάκις καὶ ἅπαντα αὐτοὶ κρίνουσιν.[4]

Aristotle's conditions did not obtain in Athens in 500 B.C., and Cloché himself demonstrated in another article[5] that even after the maturing of full democracy and the ἔμμισθος πόλις no attempt was made to reduce its powers. The boule was the city in microcosm, μικρὰ πόλις;[6] the system of appointment made it a fair cross-section of the citizen body and enabled most if not all of those who wished to serve for one year.[7] It represented the demos and so could be trusted with great powers by the demos: a deliberate reduction of its powers is conceivable only in such circumstances as we find in 410, and highly unlikely ninety years before that date. A far more attractive explanation of the bouleutic oath is that of Peremans, that the detailed working-out of Cleisthenes' reforms took several years, and the imposition of the oath on the bouleutae was

---

[1] *Representative Government in Greek and Roman History*, 15.
[2] Ibid. 18. Cf. most recently A. G. Woodhead, *Hist.* xvi 1967, 139–40 with n. 33.
[3] Phil. 328 F 140.   [4] Arist. *Pol.* vi. 1299 B 31–1300 A 4, cf. vi. 1317 B 28–38.
[5] *REG* xxxiv 1921.   [6] Schol. A. III. *Ctes* 4.
[7] Cf. Ch. I, pp. 1–7.

a measure to set the seal on the completed reorganization rather than a device to set new limitations to the power of the boule.[1]

But can we even be certain that this judicial limitation appeared in the oath of 501/0 at all? As I have remarked, it does not follow from the fact that the people had the right to make peace or war in 479 and probably earlier. The author of the *Athenaion Politeia* writes of the oath ὃν ἔτι καὶ νῦν ὀμνύουσιν, and Cloché and others have inferred that he thought the oath had remained unchanged in content until his own day.[2] The members' new obligation to sit in their allotted seats as from 410/09 is admitted as an obstacle, but is not regarded as insuperable, and Bonner and Smith went so far as to assert that 'Aristotle's statement is doubtless substantially correct'.[3] It is not obvious, however, that the author is referring to the content of the oath. It would be possible for an Englishman to say that our country has the same legislative machinery today as in the reign of Elizabeth I: enormous changes have been made in the past four hundred years, but we still have a Queen and two Houses of Parliament, and laws are still made by the Queen in Parliament—and so in a sense we still have the same legislative machinery.[4] If the essence of the bouleutic oath was a declaration of allegiance to the constitution and an undertaking to work for the good of the city, then particular clauses concerned with the actual powers of the boule could come and go without invalidating the claim that 'the same oath' was being sworn. Peremans contrasts the more specific language of *A.P.* 7. i, where a particular clause in the oath taken by the archons is thought to have persisted from the legislation of Solon to the writer's own day.[5]

We have followed the evidence for the boule's judicial powers back as far as the middle of the fifth century, and have seen that at no time except under an oligarchic regime need these powers have been unrestricted. The rejection of Mardonius' peace offer tells us nothing about the boule's judicial powers, while the oath imposed at the end of the sixth century probably involved no new limitation of the boule's power, and cannot be shown to have contained at that time the restricting clauses with which we are concerned: there are no other texts which seem to bear on the judicial work of the boule before the middle of the fifth century. In the second half of this appendix I shall try to substantiate my belief

---

[1] *LEC* x 1941, 193 sqq.; cf. V. L. Ehrenberg, *Hist.* i 1950, 545 = *Polis und Imperium*, 294; C. W. J. Eliot, *Coastal Demes of Attika*, 145–7 with n. 18.

[2] Most recently, B. R. I. Sealey, *Hist.* ix. 1960, 176 = *Essays in Greek Politics*, 29.

[3] Bonner and Smith, i. 343 n. 1.

[4] Mr. A. N. Sherwin-White has drawn my attention to T. 1. 18. i: ἔτη γάρ ἐστι μάλιστα τετρακόσια καὶ ὀλίγῳ πλείω ἐς τὴν τελευτὴν τοῦδε τοῦ πολέμου ἀφ' οὗ Λακεδαιμόνιοι τῇ αὐτῇ πολιτείᾳ χρῶνται.   [5] op. cit., cf. also *A.P.* 55. v.

that before the reforms of Ephialtes the boule had no serious judicial powers, and that Ephialtes laid the foundations of the limited jurisdiction which it can be seen to have exercised from the middle of the fifth century onwards: that is, that the *Athenaion Politeia* was mistaken to claim that the boule πρότερον μὲν ἦν κυρία χρήμασιν ζημιῶσαι καὶ δῆσαι καὶ ἀποκτεῖναι.

I begin with a closer look at the bouleutic oath and *IG* i² 114. The clauses which are known at some time to have been embodied in the oath are as follows:[1]

1. κατὰ τοὺς νόμους βουλεύσειν.[2]

2. τὰ βέλτιστα βουλεύσειν τῇ πόλει / τῷ δήμῳ τῷ Ἀθηναίων.[3]

3. οὐδὲ δήσω Ἀθηναίων οὐδένα, ὃς ἂν ἐγγυητὰς τρεῖς καθιστῇ τὸ αὐτὸ τέλος τελοῦντας, πλὴν ἐάν τις ἐπὶ προδοσίᾳ τῆς πόλεως ἢ ἐπὶ καταλύσει τοῦ δήμου συνιὼν ἁλῷ, ἢ τέλος πριάμενος ἢ ἐγγυησάμενος ἢ ἐκλέγων μὴ καταβάλῃ.[4]
   [Cf. 3A, not in Wade-Gery. 'Oath of demos and boule': μηδένα μήτε ἐξελᾶν μήτε δήσειν μήτε ἀποκτενεῖν ἄκριτον.][5]

4. ἀποφαίνειν εἴ τίς τινα οἶδε τῶν λαχόντων ἀνεπιτήδειον ὄντα βουλεύειν.[6]
   Cf. 4A, not in Wade-Gery. δοκιμασία of archons: δοκιμάσαντες τὸν ἄξιον τῆς ἀρχῆς στεφανώσειν.[7]

5. καθεδεῖσθαι ἐν τῷ γράμματι ᾧ ἂν λάχωσιν—ADDED TO OATH IN 410/09.[8]

6. ἐάν τις κόπτῃ νόμισ[μα] ἀργυρίου ἐν ταῖς πό[λεσι κ]αὶ μὴ χρῆται νομ[ίσμασιν τοῖς Ἀθηνα]ίων ἢ σταθμοῖς ἢ μέτ[ροις, ἀλλὰ ξενικοῖς νομίσμασι]ν καὶ μέτροις καὶ σταθμοῖς, [τιμωρήσομαι κα]ὶ ζ[ημιώσω κατὰ τὸ πρότε]ρον ψήφισμα ὃ Κλέαρχ[ος εἶπεν]—ADDED TO OATH c. 448.[9]

[7. γέγονα οὐκ ἔλαττον ἢ τριάκοντα ἔτη.][10]

8. οὐ δέξομαι ἔνδειξιν οὐδὲ ἀπαγωγὴν ἕνεκα τῶν πρότερον γεγενημένων, πλὴν τῶν φυγόντων—MUST HAVE BEEN ADDED TO OATH IN 403/2.[11]

[9. Oath sworn by boule and dicasts to Chalcis in 446/5, almost certainly once for all, quoted above on p. 189.][12]

?[10. μηδὲν παράνομον ἐπιψηφίζειν.][13]

---

[1] I number the clauses as in Wade-Gery's study, *BSA* xxxiii 1932–3, 113–22, and bracket those whose inclusion in the oath I doubt.　　　　[2] X. *M.* I. i. 18 (407/6).

[3] Lys. XXXI. *Phil.* 1 (soon after 403/2), [D.] LIX. *Neaer.* 4 (shortly before 339); we can perhaps trace this back to 405/4 from Lys. XXX. *Nic.* 10.

[4] D. XXIV. *Tim.* 144, cf. 147–8 (353/2). § 148 calls the oath 'Solonian'.

[5] [And.] IV. *Alc.* 3 (putative date c. 415; perhaps written early C4 but probably much later—see, most recently, A. E. Raubitschek, *TAPA* lxxix 1948 [genuine speech of Phaeax], A. R. Burn, *CQ*² iv 1954 [late school composition]).

[6] Lys. XXXI. *Phil.* 2 (soon after 403/2).　　　　[7] Lys. XXVI. *Evand.* 8 (383/2).

[8] Phil. 328 F 140.　　　　[9] M&L 45, § 12. For the date cf. Ch. III, p. 89 n. 1.

[10] In heliastic oath, D. XXIV. *Tim.* 150; same age requirement for bouleutae, X. *M.* I. ii. 35 (during lifetime of Socrates).　　　　[11] And. I. *Myst.* 91.　　　　[12] M&L 52, 4–10.

[13] X. *M.* I. i. 18 implies that as late as 407/6 *or* when Xenophon wrote this was covered by κατὰ τοὺς νόμους βουλεύειν, but this is the one clause of which there seem to be reliable traces in the oath in *IG* i² 114—cf. p. 196 below. Glotz, *The Greek City*, 183, included in the oath an undertaking 'to maintain secrecy on the affairs of the State'; but, likely as this is, I know no evidence for it.

Clauses 1 and 2 are patriotic generalities, fundamentally different from any other clauses which we know: they must surely have formed part of the original oath, and may at first have comprised almost the whole of the oath.[1] The other fragments all embody specific safeguards and assurances. 10, if this was a separate clause, is so closely related to the basic duty of the boule that it may well have been in the oath from the beginning; 7, though attested for the heliastic oath, may not have been needed as a clause in the bouleutic oath, as the selection procedure for bouleutae was more rigorous, but there is no need to doubt that the lower age limit of 30 was Cleisthenic or Solonian.[2] 5, 6, and 8 are datable additions, and 9, which was probably not incorporated in the regular oath, is also datable. This leaves only 3 and 4, the clauses concerned with the judicial powers of the boule. In section iv of this chapter I suggested that the boule always held the δοκιμασία of its successors (in which case the relevant clause may always have been in the oath), and took over the δοκιμασία of the archons from the Areopagus in 462/1;[3] in the first part of this appendix I was unable to produce any evidence for the boule's involvement before the middle of the fifth century in matters to which clause 3 could apply. There is perhaps one indication that some items may have been added to the bouleutic oath not long before the middle of the fifth century: clause 6, an undertaking to enforce a particular decree, is a surprisingly specific insertion, yet the various fragments of the decree yield enough of the text for us to be fairly certain that the insertion was made: προσγράψαι δὲ πρὸς τὸν ὅρκον [τ]ὸν τῆς βουλῆς τὸν γραμματέα τὸν τῆς [βουλῆς εἰς τὸ λοιπὸν τα]δί.[4] I find it hard to believe that this would have been done if the bouleutic oath had remained unaltered for over fifty years; but if in the past ten to fifteen years various changes in the powers of the boule had been consolidated by changes in the oath, as Cleisthenes' reorganization had been consolidated by the imposition of the oath, it could more easily have occurred to Clearchus that a similar device would provide a useful safeguard to his decree.

The only other evidence bearing on the bouleutic oath has to be extracted from *IG* i² 114. This comprises one large, one medium, and two small fragments, probably inscribed in the last decade of the fifth century, which together provide about a third of the original inscribed surface over 60 lines. The large fragment is very badly preserved indeed: Hiller

[1] Compare the summary of the archontic oath in *A.P.* 55. v: since the archons ceased to be powerful magistrates there was less need to add to this later.
[2] Cf. Ch. I, p. 1 with n. 7.
[3] Pp. 176–8.
[4] M&L 45, § 12.

von Gaertringen dismissed the whole of lines 1–16[1] with the words *pleraque deleta sunt*, and when I examined the stone in 1964 I could not confidently identify any letters in the first eight lines nor more than twelve in lines 9–16.[2] Beyond this point a few words and phrases can be made out, and we seem to be in the middle of an oath, with the verb ἐπιψηφίζω in the first person singular and οὐ for negative. But from line 29 onwards we have verbs in the infinitive and μή to indicate negation: there are references to the boule of five hundred and the bouleuterium, and perhaps to the sum of 500 drachmae.[3] This part of the inscription ends in line 34, where τάδ[ε] ἔδοχσ[ε] can be made out. After this begins a list of steps which may not be taken ἄνευ τõ δέμο τõ Ἀθεναίον πλεθύοντος (a phrase which also occurs in the earlier part of the inscription[4]): declaration of war, condemnation to death,[5] θοὰν ἐπιβαλễν, and something which involves public money, the boule, and retirement from office.

Wade-Gery claimed to detect in the first part of the inscription clauses 3 (ll. 7–10) and 2 (ll. 21–2) of the oath, and also something analogous to 10 (ll. 27–9); but his restorations are based on very meagre remains, and apart from two occurrences of the verb ἐπιψηφίζω and one of the phrase ἄνευ τõ δέμο τõ Ἀθεναίον πλεθύοντος I do not think anything of significance can be recovered from the oath's contents—though it seems likely enough that it is the bouleutic oath with which we are dealing, and the whole document is probably a part of that collection of laws which in the fourth century would have been called the νόμος βουλευτικός. Enough survives of the regulations in the second half of the inscription for it to be of some importance to know whether this is simply a re-publication at the end of the fifth century of an older law or laws, or incorporates new provisions.

Kirchhoff remarked: 'Priscae dictionis vestigia in verbis fragmentorum conspicua in eam deducunt sententiam, ut non primum illo anno haec sancta esse existimemus, verum renovatam populiscito continere antiquioris aevi constitutionem aliquam, quae hoc ipso anno denuo fuerit promulgata.'[6] Cloché wanted to link the whole document with the original imposition of the bouleutic oath in 501/0, and under his influence Hiller von Gaertringen in the *editio minor* was more

---

[1] In Wade-Gery's enumeration; in *IG* i², 1–17.

[2] A few more letters can be read 'dotted'.

[3] Line 31: I read [πεν]τακο[σ]ί[..]κ[–] (the κ seemed very doubtful and I would not rule out δ[—: cf. p. 183 n. 7 above). Hiller von Gaertringen read [πε]ντακοσίας δραχ[μάς] (*sic*); Wade-Gery [πεντ]ακοσι[..] δρα[χμ–]; Dr. D. M. Lewis tells me he would read]ντακοσι-[..] δρα[–]. 	[4] At any rate in l. 25.

[5] I could make out only [θ]α[νατ]õ[ι] (l. 36); Dr. Lewis reads θαν[α]τõι [ζεμι]õ[σαι], and in l. 37 [δ]έμο τõ Ἀθεναίον πλεθ[ύο]ντος [...] δίοχσιν ἀτιμ[ίας].

[6] Publishing the inscription as *IG* i 57.

specific: 'Priscus dictionis color saeculi initium decet.' Two phrases do seem to point to an early origin: the τάδε ἔδοχσεν of l. 34 recalls the ταῦτ' ἔδοχσεν of the Hecatompedon Inscription,[1] while θωή (θοὰν ἐπιβαλên, l. 41) seems to be an early word.[2] There are no other clear indications of antiquity, but it has been suggested that the all-pervasive ἄνευ τô δέμο τô Ἀθεναίον πλεθύοντος should be regarded in this light: there is no other occurrence of the phrase in an Athenian context,[3] and the working of the Athenian state after the fall of the Four Hundred is sufficiently well documented for it to be surprising that there should be no other mention of a legal requirement that was made or confirmed at the end of the fifth century; furthermore, we know that by the end of the fifth century capital punishment and other severe penalties were in fact within the competence of the δικαστήρια.[4] We know that the Athenians were content to retain obsolete expressions in their laws,[5] and it is quite likely that this phrase is a survival from an earlier period. Cloché suggested that δῆμος πληθύων should be regarded as a 'plenary assembly', perhaps exemplified in the body of at least six thousand which was required for an ostracism under the law of Cleisthenes,[6] and believed that by the end of the century the δικαστήρια were deemed to represent the δῆμος πληθύων in judicial matters. Against this, Sencie and Peremans argued[7] that the requirement of a plenary assembly would be more fitted to the developed democracy of the late fifth century than to the date to which Cloché assigned the original law; and they thought that ἄνευ τô δέμο πλεθύοντος ought to be rendered, 'without the people present en masse in Athens' (a requirement which would be peculiarly appropriate to the circumstances of 410). This interpretation I find very unconvincing. Cloché's is, I think, possible, but I incline to a simpler explanation, that δῆμος πληθύων means no more than 'the people in assembly'.[8] Like Cloché I have to suppose that the

---

[1] IG i² 3, 16; 4, 26 (485/4). Dr. Lewis reads the line as τάδε ἔδοχσεν ἐλ Λυκείο [τ]ôι δ[έμοι τôι Ἀ]θε[να]ίον [πλ]εθύ|[οντι].

[2] The other citations in LSJ are Od. II. 192, Il. XIII. 169, Archilochus, 109, Democritus, 262, and two fifth-century inscriptions. The verb θοάζειν is found as late as the end of the fourth century. Cf. p. 198 n. 3 below.

[3] Similar phrases occur in the Olympian bronze inscriptions, where certain matters require the approval of the boule and the δῆμος πληθύων (HMA 124 b, c [c = Buck, Greek Dialects, 64, 3–4]). Miss L. H. Jeffery dates these inscriptions c. 475? and c. 500 respectively (Local Scripts Archaic Greece, 220, nos. 9, 5).   [4] Cf. p. 169 and n. 5 above.

[5] See Lys. X. Theomn. i. 15–19 for some examples.

[6] Compare the requirement of 6,000 voting citizens at an ostracism (Pl. Arist. 7. v–vi—all relevant texts quoted at Phil. 328 F 30, and recent discussions cited by I. C. Limentani, edition of Pl. Arist., pp. xlviii–xlix). This interpretation is accepted, e.g., by V. L. Ehrenberg, The Greek State², 62.   [7] LEC x 1941, 329 sqq.

[8] Compare the use of πλῆθος as a near-synonym for δῆμος or ἐκκλησία. Larsen arrives by a very different route at a conclusion with the same practical effect, regarding the δῆμος πληθύων as the 'entire demos', as opposed to the boule (Representative Government, 15–16).

δικαστήρια came to be recognized as representative of the δῆμος πληθύων, but this is easier if what they represented was not a special body but the ordinary assembly. By 446/5 we have an oath with the shorter but (I believe) equivalent formula, ἄνευ τô δέμο τô Ἀθεναίον,[1] but there is nothing to show that the fuller expression had become obsolete half a century before this, and even at this date a more conservative drafter might have been prepared to employ it. In the present state of our evidence we may say that measures embodying the longer formula are likely to have been drafted before 450, but I do not think that greater precision is possible.

Dr. D. M. Lewis has recently introduced a new factor into the discussion.[2] In line 43 of the inscription we read:

$$[h]όπος ἂν δοκêι : : : δέμοι τô[ι Ἀ]θεναίον πλε[θύοντι].$$

The three pairs of points after δοκêι are clearly visible, and τôι is an irresistible restoration. It is amazing that τôι should never have been inscribed here, and Dr. Lewis suggests that this stone 'was carved by a careful man transcribing a damaged original with such fidelity that he preferred to mark three blank spaces which he could not read rather than make what appears to us the easiest of conjectures'. Such caution in a copyist is barely credible, but the phenomenon to be explained is a strange one and I think the explanation must stand unless a better can be found.

A word of warning is necessary about what we are dating. The publication of the laws at the end of the fifth century seems to have involved the collection in an organized code of what had previously been scattered and unconnected enactments, and the occurrence of τάδε ἔδοχσεν in the middle (l. 34) of our inscription confirms that this is likely to have happened here. In such a case, conclusive proof of the antiquity of one item would not help us to date the contents of any other part of the document. It seems likely that there is much in this inscription going back to the first half of the fifth century, including the reservation for the δῆμος πληθύων of the death sentence and the infliction of θωαί,[3] but we

---

[1] M&L 52, 9–10.

[2] JHS lxxxvii 1967, 132. I am grateful to Dr. Lewis for letting me see the manuscript of this before publication.

[3] The exact meaning of θοὰν ἐπιβαλêν is not clear. In the Hecatompedon Inscription θοâν is used of small fines, up to 3 obols (IG i² 4, 7–8, 12–13), and εὐθύνεσθαι of larger (100 dr.) (13–17, cf. 23–4); θοάζειν is used of a 50-drachmae fine in the edict of the priest of Apollo Erithaseus (IG ii² 1362) (late C4). Dr. Lewis has suggested to me that εὐθύνεσθαι may refer specifically to fines imposed at an official's εὔθυναι (cf. M&L 69, esp. 28–31, where there is some contrast between ὀφείλειν and εὐθύνεσθαι). For non-Attic instances, where θωαί seem to be punishments in general and fines in particular, see:

know of changes made in the bouleutic oath in the second half of the fifth century, and these and other changes affecting the boule ought to have been included in the consolidated νόμος βουλευτικός.³

The upshot of our inquiry is that, although judicial restrictions need not have formed a part of the original bouleutic oath as imposed in 501/0, we have some grounds for believing that the right of severe punishment had been reserved for the demos before the middle of the fifth century, and I have suggested that changes may have been made in the oath not long before Clearchus carried his coinage decree.

Though we have no evidence for judicial activity on the part of the boule in the first half of the century, we do know of some important trials. About 493 the tragedian Phrynichus was fined 1,000 drachmae for his Μιλήτου ἅλωσις by Ἀθηναῖοι,¹ and Miltiades was acquitted in a (the?) δικαστήριον on a charge of tyranny in the Chersonese;² in 489 Miltiades was prosecuted before the demos by Xanthippus: θανάτου ὑπαγαγὼν ὑπὸ τὸν δῆμον Μιλτιάδεα ἐδίωκε τῆς Ἀθηναίων ἀπάτης εἵνεκεν.³ The demos appears again in a story for which Lycurgus is our sole authority: Ἵππαρχον γὰρ τὸν Χάρμου, οὐχ ὑπομείναντα τὴν περὶ προδοσίας ἐν τῷ δήμῳ κρίσιν ἀλλ᾽ ἔρημον τὸν ἀγῶνα ἐάσαντα, θανάτῳ τοῦτον ζημιώσαντες.⁴ For the condemnation of Themistocles, Craterus found a document embodying the name of the prosecutor, who is named both in the *Lexicon Rhetoricum Cantabrigiense*⁵ and by Plutarch:⁶ the *Lexicon* regards the trial as an instance of εἰσαγγελία, while Plutarch writes of the prosecutor γραψάμενος αὐτὸν προδοσίας. Thucydides ascribes his condemnation to Ἀθηναῖοι;⁷ while the *Athenaion Politeia* has a strange story of his assisting Ephialtes'

Gortyn	*Inscr. Cret.* iv, 13m.	CC7–6
Chios	M&L 8, C 5–7: the βολὴ ἡ δημοσίη is ἐπιθώιος.	c. 575–550
Elis	Buck, *Greek Dialects*, 64, 1: an ox and full purification.	c. 500? (L. H. Jeffery, *Local Scripts*, 220, no. 5)
Miletus	M&L 43, 12, cf. 10: 100 staters.	c. 470–440
Locris	Tod 34, 9: 'double'.	c. 450
Thasos	*BCH* l 1926, 214, no. 2.	c. 415
Delphi	Buck, *Greek Dialects*, 52, D 19 (fines of 1 obol mentioned in a later clause).	c. 400

¹ H. vi. 21. ii.   ² Ibid. 104. ii.   ³ Ibid. 136. i.

⁴ Lyc. *Leocr.* 117 (Χάρμου, Wilamowitz, *Aristoteles und Athen*, i. 114–15 n. 27, from Harp. Ἵππαρχος: Τιμάρχου, codd.). His treachery probably belongs to the war with Xerxes (Wilamowitz, op. cit., i. 114–15, Burn, *Persia and the Greeks*, 352); it has, however, been suggested that this story is a 'doublet' of that of his ostracism (J. H. Schreiner, *SO* Supp. xxi 1968, 51–2).

⁵ *L.R.C.* εἰσαγγελία.

⁶ Pl. *Them.* 23. i. Both texts at Craterus, 342 F 11.

⁷ T. 1. 135. ii–iii.

attack on the Areopagus, in order to avert his own arrest and trial.[1] Finally, Cimon, when he returned to Athens from the siege of Thasos, was charged with taking bribes not to attack Macedon, and Pericles was among his prosecutors. According to the *Athenaion Politeia* Pericles κατη-γόρησε τὰς εὐθύνας Κίμωνος στρατηγοῦντος;[2] Plutarch tells us that Pericles was εἶς τῶν κατηγόρων . . . ὑπὸ τοῦ δήμου προβεβλημένος,[3] and writes of this trial, in which Cimon was acquitted, as a δίκη[4] and of Cimon's defending himself before the δικασταί.[5]

All six, except perhaps the trial of Phrynichus, could have been dealt with by εἰσαγγελία, though it would be dangerous to say that any of them could have been dealt with only by that procedure. Scholars disagree on the authority which would have heard εἰσαγγελίαι between the reforms of Cleisthenes and those of Ephialtes, but it has commonly been assumed that some at any rate of these charges were heard by the ecclesia, and that Cleisthenes must therefore have given eisangeltic jurisdiction to the boule and ecclesia, either in place of the Areopagus or as a permissible alternative to it.[6] We have no clear evidence that Cleisthenes showed any interest at all in the Areopagus, or in the powers of the boule and ecclesia as opposed to the composition of the boule,[7] though Bonner and Smith write: 'Cleisthenes was interested in trans-ferring both political and judicial powers from the oligarchic body, the Areopagus, to the democratic bodies, the boulé and the assembly.'[8] But Ephialtes, we know, was interested in transferring powers from the Areopagus to the boule and the assembly, and it is worth asking whether the six trials I have mentioned can be explained without crediting Cleisthenes with an otherwise unattested judicial reform. Another way in which trials could reach the demos at this time was by ἔφεσις from the personal jurisdiction of an archon,[9] and I am inclined to suspect that the first four were referred to the undivided heliaea in this way. The trial of Themistocles is described as an εἰσαγγελία by the *Lexicon Rhetoricum Cantabrigiense*, while Plutarch uses the participle γραψάμενος: whether the lexicographer has been misled by Theophrastus' list of charges which could be made the subject of an εἰσαγγελία, or Plutarch has used a technical

---

[1] *A.P.* 25. iii–iv, Is. VII. *Areop.*, *hyp.*   [2] *A.P.* 27. i.   [3] Pl. *Per.* 10. vi.

[4] Pl. *Per.* 10. vi, *Cim.* 14. iii, 15. i.   [5] Pl. *Cim.* 14. iv.

[6] Lipsius, 179–81, Bonner and Smith, i. 299–300.

[7] I accept the Solonian boule as historical: see Ch. V, pp. 208–9.

[8] Bonner and Smith, i. 299. Against this view see A. G. Woodhead, *Hist.* xvi 1967, 136.

[9] Cf. H. T. Wade-Gery, *E.G.H.*, 176–8, B. R. I. Sealey, *CP* lix 1964, 18 = *Essays in Greek Politics*, 51. I do not share the view of E. Ruschenbusch, *Untersuchungen zur Geschichte des athenischen Strafrechts*, 78–82, that Solon's heliaea heard all disputed cases within the purview of an archon.

term in a non-technical sense, cannot be decided with certainty, but the strange story in *A.P.* 25. iii–iv might lend some support to the view that this charge was an εἰσαγγελία heard by the Areopagus.[1] The *Athenaion Politeia* links the prosecution of Cimon with his εὔθυναι, which may be a guess but if so is an intelligent guess: it has been suggested that before 462/1 εὔθυναι were the concern of the Areopagus,[2] and it would make excellent political sense if in the 460s the Areopagus condemned Themistocles and acquitted Cimon.

In six important cases there is no mention at all of the boule, and if the boule's judicial powers were as great at this time as later in the fifth century we might have expected it to play some part in the accounts of these trials. Arguments from such small silences as these are bound to be dangerous, but our sources do mention the boule in connection with other events of this period,[3] and it is at any rate possible that the boule is not mentioned here because it had not yet acquired the powers which it was to exercise later.

Powers which the boule did not possess early in the fifth century but did possess by the middle of the century may well have been acquired through the reforms of Ephialtes, to which I now turn. The principal evidence for the content of these reforms can be set out in three short quotations. In the *Athenaion Politeia* we read that after the Persian Wars the Areopagus, though gradually weakening, dominated the state; Ephialtes became προστάτης τοῦ δήμου and began to attack this body:

καὶ πρῶτον μὲν ἀνεῖλεν πολλοὺς τῶν Ἀρεοπαγιτῶν, ἀγῶνας ἐπιφέρων περὶ τῶν διῳκημένων· ἔπειτα τῆς βουλῆς ἐπὶ Κόνωνος ἄρχοντος (462/1) ἅπαντα περιείλετο τὰ ἐπίθετα δι' ὧν ἦν ἡ τῆς πολιτείας φυλακή, καὶ τὰ μὲν τοῖς πεντακοσίοις, τὰ δὲ τῷ δήμῳ καὶ τοῖς δικαστηρίοις ἀπέδωκεν.[4]

Plutarch is at his most informative in the life of *Cimon*:

τελέως ἀνεθέντες οἱ πολλοὶ καὶ συγχέαντες τὸν καθεστῶτα τῆς πολιτείας κόσμον τά ⟨τε⟩ πάτρια νόμιμα, οἷς ἐχρῶντο πρότερον, Ἐφιάλτου προεστῶτος ἀφείλοντο τῆς ἐξ Ἀρείου πάγου βουλῆς τὰς κρίσεις πλὴν ὀλίγων ἁπάσας, καὶ τῶν δικαστηρίων κυρίους ἑαυτοὺς ποιήσαντες εἰς ἄκρατον δημοκρατίαν ἐνέβαλον τὴν πολιν.[5]

---

[1] Even on Professor White's estimate (*JHS* lxxxiv 1964) Themistocles' condemnation was at least four years before Ephialtes' reform. But the most incredible stories must originate somehow, and this one will be more intelligible if it was the Areopagus that had condemned Themistocles.

[2] B. R. I. Sealey, *CP* lix 1964, 18–20 = *Essays in Greek Politics*, 52–4. Cf. p. 204 below.

[3] The rejection of Mardonius' peace offer is ascribed to the boule (cf. pp. 191–1 and p. 191 n. 1 above); Diodorus tells rather unlikely stories of two secret meetings of the boule shortly after the defeat of the Persians (D.S. XI. 39. v, 42. v; cf. Ch. I, pp. 40–1); and Plutarch in one of his two accounts makes it the boule which by passing a decree prevented Cimon's rejoining the Athenians at Tanagra, a few years after the Ephialtic reform (Pl. *Cim.* 17. v, contr. *Per.* 10. i; cf. Ch. I, p. 36).   [4] *A.P.* 25. (i–)ii.   [5] Pl. *Cim.* 15. ii.

Philochorus credited Ephialtes with the creation of a board of νομο-φύλακες, not otherwise known before the reign of Alexander:

ἑπτὰ δὲ ἦσαν καὶ κατέστησαν, ὡς Φιλόχορος, ὅτε Ἐφιάλτης μόνα κατέλιπε τῇ ἐξ Ἀρείου πάγου βουλῇ τὰ ὑπὲρ τοῦ σώματος.[1]

Other sources have very little to add. We learn that the Areopagus retained jurisdiction in arson and certain religious cases as well as for homicide,[2] but that is all.[3]

We can at any rate recover the campaigning slogans used by Ephialtes and his opponents: the *Athenaion Politeia*'s reference to ἐπίθετα must surely be derived from anti-Areopagite propaganda, while on the conservative side there are close parallels to Plutarch's τὸν καθεστῶτα κόσμον τά ⟨τε⟩ πάτρια νόμιμα in Diodorus and Pausanias.[4] What the Areopagus lost could variously be represented as accretions or as established rights, they included an important element of judicial power, and they gave the Areopagus a φυλακὴ τῆς πολιτείας.

Despite the mention of 'accretions' in chapter 25, the *Athenaion Politeia* makes three earlier references to the Areopagus' guardianship of the laws. It occurs first in the early, pre-Draconian state:

ἡ δὲ τῶν Ἀρεοπαγιτῶν βουλὴ τὴν μὲν τάξιν εἶχε τοῦ διατηρεῖν τοὺς νόμους, διῴκει δὲ τὰ πλεῖστα καὶ τὰ μέγιστα τῶν ἐν τῇ πόλει, καὶ κολάζουσα καὶ ζημιοῦσα πάντας τοὺς ἀκοσμοῦντας κυρίως.[5]

In the so-called Draconian constitution the Areopagus is guardian of the laws, sees that the ἀρχαί rule according to the laws, and hears εἰσαγγελίαι;[6] while Solon, though creating a new boule of four hundred, was thought not to have tampered with the rights of the Areopagus:

τὴν δὲ τῶν Ἀρεοπαγιτῶν (sc. βουλὴν) ἔταξεν ἐπὶ τὸ νομοφυλακεῖν, ὥσπερ ὑπῆρχεν καὶ πρότερον ἐπίσκοπος οὖσα τῆς πολιτείας, καὶ τά τε ἄλλα τὰ πλεῖστα καὶ τὰ

---

[1] Phil. 328 F 64 b (a).

[2] Arson, D. XXIII. *Arist.* 22; sacred olives, Lys. VII. *Ol.* 22, *A.P.* 60. ii; other religious cases, [D.] LIX. *Neaer.* 79–80.

[3] I am not directly concerned with the enactment of the reforms. Some have been tempted by the mention of Ephialtes and Archestratus in *A.P.* 35. ii and by what is said of Pericles in *A.P.* 27. i and Arist. *Pol.* II. 1274 A 7–8 to postulate a reform in two or more stages: but *A.P.* 27. i may well be an attribution to Pericles of a share in the reform of 462/1, not properly co-ordinated with ch. 25, and Archestratus was a common fifth-century Attic name. See Hignett, 197–8.

[4] D.S. XI. 77. vi, Paus. I. 29. xv.
Professor Sealey has suggested (*CP* lix 1964, 13 = *Essays in Greek Politics*, 45) that the talk of ἐπίθετα derives not from the propaganda of the time but from an attempt in the third quarter of the fourth century to compare the pre-Ephialtic powers of the Areopagus with the enhanced powers which it exercised at that time, but the slogan is older than that, for the word was used of the Areopagus' powers in a lost speech of Lysias: ἐλέγετο δὲ παρ' αὐτοῖς καὶ ἄλλα ἐπίθετά τινα, ὁπόσα μὴ πάτρια ὄντα ἡ ἐξ Ἀρείου πάγου βουλὴ ἐδίκαζεν, ὡς σαφὲς ποιεῖ Λυσίας ἐν τῷ πρὸς τὴν Μιξιδήμου γραφήν (Lys., fr. 178a [Sauppe], from Harp. ἐπιθέτους ἑορτάς).

[5] *A.P.* 3. vi.   [6] *A.P.* 4. iv.

μέγιστα τῶν πολιτικῶν διετήρει καὶ τοὺς ἁμαρτάνοντας ηὔθυνεν κυρία οὖσα καὶ ζημιοῦν καὶ κολάζειν, καὶ τὰς ἐκτίσεις ἀνέφερεν εἰς πόλιν, οὐκ ἐπιγράφουσα τὴν πρόφασ ινδι' ὃ τὸ ἐκτίνεσθαι, καὶ τοὺς ἐπὶ καταλύσει τοῦ δήμου συνισταμένους ἔκρινεν, Σόλωνος θέντος νόμον εἰσαγγελίας περὶ αὐτῶν.[1]

Plutarch writes in similar terms of the functions of the Areopagus, and quotes a law from the thirteenth ἄξων to prove the existence of this council before Solon's legislation.[2] In the later chapters of the life of *Solon* he gives us further quotations from the ἄξονες and, although much that we read, particularly about the pre-Solonian state, is based on inference, I believe that ancient scholars had in these laws and in the poems of Solon enough material to guarantee that the general picture which we are given of the constitution in the sixth century is not far from the truth. In this early period jurisdiction was exercised also by the nine archons, but Solon provided for ἔφεσις from their verdicts to the heliaea.[3] In connection with Cleisthenes, as we have already noticed, the Areopagus is not mentioned, and there is no direct indication of any change in judicial machinery.

The guardianship of the laws is commonly interpreted either as some specific function of the Areopagus, a safeguard against illegal legislation or administration like that later provided by the γραφαὶ παρανόμων and νόμοις μὴ χρῆσθαι,[4] or as a comprehensive name for all the various ways in which the Areopagus could enforce respect for the laws.[5] The association of νομοφυλακεῖν with the Areopagus is certainly very old: it may be older than written laws, or it might perhaps be associated with the first codification of the laws, by Draco. Whatever its exact origin it is probably not to be associated directly with any one or more of the specific rights exercised by the Areopagus at the beginning of the fifth century: I imagine that it was intended as a comprehensive name for all the various ways in which the Areopagus could enforce respect for the laws at the time when the title was first conferred, and became the pretext on which the Areopagus based different rights which it assumed in different circumstances later. That is, by reinterpreting a general description of its judicial function, the Areopagus came to exercise insecurely based powers which could be regarded either as established rights or as accretions.

Professor Sealey in an essay on Ephialtes has claimed that the Areopagus was not deprived of its right to initiate business in the ecclesia, which it seems to have exercised on occasions in the time of Demosthenes;[6]

---

[1] *A.P.* 8. iv.   [2] Pl. *Sol.* 19.   [3] *A.P.* 9. i. Cf. p. 200 and n. 9 above.
[4] Examples cited by Hignett, 208 with nn. 4, 5.   [5] e.g. Hignett, 208–9.
[6] *CP* lix 1964, 12–14 = *Essays in Greek Politics*, 43–6. See D. XVIII. *Cor.* 134, cf. [Pl.]

and that the change from full jurisdiction of an archon with appeal lying to the heliaea, to preliminary inquiry by the archon, with regular reference to his δικαστήριον, is likely to have been a natural and gradual change rather than an abrupt and legally enforced reform[1] (with which I agree). We are left, he claims, with the transfer of εὔθυναι from the Areopagus to the board of εὔθυνοι and the courts as the only way in which the guardianship of the laws might have been destroyed, and he interprets Ephialtes' attacks on individual Areopagites περὶ τῶν διῳκημένων as prosecutions for corruption in the conduct of εὔθυναι.[2] Ephialtes must have done something, Sealey points out, or he would not have been murdered, but we may perhaps wonder whether the reorganization of εὔθυναι, important as it was, was enough to merit assassination. I believe that this was one of the ways in which the courts gained from Ephialtes' reform, but that this is only a small part of the story.

We have seen in this chapter that by the fourth century the boule was functioning as a lawcourt in a number of ways:

(i) It had a disciplinary jurisdiction over its own members, which it is likely always to have possessed.

(ii) It had an 'official' jurisdiction over most magistrates, and over private citizens who failed in their official duties.

X. Or. 850 A, Hyp., frs. 67–76 (Kenyon) also; Pl. Phoc. 16. iv. Every citizen had the right of πρόσοδος πρὸς τὴν βουλὴν καὶ τὸν δῆμον, and could hardly be prevented from stating that the view he advanced had the backing of some corporate body to which he belonged. On the enactment of decrees in general see Ch. II, and notice especially the decrees with special origins listed in Table E.

[1] CP lix 1964, 14–18 = Essays in Greek Politics, 46–52. This brings him into conflict with Professor Wade-Gery (E.G.H., 180–200) over the interpretation of the Athenian decree for Phaselis, M&L 31. Wade-Gery sees references to the archon's personal jurisdiction in the words παρ[ὰ τῶι πο]λεμάρχωι (9–10) and [ἐ]ὶ μὲν καταδικάσ[ει, ἡ καταδίκ]η ἄκυρος ἔστω (18–19), and, assuming an abrupt reform which Aeschylus celebrated in the Eumenides, dates this decree before it (his arguments are accepted by M&L); Sealey thinks this language would be entirely possible even after such a reform, and for καταδικάζειν compares Plat. Legg. XII. 958 B–C. To add to the uncertainty, Mr. W. W. Wyndham has pointed out in an unpublished essay that we could restore the more innocuous καταδικάσ[εταί τι, ἡ δίκ]η; and the decree is one of the many for which Professor H. B. Mattingly would like a much later dating (PACA vii 1964, 37–9, cf. Ancient Society and Institu tions, 216–17 n. 29).

There may well have been a law at some point, possibly enforcing a change but more probably confirming an evolution that had already taken place; but new language for new procedures does not become established overnight, and even if Wade-Gery were right in principle the decree could belong to a period of overlap when the old language was used of the new procedure. The changes in judicial procedure which I would ascribe to Ephialtes will probably have made necessary the division of the heliaea into δικαστήρια, if this division had not already (as Wade-Gery believes: E.G.H., 196) been made, but I am not convinced that Ephialtes must have abolished the archons' personal jurisdiction.

[2] I prefer to think that Ephialtes made a point of attacking those about to join the ranks of the Areopagus, in the εὔθυναι which they had to undergo on retiring from the archonship (cf. Wade-Gery, BSA xxxvii 1936–7, 169 = E.G.H., 177).

(iii) It heard εἰσαγγελίαι.

(iv) It conducted certain δοκιμασίαι.

I believe that the boule was created by Solon and reorganized by Cleisthenes primarily as a probouleutic council, and that until 462 its judicial power was limited to internal discipline and the δοκιμασία of (probably) the next year's bouleutae only. εἰσαγγελίαι were the preserve of the Areopagus, and so too was such official jurisdiction as existed at that time (less and more primitive than in the period for which we have evidence), together with some δοκιμασίαι—at any rate that of the archons. If the Areopagus lost all of these in 462/1, the boule, ecclesia, and δικαστήρια will all have benefited, and Ephialtes will have done more than enough to deserve assassination by a diehard.

Some of the powers which it was exercising the Areopagus had assumed on the basis of its position as guardian of the laws, and to be complete the reform must somehow have taken away from the Areopagus this useful title.[1] Its members, who since 487 had been appointed to the archonship by lot,[2] and who before long were to come from all but the lowest property-class,[3] were no longer to be guardians of the laws. They were not formally deprived of the right of πρόσοδος to the boule and demos, but they were formally discredited, and no one in future would pay much attention to a γνώμη Ἀρεοπαγιτῶν; no one, that is, until, more than a hundred years later, Isocrates wrote his *Areopagitic* and Demosthenes took the Areopagus into his ἑταιρεία. Only once in the intervening century did the Areopagus become prominent, when in 403/2 Tisamenus entrusted the revised law-code to it,[4] and there we can only suppose that even the democrats had been affected by oligarchic talk about the πάτριος πολιτεία.[5] Perhaps this is why our sources knew so much less about Ephialtes than about Cleisthenes and Solon: though his reform did involve the judicial changes which I have outlined, the essence of it

---

[1] I should not like to say exactly how this was done, as I find it hard to believe in the Ephialtic νομοφύλακες of Philochorus. Wilamowitz (*Aristoteles und Athen*, ii. 188) regarded a purely negative clause as impossible, but ensuring that the ἀρχαί kept the laws became one of the responsibilities of the boule (cf. *A.P.* 45. ii), and the duty of νομοφυλακεῖν may have been assumed by the boule and demos. Aeschylus' *Eumenides* (704–6) suggests to me that the issue of νομοφυλακεῖν was raised in some form at this time, and that at any rate after the event the poet thought the Areopagus ought to have retained this privilege (cf. E. R. Dodds, *PCPS²* vi 1960, esp. 22).   [2] *A.P.* 22. v.   [3] *A.P.* 26. ii.

[4] ἐπειδὰν δὲ τεθῶσι οἱ νόμοι, ἐπιμελείσθω ἡ βουλὴ ἡ ἐξ Ἀρείου πάγου τῶν νόμων, ὅπως ἂν αἱ ἀρχαὶ τοῖς κειμένοις νόμοις χρῶνται (decree *ap.* And. I. *Myst.* 84). What in practical terms Tisamenus meant by this I do not know, and I doubt whether he knew. MacDowell *ad loc.* discusses various possibilities.

[5] The fragment of Lysias, quoted in p. 202 n. 4 above, suggests that about this time the arguments about 'accretions' and 'established rights' were resurrected.

was, quite simply, that the Areopagus was no longer to be guardian of the laws.

The transfer of judicial procedures may have involved not only the enactment of new measures which could later be collected in the νόμος βουλευτικός, but also an addition to the oath sworn by the bouleutae. We are now in a position to see how what Cloché rejected as impossible could in fact have happened, that restrictive clauses were incorporated in the oath at a time when the boule's powers were not reduced but considerably increased. Ephialtes was bringing to political insignificance a body which, at any rate according to his own propaganda, had been improperly extending its powers. The boule in turn was now being given a position of great importance in the running of the state and, representative of the demos as it was,[1] there was perhaps a danger that it too might start to amass ἐπίθετα. Unless it did so, no democrat would want to reduce its powers, but some precaution against its abusing or gradually and imperceptibly enlarging its new powers will have seemed at this time very desirable. Hence the requirement that the boule's jurisdiction should be final only for routine offences; hence the acknowledgement of its limitations in the oath.

The explanation that I offer takes into account all the evidence for the boule's judicial powers except the two passages commonly regarded as fundamental:

ἡ δὲ βουλὴ πρότερον μὲν ἦν κυρία καὶ χρήμασιν ζημιῶσαι καὶ δῆσαι καὶ ἀποκτεῖναι.[2]

αἱ τῆς βουλῆς κρίσεις εἰς τὸν δῆμον ἐληλύθασιν.[3]

Since I believe that the *Athenaion Politeia* is mistaken, I must at least try to show how the mistake may have arisen. Enough modern scholars have regarded the presence of restrictions in the bouleutic oath as proof that before the oath was imposed the restrictions did not exist, for it to be perfectly credible that an ancient writer should have made the same mistake. When the *Athenaion Politeia* was written the boule swore not to exceed certain limits which had been set to its powers, and the bouleutic oath was first imposed in 501/0: the inference may have been as natural to our author as it was to Cloché, to Bonner and Smith, and to Larsen. There is also another factor which may have made for misunderstanding. There were in Athens two βουλαί, the Areopagus, and the Five (earlier Four) Hundred. The Areopagus was the older, and must for some time

---

[1] A fact doubtless far less appreciated at this time than by the political theorists of a century later.   [2] *A.P.* 45. i.   [3] *A.P.* 41. ii.

after the creation of the new council have remained The Boule *par excellence*. Scarcely any of our evidence for early history is contemporary, and when our authorities were writing the Five Hundred were The Boule,[1] but even in the *Athenaion Politeia*'s account of Ephialtes we find βουλή (alone) used of the Areopagus, while the Five Hundred are identified by their number.[2] I would suggest that fourth-century Athenians were led by the fact of the bouleutic oath and the normal usage of their own day to misunderstand a remark to the effect that ἡ βουλή had once possessed unlimited judicial powers, and that the story of Lysimachus and Eumelides, far from guaranteeing the truth of the *Athenaion Politeia*'s assertion, has been invented or misapplied to illustrate this misunderstanding.

[1] But the correct form of address to the Areopagus remained ὦ βουλή (Lys. III. *Sim.* 1, IV. *Vuln. Praemed.* 1, VII. *Ol.* 1).

[2] *A.P.* 25, *passim*.

V · CONCLUSION

In the foregoing chapters I have examined the membership and activities of the Athenian boule from the time of Cleisthenes onwards. In all probability Cleisthenes' boule was not a wholly new creation. Solon is said in the *Athenaion Politeia* and by Plutarch to have established a boule of four hundred, a hundred from each of the four old tribes, οὖς προβουλεύειν ἔταξε τοῦ δήμου καὶ μηδὲν ἐᾶν ἀπροβούλευτον εἰς ἐκκλησίαν εἰσφέρεσθαι.[1] We know scarcely anything about Solon's boule, and some scholars have refused to believe in its existence, but this scepticism seems unjustified.[2] Since the Areopagus would for some time be dominated by aristocrats who had gained admission before Solon's reforms, the creation of a second council makes sense in the light of his use of wealth as the sole qualification for office, and the fact that Pisistratus was not prevented from obtaining a bodyguard and becoming tyrant does not of course prove that there was no probouleutic council to restrain the impulses of the people.[3] It is scarcely possible that Cleisthenes' deme organization could have been completed in time for the new boule of five hundred to resist Cleomenes in 508/7, and *pace* Hignett it is surely inconceivable that an attempt should have been made to dissolve the ancient council of the Areopagus; therefore the boule which resisted Cleomenes ought to have been the four hundred.[4] A century after Cleisthenes an oligarchic constitution was for a short time set up, and a document issued by the oligarchs began with the words, βουλεύειν μὲν τετρακοσίους κατὰ τὰ πάτρια:[5] we must not automatically accept any statement made by oligarchic propagandists, but it would be surprising, I think, if at the end

---

[1] *A.P.* 8. iv, cf. 21. iii, Pl. *Sol.* 19. i. My quotation is from Plutarch: the *Athenaion Politeia* says nothing of the functions of this boule.

[2] For a full statement of the case for the Solonian boule see Cloché, *REG* xxxvii 1924, 1–26; of the case against it, Hignett, 92–6. Recent writers who believe in the Solonian boule include W. G. G. Forrest, *The Emergence of Greek Democracy*, 164–6; A. Andrewes, *Ancient Society and Institutions*, 16 with 20 nn. 26–7, and (more cautiously) G. T. Griffith, ibid. 121 with 135 n. 35; A. G. Woodhead, *Hist.* xvi 1967, 135–6. Few will follow J. H. Oliver in accepting on the basis of *A.P.* 4. iii a Draconian boule, emended to 501 members: *The Athenian Expounders of the Sacred and Ancestral Law*, 68–9, answered by M. N. Tod, *JHS* lxxi 1951, 270–1.

[3] Diogenes Laertius (i. 49) has a story that when Solon tried to warn the ecclesia against Pisistratus ἡ βουλή, Πεισιστρατίδαι ὄντες, said that he was mad.

[4] H. v. 72. ii.

[5] *A.P.* 31. i. For a brief statement of my views on the constitutional documents in *A.P.* 30–1 see Ch. I, p. 6 n. 9.

of the fifth century knowledge of the sixth was already so slight that a (surely needless) falsehood of this kind could be perpetrated. Plutarch goes on to compare the two βουλαί with a ship's two anchors,[1] and it is an attractive suggestion that here he is alluding to one of Solon's poems.[2]

The new boule is said to have been probouleutic, and I imagine that this was its only major function. It may have been given limited disciplinary powers to ensure good order at meetings,[3] and if its members were required to undergo a δοκιμασία before entering office this examination may have been conducted by the retiring boule.[4] We are not told of any prytany system in this boule: meetings were probably convened and presided over by the archon or the college of archons;[5] they need not have been frequent.

Pisistratus dominated Athens without tampering with the constitution,[6] and Solon's boule still existed in 508/7, when it resisted Cleomenes' attempt to give power to Isagoras. Cleisthenes carried his reforms, by which Attica was given a new political organization, based on the distribution of about 170 demes among ten new tribes. The membership of the boule was now increased to five hundred: each of the ten tribes had fifty seats, apportioned among the demes in proportion to their size.[7] I believe that this organization of Attica was the essence of Cleisthenes' reform of the city's government. Some modern scholars have thought that he was concerned also with the relative powers of the different bodies in the state, and attempted to strengthen the boule and ecclesia at the expense of the Areopagus,[8] but this view is to be found in none of our ancient sources. There is no allusion to the boule before 462 which need imply that it possessed more than probouleutic powers;[9] the assembly had legislative power and (as the heliaea) appellate jurisdiction; but I have tried to show that until the time of Ephialtes the Areopagus retained the

---

[1] Pl. Sol. 19. ii.

[2] K. Freeman, The Work and Life of Solon, 79 with n. 1. Of the inscriptions which have been adduced in this connection M&L 8 with its emphatic mention of a δημοσίη βολή makes it very likely that two βουλαί coexisted in Chios before c. 550; the 1938 fragment of M&L 14 makes it virtually certain that the boule was mentioned in l. 12, but this decree need not be pre-Cleisthenic.

[3] For discipline in the fifth and fourth centuries see Ch. IV, pp. 144-7.

[4] Cf. Ch. IV, pp. 176-8.   [5] Cf. Ch. I, p. 21 n. 4.

[6] See Hignett, 115-23. We do not know in what ways or to what extent Pisistratus influenced the deliberations of the boule and ecclesia.

[7] On the membership of the Cleisthenic boule see Ch. I, pp. 1-16. A. G. Woodhead's statement (Hist. xvi 1967, 135) that the members of Solon's boule were 'elected, apparently for life' seems to rest on the authority of F. E. Adcock, C.A.H., iv. 53-4.

[8] Cf. appendix to Ch. IV, p. 200. Woodhead agrees that Cleisthenes left the boule's powers unchanged, but makes the sixth-century boule a powerful body (Hist. xvi 1967, 135-6 with 135 n. 17).

[9] Cf. Ch. IV, p. 201 n. 3.

right to hear εἰσαγγελίαι,[1] to hold the δοκιμασία at any rate of prospective archons,[2] and to conduct the εὔθυναι of retiring magistrates.[3] In 501/0 the boule first swore the oath ὃν ἔτι καὶ νῦν ὀμνύουσιν.[4] Some scholars have thought that the imposition of this oath marks a departure from Cleisthenes' constitution, by which the boule lost to the people powers which it had been given by Cleisthenes, such as the right to commit the state to peace or war, and the right to condemn to death. However, the institution of an oath need not mean that the restrictions embodied in the oath are new. The year 501/0 is very close to the date of Cleisthenes' reforms, and we have no direct mention of a reform which ought to have been of as great importance as his. I prefer to believe that it took until 501 to work out the details of Cleisthenes' organization, and that the boule of 501/0 was the first to take the bouleutic oath because it was the first boule in which the demes and tribes were represented as Cleisthenes had planned.[5] It was the organization alone which Cleisthenes changed; in other respects the boule remained as Solon had established it, simply a probouleutic body. Meetings of the boule and ecclesia were perhaps more frequent in 500 than in 590, but they cannot yet have been very frequent, and I doubt whether it was found necessary to divide the boule into tribal prytanies this early.[6]

Ephialtes' reform marks a turning-point in the history of the boule. In 462/1 the Areopagus, the older council in Athens, falling in prestige since the lot had been introduced in 487 for the appointment of the archons who became its members,[7] was deprived of powers which its enemies represented as accretions, and these were given to the boule, the ecclesia, and the δικαστήρια into which the heliaea was divided.[8] Ancient writers seem to have been able to discover very little of what was involved, but the powers in question seem to have been primarily judicial or quasi-judicial. Among the changes, I have suggested, was the transfer of the right to hear εἰσαγγελίαι, major charges of public importance, to the boule and demos; also the transfer to the boule and δικαστήρια of the mechanisms through which the state supervised its magistrates. Most δοκιμασίαι were conducted by the courts, but the boule now held the first, perhaps for a time the sole, examination of the archons, and outside the strictly magisterial sphere it acquired an interest in the cavalry, in the enrolment of citizens on their coming of age, and, when the system of grants was instituted, in the examination of invalids who applied for

[1] Cf. appendix to Ch. IV, pp. 199–201, 205.
[2] Cf. Ch. IV, pp. 176–8.
[3] Cf. appendix to Ch. IV, pp. 199–201, 204–5.
[4] A.P. 22. ii.
[5] Cf. appendix to Ch. IV, pp. 190–9.
[6] Cf. Ch. I, pp. 17–19.
[7] A.P. 22. v.
[8] A.P. 25. ii.

support from the state.[1] Magistrates who passed their δοκιμασία and entered on their office had to submit their accounts each prytany to a committee of bouleutae, and the boule played a smaller part in the main examination to which they submitted at the end of the year.[2] Finally, the boule acquired the right to hear charges of νόμοις μὴ χρῆσθαι against magistrates from private citizens.[3]

Some of the functions which I have mentioned in the last paragraph may have been acquired by the boule only after the time of Ephialtes, but I believe that his giving the boule the right to hear εἰσαγγελίαι, and also some judicial powers in connection with public officials, was of crucial importance. Since the Athenians saw no reason to separate the judicial from the executive authorities, the boule because of its powers over magistrates will have become the obvious body to be charged with seeing that the decisions of the assembly on a variety of topics were carried out. Its judicial position will thus have become the basis of the boule's later development as the overseer and co-ordinator of a wide range of public activities, and this in turn will have made it better qualified to advise the assembly when new decisions had to be taken.

In this way by the late fifth century the boule had come to play a vital part in the running of the state. It retained, of course, its original pro-bouleutic function, in consequence of which it received foreign envoys,[4] heard reports from Athenians holding regular or extraordinary appointments,[5] and discussed every matter which might be the subject of a decree of the assembly.[6] It had come to be regarded as generally responsible for the financial well-being of Athens. We have seen it involved in assessing and collecting the tribute paid by members of the Delian League; we have seen it interested in the sacred treasuries which were so important to Athens in the Peloponnesian War. The boule supervised the poletae, who placed state contracts of all kinds, the apodectae (not mentioned before 418/17), who received state revenue, and the colacretae, who (until their duties were taken over in or shortly before 411 by an enlarged board of Hellenotamiae) made all payments on behalf of the state. The part which it played in finance was typical: routine work was handled by a number of separate committees, each active in a limited field, while

---

[1] Cf. Ch. IV, pp. 171–8.
[2] Cf. Ch. IV, pp. 147–8 with p. 148 n. 1.   [3] A.P. 45. ii.
[4] Cf. Ch. I, p. 43 with n. 3; Ch. II, p. 54. (In this paragraph I concentrate as far as possible on duties which the boule is known to have acquired before the end of the fifth century; but I have made use of some fourth-century material where we have no reason to believe that there had been a change in practice since the fifth century.)
[5] Cf. Ch. I, pp. 42–3; Ch. III, p. 132.
[6] Cf. Ch. II, pp. 52–81.

the boule supervised them all—the more public parts of their duty were discharged in its presence—and so was able to piece together the whole picture, and to advise the assembly if a new tax was needed, or if the money was not available for a new undertaking.[1] For the army the boule's responsibility was slight—it was involved to some extent in the enrolment of adult citizens, and conducted the δοκιμασίαι of the cavalry and other special forces—but it played an important part in Athens' naval organization. Through a sub-committee of trieropoei it was responsible for the building of new ships (though the number to be built was decided, perhaps from year to year, by the assembly), and it acted as overseer to the epimeletae who were the custodians of all that the dockyards contained. We have seen that it is difficult to define the powers of the boule and assembly in the dockyards, but it was commonly the boule that decided what was to be done with particular ships and items of equipment. The boule had important duties again when an expedition was sent out.[2] The great public buildings of the Periclean period were supervised by boards of popularly elected epistatae, but the boule was involved in the approval of plans (though the assembly sometimes claimed the right to decide even points of detail).[3] The administration of festivals was shared between the priests and boards of hieropoei, and some at any rate of the hieropoei were appointed from the boule, while the boule as a whole was involved in the Eleusinian Mysteries and the Dionysia.[4] In the fifth century and the first third of the fourth century the principal public secretary was a member of the boule, serving for one prytany.[5] The boule's position was reinforced by the fact that it was made a judge in its own causes. In finance, in naval matters, probably in connection with public works, and on certain religious questions, the boule acted as a court with limited powers of punishment; if it felt that a heavier penalty was called for than it could impose it would refer the case to a δικαστήριον for a second hearing. In this way it had jurisdiction over a great many public officials, and over private citizens in respect of their public obligations; we have seen that it could entertain a charge of misconduct against an official from any citizen, and many other cases of misconduct will have become apparent to the boule in the course of its administrative duties, in particular the interim examination of accounts made each prytany by logistae appointed from the boule.[6] Finally, charges of major offences against the state will have come to the boule as

---

[1] Cf. Ch. III, pp. 88–113.   [2] Cf. Ch. III, pp. 113–22.
[3] Cf. Ch. III, pp. 122–7.   [4] Cf. Ch. III, pp. 127–34.
[5] Cf. Ch. III, pp. 134–8.   [6] Cf. Ch. IV, pp. 147–62.

εἰσαγγελίαι, though if the procedure was not abused reference to the assembly or a court representing the demos for a heavy penalty will have been normal.[1]

The assembly remained sovereign; it took all major decisions, and elected the holders of offices in which special skill was considered necessary: but in the course of the fifth century the boule had become an essential adjunct of the sovereign assembly. Five hundred men devoted one year to the work which could not be done by an assembly of thousands, but still had to be done. They took the lesser, 'ministerial' decisions, which could not wait for the next meeting of the assembly, but had to be taken to ensure that the people's will was carried out; they watched over the activities of a wide range of public officials, and themselves punished or brought before a court men who failed in their duty to the state; and by keeping in touch with so many matters of public concern they could advise their fellow citizens in the assembly when further decisions needed to be taken. Much of this has been admirably stated in an essay by the late Professor Gomme,[2] but I cannot follow him in his conclusion that because the assembly took the major decisions it was only in the assembly that major issues were discussed.[3] It is proved beyond doubt that in the fifth and fourth centuries genuine debates were held, real decisions were taken, in the assembly; but I have tried to show that even at this time policy was discussed in the boule, and the boule was prepared in its probouleumata to make recommendations on important and controversial topics as well as on matters of routine: many decrees concerning Athens' relations with other states were published in a form showing that the basic text had been approved by the boule.[4]

We do not know how often the assembly was now meeting: an increase in the number of ordinary meetings in the year from ten to forty may have taken place towards the end of the fifth century,[5] but payment for attendance was not introduced until after 403.[6] The boule, however, was now fully occupied. The division into prytanies, to provide a standing committee to which urgent business could be taken at any time, must have been made by Ephialtes if it had not been made before, and it will soon have been found necessary for the boule to hold frequent meetings (it is uncertain how old the rule of the *Athenaion Politeia* is, that the boule

---

[1] Cf. Ch. IV, pp. 162–71.
[2] *History*[2] xxxvi 1951 = *More Essays*, 177–93.
[3] *More Essays*, 178. Cf. Jones, 117–19; Gomme, *JHS* lxxix 1959, 183, reviewing Jones.
[4] Cf. Ch. II, pp. 52–81, esp. 78–81.
[5] Cf. Additional Note A, p. 227.
[6] Cf. p. 219 n. 1 below.

met daily except on holidays[1]). Payment for attendance at meetings was being made in 411; very probably its introduction is to be dated between 461 and 431.[2] By 411 appointment was made by lot from the candidates in each deme, and about 453/2 appointment by lot to the boule was stipulated in Erythrae when Athens imposed a democratic constitution there, but it is possible that at first the Athenian bouleutae had been elected.[3] Service was for one year, and it may not have been necessary in the fifth century, as it was in the fourth, to allow men to serve twice in their lives.[4] The result was, as Gomme pointed out, that

> from a quarter to a third or more of citizens over thirty at any one time had had such political experience as membership of the council gave; the difference, that is, in experience and knowledge, between the average councillor and the average citizen in the assembly at any time was not great. Most of the citizens had had, as councillors and in one of the many minor administrative offices, some close experience of the day-to-day conduct of state affairs, none had much.[5]

In essence Gomme's statement is correct—no doubt most men who were willing to serve had the opportunity to do so, but the system could not have worked unless a fairly high proportion of citizens had been willing to serve,[6] and the boule will have played an important part in educating the citizens so that their assembly could be a responsible sovereign body[7] —but he perhaps went too far in minimizing the difference between the bouleutae for the time being and the lay citizens in the assembly. Probably most of the citizens who bothered to attend an ordinary meeting of the assembly had some experience of public office, but a comparatively small number will have had recent experience, and only those holding office at the time will have had that knowledge of the immediate situation without which responsible decisions cannot be taken. According to Gomme, 'the council is so important that it is indispensable; it is the lynch-pin of the democracy; it is the first object of attack by the enemies of the democracy; but it is not powerful. By its activity, its effective execution of its many duties, it secured the predominance of the assembly and so its own subordination.'[8] Certainly the boule was a selection of citizens taking their turn in office, not a powerful governing class with vested interests to protect, but I would say that for this very reason it

---

[1] O.O. iii. 1 sqq. (variously dated between c. 445 and c. 415: see most recently G. W. Bowersock, *HSCP* lxxi 1966, 33–8, arguing for an early date; but I should prefer to date the pamphlet after 431) emphasizes the amount of business transacted by the boule and perhaps, provides a *terminus ante quem*.   [2] Cf. Ch. I, pp. 13–14.

[3] Cf. Ch. I, pp. 6–7.   [4] Cf. Ch. I, p. 3.   [5] *More Essays*, 185.

[6] On the members of the boule cf. Ch. I, p. 3–6.

[7] This point is stressed by A. G. Woodhead, *Hist.* xvi 1967.   [8] *More Essays*, 186.

could be trusted to be powerful. When the sovereign body was a large assembly, unable to hold frequent meetings, a council with executive and judicial powers in so wide a field was bound to become powerful, not least because it was the city's centre of information, but because all citizens could take their turn in exercising this power the assembly had nothing to fear.

I cannot therefore share the view, which has often been advanced, that as the democracy came to completion the powers of the ecclesia were increased at the expense of the boule.[1] That in the course of the fifth century there was in practice a considerable advance towards ἰσηγορία, an increase in the proportion of citizens who were prepared to play an active part in running the state, I imagine no one would deny. But the men brought into politics by the spread of the view that any citizen might have something worthwhile to say in the assembly are the very men who will have responded to the doctrine that all citizens should serve the state through the boule and other public offices, and I imagine that both in 500 and in 400, and still in 200 B.C., the boule was fairly representative of those citizens who were politically minded.[2] The institution of the bouleutic oath I interpret as the culmination of Cleisthenes' reform, not as a removal of powers which he had given to the boule; and I believe that Ephialtes gave the boule judicial powers which from the start were limited because of the way in which the Areopagus was thought to have extended its powers. The sovereignty of the ecclesia was in this way firmly asserted, but as the range of public activity expanded in the heyday of the Delian League it became increasingly true that the boule was 'the instrument through which the Demos ruled'.[3] Aristotle regarded a boule as a characteristic organ of democracy, but thought that its power might be eroded in a state where generous pay gave the assembly the chance to meet frequently and attend to detailed business directly:[4] but there was no payment for attendance at the assembly in fifth-century Athens.

The failure of the democracy to win the Peloponnesian War led some

[1] Recently, D. W. Bradeen, *TAPA* lxxxvi 1955, 27, A. G. Woodhead, *Hist.* xvi 1967, 139–40, cf. G. T. Griffith, *Ancient Society and Institutions*, 129–31.

[2] The growth of ἰσηγορία in Athens is discussed by G. T. Griffith, *Ancient Society and Institutions*, 115–38, and A. G. Woodhead, *Hist.* xvi 1967. The machinery of the full democracy required the active participation of a large number of citizens, and the spread of willingness to take part in the assembly's debates must have been roughly parallelled by a spread of willingness to hold public office, each factor encouraging the other.

[3] V. L. Ehrenberg, *The Greek State²*, 63. Ehrenberg's account of the relationship between the boule and ecclesia, ibid. 62–5, is the one with which I am most in sympathy.

[4] Arist. *Pol.* IV. 1299 B 31–1300 A 4 (quoted in appendix to Ch. IV, p. 192), cf. VI. 1317 B 28–38.

Athenians to doubt the value of their democratic institutions. When news of the disaster in Sicily reached Athens, late in the summer of 413, ἐδόκει ... ἀρχήν τινα πρεσβυτέρων ἀνδρῶν ἑλέσθαι, οἵτινες περὶ τῶν παρόντων ὡς ἂν καιρὸς ᾖ προβουλεύσουσιν.[1] The πρόβουλοι were ten in number, perhaps aged forty or more.[2] Our only guide to their powers is an unreliable one, Aristophanes' *Lysistrata*.[3] There a πρόβουλος goes to the Acropolis to obtain money for the purchase of oars,[4] finds his way barred by Lysistrata and her friends, orders the τοξόται to arrest them, and finds himself heading a battle against the women;[5] defeated, the old man is arrayed for his funeral, and goes off to show himself to his fellow πρόβουλοι.[6] Later in the play he meets a Spartan herald who comes looking for the Athenian 'gerousia or prytanes', interrogates him, and orders him to go back and tell the Spartans to send πρεσβεῖς αὐτοκράτορες to Athens, while he himself will tell the boule to appoint πρεσβεῖς.[7] If his powers are fairly represented, the πρόβουλοι must have taken over some of the functions of the boule and prytanes, though the boule remained in existence, to be paid off before the end of 412/11.[8] When Pisander paid his second visit to Athens, in the spring of 411, thirty συγγραφεῖς were appointed, comprising the ten πρόβουλοι and twenty others, οἵτινες ὀμόσαντες ἦ μὴν συγγράψειν ἃ ἂν ἡγῶνται βέλτιστα εἶναι τῇ πόλει συγγράψουσι περὶ τῆς σωτηρίας.[9] At an assembly held at Colonus approval was given to the principle that citizen rights should be restricted to τοῖς δυνατωτάτοις καὶ τοῖς σώμασιν καὶ τοῖς χρήμασιν λῃτουργεῖν μὴ ἔλαττον ἢ πεντακισχιλίοις, and that there should be a boule of four hundred—κατὰ τὰ πάτρια, no doubt, but perhaps not openly authorized at this stage to enter the bouleuterium and ἄρχειν ὅπῃ ἂν ἄριστα γιγνώσκωσιν αὐτοκράτορας. A hundred men were appointed to work out the details of the constitution, and

---

[1] T. VIII. 1. iii.

[2] *A.P.* 29. ii., cf. for their number D.S. XII. 75. iv; *L.S.* 298. 25 gives their number as nine (but one from each tribe). For a discussion of the πρόβουλοι see F. D. Smith, *Athenian Political Commissions*, ch. iii.

[3] Produced in 411. I think it possible that the *Thesmophoriazusae* belongs to 410 (cf. Ch. IV, p. 190 with n. 4) and therefore cannot use that play as evidence for powers retained by the boule and prytanes during the existence of the πρόβουλοι.

[4] Ar. *Lys.* 420–3.   [5] Ibid. 430–66.   [6] Ibid. 598–610.

[7] Ibid. 980–1013.   [8] T. VIII. 69. iv, cf. *A.P.* 32. i.

[9] *A.P.* 29. ii, quoting a decree of Pythodorus, cf. T. VIII. 67. i: on debates περὶ σωτηρίας see Additional Note C, pp. 232–5.

Details of the means by which the Four Hundred came to power need not be discussed at length here; but I believe that the accounts of Thucydides and the *Athenaion Politeia* can be reconciled without great difficulty if we remember that the first is giving an account of 'what really happened' in so far as an exiled Athenian could discover that, while the second account is based, whether directly or at second hand, on the documents through which the oligarchs hoped to make their rule seem respectable. I hope to discuss the revolutions of 411 more fully elsewhere.

they perhaps nominated themselves and three hundred others as bouleutae.[1]

An oligarch who accepted the pattern of boule and ecclesia could still
differ from a democrat on two fundamental points: the qualification for
membership of the ecclesia, and the relative powers of boule and ecclesia.
In 411 limitation of the ecclesia's membership seems to have been accepted
by all the men who were behind the revolution, but the transfer of
effective sovereign power to the boule[2] seems to have been the work of
extremists, who expected opposition on this score.[3] After four months
a Spartan success off Eretria precipitated the fall of the Four Hundred,[4]
and a regime came into being which adhered to the restriction of the
citizen body, but accepted the democratic principle that the ecclesia
rather than the boule should be sovereign.[5] The ξύγκρασις which Thucydides admired[6] was achieved by combining a democratic tenet with an
oligarchic one. The size of the boule in this intermediate regime reverted
to five hundred, but the members may have been elected, and, although
the sovereignty of the ecclesia was affirmed in principle, the boule may
have enjoyed slightly greater powers than under the normal democracy.[7]
Full democracy was restored in the summer of 410,[8] but another experi-
ment with oligarchy was made with the approval of Lysander after
Athens had capitulated to Sparta in 404.[9] Thirty men, commissioned
to draft a constitution, seized power for themselves;[10] the officials whom
they appointed included a boule which was subservient to them, and the
rights of the three thousand who constituted the citizen body seem to
have been minimal.[11] The boule survived when the Thirty gave way to
the Ten,[12] but in the summer or autumn of 403 the oligarchy fell, and the
state prepared to make a fresh start.[13]

---

[1] T. VIII. 67. ii–68. i *init.*, *A.P.* 29. iv–v with 31. i *init.* Quotations are from *A.P.* 29. v on the
Five Thousand, *A.P.* 31. i and T. VIII. 67. iii on the Four Hundred. The motion may have
stood formally in the name of the συγγραφεῖς (*A.P.* 29. v), but Pisander doubtless spoke for it
(T. VIII. 68. i).   [2] T. VIII. 70. i, *A.P.* 32. iii, cf. 33. ii.
[3] Notice the assurances sent to the fleet at Samos, reported in T. VIII. 72. i.
[4] T. VIII. 89–96, *A.P.* 33.
[5] T. VIII. 97. i, *A.P.* 33. i. I cannot accept the account of this constitution given by G. E. M.
de Ste Croix, *Hist.* v 1956.
[6] T. VIII. 97. ii; for the admiration cf. *A.P.* 33. ii.
[7] On the membership and organization of the βουλαί of 411–410 see Ch. I, pp. 6–7, 28–9;
on the judicial power which they wielded, appendix to Ch. IV, p. 185 for the Four
Hundred, p. 182 with pp. 185–6 and 190 (date of the *Thesmophoriazusae*) for the boule under
the Five Thousand.   [8] For the date cf. Ch. I, p. 7 n. 3.
[9] X. *H.* II. iii. 2–3, *A.P.* 34. iii, D.S. XIV. 3. vi–vii, Pl. *Lys.* 15.
[10] X. *H.* II. iii. 2, 11, quoted in Ch. I, pp. 29–30.
[11] On the boule under the Thirty see Ch. I, p. 7 with n. 4 and pp. 29–30, appendix to Ch.
IV, p. 181.
[12] Cf. Ch. IV, p. 153 with n. 3.   [13] See especially And. I. *Myst.* 81 sqq.

In the forty years which followed the democratic restoration certain changes affecting the boule were made in the machinery of government. After two unhappy experiences of what could happen when full power was wielded by a few men we should expect the sovereignty of the demos to have been strongly affirmed, and since there is no trace in contemporary writers of further controversy on the relative powers of the boule and ecclesia I believe that this is what happened.[1] Superficial study of the evidence might suggest that for a short time the boule had the power to enact decrees which would normally require the assembly's approval,[2] or that for a short time it possessed unlimited judicial powers, and that after a while these powers were taken away and the boule reverted to its earlier position;[3] but I am not satisfied that its powers were enhanced in this way, and if the final restoration of the democracy was later than the 'restoration' of 403/2 we ought to find clearer signs of this. Changes which undoubtedly were made have been construed as an attack on the position of the boule, aimed at making it less powerful than it had been before 411. By 378/7 the presidency of the boule and ecclesia had been transferred from the prytanes to a board of proedri, comprising one man from each of the tribes not in prytany,[4] and in the course of the 360s the decision was made to appoint the principal state secretary for a year at a time from outside the boule, instead of for one prytany only from the bouleutae.[5] This is probably to be explained in terms of administrative convenience and a desire to lighten men's burdens by sharing out work more fairly: I do not believe that the boule's position in the state was seriously weakened as a result of these changes, or that anyone intended this to happen. Another change made early in the fourth century was in the field of financial organization. Whereas in the fifth century all state payments were made from a central fund, until about 411 by the colacretae (who worked under the control of the boule), in the fourth century the apodectae made a μερισμός of the revenue which they collected to various authorities who had an allowance which they could spend at their discretion.[6] Here any renunciation of power was made by the demos, which no longer claimed the right to authorize separately each item of public expenditure, and the boule through its supervision of the apodectae and through the examination of accounts which its logistae made each prytany controlled the working of the new system as it had the old. With the introduction of payment for attendance

---

[1] But some seem still to have hankered after a restrictive qualification for membership of the citizen body: see Ch. II, p. 85 n. 5.
[2] Cf. Ch. II, pp. 82–5.
[3] Cf. appendix to Ch. IV, p. 184.
[4] Cf. Ch. I, pp. 25–8.
[5] Cf. Ch. III, pp. 136–9.
[6] Cf. Ch. III, p. 103.

at the assembly[1] Athens could have approached the conditions in which
Aristotle saw that a democratic boule might be relieved of its power,[2]
but the payment was not over-generous and—more important—meetings
of the assembly were not made sufficiently frequent for the demos to be
able to rule directly instead of through the boule. I therefore believe that
in the first half of the fourth century the boule played very much the
same part in the running of the state as in the second half of the fifth
century, and had not been made less powerful.[3]

From the middle of the fourth century, however, there are signs of
a different kind of change, which affected boule and ecclesia alike.
Having made the great discovery that political wisdom is not a monopoly
of the well-born or of the rich, the first generations of Athenian democrats
had devised a system of office-sharing in which, while a great many
citizens were encouraged to take their share of work and responsibility,
no great value was set on ability and experience. To most offices appointment was by lot, and most offices a man could hold only for one year in
his life.[4] The collegiate principle and the limited scope of most offices
will have limited the harm that one dishonest or incompetent man could
do, but they will also have limited the good that could be done by an
able administrator. In some fields the cost in inefficiency was too great
to be tolerated, and in the third quarter of the fourth century ways were
found of giving extensive financial powers to men of proved ability.
Many of the details remain obscure,[5] but it is clear that from the late
350s to the early 330s an elected theoric official or board of officials
controlled a fund which provided money not only for festival distributions
to the citizens but also for a wide variety of public undertakings, so that
Eubulus and other holders of the office acquired considerable influence
in the state; and that in the 330s and 320s Lycurgus held a position which
gave him similar power and influence. According to Aeschines the theoric
officials controlled or superseded other officials,[6] and I have suggested
that their power depended first on their direct control of a fund that was
built up to considerable dimensions, and secondly on their becoming
involved, like the boule, in the work of a number of separate 'departments'. A single man or a small board, elected and able to be re-elected,

---

[1] A.P. 41. iii, dated before 392(?) by references to the τριώβολον in Ar. Eccl. 183–8, 289
sqq., etc.   [2] Cf. p. 215 with n. 4 above.

[3] For a full statement of this view, see P. Cloché, REG xxxiv 1921.

[4] The strategia, always a military office even when it was also of political importance,
was the main exception to this rule: generals were elected and could be re-elected. For
elective offices in the 320s see A.P. 43. i, 61.

[5] I have attempted to give an explanation of the view which I adopt in Ch. III, pp. 105–8,
with Additional Note D, pp. 235–40.   [6] A. III. Ctes. 25, quoted on p. 106 above.

had acquired that privilege of access to a wide range of activities which had previously been the monopoly of the boule. About 336 the theoric officials were weakened by a law of Hegemon,[1] but in the 320s they were still involved in the contract-making work of the poletae, and mentioned with them we find another elected official, the treasurer of the stratiotic fund.[2] Lycurgus' constitutional position is harder to determine, but his influence is undoubted, and I believe that he too must have been involved in the work of various boards. A new pattern was being set in financial control: various changes were tried in the decades after Alexander's death, but from the early third century the treasurer of the stratiotic fund and the board (in oligarchic periods, a single official) ἐπὶ τῇ διοικήσει controlled Athenian finance. The μερισμός to independent spending authorities seems to have been abandoned, though the central officials may have distinguished sums which they spent on different accounts; no more is heard of such boards as the apodectae and poletae.[3]

A similar move from democratic to expert control can be detected in the field of public works, though the evidence is insufficient for us to follow the development in detail. In the fifth century the ecclesia sometimes decided even small points, and each major undertaking was entrusted to the care of a popularly elected board of epistatae. Our most informative fourth-century document is the νόμος for the rebuilding of the walls, usually dated to 337/6: this provides that συγγραφαί are to be submitted by the salaried architects whom the state now employs and by anyone else who wishes, the choice of the συγγραφαί to be followed being apparently entrusted to the boule;[4] and for the supervision of the work the demos is to elect epistatae to co-operate with the tribally appointed τειχοποιοί.[5] The only serious difference between this and fifth-century practice lies in the existence of permanent state architects; but it is perhaps worth noticing as a sign of lessening public interest in the detailed control of public works that the Lycurgan period of building activity does not seem to have produced a set of documents comparable with that left by the Periclean. In the Hellenistic period we find frequent references in connection with religious works to the ἀρχιτέκτων ἐπὶ τὰ ἱερά and the στρατηγὸς ἐπὶ τὴν παρασκευήν, and it was normal for these to co-operate with the relevant priest and a lay committee on which

[1] A. III. Ctes. 25. [2] A.P. 47. ii (treasurer of the stratiotic fund elected: 43. i).
[3] Apart from their appearance in Hesp. xxxvii 23, 4–5 (assigned to beg. C2), th epoletae are last found in 307/6, combining with ὁ ἐπὶ τῇ διοικήσει to make a contract (IG ii² 463, 36, cf. 1589, 1), and the apodectae are last found in 323/2 (IG ii² 365, b 6; 1631, 324–5).
[4] IG ii² 244, 6–10. On the date see Ch. III, p. 123 with n. 7.
[5] Ibid. 28 sqq. For the appointment of τειχοποιοί by tribes see IG ii² 1658, 1 (394/3); 1660, 1–3 (393/2); cf. A. III. Ctes. 30.

some places might be allocated to Areopagites or bouleutae.[1] The decree ordering rebuilding of the walls in 307/6 shows that the boule was to be involved in some way,[2] but thereafter the boule and ecclesia did not normally concern themselves with the details of public works.

Though they were not so foolish as to disregard experts altogether, the Athenian democrats in their heyday believed very firmly that experts should be answerable to the people, and subjected their activities to close scrutiny.[3] The boule on behalf of the demos had for this reason become involved in a wide range of activities, but in finance certainly and perhaps in public works as well there seems from the mid fourth century to be a greater dependence on experts, with a move away from the view that their task was merely to help the demos make up its own mind. By placing greater faith in specialists the boule and ecclesia were together, in the interests of more efficient administration, withholding some of their constitutional power.

After the death of Alexander, pressure from outside powers helped to produce a great number of constitutional changes in Athens, particularly at the end of the fourth century and the beginning of the third. In 262, after Athens had made her last attempt at self-assertion, in the Chremonidean War, the city came under Macedonian domination again, and after a period of direct Macedonian rule a regime with oligarchic leanings was established. With the liberation in 229 came a reversion to a fuller democracy, and Athens remained free but unimportant until occupied by Sulla in 86. Diodorus' history exists only in fragments after the end of book xx (302/1), and our knowledge of Athenian history thereafter is slight: it is not possible to say much about the boule. Most if not all of the regimes in Athens retained the basic mechanism of boule and ecclesia, though some made little use of them, and on the fall of Lachares' tyranny in 295 it was felt desirable to appoint a new boule immediately, so that each tribe enjoyed a short prytany in the last three and a half months of the year.[4] Published decrees show that sovereignty normally remained with the ecclesia, though after the early third century signs of serious debate in the ecclesia are few, and it seems to have been increasingly normal for the ecclesia to adopt unaltered suggestions put to it by the boule.[5] In 307/6 the 'Macedonian' tribes Antigonis and Demetrias were created, and thereafter the number of tribes varied as new benefactors

---

[1] Cf. Ch. III, pp. 125–6.

[2] Cf. Ch. III, pp. 123–4 with p. 123 n. 12, and Ch. IV, p. 159 with n. 5.

[3] See, for example, Plat. *Protag.* 319 B 5–C 8.

[4] See W. S. Ferguson, *CP* xxiv 1929, 9, on *IG* ii² 644, and compare Professor Meritt's calendar studies, cited in Additional Note A, p. 226.   [5] Cf. Ch. II, pp. 78–81.

had to be recognized or old ones could safely be dethroned. Each tribe continued to provide 50 bouleutae, and so the changes in the number of tribes affected the size of the boule;[1] but the New Bouleuterium, built about 400 B.C., was never enlarged, and it is unlikely that there was room in it for every member of the enlarged council.[2] Now that Athens' position in the Greek world was relatively unimportant, public service must have seemed less attractive than in the fifth and fourth centuries, and even under 'democratic' regimes, when there was no property qualification for citizenship, it must have become increasingly hard to find a sufficient number of bouleutae. Restriction of service to two years in a man's life is not known to have been abandoned in this period, but the allocation of a fixed number of seats to each deme was probably found too restrictive, for this system seems to have broken down in the second century.[3]

During the Hellenistic period, as I have said, sovereignty remained with the ecclesia when it was not usurped by a single man. But in 83 Sulla enforced on the city a constitution in which the boule could take on its own authority decisions for which it would previously have asked the ecclesia's approval. Meetings of the ecclesia were revived under Caesar, suppressed under Antony, and revived again under the Empire; the Areopagus took its place beside the boule and ecclesia as one of the main bodies corporate in the state, and became perhaps more important than the other two—but as a city revered largely for its past Athens no longer had important decisions to take, and it seems that the chief business of all three bodies was to sacrifice to the gods, to award honours, and to permit the award of honours by others.[4] The attractions of a career in the boule were few, and there are signs that it became harder to find members: in A.D. 126/7, when the creation of the tribe Hadrianis again brought the number of tribes to thirteen, the boule was not enlarged to a membership of 650 but reduced to a little over 500;[5] and later in the second century we find that the ban on a man's serving more than two years in the boule had been lifted.[6] The prytany lists of the late second and early third centuries, naming with the prytanes a large number of ἀείσιτοι, many of them religious functionaries, form the last set of documents for which the boule was responsible.[7] The archaeologists must have the last word: the bouleuterium was abandoned after the Herulians' sack in A.D. 267, but the Tholos was repaired and remained in use until the beginning

[1] Cf. Ch. I, p. 1 with n. 4.   [2] Cf. Ch. I, p. 31.   [3] Cf. Ch. I, pp. 8–12.
[4] Cf. Ch. II, pp. 85–7.   [5] Cf. Ch. I, p. 1 with n. 5.
[6] Cf. Ch. I, p. 3 with n. 4.   [7] Cf. Ch. III, pp. 140–1.

of the fifth century, and the Metroum was used for a time after that before the whole of the site which the boule had occupied was abandoned.[1]

Solon had created the boule of four hundred as a counterweight to the aristocratic influence of the Areopagus: a standing committee of the ecclesia, which by its advance preparation of business could enable the ecclesia to debate more effectively on the few occasions when it met. Cleisthenes changed the organization of the boule, basing its membership on his new system of demes and tribes and so giving it the chance to become truly representative of the citizen body, but I do not believe that he changed the part played by the boule in the working of the state. The major break with the past was made by Ephialtes, who transferred various powers from the Areopagus to the boule, the ecclesia, and the δικαστήρια: the boule's gains included various powers over state officials, and on this foundation an impressive structure of executive and judicial powers was built, which in turn made the boule well informed and so well able to advise the assembly when fresh legislation was considered. The boule was a fair cross-section of the citizen body, and its membership changed every year: its interests were the people's interests, and so it could be trusted with great power by the people. In the second half of the fifth century and the first half of the fourth the boule was the instrument through which direct democracy—control by the people of all that concerned the people—was made to work. But with the rise of Eubulus to a dominant position in the field of finance we see the beginning of a change: in the interests of efficiency the people became more willing to trust an expert, and the influence of amateurs in the boule and ecclesia alike was weakened. Another change was set in motion by Philip and Alexander and continued by the dynasts who followed them: the day of the city state was over; the Greek πόλεις might be free and independent only by courtesy of a powerful ruler who hoped by a show of generosity to gain their support; and the affairs of individual cities were of correspondingly little account. In the uncertainty of the first two generations after Alexander's death the ecclesia remained active when activity was safe; but as Athens learned to live with her new status there was less need for ordinary citizens to take a keen interest in politics, and the boule ruled not by virtue of its constitutional position but because it was less troublesome if the boule did the work and the ecclesia accepted its recommendations. As a city of the Roman Empire Athens retained her traditional organs of government, including the boule, but there was no longer much government to occupy them.

[1] Cf. Ch. I, p. 32.

ADDITIONAL NOTES

A. *The Bouleutic Calendar*

Modern study of the bouleutic calendar began with Keil's discovery (published in two articles in *Hermes* xxix 1894) that for part of the fifth century the archontic and bouleutic years were not conterminous, and was given a new impetus by Professor Meritt's recognition (*The Athenian Calendar*) that the independent bouleutic year was a solar year. This led to a series of studies in which assumptions about the archontic calendar were allowed to dictate a good deal of irregularity in the bouleutic, a practice that was challenged in 1947 by Professors Pritchett and Neugebauer (*The Calendars of Athens*). Of more recent publications the most important (of which fuller details will be found in the Bibliography) are

W. K. PRITCHETT. 'Calendars of Athens again.' *BCH* lxxxi 1957.
B. D. MERITT. *The Athenian Year.* U. of California P., 1961.
W. K. PRITCHETT. *Ancient Athenian Calendars on Stone.* U. of California P., 1963.
W. K. PRITCHETT. 'Expenditure of Athena, 408–406 B.C., and the Helleno-tamiai.' *BCH* lxxxviii 1964.
B. D. MERITT. 'Athenian Calendar Problems.' *TAPA* xcv 1964.

In addition to the 'festival' or archontic calendar, in which the year, identified by its archon, was divided into twelve or thirteen lunar months, the Athenians found it convenient to use a 'civil' or bouleutic calendar, in which the year was divided into ten (or more) prytanies. For much of the fifth century the bouleutic year was wholly independent of the archontic calendar, being a solar year of 365 or 366 days (thus Meritt, *TAPA* 1964, 200; invariably 366 days, Pritchett and Neugebauer, 94–7, Pritchett, *BCH* 1957, 294): the bouleutic year 419/18 began on 16. i (Hec.) by the archontic calendar (Ant. VI. *Chor.* 44–5, with Meritt, *Athenian Calendar*, 121–2), and the bouleutic year 411/10 would have begun, but for the revolution, on 14. xii (Scir.) (*A.P.* 32. i). At some time in the last decade of the century it was decided that the boule's term of office should be the lunar, archontic year of *c.* 354 or *c.* 384 days (for the boule's serving an archontic year in the fourth century cf. schol. D. XXI. *Mid.* 114, in *BCH* i 1877, 16 = K. Latte and H. Erbse, *Lexica Graeca Minora*, 146). Meritt first used M&L 84 and Tod 92 to date the change between 410/09 and 407/6, in *CP* xxv 1930, and he now regards 407/6 as the first year under the new dispensation (*TAPA* 1964, 201, 211); Pritchett, who takes a different and to me less convincing view of Tod 92, regards the date of the change as uncertain (*BCH* 1964, 470–3). There has been much disagreement as to when the independent bouleutic year was instituted: Keil (*Hermes* xxix 1894, 74–5) and Meritt (*Ath. Cal.*, 71–2, 124–6) ascribed it to Cleisthenes;

Dinsmoor (*Archons of Athens*, 327 n. 1) and Giffler (*AJP* lx 1939) linked it with the adoption of Meton's calendar in 432; Kahrstedt (*U.M.A.*, 88) with the introduction of prytanies, which he attributed to Ephialtes. Meritt for a time thought that the independent bouleutic year might have been instituted about 450 (*Hesp.* v 1936, 374–8) but in *Ath. Yr.*, 203 n. 4, he accepted the demolition of the argument on which this was based (Pritchett and Neugebauer, 105–6) and reverted to his original opinion. Methods of dating employed in fifth-century documents (cf. below) make it very likely that the independent bouleutic year goes back at any rate to the middle of the century, and I would associate it with the division of the boule into prytanies, which I, like Kahrstedt, am inclined to ascribe to Ephialtes (cf. Ch. I, pp. 17–19): the prestige of the archons was under attack at the time, and this seems a suitable occasion for the creation of an alternative to the archontic year.

Neither kind of year is divisible into ten equal units, and the prytanies like the months must therefore have been unequal in length. For the fourth century we are told explicitly in *A.P.* 43. ii that the first four prytanies in the year were of 36 days each and the remaining six of 35. Pritchett and Meritt disagree strongly in their attitude to 'the rule of Aristotle'. Meritt now accepts that there were normally four prytanies of 36 and six of 35 days (though tampering with the calendar might sometimes lead to departures from this), but he regards the *Athenaion Politeia*'s placing of the long prytanies at the beginning of the year merely as one possibility, which was not followed every year (*Ath. Yr.*, *passim*, esp. ch. v, *TAPA* 1964, 200–12), while Pritchett insists that until positive disproof can be found this arrangement should be accepted as a binding rule (Pritchett and Neugebauer, 34 sqq., *Anc. Ath. Cals.*, 356, *BCH* 1964, 467–70), and even postulates a similar rule for the fifth century (e.g. Pritchett and Neugebauer, 94–7). We possess many documents giving 'calendar equations' between a date in the archontic calendar and a date in the bouleutic calendar: a few of these equations are intact or can be restored with certainty, but the great majority can be restored in more than one way according to the restorer's presuppositions concerning the calendar. So far Meritt and Pritchett have both been able to fit all the evidence to their own assumptions: there is no text which cannot be compatible with Pritchett's strict reliance on the *Athenaion Politeia*, and detailed and uncontroversial information for a number of years would be needed to throw serious doubt on Meritt's freer interpretation. Both scholars have found it necessary to postulate errors and irregularities in other calendar rules and in the inscription of calendar equations, and Pritchett by refusing to allow irregularities of this one kind has inevitably had to admit more and greater irregularities of other kinds (cf. D. M. Lewis, *JHS* lxxxiii 1963, 195, reviewing *Ath. Yr.*). Because his scheme is less neat than Meritt's it is not necessarily wrong, but I believe he is unwise to assume that the *Athenaion Politeia* is telling not merely the truth and nothing but the truth, but even the whole truth. The very text on whose completeness he relies makes no mention of 13-month years, in which there should normally have been four prytanies of 39 and six of 38 days (e.g. Meritt, *TAPA* 1964, 202), or of ordinary years with a total of other than 354 days (e.g. D. M. Lewis, *BSA* l 1955, 25); and there are various other matters of which the account given in that treatise cannot be accepted as the whole truth (see, for example, my Ch. IV, pp. 147 and 179–80, on *A.P.* 45. ii, and Ch. III, pp. 134–9, on *A.P.* 54. iii–v). Though the general structure of the calendars is clear, room has to be found within it for many irregularities, and it seems unwise to make one rule sacrosanct because it happens to be stated in the *Athenaion Politeia*.

The bouleutic calendar continued with modifications after the creation of new tribes. In 13-month years when there were thirteen tribes and in ordinary years when there were twelve there will have been as many months as prytanies, but it is agreed that months and prytanies were not made conterminous (*pace IG* ii² 663, 24–6, and Poll. viii. 115: Pritchett and Neugebauer, 78–9, Meritt, *Ath. Yr.*, 135–6 (misreported by E. J. Bickerman, *Chronology of the Ancient World*, 34), *TAPA* 1964, 202). Meritt believes that in 307/6 it was decided to add the intercalary month only when the year was in progress, and six prytanies of 30 days were therefore followed by six of 34 (*Ath. Yr.*, 176–8, *TAPA* 1964, 243); in 296/5 what was left of the year after the fall of Lachares' tyranny was shared among the twelve tribes (*Ath. Yr.*, 178–9, *TAPA* 1964, 244); and the bouleutic years 222/1 and 166/5 each ended a month early (*TAPA* 1964, 256–9, 242–7).

It was obviously convenient to use the bouleutic calendar rather than the archontic in connection with the proceedings of the boule and ecclesia. Our earliest public document from Athens, the decree of the late sixth century for Salamis, seems now to have borne no date (M&L 14: the 1938 fragment has made an archon-year in l. 12 unlikely), and the decrees of the Hecatompedon Inscription are dated to the archon-year 485/4 (*IG* i² 3, 16, 4, 26); but the series of decrees which begins probably in the 450s relies for dating on the bouleutic year, specifying the tribe in prytany and the secretary of that prytany (HMA 21 [*c.* 457?], M&L 40 [453/2], HMA 28 [451/0], 29 [*c.* 450], etc.; cf. Ch. I, p. 17 with n. 6), and shortly afterwards we perhaps find a previous year identified by the secretary of its first prytany (M&L 49, 15–16 [*c.* 445]: M&L doubt the restoration of πρό]το in l. 16. Other fifth-century decrees in which a year is identified by the first secretary are M&L 63, 5–6 [revised (?) 433/2]; 69, 56 [425/4]. See below for this form of dating in financial documents.) In the course of the next century more detail found its way into the prescripts of decrees, and there was an increasing tendency to give the date in both calendars, but it appears throughout that the bouleutic date was still felt to be the more important. Early in the fourth century the tribe in prytany was not only named but was given its ordinal number within the year (first found in heading, Tod 108 [394/3]; in prescript, Tod 126 [375/4]), and from the 360s a count of days within the prytany allowed greater precision (first found in prescript, Tod 136 [368/7]; in heading, *IG* ii² 109 [363/2]; in financial documents, on which see below, this manner of specifying a day is found as early as M&L 61 [433/2], but in decrees the day had previously been identified by the name of the epistates only). Mention of the archontic year became common from about 420. (On orthodox datings, there are a few earlier examples, e.g. M&L 37 [458/7?], but I do not believe they are numerous enough to lend much support to the restoration of an archon-date in M&L

40 = *ATL* D 10, 2. M&L share my doubts: they discuss the question on p. 93, but do not restore 40, 2. H. B. Mattingly by redating decrees would eliminate all archon-dates before 421/0 [*JHS* lxxxi 1961, 128 with n. 36, *Hist.* xii 1963, 272 n. 73, *Hist.* xiv 1965, 274–5 with n. 10].) The month and day are first found shortly before 350 (*IG* ii² 140 [353/2], 223 B, 6 [343/2], etc.).

A.P. 43. iii–vi reports provisions for four regular meetings of the ecclesia in each prytany, with definite items of business allocated to each; and annual matters such as nomothesia (D. XXIV. *Tim.* 20), ostracism (*A.P.* 43. v) and elections (*A.P.* 44. iv) were assigned to dates in the bouleutic year. It is uncercertain how old this practice is: elections certainly and ostracisms possibly took place before Athens had a boule divided into prytanies; but the designation of one ecclesia in each prytany as κυρία (*A.P.* 43. vi) suggests that there may have been a time when these ten were the only guaranteed meetings in the year (cf. G. T. Griffith, *Ancient Society and Institutions*, 124 with 136 n. 43). The indication ἐκκλησία or κυρία ἐκκλησία is not found in prescripts before 336/5 (*IG* ii² 330), so there is no help to be obtained from this source, but the Peloponnesian War and Cleon's courting of the people provide as likely an occasion as any for an increase in the number of regular assemblies. Many ancient commentators say that there were three regular assemblies a month, and that these were called κυρία (schol. Ar. *Ach.* 19, A. I. *Tim.* 60, III. *Ctes.* 24, D. XVIII. *Cor.* 73, XXIV. *Tim.* 20; Phot. κυρία ἐκκλησία): this yields nearly the same annual total as four assemblies a prytany, and after 307/6 there may have been three regular assemblies in each of the twelve prytanies (cf. Busolt and Swoboda, 987 n. 4), but as far as we know the term κυρία was always restricted to one meeting in each prytany. I do not think HMA 69, 8–10, need imply that there was more than one κυρία ἐκκλησία, or even more than one regular ecclesia, per prytany in the 430s; and *IG* i² 42 (*SEG* x 37), 22, is of no help in this connection.

We find both calendars used in other aspects of Athenian public life. The bouleutic year was in general the state's financial year (cf. schol. A. I. *Tim.* 104, s.v. πρυτανείας), with a general reckoning in the ninth prytany (cf. Ch. IV, pp. 148–51). The colacretae, important financial officers in the fifth century, held office for a term of one prytany (A. Wilhelm, *Sb. Wien* ccxvii. 5, 1939, 52–72), and the various boards in charge of public works in the fifth century seem to have regarded the bouleutic year as the more relevant to their activities:

PARTHENON ACCOUNTS: first ten years identified by ἀρχή (ordinal number, secretary) and boule (first secretary); remaining five by epistatae (i.e. ἀρχή) (secretary), boule (ordinal number, first secretary), and archon— *IG* i² 339–48; 349–53.

CHRYSELEPHANTINE ATHENA: by epistatae (secretary) and commonly boule (first secretary)—*IG* i² 354–62, cf. *SEG* x 257–63.

PROPYLAEA: first year by epistatae (secretary), archon, and boule (first secretary); next three years by ἀρχή (ordinal number, secretary) and boule (first secretary)—*IG* i² 363; 364–6.

It is normally accepted that the Hellenotamiae held office for a Panathenaic year (dependent on the archontic calendar): Pritchett has recently challenged this view (*AJP* lxxxv 1964, 44–6, *BCH* 1964, 455, 477–9) but Meritt upholds it

(*TAPA* 1964, 212). In the headings of most of the quota lists of the Delian League they date by years of their own ἀρχή alone, but in three late lists references are added to the archon and the first secretary of the boule (*ATL*, lists 33, 34, 39: the list published as 33 should in fact be 37—R. Meiggs, *CR²* ii 1952, 99, B. D. Meritt and M. F. McGregor, *Phoen.* xxi 1967). The inscription of the logistae, M&L 72, gives dates in the bouleutic calendar alone for sums which the state borrowed from the treasurers of Athena, and dates in both calendars for sums borrowed from the treasurers of the Other Gods (cf. J. A. Notopoulos, *AJP* lxvi 1945)—yet the beginning of the inscription defines some kind of accounting period with reference to the Panathenaea (cf. Additional Note D, p. 236). It is normally believed that the sacred treasurers held office for a Panathenaic year (e.g. Ferguson, *Treasurers of Athena*, 138–9 n. 1); Pritchett has recently suggested that the logistae's year of office was the Panathenaic year while the treasurers served for the bouleutic year (*Hesp.* xxxiv 1965, 145–7), but this can scarcely be reconciled with any interpretation of M&L 58 A, 24–9. However the interaction of calendars is to be explained, it seems clear that the sacred treasurers worked primarily on the bouleutic calendar (in addition to M&L 72, see M&L 61, HMA 79, M&L 77, 84, Tod 92; for the fourth century cf. *IG* ii² 1493); and the Hecatompedon Inscription's orders to the treasurers to check the contents of the Hecatompedon on three specified dates in each month provide one of my reasons for suspecting that in 485/4 the division of the boule into prytanies, and the bouleutic calendar based on it, had not yet come into existence (cf. Ch. I, pp. 17–19). The poletae worked under the close supervision of the boule (cf. Ch. III, pp. 96–8, 124), but their function of selling confiscated property brought them into contact with the courts, and in view of the archons' presidency we might expect the courts to work on the archontic calendar. Thus in *SEG* xii 100, a document of 307/6, confiscated property is sold on a date specified in the archontic calendar (1–39), and mines are hired out in certain prytanies (40 sqq.). The tenth of the stelae relating to the property of the Hermocopids has dates in both calendars (*SEG* xiii 21); a document of the 340s, again giving sales of confiscated property, uses the archontic calendar to date the relevant court orders (*Hesp.* v 10; cf. again *IG* ii² 1578, 1–2). In Tod 200 (325/4) we find the archontic calendar used for the sessions of a lawcourt (204–17) and to specify the day by which trierarchs must have their ships ready to sail (183–90; cf. D. LI. *Cor. Tri.* 4).

But though the Athenians were a good deal more successful than the French revolutionaries in their creation of a civil calendar, the archontic calendar remained the religious calendar, by which all festivals were fixed, and it also remained the 'natural' calendar, by which the ordinary citizen instinctively dated (cf. J. A. Notopoulos, *AJP* lxvi 1945, A. G. Woodhead, *The Study of Greek Inscriptions*, 115 with 132 n. 14). The reader of Demosthenes and Aeschines can give precise dates for many of the events of 347/6, but although these events were very much bound up with the proceedings of the boule and ecclesia our dates for them are all dates in the archontic calendar. Archontic dates occasionally appear in other places where a bouleutic date might be expected: the decree of Tisamenus *ap.* And. I. *Myst.* 83 provides a striking example of this;

and when in Tod 167 a certain item of business is reserved for debate [τῆι ὀγ]δόηι ἐπὶ δέκα (53–9), this must be 18. ix (Elaph.) 347/6 (cf. A. II. *F.L.* 61). The bouleutic calendar was well established for official purposes, but it never became more than an official calendar.

B. *M&L 69* (ATL *A 9*), *33–8*

(In this note I reproduce the Greek text of *ATL*, ii, printing in bold type those words or parts of words for which M&L adopt no restoration.)

On p. 20 I remark that the prytanes could be held responsible for ensuring that an item of business came before the boule and ecclesia. There is a clause containing such a requirement in the assessment-decree of 425/4, and the editors of *ATL* have claimed that the requirement was not carried out: that the decree ought to have been put to the ecclesia by a specified prytany but was in fact delayed until the beginning of the following prytany.

The decree was carried when a seven-letter tribe was in prytany:

ἔδοχσεν τê[ι βολêι καὶ τôι δέμοι· **Λεοντὶς**] ἐπρ[υτάνευε, κτλ.] (l. 3) (Λεοντὶς preferred to Αἰαντὶς, B. D. Meritt, *Hesp.* xiv 1945, 119.)

In the course of the decree, however, we come across a typical piece of Athenian carelessness: provisions for bringing the decree before the assembly which will have been entirely appropriate in a probouleuma but ought not to have survived in the text as ratified in the assembly (for this kind of oversight, cf. the retention of the rider in M&L 90). A certain prytany is threatened with heavy penalties if it fails to get the decree through the assembly before the end of its term of office, and there are only six letters for the name of the tribe:

ἐχ[σενε]γκέτο δὲ τ-
αῦτα ἐς [τὸν] δêμον [**he Οἰνε**]ὶς π[ρ]υτα[νεί]α ἐπάναγκες ἐπει[δὰν hέκει hε]
στρα[τιὰ] ἐς τρίτεν ἐ-
μέραν [πρôτ]ον μετ[ὰ τὰ hιε]ρά· ἐ[ὰν] δὲ [μὲ δ]ιαπ[ρ]αχθêι ἐν ταύ[τει χρεμα-
τί]ζεν πε[ρ]ὶ τούτο πρό[τ]-
ον τêι [hυσ]τεραία[ι χσυνε]χôς [hέ]ος [ἂν δ]ιαπ[ρ]αχθêι ἐπὶ τê[ς **εἰρεμένε**]ς πρυ-
τανείας· ἐὰν δ[ὲ μ]-
ὲ ἐχσε[νέγ]κοσι ἐς [τὸν δέμ]ον ἒ [μὲ] δι[απρά]χσ[ο]σι ἐπὶ σφôν α[ὐτôν εὐθυν]έσθο
μυρίασι δρ[αχμέ]-
σιν hέ[καστ]ος τôμ [πρυτάν]εον [φό]ρο[ν hος] διακολύον ἐπιδ[ôναι ἐς τὰ]ς
στρα[τι]άς.

(ll. 33–8)

If different tribes must be restored in l. 3 and l. 34, then despite the penalties with which it was threatened the prytany of l. 34 did not get Thudippus' decree through the assembly as it had been ordered.

The authors of *ATL* explain this as follows (Meritt and West, *Athenian Assessment*, 52–7, Wade-Gery and Meritt, *AJP* lvii 1936, cf. Meritt, *AJP*

lviii 1937, Wade-Gery, *AJP* lix 1938, 129–31). The expedition of l. 34 is that
with which Cleon has captured the Spartans on Sphacteria: on hearing the
news of this victory Thudippus put his decree to the boule and had it adopted
as a probouleuma, but he wanted Cleon to take part in the final debate in the
assembly, and believed that this would be possible before the end of the second
prytany of the year. Cleon had promised to bring back the Spartans alive
within 20 days (T. iv. 28. iv), and to Thucydides' surprise he kept his promise
(39. iii), but he need only have spent four days at Pylos (*AJP* 1937, 392) and
probably had ample time after his victory. Without breaking his promise he
arrived home later than expected, and it proved impossible for the prytanes
of Oeneis to discharge the duty laid on them by Thudippus: the decree was
therefore submitted to the assembly early in the third prytany, and whether
or not the threatened penalty was imposed no one saw fit to remove the clause
under discussion from the published text. Others have attempted the reverse
explanation, that by exemplary promptness the decree was carried at the end
of the prytany before that specified in l. 34 (G. De Sanctis, *RFIC* lxiii 1935,
M. F. McGregor, *TAPA* lxvi 1935): this encounters the additional difficulty
that until the very end of the prytany the tribe which was to hold the next
prytany should not have been known (cf. Ch. I, p. 19 with nn. 4–5).

The problem is now discussed by M&L (pp. 194–6), who find the survival
of this clause a serious objection to the *ATL* theory. I am not so much embar-
rassed by the clause: its survival in the decree of the demos is improper whatever the solution to our problem, and it seems to me entirely possible that if the
ATL reconstruction of the course of events is correct ll. 33–8 should have been
retained in the published text of the decree; a supplementary decree declaring
that as the delay was not their fault the prytanes concerned were after all to go
unpunished might well have been inserted, but its absence is not enough to
refute the theory. Nevertheless this is a great deal to build on a difference of one
letter between the tribe to be restored in l. 3 and that to be restored in l. 34.
Where he can be checked, the mason who cut this text was careful with his
aspirates and kept strictly to a στοιχηδόν pattern, but a glance at *The Athenian
Assessment*, Plate I, shows clearly how little of the text has survived. At another
point the editors have been able to save the στοιχηδόν pattern only by restoring
ℎοι δὲ [**νομο**]θέτα[ι δικαστέριον] νέον κα[θ]ιστάντον χ[ιλίος δικαστάς] (l. 16),
although nomothetae are not otherwise attested at this time and [θεσμο]-
θέτα[ι] though one letter longer yields a far more satisfactory sense (cf. Ch. III,
p. 90 n. 5). To postulate an epigraphic irregularity and restore the same tribe,
Leontis, in ll. 3 and 34 may strain credulity less than to insist on regular
aspirates or a regular στοιχηδόν pattern whatever the historical consequences
(cf. H. B. Mattingly, *Hist.* x 1961, 154–5). What the authors of *ATL* suggest
could have happened, but a far more secure text would be needed to demonstrate that it must have happened.

c. φυλακὴ τῆς χώρας and σωτηρία τῆς πόλεως

We possess four Athenian decrees which are said to have been enacted 'for the defence of the country':

IG ii² 435	after 336/5	(Prescript lost.) Honours for exiles from (somewhere). 13: [ταῦτα δὲ εἶναι] εἰς φυλακὴν τῆς χώ[ρας].
Tod 200	325/4	ψτδ. Colony to Adriatic. 270–1: ταῦτα δ᾿ εἶναι ἄπαντα εἰς φυλακὴν τῆς χώρας.
IG ii² 1631, 350 sqq.	324/3	ψτβ. Relaxing harsh treatment of naval debtor. 401–3: τὸ δὲ ψήφισμα τόδε ἅπαν εἶναι εἰς φυλακὴν τῆς χώρας, ἐπειδή ἐστιμ περὶ χρημάτων εἰσπράξεως.
Hesp. xi 56	247/6	E; ετδ. Appeal for contributions to stratiotic fund. 16–17: ἐπιδιδό[ναι εἰς τὴν σωτηρία]ν τῆς πόλεως καὶ τὴν φυλακὴν τῆς χώρας. 27–9: τὸ δὲ ψή[φισμα τόδε, ἐπειδὴ] περὶ πόρου χρημάτω[ν] ἐστὶν στρατιωτικῶ[ν, εἶναι ἄπαν εἰς φυ]λακὴν τῆς χώρας. Cf. also 30–2.

With these we may compare a decree of the Athenian cleruchs on Salamis, enacted in 116/15:

IG ii² 1228	15–18: τὸ δὲ ψήφισμα τόδε, [ἐ]πειδή ἐστιν περὶ ἱερῶν ἐπισκευῆς καὶ τῆς ἐπικοσμήσεως τῶν κοι[νῶν, ἐ]πειδὴ καὶ ὁ στρατηγὸς κα[ὶ οἱ ἐ]πιμεληταὶ συναποφ[αί]νονται, ἅπαν ἔ[στω] εἰς φυλακήν.

SIG³ displays similar formulae in third- and second-century decrees of Chios (SIG³ 402, 38), Erythrae (412, 13–14), and Magnesia (589, 67–8)—none of them concerned with defence.

The defence of the country is included in the *Athenaion Politeia*'s list of items which appeared on the agenda of a κυρία ἐκκλησία:

ἐν ᾗ δεῖ τὰς ἀρχὰς ἐπιχειροτονεῖν εἰ δοκοῦσι καλῶς ἄρχειν, καὶ περὶ σίτου καὶ περὶ φυλακῆς τῆς χώρας χρηματίζειν (*A.P.* 43. iv).

(Reusch, *De Diebus Contionum*, 72, noted that of the examples given above *Hesp.* xi 56 was enacted not at an ἐκκλησία κυρία but at one of the other ἐκκλησίαι.) Sandys in his commentary on the passage remarked that the defence of the country is one of the five major topics of deliberation named in Aristotle's *Rhetoric*:

ταῦτα δ' ἐστὶν περί τε πόρων, καὶ πολέμου καὶ εἰρήνης, ἔτι δὲ περὶ φυλακῆς τῆς χώρας, καὶ τῶν εἰσαγομένων καὶ ἐξαγομένων, καὶ νομοθεσίας (Arist. *Rhet.* i. 1359 B 21–3, cf. 1360 A 6–7).

It does not figure in Aristotle's expansion of τὸ βουλευόμενον περὶ τῶν κοινῶν in the *Politics*:

κύριον δ' ἐστὶ τὸ βουλευόμενον περὶ πολέμου καὶ εἰρήνης καὶ συμμαχίας καὶ διαλύσεως, καὶ περὶ νόμων, καὶ περὶ θανάτου καὶ φυγῆς καὶ δημεύσεως, καὶ περὶ ἀρχῶν αἱρέσεως καὶ τῶν εὐθυνῶν (Arist. *Pol.* iv. 1298 A 3–7, cf. 1299 A 1–2).

Defence does, however, appear in a list provided by Xenophon, when he makes Socrates, in order to curb Glaucon's desire to speak in the ecclesia, expose his complete ignorance of the city's revenue and expenditure, the strength of its own and of its enemies' forces, the φυλακὴ τῆς χώρας, the mines, and the corn supply (X. *M.* iii. vi. 1–13). But in none of these three lists do I think there is any conscious echoing of official decree-categories: the topics mentioned are matters with which any Greek city was bound to concern itself. When particular 'departments' were assigned to particular generals in the fourth century (but see Ch. III, p. 126 n. 2 for Professor Hammond's recent suggestion of an earlier division) one man was designated στρατηγὸς ἐπὶ τὴν χώραν (e.g. Phil. 328 F 155, referring to 350/49); the earliest reference to this general calls him τὸν στρατηγὸν ἐπὶ τὴν φυλακὴν τῆς χώρας κεχειροτονημένον (*IG* ii² 204, 19–20: 352/1). But the division of his duties in the first half of the third century between the στρατηγὸς ἐπ' Ἐλευσῖνα and the στρατηγὸς ἐπὶ τὴν παραλίαν shows that again φυλακὴ τῆς χώρας is to be interpreted literally. (See W. S. Ferguson, *Klio* ix 1909, 314–23.)

Since Boeckh studied the Athenian navy-lists it has been recognized that to place a decree in the category εἰς φυλακὴν τῆς χώρας ought to have given it some special importance, which would lend some point to the inclusion in this class of decrees which had little or nothing to do with the defence of the country (*Urk. Seewesens*, 467–8, commenting on Tod 200, 270–1; cf. *SIG*³ 305, note 17; 402, note 12; 589, note 23). Most recently Tod has written: 'By the final clause . . . the present decree is placed in the highest class of priority' (vol. ii, p. 288, commenting on no. 200). One clear result of a motion's being assigned to this class is that it could be discussed at a κυρία ἐκκλησία; but the classification must have meant more than this, for one of our examples is a decree of the boule, with which the ecclesia was not concerned. We should expect to find some kind of priority granted for the execution of the decree (so Boeckh, though neither he nor anyone else has been able to suggest what this could have involved): it *may* be significant that the three decrees of the ecclesia include two of the five post-403 decrees which authorize the boule to make supplementary enactments if necessary (*IG* ii² 435, Tod 200. See Ch. II, p. 82 and n. 3).

We have seen that contributions were requested in *Hesp.* xi 56 [εἰς τὴν σωτηρία]ν τῆς πόλεως καὶ τὴν φυλακὴν τῆς χώρας, and σωτηρία τῆς πόλεως is a phrase which we find elsewhere. Very close to *Hesp.* xi 56 is Isaeus, V. *Her. Dic.* 37:

εἰσφορῶν τοίνυν τοσούτων γεγενημένων πᾶσι τοῖς πολίταις εἰς τὸν πόλεμον καὶ τὴν σωτηρίαν τῆς πόλεως Δικαιογένης οὐκ ἔστιν ἥντινα εἰσενήνοχε.

(Other references to money given εἰς φυλακήν: *IG* ii² 283, 12–13; 768, 12; 798, 19–20; money given εἰς σωτηρίαν: *IG* ii² 479, 8–9.) Here the subject-matter is adequate to explain the choice of phrase, but in Isaeus and in three other passages Wilamowitz was inclined to regard σωτηρία τῆς πόλεως as a technical term (*Aristoteles und Athen*, i. 102 n. 7). In 411 the ten πρόβουλοι were joined by twenty colleagues, making a board of thirty οἵπινες . . . συγγράψουσι περὶ τῆς σωτηρίας (*A.P.* 29. ii); and Isocrates begins his *Areopagitic* with the words, πο λλοὺς ὑμῶν οἶμαι θαυμάζειν, ἥντινά ποτε γνώμην ἔχων περὶ σωτηρίας τὴν πρόσοδον ἐποιη σάμην (Is. VII. *Areop.* 1). Neither of these passages by itself compels us to accept Wilamowitz's view (though on *A.P.* 29 see below), but the principal text on which he relied was Aristophanes, *Ecclesiazusae*, 394–402:

> ΒΛ. ἀτὰρ τί τὸ πρᾶγμ' ἦν, ὅτι τοσοῦτον χρῆμ' ὄχλου
> οὕτως ἐν ὥρᾳ ξυνελέγη;
> ΧΡ.   τί δ' ἄλλο γ' ἢ
> ΕΔΟΞΕ ΤΟΙΣ ΠΡΥΤΑΝΕΣΙ ΠΕΡΙ ΣΩΤΗΡΙΑΣ
> ΓΝΩΜΑΣ ΚΑΘΕΙΝΑΙ ΤΗΣ ΠΟΛΕΩΣ; κᾆτ' εὐθέως
> πρῶτος Νεοκλείδης ὁ γλάμων παρείρπυσεν.
> κἄπειθ' ὁ δῆμος ἀναβοᾷ πόσον δοκεῖς,
> "οὐ δεινὰ τολμᾶν τουτονὶ δημηγορεῖν,
> καὶ ταῦτα περὶ σωτηρίας προκειμένου,
> ὃς αὐτὸς αὑτῷ βλεφαρίδ' οὐκ ἐσώσατο;"

This does make it seem likely that περὶ σωτηρίας was a recognized formula analogous to the Romans' *de re publica* (cf. Livy, XXII. 1. v, Varro *ap.* Gellius, XIV. vii. 9), which would permit any proposal for the general good of the state (cf. F. D. Smith, *Athenian Political Commissions*, 49: 'In such cases the Senate virtually abrogated its privilege of offering a probouleuma'). More pertinent, perhaps, than *A.P.* 29. ii is the recommendation finally produced by the thirty συγγραφεῖς, which Wilamowitz did not cite:

οἱ δ' αἱρεθέντες πρῶτον μὲν ἔγραψαν ἐπάναγκες εἶναι τοὺς πρυτάνεις ἅπαντα τὰ λεγόμενα περὶ τῆς σωτηρίας ἐπιψηφίζειν, ἔπειτα τὰς τῶν παρανόμων γραφὰς καὶ τὰς εἰσαγγελίας καὶ τὰς προκλήσεις ἀνεῖλον ὅπως ἂν οἱ ἐθέλοντες Ἀθηναίων συμβουλεύωσι περὶ τῶν προκειμένων (*A.P.* 29. iv).

Thucydides, as often, eschews technical language:

ἐσήνεγκαν οἱ ξυγγραφῆς ἄλλο μὲν οὐδέν, αὐτὸ δὲ τοῦτο, ἐξεῖναι μὲν Ἀθηναίων ἀνατεὶ εἰπεῖν γνώμην ἣν ἄν τις βούληται· ἢν δέ τις τὸν εἰπόντα ἢ γράψηται παρανόμων ἢ ἄλλῳ τῳ τρόπῳ βλάψῃ, μεγάλας ζημίας ἐπέθεσαν (Τ. VIII. 67. ii).

The appearance of περὶ τῆς σωτηρίας both in the commission of the συγγραφεῖς in *A.P.* 29. ii and in their quasi-probouleuma in § iv can hardly, I think, be accidental.

The phrase must at any rate originally have meant what it says, and have been employed in times of crisis. I should not like to guess when this form of completely open probouleuma was first used, but it appears from *A.P.* 29 and the *Ecclesiazusae* that the standard formula had come into use by the end of the fifth century. A very likely occasion for its use in the fourth century may be found in 339, when the news reached Athens that Philip had occupied Elatea (D. XVIII. *Cor.* 169–70; cf. Ch. II, pp. 54, 59); and Demosthenes himself uses the phrase περὶ σωτηρίας τῆς πόλεως in connection with the crisis brought upon Athens by the battle of Chaeronea:

μετὰ γὰρ τὴν μάχην εὐθὺς ὁ δῆμος . . . πρῶτον μὲν περὶ σωτηρίας τῆς πόλεως τὰς ἐμὰς γνώμας ἐχειροτόνει, καὶ πάνθ᾽ ὅσα τῆς φυλακῆς ἕνεκ᾽ ἐπράττετο . . . διὰ τῶν ἐμῶν ψηφισμάτων ἐγίγνετο (D. XVIII. *Cor.* 248).

Demosthenes' claim is denied by Aeschines (cf. Ch. II, p. 60 n. 1 above), but whether or not that is true it is possible that at this time the words περὶ τῆς σωτηρίας appeared in an open probouleuma, and that decrees were enacted εἰς φυλακὴν τῆς χώρας—though there can be nothing merely technical in the phrase, περὶ φυλακῆς τοῦ Πειραιέως, reported by Lycurgus from Hyperides' decree (Lyc. *Leocr.* 37). (For another Demosthenic use of the phrase, see D. V. *Pace*, 7.)

There is some temptation to link 'the safety of the city' with 'the defence of the country' (though so far as I know no one has tried to establish this link), but there are important differences to be noticed. περὶ τῆς σωτηρίας belongs to the deliberative stage, before a decree is enacted, while εἰς φυλακὴν τῆς χώρας is a classification applied to enacted decrees, as well as to a part of the agenda at a κυρία ἐκκλησία. Furthermore, περὶ τῆς σωτηρίας is an 'open' category (removal of the usual safeguards may, as Wilamowitz thought, regularly have accompanied a debate περὶ τῆς σωτηρίας, but the prytanes could only propose such a removal and ask the demos to clear the way for a free debate by ratifying it); but it appears that εἰς φυλακὴν τῆς χώρας was a 'closed' category, and there was some law specifying which decrees could be included in it: the Salaminian decree and two of the four Athenian decrees contain a clause explaining their qualification for the title (*IG* ii² 1228, 1631, *Hesp.* xi 56). Of these decrees, only *Hesp.* xi 56 (which in ll. 16–17 and 30–2 does couple σωτηρία with φυλακή) seems at all likely to have been proposed in a general debate περὶ σωτηρίας, yet here despite ἔδοξεν τῶι δήμωι we have the probouleumatic formula. The text of the decree is not complicated, and could have been produced in a hurry, but I feel that for clarity and straightforwardness it ranks well above the Athenian average. I am inclined to think that this is an ordinary probouleumatic decree (cf. Ch. II, pp. 77–8): conceivably the prytanes arranged a debate περὶ σωτηρίας in the boule, but the safety of the city is perfectly appropriate to its context, and need have no intended connection with the technical use of the phrase. There remains the possibility (which cannot be checked) that any decree which was enacted in a debate περὶ τῆς σωτηρίας would have been classified as εἰς φυλακὴν τῆς χώρας (it is not likely that the reverse was true).

We are no nearer, I fear, to discovering what was involved in this classification. The benefits must be applicable to independent decrees of the boule as well as to decrees of the ecclesia, and it is possible that the clauses authorizing the boule to stop gaps in decrees of the ecclesia are instances of a more general provision for the rapid execution of these decrees. Beyond this point we can only guess.

D. οἱ ἐπὶ τὸ θεωρικόν

In the 320s this office was certainly collegiate (in *A.P.* 43. i and 47. ii there are references to τοῦ ταμίου τῶν στρατιωτικῶν καὶ τῶν ἐπὶ τὸ θεωρικόν), and it is widely assumed that the theoric officials always formed a board (G. L.Cawkwell, *JHS* lxxxiii 1963, 47 with n. 4, G. E. M. de Ste Croix, *CR²* xiv 1964, 191; J. J. Buchanan, *Theorika*, 57–60, accepts this view without discussion). Outside the *Athenaion Politeia* there is very little evidence: A. III. *Ctes.* 24 is certainly not decisive for the existence of a single officer, but § 25 (quoted p. 106) need not be decisive for a board, if for some years the office was monopolized by Eubulus and his associates. A. II. *F.L.* 149 and D. XXIII. *Arist.* 209 likewise seem to prove little or nothing. There remains one text which does seem to me to point to the existence of a single official in the 340s, *IG* ii² 223 C, 5. This is a document relating to the boule, not to one tribal prytany, but among the officials named in the heading to the decree is Cephisophon, ἐπὶ τὸ θεωρικόν. Those who believe in a board suppose that this one member was particularly associated with the boule, but I think it may be an easier hypothesis that Cephisophon is named alone because he was the sole theoric official at that time. One of the ways in which Hegemon's law (A. III. *Ctes.* 25) weakened the position of the theoric officials will have been by substituting a college for the single officer.

The office was elective, in the time of the *Athenaion Politeia* (43. i, 47. ii) and *a fortiori* before the law of Hegemon; if *A.P.* 62. iii may be pressed re-election was forbidden during the 320s, but the scope of τὰς . . . κατὰ πόλεμον ἀρχάς was so nearly coextensive with τὰς χειροτονητὰς ἀρχάς that I would not wholly exclude the possibility that our author has formulated the ban on repetition incorrectly even for the 320s (on the claim that Lycurgus was unable to hold his office for more than one quadrennium, see Ch. III, p. 108 with n. 2), and I would certainly not rule out re-election before the law of Hegemon. Dr. D. M. Lewis has suggested that Hegemon enacted μὴ πλείω πέντε ἐτῶν διέπειν τὸν χειροτονηθέντα ἐπὶ τὰ δημόσια χρήματα ([Pl.] *X. Or.* 841 c), and that this measure, aimed at the theoric officials, was held to apply to Lycurgus (unpublished essay, cited by G. L. Cawkwell, *CQ²* xiii 1963, 135–6, *JHS* lxxxiii 1963, 55 n. 52, *CQ²* xix 1969, 169 n. 2)—but it is at any rate possible, and I should say very likely, that the law of Hegemon referred to in *IG* ii² 1628, 296–300, is a different law (*pace* Cawkwell, *CQ* 1969): I think it quite likely that this may have been among the effects intended, though I should prefer not to base any arguments on the words used to describe the officials.

The officials' term of office also has been disputed. In *A.P.* 43. i we read that all the elective financial officers, the treasurer of the stratiotic fund, the theoric board, and the epimeletes of the springs, ἄρχουσιν ἐκ Παναθηναίων εἰς Παναθήναια. This was at first interpreted as meaning the four-year period from one Great Panathenaea to the next; Ferguson (*Hellenistic Athens*, 474–5) argued that the purpose of the words was simply to define the year of office as the Panathenaic (beginning on 28. i [Hec.]) rather than the archontic or bouleutic, and most subsequent writers have ignored rather than actively disputed this; but the case for the original interpretation has been restated by F. W. Mitchel, *TAPA* xciii 1962, 220–1, cf. J. A. Davison, *JHS* lxxviii 1958, 23, 31–3. We must therefore examine the arguments.

In the fifth century the treasurers of Athena (*IG* i² 232 sqq.) and of the Other Gods (M&L 58 A, 24–7) were manifestly annual officials; when the board of the Other Gods was established this order was given:

καὶ ἐκ Παναθεναί-
ον ἐς Παναθέναια τὸλ λόγον διδόντον, καθάπερ hοι τὰ τῆς Ἀθεναίας τ-
[α]μιεύοντες.   (M&L 58 A, 27–9.)

This, coming immediately after a sentence making it clear that the office was annual, ought to be a definition of the year of office. The treasurers of Athena, though each board left its separate record, were for some purposes combined in groups of four, with the standard rubric, τάδε παρέδοσαν αἱ τέτταρες ἀρχαί, αἳ ἐδίδοσαν τὸν λόγον ἐκ Παναθεναίον ἐς Παναθέναια (*IG* i² 232 sqq., 256 sqq., 276 sqq.). A similar rubric introduces the record kept by the logistae of borrowings from the sacred treasuries during the Archidamian War: [τάδε ἐλογίσαν]το hοι λογιστα[ὶ ἐν τοῖς τέτ]ταρσιν ἔτεσιν ἐκ Παναθεναίον ἐς [Παναθέναια ὀφελόμενα] (M&L 72, 1–2). In each of these cases the four-year period is in fact a quadrennium from Great Panathenaea to Great Panathenaea, and I find it hard to resist the conclusion that this is what the rubrics mean. It must be admitted that in the inscription of the logistae the four years are preceded by seven (with no sign of subdivision), and that the fragments left by the treasurers of the Other Gods (*IG* i² 310) probably began in the non-Panathenaic year 429/8 (the only main rubric, dated to that year, heads one face); but this need not affect my argument that in the rubrics quoted ἐκ Παναθηναίων εἰς Παναθήναια refers to Panathenaic quadrennia. But Davison's view that Παναθήναια alone always refers to the major festival is difficult to maintain: M&L 58 A, 24–9 (part quoted above), and 77, 67, cannot easily be fitted to this interpretation. I am inclined to think that the phrase was left to take its meaning from its context, and that its use in fifth-century inscriptions does not therefore fix its meaning in *A.P.* 43. i.

When we turn to the actual offices whose term the *Athenaion Politeia* defines in these words, on the theoric officials themselves we have no evidence that can help us, but we are a little better informed on the other officials. The treasurer of the stratiotic fund in the last years of the century served for one year (at any rate, the office changed hands in a non-Panathenaic year), but his year was not bounded by the Panathenaea (Habron was treasurer in xii [Scir.] 306/5, Philippus on 14. i [Hec.] 305/4: *IG* ii² 1492, 118–24, 124–38), and if the date on which the office changed hands was altered the term of office may have been altered too. Callias is described as τοῦ ταμιεύσαντος στρατιωτικῶν ἐπὶ Χαιρώνδου ἄρχοντος (338/7: [Pl.] *X. Or.* 842 F) in a context where one would most naturally assume that he held office for a year only (but how would the Athenians have identified one in a series of quadrennial officers?). Demades was certainly treasurer in 334/3 (*IG* ii² 1493, restored by Mitchel after Wilamowitz: *SEG* xxi 552, xxii 133); and in an anecdote reported by Plutarch we are told that in 331 he τὰς προσόδους εἶχεν ὑφ' ἑαυτῷ τῆς πόλεως (Pl. *Praec. Ger. Reip.* 818 E; for the date cf. E. Badian, *Hermes* xcv 1967, 190–2). Mitchel combines these passages to argue that Demades was treasurer for the quadrennium 334–330 (*TAPA* xciii 1962, 219–25: he seems to bring forward the Great Panathenaea of 330 to 331). It is central to Plutarch's anecdote that Demades held a financial office which enabled him to provide money for the Choes, and the story should not be dismissed too lightly: if the office in question is the treasurership of the stratiotic fund we must therefore allow either the possibility of re-election (perhaps up to a maximum of four years' tenure— cf. p. 235 above) or a quadrennial office. On balance, however, what we know of the office makes annual appointment seem more likely than quadrennial. The same is true of the third office which ran ἐκ Παναθηναίων εἰς Παναθήναια, that of the epimeletes of the springs. The reference to Cephisodorus in *IG* ii² 215 is too generously restored for this text to carry much weight—

[Κηφισο]-
δώρο Καλλί[ο Ἀγνουσίου αἱρεθέ]-
ντος ἐπ[ὶ] Θε[μιστοκλέους ἄρχον]-
τος ἐπι[μελέσθαι τῶν κρηνῶν]

(ll. 9–12; the year in question is 347/6)—but a Panathenaic quadrennium seems unlikely in the case of Pytheas, αἱρεθεὶς ἐπὶ τὰς κρήνας, who on 9. ii (Metag.) 333/2, more than a year after the quadrennium 334–330 had begun, was honoured for what he had done in this capacity, subject to his passing his euthynae (*IG* ii² 338). Unlikely, but not impossible: once it is realized that at this time a man could be provisionally honoured, before he had presented his accounts on retirement from office (cf. Ch. I, pp. 15–16), there is no real reason why such provisional honours should not be decreed at any time; and although to us a three-year wait seems rather long the end of Pytheas' first year may have been considered a suitable occasion for such a decree. (It is even possible, I suppose, that a quadrennial officer would be required to pass his euthynae on each year separately.) Nevertheless an annual office again seems the likelier solution, and with annual appointment likely for the epimeletes of the springs and the treasurer of the stratiotic fund it is likely for the theoric officials too. But it is to be hoped that one day further evidence will allow us to decide the matter with certainty.

The most important text on the powers of the theoric officials is A. III. *Ctes.* 25, which I quote on p. 106. The sentence begins with a mention of ἀρχαί which the theoric officials ἦρχον before the law of Hegemon was passed, and ends with a list of other tasks which these officials performed. This second part need imply no interference with other offices of state: for the theoric officials to have built the σκευοθήκη and to have been ὁδοποιοί, it is enough for an orator that they should have provided the money, and perhaps have taken the initiative in having the work undertaken (though ὁδοποιός was the title of an Athenian office: *A.P.* 54. i). The first part of the sentence, however, should mean (if Aeschines is not very seriously exaggerating) that the theoric officials either replaced or at any rate became the acknowledged superiors of other officials—the antigrapheus, the apodectae, and probably the epimeletae of the dockyards (on the textual difficulty here see Ch. III, p. 106 n. 3: if Kaibel's text is adopted it can perhaps be argued that the clause concerning the dockyards belongs to the end of the sentence rather than the beginning).

We are certainly intended to think that the office of the ἀντιγραφεύς was abolished or drastically changed. Aeschines' previous sentence reads: πρότερον μὲν τοίνυν, ὦ ἄνδρες Ἀθηναῖοι, ἀντιγραφεὺς ἦν χειροτονητὸς τῇ πόλει, ὃς καθ' ἑκάστην πρυτανείαν ἀπελογίζετο τὰς προσόδους τῷ δήμῳ, and it ought to follow from *A.P.* 43. i that Aeschines' antigrapheus, if still in existence, was in the 320s no longer elected. Harpocration has the following entry (cf. Poll. viii. 98):

ΑΝΤΙΓΡΑΦΕΥΣ. ὁ καθιστάμενος ἐπὶ τῶν καταβαλλόντων τινὰ τῇ πόλει χρήματα, ὥστε ἀντιγράφεσθαι ταῦτα· Δημοσθένης ἐν τῷ κατ' Ἀνδροτίωνος (XXII. 38, 70) καὶ Αἰσχίνης ἐν τῷ κατὰ Κτησιφῶντος (III. 25—cf. above). διττοὶ δὲ ἦσαν ἀντιγραφεῖς, ὁ μὲν τῆς διοικήσεως, ὥς φησι Φιλόχορος (328 F 198—known only from this reference), ὁ δὲ τῆς βουλῆς, ὡς Ἀριστοτέλης ἐν Ἀθηναίων Πολιτείᾳ (some think this is an amalgamation of the secretaries in 54. iii–v, but I do not believe this official can be found in the *A.P.*).

I believe that the best interpretation of this passage is one rejected without much discussion by Brillant, *Les secrétaires athéniens*, app. i, that Harpocration's two ἀντιγραφεῖς did not exist simultaneously. Aeschines' antigrapheus can easily be identified with the official of that name in D. XXII. *Andr.* (355/4?— cf. Ch. I, p. 4 n. 7) and *IG* ii² 1740 (early C4?—he and the secretary are the only officials named), and this will be the man who could later be described as ἀντιγραφεὺς τῆς διοικήσεως. In the heyday of the theoric officials this office was abolished, and its responsibilities taken over by the theoric officials: thus there is no antigrapheus among the officials heading *IG* ii² 223 C (343/2), but the officials include Cephisophon, ἐπὶ τὸ θεωρικόν. (The antigrapheus of *IG* ii² 244, 23, is probably the older official, and this would strengthen Mr. G. L. Cawkwell's argument for dating the inscription earlier than 337/6: cf. Ch. III, p. 123 with n. 7). But at any rate by 335/4 the title existed again, for an antigrapheus ranks fifth among the eight officials listed in *IG* ii² 1700; he appears also in other lists of officials connected with the boule in the late fourth century, occasionally in the following three centuries, and regularly in the Christian era. This man I should like to identify with Harpocration's ἀντιγραφεὺς τῆς βουλῆς. His duties are uncertain: they may, but need not, have been financial (according to two lexica [*L.S.* 185. 16, Suid. γραμματεύς] which do not name their authority, he had secretarial duties in the boule; in the prescript of *IG* ii² 967 he is named after the eponymous secretary).

A change of this kind could mean that the title, 'antigrapheus' ceased for a few years to be used at all, and was brought back into use when a new office was created; but it could equally mean that in the one act of reorganization the title was transferred directly from one office to a totally different one. (From

321/0 to 319/18 and from 294/3 to 292/1 the title of ἀναγραφεύς, at other times used by one of the lower secretaries, was borne by the principal public secretary, who at other times was commonly called γραμματεὺς κατὰ πρυτανείαν— see Ch. III, p. 140). ἦρχον . . . τὴν τοῦ ἀντιγραφέως ἀρχήν will therefore mean that the old office of antigrapheus disappeared; but a part of his work may have been done by a similar official, now subordinated to ὁ ἐπὶ τὸ θεωρικόν, and his title will either immediately or after a few years' disuse have passed to another office.

What Aeschines says of the antigrapheus he seems also to be saying of the apodectae. In 347/6 the apodectae were ordered to advance ἐκ τῶν στρατιωτικῶν χρημάτων (which I take to mean, from the sum which they would normally have allocated to the stratiotic fund) money which was thereafter to be paid from the ecclesia's expense-account (Tod 167, 39–44), about 343 the apodectae were mentioned in connection with an adjustment to the μερισμός (IG ii² 222, 41–6; but A. C. Johnson, CP ix 1914, 424, dated the decree in or after 331), and another reference to the μερισμός performed by the apodectae occurs c. 336–4 (SEG xviii 13, 19–21); the navy-lists attest various payments to the apodectae in the 320s (IG ii² 1627, 227–9; 1628, 424–7, 628–30). If the apodectae did disappear, they did not do so for long, and there is no evidence that their powers after about 335 were less than their powers before 350. But I have suggested above that responsibility, duties, and title may be three different things; and I would suggest that in this case ὁ ἐπὶ τὸ θεωρικόν was deemed to have ultimate responsibility for revenue, while men very like the apodectae continued to do much of the routine work, and these may or may not have retained the title, 'apodectae'. It seems from the passages quoted on p. 238 above, that the ἀντιγραφεὺς τῆς διοικήσεως was concerned with revenue, and may have acted as an expert adviser to and spokesman for the apodectae: and though some work may have been left to a lower official it is likely that the more public and distinctive part of his duties passed to ὁ ἐπὶ τὸ θεωρικόν. Supersession of the apodectae, however, may have been more formal than real, and if ὁ ἐπὶ τὸ θεωρικόν had to some extent supplanted the antigrapheus, and had also (as I suggest in Ch. III, pp. 106–7) been allowed to co-operate with the financial boards in bringing business to the boule, that might have been enough to justify the claim that he ἦρχεν τὴν τῶν ἀποδεκτῶν ἀρχήν.

It is not certain that Aeschines' mention of the dockyards is parallel to his mention of the purely financial offices. But if what he says is to be understood in this way, what I have said of the apodectae must be said even more forcibly of the epimeletae of the dockyards: though responsibility may have passed to the theoric officials, much of the work must have been done by successors to the old epimeletae, and these successors may or may not themselves have been called epimeletae. Dr. Lewis has noted that the epimeletae are not directly attested between 348/7 (IG ii² 1622, 549–52) and 334/3 or later (IG ii² 1623, 1–3 [title restored, but not unreasonably]; date, l. 285), and that IG ii² 1622 is a very different document from the other navy-lists: among other things, the officials responsible, in or after 342/1 (379–85), refer to a ταμίας ἐς τὰ νεώρια who in 347/6 performed duties which would normally have fallen to the epimeletae (444 sqq.). He argues from this document (unpublished essay, cited by G. L. Cawkwell, *JHS* lxxxiii 1963, 57 n. 62) that for a time the epimeletae ceased to exist, and I would accept that the epimeletae as known at other times may have ceased to exist, though the work still had to be done and the title may have survived with the work. The transfer of their ἀρχή to ὁ ἐπὶ τὸ θεωρικόν may have had the same implications as I have suggested in the case of the apodectae, but the epigraphic evidence does seem this time to point to a more drastic change. (The reappearance of the epimeletae in *IG* ii² 1623 is in fact the last occasion on which they are named in an inscription, and they are not mentioned in the *A.P.* Dr. J. K. Davies wonders if there was a further reorganization in the 320s [cf. his note in *Hist.* xviii 1969, 316 n. 35]; but of course there must still, in the 320s as earlier, have been dockyard officials of some kind, doing substantially the same work. Davies suggests to me that other dockyard officials, who continue to be attested, such as the various ταμίαι, may have been made directly responsible to the boule and the major financial officers; but it may yet be wholly accidental that the title of the epimeletae does not appear in the texts which survive from the 320s.)

The law of Hegemon established a board, if the theoric office had previously been exercised by a single man, and it may also have set limits to any one man's tenure of a financial office. The old antigrapheus seems to have disappeared for ever, though the title survived or was revived for another office, but any major change affecting the apodectae or the epimeletae of the dockyards seems to have been reversed. The only trace in the *Athenaion Politeia* of what must have been a serious upheaval is the passage on which I have tried to base an account of how the theoric officials became so powerful, which reveals that in the 320s the theoric board and the treasurer of the stratiotic fund joined with the poletae in presenting leases and tax contracts to the boule (*A.P.* 47. ii). I have suggested that before the law of Hegemon ὁ ἐπὶ τὸ θεωρικόν by sharing in the work of the different boards was able to acquire that general knowledge of the state's finances which had previously been the monopoly of the boule, and I imagine that power which had seemed dangerous in the hands of one man was innocuous enough when divided among a board of limited tenure. At some time the treasurer of the stratiotic fund was admitted to these privileges, and in some way Lycurgus acquired great financial powers ἐπὶ τρεῖς πενταετηρίδας, but neither of these innovations need have been made by Hegemon.

TABLE A

The Size of Post-Hadrianic Lists of Prytanes

The following lists of prytanes of the period following Hadrian's tribal reform have survived complete or virtually complete. (See p. 1 with n. 5, and A. E. Raubitschek, *Γέρας Ἀντωνίου Κεραμοπούλλου*, 242–55.) All dates are A.D.

AEGEIS	*IG* ii² 1765	138/9	40 members
	SEG xiv 92	182/3	37+4 *rasurae*+πρ. βουλ.
PANDIONIS	*IG* ii² 1773	166/7	40 including γρ.
	1776	169/70	40 including γρ.
	1077	209/10	? 41 including γρ.
ACAMANTIS	1774	167/8	39+γρ.+ἐπων.+ἀείσιτοι
	1775	168/9	40
CECROPIS	1782	177/8	? 40 including γρ. but not ἐπων.
[AIANTIS	*P* 121	?	Traces of 39 names, but probably part of a list of 50, *c*. A.D. 120. Not discussed by Raubitschek.]
ANTIOCHIS	*IG* ii² 1817	*c*. 220	(no demotics) 40 including γρ.
	1783	221/2	40 including γρ.
ATTALIS	1794	180/1	40 including γρ.
	1824	221/2	(no demotics) 40?+

Notes

IG ii² 1077   'Number seems to have been 40'—Raubitschek, 252 n. 4.

1774   The list is followed immediately by the γραμματεύς, the ἐπώνυμος, and then the ἀείσιτοι. It is thus not clear that Raubitschek is right to describe the placing of the ἐπώνυμος as 'apart from panel' (248).

1782   Raubitschek describes the placing of the ἐπώνυμος as 'above panel' 251), but perhaps he should be regarded as heading the panel, to make a total of ?41.

1824   Raubitschek reports the total as 'probably only 40' (255 n. 1), but I do not think the possibility of one or two more can be excluded.

TABLE B

Men serving twice in the Fourth-Century Boule

In assembling this information for the period of the ten tribes I have compared notes with Dr. J. K. Davies, and am very grateful for his co-operation. Not all the identifications are certain.

AEGEIS

Γαργήττιοι	Androtion	*IG* ii² 61, D. XXII. *Andr.* 38 (on the dates, see p. 4 n. 7).
Ἑστιαιεῖς	Posidippus	*IG* ii² 1749 (341/0), 1700 (335/4).
Φηγαιεῖς	Polycrates	*IG* ii² 1747 (*c.* 350), *SEG* xix 149 (336/5?).
Φιλαΐδαι	Dionysius	*IG* ii² 1747 (*c.* 350), 1749 (341/0).

PANDIONIS

Μυρρινούσιοι	Aeschylides	*IG* ii² 1751 (after mid C4), *SEG* xix 149 (336/5?).
Πρασιεῖς	Timandrus	*SEG* xxiii 87 (first qr. C4), *SEG* xix 149 (336/5?).
Ὦαθεν	Eupolemus	*SEG* xxiii 87 (first qr. C4), *IG* ii² 1751 (after mid C4).

ACAMANTIS

Σφήττιοι	Timarchus	A. I. *Tim.* 109 (361/0), ibid. 80 (347/6).

OENEIS

Θριάσιοι	Cleopompus	*IG* ii² 1745 (360/59), 1698 (before mid C4).
Περιθοΐδαι	Callicrates	*IG* ii² 1745 (360/59), 1746 (*c.* 350).

CECROPIS

Συπαλήττιοι	Antidotus	*IG* ii² 337 (333/2), Ἀρχ. Ἐφ. 1917, 40–8, 92 (328/7).
	Autobulus	*IG* ii² 2384 (360–50), 1700 (335/4); see also p. 3 n. 4.

Aiantis

Ἀφιδναῖοι	Demetrius	*SIG*[3] 287 (332/1), Ἀρχ. Ἐφ. 1917, 40–8, 92 (328/7).
	Euthycrates	*IG* ii² 242/3 (337/6), Ἀρχ. Ἐφ. 1917, 40–8, 92 (328/7).
Οἰναῖοι	Phyleus	*IG* ii² 330 (336/5), 360 (325/4).

Antiochis

Παλληνεῖς	Philostratus	*IG* ii² 1700 (335/4), 410 (*c.* 330).
	Theodorus	*IG* ii² 1700 (335/4), Ἀρχ. Ἐφ. 1917, 40–8 (328/7).

TABLES C–L, *illustrating Chapter II*

In compiling Tables C–K I have examined every Athenian decree published in *IG* i² and ii², in *SEG* x–xxi, and in *Hesperia* (regular issues and supplements to the end of 1965), together with others known to me for any reason; Table L is limited to decrees published in *IG* i² and ii². Hellenistic dates have been taken over uncritically from Pritchett and Meritt, *The Chronology of Hellenistic Athens*, and Meritt, *The Athenian Year*, and within each table or category decrees are arranged as far as possible in chronological order.

In listing formulae I use square brackets to give some idea of how much has to be restored: many of the restorations are certain, and I draw attention to all serious doubts; restorations which I reject are [[enclosed in double square brackets]], and decrees for which the whole entry is so treated are not included in my statistics. Since I am inclined to place more faith in the motion- than in the enactment-formulae I stress with an ONLY in Tables C and D those decrees where only the enactment-formula is available. Where there is no entry in the Contents column of Tables C and D the decree is honorific, of a familiar type.

Abbreviations for formulae (cf. pp. 64–5):

1. Minute-headings:

βουλῆς ψηφισμα(τα)	**ΒΨ**
δήμου ψηφισμα(τα)	**ΔΨ**

2. Records of meeting:

βουλή	**Β**
ἐκκλησία *or* ἐκκλησία κυρία	**Ε**
(unusual records of meeting-place are transcribed in full)	

3. Enactment-formulae:

ἔδοξεν τῶι δήμωι	ετδ
ἔδοξεν τῆι βουλῆι καὶ τῶι δήμωι	ετβκτδ
ἔδοξεν τῆι βουλῆι	ετβ

4. Motion-formulae:

δεδόχθαι/ἐψηφίσθαι τῶι δήμωι	δ/ψτδ
δεδόχθαι/ἐψηφίσθαι τῆι βουλῆι	δ/ψτβ
probouleumatic formula	**PF**
probouleumatic formula revealing that the demos has commissioned a probouleuma	**CPF**
δεδόχθαι/ἐψηφίσθαι τῆι βουλῆι καὶ τῶι δήμωι	δ/ψτβκτδ

5. Commissioning of probouleuma   **CP**

6. Mention of probouleuma   **MP**

7. Rider-formulae:

  τὰ μὲν ἄλλα καθάπερ τῆι βουλῆι   **RP**
  τὰ μὲν ἄλλα καθάπερ ὁ δεῖνα   **RI**

An asterisk in the Contents column denotes a decree which I regard as substantial for the purposes of the discussion in Ch. II, pp. 78–81 (cf. especially p. 78 n. 3).

TABLE C

Probouleumatic Decrees

Reference	Date	Formulae	Contents
M&L 37	458/7?	RP	*Alliance with Egesta
⟦SEG x 20	c. 450/49	[RP] restored	Judicial benefits for men⟧ of Parium
M&L 44	c. 449	? [χρηματίσαι-formula]; 2 riders? (both simply ὁ δεῖνα εἶπε). (See p. 71 n. 2)	*Priestess and temple of Athena Νίκη
HMA 41	aft. 450	RP; second rider καθά-[περ Θεσπιεύς]	*Eleusinian epistatae
{HMA 69 ATL D 19}	bef. 431	R[P] both texts; second rider RI	Work on water supply
SEG x 60	c. 430	RP	*Eleusinian law
M&L 65. ii	426/5	χρηματίσαι-formula 51–6	*Second Methone decree
69	426/5	χρηματίσαι-formula 27 sqq.; RP	*Thudippus' assessment-decree
SEG x 84. i	?	RP	
ii	424/3	30–40 seem to incor-porate rider added in boule (Meritt, *Hesp.* x 1941, 320–6); RP	
M&L 70	424/3 *or* c. 386	RP	(date uncertain: see M&L and J. Pečírka, *The Grant of Enktesis*, 22–5)
SEG x 91	421/0	R[P]	
IG i² 84	421/0	RP	*Regulations for the Hephaestia
94	418/17	RP	Work on sanctuaries
IG ii² 174	c. 412	[RP]	(date, Weston, *AJP* lxi 1940, 353–4)
⟦IG i² 113+ SEG x 127	410/09	[RP] restored	Citizenship grant⟧
M&L 85	410/09	[RP]; second rider [RI]	Honours for Phrynichus' assassins
90	408/7	RP	
SEG x 136	407/6	bouleutic formula 3–6; ⟦RP wholly and wildly restored⟧ (complete text re-peated *Svt* 208 but labelled *weithin hypo-thetisch*)	*Alliance with Carthage
M&L 89. ii	407/6	bouleutic formula 56? (I would read [hὸ δέονται]: see p. 82 n. 2); RP	Second, honorific Nea-politan decree
M&L 94	405/4	δτβκτδ; RP (γνώμη and rider by prytanes; cf. Table E)	*First Samian decree

Reference	Date	Formulae	Contents
Hesp. xxi 3	end C5	RP	

Reference	Date	Formulae	Contents
Tod 97. i	403/2	[ετβκτδ]; RP (ψτδ)	Second Samian decree
ii	403/2	[ετβ]κτδ; RP	Third Samian decree
IG ii² 2	403/2	[ετ]βκτ[δ] ONLY	
7	soon aft. 403/2	[ετβκτδ]; ἐψηφίσ[θαι δὲ – 6 –] βολήν 8–9	
Hesp. xxvi 53	beg. C4	ετβ[κτδ] ONLY	?
Hesp. x 1941, 336–7	first qr. C4	RP	
Tod 103	394/3	ετβ but assembly should ratify (cf. p. 84)	*Alliance with Eretria
108	394/3	ετβ but assembly should ratify (cf. p. 84)	(Honours for Dionysius I)
IG ii² 19	394/3	[ετβκτδ]; ἐψηφίσθαι[—] *a* 6; rider κ[αθάπερ —] *b* 4; ἐψηφίσθαι δ[ὲ τῶι δήμωι] *b* 5	
Tod 110. i	aft. 394/3	[ετ]βκτδ ONLY	*Honours and privileges for Carpathus
Hesp. x 66	aft. 389	[ετ]βκ[τδ] ONLY	
IG ii² 23	388/7	ετβ[κτδ]; ἐπαινέσαι μ[έν —] 6; [ἐψ]ηφί-[σθαι δέ —] 9–10	
Tod 116	387/6	ἐὰν κα[ὶ τῶ]ι δήμ[ωι] δοκ[ῆι]; RP	(386/5, Dinsmoor, *AJA.* xxxvi 1932, 158 with n. 4: see pp. 100–1 and p. 103 n. 7)
117	386/5	[ε]τβκτδ ONLY	
IG ii² 32	385/4	ετ[β] but assembly's ratification proved by RP	
59	bef. 378/7	ετβ[κτδ] ONLY	?
60	bef. 378/7	[ε]τβ[κτ]δ ONLY	
61	bef. 378/7	[ετ]βκτ[δ] ONLY	
77. ii	bef. 378/7	ετβ κατὰ τὸ τ[οῦ δήμου ψήφισ]μα. Formula perhaps wrongly re-peated from decree i (TABLE G): See pp. 83–4 with p. 83 n. 6	(Proxeny)
80	bef. 378/7	RP	
85	bef. 378/7	[ετβκτ]δ ONLY	?
86	bef. 378/7	[ετβ]κτδ ONLY	
SEG xvii 16	C4	ετβ[κτδ] ONLY	?
Svt 255 (*IG* ii² 40)	378/7	RP (CP)	*Treaty with Thebes and Mytilene?
Tod 122	378/7	[ετβκτδ] ONLY	*Alliance with Methymna
{ Tod 124 *IG* ii² 155	378/7	ετβκτδ; PF [ετβκ]τδ; (stone ends) } (two copies)	*Alliance with Chalcis
[[*IG* ii² 95	377/6	SEE TABLE G]]	

Reference	Date	Formulae	Contents
IG ii² 76	385–376?	ετ[βκτδ] ONLY	(date, Dinsmoor, *AJA* 1932, 158 with nn. 5–6)
22	378–376?	[RP] far from certain	(date, Dinsmoor, *AJA* 1932, 158 with nn. 5–6, but *Svt* 238 still dates 390/89)
84	378–376?	RP	(date, Dinsmoor, *AJA* 1932, 158 with nn. 5–6)
79	aft. 378/7	PF (no dated example before 378/7)	
82	aft. 376	PF	(date, Dinsmoor, *AJA* 1932, 159 with n. 6)
Tod 126	375/4	ε[τβκτδ]; περὶ ὧν λέγ[ουσιν ἐν τῆι βουλῆ]ι οἱ πρεσβês]; PF	*Alliance with Corcyra and others.
[[*IG* ii² 98+*Hesp.* ix 33 =*Svt* 267	373/2	[RP] restored: no speaker	Treaty with Cephallenia]]
Tod 131. ii	369/8	ετ[β]κτδ ONLY	Praise and apologies for Mytilene
133	369/8	δ[τ]β ordering allies to submit δόγμα to ecclesia; then PF to confer honours immediately	*Relations with Dionysius I
*SIG*³ 158. i	369/8	PF; RP	
[[ii	363/2	unsatisfactory restoration includes [δεδόχθαι] *tout court*]]	
Tod 135	368/7	ετβκτ[δ]; PF	
131. i	368/7	ετβκτδ; PF; RP	Praise for Mytilene
137	367/6	[ετ]βκτδ ONLY	Concerning the Aetolian League
IG ii² 108	366/5	ε[τ]β[κτδ]; [PF]	?
109	363/2	PF (δτδ); RP	
SEG xxi 241	363/2	ετβκτδ ONLY	Ordering register of gifts to Ammon
Tod 143	363/2	ετβκτδ; PF; RP	
IG ii² 115	362/1	ετβκ[τ]δ ONLY	
SEG xvii 19	*c.* 362–355	ε[τβκ]τδ ONLY	*Judicial relations with Siphnos
IG ii² 117	361/0	[ετβκτδ]; PF	
145. ii	368–358	[ετβκ]τδ; PF (for decree i SEE TABLE D)	Giving son father's heraldship
121	357/6	[ετβ]κτδ ONLY	
Hesp. viii 4	357/6	[ετ]βκτδ; PF	Concerning Elaeus
Hesp. xiii 3	357/6	[ετβκτ]δ; proclamation ὅταν τῶι δή[μωι δοκῆι], 10–11, *not* decisive; R[P] ([δτδ])	Citizenship grant
Tod 156	357/6	ετβκτδ ONLY	Appointment of general for Andros
157	356/5	[ετ]βκτδ; PF	*Alliance with Thracian and other kings

Reference	Date	Formulae	Contents
Tod 159	356/5	$\epsilon[\tau]\beta\kappa\tau\delta$; PF	*Alliance (?) with Neapolis
IG ii² 130	355/4	$\epsilon\tau\beta\kappa[\tau\delta]$ ONLY	
248	bef. 354	$[\epsilon\tau\beta]\kappa[\tau\delta]$; CPF	(date, Johnson, CP ix 1914, 424)
136	354/3	$\epsilon\tau\beta[\kappa\tau\delta]$; PF	
137	354/3	$[\epsilon\tau\beta]\kappa\tau\delta$ ONLY	
152	bef. 353/2	$\epsilon\tau\beta\kappa\tau\delta$; CPF	
153	bef. 353/2	$[\epsilon\tau\beta\kappa\tau]\delta$ ONLY	?
155	bef. 353/2	$[\epsilon\tau\beta\kappa\tau]\delta$ ONLY	?
172	bef. 353/2	PF	On occasion of proxeny renewal, to replace lost stele
176	bef. 353/2	[PF]; R[P] ($\psi[\tau\delta]$) (reading [$\tau\hat{\omega}\iota$ $\delta\acute{\eta}\mu\omega$]$\iota$ for IG's [$\tau\hat{\eta}\iota$ $\beta o\lambda\hat{\eta}$]ι)	
180	bef. 353/2	PF	Extending proxeny to descendants
181	bef. 353/2	PF	
182	bef. 353/2	RP	
188	bef. 353/2	PF; RP	
191	bef. 353/2	PF	
192	bef. 353/2	$[\pi]\epsilon\rho\grave{\iota}$ $\hat{\omega}[\nu$ $\check{\epsilon}\delta o\xi\epsilon\nu - 18 -]s$ $\grave{\epsilon}\nu$ $\tau\hat{\omega}[\iota]$ $\delta[\acute{\eta}]\mu[\omega\iota$ $\check{\epsilon}\nu\nu o\mu a$ $\iota\kappa\epsilon\tau\epsilon\acute{\upsilon}\epsilon\iota\nu]$; PF	
199	bef. 353/2	PF	?
205	351/0	$[\epsilon]\tau\beta\kappa\tau[\delta]$ ONLY	
246	c. 350	PF	?
206	349/8	$\epsilon\tau\beta\kappa\tau\delta$; PF; RP	
208	349/8	$\epsilon\tau\beta\kappa\tau\delta$; PF	Echina; refers to $\sigma\acute{\upsilon}\mu\beta o\lambda a$
215	346/5	$\epsilon\tau\beta\kappa\tau\delta$; CPF	Honours for epimeletes of springs
218	346/5	$\pi\epsilon\rho\grave{\iota}$ $\hat{\omega}\nu$ . . . $\check{\epsilon}\delta o\xi\epsilon\nu$ $\check{\epsilon}\nu\nu o\mu a$ $\iota\kappa\epsilon\tau\epsilon\acute{\upsilon}\epsilon\iota\nu$ $\grave{\epsilon}\nu$ $\tau\hat{\eta}\iota$ $\beta o\upsilon\lambda\hat{\eta}\iota$, PF; 22 sqq. new speaker; $\pi\epsilon\rho\grave{\iota}$ $\hat{\omega}\nu$ $\check{\epsilon}\delta o\xi\epsilon\nu$ $\grave{\epsilon}\nu$ $\tau\hat{\omega}\iota$ $\delta\acute{\eta}\mu\omega\iota$ . . . $\check{\epsilon}\nu\nu o\mu a$ $\iota\kappa\epsilon\tau\epsilon\acute{\upsilon}\epsilon\iota\nu$, . . . $\psi\tau\delta$ RP	
Tod 170	c. 345	PF	
Hesp. viii (EP. NOTES) 3	345/4	$[\epsilon\tau]\beta[\kappa\tau\delta]$ ONLY	?
IG ii² 223 A	343/2	$\delta\tau\beta$ on boule's prize for best speaker, turning into PF at 8 sqq.	
Tod 173	c. 342	$\chi\rho\eta\mu a\tau\acute{\iota}\sigma a\iota$-formula 33–5; RP	
IG ii² 227	342/1	$\epsilon\tau\beta[\kappa\tau]\delta$ ONLY	?
229	341/c	$\epsilon\tau\beta\kappa[\tau\delta]$; PF	
232	340/39	PF; RP	
235	340/39	bouleutic formula 0–3; $\epsilon\tau[\delta]$, new speaker, RP ($[\psi\tau]\delta$) 4 sqq.	
SEG xvi 52	339/8	$\epsilon[\tau\delta]$; PF	?
IG ii² 243	337/6	$[\epsilon\tau]\delta\kappa\tau\beta$ (sic); CPF	

Reference	Date	Formulae	Contents
SEG xxi 340	aft. mid C4	PF	
IG ii² 255	bef. 336/5	PF	?
265	bef. 336/5	RP	?
273	bef. 336/5	PF	Praise for Byzantium
〚276	bef. 336/5	SEE TABLE D〛	
277	bef. 336/5	PF	
284	bef. 336/5	PF	
289	bef. 336/5	RP (Schweigert, *Hesp.* viii 1939, 173–5, links with *IG* ii² 372, which I place in TABLE D. See p. 72 n. 2)	
328	336/5	ετ[βκτδ]; PF	
330. iii	336/5	*E*; ετβκτδ; PF	Honours for a hieropoeus
423	aft. 336/5	PF	
428	aft. 336/5	PF	
442	aft. 336/5	PF	?
334	*c.* 335/4	(ψτδ) RP	*Regulations for Panathenaea
538	334–331	PF	Citizenship grant (date, Johnson, *CP* ix 1914, 428)
340	333/2	[*E*]; [ετβ]κ[τδ] ONLY	
*SIG*³ 287	332/1	*E*; ετδ; PF	
Tod 193	331/0	ε[τ]βκτδ; and an unlikely formula, discussed on p. 69 n. 2	
IG ii² 410	*c.* 330	PF	Honours for priests and hieropoei
415	*c.* 330	ετβκτδ; PF	Honours for ἀναγραφεύς
416	*c.* 330	PF	
Hesp. ix 41	*c.* 325	PF	?
IG ii² 373	322/1	PF. 16 sqq. complete new prescript: *E*; δτδ; speaker; RP (ψτδ)	
403	350–320	PF	Repairs to statue of Athena Νίκη

IG ii² 394	321/0–319/18	PF	Citizenship grant
SEG xxi 305	320/19	*E*; ετβ[κτδ] ONLY	?
⌈ 306	320/19	*E*; [ετβκτδ] ONLY, Dow, *HSCP* lxvii 1963, 67–75, and Meritt, *Hesp.* xxxii 1963, 431–2. But Meritt formerly restored [ετδ], and the text is far from settled, so I exclude this from my statistics	
⌊ 312	319/18	ἐ[κκ]λ[η]σία κατὰ ψ[ήφ]ισμα βουλῆς; ετβκτδ ONLY	
310	319/18	*E*; ετβ[κτ]δ; PF	Citizenship grant
IG ii² 548	318/17–308/7	ε[τβκτ]δ ONLY	

Reference	Date	Formulae	Contents
SEG xxi 341	318/17–300	[ετ]βκτδ; PF	Citizenship grant and σίτησις
Chron. Hell. Ath., 20	307/6	[*E*]; [ετβκτδ] ONLY	
IG ii² 456	307/6	[ετβκτ]δ; *E* ONLY (order sic)	Honours for Colophon
466	307/6	PF	*Judicial relations with Tenos
675+525	306/5	[*E*]; PF	*Dispatch of embassy to Antigonus (Pritchett, *AJP* lviii 1937, 329–33)
470	306/5	*E*; PF	Honours for Colophon
SEG xxi 336	aft. 306/5	PF	Honours for a bouleutes
IG ii² 557	aft. 306/5	PF	
478	305/4	*E*; [ετ]βκτ[δ]; PF	Honours for ephebi
479/80	*c.* 305/4	PF	
482	304/3	*E*; [ετβ]κτδ ONLY	
Hesp. vi (EM) 4	304/3	*E*; ε[τβκτδ] ONLY	
IG ii² 491	303/2	PF	
SEG xiv 58	302	PF	
IG ii² 691	aft. 303/2	PF	
500	302/1	PF	Honours for taxiarchs
505	302/1	*E*; ετβκτδ; PF	
562 with *Hesp.* ix 1940, 341–2	302/1	[*E*]; ε[τβκτδ] ONLY	
561	307/6–301/0	[ετ]βκ[τδ] ONLY	
566	end C4	PF	Citizenship grant
572	end C4	PF	
574	end C4	PF	
583	end C4	PF	
587	end C4	[ετ]βκ[τδ] ONLY	
591	end C4	PF	
592	end C4	[*E*]; ε[τβκτδ] ONLY	
593	end C4	PF	
Hesp. xxviii 6	C4–3	PF	?
IG ii² 716 with Add.	C3? (C4?)	PF	Confirming citizenship grant
Hesp. xxviii 8	beg. C3	PF	?
SEG xxi 359	beg. C3	PF; 8 sqq. [— εἶπεν· περὶ μὲν —]—[δτδ πάντα τὰ ἄλλα πράττειν κτλ.] cf. *IG* ii² 682, 92–5 (after 256/5)	Citizenship grant
IG ii² 693	beg. C3	PF	
708	beg. C3	PF	
717	beg. C3	PF	Citizenship grant
718	beg. C3	[PF]	Citizenship grant
721	beg. C3	PF	Citizenship grant
722	beg. C3	PF	
725	beg. C3	[CPF]	
729	beg. C3	PF	
730/1	beg. C3	PF	?
732	beg. C3	PF	
751	beg. C3	PF	?
753	beg. C3	[PF]	

Reference	Date	Formulae	Contents
Hesp. x 21	early C3	$[E]$; $[\epsilon\tau\beta\kappa\tau\delta]$; $[\delta\tau\beta$—end of stone: PF?]	Honours for [theori]
IG ii² 669	291/0	E; $[\epsilon\tau\beta\kappa\tau\delta]$ ONLY	
1534 A	291/0	E; $[\epsilon\tau\beta\kappa\tau\delta]$; PF	Ordering inventory of Asclepieum (date, *Chron. Hell. Ath.*, 50)
698	*c.* 289/8	$[\epsilon\tau\beta\kappa\tau\delta]$; PF	
650	288/7	E; $\epsilon[\tau\beta\kappa]\tau\delta$; PF	
SEG xxi 356	288/7?	$[E]$; $[\epsilon\tau\beta\kappa\tau\delta]$ ONLY	
IG ii² 652	aft. 288/7	PF	Citizenship grant
662/3 with *SEG* xvi 62	286/5	E; $\epsilon\tau\beta\kappa\tau\delta$; [PF]	
IG ii² 657	285/4	E; $\epsilon\tau\beta\kappa\tau\delta$; PF	Honours culminating in statue and $\sigma\iota\tau\eta\sigma\iota\varsigma$
659	285/4	PF	Rite of Aphrodite $\Pi\acute{\alpha}\nu\delta\eta\mu\sigma\varsigma$
660. ii	283/2	$[E]$; $\epsilon\tau\beta\kappa\tau\delta$; $\pi\epsilon\rho\grave{\iota}$ $\hat{\omega}\nu$ —$[$—$\pi\rho\sigma\beta\epsilon\beta\sigma\acute{\nu}\lambda\epsilon\nu\tau\alpha]\iota$ $\tau\hat{\epsilon}\iota$ $\beta\sigma\nu\lambda\hat{\epsilon}\iota$; PF	Praise for Tenos. See p. 69
Hesp. iv 40	283/2	E; $\epsilon\tau\beta\kappa\tau\delta$; PF	Honours for taxiarchs
Hesp. ix 48	287–278	PF	Citizenship grant
Hesp. xxviii 12	C3	$[E]$; $[\epsilon\tau\beta\kappa\tau\delta]$ ONLY	?
IG ii² 677	aft. 277	PF	Honours for agonothetes(?) of Panathenaea
Hesp. ii 5	277/6	E; $\epsilon\tau\beta\kappa\tau\delta$; PF	Honours for taxiarchs
IG ii² 710	295/4–276/5	PF	Citizenship grant
712	295/4–276/5	PF	
676	275/4	E; $[\epsilon]\tau\beta\kappa[\tau]\delta$; PF	Honours for epimeletae i/c sacrifices to $\Sigma\omega\tau\hat{\eta}\rho\epsilon\varsigma$
770	274/3	E; $[\epsilon\tau\beta]\kappa\tau\delta$ ONLY	
SEG xvi 64	272/1	$[E]$; $\epsilon[\tau\beta\kappa\tau\delta]$ ONLY	Honours for priest of Zeus $\Sigma\omega\tau\acute{\eta}\rho$
65	272/1	E; $[\epsilon]\tau\beta[\kappa\tau\delta]$; PF	Honours for astynomi
IG ii² 701	aft. 272	PF (reading $[\delta/\psi\tau\beta]$ for *IG*'s $[\delta\tau\delta]$)	
SEG xiv 64	271/0	E; $\epsilon\tau\beta\kappa\tau\delta$; PF	Honours for taxiarchs
65	271/0	E; $\epsilon\tau\beta[\kappa\tau\delta]$; PF	Honours for sitones
IG ii² 772	270/69	E; $\epsilon\tau\delta$; PF	On public doctors' sacrifices
661	269/8	E; $\epsilon\tau\delta$; PF	Honours for epimeletae of mysteries
665	268/7	E; $\epsilon\tau\beta\kappa\tau[\delta]$; PF	Honours for ephebi
666/7	268/7	E; $\epsilon\tau\beta\kappa\tau\delta$; PF	Citizenship grant
SEG xix 75	*c.* 267/6	PF	
IG ii² 685	266/5	E; $\epsilon\tau\beta\kappa\tau\delta$ ONLY	

Hesp. vii 20	258/7	E; no enactment-formula; PF	Honours for ephebi
IG ii² 682	aft. 256/5	PF; 92 sqq. $\Lambda\acute{\nu}\sigma\alpha\nu\delta\rho\sigma\varsigma$ ... $\epsilon\hat{\iota}\pi\epsilon\nu\cdot$ $\delta\tau\delta$ $\tau\grave{\alpha}$ $\mu\grave{\epsilon}\nu$ $\check{\alpha}\lambda\lambda\alpha$ $[\pi\acute{\alpha}]\nu\tau\alpha$ $\pi\rho\acute{\alpha}\tau\tau\epsilon\iota\nu$ $\pi\epsilon\rho\grave{\iota}$ $\tau\hat{\eta}\varsigma$ $\delta\omega\rho\epsilon\hat{\alpha}\varsigma$ $\hat{\eta}\varsigma$ $\epsilon\hat{\iota}\tau\eta\kappa\epsilon\nu$ $\Phi\alpha\hat{\iota}\delta\rho\sigma\varsigma$ $\kappa\alpha\tau\grave{\alpha}$ $\tau\grave{\sigma}$ $\pi\rho\acute{\sigma}\tau\epsilon\rho\sigma\nu$ $\psi\acute{\eta}\phi\iota\sigma\mu\alpha$ $\hat{\sigma}$ $\Lambda\acute{\nu}\sigma\alpha\nu\delta\rho\sigma\varsigma$ $\epsilon\hat{\iota}\pi\epsilon\nu$. Beginning of 682 not	Honours culminating in statue and $\sigma\iota\tau\eta\sigma\iota\varsigma$

Reference	Date	Formulae	Contents
		preserved, but probably L was proposer and here moves supplementary decree on later occasion.	
IG ii² 776	255/4	PF	Honours for priestess of Athena Πολιάς
792	253/2	PF	Honours for sitones
777	252/1	[*E*]; ε[τδβκτδ] ONLY	
(Add.) 768+802	251/0	*E*; ετβκτδ; PF	
(Add.) 769+441	251/0	*E*; ετβκτδ] ONLY	
SEG xix 70	C3	PF	
IG ii² 734	C3	*E*; [ετ]βκ[τδ] ONLY	
735	C3	[ετ]δ; PF	
801	mid C3	PF	Citizenship grant
804	mid C3	PF	Citizenship grant
807	mid C3	PF	Honours for epimeletae of mysteries
822	mid C3	PF	?
823	mid C3	[PF?]	
Hesp. vii 23	250/49	*E*; ετβκτ[δ]; PF	Lamian arbitration between Athens and Boeotia
IG ii² 779	250/49	PF	Honours for Lamian arbitrators
782	250/49	*E*; [ετβκτδ]; PF	?
798	250/49	ετδ; PF	
SEG iii 92	249/8	[*E*]; [ετβκτδ]; stone ends [looks as if leading to PF]	
IG ii² 683	248/7	*E*; ετβκτδ ONLY	
Hesp. xi 56	247/6	*E*; ετδ; PF	*Scheme of voluntary contributions to stratiotic fund
Hesp. vii 21	247/6	[*E*]; [ετ]β[κτδ] ONLY	?
IG ii² 1534 B	247/6	*E*; [ετβκτδ]; PF	Ordering inventory of Asclepieum
SEG xxiii 67	246/5	[*E*]; [ετβκτδ] ONLY	
SEG xxi 391	245/4	*E*; [ετβκτδ] ONLY	
392	244/3	[*E*]; [ετ]β[κτδ]; PF	Honours for ephebi
Hesp. xvii 3	244/3	*E*; ετβκτδ ONLY	Honours for sitones
SEG xviii 19. i	244/3	[*E*]; [ετβκτδ]; PF	} Honours for priest of
ii	241/0	*E*; [ε]τβκτδ; PF	} Asclepius
Hesp. xvii 24	243/2	*E*; [ε]τ[βκτδ] ONLY	Honours for ephebi
IG ii² 784	240/39	*E*; ε[τ]βκτδ ONLY	
SEG xix 78	239/8	[*E*]; ετ[βκτδ]; PF	Honours for architect
Hesp. vi 2 A	239/8	PF	Honours for σιτοφύλακες
IG ii² 786	soon aft. 239/8	PF	
787	236/5	*E*; [ετβ]κτδ ONLY	
788	235/4	*E*; ετβκτδ; PF	Honours for priest of Calliste
808	239–229	PF	
821	239–229	PF	
832	229/8	ΔΨ; *E*; PF	

Reference	Date	Formulae	Contents
SEG xix 80	soon aft. 229/8	PF	
IG ii² 836	soon aft. 229/8	PF	
837	227/6	*E*; [ετ]βκτ[δ] ONLY	?
Hesp. iv 39	226/5	*E*; ετβκτδ; PF	
IG ii² 851	bef. 224/3	PF	Citizenship grant
SEG xxi 396	bef. 224/3	*E*; ετβ[κτδ] ONLY	?
IG ii² 857	bef. 224/3	Δ[Ψ]; *E*; ετβκ[τδ] ONLY	Honours for a banker
839	221/0	[Δ]Ψ; *E*; ετβ; PF	Dedication to Hero Doctor
HSCP xlviii 1937, 105–11	216/15	βουλὴ ἐν τῶ[ι 'Ελευσινίωι καὶ ἐκκλησία]; ετ[βκτδ] ONLY	Honours for ephebi
ibid. 120–6	*c.* 215	[ετβκτδ]; PF	Refounding of Lycea
IG ii² 847	215/14	*B*Ψ; *B*; ετβκτδ; PF	Honours for epimeletae of mysteries
853	end C3	PF	Citizenship grant
858	end C3	PF	
859	end C3	PF	Concerning Cyme
861	end C3	[*E*]; [ετβκτδ]; PF 〚Meritt, *Ath. Yr.*, 166, restores [ετδ] for no apparent reason〛	
862	end C3	PF	Honours for Lamian arbitrators
SEG xxi 411	end C3	PF	Honours for ephebi
IG ii² 867	end C3?	[ε. τ. βουλ]ἐι κ[αὶ τ. δ] ONLY	
869	end C3?	PF	
871	end C3?	PF	
872	C3?	PF	?
850	shortly bef. 200	*E*; PF	Citizenship grant
Hesp. x 23	*c.* 200	PF	
Hesp. xiii 10	*c.* 200	PF	Praise for Ephesus
Hesp. xvi 55	*c.* 200	[PF?]	Honours for [epimeletae of mysteries]
IG ii² 922	beg. C2	PF	Citizenship grant
923	beg. C2	PF	Citizenship grant
927	beg. C2	PF	
931	beg. C2	PF	
936	beg. C2	PF	
926	beg. C2?	PF	
978	199/8	ΔΨ; *E*; ετβκτδ; PF	
785	196/5	*E*; ετβ[κτ]δ; PF	
Hesp. v 15	196/5	ΔΨ; *E*; ετβκτδ; PF	Honours culminating in statue and σίτησις
IG ii² 886	193/2	[*E*]; ε[τβκτδ] ONLY	
844. iii	193/2	PF	
SEG xvi 77	193/2	[*E*]; [ετβκτδ] ONLY	
IG ii² 892	188/7	[ἐκκλησία] ἀρχαιρεσίαι κατὰ τὴν μαντ[είαν τοῦ θεοῦ]; ετβκτδ ONLY	

Reference	Date	Formulae	Contents
SEG xvi 84	188/7	[βου]λὴ [καὶ ἐκκλησία ἐν τῶι] θεάτρωι μεταχ-θε[ῖ]σα ἐκ [Παναθη-ναϊκοῦ Σταδίο]υ; [ε]τβκτδ ONLY	Citizenship grant
SEG xxi 435. i	187/6	PF	
Hesp. xv 38	186/5	PF	Honours for ephebi
IG ii² 897	185/4	βουλὴ ἐμ βουλευτηρίωι σύγκλητος στρατ[ηγῶν] παραγγειλάντων καὶ ἀπὸ βουλῆς ἐκκλησία [κυρία] ἐν τῶι θεάτρωι; [ε]τβκτδ ONLY	
900	185/4	PF	Honours for ephebi
889	181/0	E; [ετβ]κτδ; PF	Citizenship grant
905	175/4	E; ετβκτδ ONLY	
Hesp. x 75	173/2?	[E]; [ε.τ.β.κ.τ.δ]ή[μωι] ONLY	?
SEG xvi 92	173/2	[ΔΨ]; E; [ε]τβκ[τδ] ONLY	Honours for epimeletae of mysteries
Hesp. xxvi 4	173/2	E; [ετβκτδ] ONLY	
SEG xix 97	c. 184–171	PF	Honours for ephebi
SEG xxi 452	173/2–168/7	E; [PF]	
Hesp. xv 40	171/0	i E; ετ[β]κτδ; PF ii E; ετβκτδ ONLY	} Honours for ephebi and cosmetes
IG ii² 907	c. 170	PF	
908	c. 170	PF	
909	c. 170	PF	
Hesp. iv (ACR) 37	c. 170	PF	
Hesp. xxxvi 6	c. 170	[E]; [ετδ]; PF	
Hesp. v 17	169/8	E; ετβκτδ; PF	
IG ii² 945	168/7	ἐκκλησία σύγκλητος ἐν τῶι θεάτρωι κατὰ τὸ ψήφισμα ὃ—εἶπεν; ετβκτ[δ]; PF	
946	166/5	E; [ετβκτδ] ONLY	
947. ii	166/5	E; ετβ[κτ]δ ONLY	
i	aft. 166/5	[ψτ]β but assembly should have ratified	(Proxeny)
949	165/4	E; ετβκτδ; PF	Honours for demarch of Eleusis (conduct of Eleusinia)
SEG xviii 22	165/4	E; ετβκτδ; PF	Honours for priest of Asclepius
Hesp. iii 20	163/2	E; ετβ[—] ONLY	Honours for taxiarch
IG ii² 956	161/0	PF	Honours for agonothetes of Thesea
Hesp. ii 16	161/0	[ετδ]; PF	Honours for cosmetes of ephebi
Hesp. xvi 64	161/0	E; [ετβκτδ]; condensed PF	Repairs to sanctuary
IG ii² 953	160/59	E; [ετβκτ]δ ONLY	
954	bef. 159	[βουλὴ σύ]γκλητος στρατ-η[γῶν παραγγειλάντων καὶ ἀπὸ τῆς βουλ]ῆς ἐκκλη-σία ἀρ[χαιρεσίαι κατὰ τὴν μαντείαν τὴν τοῦ] θεοῦ; PF	

Reference	Date	Formulae	Contents
IG ii² 955	bef. 159	ἐκκ[λησία ἀρχαιρεσίαι κτλ.] ; ετβ[κτδ] ; PF	
957	157/6	PF	Honours for agonothetes of Thesea
979	155/4	E; [ε]τβκτδ ; PF	Citizenship grant
958	152/1 ?	PF	Honours for agonothetes of Thesea
966	159–133	PF	
968. i	mid C2	[ε]τβ[κτδ] ; PF	
ii	aft. 143/2	E; [ετβκτδ] ONLY	Honours for agonothetes
980	mid C2	PF	Citizenship grant
981	mid C2	PF	Citizenship grant
984	mid C2	PF	
985	mid C2	PF	
990	mid C2	PF	
992	C2	PF	
Hesp. iv (ACR) 36	C2	PF	*Perhaps* concerned with Salamis
SEG xviii 27	C2	PF	Honours for priest of Asclepius
28	aft. mid C2	[ετβ]κτδ ONLY	Honours for priest of Asclepius
IG ii² 982	aft. mid C2	PF	Citizenship grant
988	aft. mid C2	PF	Citizenship grant
Hesp. ii (ACR) 24	aft. mid C2	PF	Citizenship grant
SEG xvi 102	c. 150–100	[ἐκκλησία ἐν τῶι θεάτρωι ἣ με]ταχθεῖσα ἐκ Πειρ[αιέως κατὰ τὸ ψήφισμα ὃ — εἶπεν] ; [ετβ]κτδ ; PF	Honours for a priestess
IG ii² 971	140/39	E; ετβκτδ ; PF	
SEG xviii 24	140/39?	PF	Honours for priest of Asclepius
SEG xix 102	139/8?	E; [ετβκ]τδ ONLY	
SEG xviii 25	138/7	[E] ; [ετβκτδ] ; PF	Work in temple of Asclepius
26	137/6	E; ετβ[κτδ] ONLY	Honours for priest of Asclepius
SEG xxi 469	129/8	ετβκτδ ; PF	*Regulations for cult of Apollo
SEG xv 104	127/6	i [E] ; [ετδ] ; PF / ii E; [ετδ] ; PF	Honours for ephebi and cosmetes
IG ii² 1006 + *SEG* xix 108	122/1	i E; ετβκτδ ; PF / ii E; ετβκτδ ; PF	Honours for ephebi and cosmetes
SEG xxi 476	c. 120	[E] ; [ετβκτδ] ONLY	Honours for ephebi and cosmetes
IG ii² 1008	118/17	i E; [ετβκ]τδ ; PF / ii E; ετβκτδ ; PF	Honours for ephebi and cosmetes
1134, 64 sqq.	117/16	ΔΨ; PF	Amphictyonic business
1009 with *Hesp.* xvi 67	116/15	i E; ετβκτδ ; PF / ii E; ετβκτδ ; PF	Honours for ephebi and cosmetes
[[*IG* ii² 1014	109/8	[B] ; ε[τβκτδ] scarcely secure]]	
IG ii² 1036	108/7	E; ε[τβκτδ] ; fathers have made πρόσοδος to boule; PF	Honours for makers of the πέπλος

Reference	Date	Formulae	Contents
IG ii² 1011	107/6	{ i E; ετδ; PF { ii E; ετδ; PF	} Honours for ephebi } and cosmetes
SEG xvi 100	104/3	{ i E; ε[τβκτδ]; PF { ii E; ετβκτδ; PF	'First' and 'second' decrees for prytanes and officials (usually i is non-prob.; ii boule alone)
IG ii² 1023	end C2	PF	
1024	end C2	PF	
1027	end C2	[ετβκτδ]; PF	Honours for cosmetes of ephebi
1054	bef. 100?	PF	Honours for theori to Thespiae
Keram., iii. A 5	c. 100	δ[τβκτδ] ONLY	Honours for treasurer of prytanes and great variety of officers

Reference	Date	Formulae	Contents
IG ii² 1028	100/99	{ i E; ετδ; condensed PF { ii E; ετδ; condensed PF	} Honours for ephebi } and cosmetes
1034	98/7	E; ετβκτδ; fathers have made πρόσοδος to boule	Honours for makers of the πέπλος
1030	aft. 96/5	δτβ very prob. to be restored as condensed PF (cf. 1028 above)	Honours for ephebi
1029	94/3	E; ετβκτδ; PF	Honours for ephebi
SEG xviii 29	94/3	B; [ετβ] but assembly perhaps ratified (cf. p. 85 n. 6)	Honours for priest of Asclepius
IG ii² 1047	49/8	[E]; [ετβκτ]δ ONLY	?
1041	mid 40s	{ i PF { ii PF	} Honours for cosmetes } and ephebi (order } sic)
1040+1025	c. 43/2	{ i [δτβκτδ] ONLY { ii E; [ετβκτδ]; [δτ]βκτδ	} Honours for cosmetes } and ephebi (sic) } (date, Reinmuth, } Hesp. xxxiv 1965)
1042	c. 41/0	{ ii PF { iii PF	} Honours for cosmetes } and ephebi (sic)

Reference	Date	Formulae	Contents
	A.D.		
IG iv² 84	38/9?	E; δτβκτδ (no. 83, with ἔδοξε tout court, is a decree of the Areopagus, with many departures from the language of decrees of the boule and demos)	
IG ii² 1072	116/17	βουλὴ ἱερὰ ἐν Ἐλευσινίωι; δεδόχθαι τῆι	

Reference	Date A.D.	Formulae	Contents
		βουλῆι τῶι ·Χ· καὶ τῶι δήμωι	
IG ii² 1077	209/10	(for early part of pre-script see p. 47); δεδόχθαι [τῆι] ἐ[ξ] Ἀ[ρείου] πάγου βουλῆ καὶ τῆ βουλῆ τῶν Φ καὶ τῷ δήμῳ τῷ Ἀθηναίων	Sacrifices for house of Septimius Severus
Hesp. iv (ACR) 34	no date offered: C4?	PF	Citizenship grant

I omit the second decree in *Hesp.* Supp. vi 31/2 with *SEG* xxi 506/5 (A.D. 229/30 or 230/1), which is thought to be probouleumatic but does not exhibit any of the older formulae (l. 29/18 describes the enactment as a δόγμα). The third decree is a resolution of the Areopagus; 31, fr. *a*, probably belongs to a decree of the Sacred Gerousia.

TABLE D

Non-Probouleumatic Decrees

Reference	*Date*	*Formulae*	*Contents*
SEG x 26	c. 450	RI	Lease of public property
M&L 49	c. 445?	RI (περὶ μέν . . . καθά-περ Δ εἶπε)	*Colony at Brea
HMA 66, 47 sqq.	c. 436?	[ετβκτ]δ; [γνόμε] στρατε-γὸν; CP (cf. *ATL*, iii. 313 n. 61, more cautious text *Svt* 186; older texts, e.g. *SEG* x 86, read [ετ]δ)	*Alliance with Perdiccas and Arrhabaeus
SEG xii 26	c. 430	CP	*Tribute collection
M&L 68	426/5	⟦No reason to restore RP before 10;⟧ RI, 26–7. See p. 71 n. 2.	*Cleonymus' tribute decree
SEG x 87	c. 423/2	[τὸς δὲ πρυτάνες τês Αἰ]αντίδος πρυτανείας [χρεματίζεν ἐπάναγκες περὶ τôν ἔργον τôν ἐ]πὶ Λαυρείοι hόπος ἂν [φσεφίσεται hο δêμος] 10–12, rest. P. J. R. and D. M. Lewis; [R]I	*Coinage
Tod 100	403?	[ετβκτδ]; ἐψηφίσθαι Ἀθηναίοις	Rewards for Phyle metics (see Hereward, *BSA* xlvii 1952, esp. 111–13)
IG ii² 145	402–399	[ετδ] (better than [ετβ]: see Ch. II, pp. 84–5) ONLY	Appointing herald
3	c. 400?	[ετδ] ONLY	(Lewis, *BSA* xlix 1954, 33, dates C5 and probably before 412 from fr. *b*; but post-403 perhaps safer)
47, 23 sqq.	beg. C4	ψτδ twice	Cult of Asclepius
26	394–387	ετδ; ἐπαινέσαι μέν, 7; ἐψηφ[ίσθαι δέ], 10–11	
51	bef. 387/6	[ετδ] ONLY	
Tod 114	387/6	ετδ; δτδ	*Regulations for Clazomenae
IG ii² 30	386/5	εὔξασθαι-formula (cf. p. 75); δτδ	*Cleruchs on Lemnos
Tod 118	384/3	ψτδ	*Alliance with Chios
IG ii² 62	bef. 378/7	ετδ ONLY	
70	bef. 378/7	[ετ]βκ[τδ]; ψτδ	
72	bef. 378/7	ε[τδ] ONLY	
78	bef. 378/7	[ψτ]δ	
83	bef. 378/7	ψ[τδ]	

Reference	Date	Formulae	Contents
Tod 123. i	378/7	ετβκτδ; ψτδ	*Prospectus of Second Athenian League
ii		the decree beginning in l. 91 seems to have been appended without an enactment- or rider-formula	
IG ii² 99	375/4	ετ[δ] ONLY	?
Hesp. iii 3	373/2	[ετδ] ONLY	
SEG xiv 45	371/0?	[ετδ] ONLY	
IG ii² 104	368/7	[ψ]τ[δ]	Reply to ambassadors
Tod 136	368/7	[ετδ]; δτδ	*Alliance with Dionysius I
139	c. 367?	RI	*Diplomatic relations with Sidon
SEG xiv 47	365/4	[ετδ] ONLY	Transfer of sacred property
Tod 142	363/2	ετβκτδ; δτδ	*Regulations for Iulis
144	362/1	ετβκτδ; εὔξασθαι-formula; mention of allies' δόγμα; MP; δ[τδ]	*Alliance with Arcadia
146	362/1	ετβκτδ; εὔξασθαι-formula; ψτδ	*Cleruchy for Potidaea
147	361/0	ετβκτδ; ψτδ	*Alliance with Thessaly
IG ii² 118	361/0?	[ετδ]; [δτ]δ	
Tod 154	357/6	[ετ]δ; [ψ]τδ; CP	*Regulations for Eretria
IG ii² 132	355/4	i ε[τδ] ONLY	
		ii ε[τδ] ONLY	
133	355/4	ε[τδ]; ψτ[δ]	
134	354/3	[ετ]βκτδ; [ψτ]δ	
177	bef. 353/2	δ[τδ]	
193	bef. 353/2	CP	
138	353/2	ετβκ[τδ]; [δτδ]	
252	mid C4	[δτδ]	
660. i	c. 350–325	δ[τδ]	(date, Johnson, CP ix 1914, 429)
207	349/8	ετδ ONLY	
209	349/8	ετδ ONLY	
Tod 167	347/6	no enactment-formula; bouleutic χρηματίσαι-formula, 55–7; RI. See pp. 73–4	
168	347/6	[ε]τβκτδ; δτδ	*Renewal of alliance with Mytilene
IG ii² 220. i	344/3	[ψ]τδ	Order to inscribe honorific decree
249	bef. 343/2	ετδ ONLY	?
225	343/2?	[ετδ] ONLY	*Alliance with Messenians and others
Tod 174	341/0	ετδ ONLY	
175	340/39	ετδ ONLY	
IG ii² 231	340/39	[ετδ] ONLY	
SEG xvi 51	340/39	δτδ	
Tod 178	338/7	ετδ; δ[τ]δ	

Reference	Date	Formulae	Contents
IG ii² 404	aft. 338/7?	ετδ; δ[τδ]	*Ratifying Chabrias' alliance with Ceos
Tod 181	337/6	[δ]τδ	
IG ii² 241	337/6	δ[τ]δ	
SEG xviii 11	337/6	[δ]τδ	
Hesp. vii (ACR) 19	337/6	[ετ]δ; δ[τδ]	
Hesp. ix 35	337/6	[ετδ] ONLY; refers to boule ll. 12, 15, 16	
IG ii² 263	bef. 336/5	[ετδ] ONLY	
276	bef. 336/5	[περὶ ὧν ἔδοξε . . . ἐν τὲι βο]υλὲι ἔννομα ἱ[κετεύειν, ψ]τδ; but RP, 23 sqq. See pp. 72–3	
283	bef. 336/5	[δτ]δ	
285	bef. 336/5	δ[τδ]	
288	bef. 336/5	δ[τδ]	
304	bef. 336/5	[δ]τδ	
436	aft. 336/5	*E*; ε[τδ] ONLY	?
330. i	335/4	*E*; ετδ; [δτδ]	Honours for a hieropoeus
SEG xxi 274	334/3	*E*; ε[τδ] ONLY	?
275	334/3	*E*; ε[τ]δ ONLY	Citizenship grant
276	334/3	[*E*]; ετ[δ] ONLY	?
IG ii² 336	334/3	*E*; ετ[δ]; MP; ψτδ	Citizenship grant
Tod 189. ii	333/2	ετδ; δτδ; published with OPEN PROBOULEUMA (for which SEE TABLE G)	Allowing Citian merchants to build temple
IG ii² 338. i	333/2	ετδ; mention of assembly's commissioning a probouleuma (which perhaps begins 32 sqq.); δτδ	Honours for a hieropoeus
RIG 106	332/1	*E*; ετδ ONLY	
IG ii² 345	332/1	*E*; ετδ ONLY	
346	332/1	ετδ ONLY	
347	332/1	ετδ; δ[τδ]	
Hesp. viii 6	332/1	[*E*]; [δ]τ[δ]	
IG ii² 350	331/0?	*E*; [δτ]δ	
SEG xxi 281	331/0	[*E*]; [ε]τδ ONLY	(date, *Ath. Yr.*, 88–9)
IG ii² 408	c. 330	[*E*]; ε[τδ]; [δ]τδ	
409	c. 330	[δ]τδ	
Hesp. ix 39	c. 330	[δτ]δ	
Tod 198	330/29	ετ[δ]; δτδ	
IG ii² 343	aft. 329	δτ[δ]	(date, Johnson, *CP* ix 1914, 425)
*SIG*³ 298	329/8	*E*; ετδ; δτδ	Honours for men chosen for ἐπιμέλεια of festival of Amphiaraus
IG ii² 353	329/8	[ετ]δ ONLY	?
354. i	328/7	*E*; [ε]τδ; [δτ]δ; published with specific PROBOULEUMA	Honours for priest of Asclepius
356	327/6	*E*; ε[τ]δ ONLY	
Hesp. iii 5	327/6	[*E*]; [ετ]δ ONLY	Honours for some board
SEG xxi 288	327/6	[ετ]δ ONLY	

Reference	Date	Formulae		Contents
IG ii² 407	330–326	[δτ]δ		
SEG xxi 289	326/5?	*E*; [ετδ] ONLY		?
IG ii² 360. iii	330/29	46–50	ψτδ	Telemachus commissions probouleuma;
iv		51–65	CPF	Cephisodotus' motion adopted as PRO-BOULEUMA;
ii		28–45	ψτδ	Telemachus' motion adopted in place of probouleuma, on which it improves.
v	325/4	66–79	PF	Phyleus' motion adopted as PROBOULEUMA;
i		1–27	δτδ	Demosthenes' motion adopted in place of probouleuma, on which it improves.

See pp. 66–7

Tod 200	325/4	ψτδ	*Dispatch of colony to the Adriatic
⌈*SEG* xxi 292	324/3	[*E*]; [ετδ] ONLY	Concerning the proedri?
⌊ 293	324/3	[*E*]; [ετδ] groundlessly restored ONLY	? ⌉⌉
IG ii² 365	323/2	ετδ; δ[τδ]	
366	323/2	ετδ ONLY. Summary only, perhaps especially liable to careless use of formulae etc., whence Johnson's argument (*CP* ix 1914, 425) for date *c.* 366/5 from absence of patronymic and demotic seems inconclusive	
367	323/2	*E*; ετδ ONLY	Concerning the Phocians
343, revised *Hesp.* ix 1940, 342–3	323/2	[*E*]; δτ[δ]	
SEG xxi 298	323/2	[δτ]δ	Citizenship grant
IG ii² 372	322/1	*E*; ε[τδ] ONLY (I dispute connection with 289: see p. 72 n. 2)	?
Hesp. xiii 5	shortly bef. 321/0	[ετ]δ; δ[τ]δ	Citizenship grant

---

SEG xxi 303	321/0	[*E*]; ε[τδ] ONLY	?
IG ii² 380	320/19	ετδ; δτδ	*Duties of agoranomi
381	320/19	*E*; ετ[δ] ONLY	Reply to ambassadors?
382	320/19	[ετ]δ ONLY	?
400	bef. 319/18	ε[τδ]; δ[τδ]	(date, *Chron. Hell. Ath.*, 3–4)
402	bef. 319/18	ετδ; [δτ]δ	Concerning Antipater
388	319/18	ε[τδ] ONLY	?
389	319/18	[*E*]; [ετδ] ONLY	?
401	321–319	δ[τ]δ	
421	bef. 318/17	*E*; ετδ ONLY	

Reference	Date	Formulae	Contents
IG ii² 422	325–318/17	ε[τδ]; [δτ]δ	(date, Johnson, *CP* ix 1914, 425)
448. i	323/2 (*sic*)	[*E*]; [ε]τδ; δ[τδ]; RIDER τάδε Πανφίλου Εὐφ[ι]λήτου	Citizenship grant made—
ii	318/17	δτδ	—and confirmed
449	318/17	[*E*]; [ετδ] ONLY	
SEG xxi 318	318/17	[*E*]; ετ[δ]; δ[τδ]	
319	318/17	[*E*]; [ετδ]; [δτδ]	Honours for ἐπίλεκτοι
320	318/17	*E* ἐν Δι[ονύσου]; δτ[δ]	Citizenship grant
IG ii² 374	318/17– 308/7	[ετδ]; δτ[δ]	Citizenship grant (date, Johnson, *CP* ix 1914, 425)
546	318/17– 308/7	[ε]τδ ONLY	
545	aft. 318/17	[ψτδ]	Decree for Thessalian exiles
552	aft. 318/17	ε[τδ]; MP; ψ[τδ]	?
549	c. 315/14	[ψ]τδ	
450	314/13	*E*; δτδ	Honours culminating in σίτησις and statue
551	bef. 309/8	δτδ	
585	bef. 307/6	[*E*]; [ετδ] ONLY	
553	c. 307	δτδ	Citizenship grant
SEG xxi 326	307/6	*E*; [ε]τδ ONLY	
IG ii² 457	307/6	ετδ ONLY on stone; no enactment-formula; but δτδ in [Pl.] *X. Or.* 851 F–852 E	
461	307/6	[*E*]; ε[τδ] ONLY	?
Chron. Hell. Ath., 16	307/6	[ἐκκλησία κατὰ τ]οῦ [δήμου ψήφισμα] ONLY	?
IG ii² 463	307/6	ετδ; [δτδ]	*Rebuilding of city walls
464	307/6	*E*; [ε]τ[δ] ONLY	?
SEG xxi 334	307/6	[*E*]; ε[τδ] ONLY	?
IG ii² 467	306/5	δ[τδ]	
471	306/5	*E*; ετδ ONLY	
(Add.) 472+169	306/5	[*E*]; [δ]τδ	
554	306/5?	*E*; [ετ]δ; δτδ	
Hesp. iii 6	306/5	[*E*]; ετδ ONLY	
IG ii² 703	305/4	*E*; ε[τδ] ONLY	
796	305/4	*E*; [ετδ] ONLY	?
797	305/4	[*E*]; [ετδ] ONLY	Concerning Mytilene
Hesp. v 1936, 201–5	305/4	[*E*]; ε[τδ] ONLY	
IG ii² 483	304/3	*E*; ετδ; δτδ	
486	304/3	*E*; ετ[δ] ONLY	
SEG xvi 58	304/3	*E*; [ετ]δ ONLY	
IG ii² 540	bef. 303/2	[δτ]δ	
558	c. 303/2	δτ[δ]	Citizenship grant
(Add.) 559+568	c. 303/2	[ετδ] ONLY	
492	303/2	[ετδ] ONLY	
(Add.) 493+518	303/2	*E*; ετδ; δτδ	
494	303/2	*E*; [ετδ] ONLY	
495	303/2	*E*; ετδ; δτδ	Citizenship grant
(Add.) 496+507	303/2	[*E*]; ετδ; δτδ	Citizenship grant
499	302/1	*E*; [ετ]δ ONLY	

Reference	Date	Formulae	Contents
IG ii² 502	302/1	*E*; ετδ; honours for a δημόσιος who ἔδοξεν ἐν τ[ῶι δήμωι ἔνν]ομα ἱκε[τ]εύειν	
503	302/1	*E*; ετδ ONLY	
Hesp. i (ACR) iv	302/1	[*E*]; [ετ]δ ONLY	?
Hesp. iv 68	302/1	[*E*]; ετ[δ] ONLY	
Hesp. ix 20	302/1	*E*; ετδ; δτδ	Honours for taxiarchs
IG ii² 640	301/0	*E*; [ετ]δ ONLY	
560	307/6–301/0	[*E*]; [ετδ] ONLY	
Hesp. vii (ACR) 25	310–300	δτ[δ]	?
IG ii² 568	end C4	[ετδ] ONLY	
573	end C4	[δτδ] *but* citations (1) [*Π*]αριανούς | [ὁ] δῆμος; (2) ἡ βου[λή] | ὁ δ[ῆμος]	
586	end C4	[δ]τ[δ]	
695	beg. C3	δτδ	
707	beg. C3	δ[τδ]	Citizenship grant
713. ii	beg. C3	δ[τδ]	Concerned with a festival
750	beg. C3	[ετ]δ ONLY	Honours (?) for ephebi
SEG xxi 361	beg. C3	[δτδ]	
362	beg. C3	[δτ]δ	
Hesp. xiii 7	301/0–295/4	δτδ	
IG ii² 641	299/8	*E*; ετδ; δτδ	
646	295/4	*E*; [ε]τδ; δτδ	Citizenship grant, σίτησις, statue
Arch. Ath., 1–15	293/2	*E*; ε[τ]δ; δτδ	Honours culminating in σίτησις and statue
IG ii² 651	288/7	*E*; ε[τδ]; δ[τδ]	
653	287/6	*E*; [ε]τδ; δτδ	
654	287/6	*E*; ετδ; δτδ	Citizenship grant
655	287/6	*E*; ε[τδ]; [δτδ]	
Hesp. ix 15	285/4	*E*; [ετ]δ; δτ[δ]	Honours for prytanes
Hesp. vii 18	284/3	*E*; ετδ; δτδ	Honours for an archon
Hesp. vii 1938, 106, A	282/1	[*E*]; ε[τδ]; [δτ]δ	
{ *IG* ii² 672	280/79	[*E*]; [ετ]βκτδ; δτδ	} Honours culminating in statue and σίτησις
Hesp. x 1941, 338–9: ANOTHER COPY		*E*; [ετδ]—stone ends	
SEG xxi 366	279/8	[*E*]; [ετ]δ; δτ[δ]	Honours for prytanes
364	279/8	ετ[δ] ONLY	Honours for prytanes
P 4	290–275	*E*; ετδ; δτδ	Honours for prytanes
IG ii² 674	275/4	ετδ; δτδ	Honours for prytanes
SEG xiv 63	c. 275	*E*; [ετδ]; [δτ]δ	Honours for prytanes
SEG xvi 63	272/1	*E*; ετδ ONLY	Honours for those elected for ἐπιμέλεια of sacrifices to Σωτῆρες
SEG xxi 369	271/0	[*E*]; [ετδ]; δτδ	Honours for prytanes
IG ii² 668	268/7	[ετδ]; [δτ]δ	Honours for archon and epimeletae of πομπή
(Add.) 687+686	267/6	*E*; ετδ; δτδ	*Alliance with Sparta
SEG xxi 372	267/6	*E*; [ετδ] ONLY	Honours for prytanes
SEG iii 94	266/5	*E*; ε[τδ] ONLY	
Hesp. vii 1938, 140–2	261/0	*E*; ετδ ONLY	

Reference	Date	Formulae	Contents
SEG xxi 376	257/6	E; $\epsilon\tau\delta$; $[\delta\tau\delta]$	Honours for prytanes
IG ii² 780. i	252/1	E; $\epsilon[\tau\delta]$; $\delta\tau\delta$	⎱ Honours for an
ii	250/49	$[E]$; $\epsilon\tau\delta$ ONLY	⎰ agonothetes
781	250/49	E; $[\epsilon\tau]\delta$; ⟦no grounds for restoring PF with IG⟧	Honours for archon
P 15	mid C3	$[E]$; $[\epsilon\tau\delta]$ ONLY	Honours for prytanes
IG ii² 680	249/8	$\epsilon\tau\delta$ ONLY	
Hesp. xiii 9	c. 246	$[\delta]\tau\delta$	Right of asylum at Smyrna
Hesp. vi 2 B	239/8	$[\delta\tau\delta]$	Honours for σιτοφύλακες
P 21	238/7	$\epsilon\tau\delta$ ONLY	Honours for prytanes
P 23+Hesp. xi 47	235/4	$\epsilon\tau\beta\kappa\tau\delta$; $\delta\tau\delta$	Honours for prytanes
P 27	234/3–230/29	$[\epsilon\tau\delta]$; $[\delta\tau\delta]$	Honours for prytanes
IG ii² 833	229/8	E; $\epsilon\tau\delta$ ONLY	
P 29	228/7	E; $\epsilon\tau\delta$; $\delta\tau\delta$	Honours for prytanes
IG ii² 838	226/5	E; $[\epsilon\tau]\delta$; ⟦$\delta\tau\delta$ restored at end of fragment⟧	
SEG xxi 400	226/5	$[E]$; $\epsilon[\tau\delta]$ ONLY	Honours for prytanes
Hesp. ix 23	223/2	E; $\epsilon\tau\delta$; $\delta\tau\delta$	Honours for prytanes
IG ii² 844. i	229/8	$\delta\tau\delta$	Grant of statue on Acropolis—
ii	221/0	$\delta\tau\delta$	—and permission to erect in τέμενος of Demos and Charites instead
843	218/17	E; $\epsilon\tau\delta$ ONLY	
SEG xiv 68	214/13	E; $\delta\tau\delta$	Honours for prytanes
P 36	212/11	$[E]$; $[\epsilon\tau\delta]$; $\delta[\tau\delta]$	Honours for prytanes
38	210/09?	E; $\epsilon\tau\delta$; $\delta[\tau\delta]$	Honours for prytanes
Chron. Hell. Ath., 104–8	204/3	$\delta[\tau\delta]$; CP (17–18 restore $[\pi\rho o\epsilon\delta\rho o\upsilon s]$ for $[\pi\rho\upsilon\tau\alpha\nu\epsilon\iota s]$?)	
SEG xvii 29	203/2	$\delta\tau\delta$	Honours for prytanes
SEG xvi 70	210/09–201/0	$[\epsilon\tau\delta]$; $[\delta\tau\delta]$	Honours for prytanes
SEG xix 91	C3–2	$[\delta\tau\delta]$	Honours for prytanes
IG ii² 884	c. 200	$\delta\tau[\delta]$	
IG ii² 922	beg. C2	$[E]$; $[\epsilon\tau\delta]$ ONLY	Honours for archon
929	beg. C2	$[\varDelta]\varPsi$; E; $[\epsilon\tau\delta]$; $[\delta\tau\delta]$	Honours for archon
Hesp. xxxii 14	beg. C2	$[\delta\tau\delta]$	
Hesp. xv 52	beg. C2	$[\epsilon\tau]\delta$; $\delta\tau\delta$	Honours for prytanes
SEG xxi 422	beg. C2	E; $\epsilon\tau[\delta]$ ONLY	Honours for prytanes
P 48. ii	199/8–189/8	$[E]$; $\epsilon[\tau\delta]$; $[\delta\tau]\delta$	Honours for prytanes
49. ii	192/1	E; $[\epsilon\tau\delta]$; $\delta[\tau\delta]$	Honours for prytanes (cf. Chron. Hell. Ath., 113–16)
51	188/7	$[\varDelta\varPsi]$; E; $\epsilon[\tau\delta]$; $\delta\tau\delta$	Honours for prytanes
52	c. 188/7	$[\delta]\tau[\delta]$	Honours for prytanes
Hesp. xv 6	188/7	$[\varDelta\varPsi]$; $[E]$; $[\epsilon\tau\delta]$ ONLY	?
IG ii² 891	188/7	$[E]$; $[\epsilon\tau]\delta$; $\delta\tau\delta$	
896	186/5	⎰ i E; $\epsilon\tau\delta$; $\delta\tau\delta$ / ⎱ ii E; $\epsilon\tau\delta$; $\delta\tau\delta$	⎱ Honours for cane-phorus and epimele-tae of πομπή
P 55	182/1	E; $\epsilon\tau\delta$; $\delta\tau\delta$	Honours for prytanes

Reference	Date	Formulae	Contents
SEG xvi 86	182/1	*E*; ετδ; δτδ	Honours for prytanes
SEG xxi 440	181/0	βουλὴ ἐμ βουλευτηρίωι σύνκλητος στρατηγῶν παραγγειλάντων καὶ ἀπὸ βουλῆς ἐκκλησία κυρία ἐν τῶι θεάτρωι; ετδ; δτδ	Honours for prytanes
442	181/0	[δτδ]	Honours for prytanes
IG ii² 888	180/79	[*E*]; [ετ]δ ONLY	?
P 64. i	178/7	*E*; ετδ; δτδ	Honours for prytanes
SEG xxi 447	177/6	[*E*]; [ετδ]; [δτδ]	Honours for prytanes
SEG xvi 89	175/4	*E*; [ετ]δ; [δτ]δ	Honours for prytanes
90	174/3	*E*; ετδ; δτδ	Honours for prytanes
91. i	173/2	*E*; ετδ; [δτ]δ	Honours for prytanes
P 71	169/8	*E*; ετδ; [δτδ]	Honours for prytanes
72	167/6?	Δ[Ψ]; [*E*]; ετδ in ras.; δτδ	Honours for prytanes
SEG xvi 95	164/3	*E*; ετδ; [δτδ]	Honours for prytanes
96. i	164/3	ΔΨ; *E*; [ετδ]; [δτδ]	Honours for prytanes
P 83	180–155	[δτ]δ	Honours for prytanes
65	153/2	[*E*]; [ετδ] ONLY	Honours for prytanes
SEG xvi 87	*c.* 182–150	[*E*]; [ετδ] ONLY	Honours for prytanes
Hesp. xvi 96	mid C2	[ετδ]; [δτδ]	Honours for prytanes
P 85	145/4	*E*; [ε]τδ; [δ]τδ	Honours for prytanes
Hesp. xvii 9. i	140/39	*E*; [ετδ]; [δτδ]	Honours for prytanes
SEG xii 101. i	135/4	*E*; ετδ; δτδ	Honours for prytanes
P 88	131/0	[ἐκκλησία ἐν τῶι] θεάτρωι ἡ μεταχθεῖ-[σα] ἐκ Πειραιέως κατὰ τὸ ψήφι[σμα ὃ — εἶπ]εν; ετδ; [δ]τδ	Honours for prytanes
SEG xxi 468. i	*c.* 130	[*E*]; [ετδ] ONLY	Honours for prytanes
SEG xv 104	128/7	iii *E*; [δ]τδ / iv [ετ]δ; [δτδ]	Honours for ephebi and cosmetes ('acceptance-decrees')
P 90	125/4	[*E*]; ε[τδ] ONLY	Honours for prytanes
91	125/4	*E*; ετδ; δτδ	Honours for prytanes
92	124/3	*E*; [ετδ]; [δτδ]	Honours for prytanes
93	122/1	[*E*]; [ε]τδ; δ[τδ]	Honours for prytanes
SEG xxi 478	118/17	*E*; [ετδ] ONLY	Honours for prytanes
IG ii² 1011	107/6	iv *E*; ετδ; δτδ / v *E*; ετδ; δτδ	Honours for ephebi and cosmetes ('accep-tance-decrees')
1020	end C2?	[ε]τδ ONLY	?
IG ii² 1038	beg. C1	δ[τδ]	
[[*SEG* xxi 490	beg. C1	[*E*]; ε[τδ] restored for no cogent reason	Honours for ephebi?]]
IG ii² 1035	C1?	δτδ	Restitution of sacred lands
SEG xvii 12. i	95/4	*E*; [ετ]δ; [δτδ]	Honours for prytanes
IG ii² 1078/9	A.D. *c.* 220	[ε]τδ; [δ]τδ	Revival of Eleusinia

TABLE E

Decree of the Demos with Special Origins

Reference	Date	Formulae	Contents
⌐M&L 40	c. 453/2?	[γνόμε τôν χσυγγραφέον] restored *ATL* D 10: possible but not necessary; not restored M&L	Regulations for Erythrae⌐
└HMA 30	450/49	[τάδε hοι χ]συγγρα[φês χσυνέγραφσαν]	Regulations for Miletus
⌐SEG x 104	417/16	χσυ[νέγραφσαν τάδε hοι χσυγγραφês] suggested as less likely possibility, Meritt, *Hesp.* xiv 1945, 125	Alliance with Argos ⌐
└M&L 73	416/15	τάδε hοι χσυγγραφês χσυνέ[γρ]αφσαν; RIDER τὰ μὲν ἄλλα καθάπερ αἱ χσυγγραφαί· περὶ δὲ τô ἐλαίο τês ἀπαρχês χσυγγράφσας Λάμπον ἐπιδειχσάτο τêι βολêι ἐπὶ τês ἐνάτες πρυτανείας, hε δὲ βολὲ ἐς τὸν δêμον ἐχσενενκέτο ἐπάναγκες	Eleusinian first-fruits
ATL D 9	410/09	[γνόμ]ε τôν συνγραφέον	Repayment of sacred moneys to Athena
SEG x 123	c. 410	[γνόμε τôν συγγ]ραφέον	Sacred Law

And compare decree of Demophantus *ap.* And. I. *Myst.* 96–8—SEE TABLE I

HMA 66, 47 sqq.	c. 436?	[γνόμε] στρατεγόν. NON-PROBOULEUMATIC DECREE: SEE TABLE D	Alliance with Perdiccas and others
IG ii² 27	416/15	γνώμη στρατηγῶν	Proxeny (date, Meritt, *Hesp.* viii 1939, 68)

M&L 94	405/4	Original motion and RP both γνώμη Κλεσόφο καὶ συνπρυτάνεων. PRO-BOULEUMATIC DECREE: SEE TABLE C	First Samian decree

---

Tod 133	369/8	Boule orders allied συνέδριον to submit δόγμα to ecclesia. SEE TABLES C AND G	Relations with Diony-sius I

TABLE E

Reference	Date	Formulae	Contents
Tod 144	362/1	συνέδριον submits δόγμα to boule, which submits probouleuma to ecclesia. SEE TABLES D AND G	Alliance with Arcadia and others

TABLE F

Decrees of the Demos moved by Prominent Fourth-Century Orators

1. Aristophon Ἀζηνιεύς

Tod 142	363/2	ετβκτδ; δτδ
IG ii² 118	361/0?	[ετδ]; [δτ]δ; [πε]ρὶ ὧν [λέγουσιν κτλ.]
121	357/6	[ετβ]κτδ ONLY
130	355/4	ετβκ[τδ] ONLY
224	343/2	(no relevant formulae survive)
289	before 336/5	A. is the author of an RP

2. Lycurgus Λυκόφρονος Βουτάδης

IG ii² 328	336/5	ετ[βκτδ]; PF
333	335/4	a religious νόμος
SEG xxi 276	334/3	E; ετ[δ] ONLY
Tod 189. ii	333/2	ετδ; δτδ (in response to an open probouleuma)
IG ii² 345	332/1	E; ετδ ONLY
Tod 198	330/29	ετ[δ]; δτδ
IG ii² 1672, 302	in or before 329/8	a decree of the boule
452, revised Ath. Yr., 95–6	328/7	E ONLY (Meritt's date accepted by Dow, *Hesp.* xxxii 1963, 438–50; rejected by Pritchett, *Ancient Athenian Calendars on Stone*, 281–3)

3. Demades Δημέου Παιανιεύς

Demades' decrees have been collected by A. N. Οἰκονομίδης, Πλάτων viii 1956, 109 sqq.: I list here only those in which relevant formulae survive or are restored, and I give in my first column the numbers of the decrees in his list:

2.	*Hesp.* ix 35	337/6	[ετδ] ONLY; refers to boule in ll. 12, 15, 16.
4.	Tod 181	337/6	[δ]τδ
5.	*IG* ii² 241	337/6	δ[τ]δ
6.	*SEG* xxi 274	334/3	E; ε[τδ] ONLY
8.	*IG* ii² 346	332/1	ετδ ONLY
9.	*SEG* xxi 275	334/3 (*sic*)	E; ε[τ]δ ONLY
10.	*IG* ii² 353	329/8	[ετ]δ ONLY
11.	372	322/1	E; ε[τδ] ONLY (dissociated from *IG* ii² 289, p. 72 n. 2)
12.	380	320/19	ετδ; δτδ

13. *SEG* xxi 306   320/19 E; [ετβκτδ] is the latest restoration of both Dow and Meritt; Pritchett declines to restore; correct text uncertain

14.   305   320/19 E; ετβ[κτδ] ONLY

16. *IG* ii² 400   ?   ε[τδ]; δ[τδ]

4. Demosthenes Δημοσθένους Παιανιεύς

     IG ii² 231   340/39   [ετδ] ONLY

5. Stratocles Εὐθυδήμου Διομεεύς

IG ii² 455, revised *Chron. Hell. Ath.*, 20	307/6	[E]; [ετβκτδ] ONLY. [Στρατοκλῆς] restored as proposer by Larfeld, *Handbuch der griechischen Epigraphik*, II. ii. 941, for no apparent reason
IG ii² 457	307/6	ετδ ONLY (no enactment-formula, but δτδ, [Pl.] *X. Or.* 851 F–852 E)
461	307/6	[E]; ε[τδ] ONLY
471	306/5	E; ετδ ONLY
486	304/3	E; ετ[δ] ONLY
SEG xvi 58	304/3	E; [ετ]δ ONLY
IG ii² 492	303/2	[ετδ] ONLY
495	303/2	E; ετδ; δτδ
(Add.) 496+ 507	303/2	[E]; ετδ; δτδ
499	302/1	E; [ετ]δ ONLY
503	302/1	E; ετδ ONLY
Hesp. i (ACR) iv	302/1	[E]; [ετ]δ ONLY
IG ii² 560	307/6–301/0	[E]; [ετδ] ONLY
568	end C4	[ετδ] ONLY
640	301/0	E; [ετ]δ ONLY
641	299/8	E; ετδ; δτδ
Arch. Ath., 1–15	293/2	E; ε[τ]δ; δτδ

TABLE G

Decrees of the Boule,
other than the Ratified Probouleumata in Table C

Reference	Date	Formulae	Contents
SEG xiv 38	409–3?	[ετβ] : [ετδ] would fit. (In either case, date in or after 403/2 perhaps safer)	?
Tod 98	soon aft. 403/2	[ε]τβ (On this formula in proxeny decrees see pp. 83–4)	To re-publish proxeny decree
[[*IG* ii² 145. i	402–399	SEE TABLE D]]	
IG ii² 49	beg. C4	ετβ	Concerning a proxeny
12. ii	399/8	ετβ	May be PROBOULEUMA relating to 12. i (whose prescript is lost)
13	399/8	[ετ]β	Concerning a proxeny
Hesp. vii 11	*c.* 398–0	[ετβ]	Concerning a proxeny
[[Tod 103	394/3	SEE TABLE C]]	
[[108	394/3	SEE TABLE C]]	
IG ii² 17. i	394/3	ετβ	Revision of publication order in citizenship decree 17. ii (see p. 83 n. 6)
[[32	385/4	SEE TABLE C]]	
58	bef. 378/7	[ε]τβ	Honorific decree
63	bef. 378/7	ετβ	Concerning transfer of proxeny from father to son
77. i	bef. 378/7	ε[τ]β κατὰ τὸ το[ῦ δήμου ψήφισμα]	To publish proxeny decree
[[ii	bef. 378/7	SEE TABLE C	(cf. p. 83 n. 6)]]
95	377/6	[ετ]β	Concerning a proxeny
Tod 133	369/8	δ[τ]β ordering allies to submit δόγμα to ecclesia; leading to PF (cf. TABLE C)	Relations with Dionysius I
IG ii² 157	bef. 353/2	ετβ ; [ψτ]β	?
223 A	343/2	δτβ ; leading to PF (cf. TABLE C)	Boule's prize for best speaker
B		i ἑλέσθαι τὴν βουλὴν αὐτίκα μάλα—not conclusive iii ψτβ	Honorific decrees
C		δτβ	
1155. i	339/8	δ[τβ]	Honours for taxiarch

Reference	Date	Formulae	Contents
IG ii² 330. ii	336/5	B; $\epsilon\tau\beta$; $[\delta\tau\beta]$; leading to OPEN PROBOULEUMA (no directly resultant decree of the ecclesia published)	Honorific decree
Tod 189. i	333/2	$\epsilon\tau\beta$; $\psi\tau\beta$: OPEN PROBOULEUMA (SEE TABLE D for resulting non-probouleumatic decree of ecclesia)	Citian merchants' request for temple
IG ii² 338. ii	333/2	$[\epsilon\tau\beta]$; B. Probably beginning of PRO-BOULEUMA mentioned in i—SEE TABLE D)	Honorific decree
354. ii	328/7	$\psi\tau\beta$: SPECIFIC PROBOULEUMA (SEE TABLE D for i, the non-probouleumatic decree which superseded it)	Honorific decree
Ἀρχ. 'Εφ. 1917, 40–8, 92	328/7	$\delta\tau\beta$	Honours for bouleutae i/c a dedication by 21 bouleutae and 10 others
IG ii² 360. iv	330/29	CPF	PROBOULEUMATA WITH OPEN CLAUSES, published with other relevant decrees (SEE TABLE D) — Honorific decrees
v	325/4	CPF	
361	325/4	B; *perhaps* $\psi[\tau\beta]$	?
1631, 350 sqq.	324/3	$\psi\tau\beta$	Relaxing harsh treatment of defaulting naval treasurer's brother
IG ii² 487	304/3	$\delta\tau\beta$	Honours for an ἀνα-γραφεύς of the laws
SEG xxi 360	beg. C3	$[\epsilon\tau]\beta$	Honours for a bouleutes
Hesp. viii 11	early C3	$[\delta\tau\beta]$	
SEG xxi 376	257/6	$[\delta\tau\beta]$	Honours for officials of prytanes
377. i	256/5	$\delta\tau\beta$	Honours for officials of prytanes
ii	256/5	$\delta\tau\beta$	Special honours for treasurer of boule
P 9. ii	256/5	$\delta\tau\beta$	Honours for officials of prytanes
22	250–230	$[\delta\tau]\beta$	Honours for officials of prytanes
SEG xxi 393	bef. 230/29	$[\delta\tau\beta]$	Honours for officials of prytanes
Hesp. ix 23. ii	223/2	B; $[\epsilon\tau\beta]$; $[\delta\tau]\beta$	Honours for officials of prytanes

Reference	Date	Formulae	Contents
IG ii² 794	216/15	βουλὴ ἐν τῶ[ι Πανα-θηναϊκῶι Σταδίωι] ; ετ[β]	? (for meeting-place cf. Pélékidis, REG lxiii 1950, 112–17)
P 31	c. 215	[δτβ]	Honours for officials of prytanes
36. ii	212/11	βουλὴ ἐ[ν βουλευτήριωι καὶ ἐκ] τοῦ βουλευ-τηρίου ἐν τῶι Ἐλευ-σινίωι ; ε[τ]β ; δτβ	Honours for officials of prytanes
SEG xvii 29. ii	203/2	B ; ετβ ; δτβ	Honours for officials of prytanes
SEG xvi 70. ii	210/09–201/0	B ; [ετβ] ; δ[τβ]	Honours for officials of prytanes
SEG xxi 409	end C3	B ; [ετβ]	Honours for officials of prytanes

Reference	Date	Formulae	Contents
P 43	c. 205–179	δτβ	Honours for officials of prytanes
SEG xxi 423	beg. C2	ε[τβ]	Honours for officials of prytanes
P 44	early C2	[B] ; ετβ	Honours for officials of prytanes
SEG xix 93	C2	[δτβ]	Honours for officials of prytanes
Hesp. ix 16	199/8	B ; [ετβ]	?
P 46 with Hesp. xxxii 15	193/2	BΨ ; [B] ; δτβ	Honours for officials of prytanes
Chron. Hell. Ath., 113–6	192/1	[βουλὴ ἐν τῶι Πανα]-θηναϊκῶι Σταδί[ωι] ; ετβ ; [δτ]β	Honours for officials of prytanes
P 48. i	199/8–189/8	[ετβ] ; [δτβ]	Honours for officials of prytanes
SEG xvi 80	c. 190	B	Honours for officials of prytanes
81. i	189/8	B ; [δτβ]	Honours for officials of prytanes
P 53	186/5?	B ; [ετβ]	Honours for officials of prytanes
IG ii² 898	185/4	B	?
P 54	185/4	BΨ ; [B] ; [δτβ]	Honours for officials of prytanes
Hesp. x 74. ii	184/3	[BΨ] ; B ; [ετ]β	Honours for officials of prytanes
Chron. Hell. Ath., 119	183/2?	[B] ; [ετβ]	Honours for officials of prytanes
SEG xxi 444	181/0	BΨ	?
P 47	181/0	B ; ετβ ; δτβ	Honours for officials of prytanes
Hesp. Supp. iv 1940, 144–7	181/0	[BΨ] ; [B] ; δτβ	Honours for 3 bouleutae i/c equipment in the Scias
P 58	before 178/7	[δτβ]	Honours for officials of prytanes
64. ii	178/7	B ; ετβ ; δτβ	Honours for officials of prytanes

Reference	Date	Formulae	Contents
SEG xvi 91. ii	173/2	B; $\epsilon\tau\beta$; $\delta\tau\beta$	Honours for officials of prytanes
P 70	182/1– 170/69	$[\delta\tau\beta]$	Honours for officials of prytanes
Hesp. ix 24	176–169	$[\epsilon\tau\beta]$; $[\delta\tau\beta]$	Honours for officials of prytanes
P 71. ii	169/8	$\delta[\tau\beta]$	Honours for officials of prytanes
73	166/5	$B\Psi$; B; $\epsilon\tau\beta$; $\delta\tau[\beta]$	Honours for officials of prytanes
IG ii² 948	166/5	B; $[\epsilon\tau\beta]$	Honours for performance of some sacrifice
P 80	164/3	$[\delta]\tau\beta$	Honours for officials of prytanes (date, Meritt, *Hesp.* xxvi 1957, 74)
SEG xvi 96. ii	164/3	$B\Psi$; B; $[\epsilon\tau\beta]$; $[\delta\tau]\beta$	Honours for officials of prytanes
IG ii² 783	163/2	$B\Psi$; $[B]$; $\epsilon\tau\beta$; $[\delta\tau]\beta$	Honours for priest of Zeus $\Sigma\omega\tau\acute{\eta}\rho$ at Piraeus
P 75	161/0	B; $\epsilon\tau\beta$; $\delta[\tau\beta]$	Honours for officials of prytanes
77	*c.* 160	$\delta\tau\beta$	Honours for officials of prytanes
78	*c.* 160	$\delta[\tau\beta]$	Honours for officials of prytanes
81	169/8– 156/5	$[\delta]\tau\beta$	Honours for officials of prytanes
84. i	155/4	$[B]$; $[\epsilon]\tau\beta$; $[\delta\tau\beta]$	UNIQUELY AS B-DECREE, honours for prytanes
ii		B; $\epsilon\tau\beta$; $\delta\tau\beta$	Honours for officials of prytanes
Hesp. ix 25	165/4–150	$[\delta\tau]\beta$	Honours for officials of prytanes
SEG xxi 462	mid C2	B; $\epsilon\tau[\beta]$	Honours for officials of prytanes
IG ii² 990	mid C2	$\delta\tau\beta$	Honours for performance of some sacrifice
1000	after mid C2	$\epsilon\tau[\beta]$; $\delta\tau\beta$	Honours for some officials
P 86	145/4	$[B\Psi]$	Honours for officials of prytanes
Hesp. xvii 9. ii	140/39	$\beta ou\lambda\grave{\eta}$ $[\grave{\epsilon}]\mu$ $\Pi\epsilon\iota\rho\alpha\iota\epsilon\hat{\iota}$ $\grave{\epsilon}\nu$ $\tau\hat{\omega}\iota$ $\Phi\omega\sigma\phi o\rho\acute{\iota}\omega\iota$; $\epsilon\tau\beta$; $\delta\tau\beta$	Honours for officials of prytanes
SEG xii 101. ii	135/4	B; $[\epsilon\tau\beta]$; $[\delta\tau\beta]$	Honours for officials of prytanes
P 95	before 104/3	$[B]$; $[\epsilon\tau\beta]$; $[\delta\tau\beta]$	Honours for officials of prytanes
IG ii² 840	end C2	$\delta\tau\beta$	Repairs to sacred objects in shrine of Hero Doctor
SEG xxi 487	99/8?	$[\beta ou\lambda\grave{\eta}$ $\grave{\epsilon}\nu$ $'E\lambda\epsilon u\sigma]\iota\nu\acute{\iota}\omega\iota$	?
Hesp. xvii 12. ii	95/4	B; $[\epsilon]\tau\beta$; $\delta\tau\beta$	Honours for officials of prytanes
SEG xxi 489	*c.* 95/4	$[\delta\tau\beta]$	Honours for officials of prytanes

Reference	Date	Formulae	Contents
⟦*SEG* xviii 29	94/3	SEE TABLE C⟧	
Hesp. xvii 13	*c.* 80	δτβ	Allowing prytanes to honour treasurer
P 97	*c.* 80?	[δτβ]	Allowing prytanes to honour treasurer
IG ii² 1039. i	83–73	*BΨ*; *B*; [δ]τβ	⎫ Honours for ephebi
ii		δτβ	⎬ and cosmetes
iii		δτβ	⎭
*ASAA*² iii–v 1941–3, 83–7, no. 6	75/4	ετβ; δτβ	Honours for hieropoei
Hesp. xvii 14	64/3	*B*; ε[τβ]	Allowing prytanes to honour treasurer
P 101	57/6	[δτβ]	Allowing prytanes to honour treasurer
IG ii² 1046	52/1	*B*; ετβ; δτβ	Allowing priest of Asclepius to rebuild shrine at own expense
1042. i	*c.* 41/0	δ[τβ]	Honours for ephebi and cosmetes ('acceptance-decree')
SEG xxi 495	Cɪ	[δ]τβ	Honours for treasurer of prytanes
IG ii² 1043. i	39/8	[β]ουλὴ ἐν τῶι θεάτρωι ἡ μεταχ[θεῖσα] ἐκ τοῦ Πα[ναθη]ναϊκοῦ Σταδίου; δτβ	⎫
ii		δτβ	⎬ Honours for ephebi and cosmetes (date, Reinmuth, *Hesp.* xxxiv 1965, 264)
iii		[δτβ]	
iv		δ[τβ]	⎭
P 111	*c.* 40–20	δ[τβ]	Allowing prytanes to honour treasurer
113	*c.* 45–20	δτ[β]	Allowing prytanes to honour treasurer
114	*c.* 30–20?	[δτ]β	Allowing prytanes to honour treasurer
Hesp. xxvi 98	22/1?	[ετβ]; [ὁπόσα μὲν πρ]ότερον ἐψηφίσατο ὁ δ[ῆμος]	Concerning Augustus' birthday
SEG xvii 46	21/0	formulae leading up to [δτβ]	Allowing prytanes to honour treasurer
P 116	*c.* 20	δτβ	Praising prytanes and honouring officials
SEG xxi 497	end Cɪ	δτβ	Allowing prytanes to honour treasurer

	A.D.		
P 119	1–19	[δτβ]	Allowing prytanes to honour treasurer
120	early Cɪ	[δτβ]	Allowing prytanes to honour treasurer
SEG xxi 499	27/8	[*B*]; [ε]τβ	Honorific decree
P 121	*c.* 120	[δτβ]	Praising prytanes and various officials
SEG xvii 35	before 138	δτβ	Honours for officials of prytanes

TABLE H

Formulae in νόμοι

In general the prescripts are modelled on those of contemporary ψηφίσματα, giving date, name of ἐπιστάτης τῶν προέδρων (cf. Ch. I, p. 28) who put the question, and name of proposer.

The following decrees contain a formula commissioning a νόμος: *IG* ii² 222, 41–6; 330, 15–23; *SIG*³ 298, 35–41 (not 39–45).

Reference	Date	Formulae	Contents
IG ii² 140	353/2	[δεδόχθαι τοῖ]ς νομο- θέταις· τὰ [μὲν ἄλλα καθάπερ τὸ]ν Χαιρη- μονίδο νό[μον περὶ τῆ]ς ἀπαρχῆς	Eleusinian first-fruits
244	337/6?	δεδόχθαι τοῖς νομοθέταις	Rebuilding of Piraeus walls
SEG xii 87	337/6	δεδόχθαι τοῖς νομοθέταις	Law against tyranny
SEG xviii 13	336–334	δεδόχθαι τοῖς νομοθέταις	Regulations for Pana- thenaea
IG ii² 333	335/4	refs. to τόνδε τὸν νόμον, 7, 11; νομο[θετῶν ἕδρα], 13	Religious laws
SEG xv 108	c. A.D. 124	κε(φάλαια) νο(μο)- θε(σίας) Ἁδριανοῦ	Compulsory purchase of olive oil

TABLE I

Decrees quoted with Formulae in Literary Texts

Reference	Date	Formulae	Contents
T. IV. 118. xi–xiv	423	ετδ (all MSS.; ε⟨τβκ⟩τδ, Gomme); ἐκκλησίαν δὲ ποιήσαντας τοὺς στρατηγοὺς καὶ τοὺς πρυτάνεις πρῶτον περὶ τῆς εἰρηνῆς ... βουλεύσασθαι Ἀθηναίους καθ᾽ ὅτι ἂν ἐσίῃ ἡ πρεσβεία περὶ τῆς καταλύσεως τοῦ πολέμου.	Year's truce with Sparta
A.P. 29. i–iii	411	(εἰπόντος τὸν μὲν πρὸ τοῦ ψηφίσματος λόγον Μηλοβίου, τὴν δὲ γνώμην γράψαντος Πυθοδώρου τοῦ Ἀναφλυστίου)· Κλειτοφῶν δὲ τὰ μὲν ἄλλα καθάπερ Πυθόδωρος εἶπεν.	To draft new constitution
[Pl.] X. Or. 833 E–F	411/10	ετβ (ἔδοξαν, MSS.)	Trial of Archeptolemus and Antiphon
And. I. Myst. 96–8	410	(quoted as ΝΟΜΟΣ) ετβκτδ; τάδε Δημόφαντος συνέγραψεν	Safeguards for democracy
ibid., 77–9	405	ψηφίσασθαι τὸν δῆμον with first clause	Reinstatement of ἄτιμοι
ibid., 83–4	403	ετδ	Providing for νομοθεσία
Ath. IV. 171 E	366/5 or 323/2	ψτβ	Boule gives itself 5 days' holiday for Apaturia
[Pl.] X. Or. 851 F–852 E	307/6	SEE IG ii² 457 IN TABLE D	
Pl. Demetr. 13. (i–)ii	307 or soon after	ἀγαθῇ τύχῃ; δτδ	Ordering election of a man to ask The Saviour about a religious matter
D.L. VII. 10–12	260/59	E; δτδ. Language bears signs of re-editing	Honours for Zeno
Jos. A.J. XIV. 150–5	106/5	E; ⟨ε⟩τδ; δεδόχθαι tout court	Honours for Hyrcanus

On the mock decrees in Lucian see F. W. Householder, Jr., *TAPA* lxxi 1940; J. Delz, *Lukians Kenntnis der athenischen Antiquitäten*, 134–50.

TABLE J

Riders to Decrees

1. *Riders proposed by mover of original motion*: *IG* i² 94 (418/17), M&L 94 (405/4), Tod 97. i (403/2) (Clisophus and his fellow prytanes), 97. ii (?) (403/2), *IG* ii² 109 (?) (363/2), Tod 143 (363/2), *IG* ii² 182 (?) (before 353/2), 206 (349/8), 334 (*c.* 335/4), pseudo-rider 682 (after 256/5). Rider by mover's son, *IG* ii² 448. i (323/2).

2. *Riders of real substance*: M&L 37 (?) (458/7?), *Hesp.* xiv 4 (?) (*c.* 450), HMA 41 (after 450), M&L 44 (*c.* 449), 52 (446/5), 49 (*c.* 445?) (for different interpretations of this rider see G. E. M. de Ste Croix *ap.* Jones, *Athenian Democracy*, 168, P. A. Brunt, *Ancient Society and Institutions*, 71), *ATL* D 19/HMA 69 (before 431), *SEG* x 60 (?) (*c.* 430), M&L 68 (426/5), *SEG* x 87 (?) (*c.* 423/2), *IG* i² 94 (418/17), *SEG* xii 32 (418/17), M&L 73 (416/15?), 85 (410/09), *Svt* 255 (378/7), Tod 139 (*c.* 367?), *IG* ii² 176 (before 353/2). An amending νόμος of substance, *IG* ii² 140 (353/2). M&L 69 (425/4) a small point, but not purely routine.

3. *Riders extending to further recipients some or all of the honours granted in the main decree*: *Hesp.* xxi 3 (end C5), Tod 97. ii (403/2), *IG* ii² 32 (385/4), *Svt* 255 (378/7), *IG* ii² 84 (378–6), Tod 131. i (368/7) (see note at end of this table), 167 (347/6).

4. *Riders making more or less routine additions* (mostly in honorific decrees; some may deal with what was intentionally omitted from the original motion, but one or two certainly and perhaps many more are repairing accidental omissions):

   PUBLICATION—*IG* i² 84 (421/0), M&L 73 (416/15?), 94 (405/4), Tod 97. ii (403/2), *IG* ii² 19 (394/3) (repeating from original motion), *SIG*³ 158. i (369/8), *IG* ii² 109 (363/2), 206 (349/8), 232 (340/39), 289 (before 336/5) (publication at private expense?), 373 (322/1).

   INVITATION TO PRYTANEUM—Tod 97. i (403/2), *IG* ii² 19 (394/3), Tod 116 (386), *IG* ii² 109 (363/2), all repeating from original motion; M&L 94 (405/4), *IG* ii² 182 (before 353/2), 206 (349/8), 265 (before 336/5).

   RIGHT OF ΠΡΟΣΟΔΟΣ AND/OR PROTECTION FROM INJUSTICE—*SEG* x 76 (425/4), *IG* ii² 80 (before 378/7), *SIG*³ 158. i (369/8), *IG* ii² 188 (?) (before 353/2), 373 (322/1).

   ΓΗΣ/ΟΙΚΙΑΣ ΕΓΚΤΗΣΙΣ, etc.—*SEG* x 84. i (424/3) (ἀτέλεια, ἄλλο ἀγαθόν) (cf. J. Pečírka, *The Grant of Enktesis*, 2–4), 91 (421/0) (ἔγκτεσις, ἄλλο ἀγαθόν) (cf. Pečírka, op. cit., 8–12), M&L 70 (424/3 *or c.* 386) (motivation, ἔγκτησις καθάπερ τοῖς ἄλλοις προξένοις), *IG* ii² 80 (before 378/7) (ἀτέλεια, ἔγκτησις, judicial privileges καθάπερ τοῖς ἄλλοις προξένοις), 265 (before 336/5) (same as 80), 373 (322/1) (olive crown, ἔγκτησις).

Perhaps likely to be genuine additions:

addition to other honours of METIC PRIVILEGES—*IG* ii² 218 (346/5);
    of status of *ΕΥΕΡΓΕΤΗΣ—SEG* x 76 (425/4);
    of PROXENY—Tod 116 (386), *IG* ii² 235 (340/39);
    of CITIZENSHIP—*IG* ii² 19 (394/3), 109 (363/2).

Certainly to be thought of as corrections:

prytanes to δοῦναι ψῆφον for citizenship grant—*IG* ii² 448. i (323/2); thesmothetae to hold a δοκιμασία δωρεᾶς—pseudo-rider *IG* ii² 682 (after 256/5); revised motivation for honours—Tod 116 (386); cf. M&L 90 (408/7)—a manifest verbal correction.

5. *Riders following up open clause in probouleuma*: M&L 89. ii (407/6), and probably Tod 173 (*c.* 342).

NOTE. The rider to Tod 97. i simply repeats two clauses, one of them καθάπερ ἡ βουλὴ προβουλεύσασα [ἐς τὸν δῆμον ἐσ]ήνεγκεν, from the substantive motion (by the same man): perhaps the rider is to repair an unintentional omission, and the secretary has altered the main decree accordingly while preserving the rider (so Jones, 115; cf. M&L 90, 7–8 with 26 sqq., 89, 7–8 with 58–9). Miller, *De Decretis Atticis*, 46 sqq., followed Reifferscheid in claiming that here and in Tod 131. i the true purpose of the rider is to delete those clauses which are *not* repeated: this I find very hard to believe. In Tod 131. i Tod thought that the purpose of the rider was to extend the honours to further recipients (vol. ii, p. 97); alternatively, if as some have supposed the ambassadors of ll. 31–3 are identical with those of ll. 24–5, I presume the point of the rider will be to have them named in the decree and/or to read 'Lesbos' for 'Mytilene'.

For *IG* ii² 19, Tod 116, and *IG* ii² 109, where the rider includes a repetition of the invitation to the prytaneum, Miller's solution (p. 51) was similar but not identical: he did not suggest that any clauses in the probouleuma were in fact to be rejected, but he nevertheless thought that the invitation was repeated to ensure that no one supposed the clause was to be rejected. I know no satisfactory explanation of these riders.

TABLE K

Clauses requiring Immediate Action (αὐτίκα μάλα)

(See Ch. II, p. 75. I use superior letters to indicate: *A* αὐτίκα or αὐτίκα μάλα, *H* ἤδη. In other decrees there is no adverb of immediacy.)

1. *In the ecclesia, indicating an open clause in an otherwise specific probouleuma or συγγραφαί or motion produced from the floor of the house, and proving nothing about the origin of the motion*: M&L 65, 5 sqq. with 29 sqq. *A*; IG i² 88, 1–5; M&L 78, *b* 2 sqq. *A*; 89, 56–8* (in manifest probouleuma); Tod 114, 13 sqq. with 22 sqq. (ετδ, δτδ) *A*; 166, 5 sqq. *A*; 173, 33–5*; IG ii² 360, 62–3 with 35 sqq., 75 with 17 sqq. (probouleumata); P 6, 18–20 (ετδ, δτδ).

   (* In M&L 89 and Tod 173 the resultant decision is presented in a rider (RP) instead of the more usual bare footnote.)

2. *In the ecclesia, ordering the herald to make a vow on the spot*: IG ii² 30 (δτδ); Tod 144 (ετβκτδ, mention of δόγμα and probouleuma, δτδ) *A*; 146 (ετβκτδ, ψτδ) *A*.

3. *In the ecclesia, proving nothing*:

   (*a*) men to be elected for some job—HMA 30, 4 sqq. (συγγραφαί) *A*; M&L 52, 45–7 *A*; IG ii² 24, *b*, 12–14 *A*; Tod 123, 72–5 (ετβκτδ, ψτδ) *A*; 156, 4–6 (ετβκτδ) *A*; IG ii² 204, 5 sqq. *A* with 74 sqq.; 244, 28 sqq. (νόμος) *A*; 360, 37 sqq. with 46–7 (ψτδ: enlarging on probouleuma); 409, 10 sqq. *A*; 555, 16 sqq. ([δτδ] unnecessarily restored); 646, 40 sqq. (ετδ, δτδ); 648, 6 sqq. with 15–16; 653, 42 sqq. (ετδ, δτδ); 672, 36–7 *H* with 43 (ετβκτδ, δτδ, but second copy has ετδ); 682, 84 sqq. *H* with 98 sqq. (PF); (Add.) 687, 48 sqq. *A* with 68–9 (ετδ, δτδ); 793, 8–11 with 21–2; 1534 B, 149–51 *H* with 164–5 (ετβκτδ, PF); Hesp. vi 3+xiii 1944, pp. 250–4, ll. 5–6 with 23; IG ii² 839, 25 sqq. with 47 sqq. (ετβ, PF); iv² 84, 38 sqq. with 45–6 (δτβκτδ); also D.L. vii. 11 *H* with 12.

   (*b*) instructions to men in an official position—T. iv. 118. xiv (ετδ, MSS.) *A*; Tod 97, 21–2 (ετβκτδ; RP) *A*; 142, 42–5 (ετβκτδ, δτδ) *A*; IG ii² 148, 11 (?) *A*; 204, 34–6 *A*. Cf. 174, 5–11 (ετβκτδ; [RP]) (herald to make proclamation [ἐν τῶι αὐτί]κα μάλα ἐν ἄστει [ἄγωνι]).

4. *In the ecclesia, giving instructions or authority to boule*: Tod 103, 17 sqq. (ετβ but ecclesia must have ratified) *A*; 137, 14 sqq. (ετβκτδ) *A*.

5. *In the boule*: IG ii² 223 B, 2 *A*, 14 *A*; 840, 19 sqq. with 32 sqq.

6. *Footnotes implying a lost clause requiring immediate action*: ATL D 21, 17–18 (my type 1); SEG xii 32, 5–6 (my type 1); Tod 121, 16 sqq. (my type 3*a*).

TABLE L

ἄλλο ἀγαθόν Clauses

Several Athenian decrees contain a clause in which further benefits are offered to an honorand: εἶναι δὲ αὐτῶι καὶ ἄλλο παρὰ τοῦ δήμου εὑρέσθαι ἀγαθὸν ὅτου ἂν δοκῆι ἄξιος εἶναι, vel simile quid (for verbal variations, see IG ii² iv. i index, p. 51. ii, s.v. εὑρέσθαι). This normally takes the form either of an OPEN CLAUSE in which the proposer provides for further benefits to be added to his own (cf. Ch. II, pp. 66–7), or of a FUTURE PROMISE of further benefits if the honorand remains loyal to Athens. The table which follows lists ἄλλο ἀγαθόν clauses in decrees published in IG i² and IG ii² only (though I cite more recent texts when available).

Reference	Date	Formulae	Contents
SEG x 84	424/3	5–7 προσα[γ]αγόν[τον αὐτὸν hοι στρατεγοὶ καὶ hοι πρυτά]νες πρὸς τὲμ βο[λὲν καὶ τὸν δὲμον εὑρέσθαι hό τι ἂν δ]ύνεται ἀγαθόν taken up in RP	
M&L 89. ii	407/6	56 καὶ νῦν hευρίσκεσθαι αὐτὸς παρὰ τ[ὸ δ]έμο τὸ Ἀθεναίον hό τι ἂν δοκêι ἀγαθ[ὸν hô δέονται] (P. J. R.; ἀγαθ[ὸν τêι βουλêι] Meritt and Andrewes) (RP takes up different point)	
Tod 97. ii	403/2	ετβκτδ	20–1 OPEN CLAUSE; taken up in RP
143	363/2	ετβκτδ; PF	17–18 OPEN CLAUSE, taken up in RP
IG ii² 169	bef. 353/2	[δ]τδ	6 sqq. FUTURE PROMISE rest. haesitanter Kirchner
223 C	343/2	decree of boule: δτβ	14–15 OPEN CLAUSE (referring to demos: almost a probouleuma)
232	340/39	PF	12 sqq. OPEN CLAUSE, taken up in RP
235	340/39		0–3 OPEN CLAUSE, taken up in 4 sqq. ετδ RP
330. ii	336/5	ετβ; [δτβ]	turning at 42 sqq. into probouleuma containing simply this OPEN CLAUSE
424	aft. 336/5		small fragment with OPEN CLAUSE
360. iv	330/29	CPF	62 sqq. OPEN CLAUSE, taken up in decree ii
v	325/4	PF	75 sqq. OPEN CLAUSE, taken up in decree i
415	c. 330/29	ετβκτδ; PF	27 sqq. OPEN CLAUSE (stone ends)
456 b	(a 307/6)		20–2 OPEN CLAUSE

Reference	Date	Formulae	Contents
IG ii² 478	305/4	[ετ]βκτ[δ] ; PF	23 OPEN CLAUSE (decree very fragmentary)
479	305/4	PF	23–5 OPEN CLAUSE
501	302/1		1–4 OPEN CLAUSE ; 5 sqq. new decree (small fragment)
567	end C4		13–14 OPEN CLAUSE (narrow fragment)
579	end C4		5 sqq. [καὶ ἄλλο εὑρέσθαι ἐ]άν του δεή[ται ἀγαθόν, καὶ πρόσοδο]ν αὐτῶι [ε]ἶνα[ι πρὸς τὴν βουλὴν καὶ] τὸν δῆμον μετ[ὰ τὰ ἱερά] : FUTURE PROMISE crossed with πρόσοδος-clause
582	end C4		4–6 FUTURE PROMISE
Hesp. vii 1938, 106, A	282/1	ε[τδ] ; [δτ]δ	17–18 beginning of clause survives: type not clear
IG ii² (Add.) 687+ 686	267/6	ετδ ; δτδ	61–3 OPEN CLAUSE for further benefit from boule or demos
IG ii² 780. i	252/1	[ετδ] ; δτδ	agonothetes praised now ; 20–2 promised further benefit after euthynae
786	aft. 239/8	PF	28 sqq. FUTURE PROMISE
844. i	229/8	δτδ	27–8 FUTURE PROMISE
851	bef. 224/3	PF	17 sqq. FUTURE PROMISE
847	215/14	ετβκτδ ; PF	48 sqq. FUTURE PROMISE
856	end C3		8 sqq. FUTURE PROMISE
861	end C3	[ετβκτδ] ; PF	24–6 OPEN CLAUSE
862	end C3	PF	8–9 FUTURE PROMISE
884	c. 200	δτ[δ]	17 sqq. FUTURE PROMISE
926	beg. C2	PF	11–13 FUTURE PROMISE
844. iii	193/2	PF	68–70 FUTURE PROMISE
891	188/7	[ετ]δ ; δτδ	15–17 FUTURE PROMISE
892	188/7	(ετβκτδ ; lacuna prob. containing beginning of fresh decree)	12 sqq. FUTURE PROMISE
SEG xvi 84	188/7	[ε]τβκτδ	23–5 FUTURE PROMISE
SEG xxi 435	187/6	PF	8–9 FUTURE PROMISE
IG ii² 907	c. 170	PF	10 sqq. FUTURE PROMISE
908	c. 170	PF	15–17 FUTURE PROMISE
909	c. 170	[ετβ]κτδ ; PF	17–19 FUTURE PROMISE
980	mid C2	PF	20 sqq. FUTURE PROMISE
982	aft. mid C2	PF	13–15 FUTURE PROMISE
SEG xix 108	122/1	ετβκτδ ; PF	96 OPEN CLAUSE (cosmetes of ephebi)
IG ii² 1023	end C2	PF	23 sqq. FUTURE PROMISE
1028. ii	100/99	ετδ ; PF	102–3 OPEN CLAUSE (cosmetes of ephebi)

The OPEN CLAUSE occurs almost always with formulae of the probouleumatic type (*IG* ii² Add. 687+686 (267/6) is the only instance with non-probouleumatic formulae : it is also unique in providing for further benefits from the *boule or* demos—so that this is not a pure open clause but looks ahead to future meetings of the boule or ecclesia). But open clauses are possible in non-probouleumatic motions, and we cannot use the clause to argue a probouleumatic origin for decrees with no other indicating formulae. The open clause, like other indications that the demos might be expected to make up its own mind on a point, is very rare after the end of the fourth century.

The FUTURE PROMISE is found principally in the third and second centuries: probouleumatic decrees predominate (as in all enactments of the period) but there are some non-probouleumatic decrees containing this clause.

BIBLIOGRAPHY

For the most part I list here only those works which are cited in the course of the book, and of them I exclude (i) standard editions of literary texts cited only for their text or translation, and (ii) publications and re-publications of epigraphic texts except when there is matter of particular relevance in the commentary.

ACCAME, S. *La lega ateniese del sec. IV A.C.* (Stud. Ist. Stor. Ant., ii.) Rome: Signorelli, 1941.

ADCOCK, F. E. 'The Reform of the Athenian State.' *C.A.H.*, iv (1926), 26–58, ch. ii.

AGORA. *The Athenian Agora: a Guide to the Excavation and Museum²*. Athens: A.S.C.S.A., 1962.

ANDOCIDES. MACDOWELL, D. M. *Andokides on the Mysteries*. O.U.P., 1962.

ANDREWES, A. 'The Government of Classical Sparta.' *Ancient Society and Institutions: Studies presented to V. Ehrenberg* (Blackwell, 1966), 1–20.

—— and LEWIS, D. M. 'Notes on the Peace of Nikias.' *JHS* lxxvii 1957, 177–80.

ARISTOPHANES. COULON, V. *Aristophane*, vol. i⁶. (Coll. Budé.) Paris: Les Belles Lettres, 1958.

—— ROGERS, B. B. *The Thesmophoriazusae of Aristophanes*. Bell, 1904, reissued 1920.

[ARISTOTLE.] LEVI, M. A. *Commento storico alla Respublica Atheniensium di Aristotele*. (Testi e documenti per lo studio dell'antichità, xix.) 2 vols. Milan and Varese: Istituto Editoriale Cisalpino, 1968.

—— SANDYS, J. E. *Aristotle's Constitution of Athens²*. Macmillan, 1912.

ATKINSON, K. M. T. 'Athenian Legislative Procedure and Revision of Laws.' *BRL* xxiii 1939, 107–50; also published separately: Manchester U.P., 1939.

BACHMANN, L. *Anecdota Graeca e Codd. MSS. Bibl. Reg. Parisin*. 2 vols. Leipzig: Hinrichs, 1828.

BADIAN, E. 'Agis III.' *Hermes* xcv 1967, 170–92.

BANNIER, W. 'Zu attischen Inschriften, XIII.' *PW* xlii 1922, 835–9.

BATES, F. O. *The Five Post-Kleisthenean Tribes*. (Cornell Studies in Classical Philology, viii.) New York: Macmillan for Cornell U., 1898.

BEAZLEY, J. D. *Attic Red-Figure Vase-Painters²*. 3 vols. O.U.P., 1963.

BEKKER, I. *Anecdota Graeca*. Vol. i, containing the *Lexica Segueriana*, Berlin: Nauck, 1814. (Vols. ii/iii, Berlin: Reimer, 1816/21.)

BELOCH, K. J. 'Griechische Aufgebote, i.' *Klio* v 1905, 341–74.

—— *Griechische Geschichte²*. 4 vols. in 8. Strasbourg: Trübner, 1912–16 (vols. i–ii), Berlin and Leipzig: de Gruyter, 1922–7 (vols. iii–iv).

BENGTSON, H (ed.). *Die Staatsverträge des Altertums*. vol. ii. Munich and Berlin: Beck for Kommission für Alte Geschichte und Epigraphik, 1962. (I have not used vol. iii, edited by SCHMITT, H. H., 1969.)

BERNEKER, E. Art. εἰσαγγελία. *Der Kleine Pauly*, ii (1967), 217–18.

BICKERMAN, E. J. *Chronology of the Ancient World*. (Aspects of Greek and Roman Life.) Thames & Hudson, 1968.

BILLHEIMER, A. 'Amendments in Athenian Decrees.' *AJA*² xlii 1938, 456–85.

BLASS, F. *Die attische Beredsamkeit*². 3 vols. Leipzig: Teubner, 1887/92/98.

BOECKH, A. *Urkunden über das Seewesen des Attischen Staates*. 2 vols. Berlin: Reimer, 1840.

BONNER, R. J. and SMITH, G. *The Administration of Justice from Homer to Aristotle*. 2 vols. U. of Chicago P., 1930/8.

BOWERSOCK, G. W. 'Pseudo-Xenophon.' *HSCP* lxxi 1966, 33–55.

BRADEEN, D. W. 'The Trittyes in Cleisthenes' Reforms.' *TAPA* lxxxvi 1955, 22–30.

BRILLANT, M. *Les secrétaires athéniens*. (Bibl. de l'École des Hautes Études, 191.) Paris: Champion, 1911.

BRONEER, O. 'Notes on the Xanthippos Ostrakon.' *AJA*² lii 1948, 341–3.

BRUNT, P. A. 'Spartan Policy and Strategy in the Archidamian War.' *Phoen.* xix 1965, 255–80.

—— 'Athenian Settlements Abroad in the Fifth Century B.C.' *Ancient Society and Institutions: Studies presented to V. Ehrenberg* (Blackwell, 1966), 71–92.

BUCHANAN, J. J. *Theorika*. Locust Valley: Augustin, 1962.

BURN, A. R. 'A Biographical Source on Phaiax and Alkibiades?' *CQ*² iv 1954, 138–42.

—— *Persia and the Greeks*. Arnold, 1962.

BUSOLT, G., revised by SWOBODA, H. *Griechische Staatskunde*. 2 vols. (HdA, iv. 1. 1.) Munich: Beck, 1920/6.

CADOUX, T. J. 'The Athenian Archons from Kreon to Hypsichides.' *JHS* lxviii 1948, 70–123.

CARCOPINO, J. *L'ostracisme athénien*. (2nd edition of *Histoire de l'ostracisme athénien*.) Paris: Alcan, 1935.

CARTER, J. M. 'Eighteen Years Old?' *BICS* xiv 1967, 51–7.

CAWKWELL, G. L. 'Aeschines and the Peace of Philocrates.' *REG* lxxiii 1960, 416–38.

—— 'Notes on the Social War.' *C&M* xxiii 1962, 34–49.

—— 'The Defence of Olynthus.' *CQ*² xii 1962, 122–40.

—— 'Aeschines and the Ruin of Phocis in 346.' *REG* lxxv 1962, 453–9.

—— 'Demosthenes' Policy after the Peace of Philocrates.' *CQ*² xiii 1963, 120–38, 200–13.

—— 'Eubulus.' *JHS* lxxxiii 1963, 47–69.

—— 'The Crowning of Demosthenes.' *CQ*² xix 1969, 163–80.

CHAMBERS, M. H. 'Notes on the Text of the *Ath. Pol.*' *TAPA* xcvi 1965, 31–9.

CHARITONIDES, S. 'The First Half of a Bouleutai List of the Fourth Century B.C.' *Hesp.* xxx 1961, 30–57.

CLOCHÉ, P. E. C. L. 'Le Conseil athénien des Cinq Cents et la peine de mort.' *REG* xxxiii 1920, 1–50.

—— 'L'importance des pouvoirs de la Boulè athénienne aux Vᵉ et IVᵉ siècles avant J.-C.' *REG* xxxiv 1921, 233–65.

—— 'La Boulè d'Athènes en 508/507 avant J.-C.' *REG* xxxvii 1924, 1–26.

—— 'A propos d'une étude sur les pouvoirs judiciaires du Conseil athénien des Cinq Cents.' *LEC* xii 1943–4, 114–17.

CROSBY, M. 'The Leases of the Laureion Mines.' *Hesp.* xix 1950, 189–297.

—— *See* LANG, M. and CROSBY, M.

DAVIES, J. K. *Athenian Propertied Families, 600–300 B.C.* 3 vols. Oxford thesis, 1965. (I have not used the published version: O.U.P., 1971.)

—— 'Demosthenes on Liturgies: a Note.' *JHS* lxxxvii 1967, 33–40.

—— 'The Date of *IG* ii² 1609.' *Hist.* xviii 1969, 309–33.

DAVISON, J. A. 'Notes on the Panathenaea.' *JHS* lxxviii 1958, 23–42.

DELZ, J. *Lukians Kenntnis der athenischen Antiquitäten*. Basle thesis, 1950.

DEMOSTHENES. GERNET, L. *Démosthène: plaidoyers civils*, vol. iii. Discours XLIX–LVI. (Coll. Budé.) Paris: Les Belles Lettres, 1959.

DE SANCTIS, G. 'Epigraphica, XIII. La τάξις φόρου del 425 a. C.' *RFIC* lxiii (= ² xiii) 1935, 52–60.

DE STE CROIX, G. E. M. 'The Constitution of the Five Thousand.' *Hist.* v 1956, 1–23.

—— 'The Alleged Secret Pact between Athens and Philip II concerning Amphipolis and Pydna.' *CQ*² xiii 1963, 110–19.

—— Review of BUCHANAN, *Theorika. CR*² xiv 1964, 190–2.

DINSMOOR, W. B. *The Archons of Athens in the Hellenistic Age*. Harvard U.P. for A.S.C.S.A., 1931.

—— 'The Burning of the Opisthodomos at Athens.' *AJA*² xxxvi 1932, 143–72, 307–26.

DITTENBERGER, W. Zu den attischen Ephebeninschriften. *Hermes* xii 1877, 1–22.

DODDS, E. R. 'Morals and Politics in the *Oresteia*.' *PCPS*² vi 1960, 19–31.

DOVER, K. J. 'δέκατος αὐτός.' *JHS* lxxx 1960, 61–77.

—— Art. Aristophanes (1). *Oxford Classical Dictionary*² (1970), 113–14.

DOW, S. *Prytaneis. Hesp.* Supp. i 1937.

—— 'The Law Codes of Athens.' *Proc. Mass. Hist. Soc.* lxxi 1953–7, 3–35.

—— 'Thucydides and the Number of Acharnian *Hoplitai*.' *TAPA* xcii 1961, 66–80.

—— 'The Athenian Anagrapheis.' *HSCP* lxvii 1963, 37–54.

—— 'Three Athenian Decrees: Method in the Restoration of Preambles.' *HSCP* lxvii 1963, 55–75.

—— 'The Preambles of Athenian Decrees containing Lists of Symproedroi.' *Hesp.* xxxii 1963, 335–65.

—— and TRAVIS, A. H. 'Demetrios of Phaleron and his Lawgiving.' *Hesp.* xii 1943, 144–65.

EDDY, S. K. 'Athens' Peacetime Navy in the Age of Perikles.' *GR&BS* ix 1968, 141–56.

EHRENBERG, V. L. 'Origins of Democracy.' *Hist.* i 1950, 515–48 = *Polis und Imperium* (Zürich and Stuttgart: Artemis, 1965), 264–97.

—— *The Greek State*. 2nd English edition, Methuen, 1969.

ELIOT, C. W. J. *Coastal Demes of Attika. Phoen.* Supp. v 1962.

—— 'Aristotle, *Ath Pol*. 44. i, and the Meaning of Trittys.' *Phoen.* xxi 1967, 79–84.

—— 'Kleisthenes and the Creation of the Ten Phylai.' *Phoen.* xxii 1968, 3–17.

FERGUSON, W. S. *The Athenian Secretaries*. (Cornell Studies in Classical Philology, vii.) New York: Macmillan for Cornell U., 1898.

—— 'The Revolution at Athens of the Year 103/2 B.C.' *Klio* iv 1904, 1–17.

—— 'Researches in Athenian and Delian Documents, 11. The Athenian Generals.' *Klio* ix 1909, 314–23.

—— 'Researches . . ., 12. Constitutional Crises in the 1st Century B.C.' *Klio* ix 1909, 323–30.

—— 'Researches . . ., Appendix.' *Klio* ix 1909, 330–40.

—— *Hellenistic Athens*. Macmillan, 1911.

—— 'The Introduction of the Secretary-Cycle.' *Klio* xiv 1914–15, 393–7.

—— 'Lachares and Poliorcetes.' *CP* xxiv 1929, 1–31.

—— 'The Condemnation of Antiphon.' *Mélanges Glotz* (Paris: P.U.F., 1932), i. 349–66.

—— *Athenian Tribal Cycles*. (Harvard Historical Monographs, i.) Harvard U.P., 1932.

—— *The Treasurers of Athena*. Harvard U.P., 1932.

FORBES, C. A. *Greek Physical Education*. New York: Century, 1929.

FORREST, W. G. G. *The Emergence of Greek Democracy*. (World University Library.) Weidenfeld & Nicolson, 1966.

—— 'Legislation in Sparta.' *Phoen.* xxi 1967, 11–19.

FOUCART, P. 'Aristote, Constitution d'Athènes. Notes sur la seconde partie.' *RPh²* xviii 1894, 244–51, xix 1895, 24–31.

—— 'Aristote, Πολιτεία Ἀθηναίων, 62. ii.' *RPh²* xlii 1918, 55–9.

FRANCOTTE, H. 'De la législation athénienne sur les distinctions honorifiques.' *MB* iii 1899, 246–81, iv 1900, 55–75, 105–23.

FREEMAN, K. *The Work and Life of Solon*. U. of Wales P., 1926.

FROST, F. J. 'Pericles and Dracontides.' *JHS* lxxxiv 1964, 69–72.

GEAGAN, D. J. *The Athenian Constitution after Sulla*. *Hesp.* Supp. xii 1967.

GIFFLER, M. 'The Introduction of the Independent Conciliar Year.' *AJP* lx 1939, 436–44.

GILBERT, G., trans. BROOKS, E. J. and NICKLIN, T. *The Constitutional Antiquities of Sparta and Athens*. Sonnenschein, 1895.

GLOTZ, G. Art. Epimélêtai, 3. Epimélêtai tôn neôriôn. DAREMBERG, C. V., and SAGLIO, E., *Dictionnaire des antiquités grecques et romaines*, vol. II. i (Paris: Hachette, 1887), 669. ii–673. i.

—— 'L'épistate des proèdres.' *REG* xxxiv 1921, 1–19.

—— trans. MALLINSON, N. *The Greek City*. Kegan Paul, 1929.

—— 'Démosthène et les finances athéniennes de 346 à 339.' *RH* clxx 1932 (ii), 385–97.

—— with COHEN, R. *Histoire Générale: Histoire grecque*. Vols. I, II, III, IV. i (IV. i by GLOTZ, G., and ROUSSEL, P., with COHEN, R.) Paris: P.U.F., 1925/29/36/39. (2nd edn. of iv. 1, 1945.)

GOMME, A. W. *The Population of Athens in the Fifth and Fourth Centuries B.C.* Blackwell, 1933.

—— Review of ATKINSON, *BRL* xxiii 1939. *CR* liv 1940, 38.

—— 'The Working of the Athenian Democracy.' *History²* xxxvi 1951, 12–28 = *More Essays in Greek History and Literature* (Blackwell, 1962), 177–93.

—— 'Thucydides, ii. 13. iii.' *Hist.* ii 1953–4, 1–21.

—— 'Thucydides, ii. 13. iii: an Answer to Professor Meritt.' *Hist.* iii 1954–5, 333–8.

—— Review of JONES, *Athenian Democracy. JHS* lxxix 1959, 182–4.

GRAINDOR, P. *Album d'inscriptions attiques d'époque impériale.* 2 vols. (U. de Gand, Rec. Fac. Phil. et Lett., liii–liv.) Ghent: Van Rysselberghe & Rombaut, and Paris: Champion, 1924.

—— *Athènes sous Auguste.* (Rec. Fac. Lett., i.) Cairo: Misr for U. of Egypt, 1927.

—— *Athènes de Tibère à Trajan.* (Rec. Fac. Lett., viii.) Cairo: Misr for U. of Egypt, 1931.

—— *Athènes sous Hadrien.* Cairo: Ministry of Public Instruction, 1934.

GRIFFITH, G. T. 'Isegoria in the Assembly at Athens.' *Ancient Society and Institutions: Studies presented to V. Ehrenberg* (Blackwell, 1966), 115–38.

GUILLON, P. 'Le décret athénien relatif aux prémices d'Éleusis et la Paix de Nicias.' *BCH* lxxxvi 1962, 467–75.

HABICHT, C. *Falsche Urkunden zur Geschichte Athens im Zeitalter der Perserkriege. Hermes* lxxxix 1961, 1–35.

HAGER, H. 'On the Eisangelia.' *JP* iv 1872, 74–112.

HAMMOND, N. G. L. 'Strategia and Hegemonia in Fifth-century Athens.' *CQ*² xix 1969, 111–44.

HARRISON, A. R. W. 'Law-making at Athens at the End of the Fifth Century B.C.' *JHS* lxxv 1955, 26–35.

HARTEL, W. VON. 'Studien über attisches Staatsrecht und Urkundenwesen.' *Sb. Wien* xc. 3, May 1878, 543–624, xci. 1, June 1878, 101–94, xcii. 1, October 1878, 87–184; also published separately: Vienna: Gerold, 1878.

HELBIG, W. 'Les ἱππεῖς athéniens.' *Mém. Ac. Inscr. et Belles-Lettres,* xxxvii. 1 1904, 157–264; also published separately: Paris: Kincksieck, 1902.

HENDERSON, B. W. *The Great War between Athens and Sparta.* Macmillan, 1927.

HEREWARD, D. 'New Fragments of *IG* ii² 10.' *BSA* xlvii 1952, 102–17.

HERODOTUS. MACAN, R. W. *Herodotus: the Fourth, Fifth and Sixth Books.* 2 vols. Macmillan, 1895.

HEYDEMANN, V. *De Senatu Atheniensium Quaestiones Epigraphicae Selectae.* Strasbourg thesis, 1880.

HIGNETT, C. *A History of the Athenian Constitution to the End of the Fifth Century B.C.* O.U.P., 1952.

—— *Xerxes' Invasion of Greece.* O.U.P., 1963.

HILL, G. F., revised by MEIGGS, R., and ANDREWES, A. *Sources for Greek History between the Persian and Peloponnesian Wars.* O.U.P., 1951.

HOPPER, R. J. 'The Attic Silver Mines in the Fourth Century B.C.' *BSA* xlviii 1953, 200–54.

HOUSEHOLDER, F. W., Jr. 'The Mock Decrees in Lucian.' *TAPA* lxxi 1940, 199–216.

JACOBY, F. *Die Fragmente der griechischen Historiker.* Vols. i–ii/iii, in fascicles. Berlin: Weidmann, 1926–30/Leiden: Brill, 1940–58 (enlarged reprint of vol. i, 1957).

JAMESON, M. H. 'The Provisions for Mobilization in the Decree of Themistokles.' *Hist.* xii 1963, 385–404.

JEFFERY, L. H. *The Local Scripts of Archaic Greece.* (Oxford Monographs on Classical Archaeology.) O.U.P., 1961.

JOHNSON, A. C. 'Notes on Attic Inscriptions.' *CP* ix 1914, 417–41.

JONES, A. H. M. *Athenian Democracy.* Blackwell, 1957. (Partly composed of essays previously published elsewhere.)

JUST, M. 'Die ἀποδοκιμασία der athenischen βουλή und ihre Anfechtung.' *Hist.* xix 1970, 132–40.

KAHRSTEDT, U. *Staatsgebiet und Staatsangehörige in Athen.* (Studien zum öffentlichen Recht Athens, i.) Stuttgart and Berlin: Kohlhammer, 1934.

—— Review of MERITT, *Athenian Financial Documents,* and MERITT and WEST, *The Athenian Assessment. GGA* cxcvii 1935, 41–54.

—— *Untersuchungen zur Magistratur in Athen.* (Studien zum öffentlichen Recht Athens, ii.) Stuttgart: Kohlhammer, 1936.

—— 'Untersuchungen zu athenischen Behörden, II. Die Nomotheten und die Legislative in Athen.' *Klio* xxxi 1938, 1–32.

—— 'Untersuchungen zu athenischen Behörden, IV. Bemerkungen zur Geschichte des Rats der Fünfhundert.' *Klio* xxxiii 1940, 1–12.

KEIL, B. 'Athens Amtsjahre und Kalenderjahre im V. Jahrhundert.' *Hermes* xxix 1894, 32–81.

—— 'Das System des Kleisthenischen Staatskalenders.' *Hermes* xxix 1894, 321–72.

—— 'Die Rechnungen über den epidaurischen Tholosbau.' *AM* xx 1895, 20–115.

—— 'Die Ἀμφιαράϊα in Aristot. Πολ. Ἀθην. 54. vii.' *Hermes* xxx 1895, 473–5.

—— *Anonymus Argentinensis.* Strasbourg: Trübner, 1902.

—— *Beiträge zur Geschichte des Areopags. Ber. Leipzig* lxxi. 8, 1919.

KIRCHNER, J. *Prosopographia Attica.* 2 vols. Berlin: Reimer, 1901/3.

KIRSTEN, E. 'Der gegenwärtige Stand der attischen Demenforschung.' *Atti del 3° Congresso Internazionale di Epigrafia Greca e Latina* (Rome: L'Erma di Bretschneider, 1959), 155–71.

KLAFFENBACH, G. *Griechische Epigraphik.*[2] (Studienhefte zur Altertumswissenschaft, vi.) Göttingen: Vandenhoeck & Ruprecht, 1966.

KOCH, E. Art. δοκιμασία. *RE,* v (1905), 1268–73.

KÖRTE, G. 'Dokimasie der attischen Reiterei.' *AZ* xxxviii 1880, 177–81.

KOLBE, W. 'Zur athenischen Marinerverwaltung.' *AM* xxvi 1901, 377–418.

—— *Die attischen Archonten von 293/2–31/0 v. Chr. Abh. Göttingen*[2] x. 4, 1908.

KRAUS, W. Art. Aristophanes (3). *Der Kleine Pauly,* i (1964), 575–80.

LAMBRECHTS, A. *Texst en Uitzicht van de Atheense Proxeniedecreten tot 323 v.C.* (K.V.Ac. Wetenschappen, Klasse der Letteren, xxxii.) Brussels: Paleis der Academiën, 1958. (In Flemish, but with summary in French.)

LANG, M., and CROSBY, M. *The Athenian Agora,* x. *Weights, Measures and Tokens.* (Comprises LANG, 'Weights and Measures', and CROSBY, 'Lead and Clay Tokens'.) Princeton: A.S.C.S.A., 1964.

LAQUEUR, R. *Epigraphische Untersuchungen zu den griechischen Volksbeschlüssen.* Leipzig and Berlin: Teubner, 1927.

LARFELD, W. *Handbuch der griechischen Epigraphik*. Vols. I, II. i, II. ii. Leipzig: Reisland, 1907/1898/1902.
—— *Griechische Epigraphik.*³ (HdA, i. 5.) Munich: Beck, 1914.
LARSEN, J. A. O. *Representative Government in Greek and Roman History*. (Sather Lectures, xxviii.) U. of California P., 1955.
—— 'A Note on the Representation of Demes in the Athenian Boule.' *CP* lvii 1962, 104–8.
LATTE, K. and ERBSE, H. *Lexica Graeca Minora*. Hildesheim: Olms, 1965.
LEPPER, F. A. 'Some Rubrics in the Athenian Quota-Lists.' *JHS* lxxxii 1962, 25–55.
LEVI, D. 'Il Pritaneo e la Tholos di Atene.' *ASAA* vi–vii 1923–4, 1–25.
LEWIS, D. M. 'Notes on Attic Inscriptions, vi. The Epistates of the Proedroi.' *BSA* xlix 1954, 31–4.
—— 'Notes . . ., ix. *IG* ii² 145.' *BSA* xlix 1954, 36–7.
—— 'Notes . . ., xiii. Androtion and the Temple Treasures.' *BSA* xlix 1954, 39–49.
—— 'Notes . . ., xxiv. The Deme Kolonos.' *BSA* l 1955, 12–17.
—— 'Notes . . ., xxv. Choregoi of Pandionis.' *BSA* l 1955, 17–24.
—— 'Notes . . ., xxvi. Elaphebolion 346.' *BSA* l 1955, 25–6.
—— 'Notes . . ., xxvii. A Bouleutai List.' *BSA* l 1955, 26–7.
—— 'Notes . . ., xxix. The Diaitetai of 330–29.' *BSA* l 1955, 27–36.
—— 'The Deme Ikarion.' *BSA* li 1956, 172.
—— 'Law of the Lesser Panathenaia.' *Hesp.* xxviii 1959, 239–47.
—— 'On the Financial Offices of Eubulus and Lycurgus.' Unpublished essay (cited by G. L. CAWKWELL, *CQ*² xiii 1963, *JHS* lxxxiii 1963, *CQ*² xix 1969), 1960.
—— 'Cleisthenes and Attica.' *Hist.* xii 1963, 22–40.
—— Review of MERITT, *The Athenian Year*. *JHS* lxxxiii 1963, 195–6.
—— 'A Note on *IG* i² 114.' *JHS* lxxxvii 1967, 132.
LIPSIUS, J. H. 'Procheirotonie und Epicheirotonie.' *LSKP* xvii 1896, 405–12.
—— *Das attische Recht und Rechtsverfahren*. Vols. I, II. i, II. ii, III. Leipzig: Reisland, 1905/08/12/15.
LOEPER, R. 'Die Trittyen und Demen Attikas.' *AM* xvii 1892, 319–433.
McDONALD, W. A. *The Political Meeting Places of the Greeks*. (Johns Hopkins Studies in Archaeology, xxxiv.) Baltimore: Johns Hopkins Press, 1943.
McGREGOR, M. F. 'Kleon, Nikias, and the Trebling of the Tribute.' *TAPA* lxvi 1935, 146–64.
MAIER, F. G. *Griechische Mauerbauinschriften*. 2 vols. (Vestigia, i–ii.) Heidelberg: Quelle und Meyer, 1959/61.
MATTINGLY, H. B. 'The Athenian Coinage Decree.' *Hist.* x 1961, 148–88.
—— 'Athens and Euboea.' *JHS* lxxxi 1961, 124–32.
—— 'Note on *IG* i² 76 (Eleusinian Firstfruits Decree).' *BCH* lxxxvii 1963, 391.
—— 'The Growth of Athenian Imperialism.' *Hist.* xii 1963, 257–73.
—— 'The Financial Decrees of Kallias (*IG* i² 91/2).' *PACA* vii 1964, 35–55.
—— 'The Peace of Kallias.' *Hist.* xiv 1965, 273–81.
—— 'Periclean Imperialism.' *Ancient Society and Institutions: Studies presented to V. Ehrenberg* (Blackwell, 1966), 193–223.

MATTINGLY, H. B. 'Athens, Delphi and Eleusis in the Late 420s.' *PACA* ix 1966, 61–76.

—— 'Two Notes on Athenian Financial Documents, 2. The Date of the Kallias Decrees.' *BSA* lxii 1967, 14–17.

—— 'Athenian Finance in the Peloponnesian War.' *BCH* xcii 1968, 450–85.

MEIGGS, R. Review of MERITT, etc., *ATL*, vol. iii. *CR²* ii 1952, 97–100.

—— and LEWIS, D. M. *A Selection of Greek Historical Inscriptions to the End of the Fifth Century B.C.* O.U.P., 1969.

MERITT, B. D. *The Athenian Calendar in the Fifth Century.* Harvard U.P. for A.S.C.S.A., 1928.

—— 'Senatorial and Civil Years in Athens.' *CP* xxv 1930, 236–43.

—— *Athenian Financial Documents of the Fifth Century* (Humanistic Series, xxvii.) U. of Michigan P., 1932.

—— 'Some Details of the Athenian Constitution.' *AJP* lvi 1935, 317–23.

—— 'Archelaos and the Decelean War.' *Classical Studies presented to E. Capps* (Princeton U.P., 1936), 246–52.

—— 'Greek Inscriptions, 4. The Statue of Athena Promachos.' *Hesp.* v 1936, 362–80.

—— 'Greek Inscriptions, 9. Sales of Confiscated Properties.' *Hesp.* v 1936, 390–3.

—— 'Greek Inscriptions, 10. Leases of Mines and Sales of Confiscated Property, including that of Philokrates the Hagnousian.' *Hesp.* v 1936, 393–413.

—— 'The Athenian Assessment Decree.' *AJP* lviii 1937, 152–6.

—— *Documents on Athenian Tribute.* Harvard U.P., 1937.

—— 'Greek Inscriptions, 22. A Decree honoring Proxenides.' *Hesp.* viii 1939, 65–9.

—— *Epigraphica Attica.* (Martin Classical Lectures, ix.) Harvard U.P., 1940.

—— 'Greek Inscriptions, 11.' *Hesp.* x 1941, 42–9.

—— 'Notes on Attic Decrees. *IG* i² 70.' *Hesp.* x 1941, 320–6.

—— 'Attic Inscriptions of the Fifth Century, 10. Athens and Chios.' *Hesp.* xiv 1945, 115–19.

—— 'Note on the Athenian Calendar.' *CQ* xl 1946, 45–6.

—— 'Greek Inscriptions, 41.' *Hesp.* xvi 1947, 150–1.

—— 'Notes on Attic Inscriptions.' *AJP* lxix 1948, 69–73.

—— 'Greek Inscriptions, 5. Law against Tyranny.' *Hesp.* xxi 1952, 355–9.

—— 'The Entrance to the Areopagus.' *Hesp.* xxii 1953, 129.

—— 'Indirect Tradition in Thucydides.' *Hesp.* xxiii 1954, 185–231.

—— 'The Archonship of Symmachos.' *AJP* lxxviii 1957, 375–81.

—— 'Greek Inscriptions, 22.' *Hesp.* xxvi 1957, 72–7.

—— 'Greek Inscriptions, 3.' *Hesp.* xxix 1960, 2–4.

—— *The Athenian Year.* (Sather Lectures, xxxii.) U. of California P., 1961.

—— 'First-Fruits at Eleusis.' *CW* lvi 1962–3, 39–41.

—— 'Greek Inscriptions, 17.' *Hesp.* xxxii 1963, 17–19.

—— 'Greek Inscriptions, 27.' *Hesp.* xxxii 1963, 26–30.

—— 'The Year of Neaichmos (320/19 B.C.).' *Hesp.* xxxii 1963, 425–38.

—— 'Notes on *Epigraphica Restituta*.' *AJP* lxxxv 1964, 412–17.

—— 'Greek Inscriptions, 37.' *Hesp.* xxxiii 1964, 186–9.

—— 'Greek Inscriptions, 53.' *Hesp.* xxxiii 1964, 201–9.

—— 'Athenian Calendar Problems.' *TAPA* xcv 1964, 200–60.

—— 'Polyeuktos and Philoneos.' *The Classical Tradition: Literary and Historical Studies in Honor of H. Caplan* (Cornell U.P., 1966), 26–42.

—— 'Collectors of Athenian Tribute.' *AJP* lxxxviii 1967, 29–32.

—— 'Greek Historical Studies.' *Lectures in Memory of L. T. Semple, First Series, 1961–5* (U. of Cincinnati Classical Studies, i. Princeton U.P. for U. of Cincinnati, 1967), 95–132.

—— and McGREGOR, M. F. 'The Athenian Quota-List of 421/0 B.C.' *Phoen.* xxi 1967, 85–91.

—— and WADE-GERY, H. T. 'The Dating of Documents to the Mid-Fifth Century.' *JHS* lxxxii 1962, 67–74, lxxxiii 1963, 100–17.

—— WADE-GERY, H. T., and McGREGOR, M. F. *The Athenian Tribute Lists.* 4 vols. Harvard U.P. for A.S.C.S.A. (vol. i)/Princeton: A.S.C.S.A. (vols. ii–iv), 1939/49/50/53.

—— and WEST, A. B. *The Athenian Assessment of 425 B.C.* (Humanistic Series, xxxiii.) U. of Michigan P., 1934.

MILCHHÖFER, A. 'Über Standpunkt und Methode der attischen Demenforschung.' *Sb. Berlin* 1887, iv, 41–56.

—— 'Untersuchungen über die Demenordnung des Kleisthenes.' *Abh. Berlin* 1892.

MILLER, H. A. E. O. *De Decretis Atticis Quaestiones Epigraphicae.* Breslau: Grass, Barth, 1885.

MILTNER, F. Art. Trieropoioi. *RE*, vii A (1939–48), 121.

MITCHEL, F. W. 'Demades of Paeania and *IG* ii² 1493, 1494, 1495.' *TAPA* xciii 1962, 213–29.

—— 'A Note on *IG* ii² 370.' *Phoen.* xviii 1964, 13–17.

NESSELHAUF, H. Review of MERITT and WEST, *The Athenian Assessment.* *Gnomon* xii 1936, 296–301.

NOTOPOULOS, J. A. 'The Conciliar and Civil Calendar in *IG* i² 324.' *AJP* lxvi 1945, 411–14.

—— 'The Date of the Creation of Hadrianis.' *TAPA* lxxvii 1946, 53–6.

OEHLER, J. Art. ἱεροποιοί. *RE*, viii (1913), 1583–8.

—— Art. κωλακρέται. *RE*, xi (1922), 1068–9.

ΟΙΚΟΝΟΜΙΔΗΣ, Α. Ν. "Δημάδου τοῦ Παιανέως ψηφίσματα, καὶ ἐπιγραφικαὶ περὶ τοῦ βίου πηγαί." *Πλάτων* viii 1956, 105–29.

OLIVER, J. H. 'Greek Inscriptions, 1–2.' *Hesp.* iv 1935, 1–32.

—— 'Greek Inscriptions (introductory note).' *Hesp.* xi 1942, 29–30.

—— 'Patrons providing Financial Aid to the Tribes of Roman Athens.' *AJP* lxx 1949, 299–308.

—— *The Athenian Expounders of the Sacred and Ancestral Law.* Baltimore: Johns Hopkins Press, 1950.

—— 'The Eleusinian Endowment.' *Hesp.* xxi 1952, 381–99.

—— 'New Fragments of Sacred Gerusia 24.' *Hesp.* xxx 1961, 402–3.

OOTEGHEM, J. VAN. 'Démosthène et le théoricon.' *LEC* i 1932, 388–407.

OSTWALD, M. *Nomos and the Beginnings of the Athenian Democracy.* O.U.P., 1969.

PEČÍRKA, J. 'Disiungenda, 1. *IG* ii² 289 and *IG* ii² 372 (cf. *SEG* xxi 300).' *LF* lxxxix 1966, 262–6.

—— *The Formula for the Grant of Enktesis in Attic Inscriptions.* Prague: *Acta Universitatis Carolinae, Phil. et Hist. Mon.* xv 1966.

PEEK, W. 'Attische Inschriften, 31. *IG* ii² 2440.' *AM* lxxvii 1942 (published 1951), 32.

PÉLÉKIDIS, CH. 'Notes d'épigraphie attique.' *REG* lxiii 1950, 107–20.

—— *Histoire de l'éphébie attique des origines à 31 avant Jésus-Christ.* (École française d'Athènes: Travaux et Mémoires, xiii.) Paris: Boccard, 1962.

PEREMANS, W. 'La juridiction pénale de la Boulè à Athènes au début du Vᵉ siècle avant J.-C.' *LEC* x 1941, 193–201. (*See also* SENCIE, J., and PEREMANS, W.)

PERLMAN, S. 'The Politicians in the Athenian Democracy of the Fourth Century B.C.' *Athen.*² xli 1963, 327–55.

PHILIPPSON, A., ed. LEHMANN, H., and KIRSTEN, E. *Die griechischen Landschaften,* vol. I. iii. *Attika und Megaris.* Frankfurt a. M.: Klostermann, 1952.

PICKARD-CAMBRIDGE, A. W., revised by GOULD, J. P. A., and LEWIS, D. M. *The Dramatic Festivals of Athens.* O.U.P., 1968.

PLATNAUER, M. Art. Aristophanes (1). *Oxford Classical Dictionary* (1949), 92–4.

PLUTARCH. LIMENTANI, I. C. *Plutarchi Vita Aristidis.* (Bibl. Stud. Sup., xlviii.) Florence: La Nuova Italia, 1964.

PRITCHETT, W. K. 'A Decree of the Year of Koroibos.' *AJP* lviii 1937, 329–33.

—— Review of Dow, *Hesp.* Supp. i 1937. *AJP* lx 1939, 257–60.

—— 'The Composition of the Tribes Antigonis and Demetrias.' *AJP* lxi 1940, 186–93.

—— 'Greek Inscriptions, 70, Titles of Officials.' *Hesp.* x 1941, 270–3.

—— 'The Tribe Ptolemais.' *AJP* lxiii 1942, 413–31.

—— *The Five Attic Tribes after Kleisthenes.* Johns Hopkins thesis, 1942 (published 1943). (Ch. i = *AJP* lxi 1940, *cit. supr.*; ch. ii = *AJP* lxiii 1942, *cit. supr.*)

—— 'An Unfinished Inscription, *IG* ii² 2362.' *TAPA* lxxxv 1954, 159–67.

—— 'Calendars of Athens again.' *BCH* lxxxi 1957, 269–301.

—— *Ancient Athenian Calendars on Stone.* (U. of California Publ. in Class. Arch., iv. 4.) U. of California P., 1963.

—— 'Epigraphica Restituta.' *AJP* lxxxv 1964, 40–55.

—— 'Expenditure of Athena, 408–406 B.C., and the Hellenotamiai.' *BCH* lxxxviii 1964, 455–81.

—— 'Gaming Tables and *IG* i² 324.' *Hesp.* xxxiv 1965, 131–47.

—— and MERITT, B. D. *The Chronology of Hellenistic Athens.* Harvard U.P. for A.S.C.S.A., 1940.

—— and NEUGEBAUER, O. *The Calendars of Athens.* Harvard U.P. for A.S.C.S.A., 1947.

PROTT, H. VON, and ZIEHEN, L. *Leges Graecorum Sacrae e Titulis collectae.* Vols. I, II. i. Leipzig: Teubner, 1896/1906.

RAUBITSCHEK, A. E. 'Notes on Attic Prosopography: Βλέπυρος Πειθάνδρου Παιονίδης.' *Hesp.* xi 1942, 305–6.
—— 'The Ostracism of Xanthippos.' *AJA*² li 1947, 257–62.
—— 'The Case against Alcibiades (Andocides IV).' *TAPA* lxxix 1948, 191–210.
—— 'Note on the Post-Hadrianic Boule.' *Γέρας Ἀντωνίου Κεραμοπούλλου* (Athens: Μυρτιδῆ, 1953), 242–55.
—— 'Demokratia.' *Hesp.* xxxi 1962, 238–43.
—— with JEFFERY, L. H. *Dedications from the Athenian Akropolis.* Cambridge, Mass.: Arch. Inst. of America, 1949.
REINMUTH, O. W. 'The Genesis of the Athenian Ephebia.' *TAPA* lxxxiii 1952, 34–50.
—— 'The Ephebic Inscription, Athenian Agora I 286.' *Hesp.* xxiv 1955, 220–39.
—— 'An Ephebic Text of ca. 43/2 B.C.: *IG* ii² 1040 and 1025.' *Hesp.* xxxiv 1965, 255–72.
REUSCH, A. *De Diebus Contionum Ordinarium apud Athenienses. Dissertationes Philologicae Argentoratenses Selectae*, vol. iii (Strasbourg: Trübner, 1880), 1–138.
ROBERT, J. and L. 'Bulletin épigraphique, 209.' *REG* lxvii 1954, 159–62.
ROBERT, L. 'Note préliminaire sur des inscriptions de Carie.' *BCH* lviii 1934, 512–17.
—— 'Sur une loi d'Athènes relative aux Petites Panathénées.' *Hellenica* xi–xii 1960, 189–203.
ROBINSON, H. S. 'The Tower of the Winds and the Roman Market-Place.' *AJA*² xlvii 1943, 291–305.
ROSSITER, S. (ed.). *Blue Guide: London.*⁹ Benn, 1965.
RUSCHENBUSCH, E. *Untersuchungen zur Geschichte des athenischen Strafrechts.* (Graezistische Abhandlungen, iv.) Cologne and Graz: Böhlau, 1968.
SCHAEFER, A. D. *Demosthenes und seine Zeit.*² 3 vols. Leipzig: Teubner, 1885/6/7.
SCHOEFFER, V. VON. Art. δῆμοι, I. Attika. *RE*, v (1905), 1–33, 35–122.
SCHREINER, J. H. *Aristotle and Perikles. SO* Supp. xxi 1968.
SCHULTHESS, A. Art. γραμματεῖς, I. Athen. *RE*, vii (1912), 1710–35.
SCHWAHN, W. Art. Strategos: Attisch. *RE*, Supp. vi (1935), 1071–81.
SCHWEIGERT, E. 'Inscriptions from the North Slope of the Acropolis, 16. An Inventory of the Treasurers of Athena, *IG* ii² 1438.' *Hesp.* vii 1938, 281–9.
—— 'Greek Inscriptions, 4. A Decree concerning Elaious, 357/6 B.C.' *Hesp.* viii 1939, 12–17.
—— 'Epigraphical Notes, 4. An Honorary Decree, 322/1 B.C.' *Hesp.* viii 1939, 173–5.
—— 'Greek Inscriptions, 42. An Honorary Decree.' *Hesp.* ix 1940, 335–43.
—— 'Greek Inscriptions, 45. A Decree in Honor of Adeimantos of Lampsakos, 302 B.C.' *Hesp.* ix 1940, 348–51.
—— 'The Xanthippos Ostracon.' *AJA*² liii 1949, 266–8.
SEAGER, R. J. 'Lysias against the Corndealers.' *Hist.* xv 1966, 172–84.

SEALEY, B. R. I. 'Dionysius of Halicarnassus and some Demosthenic Dates.'
REG lxviii 1955, 77–120.
—— 'On Coming of Age in Athens.' *CR*² vii 1957, 195–7.
—— 'Regionalism in Archaic Athens.' *Hist.* ix 1960, 155–80 = *Essays in Greek Politics* (New York: Manyland, 1967), 9–38.
—— 'Ephialtes.' *CP* lix 1964, 11–22 = *Essays in Greek Politics* (New York: Manyland, 1967), 42–58.
SENCIE, J., and PEREMANS, W. 'La jurisdiction pénale de la Boulè à Athènes au début du Vᵉ siècle avant J.-C. (suite). *LEC* x 1941, 329–37. (*See also* PEREMANS, W.)
SMITH, F. D. *Athenian Political Commissions.* Chicago thesis, 1920.
SMITH, S. B. *The Athenian Proedroi.* CP xxv 1930, 250–76.
SOKOLOWSKI, F. *Lois sacrées des cités grecques (Supplément).* (École française d'Athènes: Travaux et Mémoires, xi.) Paris: Boccard, 1962. (I have not used his *Lois sacrées des cités grecques* [1969].)
SUMNER, G. V. 'Notes on Chronological Problems in the Aristotelian *Ἀθηναίων Πολιτεία*.' *CQ*² xi 1961, 31–54.
SUNDWALL, J. *Epigraphische Beiträge zur sozial-politische Geschichte Athens.* Klio Beiheft iv 1906.
—— 'Brottstycke av en Attisk Katalog.' *Eranos* xxv 1927, 191–2.
SWOBODA, H. 'Bemerkungen zur politischen Stellung der athenischen Strategen.' *RM*² xlv 1890, 288–310.
—— *Die griechischen Volksbeschlüsse: epigraphische Untersuchungen.* Leipzig: Teubner, 1890.
THALHEIM, T. 'Zur Eisangelie in Athen.' *Hermes* xxxvii 1902, 339–52.
—— Art. *εἰσαγγελία. RE*, v (1905), 2138–41.
THOMPSON, H. A. 'Buildings on the West Side of the Agora.' *Hesp.* vi 1937, 1–226. (Metroon–Bouleuterion Complex and East Slope of Kolonos Agoraios, 115–224.)
—— *The Tholos of Athens and its Predecessors.* Hesp. Supp. iv 1940.
—— 'Excavations in the Athenian Agora, 1952.' *Hesp.* xxii 1953, 25–56.
THOMPSON, W. E. "*τριττὺς τῶν πρυτάνεων.*" *Hist.* xv 1966, 1–10.
—— 'The Functions of the Emergency Coinages of the Peloponnesian War.' *Mnem.*⁴ xix 1966, 337–43.
THOMSEN, R. *Eisphora: A Study of Direct Taxation in Ancient Athens.* (Humanitas, iii.) Copenhagen: Gyldendal, 1964.
THREPSIADES, J., and VANDERPOOL, E. "*πρὸς τοῖς Ἑρμαῖς.*" *AΔ* viii A 1963, 99–114.
THUCYDIDES. DOVER, K. J. *Thucydides, Book VI.* O.U.P., 1965.
—— —— *Thucydides, Book VII.* O.U.P., 1965.
—— GOMME, A. W. *A Historical Commentary on Thucydides*, vols. i–iii. O.U.P., 1945 (corr. 1950)/1956/1956. (I have not used vol. iv, by GOMME, A. W., ANDREWES, A., and DOVER, K. J., 1970.)
TOD, M. N. *A Selection of Greek Historical Inscriptions.* 2 vols. O.U.P., 1933 (2nd ed. 1946)/1948.
—— Review of OLIVER, *The Athenian Expounders of the Sacred and Ancestral Law. JHS* lxxi 1951, 270–1.

TRAILL, J. S. 'The Bouleutic List of 304/3 B.C.' *Hesp.* xxxv 1966, 205–40.

—— 'The Bouleutic List of 303/2 B.C.' *Hesp.* xxxvii 1968, 1–24.

TRAVLOS, J., trans. THOMPSON, H. A. 'The West Side of the Athenian Agora Restored.' *Hesp.* Supp. viii 1949, 382–93.

TRÉHEUX, J. 'Décret de Lampsaque trouvé à Thasos.' *BCH* lxxvii 1953, 426–43.

—— 'Recherches sur la topographie et l'histoire de l'Acropole d'Athènes: la Chalkothèque et l'Opisthodome.' Paris thesis, 1959.

VANDERPOOL, E. 'Tholos and Prytanikon.' *Hesp.* iv 1935, 470–5.

WADE-GERY, H. T. 'Studies in Attic Inscriptions of the Fifth Century B.C., B. Charter of the Democracy, 410 B.C. = *IG* i² 114.' *BSA* xxxiii 1932–3, 113–22.

—— Review of MERITT and WEST, *The Athenian Assessment. CR* xlix 1935, 185–6.

—— 'Themistokles' Archonship.' *BSA* xxxvii 1936–7, 263–70 = *Essays in Greek History* (Blackwell, 1958), 171–9.

—— 'Two Notes on Theopompos, *Philippika*, x. 1. Kleon and the Assessment.' *AJP* lix 1938, 129–31 = *Essays in Greek History* (Blackwell, 1958), 233–5.

—— 'Two Notes on Theopompos, *Philippika*, x. 2. Date of Jurymen's Pay.' *AJP* lix 1938, 131–4 = *Essays in Greek History* (Blackwell, 1958), 235–8.

—— 'The Judicial Treaty with Phaselis and the History of the Athenian Courts.' *Essays in Greek History* (Blackwell, 1958), 180–200.

—— and MERITT, B. D. 'Pylos and the Assessment of Tribute.' *AJP* lvii 1936, 377–94.

—— —— 'Athenian Resources in 449 and 431 B.C.' *Hesp.* xxvi 1957, 163–97.

WALLACE, W. P. 'The Public Seal of Athens.' *Phoen.* iii 1949, 70–3.

WESTLAKE, H. D. *Individuals in Thucydides.* C.U.P., 1968.

WESTON, E. 'New Datings for some Attic Honorary Decrees.' *AJP* lxi 1940, 345–57.

WHITE, M. E. 'Some Agiad Dates: Pausanias and his Sons.' *JHS* lxxxiv 1964, 140–52.

WILAMOWITZ-MOELLENDORFF, U. VON. *Aristoteles und Athen.* 2 vols. Berlin: Weidmann, 1893.

—— Review of Ἐφημερὶς Ἀρχαιολογική³ iii–iv 1897. *DLZ* xix 1898, 383–4.

WILCKEN, U. 'Der Anonymus Argentinensis.' *Hermes* xlii 1907, 374–418.

WILHELM, A. 'Diener des Rates der Athener.' *Abh. Berlin* 1939, xx.

—— 'Attische Urkunden, xxxi. *IG* i² 70, 16, 166.' *Sb. Wien* ccxvii. 5, 1939, 52–72.

—— 'Notes on the Second Decree of Kallias.' *JHS* lxviii 1948, 124–9.

—— 'Zum Ostrakismos des Xanthippos, des Vaters des Perikles.' *Anz. Wien.* lxxxvi 1949, 237–43.

WOODHEAD, A. G. '*IG* i² 95 and the Ostracism of Hyperbolus.' *Hesp.* xviii 1949, 78–83.

Woodhead, A. G. *The Study of Greek Inscriptions*. C.U.P., 1959.

—— 'ἰσηγορία and the Council of 500.' *Hist.* xvi 1967, 129–40.

Wycherley, R. E. 'Two Notes on Athenian Topography, ii. Synedrion and Ag. I 6524.' *JHS* lxxv 1955, 118–21.

—— *The Athenian Agora*, iii. *Literary and Epigraphical Testimonia*. Princeton: A.S.C.S.A., 1957.

—— 'Neleion.' *BSA* lv 1960, 60–6.

—— 'The Agora of Pericles.' *J. Hist. Stud.* i 1967–8, 246–56.

Wyndham, W. W. 'Athens in the Late Fifth Century.' (Essay submitted for Ancient History Prize of Oxford University; unpublished.) Oxford, 1963.

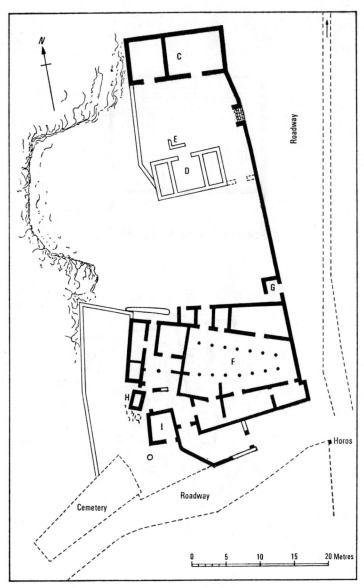

PLAN A. Area of Bouleuterium in the Last Quarter of the Sixth Century

From *Hesperia* Supplement iv 1940, fig. 13, by kind permission of the American School of Classical Studies at Athens

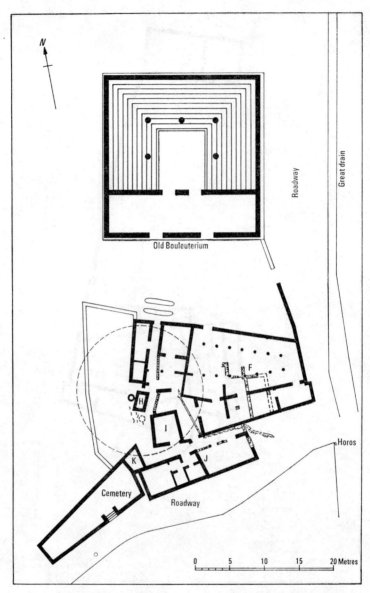

PLAN B. Area of Bouleuterium at the End of the Sixth Century

From *Hesperia* Supplement iv 1940, fig. 32, by kind permission of the American
School of Classical Studies at Athens

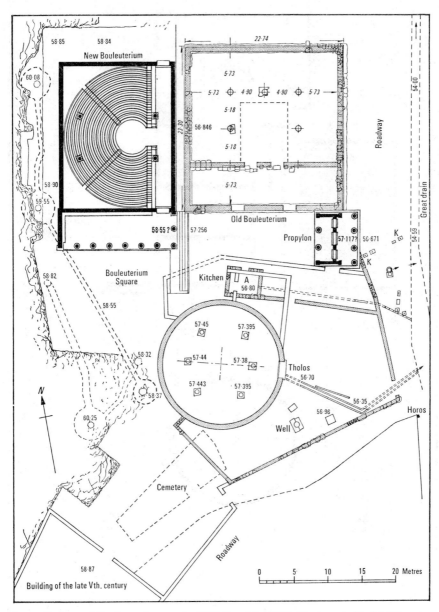

PLAN C. Area of Bouleuterium to the Middle of the Fifth Century (with Additions to the Early Third Century)

From *Hesperia* Supplement iv 1940, fig. 62, by kind permission of the American School of Classical Studies at Athens

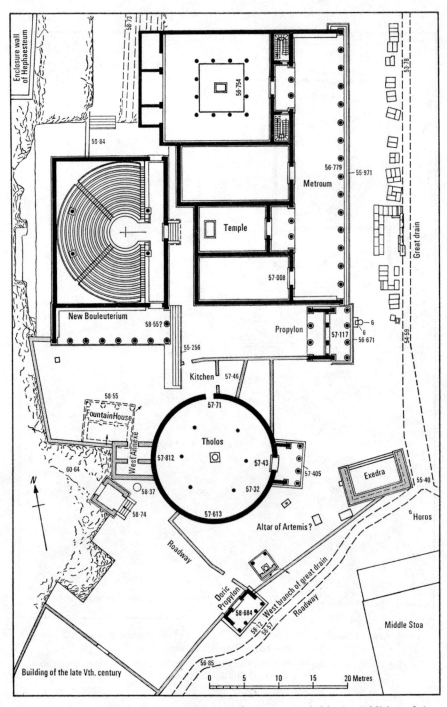

PLAN D. Area of Bouleuterium in the First Century A.D. (with the Addition of the West Annexe)

Adapted to fit the current views of the excavators from *Hesperia* Supplement iv 1940, fig. 63, by kind permission of the American School of Classical Studies at Athens

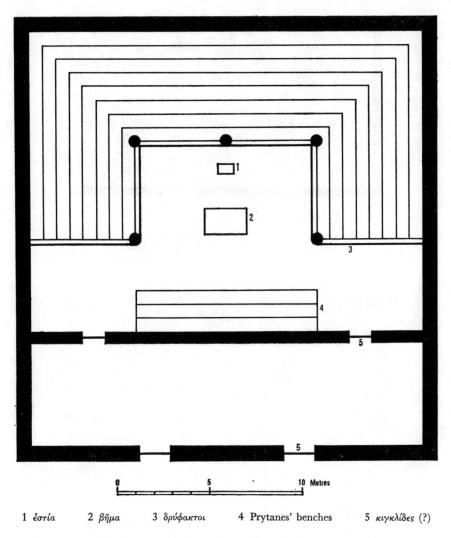

1 ἑστία   2 βῆμα   3 δρύφακτοι   4 Prytanes' benches   5 κιγκλίδες (?)

PLAN E. Old Bouleuterium: Restoration of Interior Arrangements (P. J. R.)

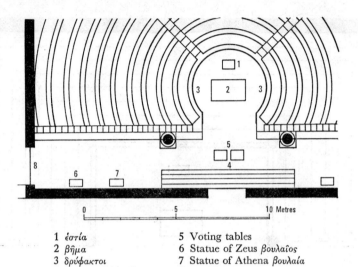

1 ἑστία
2 βῆμα
3 δρύφακτοι
4 Prytanes' benches

5 Voting tables
6 Statue of Zeus βουλαῖος
7 Statue of Athena βουλαία
8 κιγκλίς

PLAN F. New Bouleuterium: Restoration of Interior Arrangements
(W. A. McDonald)

From W. A. McDonald, *The Political Meeting Places of the Greeks*, Plate
XVIII, by kind permission of The Johns Hopkins Press

INDEX I

LITERARY TEXTS CITED

Italic numerals refer to the pages and notes of this book. Detailed discussions of a passage are listed first and are separated from other references by a semi-colon; discussions of textual problems are indicated by an obelus (†).

INDEX II

EPIGRAPHIC TEXTS CITED

'Modern' numerals (1234567890) refer to the serial numbers of inscriptions, 'old style' (1234567890) to lines of texts or to pages or dates of publication, *italic* to the pages and notes of this book. Detailed discussions of a passage are listed first and are separated from other references by a semi-colon; discussions of textual problems are indicated by an obelus (†). References marked with a double obelus (‡) are modified in the *Corrigenda*, p. vii.

Most texts cited in this book are identified by one reference only, but in this index cross-references will be found to all texts cited which have been published in *IG* or in Volume ii of *ATL* (except the texts, mostly short extracts only, published as *ATL* T 68 a–78 d).

Y

45: see M&L 49
46, 19: *16 n. 1*
47: see *SEG* x 136
48: see *SEG* x 37
51: see M&L 63
54: see HMA 69
56: see HMA 80
57: see M&L 65
59, 19: *38*
61: see *SEG* x 53
63: see M&L 69
65: see M&L 68
66: see M&L 46
70: see *SEG* x 84
71: see *SEG* x 86
— but 49–55: see HMA 66
73, 4: *116*
— 13–14: *116–17*
74: *116 n. 7*
— 23: *116*
— 31: *116*
75: *150 n. 6*
76: see M&L 73
78: see *SEG* xxi 38
79: *95 n. 3, 173 n. 3*
— 5–7: *173 n. 3*
— 7–9: *95 n. 3*†
— 9–11: *95 n. 4*
— 15–18: *95 n. 5*
80, 7–9: *102 n. 5*
81: *123 n. 1*
83: see *SEG* x 91
84: *246, 278*
— 5: *4 n. 5*
— 19–21: *128 n. 14*
— 22–3: *102 n. 5*
— 23–5: *128 n. 15*
— 38–9: *123 n. 3*
— 44: *4 n. 5*
87: see *SEG* x 80
88, 1–5: *39 n. 5, 122 n. 7, 280*
90: see Tod 68
91: see M&L 58 A
92: see M&L 58 B
94: *97 n. 6, 246, 278*
— 1–11: *97 n. 7*
— 11–13: *97 n. 5*
— 11–28: *97 n. 10*
— 15–18: *99 n. 3*
— 18–20: *97 n. 9*
— 28: *99 n. 4*
— 29–38: *98 n. 1*
95: see *SEG* xii 32
96: see *SEG* x 104

97: see *SEG* xii 26
98+99: see M&L 78
105: see *SEG* x 138
108: see M&L 89
109: see *ATL*, ii. D 9
110: see M&L 85
113+*SEG* x 127: *246*†
114*: *183–4, 195–9; 169 n. 4, 179, 183 nn.*
   6–7, 191–2, 191 n. 4, 194 with n. 13
— 1–16: *196*†
— 7–10: *196*
— 9–16: *196*†
— 21–2: *196*
— 25: *196 n. 4*
— 27–9: *196*
— 29: *196*
— 31: *183 with n. 7*†, *196 n. 3*†
— 34: *196, 197 with n. 1*†, *198*
— 35: *113; 191*
— 36: *169 n. 5, 183 with n. 7*†, *196 n. 5*†
— 37: *196 n. 5*†
— 41: *183 with n. 7*†, *196, 197, 198 n. 3*
— 43: *198*†
115: see M&L 86
116: see M&L 87
117: see M&L 88
118: see M&L 90
122: see *SEG* x 131
128: see *SEG* xxi 37
149: see *SEG* x 105
166: see *SEG* x 96
169: see *SEG* x 53
179: see *SEG* x 53
185: see *SEG* x 60
191: see *ATL*, ii. List 1
192: see *ATL*, ii. List 2
193: see *ATL*, ii. List 3
197: see *ATL*, ii. Lists 1–2
202: see *ATL*, ii. List 12
203: see *ATL*, ii. List 13
216: see *ATL*, ii. List 26
217: see *ATL*, ii. List 26
218: see *ATL*, ii. List 25
219: see *ATL*, ii. List 39
220: see *ATL*, ii. List 34
223: see *ATL*, ii. List 33
231: see *ATL*, ii. List 26
232 sqq.: *236*
256 sqq.: *236*
276 sqq.: *236*
294: see *SEG* x 226
295: see M&L 61
296: see HMA 79
299: see *SEG* x 226

* I cite by the line numbers of Wade-Gery, *BSA* xxxiii 1932–3, 113–22. To obtain the correct reference in *IG* i² 114, add one throughout.

672: *66 n. 1, 76, 264*
— 16–17: *109 n. 4*
— 35: *16 n. 2*
— 36–7: *280*
— 43: *280*
674 (*P* 6): *109–10; 100 n. 3, 264*
— 6–8: *132 n. 18*
— 13–20: *39 n. 5*
— 16–21: *104 n. 6, 109–10*
— 18–20: *280*
675: see 525
676: *252*
677: *252*
678: see *P* 10
679: see *SEG* iii 92
680: *265*
682: *72 n. 1, 252–3, 278, 279*
— 21–4: *126 n. 3*
— 84 sqq.: *280*
— 92–5: *251*
— 92 sqq.: *252*
— 98 sqq.: *280*
683: *253*
684: see *SEG* iii 94
685: *252*
686+687: *264, 282*
— 48 sqq: *280*
— 53: *1 n. 4*
— 61–3: *282*
— 68–9: *280*
687: see 686
689 (*SEG* xvi 64): *43 n. 6, 132 n. 6, 252*
691: *251*
693: *251*
695: *264*
697: see *SEG* xxi 356
698: *252*
700: see *Hesp.* vii 20
701: *252*†
702: see *P* 21
703: *263*
704: see *SEG* xvi 65
707: *264*
708: *251*
710: *252*
712: *252*
713. ii: *264*
716: *251*
717: *251*
718: *251*
721: *251*
722: *251*
725: *251*
729: *251*
730/1: *251*
732: *251*
734: *253*

735: *43 n. 6, 78, 253*
750: *264*
751: *251*
752 *b*: see *SEG* iii 94
753: *251*
766: see *SEG* xxi 392
768+802: *253*
— 12: *233*
769: see 441
770: *252*
772: *77, 252*
— 14–16: *38*
775: see *SEG* xviii 19
776: *253*
777: *253*
778: see *Hesp.* vii 23
779: *253*
780: *43 n. 6, 132 n. 13, 265*
— i: *282*
— 20: *16 n. 2*
— 20–2: *282*
781: *43 n. 6, 132 n. 14, 265*†
782: *253*
783: *43 n. 6, 132 n. 8, 274*
— 4: *35 n. 12*
784: *253*
785: *254*
786: *253, 282*
— 28 sqq.: *282*
787: *253*
788: *253*
790: see *P* 23
791: see *Hesp.* xi 56
792: *253*
— 7–9: *126 n. 1*
793, 8–11: *280*
— 21–2: *280*
794 (*HSCP* xlviii 1937, 105–11): *254*‡,
273
— 4: *35 n. 14*
796: *263*
797: *263*
798: *78, 253*
— 19–20: *233*
799: see *SEG* xxi 391
800: see *SEG* xxi 289
801: *253*
802: see 768
803: see *SEG* xviii 19
804: *253*
806: *109 n. 4*
— 1–3: *19 n. 6*†
— 6–9: *109 n. 2*
807: *43 n. 6, 253*
808: *253*
— 20–1: *19 n. 6*
809: *109 n. 4*

Z

INDEX III

GENERAL INDEX

A roman 'B' denotes 'Boule' and a roman 'E' denotes 'Ecclesia' throughout; figures in parentheses denote dates, B.C. unless otherwise stated.

Accounts. *See* Euthynae; Logistae

Acropolis. Meeting-place of B, 35; public works there, 122

Aeschines. Holds secretarial office, 139 with n. 4; accuses Demosthenes of bribery, 112; outbreak of Sacred War (340), 42, 59–60; prosecutes Ctesiphon, 15–16

Age. Of bouleutae, 1 with nn. 7–8, 172, 194–5; of ephebi, 171–3; speakers in descending order of age, 37–8

Agenda. Of B and E, 20, 36–8, 52–60, cf. 227; of nomothetae, 51 with n. 5

Agora. *See* Bouleuterium; Metroum; Stoa Basileos; Tholos

Agoracritus. Statue in Old Bouleuterium, 31

Agoratus. Arrest and trial (404), 41, 142–3, 164–5, 166, 170 n. 1, 181

Agyrrhius. Theoric fund attributed to, 105 n. 6; imprisoned for debt, 150 n. 5

Alcibiades. Profanation of Mysteries (415), 187; in 411, 6–7

— Member of cavalry (395), 174–5

Altar. In bouleuterium, 35

Ambassadors. Report to B and E, 20, 43, 54, 57–8, 60, 211, 216. *See also* Heralds

Amendments to Decrees. *See* Riders

Amphiarea. 129 with n. 8

Andocides. In Hermocopid affair (415), 41, 186–8; attempted return, 34, 41, 185; trial (400), 159–60

And(r)otion. Bouleutes twice, 4 with n. 7, 73 with nn. 4–5, 242; proposes crown for B, 15, 16, 62; embezzlement, 58–9, 149, 152, 158

Annius Pythodorus. νομοθέτης (C2 A.D.), 50 n. 4

Anticles. Secretary to epistatae of Parthenon, 139 n. 3

Antiphon. Trial (411/10), 166, 182, 190

Antoninus Pius. Dedication of ἀγορανόμιον, 127 n. 4

Antony. Ath. constitution under, 86 with n. 9, 222

Apaturia. Holiday for B, 30

Apodectae. Receivers of revenue, 98–100,

cf. 141, 148 n. 1, 211, 218, 220 with n. 3; expenditure by, 100–1, 103 n. 7; judicial powers, 147 n. 7, 150 n. 2; supervised by B, 99, 104, 211, 218; involvement with theoric officials, 106, 238–40

Apollo. Statue in bouleuterium, 34; cults of, 95, 97, 132, 133; building of shrine, 123

Apollodorus. Unsuccessful attack on theoric fund (349/8), 58, 105 nn. 4, 7

Apsephion. Takes sanctuary in bouleuterium, 34

Archebius. Trierarch, 158

Archeptolemus. Trial (411/10), 182, 190

Archers, Scythian. 21, 34, 143 n. 1, 146, 216

Archestratus. Associated with Ephialtes, 202 n. 3

— Imprisoned for proposing acceptance of peace terms (405/4), 145–6, 183 n. 3

Archinus. Has man killed ἄκριτος, 85 n. 5, 180, 181, 184 n. 1; upsets settlement with oligarchs, 180 n. 6

Architects. Regular state appointment, 95, 123, 125–6, 127, 220; for shipbuilding, 117; for allocation of theatre seats, 125–6

Archons. Appointment, 7, 205, 210; disqualifications, 3 n. 1; δοκιμασία, 171, 176–8, cf. 12 with n. 3, 36, 38 n. 10, 194–5, 205, 209–10; oath, 193, 195 n. 1, cf. 178 n. 4; preside over B and E (CC6–5), 18, 19, 21 n. 4, 209; judicial powers, 97 with n. 4, 147 n. 7, 159, 168, 200 with n. 9, 203, 204 n. 1, 228; religious duties and privileges, 132, 134; archontic calendar, 224–9, cf. 18, 135; decline of office, 195 n. 1, 203–4 with 204 n. 1, 225. *See also* Basileus; Polemarch; Thesmothetae

Areopagus. (CC7–6), 162, 202–3, 223; unaffected by Cleisthenes, 162, 200, 202–3, 209–10; attacked by Ephialtes, 201–7, cf. 19, 162, 178, 209, 210–11, 223; guardian of law code (403), 205 with nn. 4–5; used by Demosthenes (C4), 205; in later Ath., 14, 87 n. 1, 95, 126, 220–1, 222; involved in δοκιμασία, 178, 195, 209–10; in εἰσαγγελία, 162, 200–1, 202–3, 205,